GYPSIES

an English History

David Cressy

OXFORD

UNIVERSITY PRESS

OXFORD
UNIVERSITY PRESS

Great Clarendon Street, Oxford, OX2 6DP,
United Kingdom

Oxford University Press is a department of the University of Oxford.
It furthers the University's objective of excellence in research, scholarship,
and education by publishing worldwide. Oxford is a registered trade mark of
Oxford University Press in the UK and in certain other countries

© David Cressy 2018

The moral rights of the author have been asserted

First Edition published in 2018

Impression: 1

Published in the United States of America by Oxford University Press
198 Madison Avenue, New York, NY 10016, United States of America

British Library Cataloguing in Publication Data
Data available

Library of Congress Control Number: 2017952087

ISBN 978–0–19–876813–5

Printed in Great Britain by
Clays Ltd, St Ives plc

Contents

List of Figures

Map of English Counties

Introduction

Gypsies hover around the margins of English society, an elusive and sometimes menacing presence. Commentators over the ages have found them troublesome and unfathomable, fascinating and infuriating. As travelling people, wandering, roaming, here today and gone tomorrow, the Gypsies of history made intermittent contact with settled society, and occasional impact upon it. Gypsies confused the categories and offended the sensibilities of social leaders. Observers did not know what to make of them, or what to do with them, though they were sure they were undesirable. Lacking a place in the social mainstream, and not identified by status, occupation, or address, the Gypsies defied all efforts of reformation, correction, removal, or analysis. Understanding them, in the world in which they lived, poses challenges that continue today.

This book brings Gypsies out of the shadows, illuminating their doings and dealings from their first appearance in England in the early sixteenth century to the present. It seeks not only to recover the experience of the Gypsies themselves, so far as the evidence allows, but also to understand the social anxieties and political responses of the society through which they travelled. Dependent upon historical sources, the story told in these pages inevitably dwells more on their interactions with the state and society than the Gypsies' inner world. Gypsies touched a nerve in the English polity, and the cultural and legal reactions of the community reveal areas of social stress. Attending to Gypsies exposes the fears and alarms that led to their vilification, and also the processes of engagement that afforded them a niche in the economy of wayfaring. By considering Gypsies as a people whose history deserves analysis, rather than a pathology to be examined, we may also learn something about ourselves.

Popular opinion has embraced a range of opinions regarding Gypsies, as undesirable aliens, counterfeit imposters, vagrant scum, and 'all thieves and whores'. They have been idealized as free and noble, and excoriated as corrupt and loathsome. Their image is protean, unstable, and chiaroscuro. Early modern culture vilified Gypsies as idle, dirty, deceitful, and promiscuous practitioners of fraudulent fortune-telling and petty theft, a stereotype that still persists. Their itinerancy and apparent fecklessness posed challenges to the culture of order and regularity. State authorities subjected them to expulsion, mutilation, the galleys, or the gallows, though generally, in practice, they preferred to leave Gypsies alone. Tudor parliaments legislated more vigorously against Gypsies than against witches, though those laws were rarely enforced. Subsequent statutes concerning vagrancy, encampments, and the highways subjected Gypsies to harassment and arrest. Public authorities have sought to control their movement and settlement, and moral reformers have sought their assimilation. Some have even denied that they exist. The press has often sneered at them, but local attitudes were much more ambivalent than conventional summaries would suggest. Histories of prejudice and exclusion coexisted with accommodation, indulgence, engagement, and toleration.

I use the word 'Gypsy' because that was their historical denomination (corrupted from 'Egyptian', their presumed identity of origin), most commonly used in my sources. Only since the late eighteenth century have Gypsies been linked to India, and only in modern times have they been known as Rom, Roma, Romany, or in England 'Romanichals'. Only since the twentieth century have some been known as Travellers. Though many Roma activists today regard 'Gypsy' as an alien and disparaging term, worse than 'Indian' for indigenous Americans, others embrace the designation. The terms are often used interchangeably, according to context and circumstance. European activists are especially sensitive to the racist connotations of the term 'Gypsy', though others comfortably use 'Gypsies' and 'Romanies' as synonyms. The titles of *The Journal of the Gypsy Lore Society,* its successor *Romani Studies,* and the new *Journal of Gypsy Studies* reveal the variation in international approaches.[1]

Like all terminology for social identity, the choice of words invites controversy. Simply writing 'Gypsy' has political resonance, since the capital

---

1. Ian Hancock, *We Are the Romani People* (Hatfield, 2002), pp. xvii–xxi; Donald Kenrick, 'The Origins of Anti-Gyspyism: The Outsiders' View of Romanies in Western Europe in the Fifteenth Century', in Nicholas Saul and Susan Tebbutt (eds), *The Role of the Romanies* (Liverpool, 2004), 79–84; Ian Hancock, *Danger! Educated Gypsy* (Hatfield, 2010), 95–6, 152; Markus End, 'Antigypsyism: What's Happening in a Word?', in Jan Selling, Markus End, Hristo Kyuchukov, Pia Laskar, and Bill Templer (eds), *Antiziganism: What's in a Word?* (Newcastle upon Tyne, 2015), 99–113.

'G' alludes to a people, whereas lower-case 'gypsies' may merely signify a lifestyle.[2] At stake are judgements about ethnicity, social practice, and history. In this work I have standardized renditions of 'gipsy' or 'gipsey' to Gypsy, except in titles of publications or where the sense of quotations requires original usage. I prefer not to use the Romani word *gorgio* (or its variants *gaujo, gadze*, and so on) to describe non-Gypsies, a practice that risks a condescending affectation of solidarity.

I claim no Gypsy or Traveller heritage, although I grew up on the western outskirts of London among older relatives who did. The aunts on my mother's side told family stories, no doubt fanciful, of a Devonshire aristocrat whose daughter ran away with a Gypsy. The tale then turned more substantially to Caroline Parker, my great-grandmother (1859–1929), who was raised in a travelling van among Victorian Gypsy tinsmiths, basketmakers, and general hawkers. Caroline married the builder's labourer John Forward, and settled on the borders of Surrey and Kent, while her siblings continued to travel. My mother recalled visiting her Gypsy great-aunts in a caravan on Epsom Downs in the 1920s, and was impressed because they showed her a basket of gold sovereigns. The story has no bearing on my scholarly work, although it may have piqued a lifelong interest.

This is a work of history, not advocacy, nostalgia, or apologetics. It is not designed to empower or malign anyone, although it may display sympathies for a people who were excluded and misunderstood. It draws on decades of teaching and research on English social history, and an enduring interest in the relationship of the margins and the mainstream, the powerful and the powerless, the established and the insecure. It builds on my earlier work on the social order, educational disadvantage, demotic speech, and the common people in England's troubled history.

The social marginality of Gypsies, past and present, is matched by their marginality in modern scholarship. References to Gypsies are rare in works of social history, while the general literature on Gypsies in the past tends to be slight, inward-looking, and harnessed to other agendas. Research on the period before the nineteenth century is especially limited and untrustworthy. Popular fascination with Gypsies continues apace, but myths and misunderstandings abound. A comprehensive history is wanting, but the recent quickening of interest in Britain and Europe offers both a stimulus

---

2. Cf. discussion in David Mayall, *Gypsy Identities 1500–2000: From Egipcyans and Moon-Men to the Ethnic Romany* (2004), 15, and Frances Timbers, *'The Damned Fraternitie': Constructing Gypsy Identity in Early Modern England, 1500–1700* (2016), 3.

and a model.[3] Scholars have sometimes remarked on the 'isolation' of Gypsy studies, where specialists argue mainly with each other.[4] My concern is to reduce that isolation by locating Gypsies within the English historical experience.

A range of questions invites investigation. Were early modern Gypsies an ethnic group, a social amalgam, or exemplars of a lifestyle? To what extent was their identity imagined, inhabited, or culturally constructed, and how did it change over time? Did the people who encountered Gypsies, wrote about them, and pursued them in the past consider them in terms of their status or their activity, for who they were or what they did? How prejudiced, how fanciful, how trustworthy, were contemporary observations and comments? How far can we probe behind the representations to recover a history of experience and interaction? What relationship did the itinerant Gypsies of pre-modern England have to Gypsies elsewhere in Europe, and to Roma and Travellers in other historical periods and the present? What can be learned about their language, culture, and activities, in the face of prejudice, mixture, and assimilation? How did immigrants become 'Egyptians', and how did 'Egyptians' become 'Gypsies'? How were 'Gypsies' discovered to be 'Romanies', and then reidentified as 'Travellers'? In what ways were Gypsies different from other itinerants—transients and vagrants—and were they still Gypsies if they ceased travelling? How have they fared under pressure from governments and law, amid the attentions of journalists, scholars, activists, and politicians? What does their treatment say about English history, politics, culture, and society?

The following chapters examine how the state and community dealt with the Gypsies during the five centuries of their presence in England. Engaging a variety of historiographical traditions, regarding crime and punishment, law and administration, prejudice, neighbourliness, mobility, communications,

3. Other useful points of entry include Angus Fraser, *The Gypsies* (1992, 1995); Becky Taylor, *Another Darkness, Another Dawn: A History of Gypsies, Roma and Travellers* (2014); and Yaron Matras, *I Met Lucky People: The Story of the Romani Gypsies* (2014). Work on European Gypsies includes Henriette Asséo, *Les Tsiganes: Une destinée européenne* (Paris, 1994); David M. Crowe, *A History of the Gypsies of Eastern Europe and Russia* (New York, 1996); Susan Tebbutt (ed.), *Sinti and Roma in German-Speaking Society and Literature* (New York and Oxford, 1998, 2008); Elena Marushiakova and Vesselin Popov, *Gypsies in the Ottoman Empire* (Hatfield, 2001); Richard J. Pym, *The Gypsies of Early Modern Spain, 1425–1783* (Basingstoke and New York, 2007); Elisa Novi Chavarria, *Sulle tracce degli zingari: Il popolo rom nel Regno di Napoli (secoli XV–XVIII)* (Naples, 2007); Benedetto Fassanelli, *Vite al bando: Storie di cingari nella terrferma veneta all fine del cinquecento* (Rome, 2011). See also David Cressy, 'Trouble with Gypsies in Early Modern England', *Historical Journal*, 59 (2016), 45–70.
4. On 'the splendid isolation of Gypsy studies', see Wim Willems, *In Search of the True Gypsy: From Enlightenment to Final Solution* (1997), 305–9.

popular culture, ethnicity, and gender, they expose the deep roots of marginalization and exclusion as Gypsies negotiated the economy of itinerancy. I am offering a populated history, with references to named individuals as well as to the figure of 'the Gypsy'.

Chapter 1 examines classic and recent research on the Indo-Asian origins of the Gypsies, their arrival in Western Europe in the fifteenth century, and the different treatment meted out to them in the sixteenth, seventeenth, and eighteenth centuries. Examples from Germany, France, the Netherlands, Italy, Spain, and Scotland show how early curiosity about the Gypsies gave way to hostility, exclusion, and oppression. This wider survey invites comparisons to approaches and conditions in England.

Chapter 2 explores the treatment of Gypsies in English literary, satirical, and polemical texts from the sixteenth and seventeenth centuries. It shows how popular and creative writers developed a stereotype of Gypsy criminality and deceit that was plagiarized and recycled for amusement and profit. It also follows early modern debates about the origins and character of the Gypsies, and whether they possessed residual arcane 'Egyptian' knowledge. It demonstrates the persistence of representations and misrepresentations that shaped the Gypsy image.

Chapter 3 traces the experiences of Gypsies in early sixteenth-century England, and their encounters with the Tudor regime. It examines the development of legislation in 1531, 1554, and 1563 that sought to expel Gypsies or to punish them as felons. It follows the efforts of administrators from Thomas Cromwell under Henry VIII to Privy Councillors at the beginning of Elizabeth I's reign to deal with the Gypsies who had become increasingly established in England.

Chapter 4 considers how Elizabethan authorities at the local and national level coped with large companies of itinerant Gypsies who made a mockery of the law. Many officials preferred to treat the travellers more flexibly as vagrants, to be rid of them as soon as possible, rather than follow the 1563 statute that threatened death to Gypsies and 'counterfeit Egyptians'.

Chapter 5 examines responses to the Gypsy 'problem' in the seventeenth century. The evidence reveals a growing propensity to treat Gypsies more as a nuisance than as a threat. Scattered sources shed light on the mystery of the Gypsy language, the porosity of Gypsy identity, petty criminality, and the gendered practices of fortune-telling as the Gypsy community evolved. Stuart England became more tolerant, at a time when most continental regimes increased their anti-Gypsy strictures.

Chapter 6 examines the treatment of Gypsies in eighteenth-century literature and art, journalism, and the courts of law. At its centre is the case of Mary Squires and Elizabeth Canning, which divided the British public and generated scores of pamphlets and opinions. Exceptionally detailed trial testimony exposed the wanderings of a Gypsy family and their dealings with ordinary people. Renewed attention to the law led to the repeal of the Elizabethan anti-Gypsy statute in 1783, though Gypsies continued to fall foul of constables and magistrates.

Chapter 7 explores the renewed interest in Gypsies among domestic missionaries, artists, philologists, folklorists, and romanticists at the end of the Hanoverian era. It pays close attention to the work of evangelical reformers of the late eighteenth and early nineteenth centuries, whose direct experience with Gypsies yielded tracts of uncommon ethnographic value. It also includes reports from the criminal justice system that have long been hidden in the archives.

Chapter 8 contrasts the Victorian fascination with Gypsies in literature and speculative theory with their treatment in local courts and the press. The period saw an outpouring of work on Gypsies, from the fancies of George Borrow to the earnest endeavours of the Gypsy Lore Society, as well as myriad encounters with individual itinerants. Gypsies, meanwhile, defied attempts by philanthropists to reform them, efforts by census officials to count them, and pressures by local authorities to prevent their camping and travelling.

Chapter 9 investigates some of the legal, social, and political entanglements of twentieth- and twenty-first-century Gypsies, their problems with caravans and camps, and their treatment in the courts, parliament, and the press. It concludes with discussion of public policy and public perception, amid the competitive advocacy of Romany Gypsies, Irish Travellers, European Roma, and the apparent contradiction of settled itinerants.

Chapter 10 attends thematically to the lives and livelihoods of English Gypsies from the sixteenth century to the present. It considers variations, continuities, and changes in their activities, avocations, and reputations, as England became increasingly urban, populous, industrialized, and multicultural. Sections re-examine Gypsy characteristics, their 'trade of life', their language, the composition of their companies, and the myth of Gypsy child-stealing. A conclusion revisits discussion of the nature of Gypsy identity and the problem of Gypsy ethnicity. It argues that it is neither racist, essentialist, nor 'primordialist' to treat Gypsies as an ethnic group, provided we recognize ethnicity to be variable and contingent. English Gypsy ethnicity was inherited as well as constructed, fluid, flexible, and self-replicating.

A review of the interdisciplinary literature is reserved to a final section on 'Scholars and Gypsies'. My notes and bibliography cite all the sources that have gone into the making of this book. The place of publication of all printed works was London, unless otherwise indicated.

I

European Wanderers
Origins, Arrivals, and Proscriptions

No part of Europe is without Gypsies. Chroniclers first noted them in the early fifteenth century, and within a hundred years their migrations had crossed a mosaic of jurisdictions from the Balkans to the Baltic, from the Mediterranean to the Atlantic shores. European authorities were puzzled by them, wary of them, and soon devised laws and policies to punish Gypsies or be rid of them. Commentators remarked on the curious characteristics of the newcomers, including their skill in fortune-telling and their propensity for petty crime. Nobody knew where they had come from, though the myth developed that the travellers were 'Egyptians', hence the word Gypsy. Their numbers grew from hundreds to thousands, and by the modern era millions, as a dispersed and vilified minority.

This chapter examines encounters with Gypsies in several parts of early modern Europe, as both prelude and background to their experience in England. It draws on the most trustworthy documentary sources, augmented by recent historical research, to sketch a broad outline. Of necessity, it is concerned more with the impact of Gypsies on mainstream society, and reactions of states and communities to the so-called Gypsy 'menace', than with perspectives of the Gypsies themselves. It recognizes Gypsies to have been a curiosity, an anomaly, and a challenge to Western culture, an embedded 'other' that more often kept to itself than attempted to belong. Studying the reception, representation, and rejection of Gypsies in various parts of Europe exposes the complexity, the ambivalence, and sometimes the ferocity of societal responses to outsiders. Though familiar in outline to specialists on Gypsies, this narrative of contact and conflict remains untold in mainstream histories of Europe.[1]

Asian Origins

Though some scholars argue that Gypsies emerged from domestic or indigenous conditions associated with the demise of feudalism,[2] the preponderance of opinion concurs that the Gypsies reached Europe as migrants, most likely from north-west India.[3] Whether this matters depends upon the importance attached to ancestry and ethnic difference. Nobody in the fifteenth century knew that the Gypsies spoke an Asian language, and nobody before our own time had intimations of their genetic heritage.

The arrival and dispersion of a strange and mysterious people excited speculation about their identity and origins. Christian Europe entertained a hodgepodge of beliefs, conjectures, claims, and fantasies that attempted to fit the Gypsies into biblical or historical frames of reference. One recurrent story was that they were remnants of Pharaoh's scattered hosts after the biblical Exodus of the Jews, another that they had been condemned to wander since failing to assist Jesus and the Holy Family on their flight into Egypt. Claims for an Egyptian origin still had adherents in the nineteenth century, despite mounting evidence to the contrary. More common explanations for Gypsy itinerancy made them pilgrims or penitent Christians under papal or imperial protection, or refugee nobles from the land of 'Little Egypt'.[4] The widely read Renaissance occultist Agrippa von Nettesheim (1486–1535) claimed that Gypsies originated 'from a certain country between Egypt and Ethiopia, of the race of Chus, the son of Cham, the son of Noah, [and] still suffer under the curse of their progenitor'. Characteristically, he said, they lived by theft and fortune-telling, deriving 'rich spoils' from deceit of 'silly wenches and timorous women'.[5] The Italian chronicler Fra Geronimo recorded the belief in the 1420s that Gypsies may have come from India ('aliqui dicebant quod errant de India'), which proved to be a lucky guess.[6]

Observers and chroniclers sometimes remarked that Gypsies used a strange language, a 'gibble gabble' or 'Egypt speech' that nobody else could understand. Only in the eighteenth century did pioneer philologists recognize this tongue to be Romani, with remarkable similarities to Sanskrit and Hindi. Linguistic analysis not only demonstrated that the Gypsies originated in India, but also revealed, through examination of borrowed vocabulary, the cultural paths through which they travelled.[7] This research is not without controversy, but it seems most likely that the Gypsies migrated out of north-west India, through Turkic central Asia, into Anatolia and the Byzantine

Greek world, where they also absorbed Persian, Armenian, and Balkan linguistic influences. Nothing is known about the caste or social status of these migrants, so claims that they were originally defeated warriors, camp followers, entertainers, or vagabonds cannot be verified.[8] Nor can there be any certainty about the timing or circumstances of the Gypsy migration, or whether it was one migration or several, except to say that Gypsies were on the move between the tenth and fifteenth centuries. While retaining core characteristics, and elements of a distinctive Romani culture, the Gypsies acquired manners, vocabularies, and a complex genetic heritage from a variety of communities along the way. Similar processes would continue in Britain and Western Europe, as Gypsies engaged with their new host environments.

Recent work on Roma genetics confirms and complicates this history of migration and mixture. An earlier generation of scholars hoped that new kinds of tests might resolve the issue of Gypsy origins, but declared the genetic evidence inconclusive.[9] Increasingly sophisticated analysis of Y chromosomes and mitochondrial DNA now validates the Asian origin of European Roma, and renders untenable the view that Gypsies were simply a home-grown itinerant underclass. Anthropologists and sociologists who called the theory of Indian origins a 'myth', and believed that Gypsies emerged from the indigenous vagrant population after the collapse of feudalism, are now decisively answered. The Roma are proven to be genetically distinct from other populations, though subject themselves to variation. This applied to West European Gypsies, including small samples from Britain, as well as Roma from the Balkans, Bulgaria, and Romania. They clearly shared a common Indian origin, with subsequent genetic drift and admixture attributed to exchanges with peoples during their migration. Blending and divergence continued in Eastern and Western Europe, but practices of endogamy kept the Gypsies relatively isolated. Studies of mutation frequencies and haplotype divergence (markers of frequency and alteration of inherited characteristics) among the European Roma Gypsies indicate long-term maintenance of reproductive patterns and genetic structure, following an Asian 'founding event' some 800 years ago.[10] It would be unwise for historians to claim too much from this research, since samples are small and selective, and techniques are still evolving, but initial findings strongly correspond to the evidence from historical linguistics.

One widely publicized study based on genome-wide data dates the initial out-migration from India to the sixth century CE. It traces the path of the Roma through Central Asia, the Caucasus, and the Middle East to the Balkans (modern Bulgaria), where a divergence between eastern and western branches began in the twelfth century CE. Since then, in varying degrees, non-Romani Europeans have left a footprint in the Romani genome, which nonetheless retains its distinctive identity.[11] The dates indicated by this genetic analysis are earlier than those derived from other sources, and may yet be subject to revision. Despite the scepticism of some social scientists, there can now be no doubt that the ancestors of the Gypsies originated in India. What befell them later remains a matter for research.

Lords of Little Egypt

The Gypsies entered European history towards the end of the Middle Ages, the tail end of a Romani migration that worked its way across much of western Asia. But, unlike earlier waves of migrants, the Gypsies did not come as conquerors or settlers, and were not competing for authority, land, or resources. Nor were they religious exiles, or betterment migrants filling specialized economic niches, like Huguenots in Elizabethan England. The Gypsies were more like infiltrators, and remained perennial outsiders. Itinerants known as 'Egyptians' filtered into Western Europe in the century after the Black Death, and roamed through most of its kingdoms and territories. Classical antiquity knew nothing of Gypsies, so neo-Latin chroniclers had to invent a term for them. Attempting to translate local usage, they referred to the Gypsies variably as 'Aegyptii', 'Zingari', or 'Cingani', and even 'Babilonii'. The instabilities of nomenclature reflected uncertainty about Gypsy origins and identity.

German chroniclers recorded them as 'Zigeuners' or 'Zingani', which yields the Polish 'Cygan', the Hungarian 'Czigány', and the Gallic 'Tzigane'. The French knew Gypsies as 'Egyptiens', 'Bohémiens or Bohêmes', 'Saracens', or 'Tsiganes', the word 'Gitane' appearing later, influenced by the Spanish 'Gitano'. In the Netherlands they were 'Egyptenaars' or 'Heidens'.[12] People known elsewhere as 'Cingari', 'Hittani', and 'Egyptii' were 'called....by our people Gypsies', explained an author in seventeenth-century England.[13] Gypsies, declared another English authority, were 'found in all Christian countries, yet are they not in all countries alike...the French call the Gypsies Boëmie, or Bohemians...the Italians name them Zingari or Saracens, the Spaniards Itanos, as we Egyptians'. Although Gypsies everywhere shared core characteristics, it seemed reasonable to wonder 'whether they partake more of the nature of the countries whence they rise, or of those through which they pass?'[14] An answer of sorts came from the early travel writer John Ray who reported, 'there are thousands of Gypsies or Zinganies in Turkey, who live the same idle, nasty kind of life they do in Christendom, and pretend to the same art of telling fortunes, and are looked upon as the off-scouring of mankind'.[15]

A tantalizing reference in medieval Byzantine sources mentions 'Atzinganoi' snake-charmers and clairvoyants, acrobats and soothsayers, who may have been Gypsy entertainers. One source described them as 'ventriloquists and wizards... who are inspired satanically and pretend to predict the unknown'.[16] More reliable evidence from the fourteenth century shows that the diaspora had reached Greece and the Balkans, taking root in territories from the Bosporus to the Adriatic. West European pilgrims encountered 'Egyptian' fortune-tellers in the Venetian trading colonies of the Peloponnese. The town of Modon (modern Methoni) in particular, a port used by pilgrims to the Holy Land, gained a reputation for its concentration of Gypsy metalworkers, and became known as one of the places called 'Little Egypt'.[17]

Turkish expansion put pressure on eastern Gypsy populations, and stimulated their further dispersal. Bulgaria, Macedonia, and Serbia all had Gypsy immigrants by the late fourteenth century, among confused and contending ethnicities. Some Gypsies from Dalmatia may have ventured westward across the Adriatic. Others pushed north towards Bohemia. Wherever they went, the Gypsies seem to have adopted the religious practices of the prevailing local majority, though without much discipline or fervour. Itinerant, semi-settled, and semi-assimilated Gypsies were identified locally as Muslims or as different kinds of Christians. The Danubian principalities of Wallachia and Moldavia subjected large numbers of Gypsies to slavery, a condition that lasted into the nineteenth century.[18]

A spate of references and sightings in the late fourteenth and early fifteenth centuries documented the appearance of the newcomers in Europe. Chroniclers recorded Gypsies in Croatia by 1362, Serbia by 1378, Bohemia by 1399, Poland by 1401, Germany by 1407, France by 1418, Italy by 1422, Christian Spain by 1425, and the Ukraine by 1428. At Brasov, Romania, the authorities in 1416 gave food and money to the Gypsy 'Lord Emaus' and his companions, who may have been moving westward towards Bohemia.[19] Others entered German lands by way of France, the Low Countries, or along the valley of the Rhine.

German chronicles report the arrival early in the fifteenth century of 'a strange, wandering horde of people...excessively given to thievery...very ugly in appearance', with dark-skinned women wearing silver ear-rings and practising palmistry. The chronicler of Hesse mentions 'Zigeuners' or Gypsies in 1414. At Meissen in 1416 the 'Zingani, a sort of wandering, mischievous people', were driven out on account of their pilfering. They appeared in 1417 in some of the Hanseatic towns along the Baltic and in the vicinity of Hamburg, close to the mouth of the Elbe. Some of them may have been seeking letters of protection from the leaders of Christendom, who were meeting at that time at the Council of Constance (1414–18).[20]

'Ziguener, a malicious people of thieves and sorcerers', arrived at Leipzig in 1418. More 'strange people from Little Egypt' reached Frankfurt that summer, when the city provided them with food. The company comprised about 150 men, women, and children when they reached Augsburg in November 1418. Arranged hierarchically, with leaders known as 'dukes' and 'earls', they claimed to be exiles from 'Little Egypt'.[21] Related groups appeared in Franconia in 1422, and in German Switzerland, where they brandished letters of protection from Pope Martin V and King Sigismund of Luxembourg, 'the king of the Romans'. This time they claimed to be penitent apostates, condemned to a wandering pilgrimage, and told stories about their people's suffering for refusing hospitality to the refugees Mary, Joseph, and the infant Jesus.[22] Another group of Gypsies, perhaps new arrivals from Hungary, appeared at Ratisbon (modern Regensburg) in 1424. Initial offers of hospitality turned sour, as cities across Saxony and Bavaria decided that the Gypsies were no longer welcome.[23]

Gypsies paid scant attention to territorial boundaries, which in any case remained indistinct and unpoliced. Some arrived in France soon after their sighting in Germany, entering from Switzerland, Italy, the Rhineland, or perhaps via coastal havens. They travelled in family groups, sometimes numbering in the dozens. Most were on foot, though Gypsy companies were increasingly equipped with horses and encumbered with baggage.[24]

Strasbourg saw Gypsies as early as 1418.[25] A well-documented group of Gypsies, as many as 120 strong, reached the environs of Mâcon in August 1419, by way of Franche-Comté and Burgundy. Claiming to be travelling to fulfil a penance, they were led by 'Andrew, who calls himself Duke of Little Egypt', and were greeted with charitable alms and refreshments of bread and wine. Despite their imposing titles, the strangers showed few signs of nobility, and impressed some observers by their strange and dishevelled appearance. They were said to have slept in the fields 'like beasts', and to have practised the 'evil arts' of necromancy and palmistry. Their welcome at Mâcon ended in bitterness, as townsmen complained of their deceits.[26]

The Gypsies who reached Sisteron in Provence in October 1419 were initially identified as 'Saracens'. The townsmen provided them with food but would not allow them to enter.[27] Their reputation may have preceded them, and local authorities were glad to see them go. More Gypsies led by 'Andrew, Duke of Little Egypt', bearing letters of protection from the Duke of Savoy, travelled through France to the Low Countries in 1419 and 1420.[28]

The next few years saw Gypsies led by self-styled 'dukes' and lords in various parts of France, from Flanders to the Mediterranean, Alsace to Languedoc. They introduced themselves with letters enjoining hospitality and kindness, supposedly written on their behalf by 'the king of the Romans', the emperor, the pope, and other leaders of Christendom, but almost certainly forged. Some of these letters claimed that the travellers were licensed to steal, though supplies of bread, fish, and beer might meet their needs.[29]

A celebrated band of Gypsies visited the Paris region in the summer of 1427 claiming to be penitential noblemen from Lower Egypt with letters and credentials from the pope. The documentation was briefly effective, but most likely fraudulent. Their story, once again, was that they were Christian refugees who had briefly apostatized, and had been assigned to go 'about the world' for seven years without sleeping in beds. Ecclesiastical authorities were supposed to provide them with money and support. An advance guard of a dozen Gypsies arrived in Paris on horseback, followed by the rest of the company on foot, some 120 in total. They were lodged for three weeks at La Chappelle, Saint-Denys, where people were fascinated by their exotic appearance, their tawny skins, their curly hair, the rings in their ears, and strange costumes. Gypsy fortune-telling excited so much interest that the bishop of Paris declared anyone who had their hands read to be excommunicated. Some fortune-tellers sowed discord by telling people that their spouses had played them false, while others secured money by light-fingeredness and legerdemain.[30]

Another band of forty Gypsies led by a 'Count Thomas' displayed their papal letter at Amiens in 1427, and were rewarded with alms and hospitality.[31] They reappeared at Tournai in 1429, where the townsmen provided them with wine, food, and firewood.[32] There was no mistaking these exotic travellers for ordinary vagrants or vagabonds. They were not common beggars, though not averse to accepting relief from the towns through which they

Figure 1. 'Gypsy Palm Reader', in Bartolommeo della Rocca Cocles, *Complexion, Natur und Eigenschafft eines yeden menschen* (Mainz, 1534)

passed. Another troupe, perhaps led by the aforesaid 'Count Thomas of Little Egypt', obtained hospitality at Nevers in 1436, and a similar group visited Orleans in 1447. The south of France grew accustomed to the peregrinations of Gypsy companies led by alleged 'nobles' who by now had good French names such as Thomas, Michel, and Philippe. Minor conflicts reveal urban authorities divided on whether to accept or expel the 'Egyptiens', who were beginning to strain their patience as well as their resources. The eagerness of chroniclers to record the novelty of the Gypsy presence diminished in the later fifteenth century as 'Egyptiens' became increasingly familiar. Inhabitants of the diocese of Troyes who resorted to Gypsies for healing or divination became subject to penance in 1457, like the Parisians of thirty years earlier.[33]

Italians encountered Gypsies in 1422, when the company led by 'Andrew, Duke of Little Egypt', treated Bologna to a summer spree of freeloading, fortune-telling, and petty theft. Chroniclers again noted their dark complexions, flowing garments, and the rings in their ears. Relations with local inhabitants deteriorated during their two weeks in residence, amid claims of horse-theft and deceit. Curious inhabitants thronged the Gypsies, and authorities threatened fines and excommunication for anyone who went to see them.[34] The Gypsies then moved south towards Rome, by way of Forli, where, joined by another band, their numbers approached 200. They declared their intention to visit Pope Martin V, who had restored the privileges of Jews in Christendom, perhaps believing that he would look kindly on Gypsies as Christian penitents. It is doubtful whether they obtained their wished-for audience, though they somehow obtained letters of protection. When Gypsies showed up at Fermo, near Ancona, in 1430, they allegedly brandished these papal letters.[35]

Most parts of the Italian peninsula became accustomed to Gypsies by the mid-fifteenth century. They were reported at Ferrara and Reggio in the 1440s, at Modena and Milan in the 1470s.[36] If family names are indicative, the baptism of children Francesco Zingaro and Andrea Zingaro at Pisa in the early 1480s points to a Gypsy presence in Renaissance Tuscany.[37] More Gypsies settled in the southern Kingdom of Naples, and the rapidly growing city of Naples soon had its 'Zingari' district. The islands of Corsica, Sicily, and Sardinia all had small Gypsy populations by 1480.[38]

More so-called counts, dukes, and princes of Little Egypt, some with trains of a hundred or more followers, enjoyed the hospitality and tried the patience of authorities elsewhere in fifteenth-century Europe. In Spain the government of Alfonso V of Aragon gave a safe-conduct pass to 'Don Johan of Little Egypt' in 1425, and the same year instructed townsfolk near Zaragoza to return to 'Count Thomas of Egypt' two dogs they had stolen from him.[39] By 1453, the year Byzantium fell to the Ottomans, there were Gypsies in most parts of continental Europe. The Turkish takeover of Greek and Venetian settlements, like Modon, which fell in 1500, propelled some Gypsies to itinerancy yet again.[40] Further migrations followed, as Gypsies were expelled from place to place, and sought refuge and opportunity in pastures new. The reported presence of four 'Egyptians' on board the third voyage of Christopher Columbus in 1498 indicates the expansion of their world.[41]

Bans and Punishments

The curiosity and hospitality that marked early dealing with Gypsies turned sour by the end of the fifteenth century. Public policy became hostile, as anti-Gypsy prejudice hardened. Unknown numbers moved from one unwelcoming realm to another, as the powers of Renaissance Europe attempted to curtail or export their Gypsy problem. With almost every jurisdiction imposing bans and penalties, there was little place for Gypsies to find safe haven. Borders and frontiers were permeable, but Gypsies found few areas free of harassment and persecution.[42]

Later generations of Gypsies, born while travelling in Europe, lacked the plausible exoticism that had benefited earlier migrants. Writers became more scathing about their credentials. When the German scholar Sebastian Münster (1489–1552) reluctantly included 'Züginer' in his *Cosmographia Universalis*, a global encyclopedia first published in 1544, he remarked that they barely merited mention alongside more virtuous and excellent peoples. Their names in various languages—'Egyptians', 'Tartars', 'Cinganes', 'Saracens', 'Errones' (meaning wanderers), 'vagabondz', or 'diseurs de bonn aventure' (fortune-tellers)—reflected their infamy. Münster had read his chronicles, and had seen Gypsies himself at Heidelberg, so his opinions assumed some authority. He declared the belief that Gypsies emerged from 'Little Egypt' to be false. Rather, the so-called Egyptians of his day had been born in Germany or France. He found them dark, dirty, and foully dressed, of no country and no religion. They lived by thievery, and by the fortune-telling skills of their women. They spoke whatever language was locally used, although they also retained a 'jargon' among themselves. Their identity became further clouded as they allowed men and women of various vagrant origins to join them. All they deserved was condemnation and contempt.[43] English authors of the late sixteenth and early seventeenth centuries were just as dismissive of 'counterfeit' Gypsy ethnicity.[44]

The French Catholic controversialist Jean Talpin likewise excoriated Gypsies as idle vermin, and described them (through his English translator in 1574) as 'a people drawn together from many places, bearing the name of Gypsies or Bohemiens, who, much less that they ever saw Egypt, but know not where it standeth'.[45] If the Gypsies had once been immigrants or asylum-seekers, that history was largely forgotten.

The late-Renaissance polymath Philip Camerarius (1537–1624) also became convinced that 'Aegyptians (otherwise called Gypsies) or Bohemians' were frauds:

> for these gadders are none else but comrades and companions of thieves, and a rascally crew of idle, unthrifty, and cozening persons, that never came out of the East or other far countries, but from the neighbour people, and out of divers countries, who gather together by companies in the fields, and there take up their lodgings, running into villages, to markets, and other dwelling places; yea sometimes slip into towns, and into cities, where they truck, change, deceive, play at fast-and-loose, filch, fetch over finely, and making as if they were skillful in palmistry, laugh at people in their sleeves, looking upon the line of their hands, and telling them their good fortune, draw a living out of such cheating tricks, and keep themselves fat and in good liking; but all that they do is to bring them ill fortune that they come near.

The Gypsies, by this jaded account, were 'prating and cozening fellows', a 'race of deceivers', and 'players at fast-and loose, who are suffered to beguile, to steal, to rob by the highway, with all freedom from punishment'.[46] It was the duty of royal, imperial, and municipal authorities to suppress them. (Fast-and-loose was a betting game involving a belt or garter and a stick, well known for its deceptive trickery.[47])

German cities turned against Gypsies in the later fifteenth century, as local lords attempted to ban them from their lands. Imperial Diets ordered their expulsion. The Elector of Brandenburg banned Gypsies from his territory in 1482, and other jurisdictions made them outlaws. In 1497 Gypsies were accused of spying for the Ottomans, and a series of laws and edicts sought their punishment and exclusion from the Holy Roman Empire. As many as 146 German anti-Gypsy decrees have been counted between 1497 and 1774, but their repetition was a sign of failure. Enforcement was erratic until the later seventeenth century, when German attitudes towards Gypsies severely hardened.[48] Some German Gypsies moved east into Poland, where wanderers known as 'Philistines' and 'Egyptians' encountered state repression.[49]

Authorities at Lucerne, Switzerland, stiffened measures against Gypsies in the 1470s, and in 1510 and 1525 threatened them with expulsion or hanging. Geneva sought their expulsion in 1477, and again in 1514 and 1532.[50] Similar anti-Gypsy measures were enacted in Denmark in 1536, 1554, and 1561, and in England in 1531, 1554, and 1563. Moravia in 1538, Bohemia in 1541, and Poland in 1557 and 1578 also sought to expel Gypsies from their jurisdiction.[51] Dutch territories followed varying strategies, some giving Gypsies safe conduct, and others ordering their expulsion.[52] Many of these measures coincided with concerns about unemployment, destitution, and vagabondage, amid population growth and economic disruption, but Gypsies faced harsher punishments than the ordinary itinerant poor. Vagrancy was a state of moral, social, and economic delinquency, but Gypsies were condemned by their inherent condition, for who they were rather than for what they did.

In Italy, the powers of Venice and Milan took the lead in attempting to control Gypsies. Milanese edicts in 1493 and 1506 banned Gypsies from entering the Duchy and ordered the expulsion of all present. New edicts in 1517 and 1523 increased the penalties to include fines and torture, and further proscribed Gypsies in 1534 by threatening them with death. Modena, Bologna, Florence, and Savoy also passed decrees against Gypsies between 1524 and 1572, signalling that 'Cingani', 'Cingari', 'Cingali', 'Cinguli', 'Zingari', or 'Aegyptiaci' were undesirable. They were blasted as rogues, vagabonds, thieves, and sorcerers, and were blamed for problems of disorder, vagrancy, immorality, and crime, though some had permits and protection.[53] Venetian orders of expulsion in 1549, 1558, and 1588 banned 'Cingani', and in extreme cases permitted their killing with impunity. Gypsy men were liable to serve ten years in the galleys, simply for being Gypsies, and after 1588 anyone who sheltered them was also threatened with galley service. Well-behaved Gypsies were allowed to traverse Venetian territories under licence, but not to enter the city of Venice.[54] Repression intensified in many Italian territories in the 1560s, including the Papal States, which banned Gypsies from the Holy City in 1566.[55] The Adriatic city of Senigallia, controlled by the dukes of Urbino, also adopted increasingly harsh measures to expel or eliminate Gypsies between the 1550s and the 1580s.[56]

The Kingdom of Naples attempted to expel Gypsies in 1559, 1569, 1575, and 1585, but failed to dislodge those who had become semi-settled in the metalworking economy, with permits or local protection. Several Neapolitan court cases hinged on whether a 'Zingaro' had abandoned his traditional life of vagabondage and thieving, and adopted instead a 'Christian' demeanour with settled housing and stable employment. Resourceful Gypsies negotiated spaces in the economy of transit that allowed them to avoid deportation.[57] Similarly detailed cases from northern Italy in the 1580s considered the itinerary and alleged criminality of travelling 'Cingani', 'Egiziani', and 'Boemi', arguing whether they were liable to punishment under earlier edicts and bans. Lawyers, witnesses, and defendants disputed whether particular Gypsies had renounced 'la vita da Cingano', and whether Venetian or Veronese juris-diction applied. The evidence reveals the movement of bands of Gypsy travellers between the mountain lakes and the shores of the Adriatic, their exploits as thieves and fortune-tellers, and their occasional clashes with authority.[58] Governments reiterated repressive ordinances in response to incidents and alarms, but proved incapable of solving the Gypsy problem. At Modena and elsewhere, they discovered that many of the loathed 'Zingari' had been born within the province and so could not be expelled, a develop-ment similarly noted in Elizabethan England.[59]

Similar policies prevailed on the Iberian peninsula. The newly united Spain of Ferdinand and Isabella had no sooner dispatched the Marranos and the Moriscos (Iberian Jews and Moors) when it turned on the 'Egypcianos' or Gypsies, who had multiplied in recent decades. An ordinance of 1499 described 'the Egyptians who wander our realms' as families 'lacking trades or any other means of support, apart from begging, stealing, and bartering things, deceiving people and engaging in sorcery, fortune-telling, and other activities which are neither proper nor decent'. It gave the Gypsies sixty days to leave the kingdom, or else find masters and settled occupations. Those who disobeyed faced a hundred lashes and banishment for a first offence, confinement in chains and notching of the ear for a second offence, and enslavement for a third. This was an attempt at national purification, but it stopped short of the death penalty. Repeated renewals of this ordinance indicate its ineffectiveness. Some Gypsies obtained licences and dispensa-tions, but most simply evaded the law.[60]

Perceiving Gypsies as thieves and vagabonds, Spanish territories repeat-edly passed laws to expel them or punish them. 'Gitanos' or 'Bomians' were proscribed, banned, or excluded by the Cortes de Monzon in Aragon in 1510, 1512, 1542, and 1553, the Cortes de Toledo in 1525 and 1560, the Cortes de Madrid in 1528, 1534, and 1551, the Cortes de Valladolid in 1542, and by the kingdom of Navarre in 1549. If they could not be got rid of, Gypsy women were to be flogged, and the men sent to the galleys. Gypsy men aged between 20 and 50 faced six years behind the oars, a sentence that few could expect to survive.[61]

In common with other European powers, Spanish regimes identified 'Egipcianos' or 'Gitanos' as 'scandalous, footloose and unregulated' thieves and vagabonds, 'a lawless people...full of vice'. Further enactments in 1566, 1594, 1610, 1619, and 1633 sought their punishment and expulsion.[62] Advisors to the Spanish monarchs repeatedly urged bans and exclusions. The Toledo cleric Pedro Salazar de Mendoza condemned 'los Gitanos' in 1618 as false and dangerous vagabonds who spoke a vulgar jargon. Juan de Quinones in 1631 similarly berated them as anti-Christian beggars and brigands who exploited popular superstition. Several authorities likened Gypsies to 'moriscos', and wanted them similarly suppressed.[63]

Despite the bustle and bluster, these laws and campaigns had limited effect. Attempts to assimilate the Gypsies or make them lead sedentary lives were no more successful than hauling them before the Inquisition or condemning them to the galleys. Local authorities continued to treat them with ambivalence, in some cases with indulgence. When English diplomats visited Spain in 1604 to conclude a peace treaty, their hosts arranged for them to be entertained by 'a company of Gypsies...singing and dancing, playing, and showing divers feats of acuity'.[64] Though officialdom sought their removal, local patronage ensured that Gypsies were sometimes rewarded rather than punished.

A few Iberian Gypsies made their way across the Atlantic, most likely involuntarily. Portuguese attempts to expel Gypsies in 1526, 1538, and 1557 led to a few being shipped to colonial outposts in Africa and Brazil. More would follow in the seventeenth century.[65] It was not Spanish policy to transport Gypsies to the 'Indies', but several appeared in the colonial silver cities of Peru. In 1581 Philip II ordered Gypsies found anywhere in the Spanish New World to be removed, lest they contaminate the native populations.[66]

French laws against Gypsies also exhibited increasing severity. French officials had behaved courteously, even generously, towards Gypsies in the past, but the sixteenth century saw tightening of screws. Few now believed that the Gypsies were penitents, let alone itinerant aristocrats, or that they came from Egypt. Instead, the alternative myth gathered force, that they were simply vagrant ne'r-do-wells, perhaps French or Majorcan, who adopted the guise and manner of Gypsies to further their nefarious ends. The century that passed from the Gypsies' first arrival allowed time enough for some to become assimilated, and for confusion to spread about their origins. It was hard to decide whether Gypsies were a distinctive people or imposters practised in deceit.[67]

The French crackdown began in 1504, when the government of Louis XII (1498–1515) issued instructions that all so-called Egyptiens should be removed. The order was made in response to disturbances at Rouen, but applied generally throughout the realm. Henceforth, it was an offence to be a Gypsy in France, although sanctions against them were only intermittently applied. A series of edicts, ordinances, and directions sought their punishment and expulsion, with provision to send Gypsies to the galleys.[68] Gypsies were not easily rounded up, however, and many continued to travel. Local magistrates were lax in response to central direction, minor aristocrats afforded some Gypsies protection, and others were able to survive through ingenuity, intimidation, or displays of forged testimonials. As elsewhere, the Gypsies enjoyed ambivalent relationships with the communities through which they passed, being loathed for their pilfering, and feared as possible carriers of disease, but also patronized for their skills, including the telling of fortunes. Sixteenth-century sources say little about a distinctive Gypsy language, so presumably these itinerants managed to conduct their business in French.

One likely side effect of Louis XII's hard line was the migration of certain Gypsy bands across the Channel, for the first Gypsies appeared in England around 1505.[69] Turn and turn about, a generation later, Henry VIII's attempts to expel England's Gypsies may have returned some to France.[70] French measures against Gypsies included decrees in 1510 and 1539 threatening 'ces miserables voyageurs' with 'peine de la hard' or lashing with knotted thongs.[71] The regime of Francis I (1515–47), like Henry VIII's in England, banned Gypsies from entering the kingdom, and required all those present to leave.[72] Neighbouring countries were not consulted about accepting them.

French authorities made another attempt at control and exclusion in 1561 when an ordinance of Charles IX (1560–74) gave the Gypsies just two months to depart the realm; remaining Gypsy women were supposed to have their heads shaved, men would lose their hair and beards, and able-bodied men faced three years' service in the galleys.[73] This became the standard punishment for the next century or more, humiliating Gypsies by cropping their hair, and sending their men to row for the navy. Some Gypsies served as irregular soldiers and others became almost indistinguishable from brigands amid the social disturbances of the later sixteenth-century. They were often confused with homeless wanderers, beggars, and discharged soldiers, prompting magistrates at Bayonne in 1574 to require 'les bohêmes vagabonds' removed from their territory.[74] Gypsies were no longer welcome, and some authors thought the galleys too good for them.[75]

All was not darkness, however, as Gypsies still had supporters and admirers. A finely rendered contemporary drawing depicts 'l'Égyptienne quy rendist santé part art de medicine au roy d'Esoce abandonné des médecins' ('the

Egyptian whose medical arts restored to health the king of Scots, who had been given up by doctors'). It shows a handsome well-dressed woman, with a formidable turban surmounting her hanging locks, the apparent embodiment of secret knowledge.[76] Some Gypsies served as irregular troops in the French wars of religion, and it was during these troubled times that Pechon de Ruby wrote his picaresque account of Gypsy life, *La Vie généreuse des mercelots, geux et boemiens*, telling how his hero joined a company of 'Egyptiens' near Nantes and took part in their exploits.[77]

Sporadic repression of Gypsies quickened in 1606 when Henry IV (1589–1610) attempted to disperse 'les compagnies de Bohémiens' in northern and western France who wandered as vagrants and vagabonds. Echoing earlier orders, the edict of 1606 gave 'tous ceux qui s'apellent Bömiens ou Egyptiens', as well as their families and followers, two months to quit the kingdom, on pain of corporal punishment and delivery to the galleys. Gypsy bands were smaller now, as they were in England, and perhaps more adept at keeping out of trouble. They learned to play off one authority against another, sometimes exhibiting letters of protection. Gypsies risked prosecution simply by virtue of being Gypsies, but in practice, as elsewhere, their treatment varied according to local conditions and the severity of other crimes of which they were suspected.[78]

A violent dispute among French Gypsies erupted into public view at Paris in 1612 when women associated with the Gypsy captain Jean Hiérosme became involved in an affair of passion with other 'Egyptians'. One of them was found murdered in the Seine. Three Gypsy women were gruesomely executed at the Pont Saint-Michel, and the captain and his company faced perpetual banishment. The Parlement of Paris sought to generalize these penalties, ordering again that all Gypsy women should have their heads shaved and the men be consigned to the galleys. As so often happened, the entire collective was made responsible for the crimes of individuals, further souring their public image.[79]

Additional enactments in 1621, 1631, and 1640 forbade 'Egyptiens et Bohèmes' from travelling or lodging anywhere in the French kingdom. Offenders were to be scourged, branded, and banished in perpetuity, without regard to any passports or certificates that they might present. By cutting their hair and by removing their costume, the authorities attempted to strip the Gypsies of their outward distinguishing characteristics and their dignity.[80] Local governments also undertook to suppress the Gypsies, like the Synod of Saint-Malo in 1618, which condemned people called 'Bohémiens' who told fortunes. The southern dioceses of Albi and Carcassone similarly sought the expulsion of Gypsies who pillaged the local peasantry.[81] Occasional references to Gypsies in registers of baptisms and burials suggest some measure of assimilation, and some French 'Bohémiens' were known to have secured influential godparents.[82] Despite prevailing prejudices, and notwithstanding efforts to expel them, various mercenary captains 'se disant Bohémien ou Egyptiens' entered military service and gained local respectability.[83]

Little more is heard of Gypsies in France until the reign of Louis XIV (1643–1715). Another series of edicts from 1660 to 1666 stiffened the laws against vagrants, and funnelled able-bodied wanderers to the galleys. The men were supposed to serve in chains for three years, while the women were to be whipped and sent packing. Another royal decree in 1673 more specifically targeting Gypsies ('vagabonds dits Bohesmes et gens san aveu') gave them a month to leave the kingdom or else face galley service.[84] An intriguing suggestion, requiring research, is that the severity of pressure on Gypsies rose and fell with the state's demand for rowers in the galleys.[85]

The long history of attempts by the French state to bring Gypsies under control culminated in the work of Jean-Baptiste Colbert, Louis XIV's most energetic minister. A declaration of May 1682 affected Gypsies by requiring all fortune-tellers, diviners, and practitioners of pretended magic to quit the realm or else be subject to corporal punishment.[86] A weightier declaration of July 1682 sought a comprehensive solution to the Gypsy problem. In recognition of the failure of previous attempts to compel the Gypsies to quit the kingdom, the order now targeted the 'gentilshommes et seigneurs justiciers' who gave them shelter and protection. Vigorously asserting the authority of the Crown, the declaration threatened landholders who harboured Gypsies with royal disfavour and the loss of their fiefs and privileges. As for the Gypsies themselves ('vagabonds et gens appelez Boëmes'), they would be subject to a new wave of repression designed to bring them to order. Gypsy men would be rounded up and put in chains, to serve in the galleys in perpetuity. Women found leading a Gypsy way of life would have their heads shaved, and would then be removed to workhouses or poorhouses; recidivists and hard cases would be whipped and banished. Gypsy children would be taken into care, to be brought up away from antisocial influences. If Gypsies would not voluntarily give up their way of life, the state would quicken them to that end. This mixture of exclusion, domination, and assimilation was supposed to make the Gypsies disappear, though it only increased their discomforts.[87]

As usual, the bark of authority was worse than its bite. Gypsies proved impossible to eliminate or subdue, and customary protections and interactions continued to prevail. Local magistrates cooperated only patchily with the demands of the Crown, and Gypsies roamed the land with only occasional arrests.[88] By the late seventeenth century Gypsy dancers had established themselves in Paris in the faubourg Saint Germain, and in 1704 a group of Gypsies was briefly tolerated at Versailles.[89] Village communities put up with the depredations of Gypsies, or achieved a practical accommodation with them, without involving the central authorities. Some even welcomed them, as itinerant metalworkers, horse-dealers, entertainers, and fortune-tellers.[90] The French, like other powers with new-world possessions, sent some of their Gypsies into service overseas. More than two dozen 'Bohemians' arrived as forced labourers in the French colony of Louisiana in 1720, establishing a short-lived Gypsy community.[91]

European laws against Gypsies were widespread and often copied from state to state, but to little cumulative effect. Their frequent reiteration speaks to their impotence, as enforcement was weak and haphazard. Early modern regimes lacked the police power and administrative reach needed to secure compliance, and local officials were often unwilling to proceed against Gypsies. Wherever detailed records survive of cases involving Gypsies, they reveal ambiguities in the travellers' status and identity, and flexibility in the application of justice. The English experience in the sixteenth century mirrored that of Western Europe in this regard, though England did not share in the later tightening of repression. Gypsies suffered from prejudice and oppression, sharpened by instruments of law, but it would be a mistake to identify this period as one of 'intense genocidal persecution', or to see the sixteenth century as 'the first Gypsy holocaust'. Inflamed characterizations of this sort may energize contemporary constituencies, but are of little help in understanding the past.[92]

Gypsies in Early Modern Scotland

Scottish responses to the problems posed by Gypsies bear comparison to those in continental Europe and England. Gypsies reached Scotland at the beginning of the sixteenth century, perhaps a year or two before their first appearance in the southern kingdom. They most likely arrived from across the North Sea, before drifting into other parts of Britain. The reception of

Gypsies in Scotland followed a similar course to dealings elsewhere, with initial courtesy and curiosity giving way to hostility and expulsion. Detailed records from the reigns of James IV (1488–1513) and James V (1513–42) reveal some of their names and stories.[93]

The first party of Gypsies to reach Scotland presented themselves as exotic aristocrats who needed hospitality. This ruse had worked before in Germany and France, and it still yielded results. In April 1505 King James IV disbursed ten French crowns (a sizeable sum worth seven Scottish pounds) to 'the Egyptians' who visited his court at Stirling. A few months later he issued letters of protection to Anthony Gagino, 'count of Little Egypt', and his company to travel as pilgrims to the closely allied kingdom of Denmark. The Gypsies appeared to be reputable international travellers, in a circuit linking Scandinavia and Britain, but they also earned their keep as entertainers.[94]

Scottish treasury accounts from May 1529 record forty shillings given to 'the Egyptians that danced before the king at Holyrood House'. These may have been 'Count Martin, a native of Lesser Egypt, and his train', who received a royal safe conduct in March 1530. Scottish testimonials and letters of protection of this sort showed up later among Gypsies in Henry VIII's England, though some were suspected as forgeries.[95] Gypsies passed easily between Scotland, Ireland, England, and the Continent, across seas and borders that were more like zones of transaction than barriers to movement. The ready availability of shipping facilitated the circulation of goods and people among the various territories of north-west Europe. In Ireland in 1516 the earl of Kildare gave rewards to some 'Egyptians' who may have come over from Scotland. More 'Egyptians' arrived in Ireland in 1541, 'driven from Scotland by stress of weather'.[96] Few other traces survive of Gypsies in Ireland, where the government proposed in 1584 that no women should wear 'any great kerchiefs, after the Gypsy manner'.[97]

The Gypsies in Scotland lost credit when some of them became involved in crimes and scandals. When Gypsies at Aberdeen stole two silver spoons in 1527, their leader, Eken Jaks, was ordered to make restitution. When the Gypsy women Barbara Dya Baptista and Helen Andree were accused of a similar theft in 1539, their 'captain' George Faw spoke in their defence, and they were found not guilty. As troubles with Gypsies continued in February 1540, the Council of Aberdeen ordered George Faw, his brother John, and all their party to be banished from the town.[98]

The Faws, however, had friends in high places, and in that same month of February 1540 the Scottish Privy Council issued a writ enjoining authorities throughout the kingdom to assist John Faw, 'lord and earl of Little Egypt', in maintaining his authority within his company. There was, apparently, a division in their ranks, with some of the Gypsies robbing and deserting the others. The breakaway group included Sebastiane Lalow (or Lawlor), Anteane Donea, Satona Fingo, Nona Finco (or Fingo), Phillip Hatseyggow, Towla Bailzow (or Baillie), Grasta Neyn (or Nany), Geleyr Bailzow (or Baillie), Bernard Beige, Demeo Matskalla, Notfaw Lawlor, and Martyn Femine. The state was interested in maintaining order among these trouble-some 'Egyptians', and also hoped to get rid of them by 'furthering of them forth of our realm to the parts beyond sea'. The records reveal difficulties in pronouncing and writing exotic Gypsy names. These were not 'inventive tinkers', emerging from domestic disruptions, but troublesome foreigners liable to be deported.[99]

The Gypsy leader cited in February 1540 must have died soon after, for another writ in May recognized the authority of 'John Wanne son and heir of the late John Fall earl of lesser Egypt' over all the Gypsies in Scotland. (Wanne may be a scribal mistake, however, for this name was not heard again.) Division between the Faw (or Faa or Fall) group and the dissidents would resonate in north Britain for more than a decade.[100]

Official Scottish policy towards Gypsies oscillated between favour and condemnation. If there is any truth to the story that King James V, who visited France in 1536–7, was cured there by a female Gypsy healer, it would only have enhanced their reputation. No credit can be given to the legend, attractive though it may be, that James V joined in Gypsy revels in disguise, and only turned against them when they dismissed him from their festiv-ities.[101] More likely the Gypsies proved exasperating, and European anti-Gypsy legislation provided a model for their suppression. Citing 'the great thefts and skaiths [hurts] done by the said Egyptians upon our sovereign lord's lieges', an Order in Council in June 1541 cancelled all letters of pro-tection, and ordered all Gypsies to leave Scotland within thirty days, on pain of death.[102] Some of them may have drifted south.

The Gypsies, however, did not all leave Scotland, and several were recorded in the reign of Mary Queen of Scots (1542–67). In 1554 a large group of 'Egyptians' obtained 'remission for the slaughter of Ninian Small' at Linton, close to the border with England. They were named as members of the Faw clan: Andrew Faw, 'captain of the Egyptians', his sons George, Robert, and Anthony Faw, and John Faw; Andrew and Nicholas George; Sebastian, George, Julie, and John Colyne; James Haw (or Hair); and John and George

Brown'.[103] George Faw, 'Egyptian', appeared again in the records of Dumfries in June 1564, when he paid back a loan of over twenty Scots pounds, for which he had pledged some items of luxury taffeta and velvet and a couple of small gold rings. The record speaks to his integration into the culture of commerce, with good credit and good connections, and shows that sixteenth-century Gypsies were not necessarily all poor and marginal.[104]

The early part of the reign of James VI (1567–1625), when the king was a child, was a disturbed and violent time in Scottish history, but not necessarily bad for Gypsies. The authorities again sought their expulsion or assimilation, but neither goal was achieved. In 1573 the Council ordered all 'vagabond idle and counterfeit people of diverse nations falsely named Egyptians' either to settle into some honest craft or industry, or to 'depart forth of this realm' forever. Any who failed to comply would be scourged from parish to parish until 'they be utterly removed forth of this realm'. The government matched this rhetoric with another edict in 1576 ordering local authorities to prosecute 'Egyptians' for all crimes and offences of which they were suspected. Any officials who permitted the Gypsies 'to wander and remain' would themselves face sanctions 'as favourers and sustainers of thieves and murderers'. Meanwhile the Scottish parliament sent mixed signals by including 'idle people calling themselves Egyptians' among vagrants to be punished as vagabonds, rather than members of a banned group to be prosecuted as felons.[105] Similar contradictions appeared in Tudor England.

A new Scottish statute of 1579 clarified the matter and intensified the pressure on

> all idle persons going about the country of this realm, using subtle, crafty and unlawful plays—as jugglery, fast-and-loose, and such others, the idle people calling themselves Egyptians, or any other that fancy themselves to have knowledge of prophecy, charming, or other abused sciences, whereby they persuade people that they can tell their weirds, deaths, and fortunes, and such other fantastical imaginations.

Gypsies that 'have any goods of their own to live on' faced imprisonment, and the rest risked loss of their ears, followed by banishment, and death if they returned. The ratification of this statute in 1592 employed the Scottish word 'sorners' (meaning moochers or spongers), and referred again to 'counterfeit Egyptians', a phrase derived from Elizabethan English law.[106] Subsequent orders referred to 'counterfeit limmers' (rogues or scoundrels), 'counterfeit thieves', and 'counterfeit vagabonds', suggesting that deceit was central to the Gypsy character, and that they were no less real for being 'counterfeit'.[107]

The government of James VI discovered what regimes elsewhere already knew, that penal laws like these, in practice, 'received little or no effect or execution'. The Gypsies simply defied authority or received mere token punishments. The Council tried again with an ordinance in 1603, followed by a fearsome statute in 1609 that sought 'the destruction of the proscribed Egyptians'. All 'letters, protections and warrants' on their behalf were again annulled, and all 'vagabonds called Egyptians' were required to leave Scotland and never to return. Henceforth it would be legal for any of the king's subjects to 'take, apprehend, imprison, and execute to death, all manner of Egyptians, as well men as women, as common, notorious, and condemned thieves, only to be tried by one assize, that they are called, known, repute[d], and holden Egyptians'.[108] This order mirrored the measures of some contemporary European states, but went much further than the laws of Tudor and Stuart England.

As elsewhere, the Gypsies were deemed felons simply for being Gypsies. Anyone who ventured to 'reset, receive, supply, or entertain any of the said Egyptians' also risked prosecution. But, as in other parts of Britain and Europe, the impact of policy depended upon its enforcement. As the Scottish Privy Council soon realized, the Gypsies evaded the law by scattering to 'obscure places of the country', and sheltering under local protection. 'Their thievish and juggling tricks and falsities' were as bad as ever, and they continued to 'shamefully and mischantly abuse the simple and ignorant people by telling of fortunes and using of charms' with apparent impunity. The government called for their punishment and suppression, but the follow-up was weak and inconsistent.[109]

One of the first prosecutions under the act of 1609 was of Elizabeth Warrok of Edinburgh, for being 'a common vagabond and follower of the Gypsies, and taking part with them in all their thefts and juggleries these ten years past'. Her punishment was to be scourged through the city, then banned from re-entering, 'under the pain of drowning'.[110] Other victims of this crackdown included members of the Fa (or Faw) family—Moses, David, Robert, and John (known as Willie)—'for abiding and remaining within this kingdom, they being Egyptians'. Moses Faw represented himself as a semi-assimilated Gypsy who dissociated himself from 'the thievish form of doing of that infamous society'. Born and educated in Scotland, and by now a man of substance, he protested that parliament never intended the act to apply to 'honest, lawful and true persons' like himself. He even found sureties for a thousand pounds to obey the law, to appear whenever summoned, and to have no dealings with other Egyptians, so long as he could stay in the country. Notwithstanding these protestations, Moses and the others were tried at Edinburgh in July 1611 on charges of armed robbery with hagbuts and pistolets in Selkirkshire, and all four Gypsies were sentenced to be hanged.[111]

Other members of the Faw family suffered under the crackdown on Gypsies. 'Captain Harry Faw' and his son James were targets of a justiciary commission later in 1611, and James and Alexander Faa were tried as 'thievish vaga-bonds and Egyptians' in 1613. It made no difference that their mother Elspeth Maxwell (presumed partner of Captain Harry) was 'natural sister to the Laird of Newark'.[112] Some of the Faws moved north, though not beyond the reach of the law. John Faw the elder called 'Mickle' (meaning big), John Faw the younger called Little John Faw, Katherine Faw spouse to the late Murdo Brown, and Agnes Faw sister to Little John, faced trial at Scalloway, Shetland, in August 1612. They were all indicted for the murder of Murdo Brown, and for theft, sorcery, and fortune-telling. In addition to these offences, Little John was charged with incest with his wife's sister and daughter, and for adultery with Katherine Faw. Katherine, who acknowledged stabbing her husband, was sentenced to be cast off a cliff and drowned in the sea, but the rest of the family appear to have been acquitted.[113] Little John Faw lived to offend again.

Sentences of death were passed against more members of the Faw kindred in July 1616, when the 'Egyptians' John Faa, James Faa his son, Moses Baillie, and Helen Brown, spouse to William Baillie, were found guilty of 'con-temptuously repairing and abiding with the realm', contrary to the statute of 1609. All four were sentenced to hang, 'to be examples to others of their race and unhappy company to eschew the like hereafter'. They were, how-ever, reprieved to banishment, to suffer death if they ever returned.[114]

No such mercy extended to Captain John Faa, Robert Faa, Samuel Faa, John Faa the younger, Andrew Faa, William Faa, Robert Brown, and Gawin Trotter, 'all Egyptians, vagabonds, and common thieves', who were arraigned for remaining in the kingdom of Scotland, contrary to the statute, in January 1624. This time the fact of their being Gypsies was guilt enough, and all were condemned to die. Before proceeding, the court took advice of the Lords of the Council, but the next day the men were executed and their possessions forfeited to the Crown.[115]

Their wives and dependants were also arrested, and Helen the widow of the late Captain John Faa, Elspeth his niece, Lucrece wife of James Brown,

Katherine the widow of Edward Faa, Margaret his daughter, Meriore wife of James Faa, Jeane widow of Andrew Faa, Helen widow of Robert Campbell, Isobel widow of Robert Brown, Margaret Valentine widow of John Wilson, and Elspeth daughter of Henry Faa were similarly charged as Egyptians. All were found guilty, and sentenced to the gender-specific punishment of drowning. Also in court, but under age, were Edward Faa's son Alexander, John Faa's sons John and Francis, and Robert Brown's younger brother Harry. Sentence against the women was suspended, however, pending further review, and their punishment was remitted to immediate and perpetual banishment.[116] There were not many places for these Gypsies to go. They may have melted into the Scottish landscape, taken ship to the Continent, or walked south into England, where the law was not much more welcoming.

There was scant relief for Scottish Gypsies under Charles I (1625–49), though little appetite for their execution. More were sentenced to banishment in January 1626, despite the fact that they had committed no crime. (They were cleared of suspicion of fire-raising.)[117] 'Strong, able, and counterfeit limmers called Egyptians', who might technically be subject to the death penalty, would now be pressed as soldiers to fight in foreign wars. Royal orders in 1627 and 1628 sought to fill regiments for service in Denmark with Scottish Gypsies, vagabonds, masterless men, and loiterers.[118]

Trouble followed many of these 'limmers' and 'sorners'. In August 1628 the 'Egyptian' Patrick Faa was taken 'with the bloody hand' after shooting the cooper William Turnbull through the head with a pistol, and killing him. He was committed to trial, but the outcome is unknown.[119] More 'vagabond and counterfeit thieves and limmers called the Egyptians' were convicted at Haddington, east of Edinburgh, in November 1636. Deemed too 'troublesome and burdensome' to keep in prison, the men were ordered to be hanged and the women drowned, except women with children would be branded as vagrants and whipped through the town.[120] The 'Egyptian' James Faa, son of Moses Faa (perhaps the man hanged in 1611), agreed in 1637 to military service abroad rather than face banishment or execution as a Gypsy.[121]

The revolutionary decades of the mid-seventeenth century saw little improvement in the life of Scottish Gypsies. Their condition is suggested by payments recorded at Stirling in 1656 'for ropes to bind the Egyptians, 2s. 8d.'. In June 1657 'an Egyptian called Phaa [Faa] was executed upon the castle hill of Edinburgh for murder', and the following month seven Gypsies, men and women, 'were scourged through Edinburgh and banished the 'nation', with sentence of death should they ever return.[122] Other Scottish Gypsies were among the 'strong and idle beggars, Egyptians, common and notorious whores and thieves' who were transported to the New World colonies in the 1650s and 1660s.[123]

After four generations in Scotland, the Faw family of Gypsies was neither settled nor civilized, according to mainstream authorities. Alexander, Henry, Robert, Ninian, Thomas, and William Faw were among fifteen 'idle vaga-bonds' named in 1671 for 'stealing, sorning and oppressing' in the Border region. Some of these Gypsies lived like brigands, armed with swords and guns, and Scotland suffered from their depredations.[124] Violent clashes between rival Gypsy factions compounded the disorder. A battle in Tweedsdale in1676 pitched the Faws and the Shaws on the one side against the Baillies and Browns on the other. Another mêlée in October 1677 left 'Old Sandy Faw' and his wife dead, and his brother George 'very dangerously wounded'. A later chronicler reported that three infamous Gypsies were hanged at Edinburgh in 1679 as a consequence of the murders the previous year.[125]

Though harsh anti-Gypsy laws remained in force, Gypsies in later seventeenth-century Scotland were unlikely to be punished for who they were, rather than for what they did. Neither Scotland nor the rest of the British Isles embraced the new wave of anti-Gypsy sentiment that devel-oped in continental Europe. The Gypsies Gilbert, Hugh, James, John, and Margaret Baillie were among Scottish prisoners transported from Greenock to NewYork in October 1682, though their specific transgression was unre-corded.[126] When 'Captain'William Baillie and his Gypsy gang were arraigned at Edinburgh in 1698, it was because of their record of theft and violence, not because they were reputed Egyptians. Witnesses described them speak-ing 'a jargon canting Egyptian language which none but themselves can understand' (most likely some kind of Euro-Romani), but the court was more interested in their deeds, which ranged from sheep theft and armed robbery to murder. Most of the male defendants were sentenced to hang, but 'Captain William', a Gypsy with 'the character of a gentleman', was reserved for a separate trial. The court heard that he had previously been sentenced to transportation for military service, but had led a mutiny on the ship bound for Flanders, killing several men in the process. But remarkably, despite abundant evidence of a lifetime of crime, he again escaped execu-tion. William Baillie appears to have been charismatic and well connected, for all he suffered was branding on his cheek and exile to America.[127] Penal transportation took several other Gypsy criminals to the American colonies

over the next few decades, under pain of death should they return. Border
Gypsies of the Faw clan became notorious and romanticized outlaws in the
early eighteenth century, to be chased though not destroyed.[128]

Gypsy Hunts

Modern surveys and summaries concerned with anti-Roma prejudice often
mention the 'Gypsy hunts' of eighteenth-century Europe as examples of
dehumanizing persecution, when such houndings were considered sport or
public entertainment. They are described as 'notorious' episodes 'during
which the Roma were hunted like game', with bounties on their heads.[129]
There was indubitably a hardening of attitudes in many parts of Europe, but
the scale and persistence of anti-Gypsy operations are too easily exaggerated.
Having failed to rid their lands of Gypsies, or to conform them to a sedentary
way of life, regimes in Germany, France, Spain, and the Netherlands adopted
more ambitiously repressive measures in the so-called age of Enlightenment.
They found justification in dictionaries and encyclopaedias that identified
Gypsies as an incorrigible nuisance.[130] Implementation, however, was inconsistent, and the harsh rhetoric of anti-Gypsy edicts did not necessarily result
in a bloodbath.

The *heidenjachten* (Gypsy hunts) of the northern Netherlands are particularly well documented. Several states took action in the 1720s to root out
the 'zigeuners' or *heidens* haunting heathlands and woods. Large gatherings
of Gypsies were said to be moving with impunity from province to province, engaging in banditry and organized crime. Soldiers and police were sent
to round them up, sometimes violently, though the Gypsies often received
warning and moved to adjacent territories. Only when the Dutch states
coordinated their efforts did these drives against Gypsies prove effective.
International cooperation was needed to deal with Gypsies who had taken
refuge across the frontier in the German states of Cleves and Munster.[131]

Taken prisoner in one of these raids at Breda in 1723, a Gypsy woman
named Lucretia was tortured with shin screws into giving evidence against
her company. According to her testimony, the 'gang' comprised some 200–300
members; they lived by theft and deceit, and had a wide network of fences
to dispose of stolen goods. Some members had been arrested, whipped, and
branded, but most roamed free with protection from corrupt local officials.
Lucretia said that she had been orphaned in Amsterdam and then joined the

Gypsies in Brabant, taking a husband and sharing their way of life. As elsewhere, the records spoke of 'Egyptians', 'bastard Gypsies', and companies augmented by non-Gypsy vagabonds.[132]

A Dutch placard of 1725 outlawed gatherings of six or more Gypsy men, and forbade them from carrying swords or firearms. Other measures sought the whipping, branding, or banishment of any Gypsies who were discovered, and death for repeat offenders. Gypsies were forbidden to use their own language, and many of their children were removed to foster homes or orphanages. Evidence from the northern Netherlands suggests that Gypsies were gradually eliminated from areas where they had once been familiar, in a process of ethnic cleansing.[133]

Similar crackdowns occurred in German lands against well-armed bands of mounted Gypsy brigands. They were accused of intimidating villagers, murdering people, burning farmhouses, breaking into churches, and practising magic. Placards warning Gypsies that they risked being hanged or flogged were posted at the entries to some German towns.[134] As in the Netherlands, the harshest treatment was reserved for Gypsies associated with organized crime. Police and soldiers joined together in raids on Gypsies, and sometimes came off worst. At least eleven Gypsies were executed, and others tortured, whipped, and pilloried in the Habsburg territory of Carinthia in 1711, as part of a vigorous and violent campaign.[135] More Gypsies in the Palatine, Bavaria, and Saxony suffered scourging and branding in the 1720s and 1730s, and an unknown number were tortured or killed. Several were executed at Nuremberg between 1729 and 1733. Waves of persecution continued through the 1740s, as officials treated Gypsies as enemies of the state, and inscribed their authority on the bodies of offenders.[136] The Swiss too organized campaigns to track and kill Gypsies, though many escaped to more tolerant jurisdictions. Similar persecutions occurred in Lorraine in 1723, and elsewhere in France between 1765 and 1783. The problem was coming under control, one French observer remarked in 1783, because 'every Gypsy who can be apprehended falls a sacrifice to the police'.[137] Judicial authorities, however, were hard pressed to prevent Gypsies from crossing their territories, or to stop more tolerant communities from trading with 'Bohémiens'.[138]

After multiple generations in Western Europe, some Gypsies had put down local or regional roots, mingled with indigenous populations, and adopted aspects of a settled or semi-settled lifestyle. Others were as wild as ever. A report on the Gypsy problem in the Abruzzo region of Italy in 1729

emphasized their untamed lawlessness. They went about armed with arque-
buses and other weapons, and committed endless crimes, thefts, assaults,
murders, and depredations against people and animals. It was said that they
lived beyond government, ignored the Church, spread superstition, and
roamed at will. Their elimination, the ecclesiastical administrator Celestino
Galini suggested, would be a work of Christian piety, but all previous efforts
had proved ineffective.[139] So too in the Veneto, the government seemed
powerless, as renewed bans in 1690, 1692, and 1704 failed to dislodge the
'cingani'. A gang of thirty Gypsies, some armed and on horseback, terror-
ized Treviso in 1767 with 'acts of oppression and rapine'. The Venetian
Republic responded with yet another ineffective ordinance to rid the land
of 'so ill-born and accursed a plague of people'.[140]

Other territories pursued policies of forced assimilation rather than
expulsion or extermination. The Austro-Hungarian empress Maria Theresa
(1740–80) issued decrees against Gypsies in 1758, 1761, 1767, and 1773 to
suppress their way of life and convert them into decent subjects. Imperial
authorities were determined to solve the Gypsy problem, 'to win over these
poor unfortunate people, to virtue and the state', but the earnest reiteration
of these orders indicates their limited effect. Repeated decrees required the
removal of all Gypsy children aged 5 and over, to be brought up as artisans
or farmers; but, as one English commentator remarked, 'such an unnatural
and arbitrary mode of benevolence defeated its own object'. The guidelines
'de domiciliatione et regulatione Zingarorum' of the next emperor Josef II
(1780–90) went further in stripping the Gypsies of their social and economic practices, their costume, their language, and other aspects of their
culture, to turn them into civilized Europeans. They were prohibited from
dwelling in tents, from wandering abroad, and from dealing in horses. These
measures, wrote the German philologist Heinrich Grellmann in 1783, were
'intended to extirpate the very name and language of these folks, out of the
country'. It was a beneficial initiative, this Enlightenment scholar agreed, to
attempt to turn the Gypsies into useful members of society.[141]

Eighteenth-century Spain also tried to deal with its Gypsies, first by
repression and then by forced integration. Charles II in 1695 had forbidden
Gypsies to wear their costumes, to use their language, to buy and sell animals, or to possess firearms. They were supposed to take up farming or leave
the country. Enforcement, however, was predictably piecemeal and ineffective, and the Gypsies continued to thrive. In Portugal too in 1718 the authorities contemplated 'exterminating from this kingdom all Gypsies for their

thefts, serious offences, and excesses'. Hundreds were sent to the colonies, but many evaded capture.[142] Half a century later under Ferdinand VI (1746–59) the bishop of Oviedo, Gaspar Vasquez Tablada, proposed to deal with Gypsies by a combination of genocide, expulsion, and Hispanicization. Elaborate plans were made to arrest and intern the entire Spanish Gypsy population, which was thought to number as many as 12,000 men, women, and children. Implemented in 1749, the great Gypsy round-up disrupted thousands of lives, but proved impossible to administer. Hundreds of Gypsy families were imprisoned, but the state was incapable of housing or resettling them, or supervising their change of lifestyle. The government hoped that Gypsies would disappear, but a report in 1764 concluded that the kingdom was as full of Gypsies as ever. There may have been 10,000 Gypsies in Spain in the 1780s, when the state once again sought their suppression.[143]

The Bourbons of Spain may have taken notes from their Austro-Hungarian Habsburg cousins. In 1783 the regime of Charles III (1759–88) attempted to deal with Spanish Gypsies, not by expulsion or imprisonment but by suppression of their very name. Forced to assimilate, to be known henceforth as 'New Castilians', the Gitanos were afforded the rights, but also the obligations, of all of the king's subjects. They were expected to give up their language, their dress, and their way of life, and instead to settle to conventional employment, and send their children to school.[144] Some of this had been tried before, and would be tried again, with predictably unhappy results. The proliferation of such laws put pressure on Gypsies, but only intensified their marginality. The failure of European states to 'solve' their Gypsy problem exposed the underlying hollowness of their absolutist pretensions. Despite blustering decrees and draconian legislation, the powers of Europe proved unable to remove, quash, or assimilate the Gypsies. Despite widespread hostility and repeated repressive measures, European Gypsies endured. It was indicative of an alternative approach that in 1783, at a time of tightened measures in Spain, France, and Germany, the parliament in Britain repealed the penal laws against Gypsies.[145]

Images and Representations

European Gypsies presented public authorities with problems of law and order, but for creative artists they inspired the imagination. Painters and engravers cast Gypsies in pictorial morality plays, while poets and playwrights made

them subjects of fanciful tales and adventures. Literary and artistic representations responded to popular prejudices, and helped to reinforce them. Even
in regimes bent on the suppression of Gypsies, the cultural encounter was
complicated by myths that sensationalized or sentimentalized the Gypsy
way of life.

Close to a hundred visual representations of Gypsies survive in drawings,
paintings, prints, and tapestries from the fifteenth to the eighteenth centuries,
and more abound in later depictions. Renaissance artists began with por-
traits or character studies, mostly of turbaned Gypsy women; the age of the
baroque saw a fashion for visual morality dramas involving fortune-telling,
pocket-picking, and deception; and seventeenth- and eighteenth-century
painters depicted Gypsy travellers as elements in picturesque landscapes.
The execution ranged in quality from simple sketches to highly wrought
oils, as well as ornate tapestries from early sixteenth-century Flanders.[146]

One of the earliest depictions of a Gypsy family may be the drawing by
the so-called Master of the Housebook, from late-fifteenth-century Germany,
with the woman swathed and turbaned, and laden with baggage and children. It has elements in common with the engraving by Albrecht Dürer
(1471–1528) of a couple conventionally identified as Turkish or oriental,
which some art historians think are Gypsies. Dated around 1495, Dürer's
work depicts a barefoot and bare-breasted woman holding a child, a man
incongruously clutching a bow and arrow, both of them robed and wearing
turbans.[147] Less doubt attaches to the subject of 'Gypsies in the Market'
(c. 1510) by the German artist Hans Burgkmair (1473–1531), which offers a
jaunty depiction of Gypsy fortune-telling, pocket-picking, and theft. It
belongs to a north European tradition of satiric visual commentary on the
foibles and falsehoods of vagrants and beggars.[148]

Building on this tradition, a celebrated series of drawings and engravings
by the French artist Jacques Callot (1592–1635) depicts the swagger and
vitality of Gypsy companies, their poverty and panache, as they moved
through the landscape with their horses, carts, children, weaponry, and baggage.
Though possibly based on observations in Italy, Callot's designs were completed in Lorraine in the 1620s, and may depict some of the armed bands of
roving irregular mercenaries. These often-reproduced images form visual
counterparts to the picaresque tales of Pechon de Ruby, *La Vie généreuse des
mercelots, geux et boemiens*.[149]

High art had its own romance with Gypsies. The painting *Zingarella* (*The
Gypsy Girl*, in the Uffizi, Florence) by the Italian artist Boccaccio Boccaccino

Figure 2. Hans Burgkmair, 'Gypsies in the Market', *c.*1510

(*c.*1467–*c.*1525) shows a young woman with wide dark eyes, tumbling hair, a few strands of jewelry, and an elaborate headscarf. It could be a society portrait, a genre picture, or the study for a devotional Madonna. Titian's so-called *Gypsy Madonna* (*c.*1510, in the Kunsthistorisches Museum, Vienna) presents the mother of Jesus as dark-haired and dark-eyed, like many Mediterranean women, but with no obvious characteristics that could be considered 'Gypsy'.

A later generation of Mannerist and Baroque artists painted a series of images that caricatured Gypsy fortune-tellers and their victims. Caravaggio (1571–1610) was especially influential in popularizing the sexually charged scene of gullibility, exoticism, and deceit in his 1594 painting *La buona ventura* or *The Fortune Teller*. Less subtle paintings on the same theme by Lionello Spada (1576–1622) and Bartolomeo Manfredi (1580–1622) show dusky Gypsy women reading the palms of fashionable gentlemen while accomplices pick their pockets. The French artists Simon Vouet (1590–1649) and Georges de la Tour (1593–1652), and their Flemish contemporaries Nicholas Regnier (1591–1667) and Simon de Vos (1603–76), painted similar scenes involving practitioners and victims of Gypsy deceit. These works of art served as visual warnings not to be tricked or robbed by Gypsies, and scathing commentary on the dupes who let it happen.[150] Artists from Jan

Breughel the elder (1568–1625) to George Morland (1763–1804) depicted Gypsies as wild accompaniments to dramatic landscapes, or as idealized complements to natural scenes. The Ligurian artist Alessandro Magnasco (1667–1749) featured Gypsies in scenes of wild debauchery, exploring themes that have continued to the present.[151]

Creative writers over several centuries made rich use of the trope of Gypsies. The plot of children stolen by Gypsies, whose true aristocratic identity and character was later revealed, drove several plays and literary entertainments. Early examples included Gil Vicente, Farça das Ciganas (Lisbon, 1521), Gigio Artemio Giancarli, La Zingara (Mantua, 1545), and Lope de Rudea, Medora (Madrid, 1567).[152] Seventeenth-century Europe delighted in the story of 'La Gitanilla' by Miguel de Cervantes, in his Novelas Exemplares (Madrid, 1613), where the heroine Preciosa is revealed to be a long-lost Spanish noblewoman, stolen from her cradle by Gypsies. Cervantes idealized his Gypsies as free and festive wanderers, given to thievery and trickery. 'Our lightness of foot knows no shackles...no walls get in our way', proclaims one Gypsy elder. Though living in harmony with nature, the Gypsies imagined by Cervantes were also criminals, predators on the economy, and exploiters of other men's labour.[153]

Dozens of plays and poems celebrated Gypsy liberty, Gypsy trickery, and the ease of adopting a Gypsy disguise. In England the Jacobean playwrights Thomas Middleton and William Rowley reworked the story of 'La Gitinilla' in The Spanish Gypsy (1623).[154] The Restoration drama Trick for Trick by Thomas D'Urfey (1678) similarly featured an aristocrat, this time male, who was 'stolen from the nurse' by Gypsies and now 'wanders with these prophets'.[155] Several of Molière's plays included scenes with Gypsies, either prancing fortune-tellers or characters in disguise.[156] The use of stage Gypsies to display villainy, duplicity, foolhardiness, nobility, and affection was an effective literary device, but pernicious social misrepresentation.[157]

There was no recognized tradition of Gypsy music before the eighteenth century, but commentators sometimes remarked on the Gypsies' skill in dancing, and their accomplishment as entertainers. Hungarian Gypsy music and Spanish Flamenco were primarily phenomena of the nineteenth century, when they were applauded as 'deeply rooted in the Gypsy psyche and soul', with evidence of the 'integrity, individuality, and freedom' of their practitioners. They became part of the commodified framing of romantic 'Gypsyness', which fantasized about soulfulness, wildness, and freedom.[158]

Then and Now

Evidence from all parts of Europe points to the long persistence of Gypsy itinerancy, despite the forces of assimilation and repression. Though originally newcomers and anomalies, the Gypsies had arrived to stay. Despite assaults on their character, and challenges to their identity, Gypsy families and communities found ways to survive and thrive.

The westward migration of Gypsies, which created so much confusion in Renaissance and early modern Europe, continued intermittently in later generations. New groups of Gypsies arrived from time to time, driven by wars, hardships, plagues, and repression. The eighteenth-century Austro-Russian wars against Turkey triggered the movement of Bulgarian Gypsy refugees.[159] Social confusion and political upheaval from the Black Sea to the Balkans pushed more streams of Gypsies westward, especially in the nineteenth century.[160] The emancipation of Gypsy slaves in Moldavia in 1855 and Wallachia in 1856 led to more migrations.[161] So did social upheavals of the late nineteenth and early twentieth centuries. The wave of Roma migration that followed the fall of East European communist regimes in 1989 and the expansion of the European Union in the early twenty-first century precipitated legal, social, and political complexities that are still unresolved.

We need to learn more about the reception and adjustment of Gypsy migrants, and their impact on West European society. We need to know more about the differences as well as the similarities between Gypsies in various parts of Europe, in both the recent and the distant past. Questions remain about their legal status, economic activity, and social acceptance, as conditions changed over time. How various itinerant groups related to each other, as well as to different constituencies of settled society, are subjects for historical enquiry.

Though European Gypsies have long been Europeanized, they remain marginal, alien, and unfathomable. As perennial outsiders, they have long attracted hostility and suspicion. Though engaged with the economy, and confronted by the state, they have largely lived apart. The experience of half a millennium casts shadows on the present, so that Gypsies remain excluded, disparaged, and misunderstood. No attempt was made in the past to consider the Gypsy point of view, or even to imagine that there was one. Problems of stereotyping, prejudice, and hostile representation continue, despite the trappings of modernity.

Today the European Roma number between six and sixteen million people, making them Europe's largest and most vilified minority.[162] The variability of the estimates reflects the fluidity of the categories 'Gypsy', 'Roma', and 'Traveller', either as assigned labels or as self-ascription. Further confusion arises from 'the reluctance of many Roma to identify themselves as such for official purposes, and the refusal of many governments to include Roma as a legitimate category for census purposes'. Some authorities treat the Roma as an ethnic group, almost a nation without territory, but others regard Gypsies as little more than a class of people with a particularly disreputable lifestyle, or jettison the term altogether. Some use itinerancy or nomadism as an indicator, while others recognize that many Roma and Gypsies are now settled. The categories have little coherence if 'everybody is a Roma who is like a Roma', and Gypsies are everyone 'accepted by the community or who proclaim themselves to be Gypsies'.[163] The decision by the Council of Europe in 2010 that the group included 'Roma, Sinti, Kale and related groups, including Travellers and the Eastern groups (Dom and Lom), and includes persons who identify themselves as Gypsies', is politically inclusive but historically dubious.[164] It may also be subject to revision. Gypsy identity is as clouded and contested as ever, though their world and environment have changed. Investigating that history yields fresh understanding of the Gypsy experience, in ongoing counterpoint with the social and political history of the mainstream. The following chapters explore that history over five centuries in England.

2

The Rambling Roguey Gypsies of the Early Modern Page

Gypsies were a textual phenomenon as well as a social problem, appearing on the page and on the stage more vividly, and much more fancifully, than on the road and in the courts. As marginal people, outside of literate culture, they were at the mercy of other people's representations. They were demonized, categorized, satirized, and excoriated, with long-term negative effects. Early modern pamphleteers amplified the conceit of Gypsy deceitfulness in writings that were plagiarized and recycled for several centuries. A deeply entrenched stereotype—still present in some quarters—denounced the Gypsies as idle, dirty, and 'counterfeit' practitioners of fortune-telling and petty theft. Readers knew them as 'a pestiferous people', 'wretched, wily, wandering vagabonds', and 'the idle drones of a country, the caterpillars of a commonwealth, the Egyptian lice of a kingdom'.[1] If Gypsies were aware of this hostility, as seems most probable, it may have stiffened their sense of separation from the society through which they moved. It may even have helped to shape their identity. This chapter examines representations of Gypsies in print in England from Tudor times to the end of the seventeenth century, and establishes a cultural framework for later investigations of law, politics, and local policing.

Egyptians and Cony-Catchers

One of the earliest indicators of Gypsies in England appears in Thomas More's *Dialogue Concerning Heresies*, published in 1529. More refers back to the notorious scandal fifteen years earlier when the anticlericalist Richard Hunne was found dead in the Lollards' Tower in London. Amid much speculation about how Hunne came to die, More introduces the character of a gentleman who claimed to know a neighbour who in turn knew a remarkable woman who was able to 'tell many marvellous things…and therefore I think she could as well tell who killed Hunne as stole a horse'. The wise woman's insights evidently came from palmistry, the Gypsy style of fortune-telling. One party to the dialogue suggests that her powers came from the devil, but another denies it, saying, 'I could never see her use any worse way than looking in one's hand'. Though never identified by name, the fortune-teller was said to be 'an Egyptian', lodged at Lambeth, who had recently 'gone over sea'. Historical summaries repeatedly cite this episode as evidence of the earliest recorded presence of Gypsies in England. Backdated from 1529, the events of 1514 have almost canonical acceptance, mentioned in any number of surveys from Victorian Gypsiologists to modern work on Roma DNA.[2]

Close attention to the source, however, suggests that we are reading an imagined narrative rather than a record of observation. 'Famed for his gift of merry make-believe', as one modern scholar describes him, More is not a trustworthy witness, and the reliability of his tale is uncertain. More's intention was to combat heresy, not to document Gypsies, and he may have been throwing dust at his readers. It was, perhaps, a ploy to discredit critics to suggest that 'only ludicrous evidence…presented by foolish people' might implicate the Church in the murder of Richard Hunne.[3] If speculators in 1514 had consulted a Lambeth 'Egyptian'—and there might well have been one—it could suggest an even earlier Gypsy presence, since she apparently spoke sufficient English to consult with her clients, and presumably had been around for some time.

Henry VIII's court showed signs of a 'Gypsy chic', as aristocratic ladies adopted the Gypsy fashion of swirling robes and turbanned headgear. The poet laureate John Skelton described the headdress of the alewife Eleanor Rumming,

> like an Egyptian
> Capped about
> When she goeth out.

Another of Skelton's poems introduced 'Mary Gipcy, *quod scripsi scripsi*', perhaps referring to St Mary of Egypt.[4] Court ladies in 1517 are said to have adopted fancy costumes 'like to the Egyptians', and another court 'disguising' in 1520 featured ladies '[at]tired like to the Egyptians very richly'.[5] The dressing up was no more serious than when courtiers played at shepherds or outlaws of the greenwood, but it shows the development of the Gypsy mystique. The notion that Gypsies were colourful, attractive, and exotic would survive for a long time, amid more mainstream views that they were dangerous, deceitful, and loathsome. Gypsy masquerades and pantomimes would entertain gentlefolk and courtiers as well as commoners well into the nineteenth century.

The first brief attempt at analysis appeared in Andrew Boorde's *Fyrst Boke of the Introduction of Knowledge*, first published in 1542. These 'Egyptians', he wrote, 'be swarte [i.e. dark] and doth go disguised in their apparel...they be light fingered and use piking [i.e. theft]...and yet they be pleasant dancers'. Boorde's text is especially valuable, since it includes one of the earliest transcriptions of the Romani language anywhere in pre-modern Europe, discussed later in Chapters 3 and 10.[6] Parliamentary statutes were much more hostile in tone and punitive in effect. The legislation against Gypsies in 1531, 1554, and 1563 is discussed in the following chapter.

Elizabethan and Jacobean readers were charmed and alarmed by a series of publications that purported to expose the ways and wiles of low-life wanderers, criminals, and imposters. Though intended for entertainment as much as for information, these 'cony-catching' pamphlets (from conies or rabbits, the easily-caught victims of criminal deceit, but also punning on 'cunny', meaning female genitalia) became the foundational texts for early modern Gypsy studies. The most celebrated of them, often cited and anthologized, included John Awdeley, *The Fraternitie of Vacabondes* (1565); Thomas Harman, *A Caveat for Commen Cursetors Vulgarely Called Vagabones* (1567); Thomas Dekker, *The Belman of London. Bringing to Light the most Notorious Villanies that are now Practised in the Kingdome* (1608); Thomas Dekker, *Lanthorne and Candle-Light. Or the Bell-mans Second Nights Walke* (1608); Samuel Rid, *Martin Mark-all, Beadle of Bridewell: His Defence and Answere to the Belman of London* (1610); and Samuel Rid, *The Art of Iugling or Legerdemaine* (1612).[7] Most include Gypsies among the 'canting crew' of professional vagabonds, criminals, and beggars.

These publications, and several more derived from them, have often been regarded as objective observations rather than sensationalist satires. They have been plagiarized, recycled, exploited, and repackaged for several hundred years, to cumulative but misleading effect. Recent critical theorists have even used them to argue that the word 'Gypsy' was simply a 'floating signifier', and that 'real' Gypsy travellers did not exist. The cony-catching pamphlets are important as shapers and markers of early modern opinion, but their

remarks on Gypsies must be treated with rigorous scepticism. Their influence on the gentlemen and justices who enforced the law against Gypsies
is incalculable.[8]

The early Elizabethan commercial writer John Awdeley made no specific
mention of Gypsies, although he is often treated as an authority on the
subject. Awdeley's 'fraternity of vagabonds' included the 'Patriarch Co' or
Patricio, a kind of hedge priest sometimes associated with Gypsy marriages.[9]

It is in the work of the Kentish administrator Thomas Harman, published
in 1567, that Gypsies first leap from the page. Harman's introductory epistle
to the Countess of Shrewsbury employs alliterative vigour to denounce
the 'wretched, wily, wandering vagabonds calling and naming themselves
Egyptians', among the 'rowsey, ragged rabblement of rakehells' plaguing
Elizabethan England. He warned readers of their 'wicked and detestable
behaviour . . . their deep dissimulation and detestable dealing', and 'their
deep, deceitful practices, feeding the rude common people, wholly addicted
and given to novelties, toys, and new inventions; delighting them with the
strangeness of the attire of their heads, and practicing palmistry to such as
would know their fortunes; and, to be short, all thieves and whores'. Against
this nuisance, Harman commended recent legislation, the statute of 1563.
He applauded such 'redress . . . as hath been of late years', and hoped that
soon, 'thanks be to God, through wholesome laws, and the due execution
thereof, all be dispersed, vanished, and the memory of them clean extin-
guished; that when they be once named hereafter, our children will much
marvel what kind of people they were'. Harman was wrong to anticipate
the disappearance of the Gypsies, but subsequent editions, renditions, and
copying work gave his remarks an almost canonical authority.[10]

Echoing Harman, other commentators added to the battery of denigration, using the words 'Gypsy' and 'Egyptian' indiscriminately. Sir Thomas
Smith remarked in 1568 on 'that mob of rascals, prostitutes and thieves whom
they call Gypsies'.[11] William Harrison, writing a few years later, included
'Egyptian rogues' among the 'thriftless poor' who deserved the 'whip of
justice'.[12] Reginald Scot, in his *Discouerie of Witchcraft* of 1584, exposed
Gypsies as 'counterfeit Egyptians' and 'cozening vagabonds', who won 'credit
among the multitude' for their false divinations.[13] Writing in 1588, 'the great
wonderful and fatal year of our age', the year of the Spanish Armada, John
Harvey denounced 'the wizardly fortune-tellings of the runagate counterfeit Egyptians, commonly termed Gypsies'. Divination by these 'prophets of
basest condition and silliest intelligence', he charged, was simply a cover for

pilferage and pocket-picking, and its practitioners no better than witches or wizards.[14]

Just as negative was Thomas Nashe, whose satire of 1600, *A Pleasant Comedie, Called Summers Last Will and Testament*, depicts 'a company of ragged knaves, sunbathing Gypsies, lazy hedge creepers, sleeping face upwards in the fields all night, [who] dreamed strange devices of the sun and moon; and they like Gypsies wandering up and down, told fortunes, juggled, nicknamed all the stars, and were of idiots termed philosophers'. These fictional ragged wanderers were '*like* Gypsies', but whether real or counterfeit, observed or imagined, is hard to say. Following Harman, who blames 'the rude common people' for encouraging the Gypsy problem, Nashe shifts some of the responsibility to 'idiots' who credited the Gypsies with arcane knowledge and powers of prophecy. As a metropolitan wit, based in late-Elizabethan London, Nashe is more likely to have *read* about Gypsies than to have known them directly.[15]

Condemnation piled upon condemnation, entrenching an enduring stereotype. George Abbot, soon to be a bishop, remarked at the turn of the century that the inhabitants of Egypt 'are not black, but rather dun or tawny ... and of that colour do those runagates by devices make themselves to be, who go up and down the world under the name of Egyptians, being indeed but counterfeits and the refuse or rascality of many nations'.[16] Publishing in 1607, the controversial lawyer John Cowell defined 'Egyptians' as

> a counterfeit kind of rogues, that being English or Welsh people, accompany themselves together, disguising themselves in strange robes, blacking their faces and bodies, and framing to themselves an unknown language, wander up and down, and under pretence of telling fortunes, curing diseases, and such like, abuse the ignorant common people, by stealing all that is not too hot or too heavy for their carriage.[17]

These by now conventional opinions, characterizing Gypsies as 'counterfeit', were further elaborated by the Jacobean pamphleteers Thomas Dekker and Samuel Rid.[18]

Publishing with great success in 1608, Dekker alerted readers to 'idle vagabonds' and 'secret villainies', and included the 'ragged regiment' of Gypsies among the 'unruly multitude' of criminals and cony-catchers besetting England. Dekker's remarks deserve quoting at length because they have often been taken as observant commentary on the Gypsy problem. 'By a name they are called Gypsies; they call themselves Egyptians', he explained, adding that 'others in mockery call them moon-men', meaning frantic and antic wanderers, not extra-terrestrials. 'Villains they are by birth, varlets by education, knaves by profession, beggars by the statutes, and rogues by Act of Parliament. They are the idle drones of a country, the caterpillars of a commonwealth, the Egyptian lice of a kingdom... Egyptian grasshoppers that eat up the fruit of the earth.' (These last images evoke biblical plagues as well as travellers from Egypt.) The Gypsies, Dekker asserts,

> are a people more scattered than Jews, and more hated; beggarly in apparel, barbarous in condition, beastly in behaviour, and bloody if they meet advantage. A man that sees them would swear they had all the yellow jaundice, or that they were tawny Moors' bastards, for no red-ochre man carries a face of more filthy complexion. Yet are they not born so, neither has the sun burnt them so, but they are painted so; yet they are not good painters neither, for they do not make faces, but mar faces... If they be Egyptians, sure I am they never descended from the tribes of any of those people that came out of the land of Egypt. Ptolemy, king of the Egyptians, I warrant, never called them his subjects; no, nor Pharaoh before him. Look what difference there is between a civil citizen of Dublin and a wild Irish kern, so much difference there is between one of these counterfeit Egyptians and a true English beggar. An English rogue is just of the same livery.[19]

The Gypsies, Dekker insisted, were not what they claimed to be. They were therefore doubly counterfeit, dealing in deceitful practices and only pretending to be exotic. They were nonetheless notable for their 'incests, whoredoms, adulteries, and... other black and deadly damned impieties', as well as their propensity for violence and theft. Dekker, like many commentators on marginal and excluded people, betrays a prurient interest in Gypsy sexuality.

His description continues: 'They are commonly an army about four score strong, yet they never march with all their bags and baggages together, but, like boot-halers, they forage up and down countries, four, five or six in a company', with their children

> horsed, seven or eight upon one jade, strongly pinioned and strangely tied together. One shire alone and no more is sure still at one time to have these Egyptian lice swarming within it, for, like flocks of wild-geese, they will evermore fly one after another...Their apparel is odd and fantastic, though it be never so full of rents. The men wear scarfs of calico or any other base stuff, hanging their bodies like morris-dancers with bells and other toys, to entice the country people to flock about them, and to wonder at their fooleries, or rather rank knaveries. The women as ridiculously attire themselves, and, like one that plays the rogue on a stage, wear rags and patched filthy mantles uppermost, when the undergarments are handsome and in fashion.[20]

When Gypsies arrive in a parish, according to Dekker,

> the simple country people will come running out of their houses to gaze
> upon them, whilst in the meantime one steals into the next room, and brings
> away whatsoever he can lay hold on. Upon days of pastime and liberty, they
> spread themselves in small companies amongst the villages; and when young
> maids and bachelors (yea, sometimes doting old fools, that should be beaten
> to this world of villainies, and forewarn others) do flock about them, they
> then profess skill in palmistry, and, forsooth, can tell fortunes, which for the
> most part are infallibly true, by reason that they work upon rules, which
> are grounded upon certainty. For one of them will tell you that you shall
> shortly have some evil luck fall upon you, and within half an hour after you
> shall find your pocket picked or your purse cut.[21]

Finally, Dekker claims that Gypsy numbers were augmented by recruits
from among local ne'er-do-wells: 'priggers, anglers, cheaters, morts, yeomen's
daughters that have taken some by-blows...and other servants both men
and maids that have been pilferers...who running away from their own
colours, which are bad enough, serve under these, being the worst.' These
too became 'counterfeit Egyptians' who merged with the Gypsy population. Anyone, it seems, could darken their skin, don a wild costume, and
adopt a Gypsy identity.[22] Dekker's description has enjoyed several centuries of repetition and approbation. It influenced Ben Jonson's 'Masque of
the Gypsies', found echoes in later Stuart 'rogue' writings, and still influenced opinion in the Victorian period. Writing on Gypsies in 1886, the
bibliographer W. C. Hazlitt remarked that 'Dekker draws a portrait of
them, which closely corresponds with our experience of their modern
descendants'.[23] More modern commentators have not been immune to
this perception.[24]

Samuel Rid, immediately following Dekker, helped to cement the image
of Gypsies 'pilling and polling and cozening the country', living by 'dissembling and deceitful practices' and 'legerdemain, or fast-and-loose'. Rid also
remarks on their history, a matter that Dekker ignored. In *Martin Mark-all*
Rid claims that the Gypsies first appeared 'about the southern parts' of
England, and 'began to gather an head' around the twentieth year of Henry
VIII (the year of Thomas More's tract). In *The Art of Iugling* he describes
how 'a new regiment, calling themselves by the name of Egyptians', arrived
'in the northern parts' within living memory. 'Being excellent in quaint
tricks and devices, not known here at that time among us', they were at first
'esteemed and had in great admiration...insomuch that many of our

English loiterers joined with them, and in time learned their craft and cozening'. They prospered through 'palmistry and telling of fortunes, insomuch
they pitifully cozened the poor country girls, both of money, silver spoons,
and the best of their apparel, or any good thing they could make, only to
hear their fortunes'. These Gypsies roved in bands 'above two hundred
rogues and vagabonds in a regiment', he claims, with annual assemblies in
the Peak District, at Blackheath, and elsewhere. In *Martin Mark-all* Rid
names the folk characters Cock Lorel and Giles Hather as Gypsy leaders in
the reign of Henry VIII, along with Hather's 'whore' Kit Callot, 'the Queen
of Egypties'. He also remarks on their language, allegedly an artificial con-
coction, 'spun out of' Latin, English and Dutch, with a smattering of Spanish
and French.[25]

Eventually, Rid continues, after thirty or forty years of 'cozening the
country', the 'knavery' of the Gypsies was 'espied' and made subject to law.
But, despite the 'strict' statutes of the Tudor queens, and the false optimism
of Thomas Harman, Rid regrets that 'these pestiferous people' were not
properly dispatched. 'Until this day', he says, 'they wander up and down in
the name of Egyptians, colouring their faces and fashioning their attire and
garment like unto them, yet if you ask what they are, they dare no otherwise
than say they are Englishmen, and of such a shire, and so are forced to say
contrary to that they pretend.' Within a generation the Gypsies had been
transformed from exotic newcomers to counterfeit Egyptians and 'pestiferous carbuncles in the commonwealth'.[26] Caricatures like those of Rid and
Dekker bore much of the responsibility.

Idle Rogues

Gypsies were offensive to public authorities and loathsome to moral reformers
because they did no recognizably useful work. They had no lawful calling,
and performed no social duty. Instead they preyed on the foolish and credulous, and served as evil examples to anyone inclined to shirk. As 'idle drones',
given to a 'naughty, idle and ungodly life', they were offensive to God, and
a 'marvelous disturbance of the common weal of this realm'.[27] Lacking a
valid vocation, Gypsies outraged religious instructors for whom everyone
needed employment. If they saw Gypsies, they saw sin. The 'Homily Against
Idleness', read regularly in English churches, reminded parishioners that
man was born 'to labour and travail' and that idleness was 'a grievous sin'.[28]

Idleness was 'a capital plague...unseemly in a Christian...contrary to the law of God...prejudicial to human society', declared the Elizabethan moralist Henry Crosse. It was 'against the law of scripture, against the law of nature', declared the Jacobean preacher Thomas Adams.[29] The influential bishop Lancelot Andrewes taught that Gypsies and fortune-tellers were no better than 'harlots, bawds, and keepers of brothel houses', because 'they are idle and will not take pains in a calling', and 'are against the public good of mankind'.[30] The London minister Thomas Barnes preached more succinctly that 'idleness is permitted to none; employment, the devil's disquieter, is required of all'.[31]

Customary views like these shaped the preaching of John Randol in Oxfordshire, whose sermon of 1631 was published two years later. The Gypsies, for Randol, were 'a company of vagrant imps, that [do] nothing but travel from sign to sign, and never receive the sacrament in all their lives...They are a dishonour to the king, confusion to the kingdom, the off-scouring both of men and beasts, and the very scum of all the land. I fear there are some thousands of those Egyptian beggars that never were baptized.' Untouched by Christian ritual and foreign to civil society, he warned, 'the Egyptian troops of unbaptised vagrants, that are born no man knows where...offer scorn and abuse both to God and man'. Outside the market economy, with no visible means of support, 'they boast that they can make bread of beans, of acorns, nay of knots of straws rather than they will starve'.[32]

Other authors of the early seventeenth century touched occasionally on Gypsies or wandering 'Egyptians', only to echo the stereotype. Like the cony-catching pamphlets that often served as models, their work embroidered negative characteristics. Writing in 1611, for example, the chronicler Anthony Munday mentioned 'those disfigured wanderers, that walk among us with deformed faces and ill-favoured locks, using all subtle thefts, pilferies, and legerdemains they can devise, we nickname them to be Saracens, Aegyptians, or Gypsies'.[33] The linguist John Minsheu, in his dictionary of 1617, similarly identified Gypsies as masters of deceit. A 'Gypson', he said, was 'a counterfeit rogue, one that speaketh gibberish or gibble gabble'. As 'counterfeit Egyptian[s]' and 'cozening fortune teller[s]', they 'accompany themselves together, disguising themselves in strange robes, blacking their faces and bodies, and framing to themselves an unknown language'. Copying earlier authors, Minsheu writes that the Gypsies 'wander up and down, and under pretence of telling of fortunes, curing diseases, and such like, abuse the ignorant common people, by stealing all that is not too hot, or too heavy for their carriage'.[34] They were 'a vile people', the gentlewoman Dionys Fitzherbert immediately concluded, when she encountered several 'that counterfeited themselves to be Egyptians' at Oxford.[35]

Warning of Gypsy 'rogues' who preyed on 'credulous people', the critic of vulgar astrology John Melton in 1620 described their 'cunning' (a word associated with wizardry, folk-cures, and 'cunning men' or 'wise women'). Itinerants

> would appear in the village in the likeness of Gypsies, which word indeed is derived from the Egyptians, but by corruption of the tongue are called Gypsies; and that they might be thought to come of the issue of that sun-burnt generation, they with herbs and plants for the purpose would venom their skins, and with ochres discolour their faces; and then for bread, beer or bacon, cheese, especially for money, would undertake to tell poor maid-servants their fortunes, which would be sure to be good, because they would be sure of good reward; and these poor silly creatures, seeing them to be black and ill-favoured people, and it may be hearing before of some as wise as themselves of the Gypsies' cunning, would easily believe that they were cunning men, and do strange things. And it is a great folly and madness of many, who never see a tawny-visaged man with a black curled head of hair (especially if he be a scholar, or profess himself to be one) but they will think he is a cunning man and a conjurer.

The Gypsies, by this account, exploited the gullibility of simple villagers, through characteristic deception and trickery.[36] They were not just a nuisance, but stirrers of sinfulness through their 'crafty, dissembling, deceitful, flattering and lying tongue'.[37]

Guilty before being proven innocent, Gypsies were everywhere suspected of crimes. It was part of their character, their very being, that they should pilfer, steal, and pick pockets. It was, said the Jacobean writer Nicholas Breton, 'of the nature of Gypsies, cunning as the devil, to dive in to a pocket, or to pick out the bottom of a purse'.[38] The popular Restoration writer Richard Head told readers that Gypsies 'are a lazy and idle sort of people which cannot endure to take pains for an honest livelihood, but rather than labour, stroll up and down all the summer time in droves or companies, and by telling fortunes (that is, by deluding young country wenches and other foolish and credulous people) they pick up a great deal of money'.[39] Thomas Culpeper in 1670 warned readers of 'those swarms of lewd and idle persons, who prowl about in every part of the kingdom, or those gangs of Gypsies, that appear amongst us at noon-day'.[40]

The stereotype was inescapable, imprinting an image that invited disdain. It reappeared in a printed tract of 1673 that related the arrest of a company of Gypsies in Warwickshire, and the prosecution of one of their leaders for fortune-telling and theft. This derives from the cony-catching tradition, though it purports to relate a story of law enforcement. The author berates the Gypsies as 'caterpillars of commonwealths' (using Dekker's words from 1608), and also (following Dekker) blames 'the vulgar ignorance' of 'the poor credulous rabble' for succumbing to Gypsy trickery. At the heart of the story, embellished beyond credibility, is the election of a former London tradesman named Hern to be 'king' of the Gypsies. At Barford, just outside Warwick, the story goes, 'a farmer's daughter just come from market with about ten shillings in her pocket addressed herself to the Gypsy king to know her fate, who, amusing the poor girl with hard words and strange gestures, soon found an opportunity by his dexterity in legerdemain, to disburden her of her cash'. Hauled before justices, Hern denied responsibility for the crime, and rashly wished, 'that he might be burned that night, if directly or indirectly he had meddled with any of the girl's money'. Sure enough, providence so wrought that the drunken Hern allowed a candle to set fire to his prison that night, and he was 'mortally burned' in the flames. Nor is this the end of the episode, for the pamphlet relates that the remains of Hern's body were buried in St Mary's church the next Sunday evening, 'but the mayor and justices caused it to be removed a few days after'. This sensational story is presented as a moral lesson, a warning to 'all such idle extravagant persons that live by defrauding others, and use such wicked execrations to cloak their villainies'. Though the pamphlet presents itself as eye-witnessed truth, no independent evidence survives to corroborate any part of it. Among its least credible elements is the depiction of a male Gypsy fortune-teller.[41]

Stage Gypsies

The cony-catching pamphlets and similar printed works were available to playwrights and poets as they crafted their entertainments. Some of these texts may have been familiar to preachers, jurors, and magistrates as well as to theatrical audiences. They shaped, and were in turn shaped by, an image of Gypsies as deceitful tricksters, living outside the law. Skilled in legerdemain, pocket-picking, and counterfeit fortune-telling, the Gypsies were rogues and knaves, at once beguiling, mysterious, and alluring, dangerous, and false.

This is how they appear in Ben Jonson's royal entertainment 'The Gypsies Metamorphos'd', which was performed three times for the king and courtiers in 1621, and printed as *The Masque of the Gypsies* in 1640.[42] Extravagantly ragged Gypsies dance, sing, pick pockets, and tell fortunes, before they are revealed to be the Marquis of Buckingham and his noble associates in pantomine disguise, along with some professional actors. Like the vagabonds who were said to enlarge the Gypsy population, they had merely put on costume and darkened their faces. Jonson's masque adds little to our knowledge of Gypsy culture or life on the road, but shows that aristocrats at the highest levels of Jacobean society could play with quips about Gypsies, and were not averse to adopting their attire. Almost every stereotypical Gypsy attribute in *The Masque of Gypsies* can be traced to Harman and Dekker, but this has not prevented literary scholars from using Jonson's text to pronounce on Gypsy 'liminality', Gypsy 'exoticism', Gypsy 'lawlessness', Gypsy 'self-fashioning', 'the evasive character of Gypsy cultural difference', and what one has termed the 'transversal' and 'protean, "counterfeit" performativity of Gypsy identity'.[43]

Jonson's principal Gypsy appears on stage, 'leading a horse laden with five children, bound in a trace of scarves upon him; a second leading another horse, laden with stolen poultry, etc.'. The image, which would later appear in wood-cut illustrations, comes straight from Dekker.[44] There are references to stereotypical Gypsy accomplishments: 'he can thread needles on horse-back, or draw a yard of inkle [linen tape] through his nose'; Gypsy complexion: 'our tawny faces'; Gypsy costume: the rags of 'a tatter'd nation'; Gypsy cant: 'the libkins at the crackmans' and 'the boozing ken'; and Gypsy recruiting: a justice's daughter 'running away with a kinsman of our captain's'. This 'covey of Gypsies' (the word 'covey' originally applied to partridges) entertains the court by dancing and singing, by palmistry, and by acts of legerdemain, in return for hospitality. They are led by a 'Jackman' and a 'Patricio' (familiar names from Awdeley and Harman) who are skilled in reading palms and picking pockets. Among their victims' possessions to be lifted are a race of ginger, an enchanted nutmeg, a ring, a knife, some pins, and a copy of the godly tract *The Practice of Piety*. All are restored, along with harmony and mirth, when the thieves are discovered to be no Gypsies at all, but leading aristocrats in disguise.

'All your fortunes we can tell', the mock-Gypsies announce, and no less than sixteen senior members of the court and council have their palms read and fortunes told, each appropriate to their history, rank, and status. 'If you dare trust to my forecasting, | 'Tis presently good, and will be lasting', the Patricio says to the Countess of Exeter. Buckingham, who commissioned the entertainment, himself played the Gypsy captain, and audaciously read

King James's hand. Addressing his majesty as 'the prince of peace', the fortune-teller declares:

> You are no great wencher, I see by your table.
> Although your mons veneris says you are able.
> You live chaste and single, and have buried your wife,
> And mean not to marry by the line of your life.

It is little more than fluff, rogue vogue, with playful erotic teasing within the conventions of the Jacobean masque. Scholars use it to penetrate the Gypsy underworld at their peril. The 'table' mentioned here was the 'table line' or 'fortune line' that ran across the top of the palm, at an angle to the life line; the risqué-sounding 'mons veneris' referred to the pad at base of the thumb. Both are described in contemporary books on palmistry.[45]

'The Gypsies Metamorphos'd' was a courtly entertainment, but readers of literature and audiences in the theatres also encountered textual Gypsies. In *The Right Excellent and Famous Historye of Promos and Cassandra* (1578), a possible source for Shakespeare's *Measure for Measure*, the hangman threatens to play 'fast-and-loose' with a prisoner dressed 'like a Giptian', and a bystander pointing to the rope scoffs, 'how now, Giptian? . . . the hangman straight will read fortunes with this'.[46] A lover in John Lyly's *Euphues* (1580) berates his lady: 'Thus with the Aegyptian thou playest fast or loose', so that all that remained was uncertainty.[47] Antony in Shakespeare's *Antony and Cleopatra* (1607) complains, 'This foul Egyptian . . . like a right Gypsy hath, at fast-and-loose, beguiled me to the very heart of loss'.[48] Edmund Spenser's tale of *Mother Hubberd* (1591) includes a character who schemes 'to disguise in some strange habit . . . like a Gipsen, or a juggler, and so to wander to the world's end'.[49] A character in George Chapman's drama *The Gentleman Usher* (1605) reports living a disorderly life with 'a captain of the Gypsies', until 'at last I was so favoured, that they made me king of Gypsies'.[50] Similar lines would amuse audiences for decades.

James Shirley in *A Contention for Honour and Riches* (1633) referred to 'Gypsies that lived by cheating palmistry'.[51] Richard Zouch in *The Sophister* (1639) has a character rail indiscriminately at 'jugglers, cony-catchers, Gypsies, rogues, base gamesters, lying mountebanks, vile bawds, and most damned cozeners'.[52] Several playwrights played with the Gypsies' reputation for occult wisdom. The fatal handkerchief in Shakespeare's *Othello* (1602) originated with 'an Egyptian . . . a charmer', who 'could almost read the thoughts of people'.[53] A character in Thomas Middleton's *A Game at Chess* (1625) gains knowledge from 'a magical glass I bought of an Egyptian, whose stone retains that speculative virtue'.[54] Lodowick Carlell in *The Deserving Favourite* (1629) has one of his characters attribute the 'sudden curing' of a duke 'to a sovereign balm that an Egyptian gave me'.[55] The poet Robert Herrick imagined 'Love, like a Gypsy', offering to 'foretell my fortune'.[56] These playwrights imagined Gypsies as conduits of supernatural power.

Dozens of plays employed the device of the Gypsy disguise, with plots that turned on altered identities. Many were published years after they were first performed. In *The Staple of News* (acted 1625, printed 1640) Ben Jonson introduced a 'rogue . . . that speaks no language . . . but what gingling Gypsies and pedlars trade in'.[57] His play *The New Inne* (1631) introduces Lord Frampul, who would 'lie and live with the Gypsies half a year together' to stay away from his wife.[58] In Thomas Middleton's *More Dissemblers Besides Women* (performed 1614, published 1657) one character decides to 'turn Gypsy presently', because Gypsies 'lead the merriest lives' and 'never want good cheer'. A Gypsy captain invites 'come live with us', for 'he that's a Gypsy may be drunk or tipsy'. '*Ousabel, camcheateroon, pusscatelion, house-drows*', he says in the mock-Gypsy language, to which his fellow Gypsy replies absurdly, '*Rumbos stragadelion, alla piss-kitch in sows-clows*'. One prospective Gypsy remarks, 'I shall ne'er keep a good tongue in my head till I get this language'. Another, already in Gypsy disguise, declares, 'I love your language well, but understand it not'. The playwright, of course, has conjured up the entire confection out of fragments of cant and nonsense, comparable to the pastiche of gibberish and mangled English used by stage Dutchman, Irishman, or Welshman.[59] 'We are indeed from Egypt land', declare characters 'attired . . . like Gypsies', in the university comedy *Technogamia: or the Marriages of the Arts* (1618).[60]

The disguise motif appears most strongly in *The Spanish Gipsie* (acted 1623, printed 1653) by Thomas Middleton and William Rowley. Here an old lord is 'disguised like the father of the Gypsies', a count's wife is 'disguised like the mother of the Gypsies', and the heroine Constanza, a noble Don's daughter, appears 'disguised like a young Spanish Gypsy'. They are joined by a foolish young gentleman, who declares, 'we'll live as merrily as beggars; lets both turn Gypsies', and his equally foolish companion, who agrees to be 'gipsified'. Suitably transformed, the pretend-Gypsies 'frisk, they caper, dance and sing, | Tell fortunes too, which is a fine thing'.[61] *The Blind Beggar of Bednal Green* (1659) by Henry Chettle and John Day also has a character who suggests, 'let's turn Gypsies again then, and go about a fortune telling'.

Fancies and Fantasticks. 439

THE GYPSIES.

The Captain sings.

From the famous *Peak of Darby*,
And the *Devils-Arse* there hard-by,
Where we yearly keep our Musters,
Thus the *Ægyptians* throng in clusters.

Be not frighted with our fashion,
Though we seem a tattered Nation ;
We account our rags, our riches,
So our Tricks exceed our stitches.

Figure 3. 'Fancies and Fantasticks. The Gypsies', in Sir John Mennes, *Recreation for Ingenious Head-peeces* (1650)

Another proposes, 'we give him the slip, and to escape pursuit attire ourselves like Gypsies, peddlers, tinkers, or such like disguise; how like you this?'[62] Audiences, apparently, liked it very much.

The literary culture of the Restoration era was especially rich in dramatic Gypsy impostures. Three young gentlewomen in Aphra Behn's play *The Rover* (1677) are dressed like Gypsies when they offer to tell an Englishman's fortune. One of them congratulates herself on her disguise: 'we have learnt this trade of Gypsies as readily as if we had been bred upon the road to Loretta.'[63] In another production Aphra Behn publicized the exploits of a French adventurer who associated with 'tatterdemalion ingeniosoes' (*sic*), the Gypsies, 'and practiced all their tricks of legerdemain . . . to the admiration of all that saw and heard him'.[64] Similar impostures drive the plot of *The Rambling Justice* (1678), when one foolish character demands of another disguised as a Gypsy, 'tell me my fortune'.[65] In Peter Motteux's *Love's a Jest* (1696) a foolish squire insists on having his hand read by a pretend-Gypsy, while another picks his pocket. When the Gypsies are finally chased from the stage, a gentleman threatens them: 'you shall be trussed up next assizes, hanged in chains, and shown for a right Egyptian mummy.'[66] In another later-Stuart comedy one character berates another, 'Thou art as false as sin . . . as full of lies as Gypsies'.[67]

This scatter of references points to opinions about Gypsies that were generally less hostile than those of the cony-catching pamphleteers. Gypsies of the literary imagination were low and marginal outsiders, tricksters outside the law, but they could also be envied for their freedom and good cheer. They were scoundrels or rascals, rather than villains or rogues. According to a self-proclaimed expert of the later seventeenth century, it was 'customary for great persons abroad to hide themselves often in disguises among the Gypsies; and even the late Lord of Rochester among us, when time was, among other frolics, was not ashamed to keep the Gypsies company'.[68] Such 'frolics' bear no closer relation to the general Gypsy experience than those of the self-deluding 'Romany rais' of Victorian and Edwardian England.

The Gypsies who appeared in ballads—the semi-ephemeral verses that occupied the margins of oral and literate culture—were no more realistic. The ballad of *The Brave English Jipsie*, to be sung 'to the tune of The Spanish Gypsy', includes crude woodcuts of Gypsy dancers and Gypsies on horseback. It may date from the first half of the seventeenth century, but was still circulating several generations later. Giving voice to its Gypsy characters, the ballad celebrates the imagined attractions of their roving life, where

> English Gypsies all live free,
> And love, and live most jovially
>
> . . . . .
>
> Our fare is of the best;
> Three times a week we feast
>
> . . . . .
>
> To drink, be drunk and tipsy,
> Delights the English Gypsy
>
> . . . . .
>
> Great store of coin we gain,
> Yet for it take no pain.

So attractive was this fanciful regime that 'Some decayed, 'mongst gallants strives | To lead the English Gypsies' lives'. The ballad acknowledges the negative reputation of Gypsies—'Sometimes our very sight | The children doth affright'—but claimed that everywhere

> The country people run
> To see what we can do.
>
> . . . . .
>
> Whereso'er we come we find,
> For one that hates, an hundred kind.[69]

The ballad of *The Gypsie Loddy* (also known as *Gypsy Davy* or *Seven Yellow Gypsies*, among other variants) tells the tragic but romantic tale of a lord's wife who cast off her finery to run away with the Gypsies. English and Scottish versions survive from the eighteenth century, and are still in the repertoire of folk performers, but its origin may be earlier. The Gypsies here were 'brisk and bonny', but no match for the lord's retribution: 'They're to be hanged all on a row, | For the Earl of Castle's lady, O.'[70] Dozens more ballads from the nineteenth century sing of freedom-loving Gypsies, menacing Gypsies, Gypsy adventurers, and Gypsy child-stealers.[71] Sterner critics might argue that Gypsy 'liberty' was a fantasy, quite different from the disciplined liberty attributed to dutiful free-born Englishmen.[72]

Like Gypsies

The conceit of Gypsy imposture was so indelibly established that people could invoke it to shame or disparage enemies they charged with being deceitful. As early as 1583 the Earl of Surrey warned friends against his rival the Earl of Leicester, 'beware the Gypsy'.[73] In 1590 the theologian Richard

Harvey smeared Presbyterian reformers as 'frivolous atheists', like Niccolò Machiavelli and Pietro Aretino, 'both in this point very Gypsies'.[74] A Jacobean correspondent of Sir Robert Phelips described an acquaintance as 'a very Gypsy' because of his practice of deceit.[75] In the 1630s the Somerset minister Roderick Snellin 'publicly railed at his parishioners and called them Gypsies and cheating knaves'.[76] A later Stuart wit described London prostitutes as 'lustful Gypsies', while another declared, all 'women are Gypsies'.[77]

In a country divided by party and religion, the word 'Gypsy' added sting to political denigration. It joined the repertoire of insult, alongside 'Turk' and 'Jew', to indicate a racialized, exoticized disdain. The Jacobean polemicist Thomas Bell denounced Roman Catholic priests as 'thieves [and] Gypsies', and declared that 'the Jesuits, like Gypsies, have invented a trick of fast-and-loose'.[78] The preacher Thomas Thompson accused papists in general of 'dissembling and Gyptian tricks'.[79] Others attacked puritans for their 'Gypsy dialect' of hypocrisy and 'despite of all authority'.[80] Presbyterians and Independents of the 1640s branded each other 'as cunning as Gypsies'.[81] The sectarian Muggletonians were 'no better than…spiritual Gypsies',[82] while Quakers and the mystic religious community the Family of Love were 'like our wandering Gypsies in mixed seeds | Without distinction one with other breeds'.[83]

In revolutionary England John Milton attacked 'the cunning Gypsies the bishops',[84] while his opponent Fabian Philipps berated republicans as 'our new state Gypsies' for deceiving the people of England.[85] Other critics of the Interregnum denounced republicans as 'authentic Gyps(ies)' for 'fleecing the poor country',[86] and politicians of all stripes as 'Gypsies, cheats, cony-catchers, and pickpockets' for their knavery and theft.[87] A verse lament for England's troubles at the height of the revolution took the form of a 'Gypsy's prophecy', allegedly made years earlier:

> The English like heretic elves,
> Shall be the ruin of themselves.
>
> .   .   .   .   .
>
> They force away their sacred king,
> Which will destruction on them bring.
>
> .   .   .   .   .
>
> When crosses fail and church decays
> Observe well what the Gypsy says.[88]

Restoration essayists used the Gypsy slur with abandon. One described a Presbyterian as someone who, 'like a Gypsy, tells good fortune to none but those that cross his hand with . . . silver'.[89] Another imagined nonconformists as 'Gypsies in religion', skulking off like 'canting vagrants'.[90] John Tillotson, who rose to be an archbishop, demeaned two faiths with one insult, likening both Judaism and Catholicism to 'the canting of Gypsies'.[91] The Restoration controversialist Edmund Hickeringill smeared Calvinists as 'spiritual Gypsies' who beguiled the gullible by

> Telling fortunes, predestinations,
> Decrees, elections, reprobations
>
> . . . . .
>
> When spiritual Gypsy thus is at it,
> Take my advice, look to thy pocket.[92]

In 1681 an anonymous verifier satirized 'young Gypsy', the Earl of Monmouth.[93] These rhetorical barbs could be effective only if readers had some familiarity with Gypsies and the textual tradition that characterized them as rootless and disreputable deceivers. Popular parlance also had it that to undertake an impossible task was 'like those fools who think to confine Gypsies, and hope to cheat mountebanks', a saying that anyone familiar with Gypsies was supposed to understand.[94]

Gypsies also provided points of reference for exotic encounters in distant lands. In 1621, for example, settlers in the New England outpost of Plymouth Plantation reported that the local Indians 'are of complexion like our English Gypsies', and 'they sang and danced after their manner like antics'.[95] William Penn's party in Pennsylvania in 1682 found the native women 'comely, as some Gypsies are in England'.[96] Other travellers in Africa and Asia compared indigenous inhabitants to English Gypsies. There were people in Goa, for example, 'like to the Gypsies in our kingdom', and in the Gambia 'a tawny people much like to those vagrants amongst us called Egyptians'.[97] John Fryer found entertainers in Bengal 'living promiscuously, like our Gypsies'.[98] William Bruton, travelling in the lands of the Great Mogul, encountered 'very rogues, such as our Gypsies be in England'.[99] John Ray's *Collection of Curious Travels & Voyages* (1693) described Moors and Arabs 'like unto our Gypsies'.[100] Another voyager compared African Hottentots to Gypsies.[101] Even in ancient Britain, according to the Restoration antiquarian Aylett Sammes, the inhabitants coloured 'their hands, arms, faces and necks, much like to Gypsies nowadays, whereby they thought they looked more terrible'.[102]

Fortune Tales

'To speak of fortune-tellers, Gypsies, wise women, and such as pretend to tell of things lost (a profession too much suffered, as most frequently abusive in this age) would but fill much paper, and give small or no content at all to the reader', wrote Thomas Heywood in his history of women, published in 1624. These deceivers, he explained, 'pretended great skill not only in palmistry, to tell maids how many husbands they should have, and young men what wives, and how many children legitimate or bastards, with such like ridiculous and illusive conjectures; but besides this art... the knowledge of things lost, and to return any stolen goods to their true owner'.[103] Gypsies had enjoyed this reputation for more than a century, at least since the days of the wise 'Egyptian' woman at Lambeth in 1514, and would long continue to eke a living from the reading of hands. Archival reports of this activity are rare, but literary and textual sources abound with references to Gypsy divinations. The practice was strongly gendered, for Gypsy fortune-tellers were almost always female; dozens of paintings from early modern Europe depict them as dusky and deceitful readers of palms.[104] Theologians universally condemned the practice as sinful and heathen.[105]

Not all Gypsies were fortune-tellers, and not all fortune-tellers were Gypsies, but popular culture insisted on the correspondence. Critics repeatedly denounced Gypsies 'who use to pick silly women's pockets as they are looking in their hands'.[106] The fortune-teller, warned one writer, 'can with as much dexterity cozen you of your money while she only pretends observing lines in your palm'.[107] Another, discussing country fairs, wrote that 'Gypsies flock thither, who tell men of losses, and the next time they look for their purses, they find their words true'.[108] Their counterfeit palm reading, warned a later account, was only for 'milking the purses of the credulous and deceiving their expectations'.[109] Complaints of such cozening were common in Elizabethan and Jacobean accounts, and would often reappear in later Stuart publications.

The clientele for fortune-telling was almost as strongly gendered as its practitioners. Though not exclusively female, the clients of Gypsy fortune-tellers were most often described as 'silly wenches and timorous women'. Especially vulnerable were 'young wenches, that neither hope, nor wish, nor dream of anything but husbands, who must needs have their fortunes told'. Critics represented them as lovesick or love-hungry innocents who sought foreknowledge of their future husbands: 'whether kind or unkind, when they shall be married, what children they shall have, and how fortunate they shall live.'[110] These were not unreasonable concerns, when 10 per cent of young women never married, and a third of those who did were already pregnant. Fortune-tellers also told apprentices when their masters might die, and sailors' wives when their husbands would return.[111] They offered a modicum of hope in an environment of perilous uncertainty, though critics claimed that they deceived 'the poor credulous rabble' and 'impose[d] on vulgar ignorance' by 'cheating silly people' of their money.[112] Fortune-telling would continue to earn profits so long as people believed in its efficacy.

Recalling a visit to a godly household in Elizabethan Essex, the puritan Thomas Gataker described how 'some wandering Gypsies came to the house, whom the servants, as the manner of young people is, were forward and busy about to know from them their fortunes'. The lady of the house, Mrs Katherine Aylof, 'both rebuked them for doing so, and was very careful to have her children kept out of sight of those vagrants'. This was not just to protect her dependants from 'cheats and counterfeits', but rather, 'lest what they, seeing them, should say of them…and God should cause somewhat spoken by them to befall them, thereby to punish me in my children for giving so far forth heed upon them'.[113] This was complicated Christian providential reasoning, not entirely convinced that Gypsy divination was powerless. It reinforced the view that Gypsies preyed on the weaker, younger, and more dependent members of society.

A similar message could be derived from John Melton's Jacobean tale of a 'crew of these hedge-creepers trooping through Essex, telling fortunes as they went', who ended up in Ipswich gaol 'not many years since'. There, in collusion, with their gaoler, the Gypsies continued to ply their deceitful trade. In this account, which cannot be confirmed by archival sources, the imprisoned Gypsies exploited 'the simplicity of many of the townsmen's wives, daughters and servants', and told them their fortunes, based on infor-mation secretly supplied by their accomplice. The country people, 'hearing themselves named of them that never saw them before, and told them of things that had been done many years before, wondered at them, and gave them money, sent them meat every day to dinner and supper, saying it was pity such skillful people as they should not be provided for'—a generosity never extended to common vagrants. The scam continued for more than a month, by which time the Gypsies had enough money to escape the assize, and the colluding gaoler had several pounds in his pocket.[114]

Later Stuart commentators continued to embellish the image of Gypsy fortune-tellers. The Restoration-era satirist Richard Head introduces a Gypsy woman who boasts of 'how much we get by fortune-telling among the ignorant, the poor women being ready to pawn their petticoats to procure us money, to tell them how fruitful they shall be when married, or whether William or Thomas loveth them or not'. Taking advantage of vulnerable commoners, Head explained, these Gypsies 'will dexterously pickpocket whilst they are telling these simple people what shall hereafter befall them; for whilst one of these cunning Gypsies holds the hand, pretending to read therein strange things which shall come to pass, another secretly and nimbly dives into their pocket'.[115] An artless verse from the 1670s reports how

> Gypsies (some say) do understand
> By lines they read in faced and hand
> How long, when, how, where you may dwell,
> Can every way your fortune tell.
> All these mysteries, with their blessing,
> You have for sixpence, or a less thing.[116]

Another rhymester wrote of 'the rambling roguey Gypsies' who 'amaze the world by dire eclipses'.[117] Gullible women in particular were said to ask 'many strange and frivolous questions of star-gazers, fortune-tellers, figure-slingers, Gypsies, and the like, in which they throw away their money and time'.[118] There was nothing original in these observations, and not necessarily much that was true.

Writers often suggested that the Gypsies took the name 'Egyptians' in order to appear exotic. It was part of the imposture of people 'which go about and tell fortunes ... called Gypsies' to claim association with the 'most famous sorcerers of old'.[119] Readers of the Bible and history knew well that Egypt was 'once the nursery of learning', but also 'a nursery of the art of divination, a black art, far beyond the light of flesh and blood'.[120] It became a standard charge that Gypsies encouraged the belief that they were heirs to this arcane wisdom. They arrived in Christendom 'calling themselves Egyptians, as much as to say subtle and cunning people, and so took up the trade of fortune tellers, Egypt having in those days kept up the repute of such sciences. These sort of people ... in our laws provided against them are called Gypsies', explained the Restoration antiquarian Aylett Sammes.[121]

Echoing the earlier authors of cony-catching pamphlets, Richard Head claimed that Gypsies 'do endeavour to persuade the ignorant that they were extracted from the Egyptians, a people heretofore very famous for astronomy, natural magic, the art of divination, with many other occult arts and sciences'. He even claims to have heard a Gypsy 'captain' tell villagers in 1671: 'We come from a far country... and are the true children of the Wise Men of the East; we are skilled in the dark and secret mysteries of nature, and sucked from our mothers' breasts the knowledge of the stars, and can tell what hath or will befall mortals, by the lines in their hands'. Head, however, knows better, and has his hero retort: 'You... have not one drop of Egyptian blood in you.'[122]

Early modern apologists for the arts of palmistry and astrology differentiated 'true prophets' (perhaps university educated or divinely inspired) from popular 'magicians, necromancers, diviners, soothsayers, fortune-tellers, Gypsies, jugglers, prognosticators, and predictors', who were nothing but 'counterfeits'.[123] The interregnum author Thomas Ady charged that 'these arts are much abused by wandering Gypsies, who under colour of such knowledge, do commonly cheat silly people, and also rob their pockets, when they are viewing their hands and face to tell them their fortunes'.[124] According to Richard Saunders, publishing in 1663, the 'noble science' of chiromancy 'hath been much wounded' by these 'vulgar Gypsies'.[125] John Butler, writing in 1680, similarly differentiated 'the most sacred and divine science of astrology' from the falsities of Gypsy fortune-tellers, 'who as they counterfeit the feature of natural Egyptians by a mere artificial swarth wherewith they besmear their English faces, so abuse they the world with a dissembled skill of discerning secret and future things, whereas they know nothing at all but what they have learned by mere diabolical and juggling tricks'.[126] It was another charge against Gypsies that they brought predictive science into disrepute.

A few theorists, however, kept open minds about the powers of 'Egyptian' prediction. Was it possible, some wondered, that traces of ancient wisdom lingered among the Gypsies, who claimed an Egyptian ancestry? If Gypsies indeed were 'natives of Egypt, a country which anciently outvied all the world for skill in magic and the black arts of divination', could some of that knowledge have survived, however attenuated, among travellers in rural England?[127] Thomas Browne, the author of *Religio Medici* (1642), was willing to believe that 'the Egyptians, who were ever addicted to those abstruse and mystical sciences, had a knowledge [of chiromancy], to which those vagabond and counterfeit Egyptians do yet pretend, and perhaps retain a few corrupted principles which sometimes may verify their prognostics'.[128] The naval administrator and diarist Samuel Pepys was also open-minded about Gypsy prescience. After having his palm read in August 1663, he writes, 'it pleased me mightily to see how... I should look back and find what the Gypsy had told me to be true'.[129]

In an age of speculative and experimental philosophy it was not unreasonable to seek knowledge in unconventional places. The scientist Robert Boyle wrote in 1663 of a woman suffering *incontinentia urinae*, caused by a lacerated bladder, which 'was perfectly helped by wearing, as a Gypsy had taught her, a little bag hung about her neck, containing the powder made of a live toad, burnt in a new pot'. Boyle had this information from the Flemish physician Henricus ab Heer, who put the remedy to the test and published other useful 'receipts that came from mountebanks and even Gypsies'. Like other members of the Royal Society, Boyle believed that 'testimonies and observations' of this sort could be valuable for the development of natural philosophy, as if the Gypsies had knowledge worth knowing.[130]

The savant Joseph Glanvill was also willing to consider that the Gypsies 'were not such imposters as they were taken for, but that they had a traditional kind of learning among them, and could do wonders by the power of imagination'. Glanvill told the story of 'the scholar Gypsy' (the basis of Matthew Arnold's Victorian poem), who dropped out of Oxford to live with 'vagabond Gypsies' and acquired their 'traditional kind of learning'. The Gypsies taught him 'the power of advanced imagination', a kind of mind meld or remote sensing, which could prove valuable for modern science. Sir Isaac Newton evidently thought as much, for he referenced Glanvill's story in his 'Philosophical Questions'.[131]

Joining the Gypsies

The curious 'scholar Gypsy' was by no means the only vagabond imagined to have cast his lot with the Gypsies. The cony-catching pamphleteers and their imitators insisted that runaways with artificially darkened faces 'joined with them, and in time learned their craft and cunning'.[132] Playwrights and satirists also devised scenes involving characters who joined the Gypsies. Creative writers presented a Gypsy culture that was willing to absorb outsiders, because it was largely composed of counterfeits and impostors. Modelled on continental 'rogue' literature, this was a fantasy that grew in the telling.[133] Early modern dropouts, deserters, ne'r-do-wells, renegade schoolboys, and even London tradesmen were said to 'keep company with Gypsies', and could rise to become Gypsy 'princes', Gypsy 'kings', or the 'Infanta of the Gypsies', as if such figures really existed.[134] Becoming a Gypsy could be imagined as an extreme and perverse self-fashioning.

The most extensive and most fanciful representation of later Stuart Gypsies appears in the work of the prolific Restoration popularizer Richard Head. Drawing on Dekker and other Jacobean authors, as well as continental models, Head associates the self-made 'Gypsy' with the picaresque 'English rogue'. In *The Canting Academy, or, the Devils Cabinet Opened* (1673) he presents an elective community of home-grown wanderers who 'are admitted into their fellowship'. From otherwise ordinary backgrounds, these neophytes *joined* the Gypsies, and were incorporated into their company, so Head imagined, with an oath 'which these Gypsies and other strolling canters take when they are first admitted into this society'. The author invents a ritual of initiation comparable to that which bound apprentices to their master, or witches to the devil, 'that everyone must take before he is admitted into this ragged society'. Once incorporated, the new-made Gypsy exchanges his clothes for tatterdemalion rags, darkens his face with a 'tawny dye', and adopts the underground vocabulary of canting.[135]

In *The English Rogue Containing a brief Discovery of the most Eminent Cheats, Robberies, and other Extravagancies, by him Committed* (1688), Head's leading character tells how he sheltered with Gypsies early in his life of crime, and then became one of them: 'They told me that they were Gypsies, and if I would be of their gang and take part of their fortunes, they would be glad of my company; to which I consented, and the next day, being stripped out of my holiday habit into tatters and rags, I became one of their fraternity, having my face to be be-daubed with green walnuts, that I looked as much like a Gypsy as the best of [th]em.'[136] The Gypsy 'captain' in this story turns out to be a grammar-school-educated English runaway apprentice, once transported to Virginia and then returned, who relates how 'I resolved to follow the life of a strolling Gypsy, into which society I was joyfully received'.[137] With stories within stories, one counterfeit Gypsy presides over the acculturation of another.

Offering more detail than Dekker, Head also offers readers a prurient fantasy of Gypsy promiscuity, of the sort applied earlier to religious sects such as the Adamites, the Ranters, and the Family of Love (and sometimes also to New World indigenous people and the Irish). His counterfeit 'captain' relates that 'our females are all in common among us, and though their skins be discoloured, they have as good flesh as can be coveted by a youthful appetite'. Head asserts that, 'as they live together, so they lie promiscuously one with another; so that as they know not how to claim a propriety in the children begotten, the mothers only being sensible whose they are by conception, so all things else are in common among them'. But, far from free love and community of offspring being socially damaging, 'this general interest ties them more firmly together, than if all their rags were twisted into ropes to bind them indissolvably from a separation'.[138] This communal spirit also applied apparently to the provision of alcohol and the proceeds of crime, 'all things being in common amongst them; this it is which makes them take such delight in this villainous way of living'. And, 'having eaten more like beasts than men, they drink more like swine than human creatures'.[139] These imagined features of Gypsy life were supposed to horrify polite society, though they also helped to explain why work-shy and lecherous young men might be drawn to associate with the apparently carefree Gypsies.

The Gypsies, by this conceit, formed an open community, which almost anyone could join. Newcomers could adopt their manner, learn their trade, and pass as counterfeit Egyptians. They could thereby share in the Gypsies' 'good cheer', while also risking the penalties to which Gypsies were exposed by law. That this was almost entirely a fantasy has not stopped writers past and present from depicting the Gypsies as a 'counterfeit' amalgam of volunteer vagabond rogues. So-called true accounts of the lives and deaths of notorious criminals often related how their heroes joined the Gypsies and rose to 'be made much of amongst them'.[140] Pseudo-autobiographies of the eighteenth century plagiarized and embellished these stories. None of them paused to wonder why Gypsies would welcome outsiders who were unfamiliar with their ways, and who would be additional mouths to feed, or why such a person would become their 'king'. There were undoubtedly adventurers who spent time in the company of Gypsies, but the Gypsies were primarily a closed society, estranged from the rest by culture, heritage, and law.

A final condemnation, obviously indebted to Jacobean texts, appeared in *A New Dictionary of the Terms Ancient and Modern of the Canting Crew*, published in 1699. The author, known only by his initials B.E., described Gypsies as

> a counterfeit brood of wandering rogues and wenches, herding together and living promiscuously, or in common, under hedges and in barns, disguising themselves with blacking their faces and bodies, and wearing an antic dress,

as well as devising a particular cant, strolling up and down, and under colour of fortune-telling, palmistry, physiognomy, and cure of diseases, impose always upon the unthinking vulgar, and often steal from them, whatever is not too hot for their fingers, or too heavy to carry off.

As notorious members of 'the canting crew', they shared the road with such 'wanderers of fortune' as 'beggars, peddlers, hawkers, mountebanks, fiddlers, country-players, rope-dancers, jugglers, tumblers, showers of tricks, and raree-show men'.[141]

Drawn from a century's worth of stereotyping, pejorative descriptions like these would influence popular perceptions for another three hundred years. Written to amuse or alarm, they dealt in categories and constructs that were always artificial and usually out of date. Generally lacking particulars of name, place, and date, the Gypsies of the textual tradition were generic figures, generally loathsome, though sometimes endowed with rascally charm.

3

Tudor Gypsies against the Law

No reliable evidence survives of the Gypsies' first arrival in England, but it seems to have been in the reign of Henry VII (d.1509). Some may have sought refuge after the French expulsion order of 1504, and more may have followed on discovering England to be a relatively safe environment.[1] The earliest traces appear in gentry account books, such as those of Sir John Arundell of Lanhere, Cornwall, who paid twenty pence in 1504 or 1505 'to the Egyptians when they danced afore me'.[2] These Gypsies travelled as entertainers, capitalizing on their novelty, and were rewarded for being skilful, and interesting. Similar entries from the 1510s and 1520s show payments to 'Gypsions' at aristocratic establishments at Tendring Hall, Suffolk, and Thornbury, Gloucestershire.[3] An entry in the Cambridge treasurer's book for 1515 records 6s. 8d. paid 'for leading up the Egyptians to London to the king's Council', though whether to be rewarded or punished is unclear.[4] By this time the 'Egyptian' fortune-teller at Lambeth, south of London, had reportedly left the country.[5] Tudor sources refer to 'Gypsions', or 'Gypcyans', as well as Gypsies and Egyptians, and the terms were used interchangeably.

By 1530 they had clearly outstayed their welcome. The novelty had become a menace. Gypsies who arrived as entertainers or fortune-tellers— or perhaps as early modern asylum-seekers—acquired reputations as pickpockets and thieves. At Hereford in 1530, for example, the mayor detained a group of nineteen Gypsies, 'men, women and children . . . with bag and baggage', after a gentleman of Ludlow claimed they had robbed him of £4 7s. 6d.[6] No longer well received, the Gypsies were charged with idleness, immorality, falsehood, and crime—a reputation that continues internationally today.

Henry VIII's parliament attempted to deal with the problem in 1531 by banishing the 'outlandish people calling themselves Egyptians'. All Gypsies were to be expelled from England. The problem they posed was said to be threefold. First, by 'using no craft nor fact of merchandize', and by moving from 'place to place in great company', they fell outside the moral order, the economic hierarchy, and the social chain of being. Second, by claiming 'that they by palmistry could tell men's and women's fortunes', they 'by craft and subtlety have deceived the people of their money'. And third, in the course of these activities, they 'committed many and heinous felonies and robberies, to the great hurt and deceit of the people that they have come among'. Perceived as people without roots and without honesty, the Gypsies were a danger to society, an affront to the state, and offensive to God. Parliament's remedy was to remove them as quickly as possible by shipping them overseas. No more 'Egyptians' would be permitted to enter the realm, and those already in England would be rounded up and deported. If they did not leave within sixteen days, they faced imprisonment and forcible expulsion, with their goods and chattels forfeit to the state. Victims of Gypsy crimes could then sue for return of items 'craftily or feloniously taken or stolen' from them. Several writers on Gypsies misdate this legislation to 1530, though the parliament sat from 16 January to 31 March 1531.[7]

The measures of 1531 formed part of a programme of reformation targeting monks and nuns, as well as Gypsies, who preyed on the credulity of the faithful.[8] The reformation of the commonwealth went hand in hand with the reformation of morality and religion. The reformer Simon Fish had denounced the clergy as 'puissant and counterfeit holy and idle beggars and vagabonds', using language similar to that applied against Gypsies.[9]

In a companion piece of legislation, parliament associated 'Egyptians' with the larger social problem of 'persons being whole and mighty in body and able to labour' who refused to work. 'Idleness', the lawmakers noted, was the 'mother and root of all vices', from which sprang 'heinous offences and great enormities, to the high displeasure of God' and 'the marvellous disturbance of the common weale of this realm'. Offenders were to be whipped and placed in the stocks, then sent to their place of birth or last residence. Though not specifically directed against Gypsies, the vagrancy act of 1531 included as malefactors those travellers 'using divers and subtle crafty and unlawful games and plays, and some of them feigning themselves to have knowledge in physic, physiognomy, palmistry, or other crafty sciences, whereby they bear the people in hand, that they can tell their destinies, deceases and fortunes, and such other like fantastical imaginations, to the great deceit of the king's subjects'. Fortune-tellers of this sort were liable to be scourged by whipping, and repeat offenders could have their ears cut off at the pillory.[10] Further legislation in 1536 against 'valiant beggars and sturdy vagabonds' provided for repeat offenders 'to suffer pains and execution of death as a felon and as enemies of the commonwealth'.[11]

Gypsies were therefore subject to two sets of laws, one that treated them as vagrants to be punished, the other as aliens to be removed. The state conceived of Gypsies as 'outlandish' immigrants, with no business being in the king's dominions; but their social offence was to engage in deceitful disorders and to have no lawful calling. There was already a blurring of lines between the law's 'Egyptians', the community's 'Gypsies', and other kinds of disreputable wanderers. They could be aliens without being vagabonds, and some of them evidently had financial resources. When one of the 'Gypcons' died on the south coast at Lydd, Kent, in 1533, his companions paid nine shillings for a ceremonial church burial, and were otherwise unmolested.[12]

Tudor authorities expected the law to be enforced. Thomas Cromwell wanted 'Egyptians' shipped abroad by the first available wind. But the Gypsies proved uncooperative, hard to pin down. One group of travellers, led by Paul Faa, 'a native of Egypt in parts beyond seas', caused complications in June 1537 when a murder was committed in their company. The victim was described as 'an Egyptian called Sacole Femine'. Faa was arrested, but instead of being tried he was pardoned, conditional on departing the realm. He and 'his wandering associates called Egyptians' were given fifteen days to leave England.[13] These may have been the same 'Gipsons' allowed 'to tarry in the town [of Southampton] three of four days' in 1537, with temporary permission to trade in linen, satin, and silk cloth.[14]

State policy was to export the problem, but ordering did not mean accomplishment. The Gypsies still awaited deportation half a year later, and in the meantime committed more enormities. In October 1537 the Council called on justices, mayors, and sheriffs to apprehend certain 'Egyptians...for having robbed one Martin Femyne, the king's servant, who, with his wife and servants, were wounded and their lives endangered by the said Egyptians'.[15] Some of these Gypsies had apparently obtained letters of protection that the Council now revoked. It seems likely that the state became concerned about a feud between rival groups of Gypsies, and wanted to be rid of the lot of them.[16] The relation of Sacole Femine and Martin Femyne remains obscure, as is Martin's status as 'the king's servant', but Scottish records from 1540 name 'Martyn Femine' among a group of

'Egyptians' in dispute with others in their company, including leaders named Faa or Faw.[17]

A letter from Thomas Cromwell to Rowland Lee, President of the Council of the Marches, dated 5 December 1537, sheds light on the matter. The king, Cromwell said, had given 'pardon to a company of lewd persons within this realm, calling themselves Gipcyons, for a most shameful and detestable murder committed among them'. All had agreed 'that unless they should all avoid this his grace's realm by a certain day long since expired, it should be lawful to all his grace's officers to hang them, in all places of his realm where they might be apprehended, without any further examination or trial after form of law'. In other words, all remaining 'persons calling themselves Egyptians' risked summary execution. Unfortunately, Cromwell continued, the king had learned 'that they do yet linger here within his realm, not avoiding the same according to his commandment and their own promise, and that his poor subjects be daily spoiled, robbed, and deceived by them'. Local authorities, 'little regarding their duties towards his majesty, do permit them to linger and loiter in all parts, and to exercise all their false-hoods, felonies, and treasons unpunished'. There must be no further delay, Cromwell insisted, and any magistrate, knowing of any Gypsies, should 'compel them to depart to the next port of the sea to the place where they shall be taken; and...upon the first wind that may convey them into any part beyond the seas, to take shipping'. Anticipating that the Gypsies might have forged letters of authority, Cromwell ordered the officials to proceed, 'without sparing upon any commission, licence or placards that they may show or allege for themselves to the contrary'. Any Gypsies who 'shall in any wise break that commandment' should be 'executed according to the king's highness's said letters patent'.[18]

Despite these strictures, travellers 'naming themselves Egyptians' continued to cause trouble. Some wandered with impunity, and if they were shipped overseas might easily slip back. Reports of Gypsy deceits and depredations spread from Kent to Lincolnshire, from the West Country to East Anglia. One group was traced from the Cotswolds in Gloucestershire to the Chilterns in Buckinghamshire, where they tried to dispose of a parcel-gilt salt cellar, valued at £6 13s. 4d., apparently acquired 'by subtle and crafty means'. John Straunge of Cirencester reported being robbed by 'strangers called Egyptians', and under the statute of 1531 sued for return of items 'craftily or feloniously taken or stolen'. By the time the Gypsies were apprehended at Wycombe, however, the silver had changed hands several times, and the Gypsies had no traceable assets.[19]

Led by George Faa and Michael Meche, 'two Egyptians as they say', another large band intercepted in Staffordshire in February 1539 boasted little more than 'an old cushion of crimson velvet, an old gown of black velvet, an old torn gown of tawny satin', a grey horse worth 6s. 8d., and 'a little black horse called a nag', also worth 6s. 8d. When the sheriff examined them for being in the king's realm, potentially a capital offence, the Gypsy leaders produced a box of writings and testimonials that seemingly gave them safe passage. These included authorizations from the mayor of London, the sheriffs of Yorkshire and Worcestershire, the commissioners in the Marches, the king of Scotland, and the abbot of Holyrood, none convincingly authentic.[20] Though most likely themselves illiterate, the Gypsies evidently recognized the power of writing, which sufficed to impress gullible officials. Their journeys apparently ranged from southern Scotland to the English Midlands.

A few months later Kentish authorities stayed another group of 'Egyptians' in Romney Marsh. They too displayed a kind of passport, supposedly a patent under the Great Seal 'in behalf of John Nany, knight of Little Egypt, and his company', which officials referred to Cromwell.[21] Cromwell's 'Remembrances' for 1539 include the note, 'to advertise of the sayings of the Egyptians, and special letters to be written for their apprehension and punishment'. Government expenditure for the year included £6 13s. 4d. for 'costs and charges... for the apprehension of certain lewd persons calling themselves Egyptians'.[22] The travellers played a cat and mouse game with the authorities, which the Gypsies usually won.

Inventories of confiscations display Gypsy resources as well as Gypsy enterprise. When constables at Boston, Lincolnshire, searched a contingent of some eighty Gypsies in May 1540, and set some in the stocks as vagabonds, they found 'not so much as would pay for their meat and drink, nor none other baggage but one horse not worth four shillings'. Unless they had hidden their wealth, these Gypsies had little to show for their efforts. They claimed that they were trying to leave the country, had tried the port of King's Lynn, and were come to Boston in search of shipping. Town officials sent four of their leaders to London for examination, and herded the rest towards Newcastle and Hull to seek passage for Norway.[23] Another group of Gypsies needed charitable relief in June 1540 after officials at Canterbury confiscated their money and goods. The city chamberlain's accounts record £3 11s. 'received of the sale of the proceeds of the Egyptians attached and seized', plus 9s. more 'in money of the men Egyptians' and 4s. 9d. taken from 'the women Egyptians'. One of the appraisers was the keeper of the gaol where the Gypsies were temporarily housed. The city paid twelve pence to move them on towards Dover.[24]

Other 'people calling themselves Egyptians' were comparatively wealthy. One company caught at Bishop's Lydeard, Somerset, in October 1542 possessed six yards of black camlet (a luxury fabric), two ells of black worsted, and seventy-two ounces of silver plate and parcel-gilt, valued at more than £18, besides five good-quality horses worth 10s. each. Their haul also included 'a piece of silver plate weighing thirty-two ounces at 3s. 6d. the ounce', presumed stolen, which was taken from them and entrusted to the bishop of Bath and Wells.[25]

Officials in Huntingdonshire stayed another band of Gypsies with seventeen horses in the summer of 1544, and sought to know the king's pleasure regarding these 'lewd persons naming themselves Egyptians, who have long wandered in this realm... lately apprehended for robberies about Huntingdon'. On the king's behalf, Lord Chancellor Wriotheseley instructed that 'such of them as could be proved felons' should be arraigned according to the statute, and any others 'reported to be Englishmen' to be 'well whipped like vagabonds and so remitted to their countries'. Their horses could be sold to defray the cost of keeping them in custody. The Gypsies evidently constituted a composite band, immigrant and native-born, but their demography was changing. Two of the leaders were sentenced to be hanged, but the Gypsies surprised everyone by offering three hundred pounds to save them from the gallows. This was a huge sum of money, as much as an aristocrat's income, which suggests that some Gypsies, at least, had wealthy friends or deep pockets. The cash-strapped Council acknowledged 'it would be hard to attain this money otherwise'.[26]

Writing from Boulogne, in the midst of his war with France, Henry VIII instructed his Council that 'the Egyptians you wrote for are to be pardoned and the rest banished'. The Council recorded that 'we have taken such order that all the lewd people of this sort shall be dispatched out of the realm with all diligence, and doubt not but this example will make that neither they nor any other like will much covet hereafter to come hither'. And, lest any Gypsies attempted to root themselves in the English enclave on the Continent, they sent instructions to Calais 'for the ridding them out of the king's majesty's pale there'.[27] Nothing more is known of them, nor of the 'large troops of Egyptians' inhabiting the Scarsdale district in Derbyshire, who refused to serve in Henry

VIII's wars.[28] Parliament considered a new bill in 1545 for the punishment and expulsion of Gypsies, but the legislation came to nothing.[29]

A final burst of administrative energy in the waning years of Henry VIII's reign generated more documentation about Gypsies in England. In January 1546 the Council approved a passport 'for the Egyptians to pass with their bags, baggages, and other necessaries belonging to them, under the conduct of Philip Cazar, their governor, without impediment ... to embark at London' according to the Lord Admiral's orders.[30] (The Lord Admiral at this time was the high-flying John Dudley, Viscount Lisle, later to become Earl of Warwick and Duke of Northumberland.) By the end of March Cazar's contingent had reached Dover, to await shipping, when overly zealous local officials committed two of their leaders to gaol. The main group refused to depart without the others, and the Privy Council had to intervene to resolve the impasse. The government judged it more important to rid the realm of Gypsies than to mete out exemplary punishment, and the Council would 'rather see them dismissed than that their company should any longer tarry there for them' at public expense. However, 'if the offence were such as should require the course of the law to be executed, they should cause their train to embark out of hand and be dispatched without further tarrying for their leaders imprisoned'.[31] Later in the year the Council arranged for 'a vessel for the avoiding of the Egyptians, and letters to the deputies of Calais and Boulogne to avoid them at their arrival there'. Justices of the peace in Kent, East Anglia, and the Home Counties had instructions to deport all 'idle men called Egyptians', and to punish 'such as should offend the law'. The knight marshal Sir Ralph Hopton was reimbursed twenty pounds that year 'for the conveyance of the Egyptians out of the realm'.[32]

There may have been more circulation of Gypsies between England, Scotland, Ireland, and France than is generally recognized. As early as 1516 the Earl of Kildare presented a horse to 'the earl of Little Egypt', and may have taken Gypsies under his protection. A mysterious Melour Faa appeared in 1528 as a consultant to the earl, and declared it 'an evil sign' when Kildare's daughter returned to Ireland before him. More 'Egyptians driven from Scotland by stress of weather' found refuge in Dublin in 1541. These included 'Powyell Fayoff of Little Egypt', who may have been the Paul Faa expelled from England in 1537, and 'John Naune and his company', most likely John Nany's group of Gypsies pursued by Cromwell in 1539. Members of the Faa kindred were especially prominent among Gypsies who criss-crossed the border between England and Scotland.[33]

Mid-Tudor Restraints

The parliament of EdwardVI addressed the Gypsy problem again in late 1547 but achieved nothing substantive.[34] Much has been made among modern Roma activists of the statute of EdwardVI that allegedly subjected Gypsies to branding and slavery. It is often discussed alongside references to Gypsy slavery in eighteenth-century Wallachia and slave labour under the Nazis, as an example of state persecution.[35] But anyone who reads the 1547 law will see that it is called 'an act for the punishment of vagabonds and for the relief of the poor', and that Gypsies are nowhere mentioned. The law does indeed take harsh measures against vagrants and idle wanderers. Uniquely, among English social legislation, it provided for such loiterers to be 'marked with a hot iron in the breast the mark of V' (for vagabond) and enslaved for two years. Runaways and repeat offenders were to be branded on the cheek with an 'S' (for slave), and enslaved in perpetuity. But three points need to be made. First, this was an extreme and experimental response to the problem of vagrancy and poverty, not an attack on Gypsies per se. Second, the law specifically exempted foreign-born vagrants, such as 'Egyptians' were presumed to be, from the physical penalties of branding, requiring only that they be conveyed into their own countries at community expense. And, third, the law was of short duration and minimal execution, and was repealed in 1550. It was, the historian Paul Slack observes, 'the most spectacular failure'.[36]

The Edwardian regime did concern itself with Gypsies, but with no great outlay of originality or energy. The young king noted in June 1549 that 'there was a privy search made through Sussex for all vagabonds, Gypsies, conspirators, prophesiers, all players, and such like', but this was more a routine security sweep than a targeted attack on travellers.[37] In January 1550 Sir George Conyers informed the Council of the North about John Roland, an 'Egyptian' who had counterfeited the king's Great Seal, an offence akin to treason. Informing against Roland, and attempting to dissociate themselves from his crime, were fellow Gypsies George, Amy and Baptist Fawe, from the well-known Anglo-Scottish family of Faa or Faw. All were held in Durham prison while the Earl of Shrewsbury, the president of the Council, decided what to do with them. None of them was enslaved.[38]

The government still hoped that 'Egyptians...may be sent out of the realm with all convenient diligence', but hoping was not enough. Repeated orders 'that the Egyptians...may be used according to the order of the law, and the country unburdened of them as soon as may be', proved ineffective. In April and May 1552 the Privy Council again instructed justices in Bedfordshire, Buckinghamshire, Norfolk, and Suffolk 'to cause all such idle persons as name themselves Egyptians to be conveyed from place to place ... till they shall come to the next haven or port, and thence to be without any manner delay dispatched and sent out of the realm, not suffering them in any wise to wander or stray abroad in the country in this their conveyance'.[39] One such Gypsy whose journey was interrupted was 'Anthoine an Egyptian', who was buried at Gravesend, Kent, in May 1553.[40]

Fragmentary as it is, the evidence leaves the impression that Gypsies could travel around England with little risk of molestation. Holding or herding them was like trying to divert a river or move water with a sieve. Central government waxed indignant, but interceptions and arrests were rare. The administrative effort was fierce but fickle, and only the most troublesome 'Egyptians' faced deportation. Notably distinct from ordinary vagrants and beggars, the Gypsies moved on foot, or with small strings of horses, following the geography and calendar of markets and fairs. They lived as entertainers and fortune-tellers, and also by trading in animals and textiles. Some many have set up as travelling cunning folk, offering cures and advice as well as divinations and deceptions. There may have been two or more main contingents in mid-Tudor England, one working a south-eastern circuit and another based in the north and west.

Banded in groups of a dozen or so members, and occasionally gathering in companies of a hundred or more, the Gypsies must have seemed intimidating as well as strange. Though most likely themselves illiterate, some of them recognized the power of writing, and were sophisticated enough to amass papers that seemingly gave them protection. Some, at least, spoke a distinctive Gypsy language, a dialect of Romani, with sufficient English to tell fortunes and outwit the authorities. Andrew Boorde's celebrated treatise *The Fyrst Boke of the Introduction of Knowledge*, first published in 1542, included thirteen phrases of 'Egypt speech', with such useful Romani expressions as 'lachittur ydyves' ('good morrow'); 'cater myla barforas' ('how far is it to the next town'); and the essential instruction 'achae da mai manor la veue' ('maid, give me bread and wine'). Where these fragments were found, and who was speaking, were never specified. They could have come from a Sussex alehouse, or the English enclave of Calais, or from Boorde's extensive travels in continental Europe. Historical linguists recognize them as one of the earliest documented transcriptions of the inflected Romani dialect.[41]

The total population of Gypsies in mid-Tudor England is impossible to calculate, but it is unlikely to have been more than a thousand. Claims of ten thousand Gypsies in 1528 or 1577 are entirely fanciful, though often repeated in popular surveys.[42] State policy was deportation, but the problem grew complicated as Gypsies reproduced themselves, and ordinary English vagrants apparently attached themselves to Gypsy bands.[43]

A quarter of a century after Henry VIII's legislation, the parliament of Philip and Mary returned to the Gypsy problem. Notwithstanding past attempts to rid England of 'certain outlandish people calling themselves Egyptians', such people had 'enterprised to come over again into this realm, using their old accustomed devilish and naughty practices and devices, with such abominable living as is not in any Christian realm to be permitted'. The legislation of 1554 raised the rhetorical temperature—the Gypsies were now 'devilish' as well as 'outlandish'—and added punitive weight. The new law called again for their forced removal, imposed fines on facilitators of Gypsy immigration, and death for any Gypsy lingering over a month. Henceforth it was a felony to be a Gypsy in England, but a proviso offered an exception to 'any of the said persons commonly called Egyptians' who 'shall leave that naughty, idle and ungodly life and company, and be placed in the service of some honest and able inhabitant... or that shall honestly exercise himself in some lawful work or occupation'—in other words, to cease living as a Gypsy. The choice was expulsion, the gallows, or assimilation, providing the law could bring them within reach.[44]

Enforcement, as ever, was piecemeal and half-hearted. One of the first implementations of the law was in October 1555, when the sheriffs of Norfolk and Suffolk imprisoned people 'such as name themselves Egyptians', and confiscated their 'passports and licences'. The Council instructed local officials 'to examine the truth of their pretended licences', to see the offenders punished 'according to the statutes', and to hasten 'their transportation out of the realm'.[45] A few years later another group of 'Egyptians', held in the White Lion prison at Southwark, sought release on the grounds that they would perish for lack of sustenance, and would lose the use of their limbs if their misery continued. Whoever drafted their petition knew that it would help if they acknowledged their 'transgression', agreed to amend their lives, and showed willingness to depart 'home into our country' under penalty of death.[46] Perhaps more compelling was the argument that keeping the Gypsies in gaol cost money, and the community was better served by letting them leave.

As before, the Gypsies proved slippery and elusive. Laws against them were no more effective than the laws against sumptuous apparel, although potentially more lethal. Gypsies continued to arrive, to proliferate, and to travel around England, living, it was said, 'upon the spoil of the simple people'. One offender, 'Lawrence Valentine, a Gypsy' (*Aegyptius*), was 'examined and punished' by the London College of Physicians in 1556, not for violating laws against Egyptians but for providing irregular medical services.[47] The exotic was becoming domesticated, as Gypsies established themselves in the wayfaring culture of early modern England.

Early Elizabethan Encounters and Responses

From its very beginning the Elizabethan regime was concerned about 'vagabonds, unlawful beggars, rogues, and Egyptians'. Responding in 1559 to the arrest in Dorset of 'a great number of vagrants having the manner of Egyptians', the Council instructed Lord Mountjoy, the Lord Lieutenant, how to proceed against these people of 'horrible and shameful life'. The government thought it 'very convenient that some sharp example and execution should be made according to the order of our laws upon a good number of them . . . that no favour otherwise than the law permitteth may be moved to any such as may be proved felons or such like malefactors, or that have been before time apprehended . . . or set at liberty upon compassion, or put out of the realm at any time for the like offence heretofore, nor to such as have from their youth of long time ha[u]nted this lewd life, nor to such as be the principal captains and ringleaders of the company'. The worst offenders were to be charged as felons at the assizes, while the rest would be speedily 'conveyed out of the realm'. Compassionate treatment, however, was recommended for nursing mothers, children under 16, and 'such as very lately have come to this trade of life'.[48] One such innocent, 'Joan the daughter of an Egyptian', was baptized at Lyme Regis early in 1559.[49]

When the Gypsies appeared before Dorchester assizes in September 1559, a technicality cast a cloud on their indictment. Justices Richard Weston and Richard Harper explained to the Council that 'touching their coming into this realm, that they in December last came out of Scotland into England by Carlisle, which is all by land, and were not transported or conveyed hither by any according to the statute'. The law of Philip and Mary assumed that Gypsies arrived from overseas, whereas this group had migrated overland

within Britain. The assize court 'proceeded to their deliverance', while asking London for advice 'touching punishment for their idle and naughty life
and dispatch out of this realm'.[50]

Free again, the Gypsies drifted slowly northward, reaching Gloucestershire
by late October. Lord Mountjoy, the Dorset Lieutenant, was unwilling to
see 'that idle and ill kind of people' unpunished, and sent the bailiff of
Blandford to his counterpart at Longhope, Gloucestershire, further to harass
them. Eight individuals 'naming themselves Egyptians' were taken to Gloucester, where their treatment can be inferred from records of payment 'for birch
to make rods to beat the Egyptians naked about the castle', and for the rent
of the cart 'whereat the said Egyptians were tied and so brought about the
city and scourged' before being released.[51]

The story was not all violent harassment, however, as fragmentary evidence suggests that some Gypsies found temporary welcome. It appears that
the 'Jepsiyans' who used the church house at Stratton, Cornwall, in three
successive Februaries from 1559 to 1561 were travelling Gypsy performers,
given hospitality in exchange for entertainment. Not quite knowing what
to make of the newcomers, the wardens first recorded them as 'Jewes' before
altering the entry to 'Jespsiyans'.[52] The London diarist Henry Machyn heard
the rumour in 1561 that certain outcasts from Egypt (presumably Gypsies)
were 'ready to set on the Great Turk with great armies of men'. Association
with Christendom's great struggle against the Islamic Turks might secure
some tolerance for local 'Egyptian' travellers.[53]

More complications arose in 1562 when another group of Gypsies was
arrested in Oxfordshire. The sheriff gaoled various 'vagabonds naming
themselves Egyptians' at Oxford and Wallingford, but could not decide what
to do about 'their children, whose years may make declaration that they
were innocent of their parents' lewdness'. The Council kicked the problem
back to the locality, commending the magistrates for their 'travail in appre-
hending and committing the Egyptians passing through the county', and
instructing them 'to do as they shall think requisite'.[54] It was apparent that
the Gypsy population had changed, and existing measures were ineffective.

Elizabeth I's parliament addressed the problem in 1563, with a new act
'for the punishment of vagabonds calling themselves Egyptians'. (Parliament
met from 12 January to 10 April 1563, although historians commonly misdate this legislation to 1562, apparently not realizing that the calendar year
changed on 25 March.) Against the background of anxiety over religion,
uncertainty about the succession, and the queen's recent brush with small-

pox, members addressed the 'dangers, perils, and mischiefs' affecting 'the lamentable estate of this commonwealth'. The Lord Keeper Sir Nicholas Bacon recommended 'sharp laws... for the banishing of sloth, corruption and fear', and parliament responded with major legislation concerning poverty and work (the 1563 poor law and the statute of artificers), as well as acts against perjury, buggery, witchcraft, and Gypsies.[55]

The Elizabethan statute concerning 'Egyptians' renewed the Marian legislation against 'that false and subtle company' while addressing more recent developments. Earlier Tudor law had assumed that the Gypsies 'calling themselves Egyptians' were 'strangers', born overseas and transported from abroad. But now 'there is a scruple and doubt risen whether such persons as being born within this realm of England or other [of] the queen's highness's dominions, and are or shall become of the fellowship or company of the said vagabonds, by transforming or disguising themselves in their apparel or in a certain counterfeit speech or behaviour, are punishable by the said act'. Henceforth, it was enacted, anyone 'seen or found within this realm of England or Wales, in any company or fellowship of vagabonds commonly called or calling themselves Egyptians, or counterfeiting, transforming or disguising themselves by their apparel, speech or other behaviour like unto such vagabonds', and continuing so for one month, 'shall by virtue of this act be deemed and judged a felon', liable to pains of death. It was henceforth punishable by hanging to be a Gypsy, to look like a Gypsy, or to consort with Gypsies—a crime of status rather than activity that applied as much to native-born as to alien 'Egyptians'.

Once again, the law offered Gypsies the choice of entering 'some honest service' or taking up 'some lawful work', so long as they 'utterly forsake the said idle and false trade, conversation and behaviour of the said counterfeit or disguised vagabonds, commonly called or calling themselves Egyptians'. To emphasize this point, the statute stressed that it was not intended 'to compel any person or persons born within any of the queen's majesty's dominions to depart out of this realm of England or Wales, but only to constrain and bind them... to exercise themselves... honestly in some lawful work, trade or occupation'. Children under the age of 14 were exempt, as were Gypsies already in prison awaiting expulsion. None of the English laws adopted the French practice of shaving the heads of Gypsy women and depriving the men of their beards.

The anti-Gypsy legislation of 1563 remained technically in force until 1783, but, as we shall see, it was rarely rigorously enforced.[56] The Jacobean character-writer Sir Thomas Overbury imagined that some travellers 'recanted Gypsyism' because of this 'terrible statute',[57] but there is no evidence to this effect. Later reformers looked back on the act as 'the most barbarous...that ever disgraced our criminal code', and modern Romani activists have cited it as the apogee of legal savagery. The Victorian Gypsy enthusiast George Borrow described how 'the gibbets of England groaned and creaked beneath the weight of Gypsy carcasses', and another nineteenth-century expert imagined Tudor authorities 'hunting the women and children with bloodhounds, and dragging the Gypsy leaders to the gallows'. The claim has often been repeated, that 'very great numbers were executed for no other crime but being Gypsies'.[58] In practice, however, the application of the law never matched its rhetoric. There were executions, but not as many as has been suggested. A recent 'history of Gypsies' explains 'the mismatch between intention and action', in England and elsewhere, by reference to 'the limitations of state power, and the resilience of Gypsy culture in the face of oppression';[59] but it is just as likely that local authorities themselves exercised discretion and preferred less sanguinary solutions. Later chapters further examine dealings with Gypsies under Elizabeth I and the Stuart monarchs.

The word 'counterfeit' in the statute of 1563 has caused endless problems in discussions of Gypsy identity, persuading some people that 'counterfeit Egyptians' were not really Gypsies at all. Rather, it is suggested, they were volunteer vagabonds who mimicked, acquired, or otherwise inhabited the manner of 'authentic' Gypsies. 'Egyptians' or 'Gypsies', by this argument, were a constructed category of criminal imposters, rather than an identifiable people.[60] This is an important topic in Romani politics and scholarship, where Gypsy ethnicity is hotly contested. The leaders of Elizabethan England may have been anxious lest some of the queen's subjects should be seduced into a pernicious way of life, but the state's main concern was with Gypsies known as Egyptians, not vagrants who pretended to be Gypsies. The word 'counterfeit' meant forged, imitated, or sham, but in sixteenth-century usage it could also mean false and deceptive, the opposite of 'honest', as in 'counterfeit rogues',[61] 'counterfeit witches',[62] and the 'counterfeit' priests of the 'fond, fained, and counterfeit' Roman church.[63] Such people were no less rogues, witches, or priests for being 'counterfeit'.

Applied to Gypsies or 'Egyptians', the word intensified rather than questioned their identity as practitioners of deceit. They were 'counterfeit' because of their fraudulent practices, and because they passed themselves as

'Egyptians'. Few people believed that Gypsies actually came from Egypt, though some speculated that they may have inherited some of the wisdom of that ancient people. When constables and magistrates subsequently cited 'counterfeit Egyptians', it was to secure prosecution in accord with the statutes, not just to allude to ne'er-do-wells who became Gypsies by association. The law preserved and perpetuated the terms 'Egyptian' and 'counterfeit Egyptian' for people commonly described as Gypsies. The usage continued into the eighteenth century, more a stock phrase than a reasoned assessment.

In 1571 some councillors proposed to extend the anti-Gypsy law to fugitive Catholic priests who travelled in disguise as serving men, because they too were counterfeit vagabonds.[64] This may be the basis for the otherwise false claim that 'the Tudor state blamed Gypsies for plots against Elizabeth I and of harbouring Spanish spies in their midst'.[65] However, there is no evidence to suggest that 'agents of the Pope' found 'a cloak for their subversion in the camps of travellers and Gypsies', as one recent study posits.[66]

No Tudor proclamation specifically addressed Gypsies, but the Privy Council periodically urged sheriffs and justices to enforce existing laws against rogues, vagrants, beggars, and 'Egyptians', who 'use no ordinary and daily trade of life to get their living'. The Council warned the Sheriff of Surrey that such offenders were 'not only abominable in the sight of almighty God, but very harmful, slanderous and dangerous to the common weal'.[67] Echoing the earlier Tudor vagrancy laws, the statute of 1598 'for punishment of rogues, vagabonds and sturdy beggars' also encompassed 'persons . . . wandering and pretending themselves to be Egyptians, or wandering in the habit, form or attire of counterfeit Egyptians', as well as tellers of 'destinies, fortunes or such other like fantastical imaginations'. All such people were to be whipped, and sent back to their parish of birth or residence (if such could be determined), and especially 'dangerous' rogues faced imprisonment, banishment, or consignment 'perpetually to the galleys of this realm' (even though galleys had all but disappeared from the late Elizabethan navy).[68] By the end of the Elizabethan age, then, Gypsies had found their way into every corner of rural England, where they were menaced by the law but only occasionally drawn into its meshes.

4

Gypsies and Counterfeits
in Elizabethan England

Tudor statutes vilified the Gypsies as crafty and subtle, thievish and deceitful, devilish, naughty, and 'counterfeit'. They were rootless and unchurched, their 'difference' a matter of 'trade of life' as well as cultural heritage and evil character. The legislation of 1563 gave the authorities a powerful weapon to inspire fear in 'Egyptians', 'counterfeit Egyptians', and people who consorted with them. Making Gypsies felons and threatening them with death, it was unique in criminalizing people for who they were rather than for what they did. Commending this recently passed legislation, the Speaker of the House of Commons reminded members that 'laws without execution be as a torch unlighted or a body without a soul. Therefore look well to the execution.'[1] The charge applies as much to modern historians as to early modern administrators.

This chapter reviews encounters between travelling Gypsies and local authorities in Elizabethan England. It gathers evidence from a variety of documents to show how the law was applied, ignored, or circumvented from the 1560s to the beginning of the seventeenth century. The records are not only external to Gypsy culture, but often hostile to it and baffled by it, but they constitute our most fruitful source. They shed light on the attitudes and understandings of constables and magistrates who were responsible for policing and discipline, and also, less directly, on the doings of the Gypsies themselves.

Egyptian Vagabonds

Surviving records reveal varying responses to Gypsies and 'counterfeit Egyptians'. In Yeovil, Somerset, in 1564, the churchwardens continued to deal amicably with the 'Gipsians', allowing them use of the parish house.[2] Elsewhere relations turned hostile. Early in August 1566 the constables of Great Chesterford, Essex, apprehended fourteen 'vagabonds otherwise called Egyptians', with a dozen or so children travelling with them. But, rather than dealing with them according to the 1563 statute, they handed them over to their counterparts at Ickleton, Cambridgeshire. For the next few weeks the Gypsies were shuttled from parish to parish, even county to county, forcibly itinerant, while the authorities decided what to do with them. Cambridgeshire officials returned them to Essex, where they were herded by the constables of Wimbish to town authorities at Saffron Walden, on to Littlebury, and then back to Little Chesterford, close to where they had first been intercepted. The Gypsies eventually appeared before the Essex Quarter Sessions, and were either dismissed or remanded to the assizes. Reports by different officials refer to these same travellers as 'ejepcyanse', 'egipsyens', 'counterfett egypcyans', and 'Gypsyas', indicating yet again the interchangeability of the terms.[3]

The names of the adults in the company, spelled variably in different lists, included Christian Laurence (or Larduke), Edmond Laurence, John Laurence, Dorothy Laurence, Christopher Laurence, Katherine Peter (or Pettit), Elizabeth Peter, William Balsebane, Agnes Penko, Barbara Dego (or Ego), Jacken Dego (or Sego Gaxon), Mary Symond (or Symon), Margaret Roberts, and William Roberts. Six more men—George and Christopher Salmon, Henry Bastian, John Charles, William Atkinson, and Christopher Lawrence— were charged with feloniously consorting with so-called Egyptians, contrary to the statute, but the Chelmsford Assize jury found them all 'not guilty'. Others in their company included Thomas Williams the elder, Thomas Williams the younger, Katherine Williams, Margaret Amy, and Davy Rumpull. They evidently comprised several kin-connected groups, with a mixture of English and exotic-sounding names. Ejected from Essex, these 'counterfeit Egyptians' and their associates were transferred across the Thames from East Tilbury to the constables of Gravesend, who moved them southward through Kent into Sussex.[4] Local authorities apparently preferred removal to prosecution, essentially nullifying the statute that made Gypsies felons.

Less fortunate were David and Nicholas Fawe, perhaps descendants of the Faa family that had troubled Thomas Cromwell, who were convicted at the Kent assizes in July 1569 of consorting with Egyptians, and were sentenced to hang. But other so-called Egyptians in their company were acquitted. Among them were William Bastyan, James Valentine, and John Valentine, whose names were already familiar.[5] Thirteen more counterfeit 'Egyptians' indicted at the Essex summer assizes in 1570 were found guilty but secured pardons, a reminder that sentencing was a stage, not an end, with multiple opportunities for alternative outcomes. The group included William and George Fawe, who were almost certainly kin to the Fawes who had been condemned the previous year in Kent.[6]

Wandering Gypsies found a friend, or at least an accomplice, in Richard Massey, a Cheshire schoolmaster, who used his literacy to forge licences and passports that purportedly authorized their travel. Massey's fake licences showed up among Gypsies as far south as the Thames Valley. When 'certain lewd vagabonds, men and women, naming themselves Egyptians', were apprehended in Berkshire in March 1577 they displayed 'a counterfeit licence', allegedly granted by the Council at York. Under examination they confessed that the paper was the work of 'one Massey, a schoolmaster dwelling... within a mile of Whitchurch' in Cheshire, close to the Shropshire border.[7] (There was evidently a black market in documents and seals, which some Gypsies used to fool gullible officials. One vagrant later claimed 'that he gave 20d. for them to a man whom he met on the road, and who wrote them on his knees'. Another traveller arrested in Wiltshire obtained his forged pass from a schoolmaster at Lye, near Bristol.[8] Essex authorities learned in 1581 of the work of Davy Bennett, who could copy any justice's seal, 'and so he will do their hands, for that he writeth sundry hands, and hath most commonly about him a little bag full of those counterfeit seals'.[9] The cony-catching 'fraternity of vagabonds' allegedly included the literate 'Jackman', who 'useth to make counterfeit licenses... and sets to seals'.[10])

Massey was quickly arrested and imprisoned. Under examination in April 1577, he confessed to forging a grant from the Council at York 'unto certain rogues naming themselves Egyptians'. The Privy Council instructed the sheriff of Chester to transport the schoolmaster to the Marshalsea prison in London, 'under safe guard, and to be kept from conference by the way'. Counterfeiting licences under the Great Seal was a capital offence, and Massey spent a miserable few months in prison while his wife became 'an humble suitor unto their lordships for him'. He was eventually released and bound over in the sum of forty pounds (more than a year's income for a schoolmaster) to appear at the next Gaol Delivery in Shropshire, where he had allegedly committed his crime. What befell him is unknown.[11]

Meanwhile, the Gypsies taken in Berkshire with Massey's forged papers faced a special commission of Oyer and Terminer (to hear and determine the matter). Some of the 'rogues' of their company were traced to the adjacent counties of Buckinghamshire and Oxfordshire, where they were charged with 'naming themselves Egyptians' and 'deceiving her majesty's subjects under colour of a counterfeit licence'—a double counterfeiting of identity and documents. Their leaders were tried at Aylesbury for high treason, for falsifying warrants under the Great Seal, though one, Philip Bastien, was set aside 'because he may give evidence against others'. Roland Gabriel, Thomas Gabriel, William Gabriel, Lawrence Bannister, Christopher Jackson, George Jackson, Richard Jackson, and the widow Katherine Deago were all found guilty of 'counterfeiting, transferring, and altering themselves in dress, language, and behaviour to such vagabonds called Egyptians, contrary to statute'. All were sentenced to be hanged, though whether all went to the gallows is uncertain. Katherine Deago was most likely reprieved, for a Gypsy with that name appeared in Essex a year later.[12]

Certain surnames became familiar to judicial authorities, though increasing numbers of Gypsies shared names no different from ordinary English men and women. Bannisters, Gabriels, Jacksons, and Valentines were especially prominent in the Elizabethan era. The Philip Bastien who gave evidence in 1577 was probably related to the Henry Bastian indicted in Essex in 1566 and the William Bastyan indicted in Kent in 1569. 'Egyptians' committed at the summer assizes at Horsham, Sussex, in 1577 included the widow Agnes Bannister with Elizabeth, Margaret, and another Agnes Bannister; Thomas Balmer alias James Follentyne (or Valentine) and Margaret Follentyne his wife; George Follentyne and Margaret his wife; Henry Follentyne and Margaret his wife; yet another Margaret Follentyne, widow; William Jackson, Dorothy Jackson, Catherine Jackson, and the widow Catherine Jackson; William Harvey and Charity his wife; and single women Eleanor Thomas and Margaret Mose.[13] Edmund Sheres, Lettice Jackson, four members of the Bannister family, and three surnamed Gabriel were among the Gypsies indicted at the Essex assizes at Brentwood in 1578, along with Katherine Deago, and all were found 'not guilty'.[14] Victorian Gypsylorists and some of their successors searched for characteristic 'Gypsy names', but every one was shared with members of the larger settled community.

The government at Westminster wanted the nation's laws enforced, but too often discovered 'a universal negligent and willful permission of vagabonds and sundry beggars commonly called rogues and in some parts Egyptians'. The Privy Council threatened action against justices who failed to punish such 'disordered persons', but central direction was inconsistent.[15]

Local justices often asked the Council what to do when they encountered 'certain assemblies and companies of lewd persons calling themselves Egyptians'. The answers were not always helpful. When magistrates in Herefordshire informed London about 'certain assemblies and companies of lewd persons calling themselves Egyptians' in 1573, the Council instructed them to 'try and execute according to law the principal heads and ringleaders for terror and example; and for the rest, proceed against them as rogues and send them home into their countries, or use such moderation as they shall think good'.[16] When they reported the arrest in 1589 of 'certain lewd and bad persons terming themselves Egyptians, that lived by deceitful shifts, pilfering and abusing of the people, going from place to place…with a counterfeit passport, thereby increasing their offence and lewdness', the Council advised them to do everything 'meet for their correction, and to rid and ease the country of those bad and lewd kind of people'.[17] When the sheriff of Radnor, Wales, apprehended forty 'vagrant persons terming themselves Egyptians' in 1579, he asked the Privy Council for a special commission to bring them to immediate trial, rather than face 'the charges that might grow by the feeding of so great a number in prison till the next assizes'.[18] Confronting a similar problem with Gypsies in Nottinghamshire, the Council advised that 'such punishment may be inflicted upon them as shall be fit for their deserts'.[19]

From 1581 onwards magistrates could also turn to William Lambard's *Eirenarcha: or of the Office of the Iustices of Peace*, which offered a convenient recapitulation of the statutes. Lambard reminded readers that a felony had been committed 'if any strangers, calling themselves, or being commonly called Egyptians, have remained in the realm one month; and if any person (being fourteen years of age)…hath been seen, or found in the fellowship of such Egyptians, or…hath disguised himself like to them…by the space of one month'. The same handbook explained that justices could 'seize all the goods of any outlandish persons (calling themselves Egyptians) that shall come into this realm', so long as they made account thereof to the queen in the Exchequer. *Eirenarcha* offered little advice for difficult local circumstances, and held to the view that the Gypsy problem was related to immigration.[20] Lambard himself 'joined in the examination of eight persons that counterfeited their apparel and language as the rogues called Egyptians were wont to do' in August 1581, and consigned them to the local gaol in Kent.[21]

The Tudor statutes, as Lambard noted, allowed sheriffs to confiscate the goods of Gypsies, in order to compensate those from whom they had 'craftily or feloniously taken or stolen' them. Records of confiscations add to our knowledge of Gypsy itinerancy, despite the fact that inventories were notoriously imprecise and incomplete. 'Egyptians' in Northumberland suffered losses around 1573 when the bailiff of Shotton confiscated their gear 'concerning the coursing of a horse'.[22] In 1579 the sheriff of Lincolnshire accounted for 'certain Egyptians' goods seized into his hands', including two horses and a mare of divers colours, and a few small eyelets of gold, worth 32s. 6d. in all. Another party boasted little more than two old mares, one lame nag, and 'certain old silver', worth in total £2 3s. 4d.[23] A similarly sad collection of scrawny beasts was all that remained with the sheriff of Cambridgeshire in May 1588, after certain 'Egyptians' had moved on. Their equipage included 'a dark sorrel nag; a grey mare; two old jade mares; one white old jade; one blind curtail; one sorrel dun lame jade; two white jades being lame geldings; one little stone nag; one brown mare; a brown spavined gelding'. These were horses, indeed, but poor ones, long past their finest condition. The sheriff valued the best of them at 6s. 8d., the old jade mares at 4s. 2d. each, and the lame jade geldings at only 3s. 4d., at a time when more favoured horses cost two pounds or more apiece.[24] Other evidence suggests that some Gypsies were adept at hiding their wealth, perhaps storing it with associates or colluding with local officials. Gaolers and justices sometimes took their possessions to pay for their keep in custody. The Gypsies were rarely destitute, until their goods were confiscated, and usually had means of repairing their fortunes.

A Star Chamber Story

A complex episode from Nottinghamshire shows Gypsies in collision with the law, and magistrates in conflict with each other, as they wrestled with the Gypsy problem. As often happens in such cases, the documents shed more light on the authorities themselves than on those they attempted to govern.

The difficulties arose around Easter 1591, when villagers from Elkesley, East Markham, and Tuxford complained about more than a hundred Gypsies, 'called of some Egyptians', who had gathered on the Great North Road. Apparently they were heading towards Lincolnshire for Gainsborough fair, which was held on the Monday after Easter, this year on 5 April. Their leader, Thomas Jackson, stood out with his distinctive blue coat, a sign, perhaps, of status and wealth. (Only the year before magistrates in Essex interviewed a Thomas Jackson, possibly the same man, who led a band of transients accused of stealing chickens; he was said to be skilled in the canting language of 'pedlars' French', and claimed to have served the Lord Stafford. At that time Jackson belonged to a company of more than thirty men, women, and children, who travelled through Yorkshire, Nottinghamshire, Northamptonshire, Rutlandshire, Bedfordshire, Hertfordshire, Essex, Cambridgeshire, Norfolk, and Kent, before falling foul of the authorities. Edward, baron Stafford (1553–1603) was patron to travelling players and bear-keepers, and may have offered protection to Gypsies.[25])

Responding to complaints of pilferage and robbery, Nottinghamshire justices William Cardinal and Anthony Neville performed their duty and set the principal offenders in stir. Before the Gypsies could come to trial, however, fellow justices Peter Roos (or Rosse), William Sutton, and a Mr Basset set them all free and allowed them to continue their journey. Cardinal and Neville complained that they were crossed and disgraced, and referred the matter to the Quarter Sessions at Retford and to higher authorities in London. The dispute was no longer only about Gypsies, but about gentry honour, legality, and magisterial power. It may even have been a surrogate struggle for aristocratic factions competing for regional ascendancy. Disagreement about how to deal with Gypsies developed into a legal and political tussle, involving suits and counter-suits in the court of Star Chamber, and intervention by the Privy Council.[26]

Justices Cardinal and Neville recited 'the lewd behaviour of those vagrant persons terming themselves Egyptians, that have committed sundry outrages on her majesty's good subjects', and complained to the Privy Council that the other justices 'did set at liberty such malefactors and seditious people'. The Council responded by recommending 'the apprehension and committing to prison of so many of those disordered and tumultuous people as shall be yet found in those parts, to the end such punishment may be inflicted upon them as shall be fit for their deserts'. They also summoned Roos to explain himself in London.[27]

Queen Elizabeth's attorney general, Sir John Popham, grilled Roos in Star Chamber. As an experienced lawyer, 'a double reader in court', surely Roos knew better than to set free 'such a loose and lewd band of vagrant and idle rogues'. As 'a man learned in the law', he surely should 'have first conferred with his fellow justices, that committed the said Egyptians, to have known the cause', rather than yielding to 'humours and persuasions' to set them at liberty. The Gypsies, as everyone knew, were 'lewd . . . vagrant . . . idle . . . seditious . . .

disordered...tumultuous...and notorious', and were felons under the terms of the statute. State authority and popular culture concurred in vilifying Gypsies. What could lawyer Roos have been thinking by allowing them to depart unpunished?

Peter Roos offered several explanations for his actions. He said he took account of the concerns of local freeholders, who did not want responsibility for holding a hundred or more Gypsies in custody. In particular he was pressed by 'one James Bellamy' (whom Popham characterized as 'a very mean and simple man'), who 'had the charge to carry the said Egyptians to prison, which he was loath to do because the prison was about seventeen or eighteen miles from him'. The logistics of moving so many Gypsies to Nottingham castle, and then caring for them while they awaited trial, were simply overpowering. In any case, Roos continued, the county gaol was already overcrowded, and he feared 'that if any more should come thither it were very like to breed an infection of sickness in the town of Nottingham'. To this Popham responded that the justice should have bailed lesser offenders to make room for 'such great and dangerous thieves, not fit to go at liberty, as the said Egyptians are notoriously known to be'.

The main reason for releasing the Gypsies, so Roos told the court, was 'for the good of the country, to avoid such a great company of the Egyptians then at liberty out of that part of the country, who otherwise would still there remain, to the great annoyance and disquietness of her majesty's good subjects'. It was evidently a strategy used elsewhere, to hasten the departure of Gypsy bands who might otherwise cause cost and complications while waiting for their leaders to be tried or released. In this case Roos ordered 'the whole company of the said Egyptians to be transported to the other side of the Trent', into the next county, to be rid of them.

Attorney General Popham castigated Roos for his poor judgement, 'in that he conceiveth of no other ways so fit to rid the country of other Egyptians, then being at liberty, as to set at liberty all the ringleaders and captains of them'. The effect, he continued, was 'to reunite them all to their full strength again, to make them able to rob and spoil again her majesty's good subjects, as after their said bailment they did'. Reason and experience should have taught Roos

> that a people weakened by having their ringleaders and leaders taken from them might sooner be dispersed into small companies, and with less danger to the country, than when they were all united to their full strength again; for they being so dispersed, if after they had committed any theft or outrage, any

poor village had been able to have resisted them; whereas now, they being restored by the said Peter Roos's bail to their full strength again, three or four of the best towns in Nottinghamshire and Lincolnshire, whither they were sent, were scarce able to resist or suppress them.

Popham, for the Crown, was indignant 'that such strong and notorious thieves, coming together in such great troops, and committing such notorious robberies and outrages', should be free to leave on bail. And because they had left no 'good and sufficient sureties for her majesty's use', the Crown was now 'utterly defrauded'. There was little to be done besides wringing of hands and issuing of rebukes, for the people led by the man in blue had gone. Sterner measures might be resolved for the future, but there was no mention here of deportation or punishment by death. Any truth to the legend that Sir John Popham himself, as a child in the 1530s, had been kidnapped by Gypsies who branded him with 'a cabalistic mark' would add poignancy to this story.[28]

Late Elizabethan Rogues and 'Egyptians'

The well-known stresses of the late Elizabethan era intensified pressures on the marginal and poor. Vagrancy increased in the 1590s, in a decade of dearth and disease, uncertainty about the succession, and continuing war with Spain. It would not be surprising if some enterprising or desperate wanderers threw in their lot with the Gypsies, though evidence of this is minimal. There are, however, increasing signs of anxiety among the propertied classes about the dangers of idleness and disorder. The statutes of 1598 'for the relief of the poor' and 'for punishment of rogues, vagabonds, and sturdy beggars', were belated responses to the problem.[29] Magistrates conducted occasional sweeps of 'rogues, beggars, Egyptians' and other 'lazy and unprofitable members of the commonwealth', sometimes under pressure from London. The local judicial response was inconsistent, with little appetite for executing 'Egyptians'. Those few condemned for 'counterfeiting themselves to be Egyptians', or being 'found in the consort or society of vagabonds commonly called Egyptians', had usually committed more serious criminal offences.[30]

Robert Hilton, late of Denver, Norfolk, was sentenced in December 1591 for the felony of 'calling himself by the name of Egyptian', but was then pardoned. Five more unfortunates 'counterfeiting themselves to be Egyptians' were judged guilty at Durham in August 1592, and were condemned to the gallows.[31] In October 1592 Gloucestershire magistrates intercepted 'certain vagrant persons that go under the name of Egyptians, to the number of 49 and upwards', and sought advice from the Privy Council. The Council shared their frustration that 'by reason you cannot hear the certainty of their several births, you are not able to bestow them according to the tenor of the statute'. All they could suggest was to 'take the advice of some learned and sufficient counsellor at the law what course may conveniently and lawfully be taken both for the disposing of the children and due punishment of the rest, and accordingly forthwith to proceed to the examination thereof, that the country be no more pestered with them, being such evil members'. Though evidently English born, few of the Gypsies could be tied to particular parishes.[32] Two years later the Middlesex sessions charged five men, late of London, with being 'seen and found' on Hounslow Heath 'in the consort or society of vagabonds commonly called Egyptians'. William Standley, Francis Brewerton, and John Weekes pleaded 'guilty' to calling themselves Egyptians, and were sentenced to be hanged, but were subsequently pardoned for 'feloniously counterfeiting of themselves as Egyptians'.[33] Their companions John Browne and Robert Ambrose also managed to avoid punishment.

Central and local authorities maintained an intermittent pressure against 'Egyptians and other rogues ... whereby they may be driven by punishment to change that wicked and dangerous course of life'. When one such party of eighty 'lewd persons ... calling themselves Egyptians and wanderers through divers counties' was arrested in Northamptonshire in 1596, the most prominent among them were sent up to London to be questioned. The Privy Council instructed the Recorder of London that, 'if you shall not be able by fair means to bring them to reveal their lewd behaviour, practices and ringleaders, then we think it meet they shall be removed to Bridewell and there put to the manacles, whereby they may be constrained to utter the truth in those matters concerning their lewd behaviour that shall be demanded of them'. A touch of torture would be applied to make the uncooperative Gypsies talk.[34]

Yorkshire justices faced a larger problem in the spring of 1596 when they apprehended 'one hundred, four score and sixteen persons of men, women and children ... some of them feigning themselves to have knowledge in palmistry, physiognomy, and other abused sciences, using certain disguised apparel and forged speech, contrary to the laws and statutes of this realm'. Most were described as 'idle persons, the queen's natural born subjects, and some of them descended of good parentage', but at least nine were 'strangers, aliens born in foreign parts beyond the seas', who may have been immigrant Gypsies. The justices committed the entire 'lewd' crew of 196 souls to gaol, and the 106 adults among them were arraigned as felons. The nine 'most valiant' immigrant strangers, apparently the leaders, went to the gallows, and the rest were set to follow. Had the sentences been carried out, this would have been the largest mass killing of Gypsies in English history. But such 'doleful' and 'piteous' cries went up from the infants and young children that the court 'reprieved the residue of their condemned parents' and sent them back to gaol. There they stayed for two months, at county expense, until the Council of the North obtained their pardon. They would be free to depart, so long as they promised 'to reform their lives' and 'to demean themselves in some honest faculty'. Not surprisingly, the Gypsies accepted this offer, and the court arranged for a conductor, William Portyngton, to escort them back to their parishes of origin, if such could be found. The court allowed eight months to complete the resettlement, and any who escaped or defaulted would again be deemed felons. Details of these arrange-ments survive in a copy of Portyngton's warrant that reached Glamorganshire, indicating a slow journey westward from Yorkshire across the Pennines and into Wales. Like the company in 1566 that was herded from Cambridgeshire and Essex into Kent and Sussex, these northern Gypsies thirty years later were compelled to travel from county to county and pillar to post under escort.[35]

While this drama was unfolding in the north, magistrates in Somerset faced a similar problem, they said, of 'infinite numbers of the wicked wan-dering idle people of the land'. The problem with these people, Edward Hext told Lord Burghley in September 1596, was that 'in truth, work they will not... they will rather hazard their lives than work'. Hext reviewed the usual litany of 'rogues and vagrant suspicious persons', thieves, tinkers, and wandering soldiers, then made the following observation about Gypsies: 'Experience teacheth that the execution of that godly law upon that wicked sect of rogues the Egyptians had clean cut them off; but they seeing the liberty of others do begin to spring up again, and there are in this country of them.' Law and government had apparently come close to solving the Gypsy problem, with threats of the death penalty, but their numbers were again increasing. There were, Hext guessed, 'three or four hundred in a shire', who wandered in bands too strong to be apprehended. The Gypsies, he claimed, 'laugh in themselves at the lenity of the law, and the timorousness of the executioners of it'. 'Inferior officers' were more afraid of the Gypsies than the Gypsies feared the state. As in Nottinghamshire, so in Somerset, Gypsies became adept at manipulating the system, though some justices took a harder line than others.[36]

Records from the final years of Elizabeth's reign reveal a few more encounters with Gypsies. Charles, Oliver, and Bartholomew Baptist were committed in Devonshire early in 1598 for 'wandering like Egyptians'.[37] Arrested at Knightsbridge, Middlesex, in May 1599, William Fetherstone and his wife Elizabeth were charged with calling themselves Egyptians, but the court found the indictment insufficient. In January 1601 the same Middlesex sessions court proceeded against Joan Morgan and Anne Simpson, spinsters, who 'were seen and found' at Hammersmith 'in the company of a society of vagabonds commonly called Egyptians, and call themselves Egyptians'. Both women pleaded guilty, but claimed pregnancy to escape hanging. A jury of matrons found that Anne was indeed pregnant, so she was reprieved, but Joan was 'not pregnant' and cleared for execution.[38] In October 1602 another group of eighteen Gypsies led by George Portingall, labourer, 'otherwise called Captain of Egyptians', appeared before the Lancashire Quarter Sessions, but the disposition of the case is unknown.[39] There may be more cases, still buried in the archives, but they are unlikely to alter the overall picture.

Wayfaring Gypsies cost some communities more than a few stolen chickens and deceptively-told fortunes. Parishes were responsible for the welfare of distressed travellers, and for the upkeep of people they arrested. The Gypsies put pressure on parish resources, and local authorities on major routes became accustomed to their passage. Officials at Sheffield, Yorkshire, for example, paid the watchmen two shillings 'when the Gypsies were in the town' in February 1596. The following year they gave the Gypsies 6d. towards their sustenance, and in 1599 12d. 'to certain Gypsies'. In 1602 the constables of Repton, Derbyshire, paid 20d. 'to Gypsies . . . to avoid the town'. Records of this sort became common in the seventeenth century, combining welfare and policing.[40]

The willingness of at least a few Gypsy parents to seek (or allow) baptism for their children points to interactions that were not necessarily deceitful, hostile, or confrontational. Church of England parish registers record several Gypsy burials and a scatter of Gypsy baptisms, though most Gypsies remained unchurched.[41] Gypsy children were baptized at Lyme Regis in 1559, at Bedford in 1567, and at Barnstaple in 1568.[42] 'Elizabeth, child of Anthony Smalley, the Egyptian', was baptized at Leeds in June 1572. John the son of 'Charles the Egyptian' was baptized at Didsbury, Lancashire, in August 1579, and John the son of 'Charles Baptis, Egyptian', was buried there the next day.[43] Other recorded baptisms of Gypsy children include Margaret Bannister, the daughter of William Bannister, 'going after the manner of roguish Egyptians', baptized at Loughborough, Leicestershire, in April 1581;[44] Nicholas, the son of 'James Bownia, an Egyptian rogue', at Launceston, Cornwall, in March 1587;[45] and twin children of George Jackson, 'an Egyptian', who received baptism at Brough-under-Stainmore, Westmorland, in September 1588.[46] The extraordinarily named 'Pharao the son of William Valentyn a counterfeit Egyptian' was baptized at Trinity Church, Hull, in March 1595.[47] Leticia the daughter of 'Willm Voclentine Egiptian', baptized at Blackburn, Lancashire, in December 1602, may have been his sister.[48] All these children, and others like them, secured settlement rights in their parishes of origin, if ever they decided to give up life on the road. They also acquired godparents, who may have brought them some passing benefit. They belonged to the third generation of English Gypsies, embedded in the cultural environment of Elizabethan England yet perennially alien to its principles of hierarchy, order, discipline, and inclusion.

Fortune Trickery

An extraordinary tale of cozenage and gullibility survives in the papers of the late Elizabethan administrator Sir Robert Cecil, and was retold in a pamphlet in 1595. It concerns the trickery of 'Doll Pope', who wandered with persons calling themselves 'Egyptians', and 'practiced many cozening sleights and devices to deceive the simpler sort of people in the country'. Primed with information previously and secretly obtained from accomplices, she looked into the faces or hands of her victims to announce their impending good fortune. 'You will come to be exceeding rich', she told one couple in Hampshire, with fanciful tales of hidden treasure exposed by the queen of the fairies. She then robbed them blind, to their 'utter infamy and shame'. Arrested at Salisbury, she was condemned to die, but was afterwards pardoned. She then married John Phillips, 'a poor laboring artificer', gave up her Gypsy wandering, and took the name Judith. She had not, however, abandoned her craft of fortune telling.[49]

According to the manuscript, a wealthy London widow named Mascall, who had several suits for remarriage, sought to know the future from Judith

Phillips (formerly Doll Pope), who was recommended as a 'wise woman' who 'could do her great good'. Judith (as we should now call her) persuaded the widow that she 'could help her to a husband of mighty revenues and great wealth', explaining, 'I see by the art of palmistry in your hand, and by mine own skill, that you are born to good fortune'. Well primed with inside information, the fortune-teller claimed to know the source of noises heard in the house. 'How know you that?' asked the widow. 'I know it well', quoth Judith, 'and the cause too, for there is money hid in your house', with spirits troubled by unclaimed gold.

With the bait set, 'the widow did earnestly desire' Judith's assistance. To secure the hidden hoard, Judith instructed widow Mascall to 'fetch as much gold, rings, jewels, and chains, to the value of one hundred pounds, and put them into a purse' to be bound up with wool, and then 'lock this up very sure, and look not at it until I come again'. The packet was supposed to lie thus for two days, until, assisted by the queen of the fairies, it would be mysteriously multiplied. Gloating in her trickery, and perhaps over-confident, Judith 'also told the widow she must have a turkey and a capon to give to the queen of the fairies, which the widow provided. Also, she made the widow say certain prayers in sundry places of her house, and then departed.' Judith, however, had switched the gold and jewels for a similar purse full of stones, and had no intention of returning.

This was a classic confidence trick, predicated on the victim's greed and gullibility. It was premised on the principle of like attracting like, of precious metal multiplying itself, as well as the greed of all parties, and would be often repeated. The pamphlet of 1595 excoriated both fortune-teller and victim for 'the grievous sin of covetousness', and declared that 'the like was never in any age committed by a woman', though it was not, in fact, unique. Both Judith and her husband were committed to Newgate, but were not convicted as felons. Judith was indicted, not for being a Gypsy or counterfeit Egyptian, but rather for deceiving the widow of her money and her plate. According to the pamphlet, 'she had judgement for her offence to be whipped through the city', and no more of her story is known.

Perceptions of Gypsies changed over the course of Elizabeth's long reign, from an exotic menace to exemplars of an indigenous social problem. Earlier legislation treated Gypsies as strangers, subject to deportation, but the statute of 1563 made felons of home-bred 'Egyptians', 'counterfeit Egyptians', and those who consorted with them. The law gave the courts a powerful weapon, but local authorities were reluctant to wield it to the limit. In this regard the state spoke loudly, but carried a little stick. Spurts of enforcement led to arrests and occasional hangings, but typically when Gypsies were apprehended their leaders were subjected to examination, and the rest sent on their way. The harshest of laws remained in force, but most constables and magistrates exercised a more tolerant discretion. Few wanted to proceed under a capital statute unless the Gypsies could be shown to have stolen a horse or committed a robbery. Even those accused of deceptive fortune telling might find favour from authorities who set more blame on the credulity of their victims.

Judicial proceedings were negotiable, and by no means necessarily successful. Courts might hesitate to bring indictments against Gypsies, and indictments did not always stand. Juries might disregard evidence and declare defendants 'not guilty'. Even if convicted and condemned, offenders might still avoid the gallows, through processes of mitigation, mercy, appeal, and pardon. Though numbers are uncertain, it appears that no more than a few dozen Gypsies actually went to the gallows.

Judicial authorities could afford to sidestep the anti-Gypsy laws because they had other instruments at their disposal. They could choose, in effect, whether to treat Gypsies as notorious felons, or as tolerable nuisances, or ignore them altogether. It usually proved simpler to proceed under the vagrancy laws, revised under Elizabeth, which treated Gypsies like rogues, vagabonds, and other disorderly itinerants. The Gypsies suffered harassment, delay, and sometimes imprisonment and loss of their goods, but, as popular wisdom held, it was better to be whipped a hundred times than to be hanged once. The late Elizabethan evidence cannot be construed as indulgence towards Gypsies, or condoning of their lifestyle, but officials often reached a practical accommodation that allowed the travellers to go about their business and then move on.

5

Gypsies in Stuart England

Gypsies were familiar travellers in every region of seventeenth-century England. They practised a restless mobility, from the south-west to East Anglia, from the Thames valley to the Welsh marches, from the Channel coastline to the borders of Scotland. They may have been joined occasionally by new Gypsy immigrants, propelled by continental wars and persecution, but no firm evidence survives to that effect. English Gypsy numbers may have grown to several thousand, possibly incorporating a fringe of vagabonds who adopted their manner of life. Most Gypsy companies included clusters of children who reproduced the culture of their elders. By the Stuart era they were heavily anglicized, though not assimilated, integrated, or accepted. Gypsies continued to be unchurched outsiders, unattached to place or parish, and untrammelled by reputable occupations. Malignant stereotypes continued to shape their image. This chapter examines how the settled communities of seventeenth-century England coped with the legal, social, and administrative difficulties posed by the Gypsies in their midst.

The Tudor statutes that criminalized 'Egyptians' still applied under the Stuarts, but the era saw no new legislation regarding Gypsies, and no more than intermittent efforts to bring them to order. Parishioners, constables, and justices of the peace dealt with the Gypsies warily, but rarely invoked the utmost rigour of the law. Seventeenth-century handbooks for justices and constables built on William Lambard's *Eirenarcha* (1581), which was frequently republished up to 1619. Its successor, Michael Dalton's *Countrey Justice* (1618, and many later editions), reminded magistrates that it was a felony, by the statute of 1563, if anyone 'shall call himself an Egyptian, or shall be in the company of such, or shall disguise himself in apparel, speech, or otherwise like such', and shall continue so for one month. Dalton also noted, by reference to the Elizabethan vagrancy statutes, that 'all persons wandering and pretending themselves to be Egyptians, or wandering in the habit or form of Egyptians, not being felons', should be treated as rogues and vagabonds.[1] Local officials had no excuse not to know the law, but exercised discretion in applying it. A character in the Jacobean comedy *The Coxcombe* refers to 'wandering Gypsies, that every statute whips', as if that was the only fate that befell them.[2] By the Restoration era the capital laws against Gypsies could be regarded as 'a dead letter'.[3] Only the echoes and rhetoric of the Tudor legislation remained.

Jacobean 'Egyptians', 1603–1625

Local administrative records provide occasional glimpses of Gypsy travels in the early seventeenth century, but scant information about their activities or way of life. Gypsy culture remained mysterious and impenetrable. When Gypsies appeared in records of criminal prosecution, or as recipients of parish poor relief, the entries shed more light on the anxieties of local officials than on the Gypsies themselves. Jacobean Gypsies no longer travelled in large groups, and either learned to avoid officialdom or became less troublesome to the authorities they encountered. When constables or magistrates demanded they account for themselves, they may have responded with practised dissembling.

Local and regional officials dealt occasionally with Gypsies, with varying degrees of irritation, but traces of their transactions are few. Those who came to judicial attention were typically described as lewd persons 'going after the manner of roguish Egyptians', people 'counterfeiting themselves to be Egyptians', 'miserable poor people of the quality of runagate Gypsies', or vagrants 'travelling about and telling fortunes and calling themselves Egyptians'. Officers familiar with the statutes continued to refer to 'Egyptians' or 'counterfeit Egyptians', while ordinary witnesses talked of 'Gypsy people as they are usually called'. The markers of Gypsy identity remained indeterminate, though people seemed to know them when they saw them. Rather than arresting Gypsies, in accord with extant legislation, local officials sometimes hastened their departure, or colluded in securing them temporary shelter.

Often the Gypsies had moved on before magistrates became aware of them. All that was left was recrimination. Justices in the North Riding of Yorkshire reprimanded the constables of Sutton in 1605 for permitting four

Gypsy women ('vagrantes more Egyptianorum') to stay in their village and then depart unpunished. They cited an alehouse-keeper at Borrowby for permitting five men and boys 'being Gypsies' to stay several nights around Epiphany, 'to the great terror of his neighbours, against the form of the statute'. They also rebuked villagers 'for denying to aid and assist the constable of Bainbrigg to arrest certain wandering Egyptians troubling the country by filching and stealing'.[4] In Nottinghamshire too, the Gypsies found measures of protection and accommodation. Magistrates brought charges against alehouse-keepers 'for harbouring lewd and uncivil company and Gypsies', and against constables for permitting 'Gypsies to remain in the townships longer than was necessary'. They charged parish officers 'for permitting vagrants called Egyptians to escape... unpunished', and in January 1616 they prepared a warrant against Gabriel Elston of Chilwell, 'because he procured two Egyptians to deliver from custody' somebody who had been arrested.[5]

Local records commonly show Gypsies as recipients of parish funds rather than targets for prosecution. Constables at Market Harborough, Leicestershire, paid two shillings to a group of 'Egyptians' in 1606 to speed them on their way towards Cumberland. Constables at Melton Mowbray similarly shelled out a shilling to Gypsies in 1613, explicitly 'to rid the town of them'.[6] The chamberlain's accounts for Woodstock, Oxfordshire, note sixpence given 'to certain Egyptians' in 1623, after an earlier group of Gypsies left behind two silver rings and a cloak that had probably been confiscated from them.[7] The early Stuart 'town book' of Lymington, Hampshire, records two shillings 'given to the Egyptians', most likely to speed their passage.[8] Combining provisions of the poor law, traditions of charity, and local self-interest, these communities dealt with the Gypsies by paying them to go away. The amounts expended matched local resources to the numbers and needs of the travellers. Prosecution and incarceration were more expensive and more cumbersome than simply moving them along.

As in earlier decades, a rare few Gypsies left their names in parish registers. We learn, for example, that George Leister, son of Nicholas, a Gypsy, was baptized at Ormskirk, Lancashire, in October 1607.[9] 'Anne, the daughter of an Egyptian', was baptized at Northampton in August 1620 after her father had been executed at the assizes. Elizabeth, also daughter of an 'Egyptian', was baptized at Martock, Somerset, in October 1624.[10]

Though Gypsies travelled everywhere in England, they often avoided official attention. The Dorset justice Sir Francis Ashley kept detailed case records from 1614 to 1635, but none of his entries concerned Gypsies.[11]

Oxford Quarter Sessions orders for the same period include multiple citations of 'wandering rogues' and 'idle vagrants' but not a single reference to Gypsies or Egyptians.[12] Justices in the West Riding of Yorkshire watched out for 'wandering, idle, and strange beggars', but documented no Gypsies.[13] Detailed Assize records survive from Jacobean Hertfordshire, Kent, Surrey, and Sussex, but none mentions Gypsies or Egyptians. Gypsies who travelled in those counties evidently kept a low profile, and the authorities refrained from prosecuting them.

From time to time, however, zealous magistrates exercised their office *in terrorum*, to instill fear, and proceeded against Gypsies as felons. It is hard to explain how rigorous enforcement coexisted with degrees of tolerance and accommodation, but judicial personalities and local circumstance were likely factors. Felony indictments were rare, and convictions even rarer, since juries often declared defendants 'not guilty'. No accurate estimate of executions is possible, but several dozen Gypsies may have been condemned to death in the course of the reign of James I.

The summer assizes in Essex in 1608 sentenced two men and two women to death for impersonating or disguising themselves as 'Egyptians'. Those condemned were William Poole, labourer, George Portingale, farrier, and Honor and Elizabeth Johnson, spinsters. Their occupational labels suggest that the men may not have been lifetime Gypsies, though the designations could have been adopted by the defendants or made up by the court. The indictment was framed to fit the Elizabethan statute. No record indicates that they had committed any other crime. If the George Portingale here was identical with the George Portingall, 'captain of Egyptians', cited in Lancashire in 1602, he was a notorious and much-travelled Gypsy. His name suggests that he or his forebears was Portuguese. The women both pleaded their bellies, but a jury of matrons determined that neither was pregnant and cleared them for the gallows.[14]

George Portingale may have lived to offend again, for a Gypsy of that name was 'seen and found' among 'the company of vagabonds called Egyptians' apprehended at Rochford, Essex, in September 1611. George and Elizabeth Portingall, George and Mary Brooke, Robert, Sarah and Mary Newman, Sarah Johnson, and Ann Valentine were among Gypsies suspected of stealing a purse worth eightpence containing five shillings in coin, but all were acquitted at the Quarter Sessions.[15] Two years later prisoners at Colchester castle included Joan Arrundell and Mary Lacie, committed to the assizes 'for being Gypsies'.[16]

In 1613 the Earl of Huntingdon sent forces against another group of Gypsies in Leicestershire who refused to disband. The incident came to the attention of the diplomat Dudley Carleton, not because of his interest in Gypsies, but owing to false reports that the Papists were arming.[17] Several glimpses of seventeenth-century Gypsies come indirectly like this, when the authors or authorities were primarily concerned with something else. In 1615 the archbishop of Canterbury informed the Lord Mayor of London of the king's 'detestation' of fortune-tellers and persons who 'reveal past and future secrets', but did not name them specifically as Gypsies.[18] The great fire at Wymondham, Norfolk, which burned 300 houses in June 1615, was allegedly started by Gypsies who set light to straw in a barn. Those charged as culprits included Francis Brewerton, named as 'king of Egyptians that rogued about', and others who were said to be 'Scots, but went under the name of Egyptians'.[19]

The most remarkable record of Gypsies in the early Stuart era comes from Hampshire in 1616, when magistrates cracked down on 'counterfeits and false writers of the king's majesty's letters patent and broad seal', and imprisoned several dozen offenders in the house of correction at Winchester. The detainees included a mixture of vagabonds, rogues, and Gypsies, including Walter Hindes, who claimed only to have fallen in with 'the company of counterfeit Egyptians'. Singing for his life, to deflect charges of felony, Hindes testified about his recent travels. Most interesting of all, he helped to compile 'a note of such canting words as the counterfeit Egyptians use amongst themselves as their language', with English translations. Hindes's list of over 100 words and phrases reveals a vocabulary that linguists identify as Angloromani, combining a Romani vocabulary and an English colloquial structure. Most of the expressions refer to parts of the body, items of clothing, food, drink, money, weapons, crimes, and punishment. *Toner moy*, for example, meant 'wash your face'; *cubney gaggey* was 'a woman great with child'; *chrin kessey* was 'to cut a purse'. The Winchester word-list supports claims for the Gypsies' distinctiveness, and explains why witnesses sometimes reported them to use a language that nobody else could understand.[20]

Being demanded how long he had continued in their company, [Hindes said] that it is a month since or thereabouts [the minimum time spent as a Gypsy to qualify as a felony, as specified in the Elizabethan statute], and he being travelling to London met with one Henry Mannering of that company, who told him if he would carry certain pillage for him he would bear his charges for him till he came to London, which he consented unto and kept them company until they were apprehended at Farnham and sent to the gaol aforesaid ... Being demanded what the names of the said Egyptians were, he sayeth that the captains of their company are these, viz: William Poynes, the aforesaid Mannering, and one William Clifford.

Being demanded what the women were that were in their company, he sayeth that three of them were wives to the forenamed men, and the rest of the company were their children and servants. Being demanded whether he had been formerly acquainted with them, he sayeth that he had, and that their course of life is to travel the country all the summertime, telling fortunes and deceiving the country, and in the wintertime they repair to London, and there they spend their time till the spring.

Being demanded in what part of London their chief place of report was, he sayeth in Kent Street, at one William Lacy's, near unto the sign of the White Horse; the which Lacy is one that sells diaper and damask, and in times past was one of their company, but now he lieth still in London and receiveth such commodities as they either bring or send him; for he sayeth that if he had not been apprehended when they were the next day, they had sent up both money and gold with other pillage to London to the forenamed Lacy, who is uncle to this examinate. He sayeth further that the forenamed Mannering was in Salisbury gaol for the like offence.

Hindes's words, if reliable, add considerably to our knowledge of early modern Gypsies. The band he travelled with seems to have been a dozen or so strong, following a circuit through south-west England to London. His report of seasonal wanderings, fortune-telling, criminal transactions, and the accumulation of gold and money is unparalleled. The London fence William Lacy was apparently once 'of the company', and was Hindes's and the Gypsies' kinsman, so his connection to the travellers may not have been as casual as depicted. The informant's detailed knowledge of Anglo-Romani suggests a deep immersion in their culture. Gypsies were different from ordinary itinerants, but the evidence points to porous borders between their world and more settled communities. Nor should this be especially surprising. Popular commentary had long claimed that Gypsy bands incorporated vagrants and runaways, even if it exaggerated the degree to which 'counterfeit Egyptians' were imposters.

In another case from northern England, a witness before the Lancashire sessions at Manchester in November 1618 deposed that the previous summer, 'he going towards Heptonstall fair in the county of York did meet a company of counterfeit Egyptians', including one now calling himself William Waller. Appearing before the court, Waller, identified as a shoemaker, late of Newcastle upon Tyne, confessed that he had 'travelled under the pretence of a counterfeit Egyptian', though only for a short period of time, and at Ashton under Lyne he met up with 'his wife and child, and divers other strangers, who also travelled as counterfeit Egyptians'. The Manchester constables' accounts for 1619 include payments of 2s. 8d. 'for whipping of eight counterfeit Gypsies that were taken with a privy search', which was presumably the fate of Waller and his wife.[21] The uncertainty of Waller's status and the shiftiness of his story are typical of documentary records involving Gypsies.The midland parishes of Pattingham, Staffordshire, Brantham, and Waltham, Leicestershire, made repeated payments 'to rid the Egyptians out of town'.[22] The Gypsies faced harassment and discomfort, but rarely the shadow of execution.

Evoking God's law 'against begging and laziness', and the kingdom's laws against 'beggars, rogues, vagabonds, Egyptians, and such lazy and unprofitable members of the commonwealth', Lord Keeper John Williams, who was also bishop of Lincoln, instructed magistrates in September 1622 'forthwith' to undertake 'the punishing, employing, chastising, and routing out of these idle people', who did 'exceeding great damage' to 'many of his majesty's poorer subjects'. Gypsies were not the main target of this directive, but they shared in the frown of authority against vagrancy, idleness, and misrule. Typical of the Jacobean regime, there was little follow-up to this intended crackdown, though authorities in several counties acknowledged the instructions.[23]

One final glimpse of Jacobean Gypsies comes from the church court records of Wimborne Minster, Dorset, where 'Egyptian' fortune-tellers had told Elizabeth Rivers that she had one bastard child and was 'in possibility of another'. This led to local acrimony and protest, and a defamation case heard in 1623. Another woman, Julian Gurde, reported that she too had paid to have her fortune told, but 'because the Egyptians did not tell her fortune to her mind, she took away her money again'. The 'Egyptians' are only incidental to this record, which dealt mainly with village women who were discerning clients of Gypsy fortune-tellers. It suggests at least that Gypsies did not always tell people what they wanted to hear.[24]

Gypsies under Charles I, 1625–1642

In pursuit of order and discipline, the government of Charles I took a hard line against vagrant travellers, but was not especially concerned with Gypsies. The principle guiding social policy was that 'the truly poor and impotent should be relieved, those of able bodies should be set on work and employed in honest labour, and sturdy, idle, and dangerous rogues and vagabonds should be repressed and punished'.[25] A handbook for constables and over-seers of the poor reminded officers of their duty to arrest and examine

> all persons wandering and misordering themselves, all persons which cannot render a lawful account of their travel, all Irish people wandering and beg-ging... all idle persons going either about begging or feigning themselves to have knowledge of physiognomy, palmistry, or other like crafty science... all jugglers, tinkers, peddlers, petty chapmen... and all persons wandering in that habit, form, or attire of counterfeit Egyptians.[26]

Gypsies were swept into the mix, and occasionally appeared in court records, but were not particular subjects of attention. One justice of the peace reminded himself in his notebook in 1627 that 'if any Egyptians shall continue within this realm one month, or if any person disguise himself like an Egyptian, and so continue for a month, it is a felony', but the Elizabethan statute to which this referred was only intermittently enforced.[27] Rootless Gypsies remained a living rebuke to the ordered arrangements of Charles I's England, but few faced prosecution simply by virtue of their status. Gypsies were often suspected of crimes and deceits, but officials did little in practice to differen-tiate them from other offenders. Caroline proclamations called for enforce-ment of the laws against rogues and vagabonds, who 'do much more abound than in former times', but made no specific mention of Gypsies or Egyptians.[28]

Expanding on Jacobean practice, Caroline authorities instructed county officials 'to apprehend and punish such vagrants and idle persons as live not in any lawful vocation, and in time of trouble may either by tales or false rumours distract the people's minds and commit insolences'.[29] They warned the justices at Quarter Sessions about 'the great number of rogues and vaga-bonds and sturdy beggars wandering and lurking in the country', and demanded efforts, from time to time, against the people who harboured them.[30] In 1626 and 1627 the Privy Council ordered justices 'to search for and apprehend all such misliving people' as rogues and idle vagabonds, and instructed military provost marshals to search for runaway soldiers among such 'loose persons'.[31] Similar orders in 1629 encompassed 'suspect persons, rogues, both sturdy beggars and begging vagrants', including 'palmisters, fortune-tellers, Egyptians, and the like'. Parish constables were required to make weekly searches, and magistrates were supposed to send reports to London. Documentation of this activity is abundant, but Gypsies are rarely mentioned.[32] Similar orders in Lancashire in 1633 'for restraint of wanderers and foreign beggars' likewise failed to rein in Gypsies.[33]

In September 1625, in the opening year of Charles I's reign, a group of Gypsies at Bramcote, Yorkshire, 'committed an uproar, and had lost two pieces of gold'. Nothing more is known of them, but they could not have been paupers if they had gold to lose.[34] No less than 'seven lewd persons...being apprehended for Egyptians cozening the country of their money', were gaoled in Essex in January 1627 in advance of the county Quarter Sessions. Four of these so-called Egyptians—John Dawson and Francis his wife, John Baker and Elizabeth Jackson—succumbed to gaol fever and died in prison, but the others—Robert Smith and Rose his wife, and Ann Dawson, sister to the late John Dawson—were remanded to the assizes, where it was charged that 'of long time they wandered and cheated his majesty's people'.[35] These Gypsies, like most at this time, had ordinary English names, and, like most people cited before the early modern courts, their subsequent disposition is unknown.

Less doubt attaches to the fate of Nicholas Clifton, originally from Derbyshire, who was found 'wandering as a counterfeit Egyptian' at Stansted Mountfitchet, Essex, in June 1627. Other disorderly vagrants taken that summer were whipped and sent back to their parishes of origin. Clifton, however, was lodged in gaol to await the assizes, where it was charged that he, in company with William Spencer and William Smith, labourers of Ridgewell, Essex, 'disguised themselves as Gypsies and frequented the fellowship of divers vagabonds called Egyptians'. As far as the law was concerned, they were felons, whether they were hereditary Gypsies or newcomers to that trade of life. Clifton confessed, and was hanged at Chelmsford, while his confederates Spencer and Smith remained 'at large'.[36]

The last recorded executions under the Elizabethan anti-Gypsy statute appear to have been in 1628. Several modern accounts mistakenly date this to 'Cromwell's time' in the 1650s, when, so they say, 'very great numbers were executed for no other crime but being Gypsies', exaggerating the bloodbath and misdating it by a quarter of a century.[37] The source of this confusion is Sir Matthew Hale's *Historia Placitorum Coronae. The History of the Pleas of the Crown*, written around the time of the Regicide in 1649, but not published until 1736. Discussing the punitive Tudor statutes, Hale recalled that 'about thirteen Gypsies were condemned and executed' at the assizes at Bury St Edmunds 'about twenty years since'.[38] Suffolk assize records do not survive for this period, but the episode can confidently be dated to 1628. Local sources report that John Agglinton, a runaway apprentice, was caught that year 'in the company of certain counterfeit Egyptians that were tried and executed at the last assizes in Suffolk'. Rather than being condemned as a felon, or otherwise punished according to the statutes, Agglinton was sent back to his master, a Colchester say-weaver, then reapprenticed to a ship-wright. His brief sojourn with the Gypsies, and his forced return to settled society, indicates once again the porosity of the boundaries between migrant and mainstream populations.[39] It remains a mystery why thirteen Gypsies or 'counterfeit Egyptians' were so harshly treated in 1628, and why such punishments were abrogated in the years that followed.

Local residents in Caroline England sometimes claimed to live 'in fear' of 'straggling rogues and vagabonds' and other 'suspicious persons' who wandered back and forth.[40] It was widely believed, though seldom documented, that 'idle, lewd, and roguish' travellers were responsible for 'many thefts and felonies... daily committed', and that plague 'may be feared to be brought by such wandering persons'.[41] Some towns kept watch for bands of wandering vagrants and denied them entry, especially in times of crisis. A broadsheet of 1630 called for suspected carriers of the plague to be 'kept out at the town's end, as Gypsies have been in time past'.[42]

A growing problem in Charles I's reign concerned Irish beggars, entering through Bristol, south Wales, and western Scotland, whose 'concourse' and 'multitude' were said increasingly to have 'infested' the kingdom. Irish travellers were uncommon in England before the 1620s but commonplace thereafter. More than 200 arrived at Bristol in 1628, much to the consternation of local authorities. Officials in Essex complained to the Privy Council in March 1629 that 'our country is now very full and much troubled with a multiplicity of Irish men, women and children beggars, of whom we cannot learn at what port or haven they were landed, or the cause of their landing'. Inhabitants of Pembrokeshire, south Wales, were similarly 'much infested with the continual concourse of Irish beggars', and believed that 'multitudes' came ashore in night-time landings in the coves around Milford Haven.[43]

More Irish beggars moved from Ulster to Scotland, and may have travelled south. Some were followers of Irish military recruits, but most were driven by the scarcity of corn. Efforts to remove them had only limited effect. The government of Charles I issued proclamations in 1629 and 1634 'for the speedy sending-away of the Irish beggars... who live here idly and dangerously, and are an ill example to the natives of this kingdom'.[44] They showed up occasionally in constables' accounts, such as those from Manchester, where six poor Irishmen and seven poor women were given payments in 1634 to speed them on their way.[45] Irish travellers in bands a dozen or more strong troubled communities as far apart as Salisbury and Colchester.[46] The Irish rebellion in 1641 drove more Irish men and women onto English roads as refugees needing relief. Nobody in the seventeenth century confused Irish travellers with Gypsies, though elements of these groups may have grown to resemble each other over time.[47]

Gypsies and 'counterfeit Egyptians' remained exposed to still-extant statutes, but the Caroline crackdown on vagrancy reined in relatively few of them. Some attracted judicial attention for being vagabonds or fortune-tellers; some fell foul of hard-line magistrates; but most avoided trouble unless they were suspected of serious crimes. The town of Dorchester did its best to be rid of 'vagrant rogues' and wanderers 'living incontinently', but its records mention no Gypsies.[48] The Oxfordshire town of Banbury was one that congratulated itself in 1631 that, 'as for rogues and vagabonds, we are little troubled with them, they like their entertainment so ill'.[49]

Magistrates in Devonshire were 'credibly informed' in 1631 that 'palmisters, fortune readers, Egyptians and the like' were among the roving rogues and sturdy beggars who 'prejudiced' and 'terrified' his majesty's 'better subjects' by meeting in companies thirty strong upon the highway. Responding again to directives from London, they ordered the watch to 'make a diligent search' to bring 'the evil members' to be punished 'as the law biddeth', and to send them back to their parishes of origin. The crackdown was not specifically aimed at Gypsies, but rather at the vagrants who travelled 'by thirty in a company' and frequented 'houses of evil report'.[50] These vagrants were likely to have included veteran soldiers and sailors, discharged after the end of Charles I's European wars, as well as casualties of distress in the cloth industry, though so-called Egyptians might have been among them.

In June 1631 the bailiff and justices of Leominster, Herefordshire, reported that they had 'punished twelve wandering persons, men and women, who termed themselves Gypsons, and sent them towards the town of Berwick [at the opposite corner of England] where they said they last dwelt'. These travellers would now have written authorization for their passage from the Welsh marches to the Scottish border. But nobody could guarantee that their passage would be orderly or direct, or that the Gypsies would behave as instructed.[51] Another return by justices of the peace in Norfolk in 1634, pursuant to 'his majesty's late directions and orders', reported the arrest of thirteen women and children at Rollesby in Flegg hundred, 'miserable poor people and of the quality of runagate Gypsies, for that they took upon them palmistry'.[52] The usual procedure was to round them up, feed them as necessary, and then send them on their way with a whipping. In October 1637 the constable of Ugthorpe, Yorkshire, faced censure 'for not punishing certain rogues and vagabonds... calling themselves Egyptians, who were loitering about the said township, and begging'.[53]

Charitable relief went hand in hand with punishment. The parish records of Shillington, Bedfordshire, noted three shillings 'given to Gypsies' in 1626.[54] At Stathern, Lincolnshire, 'a great company of Gypsies' shared a shilling in aid in 1632.[55] At Leverton, Lincolnshire, in 1635, the constables distributed a penny each to eighteen Gypsies for their temporary relief, and to induce them to leave.[56] The parish of Chawton, Hampshire, likewise spread fourpence among 'a company of Gypsons' in 1638.[57] Ecclesfield, Yorkshire, more generously paid three shillings 'to fifteen Egyptians and four men with them' in 1639, and three shillings more 'to twenty-five Egyptians also and [a] guide with them', to see them hence. Twelve more Gypsies passed through the parish in 1640, and in 1642 local officials paid four shillings to 'thirty-seven "Gyptians" and three men going with them to Brightside', north-east of Sheffield. Six more 'Gieptians' received handouts of a penny a piece at Upton, Nottinghamshire, in 1642. At Northampton the churchwardens paid small amounts to support an 'Egyptian maid' in 1642, and three shillings the year following 'for a sheet and burying the Egyptian'.[58] Travelling where they pleased, and rarely pausing, these Gypsies appeared more like indigents in need of assistance than bearers of exotic wisdom or dangerous perils.

'Tellers of destinies' locked horns with the law in December 1638 when Richard White, Mary his mother-in-law, Jane White, and Alice White, with two little children, appeared before the Essex Quarter Sessions. The family was said to have originated at Yarmouth, Norfolk, had lived ten years in Wales, and had 'wandered up and down in the kingdom since about September last, and now were taken at Brentwood as vagrant and with a counterfeit pass'. They were to be indicted as 'incorrigible rogues', to be 'well whipped', and sent back to their parish of origin, as the statute required. Though not described as Egyptians, the family lived a Gypsy life, but it was their pass, not their identity, that was counterfeit.[59]

Similarly punished were Richard Bannister, Elizabeth his wife, and Simon and Michael Bannister, who were arrested by constables in Middlesex in June 1640. They shared a name, and perhaps a heritage, with the Gypsy Bannisters of the Elizabethan era, and were committed to the house of correction for wandering and begging as 'counterfeit Egyptians'. By statute they could be charged as felons, but instead they were convicted of 'vageing' and wandering, sentenced to be whipped naked, and sent to Bodmin, Cornwall, their reputed place of origin.[60] They may have been connected to the two companies of 'Egyptians' given charitable relief at Lapford, Devon, that summer.[61]

Another band of travellers, intercepted by Devonshire magistrates in 1642, was found to be 'using also a canting language, and eating cats like Egyptians, which renders them more suspicious'. Some of these men had swords and 'seemed to be very dangerous and desperate and a terror to the country people', but on examination they proved to be discharged soldiers, returning from service in Germany, on their way from London to Cornwall. 'Like' Gypsies, they were exotic and menacing outsiders, allegedly given to distasteful practices, but in reality they were just outlandish Englishmen.[62] Constables and magistrates could usually tell the difference.

Gypsies in Revolutionary England, 1642–1660

Traces of Gypsies faded from view in the mid-seventeenth century, amid the drama of civil wars and revolution. We should not imagine that Gypsies disappeared at this time, but rather that the authorities had more pressing matters of concern. References appear more frequently in the years of the Interregnum, when routine administrative order was to some extent restored.

Amid post-war disturbances at Plumbland, Cumberland, in October 1647 a neglected church 'became a lodging place to vagabond people going under the name of Egyptians, and was in danger of being burnt by the fires made in it'. This incident reveals the use by Gypsies of outbuildings, barns, and vacant structures, but it came to light only when one faction in the parish pinned responsibility for the damage on another.[63] The culprits may have been associated with the band of forty-six 'Egyptians' who secured relief at Uttoxeter, Staffordshire, in 1647, allegedly with a pass from parliament.[64] More Gypsy bands, ten to twenty in number, received payments from the constables of Repton, Derbyshire, Helmdon, Northamptonshire, and Upton, Nottinghamshire, in the middle decades of the seventeenth century.[65] At Uplyme, Dorset, in 1650 the churchwardens paid a shilling and sixpence 'unto twelve Egyptians which the tithing man brought', presumably to assist them on their way.[66] In the same year 'Susanna Heyron daughter of Peter Heyron one of the Gipsies' was baptized at Killington in the parish of Kirkby Lonsdale, Westmorland.[67]

Autobiographical fragments also shed occasional light on the presence of Gypsies. The Oxford-educated Ranter Abiezer Coppe abased himself, so he said, by keeping company with 'beggars, rogues, and Gypsies', and wrote enigmatically of 'that notorious business with the Gypsies and gaol-birds (mine own brethren and sisters, flesh of my flesh, and as good as the greatest lord in England) at the prison in Southwark near St George's church'. The 'notorious business' refers to Coppe's ostentatious Christlike embrace of the wretched of the earth, in hopes of turning the world upside down. Why the Gypsies were in Southwark gaol is unknown, but Coppe is candid about his intimacy with them: 'I chose base things when I sat down and eat and drank around on the ground with the Gypsies, and clipped and hugged and kissed them, putting my hand in their bosoms, loving the she-Gypsies dearly.'[68]

Quaker sources also mention encounters with Gypsies in prison. Barbara Blaugdone, a suffering Quaker who fell foul of authorities at Exeter, reported being housed 'among a great company of Gypsies that were then in the prison'. The next day she was turned out and set free 'with all the Gypsies'.[69] Harassment and incarceration were tribulations for Quakers to endure for the sake of the Lord; but the anonymous Gypsies were probably more familiar with routine arrests at the hands of beadles, constables, and local magistrates. Without the Quaker witness, however, their presence in Interregnum Devonshire would be obscured.

A group of wanderers 'in the habit and carriage of Gypsies' was apprehended at Bransby and Normanby, Yorkshire, early in 1650 and held in the castle at York. A constable reported that 'divers of them did tell fortunes to children and others, and asked them money. They did sometime speak in languages which none who were by could understand.' The party was led by a man named Grey, and included his wife Elizabeth Grey, Richard Smith, Barbary Smith 'who pretends to be his wife' (and who was apparently the principal fortune-teller), Francis and Elizabeth Parker, and several unnamed children. Richard Smith confessed that they had earlier been arrested in London 'as suspicious persons, for highway robbers, and were...ordered to be sent to their several dwellings or countries, conducted by one Grey'. They were now on their way to Northumberland, having travelled through Herefordshire, Staffordshire, Shropshire, Cheshire, and Lancashire, and most recently the East Riding of Yorkshire, with a pass that may have been forged.[70]

The imprisoned Gypsies petitioned the North Riding magistrates for their release, in a document that testifies to their rhetorical acuity and to their ability to appeal to law and sentiment. Identifying themselves as 'distressed wandering persons, calling themselves by the name of Gypsies', they claimed that their 'poor infants' were 'almost famished for want of livelihood'. The officers who arrested them, they complained, 'contrary to all equity and Christianity, and as we are informed, contrary to the law of this kingdom, bereft us, and took from us our mare and many things of great note and value'. (How were they to know that England was now a commonwealth, not a kingdom, a year after the execution of Charles I?) The petitioners then declared themselves 'sorry for their former lewd course of life', and promised hereafter to direct their lives to 'the will of God and laws of this land', if only the court would restore 'our goods so unjustly taken from us'. In other words, they would cease to be wanderers as soon as they were allowed to wander on their way.[71]

This plausible story was undermined by the testimony of the Yorkshirewoman Jane Savage, wife of Thomas Savage, who exposed their fraudulent practices. Jane Savage said that she visited the house where the Gypsies were first held, and one of them named Barbary Smith 'did wag her hand of her and did draw her to a side, and told her she would help her to three score pounds in money, three silver spoons, and two gold rings, if she might have half'. The Gypsy woman said that the hoard was hidden in a sheet in the ground, but to release it she needed Jane to supply her with a shilling and fourpence, a linen sheet, and a linen pillow case 'and upon this she told her she should find this money, plate and rings abovesaid'. Jane Savage reportedly followed the Gypsy's instructions, and handed over the money and textiles, in expectation of good fortune. But, not surprisingly, no hidden treasure materialized, and the fortune trick had found another victim.[72] No record survives of the outcome of this investigation.

More 'vagabonds, commonly calling themselves Egyptians', passed through Shropshire early in 1653, apparently enticing several local labourers 'to keep company with them'.[73] A similar ensemble was indicted in Middlesex in April 1653 'for being counterfeit Egyptians', which was still a crime by extant statutes. They were named as George Brewer, Matthew, Elizabeth and Anne White, Richard and Mary Standley, Thomas and Mary Arrington, and Margaret Wood. The court found them 'not guilty' of counterfeiting themselves as 'Egyptians', but 'guilty' of being vagabonds, to be whipped and returned to their places of birth. Matthew White, however, was respited on grounds of being extremely feeble. The court treated these travellers as part of the general vagrant problem, rather than a problem specific to Gypsies.[74]

A similar policy applied at London's Bridewell, where four more wanderers—Robert, John, Margaret, and Elizabeth Powell—were briefly held in January 1654. Two more women of the Powell family—Mary and Jane, this time described as Gypsies—came before the Bridewell court in October 1654, and were sentenced to work. Bridewell's business was with the vagrants and petty criminals who crowded London, but these were the court's only seventeenth-century cases specifically naming Gypsies.[75]

Gypsies passing through north Norfolk also fell foul of local authorities, and suffered brief incarceration. In July 1654 the Quarter Sessions at Swaffham ordered the constables of Wiggenhall St Mary Magdalen to hand over 'all goods in their hands belonging to the Gypsies late in the house of correction'.[76] In Wiltshire too the records from 1654 refer to a 'company of rogues who went up and down cheating the country in the nature and fashion of Gypsies'. They were committed to the house of correction after telling fortunes at Bradford-on-Avon and taking almost ten pounds from gullible villagers.[77] Four years later another group was committed at Marlborough, Wiltshire, for travelling up and down 'in the [at]tire of Egyptians'. Among them were Robert Poole and his wife Mary, said to have originated in Kent (perhaps the Robert and Mary Powell previously held at Bridewell), and William Finch and his wife Madlyn, said to be from Devon. All were eventually released with passes, though where they went next is uncertain.[78]

In 1655 an inhabitant of Hertfordshire named John Bourne was ordered to appear at the Quarter Sessions for 'entertaining and harbouring several Egyptians in his house, who go robbing people of their goods'.[79] This may have been related to the order in October 1655 that five men taken as 'Egyptians' and committed to the Hertfordshire House of Correction should be 'well whipped' and sent with passes to their places of origin. The offenders were George Brugman, late of Little Malvern, Worcestershire ('where he has a dwelling house as he declares'), Henry Hall, born at Fairfield, Derbyshire, and Edward Morrell, William Morrell, and Alexander Morrell, born at Calne, Wiltshire, each of whom had, or was conceived to have, settlement rights in a particular parish.[80] Ten more 'Egyptians' were reportedly moved out of Macclesfield, Cheshire, in 1656.[81]

Not specifically named as Gypsies, but acting suspiciously like them, were Margaret Sergeant and her father, who wandered between Surrey, Somerset, and Devon during the Interregnum. They were arrested at Barrington, Somerset, in July 1656 after 'telling of people's fortunes' for money. The old man escaped, but his daughter was questioned by magistrates. 'Being demanded where they learned that strange language that they spake', she answered, from her father. Asked about the horse that accompanied them, she said they had acquired it in Devon. When asked to set her name to her testimony, she signed it with a cross. The authorities may have been satisfied with these remarks, for there is no record of any prosecution. Nor was there any gloss on that mysterious 'strange language', which may have been Anglo-Romani.[82]

The parish register of Malmesbury, Wiltshire, includes the most extraordinary note of a Gypsy burial:

> John Buckle, reputed to be a Gypsy, deceased September 21 at John Perin's house upon the Fosse at Shipton parish in Gloucestershire, was buried in King Athelstone's chapel, by King Athelstone and the Lady Marshall within the abbey church of Malmsbury. This burial was September 23 1657. Howbeit, he was taken up again (by the means of Mr Thomas Ivye, esquire, who then lived in the abbey, and by the desires and endeavours of others) out of the said chapel; and was removed into the churchyard, and there was reburied near the east side of the church porch, October 7 1657, in the presence of Mr Thomas Ivye of the abbey, esquire, Mr Pleadewell of Mudgell, esquire, Richard Whitmour of Slaughter in the county of Gloucester, and Dr Abia Qui of Malmesbury, with very many others.[83]

The registration of Gypsy burials is extremely rare, and in this case it seems that death did not end this Gypsy's wanderings. The village of Shipton Moyne sits barely a couple of miles from Malmesbury, across the county boundary, and it would have been easy to transport a corpse that distance. Why John Buckle should deserve such a grand burial site, adjacent to the great Anglo-Saxon king, is unknown, but it was, apparently, quickly resented. Malmesbury had been the site of intense civil-war fighting, the church had been used to store gunpowder, and local political divisions still festered. The Gypsy's body had been buried barely a fortnight before leading parishioners (with some outsiders) had it removed from the abbey church and reburied outside. Robert Harpur, vicar of Malmesbury from 1649 to 1662, served as registrar, and most likely penned the entry, but his role in the two interments is unknown.

A final reference to Interregnum Gypsies appears in the 1659 Order Book of the Surrey Quarter Sessions. Francis Squire and Robert Poole (perhaps the same Robert Poole held in Wiltshire in 1658) were apprehended at Limpsfield 'as vagrants and going under the name of Egyptians'.

Parish officers confiscated their possessions, including a mare and a 'panel' (a saddle cloth), and installed the offenders in the house of correction to await the Sessions. Before the court could act, however, the Gypsies were released or escaped, and their captor put in a claim of £4 14s. 8d. for his expenses for their care. It was this claim, rather than a record of prosecution, that generated the documentary record.[84]

The moral indignation behind these enquiries and indictments changed little from previous generations. Though Christians were obliged to care for 'God's poor', according to the Interregnum author Richard Young, 'sturdy beggars and vagrant rogues' deserved rebuke and correction. Young made no specific mention of Gypsies, though they were presumably included among those 'men without religion, order, ordinances, faith, hope, etc. ... without God in the world', who had 'nothing in propriety but their licentious life and lawless condition'. Like Gypsies, they were denounced as 'idle drones that feed upon the common spoil ... They come to pilfer, not to beg.'[85] It was part of an old argument, still current in our own day, that the moral failing of indigence was encouraged, rather than corrected, by charitable relief.

Later Stuart Rogues and Gypsies, 1660–1700

The Restoration era is rich in textual commentary on Gypsies, but archival traces are relatively spare and thin. This was the period of Richard Head's fanciful 'English rogue', of the Earl of Rochester's Gypsy romps, Joseph Glanvill's 'scholar-Gypsy', and Aphra Behn's theatrical Gypsy imposters.[86] Gregory King's famous 'Scheme of the Income and Expence of the Several Families of England, calculated for the Year 1688' estimated 30,000 'vagrants; as gipsies, thieves, beggars, etc.' but offered no basis for this figure nor any disaggregation.[87]

Gypsies appear frequently in later Stuart drama and fiction, but only occasionally in the records of law and policing. A rare glimpse appears in the notebook of the Cambridgeshire justice Sir Thomas Sclater, who recorded in October 1663 that the constable of Linton arrested a man and three women 'like Gypsies ... and having no pass, and being about fifteen in company, and giving no good account of their settlement', who were presented to the Quarter Sessions as 'incorrigible rogues'. The court found them guilty, and ordered them 'branded in the left shoulder with a hot iron with a Roman R', a bodily disfigurement reserved for rogues. Sclater noted that one of the Gypsies had been branded before, and that one of the women so punished was 'big with child'.[88]

The diarist Samuel Pepys made two remarkable references to Restoration Gypsies. Pepys recorded in his diary in August 1668 that his wife and her companions went 'to see the Gypsies at Lambeth and have their fortunes told; but what they did I did not enquire'. His discretion on this occasion was perhaps well advised, for two of the party, Mary Mercer and Deb Willet, had been subject to the diarist's sexual attentions.[89] More revealing is Pepys's commentary on his own dealings with Gypsies a few years earlier. On 22 August 1663, he writes: 'I walked to Greenwich, and in our way met some Gypsies who would needs tell me my fortune.' (Whether the initiative came from him or them is uncertain.) Pepys paid the fortune-teller ninepence (a generous sum), and she 'told me many things common, as others do, but bid me beware of a John and a Thomas, for they did seek to do me hurt, and that somebody should be with me this day sennit [seven nights] to borrow money of me, but I should lend them none'. The diarist thought no more of this, he says, until 3 September, when he overtook some beggars 'that looked like Gypsies, and it came into my head what the Gypsies eight or nine days ago had foretold, that somebody that sennit should be with me to borrow money, but I should lend none'. Sure enough, on arriving home Pepys found 'that my brother John had brought a letter that day from my brother Tom to borrow £20 more of me, which had vexed me'. The diary continues, 'it pleased me mightily to see how . . . I should look back and find what the Gypsy had told me to be true'.[90]

Routine interactions generated more laconic commentary. At Upton, Nottinghamshire, in May 1663, the constables recorded their payment of sixpence 'to four Egyptians that came out of Portingal [Portugal] with a pass'. The only thing remarkable here was the intimation that these particular Gypsies were newcomers from the Iberian peninsula, the homeland of Charles II's queen Catherine.[91] At Hungerford, Berkshire, in 1667 the constables paid for 'lodging a company of Jipsons'.[92] The constables of Grandborough, Warwickshire, expended ten shillings in 1688 when 'a company of passengers in the habit of Gypsies' passed through the parish. Other groups of a dozen or more moved through in subsequent years.[93] More Gypsies (perhaps the same Gypsies) received relief at Helmdon, Northamptonshire, twice in 1689: southbound towards Essex in January, and passing northwards towards Cheshire in May.[94]

Seventeenth-century Gypsies were not necessarily law-breakers, although the criminals among them shaped the reputation of the rest. They all risked falling foul of the authorities, for statute law still made it a crime to be a Gypsy, to consort with Gypsies, or to go about as a 'counterfeit Egyptian'. Enforcement, however, remained lax and haphazard. Gypsies in general were suspected of deception and petty theft, but the courts were reluctant to press felony charges unless more serious crimes were involved. For the most part the authorities ignored Gypsies, or treated them as 'rogues and vagabonds', to be disciplined and sent on their way.[95] It was a relative rarity in August 1693 when eight people 'calling themselves Egyptians' faced indictment at the Devonshire assizes, for 'wandering as, or in the manner of Gypsies'. This was no longer a charge with much force, but despite their acquittal the travellers stayed in prison until the authorities decided what to do with them.[96]

Sometimes, as in earlier periods, the only trace of Gypsies was a charge against someone for failing to deal with them strictly. One local constable was cited at the Kent assizes in March 1670, 'for failing to arrest thirteen Gypsies who were begging at Harrietsham' the previous summer. The Gypsies themselves had long since departed, but the officer responsible for their detention was made to answer for his neglect.[97] At Nettleton, Wiltshire, in 1672 an innkeeper was presented for entertaining 'people commonly calling themselves Egyptians, who did behave themselves very barbarously', though the Gypsies themselves escaped prosecution.[98] Enforcement was more thorough at Eling, Hampshire, where the churchwardens were reimbursed £1 19s. in 1672 for 'expenses that arose on the parish by a company of "Giptions" that were taken by hue and cry and committed to prison for a fact at Portsmouth'.[99] At Holwell, Dorset, in 1690 the overseers of the poor allowed 10s. 6d. 'to Thomas Eyers for entertaining sixteen Gypsies and carrying them to Wootton', an expenditure of eightpence per person.[100] In Lincolnshire the Quarter Sessions fined William Newton, an innholder at Ancaster, a shilling in October 1694 because, 'contra formam statuti babbolonios (anglice Gipseys) servit et harboravit infra domum suum ad detrimentum inhabitium ibidem' ('against the form of the statute, he served and harboured Gypsies in his house, to the detriment of the inhabitants there'). The only thing unusual here was the word *babbolonios* instead of the more common Latin *Aegyptii*.[101] Surely nobody imagined Babylonians in Stuart Lincolnshire. In Somerset the blacksmith John Sedgeburrow faced charges in 1693 for giving Gypsies shelter and furthering their purposes. Sedgeburrow

allegedly entertained vagrants and vagabonds every week, including 'eight
or ten persons in the habit of Gypsies for the space of one week or ten days,
and during that time exchanged several pieces of gold for the said Gypsies
with the inhabitants of Brushford'. He seems to have operated as a fence for
travelling thieves, for several local inhabitants suspected him of handling
pieces of iron that were stolen from their gates and tool sheds. There was no
firm evidence that the Gypsies were responsible for the thefts, but neighbours knew that Gypsies behaved that way, and that Sedgeburrow was their
friend and likely accomplice.[102]

County governors still expressed periodic outrage at the presence of
idle wanderers, and reminded lesser officials of their duty. They ordered
Wiltshire constables in 1678 to search 'all ale-houses, victualling houses,
barns, and other suspected places' for 'rogues, vagabonds, sturdy beggars,
wandering and idle persons', who were 'menaces' to their neighbours,
though Gypsies were not specifically mentioned.[103] In Gloucestershire,
however, the Quarter Sessions in 1681 issued orders for the suppression of
'Egyptians'.[104] It was a burst of zeal in Somerset that led to the citation of
Elizabeth White for reading futures at the Hare and Hounds alehouse in
Ashill, and Elizabeth Buckley for plying a similar trade at the Hag's Head
in Ilminster. Both were reported to the Quarter Sessions in 1675, but neither was specifically identified as a Gypsy, and they seem not to have been
severely punished.[105] A Middlesex jury heard in 1694 that the notorious
Jacobite bigamist John Lunt had plotted with one of his wives 'to black
her and their child, and to go as Gypsies and tell fortunes, but that wife
being fair or conceited would not be blacked'. The testimony speaks to
the presumed distinctive appearance of Gypsies, and to the view that
Gypsy identity could be faked.[106]

By this time criminals, vagrants, and beggars were routinely transported
to the American plantations, and Gypsies were sometimes among them.
They were not condemned to 'slavery', as some sensationalist historical
sketches suggest, though prospects for survival in the southern and Caribbean
colonies were unpromising. Roger and Robert Bates, two felons convicted
in 1669 'for wandering up and down the country as vagabonds, with other
lewd persons calling themselves Egyptians, and pretending to tell fortunes',
were reprieved at the Old Bailey 'on security to transport themselves to the
foreign plantations, and there to remain during the time prescribed by their
pardon of transportation'.[107] When a woman named Joan Scot was examined in Henrico County, Virginia, in 1695 for 'the filthy sin of fornication',

she was discharged on the technicality that the act against fornication 'does not touch her, being an Egyptian and no Christian woman'. It appears that she had borne a bastard, and either collided with, or sought relief from, Virginia's 1662 anti-miscegenation law. In this case, it seems, Joan Scot obtained advantage from her apparent status as a Gypsy.[108] English Gypsies commonly faced detention and whipping, if the authorities were in a punitive mood, but justices generally exercised a calculus of discretion, amid conflicting social pressures and the ambiguities of the law.[109]

The remarkably detailed Old Bailey records of the later seventeenth century illuminate dealings with Gypsy criminals in the London area. In May 1680, they report, 'two women of the unlucky gang, commonly called Gypsies, were tried for robbing of a country maid of a silver bodkin and some other small things; but there being so many of them when they came to the house where she lived in the country, she was not able to swear these were the persons that did it, and so they were acquitted'.[110] The report hints at the advantage of safety in numbers, and perhaps too at a view among victims that Gypsies all looked alike, and that bad luck followed those who testified against them.

Less fortunate were Francis Buckley and Peter Lawman, condemned at the Old Bailey as 'Egyptians' in 1695, who may have been Gypsy highwaymen. Buckley was arrested at Hampstead, Middlesex, that June with a pistol and a mare worth twenty shillings, when authorities found him in a barn, 'covered over with straw, and two Egyptian women sitting upon him'. Buckley declared to his captors that 'he was an Egyptian, and king of the Egyptians', though he later denied this in court. Lawman 'was seen to wander up and down, calling himself an Egyptian', thereby incriminating himself. In court he declared himself to be a German, not an Egyptian, though the evidence for the Crown was 'very positive against him'. Both men were judged 'guilty', and were sentenced to hang. Deeming them 'aliens from God's covenant', the chaplain of the Old Bailey 'endeavoured to make them sensible of their wicked lives, and how great a sin it is to pretend to tell people their fortunes, but they were not affected with their sinful courses'. Both were executed at Tyburn on 18 September 1695, in company with other felons.[111]

Another Old Bailey trial dealt with Elizabeth Johnson, who was indicted in July 1695 'for pretending herself to be an Egyptian, and having familiarity with evil spirits, and pretending by magic arts she could discover where treasure was hid'. She seems to have been a trickster, in the venerable tradition of the fortune trick, who played on the gullibility of her victims. One day she persuaded a Mr Richardson's daughter

> that there was treasure hid in the house. She likewise desired she might see some of Mr Richardson's goods, and his daughter let her see three gold rings, a silver-hafted knife and fork, a silver bottle and a silver box; which she bid the young damsel put under her apron, and carry them into the cellar, where she said the treasure was hid; but she secretly took the things from under her apron, and when the young woman was gone to find her supposed treasure, she made her escape with the goods.

Richardson's daughter was faulted for her folly, and Elizabeth Johnson was fortunate to be found 'not guilty'.[112]

In 1696 the Somerset Quarter Sessions heard complaints against the Gypsies Rachel and Elizabeth Jones, 'Egyptians as they termed themselves', who were suspected of fraud and theft. Several witnesses told how they 'heard that there were Egyptians at the house of Simon Hellier of Trent', where neighbours gathered to buy and drink beer. Curiosity about the travellers stimulated trade, for the women 'owning themselves to be Egyptians' offered to tell people's fortunes. Rachel Jones told James Hellier, a kinsman of the host,

> that if he would cross her hand with a piece of silver she would tell his fortune. Upon which he gave her sixpence, and then she replied and told him that he must show her all his silver, then she would tell him his fortune. Upon which he took out of his pocket in his hand twenty shillings and showed it in his hand. Upon which she took nine shillings out of his hand and unjustly detained it from him, although he often requested her to have it again. [She] at length bid him get his money where he could

and returned to her drinking.[113]

Another neighbour, Jeffrey Caple, was also keen to know his fortune, and succumbed to similar trickery. In exchange for a flagon of beer, Elizabeth Jones took Caple to an upstairs chamber, 'and there she told him he must take out a piece of silver and cross her hand'. Caple accordingly held out a sixpence, but the fortune-teller demanded more, insisted on holding the money herself, and 'juggled' the coins out of his hand. She said that she knew he had four pounds more at home, and offered, 'if he would fetch her that four pounds and a piece of dirt from the biggest apple tree that he had, she would tell him where he should find four hundred pounds in gold and four score pounds in silver'. Caple's greed and credulity were aroused, for he told the court 'that he had exactly four pounds at his own house as she told him, and found it to be true'.[114] These depositions were grounds for indictment, if the women could be found and arrested, but they had already slipped away. Beyond this the record is silent.

In one last seventeenth-century case from metropolitan Middlesex, the Old Bailey court recited the deeds of Mary Poole, a Gypsy of the parish of St Giles in the Fields. (She may have been related to the Pooles or Powells encountered earlier, and was perhaps using London as a winter refuge.) Mary Poole was indicted in December 1699 for stealing ten pounds in money from a gentleman's house near Lincoln's Inn Fields. The victim, Richard Walburton, testified that, when Mary knocked at his door, 'she desired him to cross her hand with some silver, which he did with a six-pence. Then she told him that some of his servants had a mind to put him out of his place, upon which he seemed to be something concerned.' Mary then 'desired him to let her have the sixpence, and she would bring it again within the hour, and she would put him in a good way of living and tell him more', this 'with much persuasions of her canting dialect'. Gullible, anxious, and hopeful, like victims across the ages, Walburton agreed to the Gypsy's instructions to 'get all his money together, against she came'. When they next met Mary 'showed him some juggling tricks, till she had juggled away his money'. She then instructed him to search for hidden treasure, but while he was looking both the Gypsy and the gold disappeared. Mary Poole tried versions of this trick on several occasions, usually desiring a victim 'to cross her hand with a piece of silver', and as soon as he did so the money van-ished. Several witnesses charged that Mary had 'juggled' them out of their money, and one accused her of being a witch. The Old Bailey jury found her guilty, but her only punishment was to be burnt in the hand (a com-paratively mild sentence by the standards of the time).[115] Judges commonly rebuked victims for their gullibility, and warned them not to trust in fortune-tellers, but their remarks were just as often ignored.

This scatter of references from seventeenth-century England reveals a variety of encounters with Gypsies. Townsfolk and villagers allowed Gypsies to tell their fortunes, or sought them out for that purpose. A few were gul-lible enough to entrust 'tellers of destinies' with their valuables as well as their secrets, expecting multiplied riches or the rewards of hidden treasure. Gypsies were occasionally found lying in barns or outbuildings, and some were accused of crimes against property or of accidentally starting fires. Their companies ranged across counties and regions, usually self-sufficient but sometimes needing assistance. Apart from their women's practice of fortune telling, their continuing use of a baffling language, and their travel in large family groups, there was little to distinguish Gypsies from other itinerant and marginal people. Nonetheless, the stereotype and persona of Gypsies survived. Prejudice against them was undiminished, but Stuart authorities made no special effort to subject Gypsies to the law. Later seventeenth-century England saw none of the state-sponsored crackdown that targeted Gypsies elsewhere in Europe.

6

The Trials and Travels of Eighteenth-Century Gypsies

Gypsies generally maintained a low profile in eighteenth-century England. The authorities regarded them more as a minor irritant than as a major problem, and the long-ignored Tudor statutes were almost forgotten. Uncountable, and sometimes invisible, unfathomable, and sometimes menacing, the Gypsies remained separate from the established order of hierarchy, settlement, and discipline. They travelled about the country as horse-dealers, pot-menders, fortune-tellers, and petty traders, mostly staying out of trouble. Prejudice against Gypsies in England was largely low-key and latent, though subject to manipulation by the press. This relatively benign condition contrasted with the situation in eighteenth-century Germany, the Low Countries, France, and Spain, where Gypsies were persecuted as never before.[1]

This chapter attends to Gypsies in Hanoverian England, and explores their relationship to mainstream society. It reviews their treatment in literature and in law, and uses evidence from court cases and commentary in the press to contrast lingering public anxiety about Gypsies with more tolerant local interactions. At its centre is the case of Mary Squires, an aged Gypsy who was falsely accused of kidnapping and robbery, a case that divided the British public and generated reams of pamphlets, testimony, and opinion. It closes with court cases and published reports from the end of the eighteenth century, following the repeal of the Elizabethan law that made Gypsies felons. There is little historiography on which to build, since, as several scholars have recognized, eighteenth-century English Gypsy studies constitute a 'largely untrodden world'. Among historians the subject suffers from 'almost total neglect', though historically minded literary critics have opened fruitful pathways.[2]

Rogues and Wenches

Two discursive images of Gypsies lingered from the seventeenth century: one that they were loathsome for their deceits and depravities, the other that Gypsies were enviable for their freedom. Both views were artful, archaic, and prejudicial, being derived more from texts than from actual encounters. Both survived the eighteenth century, with some softening and modification. Few of these impressions were based on close observation, but reflected a range of profound misperceptions that have not entirely dissipated today.

Conventional anti-Gypsy prejudice appears in Joseph Addison's *Spectator* in 1711, in which Sir Roger de Coverly terms Gypsies 'a band of lawless vagrants', responsible for 'mischiefs ... in the country, in stealing people's goods and spoiling their servants'. He further denounces 'this race of vermin' for speaking 'uncouth gibberish', and for using palmistry as a cover for pocket-picking. Addison himself remarks that 'this idle profligate people infest all the countries of Europe, and live in the midst of governments in a kind of commonwealth by themselves'. In a later issue he condemns 'wizards, Gypsies, and cunning men' who thrive on the curiosity of the gullible.[3]

The long-established tradition of vilification was encapsulated (and heavily plagiarized) in *A New Canting Dictionary: Comprehending All the Terms, Antient and Modern, Used in the Several Tribes of Gypsies, Beggars, Shoplifters, Highwaymen, Foot-Pads, and all other Clans of Cheats and Villains* (1725). The Gypsies are imagined here as members of the 'canting crew' of professional rogues and vagabonds.

> They endeavour to persuade the ignorant that they derive their origin from the Egyptians, a people heretofore very famous for astronomy, natural magic, the art of divination, etc., and therefore are great pretenders to fortune telling. To colour their impostures, they artificially discolour their faces, and rove up and down the country in a tatterdemalion habit, deluding the ignorant vulgar, and often stealing from them what is not too hot for their fingers, or too heavy to carry off ... They stroll up and down all summer time in droves, and dexterously pick pockets, while they are telling of fortunes.[4]

The Thief-Catcher; or, Villainy Detected (1753) similarly depicted Gypsies 'continually wandering from one place to another, under pretence of fortune telling; they pilfer and steal, and living in sloth and idleness, they bring their children up in the same manner, and who consequently become the most despicable of thieves'.[5] 'Idle Gypsies, rogues in rags' was Alexander Pope's poetic condemnation.[6]

Alongside this negative representation was an alternative fancy, also long enduring, in which 'English Gypsies all live free, | And love, and live most jovially'.[7] The compendium of *Poetical Reflexions Moral, Comical, Satyrical* of 1708 includes a speech in 'praise of liberty...suppos'd to be spoken by the King of the Gypsies', in which he commends his brothers 'who live at large, and nature's law renew, a thousand joys attend our happy lives'.[8] The Gypsies, by this tradition, were wild and free, and therefore enviable. A new version of the *Jolly Gipsies* ballad appeared about 1770, presenting Gypsies as 'merry souls' who 'never want good cheer'.[9]

Literary characters drawn to the Gypsy life of 'strolling' present a mixture of delight and disgust. A heroine in Jane Barker, *The Lining of the Patch Work Screen* (1726), is tempted to join the Gypsies and, 'disguised both in habit and complexion', is readily received 'into their clan' as a volunteer recruit. She soon grows tired, however, of 'the fatigue of wind and wet, heat and cold, bad food, bad lodging, and all things disagreeable to her constitution and education', and regrets her 'folly...misery and disgrace'. She concludes by denouncing 'the wicked ways in which these vile wretches lived, cheating, stealing, lying, and all sorts of roguery', in a life she judges 'abominable'. Another of Jane Barker's romantic stories relates how a former soldier decided to join the Gypsies, and was readily received into 'their gang'.[10]

Picaresque adventures were incomplete without an episode with Gypsies. In *The Life and Humorous Adventures of William Grigg* (1733) the hero is embraced by 'strolling' Gypsies who welcome him into their company, in the manner of Richard Head's *English Rogue*. These Gypsies appear as 'a wanton, disorderly set of people, despising laws, without the least principles of honesty or honour', but that, of course, was what made them fascinating and attractive.[11] The *Memoirs of Mary Saxby, a Female Vagrant* (1807) also recalled incidents from the eighteenth century when the title character 'met with a gang of Gypsies', acquired their manners, and for a season 'liked it well'. These Gypsies, she relates, 'lived by stealing sheep, or anything they could get their hands on, or getting money from young people under a pretence of telling their fortune'. In her case, so the tale goes, it was an improvement to quit the Gypsies and become a sailor's doxy.[12]

Building further on the 'rogue' tradition, the pseudo-autobiographical *Life and Adventures of Bampfylde-Moore Carew* (1745) presents a 'well born and tenderly bred' adventurer who is so impressed by the 'feasting and carousing…merriment and jollity…mirth and pleasure' of 'a gang of Gypsies' that he and his school friends conceive 'a sudden inclination to enlist in their company'. Their wish is readily granted, this being fiction, and so, with their skin darkened by 'a liquour made of the green shells of walnuts', they share in the Gypsy 'bounty', and sample the delights of the 'brisk' Gypsy girls.[13] In Henry Fielding's *History of Tom Jones, a Foundling* (1749) the hero and his companion Partridge fall in with a roistering community of Gypsies, to enjoy their hospitality, their abundance, their sexual freedom, and their justice. The 'Egyptians, or as they are vulgarly called, Gypsies', are found in a barn, 'merry making…and diverting themselves with much apparent jollity'. The adventurers find this irresistible, and are readily welcomed. They delight in 'the utmost mirth' of the Gypsies, their 'good store of bacon, fowls, and mutton', and, above all, the ability of young female Gypsies 'to inflame inordinate desire'. Partridge's dalliance with a married Gypsy causes turmoil, which the 'Gypsy king' resolves with Solomon-like authority. Fielding's remarks on the happiness of the Gypsies 'under this form of government' offered a satiric contrast to the manners and justice of Hanoverian England.[14]

Several of the most successful novels of the eighteenth century make use of Gypsy fortune-tellers to advance their plot. When 'a Gypsy-like body' appears in Samuel Richardson's *Pamela: Or, Virtue Rewarded* (1740), one character tells another: 'I don't like these sort of people, but we'll hear what she'll say.' The Gypsy woman tells the heroine's fortune, and warns her, 'take care of yourself', and then becomes a conduit for Pamela's secret correspondence.[15] In Oliver Goldsmith's *Vicar of Wakefield* (1766) the family is visited by 'a fortune-telling Gypsy', a 'tawny Sybil', who tells one daughter that she will be married to a squire, and the other that she is to have a lord. Many setbacks have to be endured before these prophecies come true.[16] The Gypsies in these fictions are neither romantic nor threatening, but simply familiar devices for telling a story. They appear as solitaries, presumably from some camp nearby.

Elite voyeurs were drawn to the Gypsy spectacle, so long as it was sufficiently sanitized. At Norwood, Surrey, where main roads branched from London to the south, Gypsies became subjects of polite fascination. 'Spectators from the highest rank of quality' came to see the famous fortune-teller Margaret Finch, so-called Queen of the Gypsies, who was shown in engravings smoking her pipe, 'sitting on the ground, with her chin resting on her knees'. When Margaret died in 1740, after 'a course of travelling the kingdom', two mourning coaches and 'a great concourse of people' attended

Figure 4. 'Margaret Finch, Queen of the Gypsies at Norwood', *c.*1740

her funeral; it was noteworthy that her body was so 'contracted' that she had to be buried in 'a deep square box'.[17] More celebrity Gypsies attracted the attention of royalty in June 1750, when the Prince of Wales and his party 'went in private coaches to Norwood Forest to see a settlement of Gypsies'. Others followed on journeys of pleasure 'to see the Gypsies at Norwood'.[18] Visitors there in 1761 observed 'a new sort of Gypsies; they are blacker than those who formerly used to be there, and speak very bad English'. Though the origins and language of the newcomers remain mysterious, they may well have included recent arrivals from the Continent, perhaps carriers of a deeper or more traditional Romani.[19]

Vagrants and Criminals

The eighteenth-century public had generally forgotten that Gypsies were illegal, made criminals by Tudor statutes that made it a felony to be a Gypsy, to look like a Gypsy, or to associate with 'counterfeit Egyptians'. The law of 1563 described them as a 'false and subtle company of vagabonds... transforming or disguising themselves by their apparel, speech or behaviour', and engaged in an 'idle and false trade'. Their crime was rootless itinerancy and deceitful separation from the structures of status, occupation, religion, and address.[20] This law was technically still in force until 1783, but had long fallen into disuse. Sir Matthew Hale's classic *History of the Pleas of the Crown* (1736) summarized the sixteenth-century legislation but observed: 'I have not known these statutes much put in execution.'[21] Unless they checked old law-books, constables and magistrates might not know that Gypsies could be liable to the death penalty. Instead, for more than 100 years, local authorities had regarded Gypsies as merely part of the vagrant stream, albeit as disreputable and sometimes troublesome wanderers.[22]

While reminding magistrates that it was a crime for anyone to 'call himself an Egyptian', and that by law 'Egyptians' were 'all deemed felons', eighteenth-century editions of Michael Dalton's well-worn handbook *The Country Justice* (first published in 1618, but repeatedly reprinted to 1746) observed that 'at least they are all incorrigible rogues'. Readers were advised that 'these manner of persons are besides all of them for the most part thieves, cut-purses, cozeners, or the like; and therefore the Justice of Peace shall do well to be careful, not only in examining of them, but also to cause them to be well searched for counterfeit passes, stolen goods, and the like'.[23] Jacob Giles, *The Compleat Parish Officer* (1718 and many later editions), listed 'Gypsies' among vagrants, rogues, and vagabonds. The index to Richard Burn, *The Justice of the Peace, and Parish Officer* (1755), which replaced Dalton, simply said of 'Egyptians': 'see Vagrants'.[24]

Sixteenth-century language survived in eighteenth-century legislation—for example, in an amendment to the poor law in 1714 that listed 'persons pretending to be Gypsies or wandering in the habit or form of counterfeit Egyptians, or pretending to have skill in physiognomy, palmistry or like crafty sciences, or pretending to tell fortunes or like fantastical imaginations', among 'rogues, vagabonds, sturdy beggars and vagrants' to be whipped and sent packing.[25] The Vagrancy Act of 1744 similarly included 'persons pretending to be Gypsies, or wandering in the habit of Egyptians' among wanderers 'not giving a good account of themselves', who were liable to be called before justices of the peace.[26] The phrasing was antique boilerplate, adapted from Tudor statutes.

Though sure that Gypsies were disreputable, local authorities had difficulty clearly naming or describing them. Hertfordshire Quarter Sessions in 1703, for example, made out a warrant for the arrest of a some fifty Gypsies 'travelling about and telling fortunes and calling themselves Egyptians'.[27] Other jurisdictions registered 'people commonly called Gypsies', or 'persons pretending to be Gypsies', at a time when 'pretending' could mean 'presenting oneself' or 'being taken for', not necessarily falsifying.[28] One such was Elizabeth Bicknell, 'a travelling person commonly called a Gypsy', examined in Essex in 1707, who was unable to give 'any good account of herself and her manner of living'.[29] Another was Paccata Boswell, a vagrant 'pretending to be a Gypsy and wandering in the habit and form of an Egyptian and lying in the field and outhouses', who was apprehended some time later in Bedfordshire.[30] The brothers Valentine and Solomon Draper, 'Gypsy people as they are usually called', were found guilty of highway robbery at the Southampton assizes in 1739, and recommended for transportation.[31] Similarly sentenced for theft in 1751 was Mary Norman, who 'went under the character of a Gypsy'.[32]

Courts of Quarter Sessions took occasional notice of Gypsies suspected of minor pilferage who were unable to give good account of themselves. Missing horses and stolen sheep were often blamed on 'idle', 'loose', or vagrant Gypsies, who were also accused of damage to property and setting of fires.[33] Gypsies were occasionally whipped for vagrancy, as they had been earlier, and a few found guilty of serious crimes were sentenced to prison, the gallows, or transportation. When four members of the Lee family were arrested in Surrey in 1713 for 'pretending themselves to be Egyptians or fortune tellers', they were held in the house of correction, and then discharged.[34] Edward Boswell, another so-called king of the Gypsies, was executed for horse theft at Aylesbury in 1740.[35] But the previous year, when Gypsies in Hampshire were accused of highway robbery, witnesses testified that they 'behaved civilly like honest men', while camping in the vicinity.[36] The worst that could be said of the three 'Egyptians' seen at Worplesdon, Surrey, in 1764 was that they were 'lying about in a loose disorderly manner in the open air'.[37] The occasional indictment of ordinary villagers 'for harbouring and entertaining Gypsies and...other loose people' points to

levels of local tolerance not necessarily shared by state authorities. Such citations, like the one directed against David Bristow of Monks Risborough,
Buckinghamshire, in 1714, were intended more for the suppression of disorderly alehouses than the repression of Gypsies.[38]

Readers of the eighteenth-century press found repeated opportunities to
inform themselves about the misdeeds of Gypsies. They could learn, for
example, about the 'evil practices' of the 'notorious sturdy vagrants calling
themselves by the names of Baileys, Shaws, Falls or Faws', all generally regarded
as Gypsies, whose depredations along the Northumberland borderlands
included theft and burglary, house-breaking, house-burning, and pocket-
picking. Other Gypsies with the ancient name of Faa held sway on the
Scottish side of the border. Some were arrested in a crackdown in 1712, but
several imprisoned at Morpeth, Northumberland, escaped.[39]

New legislation in 1718 expanded the possibilities of criminal transportation, and Gypsies were included among the felons shipped overseas. They
were transported, not because they were Gypsies but because they were
convicts who happened to be Gypsies. Several of the border Gypsies who
were sent to America managed to return in the 1720s. Others moved south,
to reappear later in the eighteenth century as 'the Coventry gang'.[40] The
three Gypsy convicts who escaped from servitude in Maryland in 1767 may
also have had Coventry connections. The notice of reward for their capture
identified 'Joseph Smith, an old man, a Gypsy, very much resembling a swarthy
mulatto in colour', his brother William Smith, and his son John Smith, 'a
strong hearty young fellow, nearly of the same complexion with that of his
father and uncle'.[41] The 'swarthy' complexion of some immigrant Gypsies
would confuse American racial classifications for more than 100 years.

Another Gypsy 'gang' in the London area drew comparable media attention. The metropolitan newspaper *Mist's Weekly Journal* reported in March
1726

> that there are several idle vagabond people called Gypsies, and distinguished
> by the name of Powell's gang, about fifty in number, and are lodged and enter-
> tained at a house in Kent Street, and in Bird Cage Alley opposite to the King's
> Bench, that go about the City and suburbs pretending to tell fortunes, and
> thereby cheat and impose upon young people and the ignorant and unwary.

An enterprising thief-taker named William Jones, resident 'at the Raven and
Bottle in the Old Mint', now invited 'any person that has been defrauded or
cajoled out of money' by these Gypsies to apply to him, 'who will help you
to them' and promote their prosecution.[42] Other newspapers from time to

time reported the deceits of 'pretended fortune-tellers', and cautioned readers 'against the practices of such vile imposters' as pretended Gypsies.[43] County courts took occasional notice of Gypsies lying out in barns, as in Hampshire in 1742 and Dorset in 1748, but seem not to have been greatly troubled by them.[44] In 1748 the overseers of Hatfield Broad Oak, Essex, confiscated a mare and a colt belonging to some travelling Gypsies, to offset their 'charges'. Among them were Charles, Frances, and Peranus Blivet, whose names suggest a Gallic origin.[45]

Public trials exposed the manipulations of deceptive fortune-tellers. Elizabeth Farrel and Martha Norman told a victim in Middlesex in 1713 that 'she was born to a very good fortune; but the thing could not be accomplished if she did not give them her money and clothes, which if she did, a pot filled with diamonds and gold rings should arise out of the earth to her use'. They further told her that 'she could not have the benefit of her fortune without she let them have her master's plate too, for the pot would not arise so long as there was any plate in the house'. Needless to say, no such miracle happened when the gullible young servant complied. Found guilty of theft and falsehood, Elizabeth and Martha were burned in the hand and sent to hard labour.[46] In an imaginative version of the fortune trick, included in a rogue tale in 1745, the Gypsies netted twenty guineas after persuading their victim to dig for 'a large pot of money' beneath a garden tree.[47]

Mary Norman (perhaps related to the Martha Norman of the previous episode), who 'went under the character of a Gypsy', was indicted in 1751 for a similar deception, which netted her eight silver tablespoons, two silver teaspoons, two silver salts, and one silver pepper box, the entire haul valued close to five pounds. According to testimony at the Old Bailey, she entered a house in Edmonton and asked a servant if she wanted any matches, 'and begged some small beer'. The servant, Sarah Bington, testified that,

> after she had drunk it, she asked me if I would have my fortune told. She told me it would be a very lucky house to me, and told me also that there was money, upwards of seventy pounds, buried in the cellars. She named twenty-five large pieces of gold, some large pieces of silver, three gold rings, silver spoons, and other things, which were buried by an old man and woman, and that they were buried for me, and that I was the person who was to have them.

A few days later the Gypsy returned for more small beer, and told Sarah that, in order to obtain the treasure, 'I must get a quantity of silver or gold, four or five pounds value, and put into my right side pocket till such time this money was brought'.

Anyone familiar with the trick could guess what happened next. Sarah obligingly laid out the spoons, salts, and pepper box on the kitchen table, and helped the Gypsy wrap them in cloth. She 'ordered me to go and put some salt in the fire. When I came again the cloths were rolled again... She then ordered me to get a piece of packthread, with which she tied it up at the end where the spoons were, as I thought.' The Gypsy added some linen to the parcel, and together they laid it in the cellar, with an air of mystery and ceremony. 'She told me I must not go near it till she came again, which would be in about two hours', but of course she never returned. Later, when the wrapped items would be wanted for dinner, Sarah 'untied the parcel to take out the plate, there was nothing in the cloth but a wooden spoon, a flint, and some powder, I believe gunpowder; it was tied up as it was she left it'. Notices went out to advertise the theft, and Mary Norman was arrested when she tried to pawn the stolen items. In her defence, she proclaimed: 'I know nothing of the things, I never saw them in my life.' Found guilty, she was sentenced to transportation.[48]

Following yet another case in which a Gypsy made off with six silver spoons 'under pretence of working some miracle with the planets', the Old Bailey judge advised the victim 'to let this be a warning to her how she trusted pretended fortune-tellers again. It was surprising persons should be found so weak as to imagine a set of vagabond Gypsies gifted with that knowledge of futurity, which God had denied to those of a superior rank in life.'[49]

The Gypsy Mary Squires

The generally low profile of eighteenth-century Gypsies changed dramatically in 1753 and 1754 when a sequence of controversial trials made 'a great deal of noise in the country', and stirred opinion on Gypsies 'wherever the English language is understood'. The reading public of mid-Georgian England was transfixed by a story of crime and deception involving kidnapping, robbery, assault, and perjury. Exposing the vulnerabilities of age, gender, and ethnicity, the social psychology of victims and advocates, and the uncertainties of evidence and truth, the allegations, counter-allegations, rumour, and testimony in the case of Elizabeth Canning and Mary Squires became 'the subject of universal controversy'. Observers became 'strangely perplexed and divided' in their views.[50] One strand of popular opinion even became known as 'Gypsyites', because they took the side of a particularly unfortunate Gypsy woman. Commentators speculated on the Gypsies' history, their character, and their status in law, as old stereotypes and prejudices were revived.

Several scholars have remarked on this famous case, with reference to jurisprudence, class, feminism, and the public sphere, but few have noted its potential for exposing the experience of Gypsies.[51] Recorded transcripts, over 400 pages long, yield more information about one family of Gypsies than any previous travellers in British history.[52] Recent generations had paid Gypsies relatively little heed, but suddenly they were subjects for conversation, journalism, and polemic. Public anxieties may have been heightened by recent social disturbances and 'mayhem' among the lower orders and the unemployed. Historians have discerned signs of a moral panic at that time around the nexus of gender, class, and crime.[53]

The case erupted after Elizabeth Canning, an 18-year-old servant to a carpenter in London, claimed that 'two lusty men, both in great coats, laid hold of her' and robbed her as she was walking through Moorfields, late on New Year's Day 1753. They dragged her to a house at Enfield, Middlesex, owned by a Mrs Wells, where, before dawn on 2 January, she encountered 'the Gypsy woman Mary Squires', who allegedly 'took her by the hand, and asked her if she chose to go their way, saying that if she did she should have fine clothes'. Described by lawyers as 'a weak illiterate woman', Elizabeth Canning could not immediately say what the expression 'go their way' meant, but a witness on her behalf explained that it was an invitation 'for her to turn whore'. Court clerks and commentators understood the expression 'go their way' to mean 'to become a prostitute'. The widow Mary Squires, by this representation, was a Gypsy procuress and her landlady Mrs Wells the hostess of 'a very bad and disorderly bawdy house'. Some interpreted the phrase as an invitation 'to increase the family of Gypsies', as if that was how Gypsies augmented their company.[54]

When Elizabeth vehemently said 'no' to this proposition, her report continues, the Gypsy woman drew a knife from a dresser drawer and 'ripped the lacing of her stays' (corset-like undergarments, in this case worth ten shillings, enough to make their theft a felony) and took them from her, slapped her face, pushed her upstairs, and threatened to cut her throat. Elizabeth's tormentors held her confined for a month, on short rations, until she managed a daring escape. She walked home, famished and dishevelled, to be reunited with her distraught mother. Though questions arose about her month of absence, the authorities immediately believed Elizabeth's story and rushed to arrest those responsible for her ordeal. Confronting the

Figure 5. 'Mary Squires the Gypsy', 1753

suspects in the house at Enfield, Elizabeth Canning identified the old Gypsy woman as the person who had robbed her and kept her imprisoned.

Reports of this episode 'in the daily papers and in printed bills' made Elizabeth Canning an 'object of almost universal compassion'. Her story, convincingly told at the Old Bailey in February 1753, led to a felony conviction and sentence of death for Mary Squires. Found guilty as the Gypsy's accomplice, Mrs Wells was branded on the thumb and imprisoned for six months. London gallantry rose to the defence of English girlhood, and cast opprobrium on her attacker. One author reported that the mob of 'people without doors...zealots for Canning', voiced 'spite and malice against the Gypsy'. Another related that the opinion 'of the common people in her favour had risen to such a pitch of enthusiasm, that the most palpable truths, which appeared on the other side, had no other effect than that of exasperating them to the most dangerous degree of rage and revenge'.[55] Potential witnesses who might have exonerated Mary Squires were intimidated by crowds in the Old Bailey yard and were not allowed into court. Three men who offered an alibi for the Gypsy themselves faced prosecution.[56] The case revived popular prejudice against Gypsies, and drew attention to the forgotten sixteenth-century laws.

Fortunately for Mary Squires, before she could be hanged, doubts arose about the soundness of her conviction. Confidence in the Old Bailey verdict began to erode as reports of the Gypsy's alibi became known, and inconsistencies in Elizabeth Canning's testimony became increasingly apparent. Even Henry Fielding (the author and at this time London's chief magistrate) acknowledged that Canning's account was 'scarce credible... resembling rather a wild dream than a real fact', though his sympathies and prejudices cemented him to her side. Fielding's widely circulated opinion judged Mary Squires guilty, and represented Elizabeth Canning as 'a poor, honest, innocent, simple girl, and the most unhappy and most injured of all human beings'.[57] More cynical sceptics wondered whether Elizabeth Canning had engineered her own disappearance 'to conceal a scene of wickedness that has yet escaped the vigilance of justice', such as elopement, bastard-bearing, or abortion.[58] The Lord Mayor of London, Sir Crisp Gascoyne, sensed a miscarriage of justice, and petitioned for respite of the death sentence. The Attorney General and Solicitor General concurred, and in April the Crown gave Mary Squires a free pardon. Charges of perjury were prepared against Elizabeth Canning, and in May 1754 it was her turn to come to trial.

Ambiguities, doubts, and rumours continued, however, and impassioned arguments agitated a deeply divided public. One strand of commentary saw Elizabeth Canning as a frail and innocent maiden, who was cruelly abused, deprived of her underwear, and barbarously held against her will with no more sustenance than bread and water. Another came to see her as a manipulative fantasist, who exploited anti-Gypsy prejudice and played on sympathies for damsels in distress. Opinion was divided between 'Canningites' (sometimes rendered as 'Canaanites'), who supported their virtuous victim, and 'Gypsyites' or 'Egyptians', who believed that the old woman was wrongly accused. In a reversal of roles and fortunes, the young Londoner would become the face of deceit, and the Gypsy crone's innocence would be vindicated. Elizabeth Canning would emerge as a 'vile and abandoned impostress', while the 'hideous' Mary Squires earned sympathy from a public previously prejudiced against her. The drama played in the press as well as in the court, putting 'justice' as well as womanhood and Gypsydom on trial.

No longer gathered in large collectives, like their Elizabethan forebears, and not yet equipped with horse-drawn caravans, like some of their Victorian successors, the Gypsies of mid-Georgian England travelled in small family clusters. Mary Squires and her adult children George, Lucy, and Mary journeyed mainly over southern and south-west England. They belonged to an extended Gypsy kindred that included settled and semi-settled members, as well as travellers on the road. They made their living by trading fabrics and smuggled goods, as well as by mending broken china and telling fortunes. Mary Squires herself had a sideline in 'old clothes and silver lace'. Her son dealt in handkerchiefs, waistcoats, aprons, worked gowns, nankeens (printed cotton), 'and such things'. George Squires claimed a residence at Newington Butts, Surrey, and relations in Kent who 'sell goods in the country, and travel about as we do'. Like other Gypsies before and since, they often spent part of the winter around the outer suburbs of London. George's wanderings towards the end of 1752 took him through Kent and Sussex, Hampshire and Wiltshire, before he rejoined his family in Somerset. Nothing is known of their previous history, or of Mary Squires's late husband, but Gypsies with that surname had been recorded in England since the seventeenth century.[59]

Mary Squires was considered to be memorably ugly, a fact that helped establish her alibi. One of the lawyers described her as 'an ugly, old, decrepit hag'. She may have been disfigured by scrofula. Confirming her presence in their parish, the churchwardens of Abbotsbury, Dorset, described her as 'about seventy years of age . . . five feet seven or eight inches high, of a very black rusty complexion, with black eyes, a large nose, and an uncommon thick under lip'.[60] The Abbotsbury schoolmaster Hugh Bond affirmed: 'this old woman is the very same person; whoever sees her once can never mistake her again.' Another Dorset witness 'was so struck with the old woman's hideous face, that she compared her to a picture in her house of old mother Shipton' (a notoriously misshapen witch and prophetess, familiar from seventeenth- and eighteenth-century prints). Another claimed to have known Mary for thirty years, saying: 'I have seen her face often before.' William Tredget, who took notice of Mary Squires at Tottenham, Middlesex, told the court she was 'a woman not common to be seen'. Fortune Natus, who met her at Enfield, described her face as 'frightful'. Mary Squires herself declared, when she was first accused by Elizabeth Canning, 'if you have once seen my face, you cannot mistake it, for God never made such another!' Printed depictions of the Gypsy accompanied several popular accounts of the trials and emphasized her grotesquery.

The London newspapers presented Mary Squires as the quintessential Gypsy, for 'no woman ever possessed the colour and character of that singular people so strongly'. As a member of 'the clan and fraternity of Gypsies', and 'a person traditionally and hereditarily versed in the ancient Egyptian cunning', she was naturally untrustworthy and probably guilty of other enormities.[61] Henry Fielding, who was deeply involved in the case, excoriated the Gypsy class in general as 'wretches, very little removed, either in their sensations or understandings, from wild beasts'.[62] It was 'well known', claimed another author, that Gypsies 'never act from principles of honesty' and 'are capable of perpetrating the worst kinds of villainy'.[63] They were well known as pickpockets, being 'a sort of people whose very professions generally speaking entitle them to the gallows'.[64] The Gypsies, one commentator asserted, lived by 'cunning, artful deceits', and were 'constantly shifting their quarters to escape the lash of justice'; though 'sometimes they do penance in the stocks, or at the cart's tail, 'tis but rarely we see any of them swing on a gallows', a remissness he hoped to see remedied.[65] Sentiments like these were rarely heard in the eighteenth century, before the case of Squires and Canning inflamed public opinion.

The lawyers for Elizabeth Canning referred repeatedly to the Gypsies as a 'gang' of 'vagrants' and 'vagabonds', who were inherently devious and no fit companions for respectable society. One of them suggested in court that all Gypsies were felons, 'for so they are by law' according to the still-extant statute of 1563. Champions of Elizabeth Canning drew on old publications to whip up anti-Gypsy frenzy, and her attorney John Miles fed notices to the press about the near-forgotten laws that made Gypsies criminals. These Tudor statutes, one commentator declared, were 'just, good, and wholesome laws' that ought to be put into execution.[66] When London newspapers helpfully published summaries of the 'statutes concerning Gypsies', it was not, they, declared, 'with any desire to prejudice the public against Squires: for whatever she may deserve to suffer as a Gypsy, she ought not to suffer for what she is not guilty of'. But simply being a Gypsy was enough to put her in peril, according to the strictures of the law and some streams of opinion.[67]

To win their case against Elizabeth Canning, the prosecutors in the 1754 trial needed to present Mary Squires and her children in the best possible light, as poor but honest victims of a 'wilful and corrupt perjury'. Proving this was important, declared the Crown lawyer Edward Willes, because the case had become 'the cause of great uneasiness and distraction in this country', and 'the deluded multitude' needed to learn 'the truth'. Mary Squires, explained his colleague William Davy, was 'one of that tribe of people called Gypsies, and strolls about the country as a hawker and peddler'. There was nothing exotic or threatening about her, except for her distinctive visage. Nearly every reference to Mary Squires in the court and in the press identified her as 'the Gypsy', though one well-intentioned pamphlet erased her membership in 'the clan and fraternity of Gypsies' and made her simply a peddler, licensed 'to travel the country and sell goods in the peddlery way'.[68] Ordinarily unlicensed, the Gypsies were distinguished from common peddlers by their mystery, their heritage, their aspect, and their practice of divination. It is unlikely that the Squires family had licences of any kind.

Though popular opinion held Gypsies to be outcasts, few who encountered Mary Squires and her children found them alien or threatening. James Harris, the vicar of Abbotsbury, Dorset, told the court that the Gypsies came frequently to his parish with goods to sell, 'and always paid him very justly for what they had'.[69]

Witnesses who had seen the Gypsies in the vicinity of Enfield, just before Mary Squires's arrest, gave vivid accounts of their dealings. Several recalled seeing the old Gypsy woman, wrapped in her cape, sitting by the fire, and smoking her pipe in the house of Mrs Wells. The publican John Cantril recalled Mary Squires lighting her pipe, and her son George buying 'a half-pennyworth of gin'. Mary Larney, who kept a nearby chandler's shop, remembered the Gypsies because she supplied them with small necessities, such as bread and cheese, tobacco, small beer, and tea. She was especially careful when the Gypsies paid her, because, she said, she 'had heard they can get the money again'. She apparently shared the belief that Gypsy money was 'nimble', and had to be purified 'lest it might be conjured from them by this left-handed kind of divinity'. Mary Larney was especially wary of Mary Squires, and put the old woman's money 'into a pail of water' to keep it safe, but she found young Lucy Squires less threatening and put the money she tendered into her pocket. Fear of deceit did not prevent these traders from accepting Gypsies as cash customers.

A more wary Enfield resident, a Mrs Howard, said that she first noticed the Squires family when her servants 'told me they were Gypsies; then I bid them not to unbolt the door'. She was willing to allow the Gypsies to take water from her pump, but drew the line at them entering her house. Sarah Star of Enfield testified that Mary Squires 'asked at the door, if I had any Delft to mend or china', then pushed her way into the kitchen, where 'she offered to tell my servants' fortunes, and to tell me mine'. Star reported that she wanted to get rid of her visitor, 'for I was terribly scared of seeing such a strange Gypsy woman, though I have seen hundreds of Gypsies at one time or other'. Mary allegedly told her, 'don't be scared of me, for I have been before dukes, lords, and earls, and I hurt nobody, madam, I will not hurt you'. Another Enfield witness, Tobias Kellog, said that Mary Squires came to his barn to ask for 'a bit of tobacco', and then asked a young man 'to cross her hand with four half-pence to tell him his for-tune'. The Enfield housewife Wise Bassett recalled that the Gypsy woman 'asked me to let her light her pipe; I gave her a penny for telling my for-tune', which was 'a little foolishness that belongs to woman kind'. According to another witness, Mary Squires 'asked at the door if we had any china to mend', and when she said 'no', the Gypsy prophesied, 'you will not live long'. These are extraordinary glimpses of eighteenth-century Gypsy encounters, but much more detail would follow. The descriptions of dress, complexion, demeanour, eating, drinking, smoking, socializing, working, and sleeping in the Old Bailey transcript yield unparalleled ethno-graphic riches.

A few witnesses from the area around Enfield recalled seeing 'a parcel of Gypsies' who 'used to have two asses and a little horse', but these could not have been Mary Squires and her family, who travelled on foot. The farmer William Smith testified that Gypsies lodged from time to time in his cow-house and barn, and others mentioned a Gypsy family with small children who were trying to find their strayed horse. The Enfield shopkeeper Jane Dadwell said she had often seen 'such as are called Gypsies', and she was sure one of them was Mary Squires, but it is likely that several families roamed the Lea valley, and some witnesses could not tell them apart.

The most compelling evidence that Elizabeth Canning had committed perjury was that Mary Squires was over 120 miles away in Dorset at New Year 1753, when the alleged theft and kidnapping occurred. Over forty witnesses would speak to the Gypsy's whereabouts, exposing Elizabeth Canning's account as a perjured fabrication.

Christmastide 1752 found Mary, George, and Lucy Squires at Queen Camel and Yeovil in Somerset. They reached the village of South Parrot, Dorset, on 29 December, and lodged overnight in 'a little inn' known as the Red Lion. (The younger daughter Mary, known as Polly, was ill at this time, recovering with relations in Middlesex.) The next day they took refreshment at the Three Horseshoes at Winyard's Gap, Dorset, where the housekeeper recalled telling her mother that she had 'met three Gypsies', who asked in reply if she 'was not affrighted'. When one of the lawyers enquired, 'what made you think they were Gypsies?', she answered that it was their style of travelling on foot, the man carrying a bag in his hand. The old woman appeared to be 'very unhealthy', but she walked behind the others without assistance. The witness noted Mary Squires's 'great nose and lips', in contrast to the looks of her daughter Lucy, who seemed to be of 'a very clean sort of body, and of a black [i.e. dark] complexion'. The old Gypsy was dressed in 'a sort of drab-coloured cloak' and 'a sort of serge gown', neither of them ragged. Her daughter 'had a white gown on and a red cloak; it was a sort of Holland gown, very clean and neat', and she 'did not look like a traveller or a Gypsy by her dress'. George Squires too was well attired—'in a blue coat and a red waistcoat' according to one witness, altogether 'clean and fitty'. The very ordinariness of their apparel belied the stereotype of 'odd and fantastic' garb that Gypsies were believed to affect.[70]

On New Year's Day 1753, pressing south through Dorset, the Gypsies came to an alehouse at Litton Cheney, where the bell-ringer Francis Gladman was taking liquid refreshment after ringing a celebratory peal. He found Mary Squires sitting silently and smoking her pipe, and immediately identified her as a Gypsy: 'I sat down close by her and asked her if she could tell fortunes. She said no, she was no fortune teller.' Gladman tried other conversational gambits, but received no answer. 'Upon this an old gentleman said, you must cant to her, talk Gypsy to her, and she'll answer you. Then I said, you are one of the family of the Scamps; she said, no I am no Scamp; and a young man in the room said her name was Squires.' (It is worth trying to unpack this exchange for its nuance and implications. The word 'scamp', meaning rogue, first appeared in the eighteenth century, and grew to mean rascal, cheat, or wastrel. Several Gypsies surnamed Scamp appeared in eighteenth-century records, including John Scamp and his wife Angelette who had been apprehended at Litton Cheney five years earlier and sent to the local Bridewell. A Lazarus Scamp, sentenced for sheep-stealing in Hampshire in 1788, was reputedly the first Gypsy transported to Australia.[71] This family history may have helped fix the meaning of the word 'scamp', which was not much used before the later eighteenth century. Also intriguing is the suggestion that communication in the alehouse would improve by talking 'Gypsy', though whether any of the drinkers knew Romani is doubtful. The drinkers also jestingly suggested that the Gypsy might respond to Spanish, Portuguese, French, or Dutch.)

On the evening of 1 January the Squires family reached Abbotsbury, Dorset, 'where they were very well known by a great many people, having been there often before', and rested there for over a week. While at Abbotsbury the Gypsies took part in seasonal festivities with local villagers, and were 'present at several dancing matches', where they 'danced country dances till about eleven or twelve at night'. Lucy Squires danced with William Clarke, the Abbotsbury shoemaker, who thought her 'as honest a girl as any in the world'. George Squires danced with the landlady's daughter. The carpenter John Ford shook Mary Squires by the hand, drank with her son, and gave her daughter a kiss. Entertained by the local blacksmith, the splendidly named Melchisedech Arnold, who played the fiddle and sold cider, the company seemed untroubled by the presence of Gypsies. George Squires shared a room one night with a local excise officer, Andrew Wake, who seemed equally unperturbed, and borrowed the Gypsy's great coat. Wake's notebook and testimony further supported Mary Squires's alibi (although he himself would soon leave the service for dereliction of duty).

One of the lawyers for Elizabeth Canning expressed amazement that, 'instead of being Gypsies that everyone avoids, except such as want to deal in fortune-telling and smuggled goods, they are now companions of those in the best rank in the place, and at two balls in one week!' Openly sceptical of the Abbotsbury evidence, he could only imagine that the villagers and Gypsies were in cahoots, in conspiracy to defy the law. Though this suggestion appealed to the Canningites, and has found some modern support, it gained no traction with the Old Bailey jury.[72]

With Christmastide behind them, the Squires family moved towards London. They were at the Chequers alehouse at Portersham on 9 January—'a very bad rainy day'—then at the Sloop Aground at Ridgeway on the 10th, where George Squires left some Nankeen cloth as surety for the reckoning. Reaching Dorchester on the 11th after 'terrible' rains, they found the way flooded. A local miller's man helped Lucy Squires to cross the swollen River Frome by sitting her behind him on his horse, while George Squires carried his mother on his back. They did not seek lodging that evening but pressed on through the night, anxious to rejoin the younger sibling Mary, who was said to be 'extremely ill'.

On 12 January they paused for 'some bread and cheese and a pint of beer' at a roadside alehouse at 'a place called Tawney Down', and spent the night sleeping rough a few miles past Blandford Forum in Dorset. On Saturday, 13 January, they found shelter in a farmer's barn at Martin, just inside Hampshire. Asked by a lawyer to describe the night at Martin, George Squires related that 'we all three lay upon straw; we don't carry sheets or blankets with us; we all sat up in our clothes'. The next morning, however, they received better welcome, one witness seeing 'the old woman' in farmer Thane's house 'by the fire, and her daughter was joining china for them'. This was a Sunday, but there was no question of them going to church. On the night of the 14th they lodged at a widow's house at the sign of the Lamb at Coombe Bissett, Wiltshire. Several Coombe witnesses had their fortunes told, including the farm servant Richard Merchant, who recalled that 'the old Gypsy-woman cheated him out of sixpence, for which he wished her hanged'.[73] This was hostile testimony, but it helped to corroborate Mary Squires's alibi.

By 18 January the family had reached Basingstoke, Hampshire, where they drank at an alehouse and lodged at the Spread Eagle. There the illiterate Lucy Squires dictated a letter to her Abbotsbury sweetheart William Clarke. This too, with its dated postmarks, would later be produced in court to confirm the travellers' itinerary. On 19 January they reached Bagshot, Surrey, and spent the night 'at a little tiny house on the heath'. Reaching Brentford, Middlesex, on the 20th, they lodged a few nights 'at Mrs Edward's, who sells greens and small beer'. There they were reunited with the younger daughter Mary, who was now fit enough to travel. On 23 January all four sought to spend the night at the Two Brewers at Tottenham, but were referred instead to a farmer at nearby Page Green. The next day they arrived at Enfield Wash, where their troubles began. 'Here they were strangers, and inquiring for lodging, had the ill luck to be recommended to Susannah Wells', who kept the house where Elizabeth Canning said she was imprisoned. There they stayed until Mary Squires was arrested, on Canning's evidence, on 1 February 1753.

The West Country testimony speaks to the pace and range of the Gypsies' travels—ten miles a day on foot quite commonly, and occasionally twice that distance. It shows them, for the most part, paying for their lodgings, and only *in extremis* sleeping rough or lying in hay or straw. They lived on beer, bread and cheese, tea, and the occasional fish or boiled fowl, and scrupulously paid their reckoning. There might even be beef when funds were flush. When a sceptical lawyer suggested that two fowls made 'a very remarkable dinner for three Gypsies' at Abbotsbury, George Squires responded that he bought them for sixpence apiece, and that fowls were cheaper than beef or mutton. A correspondent just a few years later found it 'no uncommon sight...to see the Gypsies, their trulls and children, sitting under a hedge drinking of tea', which was formerly a luxury beverage.[74]

Though poor and marginal, these Gypsies were not outcast, and enjoyed some sociability with people they met on their journeys. They were, said one witness, 'what we call Gypsy people', but they were neither criminal wanderers nor idle vagrants. Rather, they were familiar itinerants who filled a niche in the networks of service, entertainment, and distribution. People bought their goods and accepted their services, and were content to sit with them, dance with them, and assist them in their travels. In normal times the authorities left Gypsies alone, and history has no view of them. The Squires family was only unusual for the scrutiny it received in the courts and in the press. Homeless, but by no means destitute, they eked out a living from their travelling life.

Acquaintances and strangers treated the Gypsies with caution and curiosity, but not as pariahs. Only one witness declared that 'I don't like to have to do with them'. Most villagers expected them to tell fortunes, and the Gypsy women sometimes obliged. The Abbotsbury weaver John Hawkins remembered asking Mary Squires 'about telling of fortunes', to which she replied, 'she was no fortune-teller'. But Richard Aimer, a Wiltshire farm servant who met the Gypsies at Coombe Bissett, recalled talking with her 'in the way of bantering and telling of fortunes'. On this occasion Mary Squires read the young man's hand in exchange for twopence. When one of the lawyers asked sarcastically, 'All is come true, I hope?', he replied: 'I did not think anything was true when it was done.' Nobody accused Mary Squires of the kind of trickery attributed to more manipulative fortune-tellers.

The jury at the Old Bailey in May 1754 found Elizabeth Canning guilty of wilful and corrupt perjury (though two jurors dissociated themselves from the words 'wilful and corrupt'). One contemporary observer remarked with frustration that, 'in short, nothing is discovered'.[75] The court sentenced Elizabeth to transportation to America for a term of seven years, and her supporters ensured that she went to New England, rather than the harsher penal environment of the southern plantations or the Caribbean. Friendly letters, testimonials, and subscriptions eased Elizabeth Canning's exile, in a land of second chances, and found her a place in the household of the Revd Elisha Williams at Wethersfield, Connecticut. There she recovered her respectability, married the well-connected John Treat, and bore him four children, before dying in 1773 as a colonial American matriarch.[76]

Scrupulous public officials saved Mary Squires's life and prevented a miscarriage of justice. But the legal process by no means settled the matter, and public opinion remained divided. According to Tobias Smollett, 'people of all ranks espoused one or other party with as much warmth and animosity as had ever inflamed the Whig and Tories'. Both 'Canningites' and 'Gypsyites' could claim that 'falsities innumerable have been, indeed, devised by the interested, received by the credulous, and propagated by the malicious'.[77] Some explained the apparent discrepancy between the events at Abbotsbury and Enfield by reference to the recently reformed calendar, and confusion between 'new' and 'old' New Year's Day, which were eleven days apart. More imaginative wits suggested that Mary Squires could have been in two places at the same time by practising witchcraft, 'and flew backwards and forwards by night upon a broomstick'. Engravings depicted her airborne with her distinctive cloak and pointed hat.[78] 'The most general opinion', according to Horace Walpole, was that Elizabeth Canning had indeed been robbed, 'but by some other Gypsy'.[79]

The spate of publications produced no agreement concerning 'the truth', no consensus regarding Gypsies, and no better account of Elizabeth Canning's missing days. The Canningites continued 'to raise a general indignation against the Gypsies', one publication claiming that, as a member of 'that atrocious race of vermin', Mary Squires deserved execution as 'an example to all other Gypsies, and for the safety of society in general'.[80] Faced with evidence that Mary Squires could not have committed the crime in question, one journalist remarked that, 'if she were hanged, though innocent, what might matter, she was but a Gypsy'. The only consequence, declared another, 'would have been, that here had been in the nation one vagabond less'.[81]

When all the fuss died down, Mary Squires and her family returned to obscurity, presumably to life on the road. Mary's subsequent history has never warranted comment, but we can at least know its ending. Two London newspapers reported that, on 26 January 1762,

> Mary Squires, the Gypsy woman who was tried with Mrs Wells at the Old Bailey, for concealing Elizabeth Canning at Enfield, was buried at Farnham in Surrey. There were near one hundred lights, and forty of the Gypsy sort were mourners. She had lived at the above place about six months, and went by a

fictitious name. She died in great agony, her limbs being so much distorted that her coffin was made much deeper than usual [reminiscent of the burial of Margaret Finch at Norwood]. It is imagined she died worth a considerable sum. A Gypsy fellow at this burial had a pair of silver buckles that very near covered his shoes, and were imagined to be worth upwards of five pounds.[82]

Inspection of the parish register of Farnham reveals the burial that day of 'Mary Moor, stranger', a fitting name for a briefly famous Gypsy.[83] An early Victorian newspaper did poor service to her memory when it related the garbled tale of 'Lady Mary Squires, Queen of Bohemia', who was 'hanged at Tyburn' for imprisoning Elizabeth Canning, and claimed she had blood of 'the tide which circulated in the veins of the Pharaohs'.[84]

Changing Attitudes

Publicity surrounding the Squires–Canning affair renewed interest in the history and condition of Gypsies and may have brought them sympathy. Thomas Gainsborough's painting *Landscape with Gipsies*, the first major study of this subject by a British artist, dates from the height of the scandal in 1754 and offers a sentimental view of Gypsies at rest. Viewers can imagine them as simple countryfolk, the Madonna with child, or the Holy Family in its flight to Egypt, by no means sinister or threatening.[85] The swirl of attention, however, did little to clarify understanding of Gypsy culture, or to improve their material condition. Several publications tried to explain where Gypsies came from, what the law said about them, and why they were a problem. But, rather than pressing for outdated laws to be implemented, the weight of public attention hastened their repeal. Mary Squires was never charged under the still-extant Tudor statutes, but her ordeal became a precipitant for their abrogation.

Lecturing at Oxford in 1754, amid feverish interest in the Squires–Canning case, the jurist Sir William Blackstone observed that 'outlandish persons calling themselves Egyptians or Gypsies' still suffered from 'the severity of some of our unrepealed statutes'. He cited cases of Gypsy executions from the early seventeenth century, related by Sir Matthew Hale, but asserted with pride, 'to the honour of our national humanity, there are no instances more modern than this of carrying these laws into practice'.[86]

The reformer William Eden (Lord Auckland) pointed to the legislation of 1563 as part of the 'dismal catalogue' of 'obsolete and useless statutes' that

Figure 6. Thomas Gainsborough, 'Gypsy Family', c.1753

discredited the laws of England.[87] Other reformers blasted it as 'the most barbarous statute, perhaps, that has ever disgraced our criminal code'.[88] Taking up the matter in 1772, the House of Commons debated whether the anti-Gypsy statutes should be repealed. Mr Harbord Harbord, the member for King's Lynn, argued that these obsolete laws 'hung as terrors over the heads of the innocent, as spite, malevolence or wantonness might at pleasure put them still in force'. They also rendered the law 'ridiculous', he said, making it 'the object of disgust rather than veneration'. The Tudor laws were especially unjust because they penalized a class of people, rather than particular offenders; and, if the law was to be respected, it had to be maintained. When one Member of Parliament worried that 'the obscure and mystical language' of 'certain Gypsies' made it difficult to bring them to prosecution, another rose to say 'that he hoped the gentleman would not have even a Gypsy hanged for suspicion'. The House agreed on reform, but the bill died in the House of Lords. Repeal had to wait until 1783.[89] Gypsies were 'until within the period of the last year, an object of the persecution, instead of the protection of our laws', observed a fellow of the Society of Antiquaries in 1785.[90] The forgotten earlier law of 1554, which sought the removal of all Gypsies and death for any who remained, stayed on the books until 1820.

By that time a Member of Parliament could express satisfaction that Gypsies in England, 'who were the vilest of the vile', could find protection from the nation's laws, 'so long as its laws were respected by them'.[91]

These proceedings in the so-called age of Enlightenment mark a growing divergence of policy and opinion between Britain and the rest of Europe. Sixteenth-century England had imposed penalties against Gypsies similar to those on the Continent. But, while seventeenth-century England relaxed its laws, and in the eighteenth century worked to repeal them, state persecution of Gypsies intensified in France, Germany, Spain, and elsewhere. The France of Louis XIV again sought the expulsion of Gypsies; Gypsies in Germany risked branding, deportation, and execution; and in Spain, after attempting a round-up in 1749, the government tried in 1783 to suppress the very name *gitano* and ban all Gypsy activity.[92] Refugee migrants from these societies may have added to the English Gypsy population.

Eighteenth-century England could marvel at Gypsy funeral observances. The burial of Margaret Finch at Norwood in 1740 and Mary Squires at Farnham in 1762 had been remarkable for the number and extravagance of Gypsy mourners. Other notable funerals revealed a practice that left witnesses baffled and disconcerted. After the burial of a Gypsy woman at Tring, Buckinghamshire, in 1769, 'the survivors took all of her wearing apparel and burnt them, including silk gowns, silver buckles, gold ear-rings, trinkets, etc., for such is their custom'. The burning of the property of the deceased was recorded again in 1773, when the clothes of Diana Boswell, late 'queen of the Gypsies', were incinerated in Southwark, 'according to ancient custom'. Market-minded observers found the destruction of valuable property strange, and had no inkling of its roots in Gypsy concepts of pollution.[93]

A few Gypsy weddings also gained public attention. One such celebration at Isleworth, Middlesex, in August 1771 proceeded from the inn to the church, and thence to a dinner on Hounslow Heath, where 'forty Gypsies sat down together... The bridegroom's pockets were well lined with gold, and the father declared he could give him a thousand pounds.' Another church wedding at Leicester in July 1785 joined 'a youth belonging to Boswell's gang of Gypsies' to a daughter of 'Mr Boswell, king of this fraternity'. These were celebrity weddings among the Gypsy aristocracy, a far cry from the informal unions of most Gypsy couples. The free-spending propriety of these occasions encouraged some observers to hope that Gypsies could be made genteel.[94]

Gypsy baptisms were relatively rare, but a few stand out in parish records. The register for Wing, Buckinghamshire, records the baptism on 9 February

1772 of 'Plato, son of Peter and Dorothy Buckley, a gipsy, born under the hedge in Crafton Field in the great snow'. 'Ammariah Burden a Gypsies child' was baptized at Yetminster, Dorset, in 1799. Other entries recorded the baptism of babies born to people 'who go by the name of Gypsies', 'travelling Gypsies', 'vagrant Gypsies', or 'Egyptians'.[95] These were not children of settled parishioners, but baptismal registration gave them rights in the parish, under the poor law, and made their welfare 'likely to be chargeable' to local taxpayers.[96]

Attitudes towards Gypsies changed further in the late eighteenth century with the discovery that their private language was rooted in Sanskrit or Hindi. European travellers in India had discovered that some of the languages spoken in the subcontinent were remarkably similar to those of European Gypsies. Officers of the Bengal Infantry heard words and expressions like those of the Gypsies in Georgian Hampshire. Members of the Society of Antiquaries in London learned in 1785 that 'a dialect precisely similar to that spoken at this day by the obscure, despised and wretched' Gypsies in England could clearly be identified as Hindustani. William Marsden, the famous surgeon, shared his observations with the renowned botanist Sir Joseph Banks, prompting others to contribute their own comparisons of vocabulary. The Gypsy language had long 'been considered as a fabricated gibberish, and confounded with a cant in use among thieves and beggars', but now it could be shown to be both ancient and exotic.[97]

The Indian affinities of the Gypsy language were demonstrated more fully in Heinrich Moritz Gottlieb Grellmann's *Dissertation on the Gipsies* (published in German in 1783 and in English in 1787). Drawing on philological evidence (much of it plagiarized from the linguist Johann Rüdiger), Grellmann showed that a surprisingly large proportion of the words used by Gypsies had counterparts in Hindustani. The only compelling explanation was that ancestral Gypsies had migrated out of India, and that successive generations had kept their vocabulary alive. The dates and paths of that migration remained conjectural, but the oriental origin of the Gypsies seemed uncontestable. Grellman set out to understand 'the manner of life, economy, customs and conditions of these people . . . and their origin'. He found them both familiar and exotic, for, despite centuries of sojourning in the West, 'they remain ever, and everywhere, what their fathers were— Gypsies . . . for the most part, unsettled wandering robbers'.[98]

Grellmann's work stimulated interest in the economy and customs of European Gypsies. It made them a people to ponder, rather than simply subjects of denigration. Gypsies were suddenly interesting. Indian origins gave them a veneer of respectability, and their strangeness could be attributed to their exoticism. Several newspapers broadcast the news that 'the Gypsies are proved to be of Eastern origin'.[99] The rapid adoption of this theory is shown in the baptismal register of Hawkhurst, Kent, which recorded on 19 September 1790 the christening of 'Joseph son of Manfield and Luctatia Leo reputed Gipsies perhaps Hindees'.[100] 'It is now, I believe, pretty generally agreed, that they came originally from Hindustan, since their language so far coincides with the Hindustani', wrote a Scottish commentator in 1797.[101] A long-familiar community was newly orientalized.

Other indicators point towards a more sympathetic engagement with Gypsies. One summer evening in 1789, the *English Chronicle* reported, a gentleman in Kent encountered 'a large body of Gypsies...carousing under the shade of a large oak tree' near Chiselhurst common. He joined them in drinking 'excellent Rhenish wine', with toasts to King George, the Prince of Wales, and Charles Fox. 'Elizabeth Winifred, the present reigning queen of the Gypsies, pledged "success to the Gypsies of England, particularly those of Kent"...after which they gave him three huzzas, and conducted him safe to the road.'[102] When Gypsies were suspected of 'divers footpad robberies' in the neighbourhood of Norwich in 1795, 'a respectable person upon oath' assured the magistrates 'that this tribe were regarded more as a protection to the neighbourhood than objectionable as a nuisance'.[103] Among other relatively benign interactions, villagers at Flitton, Bedfordshire, at the end of the eighteenth century developed 'a custom to provide a dinner for Gypsies'.[104]

Several major artists portrayed Gypsies in picturesque scenes, at ease in a wooded landscape. Thomas Gainsborough's *Gypsy Encampment, Sunset* (*c.*1779), George Morland's *Gypsies by a Campfire* (1792), and the same artist's *Gypsy Encampment* (1795) set the style.[105] Diarists rarely mentioned them, although, in October 1783, while riding near Enfield, Middlesex, Thomas Fenwick encountered 'some Gypsies lying, which frightened my mare very much'.[106] The Norfolk parson James Woodforde noted on Maundy Thursday, 1799, 'a troop of Gypsies went through the parish today', but made no other reference to Gypsies in more than four decades of diary-keeping.[107] The poet William Cowper in *The Task* (1785) depicted Gypsies as 'a vagabond and useless tribe', but also memorialized their outdoor pleasures:

> Such health and gaiety of heart enjoy,
> The houseless rovers of the sylvan world;
> And breathing wholesome air, and wand'ring much,

Need other physic none to heal th'effects
Of loathsome diet, penury, and cold.[108]

Polite society delighted in Gypsies, so long as they were romanticized, sanitized, and artificial. Northern newspapers reported in 1773 that 'a group of
Gypsies were well supported and afforded much entertainment' at Lord
Coventry's masked ball at the Pantheon in York.[109] London was entertained
in 1777 by 'a new pantomime called The Norwood Gypsies', complete with
Harlequin and runaway lovers. David Garrick's May-Day: or, The Little Gipsy
that season was a 'musical farce' in which an heiress impersonated a Gypsy
to tell fortunes.[110]

Audiences the following year could laugh at The Gipsies. A Comick Opera,
in Two Acts at the Theatre Royal in the Haymarket. True to its roots in com-
media dell' arte, with romantic disguises and long-lost changelings, 'these
ragamuffins turn out to be princes after all'.[111] The 1795 season featured The
Wandering Gipsy: A Ballad, Sung by a Young Lady in the Character of a Gipsy, at
the Ranelagh Masquerade, and by Mrs Clendening at the Theatre Royal Covent
Garden.[112] King George III and his family met Gypsies at Windsor Castle, at
least stage Gypsies, with the season's leading actress 'fantastically dressed' and
singing 'a Gypsy song with uncommon vivacity and sprightliness'.[113] A few
years later 'a new musical piece called The Little Gipsies' was performed at
Sadler's Wells, under the patronage of the Duke of Clarence.[114] The late
Hanoverian court found amusement in Gypsies, as did some of its predecessors
and successors. Fashionable ladies waved fans imprinted with images of Gypsy
fortune-tellers.[115]

Gypsies in England at the end of the eighteenth century still faced harassment, and were often suspected of serious offences. They were still subject
to laws against vagrancy, and would be dealt with harshly for involvement
in sheep-stealing or horse theft. One newspaper reported in 1789 that 'the
race of Gypsies are a good deal on the decline in this country', but several
magistrates thought a crackdown was needed, especially in the era of the
French Revolution.[116] Parish officers at Pitcombe, Somerset, charged
William and Ambrose Cooper, Penelope, Sabrina, and Trinetta Cooper in
1792 with 'lodging in the open air, not giving a good account of themselves,
and pretending to be Gypsies, and wandering in the form of Egyptians, and
not having a visible means of gaining their livelihood'. The denunciation
echoed the words of the vagrancy act, to secure the attention of magistrates
who were anxious about wanderers and outsiders.[117] Judges at Quarter
Sessions reminded constables that Gypsies were targets for prosecution.[118]

Few officials were as explicit in their anti-Gypsy prejudice as Sir Richard Perryn, the presiding justice at the Buckinghamshire assizes, who refused to substitute transportation for a felon condemned to death in 1794, 'the convict being a Gypsy' and the country much troubled by the 'frequent injurious offence' of sheep-stealing. The criminal James Eyres, Sir Richard explained, belonged to

> the people known by the denomination of Gypsies or Egyptians, who have no visible means of gaining an honest subsistence, and can only support them-selves by rapine... I thought I should not do my duty to the country if I was to reprieve him, though applied to by the prosecutor for that purposes, hoping and conceiving that such an example might put this race of people on their guard.[119]

The Gypsy Tobias Smith

In 1792 the Methodist circuit preacher Thomas Tattershall (1754–1822) published two editions of a pamphlet memorializing the life and death of the runagate Gypsy Tobias Smith.[120] These texts were intended to display the power of Christian charity, through which even the most desperate character could find redemption. In order to exhibit his own evangelical credentials, Tattershall found it useful to document a Gypsy's career.

Tobias was the 'son of James and Jemima Smith, of that sort of people called Gypsies, who live an uncommon vagrant life, having no method of procuring a subsistence but by selling small articles from place to place: fortune-telling, fiddling, or such other loose and unwarrantable practices'. The description could have fitted Mary Squires and her family. Born at Southwell, Bedfordshire, in 1773, Tobias 'was brought up in this vagrant way, in a total ignorance even of the form of religion'. His mother, how-ever, was not Gypsy born, but had 'lived several years in service' before she 'took up with a Gipsy' and adopted an itinerant life.[121]

At the age of 18, in November 1791, Tobias was arrested 'for stealing a mare'. He was tried at the Lent assizes at Bedford in March 1792, was found guilty, and was sentenced to hang. Tattershall visited him several times in his condemned cell, and seems to have secured his religious conversion. He published his 'extraordinary account of Tobias Smith' as a cautionary tale 'for the information of the Gypsies', but also for self-advertisement.[122] Though Tattershall was primarily concerned with Christian salvation, his work sheds incidental light on the doings and dealings of Gypsies. The evangelist was disparaging of Gypsy rootlessness, though he himself was an itinerant preacher, ministering throughout northern and eastern England.

Tobias Smith, it transpired, was the second son of a family of sixteen children, eight of whom were still alive, 'wandering as vagabonds over the earth'. Though small in stature he was well formed and agile, excelling in

> leaping, running, fighting, etc. From his infancy he never knew any other way but wandering from place to place; to fairs, feasts, races, and other places of public concourse and diversions. He was taught to play on the fiddle as soon as possible, for the purpose of getting money at such times, when the people are intoxicated, and often unguarded in what they do; and many very materially hurt themselves and families by falling an easy prey to such companies of depredations.[123]

Like many a modern social worker, Tattershall the prison visitor emphasized the violence and neglect of the Gypsy's upbringing, in which his father often beat his mother, 'and took up with other women and other gangs of Gipsies; and at other times turned out the children to provide for themselves'. Having been brought up in 'vicious habits and continual scenes of iniquity', Tobias not surprisingly drifted into crime, on one occasion robbing his parents of a guinea, on another assisting in the theft and butchery of some sheep. He also gained experience as a prize-fighter, which may explain why 'he was so deaf at the time of his trial that he never heard one word from the counsel, witnesses, jury, nor judge'.[124]

The account of the horse theft that brought Tobias to the gallows is marked by violence and folly. He was, Tobias confessed, 'full of liquor' when he stole Mr Curtis's mare from a field near Potton, Bedfordshire, and rode her into Essex. He intended to sell the horse at Saffron Walden fair, but forgot that it had finished the week before. He then rode back to Bedfordshire and attempted to sell the horse, without success. 'Being much afraid lest he should be found out, he went into the field where he had left her, and stabbed her in two places with his knife.'[125] Justice descended, and he was taken to prison, trial, and condemnation.

The rest of Tattershall's twenty-four-page publication is taken up with his own efforts at evangelical instruction. 'I conversed with him, striving to turn his mind to God to seek pardon for his numerous sins; but he did not appear to have the least knowledge or idea of the being of a God.' Several days of intensive counselling apparently had their effect, and one of Tattershall's colleagues rejoiced that Tobias's soul 'shall take its flight from the gallows to

Paradise'. Like most Gypsies he was illiterate, and 'never could learn the right end of a book nor a letter in it'; but under instruction, awaiting execution, he 'soon got the words God, Lord, Jesus, Christ, Holy Ghost, Saviour, etc.'. 'This is one of the most wonderful things', Tattershall exalted, 'that God should teach him his letters in so miraculous a way'. It was not just Tobias's soul that was cleansed, however, for he went to the gallows with 'not the least of that tawny look which the Gypsies generally have', the lighter skin tone suggesting assimilation, his death in Christ 'a miracle of grace'.[126] Elite opinion remained divided, however, whether Gypsies most needed harsh punishment or Christian ministration.

Tobias's mother visited him in prison, giving Tattershall more opportunities for moralistic social intervention. 'I talked to her about her vagrant life, and advised her to go to her parish and settle, showing her the evil of it... With difficulty I brought her to confess she had been dishonest in her dealings, but could make no impression upon her to consent to settle.'[127] Not mentioned in Tattershall's account was Tobias's thwarted intention to marry. The parish register of Haynes, Bedfordshire, has the remarkable entry that on 17 and 24 April 1791 the banns of marriage (announcing the intention) were read on behalf of Tobias Smith, Gypsy, and Elizabeth Dines, spinster. But before the banns could be read for the third time they were 'withdrawn at the insistence of Elizabeth Dines (a minor) and her mother'. This was six months before Tobias was arrested for horse-stealing, when Mrs Dines decided that a Gypsy would not be a good match for her daughter. Other sources mark the end of the affair, when local officials charged twelve shillings for 'a coffin for Tobias Smith', three shillings 'for cap and wool' to clothe him, and two shillings and sixpence for repair of the gallows and the seat in the cart to transport him.[128] Tobias Smith's life and death could be blamed on his Gypsy condition, but influential writers thought his story worthy of literary and evangelical attention. Like Mary Squires, though with much less publicity, he became the Gypsy of the moment, a stand-in for all who were assigned that name.

7

Reformers and Enthusiasts
in the Early Nineteenth Century

The opening decades of the nineteenth century saw a burgeoning interest in Gypsies, and increased curiosity about their condition. Gypsy culture remained as mysterious as ever, but a growing number of moralists, philanthropists, and social enquirers sought to uncover their circumstances, to learn their language, and to reform their character. Old prejudices jostled with new sympathies, as Gypsies became subjects of literary, religious, and ethnographic attention. The London writer James Peller Malcolm commented in 1811 on 'the Egyptians, or Gypsies, who have long infested the environs of the metropolis', describing them as 'a distinct people, despised and rejected', who offended polite society by 'their vicious habits, and their wretched mode of living'. The Gypsies, however, could rouse sympathy as well as distaste, for 'those who have seen them seated by their scanty fires on the wastes near villages, shivering with cold, wet, and objects of scorn on all sides, may almost be tempted to forgive their artifices in telling fortunes, though certainly not their thefts'.[1] A writer in *The Christian Guardian* in 1812 described English Gypsies as 'so pitiable a race', and urged 'their conversion to the Gospel'. Another writer in 1816 recommended that 'the government may act by the application of penal and compulsive measures', by 'bringing Gypsies under the observation of our provincial police', and by 'compelling them to let their children receive education'.[2]

Gypsies continued to elicit mixed reactions. Though sometimes menaced by magistrates, and 'routed' (moved on) by local officials, early nineteenth-century Gypsies were just as likely to be bothered by evangelists, romantics, and seekers of the picturesque. Reformers sought their moral and material improvement, while disparaging their way of life. This chapter examines dealings with Gypsies in the late Hanoverian period, in the decades preceding the accession of Queen Victoria (1837). It reviews reports in the press, representations in literature, and commentary by religious activists. These works reveal the continuance and modulation of deep-seated prejudices, as well as naive and sometimes generous enthusiasms. By reading these texts against the grain, for their incidental descriptions as well as their stated purpose, it may be possible to retrieve elements of a lost ethnography.

Several commentators believed that Gypsies were 'fast disappearing', that their numbers had 'decreased', or that there were 'not so many of them with us as there used to be'.[3] Some observers attributed the decline to application of the vagrancy laws, or thought enclosure had driven Gypsies from the commons. (More than three million acres of land were enclosed for cultivation during the first two decades of the nineteenth century, to the considerable benefit of major landowners.[4]) Others blamed the Gypsies themselves, believing that their way of life condemned them to decline.[5] There is no telling, however, whether any of these conjectures was valid.

The country was rapidly changing, with increased commercial, agricultural, and industrial activity, which put pressure on itinerants. The population of England and Wales grew from a little under nine million in 1801 to close to fifteen million in 1841. Estimates of the number of Gypsies are elastic and unreliable, plagued by the perennial problem of who is to be counted and how. One member of parliament in the reign of George III ventured the figure of 'not less than thirty-six thousand', though more knowledgeable authorities suggested half that number or 'about 18,000 in this kingdom'.[6] One writer in 1828 estimated 'above 100,000, and all of these necessarily living by means of fraud, theft, robbery, or some species of crime and imposture', but neither the number nor the assessment is persuasive.[7] Gypsies were mostly absent from the early censuses, though enumerators for Essex reported in 1821 that 'the return of Sewardstone hamlet includes a gang of Gypsies to the number of 45'. Census officials made no concerted effort to record travellers, but nonetheless took note of 'a gang of 13 Gypsies' in the parish of Barming, Kent, another 'gang of 13 Gypsies' at Stanstead, Suffolk, and 'upwards of 50 Gypsies' at West Walton, Norfolk.[8]

Encounters and Reports

Gypsies were familiar figures in the late Hanoverian landscape. Like other poor and marginal itinerants, they were subject to the vagrancy laws, and were often suspected of crimes. Villagers approached Gypsies with caution and curiosity, and made occasional use of their services. Never quite sure what to make of them, local courts of justice described them as 'Gypsies wandering in the form or habit of Egyptians', 'people known by the denomination of Gypsies or Egyptians', or 'a gang of vagrants called Gypsies'.[9] The infamous Elizabethan statute that made all Gypsies felons had been repealed in 1783, but echoes of its rhetoric remained. Sentencing the Gypsies Newcombe Boss and George Young to transportation at the Peterborough Quarter Sessions in 1819, the reverend magistrate Samuel Hopkinson declared that 'this atrocious tribe of wandering vagabonds ought to be made outlaws in every civilized kingdom and exterminated from the face of the earth'.[10] Another judge at the Winchester assizes in 1827 promised to give no mercy to 'horse-stealers, especially Gypsies'.[11] Prejudices like these were not easily altered.

Isaac Gregory, constable of Frome, Somerset, recorded encounters with Gypsies in his journal. In June 1814 a neighbour brought him news of 'a strong camp of Gypsies at Oldford Hill', so Gregory 'collected a party of men and went and routed them at 8 o'clock in the evening'. It was close to midsummer, so still light for several more hours.

> Their numbers of children, tents, etc., made the lane the appearance of a small village. They were in number men, women, and children about forty—with five or six asses and as many foals, and one prime mare and foal. They had five tents and their fires burning. They was dreadfully afraid, and it was wonderful to see their dispatch in striking their tents—although many of them was naked when we discovered them—they had packed up all and was off in the course of half an hour.

Gregory and his posse followed their track for a short while, finding evidence that the Gypsies had plundered a hayrick for bedding, but they made no arrests. It was enough to dislodge the camp, and send the Gypsies into the night.[12]

Parliamentary legislation in the 1820s gave local authorities further means to make life difficult for Gypsies. The Turnpike Act of 1822 made it an offence 'if any hawker, haggler, Gypsy, or other person or persons travelling with any machine, vehicle, cart, or other carriage, with or without any horse, mule, or ass, shall pitch any tent, booth, stall, or stand, or encamp upon or by the sides of any turnpike road'. Stopping along 20,000 miles of the nation's highways now risked a forty shilling fine.[13] Borrowing language from previous legislation, the Vagrancy Act of 1824 imposed broad sanctions on 'idle and disorderly persons...pretending or professing to tell fortunes, or...wandering abroad and lodging in any barn or outhouse, or in any deserted or unoccupied building, or in the open air, or under a tent, or in any cart or wagon, not having any visible means of subsistence, and not giving a good account' of themselves.[14]

Enforcement, as ever, was erratic, but the law empowered magistrates to proceed against itinerants they deemed a nuisance or threat. Gypsies were only a small minority of persons gaoled under the vagrancy laws, as parliamentary reports attest. Only 10 of the 303 vagrants committed to the House of Correction at Wisbech, in the Isle of Ely, and only 3 of the 137 committed at Gloucester, between 1820 and 1823 were described as Gypsies. At Norwich, however, either the concentration of offenders or the system of classification was different, for 54 of 114 vagrants committed there were described as Gypsies.[15]

The journalist William Cobbett encountered Gypsies in Hampshire on one of his rural rides in October 1822:

> At Cheriton I found a grand camp of Gypsies just upon the move to Arlesford. I met some of the scouts first, and afterwards the advanced guard, and here the main body was getting in motion. One of the scouts that I met was a young woman, who, I am sure, was six feet high. There were two or three more in the camp about the same height, and some most strapping fellows of men. It is curious that this race should have preserved their dark skin and coal-black straight and coarse hair, very much like that of the American Indians. I mean the hair, for the skin has nothing of the copper colour as that of the Indians has. It is not, either, of the mulatto cast; that is to say, there is no yellow in it. It is a black mixed with our English colours of pale, or red, and the features are small, like those of the girls in Sussex, and often singularly pretty. The tall girl that I met at Tichbourne, who had a huckster basket on her arm, had most beautiful features. I pulled up my horse, and said, 'Can you tell my fortune, my dear?' She answered in the negative, giving me a look at the same time, that seemed to say, it was too late; and that if I had been thirty years younger, she might have seen a little what she could do with me. It is, all circumstances considered, truly surprising, that this race should have preserved so perfectly all its distinctive marks.[16]

The Gypsies, for Cobbett, were a phenomenon to be observed rather than a people to be reformed. Their apparent distinctiveness had survived the passage of time. It is telling that the initiative in this encounter lay with the horseman—'Can you tell my fortune, my dear?' with its sexual undertones— and that the Gypsy demurred. Cobbett's expectations and assumptions coloured his reactions. Remarkable too is Cobbett's reflection on the Gypsy visage, his tortured effort to describe their complexion, and his fascination with the beauty and stature of the female Gypsies.

An extraordinarily detailed account of Gypsy activity and Gypsy sociability appears in the Quarter Session records for Huntingdonshire in September 1822. The constable of Kimbolton had apprehended a cluster of Gypsies 'for an act of vagrancy committed by them, in wandering abroad and lodging in...tents' in Honeyhill Lane. Transcribed statements by John Buckley, Edmund Hearn, and Humphrey Smith named their companions and explained their circumstances. Though framed by judicial procedures, the record of their examination brings one as close as is possible to the utterances of Gypsies themselves. They appear to have been explaining why they should not be prosecuted as vagrants. The campers were all related to each other, and had three tents between them. John Buckley shared his tent with his mother Quality Buckley and his sister Charlotte Smith. The next tent housed Siverency Hearn (alias Buckley or Butler), her son Humphrey Hearn, Humphrey's wife Charlotte Hearn, and the children Sagy Hearn aged 12 and Edmund Hearn aged 9. Humphrey Smith and his wife (Nancy Butler?) shared the third tent, and looked after the animals. They had a horse, three asses, three dogs, and two puppies between them, and were delayed in Kimbolton while looking for a lost donkey. The group had visited several villages along the Bedfordshire–Huntingdonshire border, and had dealings with other Gypsies, including the basket-maker Thomas Loveridge from Towcester, and their kinsman Benjamin Smith. All had been at Tilbrook Fair in Huntingdonshire, where John Buckley had been engaged in chair-mending, and the others had been involved in fairground entertainment, skittles, and beating of tambourines and drums. The men wore frock smocks, of the sort then favoured by working countrymen. Their subsequent history is unknown, but the following year Mary Welch, Jemima Shaw, Elisha Gray, and Moses Shaw were convicted at the Huntingdon Quarter Sessions for 'having wandered around Eynesbury pretending to be Gypsies and sleeping in the open air'.[17]

An even more remarkable episode emerged from the archives of the Home Office, the criminal courts, and the provincial press later in the reign of George IV. The Gypsy Matthew Broadway was convicted of highway robbery at the Salisbury summer assizes in 1828, and was condemned to hang. This sentence was quickly commuted to transportation for life, and he was moved to the hulks at Portsmouth to await shipment to Australia. This might have been the end of the story, had not doubts arisen about the safety of Broadway's conviction. The record reveals a miscarriage of justice, founded on prejudice and suspicion.[18]

Thomas Eatwell of Winterbourne, Wiltshire, claimed that Broadway and an unnamed companion robbed him at pistol point on the Devizes road at Beckhampton, on Easter morning, 6 April 1828. He had been intending to get married, he said, and Broadway robbed him of his savings of £8 10s. Suspecting that the criminals would frequent Devizes fair, Eatwell kept watch there two days, and eventually discerned Broadway among spectators to a fight. He followed him into a public house, and 'then procured a constable for his apprehension'. Broadway was found to have a suspicious amount of money in his possession—four pounds in notes and two gold sovereigns—which appeared to be the proceeds of robbery. When challenged, the Gypsy allegedly threw the money down and said, 'if that's yours, damn your eyes, take it', and the money was returned, or given, to his alleged victim.

The assize jury in July found Broadway guilty, despite claims that he was twenty-five miles away at the time of the offence. Villagers who spoke on his behalf were disbelieved. A petition on his behalf described the Gypsy as 'a quiet, inoffensive, and sober man' who 'in all ways bore a very honest character', while his prosecutor, Thomas Eatwell, was 'a very abandoned and wicked man, and the general belief in his residence is that he suffered no robbery'. The court, however, was unmoved, and Matthew Broadway was still on board the *Leviathan* hulk at Portsmouth half a year later in February 1829 when local report convinced Thomas Goodlake, the magistrate who had taken first reports of the case, that Broadway's conviction was unsound. Sworn affidavits from 'persons whose testimony is worthy of credit' told a different story of benign interactions, and gave good evidence of Broadway's innocence. Like Mary Squires several generations earlier, though without the press frenzy in that episode, the Gypsy had been the victim of malicious prosecution and perjury, which almost cost him his life.

William Appleford, a farm labourer of Letcombe Bassett, Berkshire, testified that on Good Friday morning, 4 April 1828, he saw Matthew Broadway, with his father and mother, 'pitching a tent in the manner of Gypsies' on Letcombe downs. He saw them frequently over the next few days, and each time he passed the Gypsies asked him what hour it was. He distinctly recalled seeing them on Easter Sunday morning, 'sitting in a tent at breakfast on a hedgehog', when the Gypsies invited him 'to partake of some hedgehog which they were eating'. There could be no doubt about the identification, he was confident, because Broadway lacked the first joint of his right thumb, 'and he seemed to handle the knife with which he was eating the hedgehog very awkwardly'.

Also that morning the maltster Jacob Fidler of East Challow rode his grey horse across Letcombe downs, and stopped by the Gypsies to tighten his girth. He knew the time, ten on Easter Sunday, by the ringing of the bells at Letcombe church. Matthew Broadway then looked in the mare's mouth and asked if he would be willing to sell it, which the maltster declined. Fidler too noticed the distinctive damage to the Gypsy's right thumb. They exchanged cordial greetings, wished each other good morning, and the Gypsies informed him that they would soon be at Wadley fair.

Further evidence that the Gypsies were on Letcombe downs in Berkshire, twenty-five miles from the scene of the crime in Wiltshire, came from the gamekeeper Philip Self, employed by the magistrate Thomas Goodlake, who recalled seeing the Gypsy tent on Easter Sunday, where the occupants greeted him with 'Good morn to you'.

Goodlake also secured affidavits about the Gypsy's incriminating money. Matthew Broadway the elder, described as a 'travelling brazier', swore that 'the four one pound notes and two sovereigns which were found upon his son when he was apprehended at Devizes fair... was the same money which was paid him for a pony he sold to Mr Henry Shannon of the Rising Sun public house at Devizes the same morning'. And, to substantiate this, he secured another affidavit from Henry Shannon, that 'I did buy of Matthew Broadway a pony, for which I paid him six pounds—two sovereigns and four notes... to take care of till the morning for his father', who at the time was overmuch in liquour.

Goodlake wrote to the assize judge, Justice Park, and also appealed to Richard Hart Davis, MP, and to the Home Secretary Robert Peel, declaring it 'impossible that the prisoner Broadway...could be one of the persons who robbed the man in Beckhampton downs'. Recommending pardon, he revealed both the prejudice and the ideals of his class and profession: 'I abhor Gypsies myself and often threaten to have them apprehended, but I am the last person that would like to see any fellow creature suffer wrongfully.' Though loathsome, by this account, the Gypsies at least shared common humanity.

At Goodlake's request, Justice Park reviewed his notes of the trial, and deemed it lawfully conducted. But he revealed that he had been influenced

by the defendant's status as a Gypsy, as well as his alleged criminality: 'The
jury having found him guilty, which was their province, and the prisoner
leading at all events a wandering life, I thought he might as well be sent out
of the country.' However, in light of the evidence that Goodlake had collected, the judge now thought it 'a case not unworthy of his majesty's royal
commiseration'.

Matthew Broadway was pardoned on 19 February 1829, after ten months
of incarceration. He presumably returned to his family, and to his life of
itinerant tinkering and horse-trading, with no compensation for his losses.
Newspapers in Wiltshire and nearby counties had reported his arrest and
conviction, but there was no press coverage of his exoneration. Only in the
archives was there testimony of the injustice he had suffered. These records
show Gypsies like the Broadways to have been sociable and unthreatening,
subject both to disapproval and toleration. They were reputedly of good
character, and honest in their dealings, and were likely to say 'good morning'
and to invite strangers to share meals. They were also vulnerable to a long
legacy of prejudice and suspicion that could upend or take away their life.

More glimpses of Gypsies appear in reports of the Poor Law commissioners concerning problem cases. One commissioner told a parliamentary
committee in 1835 about 'a man named Gray, a tinker and Gypsy, living at
Cambridge; he is an old man with numerous offspring, all deriving their
settlement through him'. The children and grandchildren of this Gypsy, the
report continued, 'have troubled us frequently for relief. We are obliged to
buy them off. They come and pitch their tent by the roadside, and say they
are come to settle.'[19]

At Sulgrave, Northamptonshire, reported another commissioner,

I found a clan of Gypsies fixed like horse-leeches on the shoulders of the parish. How they came there was a matter of tradition; the patriarch of the family
had acquired a settlement 70 or 80 years back, and nothing was heard of him
for 50 years, when one of the sons, one Aaron Smith, came back. The magistrates of that day obliged the overseers to find the man a house, although he
confessed he had never slept in a house before; and the consequence is, that
when any of the man's brethren, or brethren's children, now a numerous and
widely-spreading family, are refused their guinea or two guineas, they threaten
to come and make the overseers find them houses also...In general, what
they ask for is given without much inquiry, so little, that a Gypsy woman who
came to ask for money for her husband's burial, was furnished with the means
and went away; and the husband himself, who came to life again about a
month before my visit, received almost £3 to get rid of him again.[20]

As in earlier eras, the Gypsies proved adept at exploiting local resources and systems of parish relief.

National and provincial newspapers spread reports of Gypsies throughout the kingdom, repeating nuggets of news in different publications. Press accounts provided no reliable mirror of Gypsy activities, but tended to sustain their dark reputation. Journalists, as ever, thrived on popular prejudices, and sought out newsworthy accounts of outrages and curiosities. Reports of criminality, trickery, or imposture were common fare, and accounts of Gypsy weddings, fights, and funerals offered items of human interest.[21]

There was nothing remarkable in the report in *The Times* in September 1816 that the Gypsies Solomon and William Hearn had been sentenced to transportation for theft. What piqued the paper's attention was the escape of one of them while being conveyed by coach from Rutland to London. Somewhere near Biggleswade 'it was discovered that William Hearn was missing, and the night being wet and dark he got clear off, notwithstanding his irons, and notwithstanding the vigilance of the gaoler... and his assistant, and of the guard of the coach, all of whom were armed'.[22] Of such exploits were legends born. Provincial papers reported the escape of another 'suspicious looking character of the Gypsy tribe', in January 1832, who, though 'bolted and gyved', managed to outwit a constable.[23]

The *Morning Post* reported in October 1822 the suspected involvement of Gypsies in a theft from a farmhouse at Helston, Cornwall. Their offer to tell fortunes was just a cover for their crime. By the time the theft was discovered the Gypsies—two men and two women, with three children between them—'had struck their tent, and departed', but the victim managed to track them 'in a zig-zag course 150 miles' to Newbridge, Devon, beyond Dartmoor. Incriminating coins and bank notes were found in their possession, and it seemed likely that they had recently purchased horses with stolen money. More suspicion attached to the Gypsies' baggage, which was found to contain 'a great variety of children's clothes of a superior quality, several pieces of cotton goods, a number of gown pieces, flannels, a handsome gold seal, etc.'. This was not much different from the stock of the Squires family seventy years earlier, but was interpreted as evidence of criminality. The whole party was committed to Exeter gaol, but their subsequent disposition is unknown. Newspaper readers could regard the incident as typical of Gypsy depredation, but the report also yields ethnographic detail of the composition, movement, and equipage of a small Gypsy company.[24]

Also typical was the report from Lincolnshire in January 1832 of the theft of 'a beautiful ewe in lamb'. The night-time 'villains' butchered the animal in an adjacent field, 'and after picking the meat from various parts, left the bones'. The writer editorialized that 'the thieves are supposed to be Gypsies, who, whilst perambulating the country under pretence of telling fortunes, make it their business to kill their own mutton'.[25] Critics of Gypsies had been saying as much for more than 200 years.

More enormities in March 1832 were attributed to 'a most extensive and formidable horde of Gypsies' who menaced passing gentlemen on the roads near Taunton, Somerset. According to the *Bath Chronicle*, 'the gang...had a regular encampment—fourteen or fifteen horses and donkeys, and a cow, were observed among them—all honestly acquired, no doubt'. One of the Gypsies had blocked the road with his white horse, and was later observed 'with a large blunderbuss in his hand', no doubt intended for 'base purposes'. The report concluded by recommending, 'it is high time that parish officers exerted themselves more in these matters than they do'.[26]

Early nineteenth-century journalists continued to affect surprise that people should fall victim to the trickery of fortune-tellers, especially 'in England at this day'. A report in the *Morning Post* in November 1821 noted all the elements of the classic fortune trick: a naive simpleton, cunning Gypsies, promises of buried treasure, the wrapping and hiding of money, mystifying incantations, and the 'unspeakable surprise and dismay' of the victim, in this case a carpenter in Cornwall, when he discovered he was cheated of £31 6s. Once again, the Gypsies promptly 'decamped...and conducted their march so secretly that no trace of them could be discovered by their nearly distracted dupe or his friends'.[27] A similar report in the *Westmorland Gazette* in May 1826 mocked the credulity of a farmer who was charmed out of £40 'by palmistry, physiognomy, and incantations'.[28] A villager near Manchester was similarly defrauded of £92 6s. 6d. in 1833, when Gypsies persuaded him that his garden hid treasure from the time of Oliver Cromwell.[29] The mechanics of the deception were almost identical, though it is noteworthy that in each of these cases the victim was a man.

Gypsy weddings were almost as newsworthy as Gypsy crimes. Several papers reported the wedding at Doynton, Gloucestershire, in May 1815, between a Mr Wilson, a resident near Stroud, and Sarah Lock, 'a young Gypsy girl belonging to a gang now hutted on the common'. It was accompanied by church bells, a handsome dinner, and a ball, with 'the whole of the Gypsy corps' in attendance. Readers were left to their own reflections on this unusual union between a local inhabitant and a Gypsy, but could not ignore the apparent extravagance of Gypsy customs. 'At eleven o'clock the dingy tribe retired, but not before the father of the bride called for a pint pot, which he filled with guineas and presented to the bridegroom.'[30] A similar report of a wedding between two Gypsies in Lincolnshire in January 1832 was offered to readers 'as a kind of commentary on the manners and habits of that separated community at this part of the nineteenth century'. Though the ceremony was performed in church by a reputable minister, the merriment and gaiety of the participants made it 'a very different affair to the melancholy of the weddings of the more civilized community'.[31]

'Wild Outcasts of Society'

Scholarship on Gypsies in the Romantic era cleaves closely to the writings of canonical authors. Literary scholars in particular tease meaning from the poetry of William Wordsworth (1770–1850) and John Clare (1793–1864), and from novels by Walter Scott (1771–1832) and Jane Austen (1775–1817). The key texts in this regard are Wordsworth's 'Gipsies', Clare's 'Gypsy' poems, Scott's *Guy Mannering*, with its memorable figure of Meg Merrilies, and Austen's *Emma*, with its scene of deliverance from a menacing Gypsy camp. Representations of Gypsies in these works reveal imaginative conceptions of England's itinerant underclass that influenced popular perception for decades.

The poet William Wordsworth meditated on 'Gipsies' in his poem of 1807, to which he returned in 1820. Reversing roles, it is the poet who is the wanderer, while the Gypsies lie static, 'the same unbroken knot of human beings, in the self-same spot!' The poet's disapproving contrast of the Gypsies' unproductive lethargy and his own ambulant energy is modified in the 1820 version:

> In scorn I speak not;—they are what their birth
> And breeding suffer them to be;
> Wild outcasts of society.[32]

Criticizing this poem, Wordsworth's contemporary Samuel Taylor Coleridge (1772–1834) pointed out that these 'poor tawny wanderers might probably have been tramping for weeks together through road and lane, over moor and mountain, and consequently must have been right glad to rest themselves,

their children and cattle, for one whole day'. The poet is rebuked for his lack
of empathy with the subjects of his verse. They are subjects of his gaze, not
his knowledge.[33]

John Clare famously socialized with Gypsies, and entertained notions of
adopting their way of life. 'To me how wildly pleasing is that scene... | A
group of Gipsies, centr'd on the green' ('The Gipsys Evening Blaze', 1809,
published 1820). In 'The Gipsies Camp' (1820) he recalls 'How oft on
Sundays, when I'd time to tramp, | My rambles led me to a gipsy's camp'.
There, in the lanes of Northamptonshire, he observed their crafts, learned
their music, experienced their fortune-telling, and sampled their foraged
food. In 'The Village Minstrel' (1821) Clare finds beauty in the Gypsy camps,
and defends their residents—'poor ragged outcasts of the land'—against
false charges of petty theft. The Gypsies were not past pilfering, as Clare
acknowledged in his poem of 'Langley Bush' (1821), but seemed to be at
one with the traditional landscape. 'The Gipsy's Song' (before 1832) celebrates Gypsy 'liberty' and merriment. Only in the late poem 'Gipsies' (1841),
written in Clare's mental asylum, has the camp become 'squalid', and its
inhabitants more pathetic than picturesque: ''Tis thus they live—a picture to
the place; | a quiet, pilfering, unprotected race'.[34]

Walter Scott's novel *Guy Mannering* (1815) is dominated by the figure of
its formidable heroine, the Gypsy Meg Merrilies. Her foreknowledge of the
fate of the heir of Ellangowan drives the complex plot. The Gypsies, Scott
informs his readers, were once 'a distinct and independent people', but had
become 'a mingled race' with 'greatly diminished' numbers. Some in
Scotland were semi-settled or seasonally itinerant, the men engaged in 'rude
handcrafts' and 'out-of-door sports', the women in petty trade and fortune-
telling. Though often reputed 'idle and vicious', some Gypsies, most notably
Meg herself, exhibited wisdom and generosity 'amounting almost to hero-
ism'. Meg, however, is 'true bred', tall, dark, and disfigured, so that, like Mary
Squires in the 1750s, 'naebody that's seen her will ever forget her'. Scott's
sympathetic treatment of his imagined Gypsy prophetess offered an alternative stereotype, and may have encouraged some readers to give credence to
Gypsy predictions.[35]

In Jane Austen's *Emma* (1816), a novel of very different sensibility,
unaccompanied young ladies panic at the sight of a party of Gypsies beside
the Richmond road. 'Exceedingly terrified', though with no real cause for
alarm, Harriet Smith fears attack by 'half a dozen children, headed by a stout
woman and a boy'. In her eyes, the 'trampers' are 'clamorous, and impertinent

in look', then 'loud and insolent', but the danger is entirely imagined. Harriet's quick rescue by Frank Churchill leaves the Gypsies where they were found, on the secluded greensward, separate from civil society. Jane Austen's Gypsies are total strangers, yet not out of place within their woodland setting. Though little more than a plot device, the incident has occasioned reams of commentary on the illumination of Gypsy character.[36]

Despite creative attention, the Gypsies of the literary imagination remained mostly anonymous, generic, and enigmatic. They could be merry or mysterious, dangerous or sublime, but, except for some of John Clare's associates, they remained remote and unknowable. It fell to a different community to concern themselves more closely with the moral, material, and spiritual circumstances of England's Gypsies.

Evangelical Ethnographers

The evangelical movement of the late eighteenth and early nineteenth centuries constituted an ecumenical religious revival, involving benevolent activities at home and abroad in the name of the Christian gospel. Its agents included Quakers, Methodists, and Dissenters, as well as members of the established Church of England. The philanthropic projects of leading evangelicals are well known, especially their work against slavery, poverty, and prostitution.[37] Lay and clerical activists sought to spread religion among marginal communities, including, in some cases, Gypsies. This was the great age of missionary endeavours, but one evangelical sympathizer in the 1820s remarked that it was easier to fund missions at the ends of the earth than among 'the poor Gypsies' in England.[38] Another cited the 'hundreds of thousands of pounds...devoted to the moral and religious reformation of the natives of Otaheite...while this wretched and unfortunate race of our own countrymen'—the Gypsies—lived 'in open violation of law and religion'. It was a 'foul reproach' that the Gypsies were so neglected in a country committed to 'the civilization and instruction of mankind'.[39]

The English Christian evangelists who strove for the 'improvement' of Gypsies in the first third of the nineteenth century are easily dismissed as ignorant and prejudiced interferers. They endeavoured to change Gypsies, not to understand them. Even those well-wishers who constituted themselves as the 'advocate' or 'friend' of the Gypsies harboured deep-rooted stereotypes about Gypsy fecklessness and disorder. By leading Gypsies to

godliness and teaching them the paths to salvation, these domestic missionaries sought the end of the Gypsy way of life. Historians have generally
recognized their work as 'moralistic', 'manipulative', and condescending,
and have put little store by their efforts. Most of their missionary activities
failed, but their writings preserve valuable observations about the lives of
pre-Victorian Gypsies.[40]

Foremost among these reformers were the Quaker John Hoyland (1750–
1831), the Church of England cleric Thomas Blackley (1783–1842), the lay
philanthropist Samuel Roberts (1763–1848), and the Methodist James Crabb
(1774–1851). Hoyland's work on Gypsies is well known, Roberts and Crabb
have received scholarly attention, but Blackley's contribution to Gypsy
studies has not been previously acknowledged. Their work was stimulated
by a series of published articles and correspondence. A contributor to the
Christian Guardian in 1812 recommended that, 'in order to do any good
amongst the Gypsies, we must conciliate their esteem, and gain their confidence'.[41] The following sections examine their activities, impressions, and
influence, as they went about this project.

John Hoyland's Gypsy Survey

The Quaker John Hoyland, who published *A Historical Survey of the Customs,
Habits and Present State of the Gypsies* in 1816, shared the common view of
Gypsies as 'filthy and disgusting', with a 'depraved and fraudulent character',
but hoped nonetheless for 'the amelioration of their condition'. Moved by
notions of Christian charity, and finding Gypsies in 'a state so derogatory to
human nature...so repugnant to the mild and genial influences of the
Christian religion', he resolved to advocate for 'their improvement'. Hoyland
drew heavily on Heinrich Grellmann's *Dissertation on the Gipsies*, available in
English since 1787, but incorporated contemporary observations on the
'destitute and abject condition of the Gypsy race'.[42]

Hoyland first visited a Gypsy camp near Rushden, Northamptonshire, in
the summer of 1814. Most of the adults were away at feasts and fairs, leaving
only an elderly woman weaving a cabbage net, a middle-aged woman nursing an infant, and three Gypsy children engaged in camp chores. These were
his first informants. Hoyland found the 'very tattered and squalid appearance' of one 12-year-old girl, who was boiling water for washing, to be
'truly affecting'. There were five tents, home to several branches of the

Smith and Loversedge families, who dealt in asses or donkeys and performed as musicians. In answer to Hoyland's questions, the old woman indicated that all were ignorant of the Scriptures, and none of the children
could read. Prompted by his study of Grellmann, he asked her whether the
Gypsies ever ate 'animals they might find dead on the road'. He was excited
by her answer, that 'those that have died by the hand of God, are better than
those that have died by the hand of man', because it corresponded 'exactly
with that of the Continental Gypsies', as related in Grellmann's
publication.[43]

Hoyland mused on the effect of 'the torrent of invective and abuse, almost
universally poured upon this people', and suspected that it affected his relationship with his informants. 'Despised and ill-treated as they often are, have
they not reason to imagine the hand of every man to be against them? Who
then can wonder at their eluding, as much as possible, the inquiries of
strangers!'[44]

To find out more, hoping to 'enable the rising generation to correct the
errors of Gypsy habits', Hoyland devised a survey, which he called a 'circular'. He asked his correspondents a series of questions:

> From when is it said the Gypsies first came? How many is it supposed there
> are in England? What is [their] circuit in the summer? How many Gypsy
> families are supposed to be in it? What are the names of them? Have they any
> meetings with those of other circuits? And for what purpose? What number
> of Gypsies are there computed to be in the county? What proportion of their
> number follow business, and what kind? What do they bring their children
> up to? What do the women employ themselves in? From how many generations
> can they trace their descent? Have they kept to one part of the country, or
> removed to distant parts? How long have they lived in this part? Have they
> any speech of their own, different to that used by other people? What do they
> call it? Can anyone write it? Is there any writing of it to be seen anywhere?
> Have they any rules of conduct which are general to their community? What
> religion do they mostly profess? Do they marry, and in what manner? How
> do they teach their children religion? Do any of them learn to read? Who
> teaches them? Have they any houses to go to in winter? What proportion of
> them, is it supposed, live out of door in winter, as in summer?[45]

These were thoughtful enquiries, before the establishment of the discipline
of anthropology, yet they revealed stark ignorance about a people who had
lived in England for some 300 years.

The original returns to Hoyland's survey are not known to survive. They
might have yielded detailed ethnographic information, of the kind sent in

by a friend of his in Essex: 'The construction of their tents, is well known to be wooden hoops fastened into the ground, and covered with an awning of blankets or canvas, which resembles the tilt of a wagon; the end is closed from the wind by a curtain.' The residents here were scissors-grinders and tinkers, said to be from Staffordshire, but they spoke 'the language of Gypsies' among themselves. This was not 'cant' or 'the slang of beggars', but a Hindu-based language made accessible by 'Grellmann's vocabulary'. It was 'astonishing', Hoyland remarked, that these people, though 'scattered on the face of the earth, have preserved, spoken, and transmitted the same language to their descendants'.[46]

Hoyland's printed summary of returns to his 'circular' sets forth the state of knowledge in the summer of 1815: 'All Gypsies suppose the first of them came from Egypt.' Their total numbers in England are unknown. Gypsies in various counties continually made circuits, but either did not know or would not tell the numbers of other Gypsies in those counties. 'The most common names are Smith, Cooper, Draper, Taylor, Boswell, Lee, Lovell, Loversedge, Allen, Mansfield, Glover, Williams, Carew, Martin, Stanley, Buckley, Plunkett, Corrie' (all unexceptional British surnames). The various groups or 'gangs' have little regular connection or organization, 'but those who take up their winter quarters in the same city or town, appear to have some knowledge of the different routes each horde will take'. 'More than half their number follow no business; others are dealers in horses and asses, farriers, smiths, tinkers, braziers, grinders of cutlery, basket-makers, chair-bottomers, and musicians.' (In Kent, Surrey, and Sussex, Hoyland added, they 'assist sometimes in hay-making and plucking hops'.) 'Children are brought up in the habits of their parents, particularly to music and dancing, and are of dissolute conduct.' 'The women mostly carry baskets with trinkets and small wares, and tell fortunes.' 'When among strangers, they elude inquiries respecting their peculiar language, calling it gibberish.' No written versions of this language are known. 'Instances of their attending any place for worship are very rare.' 'They marry for the most part by pledging to each other, without any ceremony.' 'They do not teach their children religion.' 'Not one in a thousand can read.'[47]

Hoyland had nothing to say about Gypsy criminality or Gypsies' reputation for theft and pocket-picking. Rather he saw them as candidates for improvement, by which he meant assimilation. It caught Hoyland's attention that some Gypsies moved back and forth between itinerant, semi-settled, and settled modes of life, but did not cease to be Gypsies. They were distinguishable, he believed, from other travelling 'hordes', such as the 'potters', who 'traverse most of the nation with carts and asses, for the sale of earth-enware, and live out of doors great part of the year, after the manner of Gypsies'. Identification was complicated, however, because 'Gypsies have intermingled with them, and their habits are very similar'. Without evidence, he implied that much of the bad reputation of Gypsies stemmed from other vagrants who looked like them.[48]

Hoyland's survey may be considered naive and superficial, but it repre-sented the most sophisticated social knowledge of its day. It was widely reviewed, and proved a stimulus to contemporary evangelists and others who took up their mission. Hoyland's account is sprinkled with details that are unobtainable elsewhere, and serves as a window into the *gorgio*'s view of Gypsy culture in the early nineteenth century. One of his early readers, Daniel Copsey, of Braintree, Essex, contributed his own observation of the Lovell family of Gypsies in 1818. 'The man called himself a tinker, and the woman said she sold earthenware, but... denied practising fortune-telling.' All enjoyed 'very vigorous health'. Using Hoyland's word-list, Copsey was able to extract from these Lovells a vocabulary of more than sixty Romani words and phrases that they used with other 'tribes'.[49]

Thomas Blackley's 'wandering and scattered people'

Another who 'derived much pleasure' from Hoyland's survey was Thomas Blackley, the curate and later vicar of Rotherham, Yorkshire. Blackley was a prolific religious essayist, sermonizer, and versifier who published his own tract in 1822 in 'commiseration for the moral degradation of the neglected Gypsies'. This anonymous publication enjoyed a small local circulation, but gained national prominence when both James Crabb and Samuel Roberts incorporated it into their own treatises.[50]

Primed by his reading of Hoyland, when Blackley encountered a Gypsy child he remarked that 'its swarthy face, its black hair and eyes, plainly bespoke its family and its people'. He soon caught up with the travelling company, who 'were scattered in their march like a flock of sheep: the main body with the baggage at some distance in front, some females and children in detached groups behind. I thought, here is an opportunity of instructing these wanderers.' Seeing the Gypsies with their 'asses, horses, carts, pack and package', he found the ensemble 'altogether highly picturesque'. This was a conventional aesthetic reaction, though irrelevant to the evangelistic mission. Entering another Gypsy camp, Blackley observed that 'the waste ground was occupied with tents and packages; their horses and asses feeding by their side, while a fire from collected broken branches' sent forth smoke. This offers a sense of verisimilitude, though it may also be shaded by fiction. This travelling company comprised 'sellers of earthen pans and pots', indistinguishable from the 'potters', who Hoyland claimed were only similar to Gypsies.[51] A contemporary contributor to the *Lonsdale Magazine* thought that the itinerant 'potters' were 'like the true Gipsy race' and 'of their fraternity', and shared with Gypsy 'heathens' a lack of acquaintance with God.[52]

Entering this 'picturesque' assembly, Blackley remarked on 'a female, apparently about eighteen years of age, dressed in a tidy and neat manner, with a sweet baby at her back: her features were particularly dark and handsome, with fine expressive black eyes'. To the evangelist's surprise, this woman seemed to have some knowledge of religion. He responded, unctuously, 'I will not fail to pray for thee, thou lovely wandering Gypsy female, thou young pilgrim!' Meeting another group of 'knife-grinders, chair-bottomers, and china-menders', known as 'Bosvile's gang' (the Boswell family), he was again most struck by the 'fine-looking young females, with true Gypsy features and dressed in the highest order of Gypsy fashion. One of them wore a loose dress of large printed cotton, with rolling collar, with deep flounce, and apron to match.' Another caught the evangelist's attention with her 'expressive eyes' and 'big tears rolling down her cheeks, wiped away with her long black tresses', so moved was she by his preaching.[53] Like other early ministers among the Gypsies, Blackley was affected by the 'wretchedness of this lost people', but was also convinced of their potential for Christian conversion. Inflating his own credentials, he noted that they listened 'with evident interest' when he began to preach. Visiting 'Bosvile's gang', with eyes not only for the women, he remarked on 'the civility and etiquette of my reception. Never was a king received with more hearty welcome, or with greater attention and respect.' One would love to hear this from Bosvile's (or Boswell's) point of view.[54]

Doctor Syntax Visits the Gypsies

Satirizing the evangelical encounter and the quest for the picturesque, the poet William Combe and the artist Thomas Rowlandson collaborated to

Figure 7. Thomas Rowlandson, 'Dr Syntax and the Gypsies', in William Combe, *The Second Tour of Doctor Syntax: In Search of Consolation* (1820)

create the fictional Dr Syntax. The illustration of 'Dr Syntax and the Gypsies' (1820) shows the well-intentioned but self-absorbed clergyman lecturing a family of Gypsies, while his companion has his fortune read and his possessions rifled.[55] The celebrity of Rowlandson's print has overshadowed its original context accompanying Combe's hack verse. In the episode with the Gypsies the bumbling clergyman espies:

> A medley troop, that lay at ease
> Beneath a wood's embow'ring trees.
> Some slept upon the naked ground,
> With one poor blanket wrapp'd around;
> Scarce shelter'd from the open sky,
> But by the leaves green canopy.

He stumbles on a scene that could have come from a painting by Gainsborough or Morland, with a cluster of families resting, with children playing, and food in preparation:

> And, as the aged crones sat smoking,
> The young were laughing, singing, joking
>
> .　　.　　.　　.　　.
>
> But through the scene seem'd to express
> The outward shew of wretchedness,
> No visage marked that heartfelt care
> Had taken up its dwelling there.

Dr Syntax's companion Patrick explains about the Gypsies:

> They have no trade, nor buy, nor sell,
> But when they're paid, will fortunes tell.

They live, says Patrick, by theft and cunning, by raiding orchards and hen roosts, and stealing linen and sheep. As for their language:

> 'Tis said, that their strange gibb'rish tongue
> Does to themselves belong .
>
> .   .   .   .
>
> It is not English I declare,
> And 'tis not Irish, that I'll swear.

Drawn toward the picturesque, and seizing the opportunity to spread the gospel, Dr Syntax determines 'to confer with this vagrant nation'. Insisting on being heard, he lectures the Gypsies on the depravity of their way of life and the foolishness of fortune-telling. A Gypsy patriarch responds by explaining the timeless preservation of his people's 'ancient nature':

> In customs, manners, and in feature
>
> .   .   .   .
>
> While we in character and name
> Continue through all time the same
>
> .   .   .   .
>
> Expos'd to insult we remain,
> A wandering persecuted train.

Like many a clerical outsider, like Hoyland and Blackley, Dr Syntax is eager to learn the 'secrets' of the Gypsies. To his disappointment, the Gypsy patriarch explains:

> But that's a branch of Gypsy art
> That nought will bribe us to impart
>
> .   .   .   .
>
> We this strange mode of living choose,
> And all your social good refuse.

None the wiser, but a few silver coins lighter, Dr Syntax has learned nothing. Old stereotypes are confirmed. The Gypsies remain a 'wandering people' with 'strange habits', separate from the religion and morality of the mainstream. Resistant to instruction and hostile to reform, the Gypsies will be left by the road as the minister goes in search of his next picturesque adventure.

Samuel Roberts's Dispersed Egyptians

Like many lay evangelists of the early nineteenth century, the Yorkshire manufacturer Samuel Roberts was active in the anti-slavery movement as well as domestic philanthropy. Moved by his reading of Hoyland, he included 'A Word for the Gipsies' in an anonymous tract of 1816 and in subsequent publications. Roberts could not accept claims for the Indian origin of the Gypsies. 'It is well known', he remarked, that their putative ancestors, the Suders or low-caste Hindus, 'were one of the most abject, oppressed, and spiritless people on the face of the earth' and 'creatures of an inferior order'. The Gypsies, by contrast, were 'distinguished by an untamable love of liberty, and an unconquerable spirit of independence'.[56] Bible study convinced Roberts that the Gypsies were in fact 'descendants of the ancient Egyptians'. Especially persuasive was the verse from Ezekiel 29:12, 'I will scatter the Egyptians among the nations, and will disperse them through the countries'. It was God's plan, he believed, that the Gypsies should be brought to know the Lord, as a prelude to the conversion of the Jews.[57]

Though he had yet to make their acquaintance, Roberts believed that Gypsies in Britain were victims of 'prejudice and cruelty'. He urged readers in 1816 to learn more about these 'wandering vagrants': 'Let their habits, their manners, their sentiments, and their language be carefully studied.' This was an invitation to ethnographic enquiry that Roberts himself would adopt.[58] Over the next two decades he embraced every opportunity to meet Gypsies, mostly in Yorkshire and Derbyshire, and presented them with copies of his tracts. These publications often repeated the same stories and observations, and incorporated material from other evangelists. Though filtered, selective, and sometimes misperceiving, they nonetheless constitute a valuable record.

Roberts's tract of 1830 describes the tents and clothing of some members of the Boswell family. Their single tent,

> pitched in a retired green lane . . . had the appearance of a long tilt for a huckster's cart. One third of it, in the middle, being uncovered, the open space served as a kitchen, the fire being made in it, and the two ends as separate sleeping rooms . . . Two feather beds (with bed clothes good, and exceedingly clean) laid on dry straw, occupied the two ends of the tent.

Seeing newly-washed clothes hung out to dry on the hedges, Roberts was 'greatly surprised to see them equal in quality and colour to what one would expect to be worn by decent trades-people'. The visitor was especially

Figure 8. John Augustus Atkinson, 'Gipsy Encampment', c.1830 (detail)

impressed by a young Gypsy woman who, though 'busily employed, was neat and clean; and though her dress was not modern, it was strikingly graceful; particularly the disposing of the coloured handkerchief as a kind of bandeau or turban round the head'. Her eyes were 'remarkably good, dark and piercing'.[59] The observer's expectations of exotic costumes and filthy conditions, in this case, were belied by closer inspection.

Aware of popular prejudice, if not his own, Roberts averred that the Gypsies were 'much less objectionable than is generally imagined' and 'more sinned against than sinning'. In his opinion, 'rogues and vagabonds of the worst description, personating Gypsies, and often passing for them', were responsible for their bad reputation.[60] Visiting their camps, he found them 'a silent and reflecting people' with strong family values. Without using the word 'endogamy', he observed that 'they marry within the line of consanguinity, and that they sleep the whole family promiscuously together under the cover of their little tent'.[61] Some of these judgements were clichéd and derivative, but that does not necessarily make them invalid.

Roberts recognized that the Gypsies 'can speak the language of every country in which they reside, but in no instance have they been known to substitute it for their own'. In Yorkshire 'they spoke English and Gypsy indiscriminately among each other', and 'all the children' learn the Gypsy language. They evidently used a version of Romani, though Roberts did not know that name. In 1830 he recommended that the British and Foreign Bible Society translate the New Testament into 'the language of the Gypsies', anticipating later efforts by the author George Borrow and others. Furthering this end, he enlisted his own daughters in transcribing the vocabulary of the 12- year-old Gypsy Clara, an orphan daughter of the Boswell clan, who briefly stayed in his house. The resulting word-list, though not expertly transcribed, augmented nineteenth-century knowledge of Romani linguistics.[62]

James Crabb and the Way to Heaven

Moved by similar evangelical impulses, the Methodist preacher James Crabb belonged to a group of Christian activists around Southampton who sought to save the souls of Gypsies, prostitutes, and the feckless poor. In 1827 he helped to found a committee 'for taking into consideration the condition of the Gypsy race, and devising some means for their moral and spiritual development', and took to visiting camps on Shirley Common near Southampton and at Epsom Downs in Surrey. Through 'familiar visits to their tents', he acquired 'a general knowledge of their vicious habits, their compara-tive virtues, and their unhappy mode of life'. Influenced by Hoyland, Crabb's group circulated a list of questions concerning the numbers, condition, edu-cation, occupation, habits, and character of the Gypsies.[63] He later boasted of his intimacy with Gypsies: 'no man ever had such an opportunity of describ-ing their actual situation...There is not a secret in their habits but I know.'[64]

Crabb's treatise of 1832 positions him as the 'Advocate' of the Gypsies. Its subtitle, *Observations on the Origin, Character, Manners, and Habits of the English Gipsies: To Which are Added many Interesting Anecdotes*, suggests a journalistic or anthropological curiosity. Unlike Roberts, Crabb accepted the theory of the Gypsies' Indian origin, but his primary interest was in the improvement of their current condition 'and their conversion to Christianity'. He invited readers to share his 'feelings of pity, mercy, love and zeal, for these poor English heathens'. George Borrow and the young Princess Victoria were among those he influenced.[65] When Crabb visited Gypsy camps, he insisted on the importance of his own status and message. 'Make room for me,' he instructed one Gypsy family at Epsom, 'for I must sit down with you, and tell you the way to heaven'.[66]

Crabb's incidental observations, included to support his evangelistic purpose, illuminate the economy, culture, and family life of early nineteenth-
century Gypsies. His comments oscillate between approval of certain Gypsy
traits and sharp distaste for others. He frowned on their 'aversion to labour'
and 'propensity to petty thefts', but heartily approved of 'the fervour and
tenderness of their conjugal, parental, and filial sensibilities'. Crabb observed
that 'it has been the lot of Gypsies in all countries to be despised, persecuted,
hated, and have the vilest things said of them', but he believed that their
condition could be remedied by instruction and prayer. Like others, he
noted that 'many persons pass for Gypsies who are not', but believed it possible to identify 'real Gypsies'. The key marker, from his point of view, was
their potential receptiveness to his Christian message.[67]

Crabb described the Gypsies' clothes (colourful, with silver buttons and
gold rings), their diet (including, in winter, 'snails, hedge-hogs, and other
creatures not generally dressed for food'), and their knowledge of medicinal
herbs. One old Gypsy, Crabb relates, 'put a hundred and fifty sovereigns into
his kettle, to treat himself with what he called gold water, for his tea'. Crabb,
like Hoyland, recognized that Gypsies were not all alike, and pursued a variety
of activities. They were integrated into the commercial economy, worked
seasonal jobs in the hop fields and market gardens, and were punctual in
paying their debts. 'The trades they follow are generally chair-mending,
knife-grinding, tinkering, and basket-making, the wood for which they
mostly steal.' Their women, he added, supported their families 'by swindling
and fortune-telling'. To the list of Gypsy surnames given by Hoyland, Crabb
added Baker, Blewett, Broadway, Light, Scamp, and others.[68]

Crabb understood that Gypsies were not always itinerant, though, 'when
they leave their tents to settle in towns, they are generally ill for a while'.
This is a remarkable and important observation, almost a warning against
assimilation. Many Gypsy families spent winters in London, Westminster,
Bristol, and other large towns, and Crabb thought this provided a good
opportunity to teach them 'the elements of reading and the principles of
true religion'. Besides seasonal haunts in Tottenham Court Road and other
parts of the metropolis, they camped on commons around the suburbs. 'On
Wimbledon common alone there were seventy of them at Christmas 1831.'
Crabb also mentioned 'their ancient haunt, Norwood', south of London,
which was once so famous that the Prince of Wales went there expressly to
see the Gypsies. Crabb seems not to have shared Hoyland's observation that
the Gypsy presence at Norwood had greatly shrunk, owing to the enclosure

of the land they formerly used. He concluded his treatise with pious verses, composed by fellow Christian ministers, with the refrain, 'pity, oh, pity the poor Gipsy race'. This rhymed with 'wretched and base', but also, hopefully, with 'infinite grace'.[69]

The Princess and the Gypsies

These printed surveys, accounts, and treatises have long been accessible to scholars, and should not be expected to contain surprises. For the most part they confirm or embellish existing impressions. Yet the detail they offer, and the sensibility with which it is presented, deserves fresh attention. Evangelical activists under the late Hanoverian monarchs sought the conversion of Gypsies, and in the process touched on enduring topics of livelihood, language, and identity. As informal and unwitting ethnographers, they did not ask all the questions we might want answered, but they generated a valuable pool of information.

All these writers were confident in identifying people as Gypsies. They were aware that Gypsies sometimes mingled and even married with settled parishioners, and that there were others travelling on the roads who only mimicked a Gypsy lifestyle. Nonetheless they knew a Gypsy when they saw one, recognized their informants to be Gypsies, and wrote about them both individually and collectively. Though disdainful of the 'wretchedness' of Gypsy life, the evangelists remarked positively on the politeness and cleanliness of the Gypsies they encountered, and the possibilities of their redemption. They sought to make the Gypsies devout and settled, but recognized the obstacles confronting that nigh impossible task. The dream that Gypsy children could be 'carefully instructed in reading, knitting, sewing, and household work, with the view of qualifying them for service', had little chance of realization.[70] Perhaps, like other observers past and present, they saw mainly what they expected to see.

The project to reform and evangelize the Gypsies bore few enduring fruits. One reverend gentleman, sceptical of domestic missionary efforts, insisted in November 1827 that 'those roving tribes called Gypsies' were 'an idle worthless set of wanderers, that are a reproach to the police of this country, and ought first to be brought under the cognizance of the civil magistrate, before any effectual means can be provided for their religious improvement, or future spiritual good'.[71]

Less dismissive was the young Princess Victoria, soon to be queen, who visited a Gypsy encampment in southern England on Christmas Day, 1836. 'Anxious to know how our poor friends were after this bitterly cold night', she was pleased when the royal party dispensed fuel, broth, blankets, baby clothes, and a gold sovereign to 'these poor wanderers'. The princess was worldly enough to observe 'that whenever any poor Gypsies are encamped anywhere and crimes and robberies etc. occur, it is invariably laid to their account, which is shocking'. The Gypsies in the vicinity of the court at Claremont, Surrey, by contrast, were deserving and picturesque. Victoria confided in her diary:

> I cannot say how happy I am that these poor creatures are assisted, for they are such a nice set of Gypsies, so quiet, so affectionate to one another, so discreet, not at all forward and importunate, and *so* grateful; so unlike the gossiping, fortune-telling race [race-course] gypsies; and this is such a peculiar and touching case. Their being assisted makes me quite merry and happy ... knowing they are better off and more comfortable.

She even recorded a sketch of her Gypsy friends. A few days later, reflecting on her reading of James Crabb's *The Gipsies' Advocate*, she wished she could 'do something for their spiritual and mental benefit and for the education of their children ... I am sure that the little kindness which they have experienced from us will have a good and lasting effect on them'.[72]

Victoria's sentimental interest in charming but vulnerable Gypsies did not usher in a new dispensation for their treatment, but within months of her accession to the throne the newspaper-reading public knew that their queen had visited 'an encampment of the Egyptian tribe'. One of the Gypsies became a local celebrity after offering to tell Victoria's fortune: 'you were born to good luck; you shall have a lord across the seas now; you shall have seven children and a carriage to ride in', all of which came true.[73]

By the time Victoria became queen in 1837 the Gypsies were more studied and better documented than ever before. They had friends and advocates as well as traditional enemies and opponents. Some of Victoria's subjects would champion the Gypsies, and shroud them with sentiment and nostalgia. Others would disparage them or wish them eliminated. Many questions remained about the identity and character of these 'interesting' and 'mysterious' people. Was it possible to make Gypsies sedentary, settled, devout, and industrious, and if one succeeded in this end would they still be Gypsies? What was the difference between the charming Gypsies who delighted Princess Victoria and the horrid race-course Gypsies of whom she disapproved? Was

it the eye of the beholder or the circumstance of the subject that determined opinion? How many varieties of Gypsies were there, and what was
their relationship to the settled social mainstream and to other streams of
itinerants? Were they, indeed, a race, an ethnicity, or 'merely' followers of a
lifestyle? Were their numbers increasing or decreasing, and how was Gypsy
culture changing in the face of modernity? These and similar questions
were all addressed in nineteenth-century England, and continue to pose
problems in the present.

8

Victorian Encounters

This chapter examines interactions with Gypsies in the reign of Queen Victoria (June 1837 to January 1901). It uses newspaper accounts and government documents, as well as fictional and non-fictional texts, to consider their employments, encampments, travels, and brushes with the law. It attempts not only to review representations, but to get closer to the Gypsy experience. But, despite the proliferation of materials, Gypsy voices remain hard to hear. As in previous ages, our sources are external to Gypsy culture. They reveal far more about the wishes and anxieties of non-Gypsies, the general public, and the state than about the Gypsies themselves. Nevertheless, some traces may be discerned by reading across the grain and between the lines.

Unlike earlier periods, the nineteenth century yields abundant documentary material, and is well served by scholarship on Gypsies. Historians, literary scholars, and historically minded social scientists have laid a firm foundation on which others can build. George Behlmer's pioneering essay on 'The Gypsy Problem in Victorian England' (1985) examined conflicting views of Gypsy culture among journalists, philanthropists, romantics, and genteel enthusiasts.[1] David Mayall's indispensible *Gypsy-Travellers in Nineteenth-Century Society* (1988) probed more deeply into Gypsy interactions with moralists, reformers, local authorities, and the police. His *Gypsy Identities 1500–2000* (2004) re-examined the cultural construction of Gypsy ethnicity.[2] This later study was influenced by Wim Willems, *In Search of the True Gypsy: From Enlightenment to Final Solution* (1997), an exercise in historical sociology, with central sections exposing the deficiencies of nineteenth-century romantics, racial theorists, and Gypsylorists.[3] While deconstructing the Gypsy 'image', and showing how settled society represented or misrepresented travellers, these works are much more concerned with the figure of 'the Gypsy' than with particular Gypsies, and remain remote from life on the road. Similarly attending to Victorian authors, the cultural theorist Jodie Matthews suggests that 'there is no complete, neutral, historically accurate picture of "the Gypsy" waiting to be uncovered' that cannot be illuminated by doses of Derrida, for those with a taste for French cultural theory.[4]

Significant studies in English literature include Deborah Epstein Nord, *Gypsies and the British Imagination, 1807–1930* (2006), and Sarah Houghton-Walker, *Representations of the Gypsy in the Romantic Period* (2014). Both explore depictions of Gypsies by nineteenth-century poets and novelists. They show how authors used the image of exotic, menacing, or carefree itinerants to develop fictional plots, and to expose the foibles or fortitude of central characters.[5]

Major works of literature feature Gypsy elements or episodes. John Ruskin's poem *The Gipsies* (1837) celebrates the 'lovely liberty' of 'the earth's wide wanderers'.[6] In Charlotte Brontë's *Jane Eyre* (1847) a Gypsy fortune-teller who disrupts a domestic gathering turns out to be the householder Mr Rochester in disguise. In Emily Brontë's *Wuthering Heights* (also 1847) the hero Heathcliffe has 'a dark-skinned Gypsy aspect', and possible Gypsy origins. Matthew Arnold's contemplative poem 'The Scholar-Gypsy' (1853) muses on an Oxford scholar who 'went to learn the Gypsy lore . . . with that wild brotherhood . . . the Gypsy crew'. In George Eliot's novel *The Mill on the Floss* (1860), the 'half wild' heroine Maggie Tulliver attempts to join the Gypsies, with hopes of becoming their queen, and is surprised by their kindness and their poverty. In her verse romance *The Spanish Gypsy* (1868), Eliot presents Gypsies as 'a race more outcast and despised than Moor or Jew . . . so despised, it is not persecuted, only spurned'. The picaresque hero of George Meredith, *The Adventures of Harry Richmond* (1871), falls in with a girl of 'Gypsy blood, true sort', whose people were different from 'tramps' and 'mumpers'.[7] These works, and many others long forgotten, offer images of Gypsies for moral, imaginative, and sentimental reflection.

Gypsylorists and Romany Rais

More was written in English about Gypsies between 1840 and 1900 than in any previous period in history. Creative writers, social reformers, reporters, folklorists, philologists, and self-declared experts bombarded the reading public with texts on 'Gypsydom'. Following the evangelists of the late Hanoverian period, who sought the Gypsies' religious redemption, romantic Victorian writers championed the Gypsy way of life. Others worked for the Gypsies' social improvement, or attempted to place Gypsies within the sweep of linguistic and ethnographic history. Several worked hard to learn the Gypsy language, collected vocabulary, and boasted of their skill in Romani. Whether they sought to nurture the Gypsies or transform them, or just to spin stories of Gypsy adventures, most of these authors wanted to be admired as the friend and confidante of real Romanies. Several adopted the persona of a 'Romany rai' (or *rye/rya*), meaning a gentleman recognized by Gypsies for his knowledge of their language and culture.[8] It was during this period, from the middle of the nineteenth century, that Romani words like *didicoy* or *didakai* (half breed), and *gorgio* or *gadze* (non-Gypsy) began to filter into Gypsylorist writings.

The Romany rais could not help carrying their gender, class, and ideological comportment into interactions with informants. They could not shed assumptions about the nature and circumstances of Gypsies. Simply classing an interlocutor as an informant, and recognizing him to be a Romany, could influence the conversation. They invited what modern ethnographers call the 'observer-expectancy effect', whereby the outsider gathers information of the sort that he or she expects to find. A succession of Romany rais plied Gypsies with questions and tobacco, earnestly recording answers that the Gypsies knew would be rewarded. Who could tell how artful or self-conscious those Boswells and Loveridges, Woods and Lees, became when a Gypsylorist sat down with them, and whether they set out more to please than to tease? It is well to be reminded of 'the facility with which real Gypsies got to know the tropes that were being circulated about them', as one historian has put it.[9]

A related problem is that Gypsy culture itself might be affected by the exchange. The participant–observer may inadvertently influence the environment under study and alter the very culture in question. Something of this sort may have happened when Gypsylorists taught Gypsies about their Indian origins, and shared their views of the Romani heritage and language. It is at least worth wondering to what extent Gypsy dealings with the police, the public, and the press since the mid-Victorian period have been influenced by their knowledge that their culture was ancient, exotic, and 'interesting'.

Victorian Romany enthusiasts assembled a shelf of books on Gypsies, many of them still valuable today. Like some of the earlier evangelicals, these authors included details that constitute an unwitting ethnographic record. Rather than dismissing them as naive and prejudiced, responsible only for racial constructions of identity, the tracts and treatises of the nineteenth century can be read for insight into the activity and condition of Gypsies. By treating these authors as witnesses, rather than simply outmoded racists or romantics, we may augment our understanding of nineteenth-century English Gypsies.

The fanciful romantic fixation with Gypsies appeared most fulsomely in the writings of George Borrow (1803–81). In *The Zincali* (1841), *Lavengro* (1851), and *Romany Rye* (1857) he introduced the Gypsies as wise and worthy wanderers, and himself as their patron and interpreter. Borrow informed his readers that 'strange things are every day occurring, whether in road or street, house or dingle', and that he, with 'something of the Gypsy manifest in the scholar', would bring them to light. Borrow presented Gypsies as dark and mysterious itinerants, who were delighted to have him as their gentleman friend. *Romano Lavo-Lil* (1874) purported to outline the English Gypsy language and their way of speaking and thinking.[10] Borrow's books have been criticized as slapdash, pretentious, and inauthentic, but for several generations they opened a window into Gypsydom.[11]

Building on Borrow, at first by invoking his authority, later by citing his inadequacies, a series of publications discussed the origins, history, capabilities, and plight of England's Gypsies. The Methodist minister Henry Woodcock, in *The Gipsies: Being a Brief Account of their History, Origin, Capabilities, Manners and Customs; with Suggestions for the Reformation and Conversion of the English Gipsies* (1865), offered a mostly derivative account of the Gypsy condition. Although he praised those 'moralists and Christian philanthropists' who 'pushed their way into the Gypsies' camp' to decipher 'the life, manners, and customs of those we knew not before', there is little evidence of Woodcock's own encounters with Gypsies in the lanes and byways of Kent.[12]

More insightful was the government health officer Walter Simson, who followed English Gypsies to the Scottish borderlands in search of the 'true' Gypsy soul. His treatise, expanded and published by his son as Walter and James Simson, *A History of the Gipsies: With Specimens of the Gipsey Language* (1865), is rich with historical extracts, philological speculation, and occasional direct observations. 'Gypsy-hunting', he avowed, 'is like deer-stalking . . . it is necessary to know the animal, its habits, and the locality in which it is to be found'.[13]

Simson recalled that he

> once inspected a horde of English Gipsies, encamped at the side of a hedge, on the Jedburgh road . . . Their name was Blewett, from the neighbourhood of Darlington. The chief possessed two tents, two large carts laden with earthenware,

four horses and mules, and five large dogs. He was attended by two old females and ten young children. One of the women was the mother of fourteen, and the other the mother of fifteen, children. This chief and the two females were the most swarthy and barbarous looking people I ever saw. They had, however, two beautiful children with them, about five years of age, with light flaxen hair, and very fair complexions... Apparently much care was taken of them, as they were very cleanly and neatly kept.

This was first-hand observation, with verisimilitude akin to a field report, though others might have identified the Blewetts as 'potters'.[14]

The Gypsies, the Simsons insisted, 'take a pride in being descended from a race so mysterious, so ancient, so universal, and cherish their language the more for its being the principal badge of membership'. That language, the Simsons believed, had roots in Hindustan, though their reading of the Bible suggested that the Gypsies reached India after leaving Egypt. They recognized that the Gypsies they met in Britain had mixed blood, with both dark and fair complexions, and that some were 'tented' and others settled; yet they believed that the 'soul' and 'spirit' of the Gypsy 'caste' survived in all descendants of this 'ancient' and 'mysterious' race. It was, for them, a regrettable fact, though perhaps remediable, that Gypsies throughout Europe and throughout history had 'an hereditary propensity to theft and robbery', including the stealing of children.[15]

The American Charles Leland produced a seemingly authoritative treatise, *The English Gipsies and their Language* (1873), which went through four editions in twenty years. Leland visited Gypsies in caravans as well as tents, testifying to the advance of these mobile dwellings. Every word, story, or saying, he says, 'was taken from Gypsy mouths...fresh from nature'. Like other Gypsylorists, he was fascinated and charmed by his subject: 'There is a strange goblinesque charm in Gipsysdom—something of nature, and green leaves, and silent nights—but it is ever strangely commingled with the forbidden.' Like most of the Romany rais, Leland believed in a gradient of dark blood, full blood, half blood, and weaker mixtures, and held that 'true' or 'pure blooded' Gypsies were becoming rarer. He assured readers, however, 'that Gypsy blood intermingled with Anglo-Saxon when educated, generally results in intellectual and physical vigour', making the modern English Gypsy far more 'courageous' than his Hindu ancestors.[16]

Hoping to improve on the 'picturesque mannerism' of George Borrow, without Charles Leland's concessions to 'the popular element', the philologists Bath Charles Smart and Henry Thomas Crofton collaborated in 1875 to produce the first 'scientific' survey of *The Dialect of the English Gypsies*. Documenting the 'deepest' Romani derived from the most authentic informants, they expounded 'the Gypsy language, as we have actually heard it'. Like other Gypsylorists, Smart and Crofton believed they were collecting 'relics of extinct forms' and 'the broken utterances of an expiring language'. One of their samples of Romani was actually a lament for its loss. Their work also illuminated such day-to-day activities as doctoring a horse, choosing a campsite, pitching a tent, and preparing a meal. The work had some circulation among Gypsies as well as scholars, for the Gypsy Sylvester Boswell was said to have erased in his copy every word and sentence 'that did not emanate from his own "great knowledge"'.[17]

Also tackling the subject was Samuel Benjamin James, vicar of North Marston, Buckinghamshire, whose monograph 'English Gipsies...In Five Chapters' appeared serially in the *Church of England Magazine* from August to December 1875. Broadly sympathetic, and not particularly original, James believed that Gypsies 'have now entered upon a stage of gradual amalgamation with the *gorgio* [non-Gypsy] race'. Pure-bred Gypsies were hard to find, and 'the confusion becomes worse confounded' when 'posh mumpers and tramps' (half breeds and vagrants) possessed 'a little Romany blood, and...picked up a few Romany words'.[18] About this time the Northamptonshire writer David Townsend advanced the claim that Gypsies themselves looked 'with scorn' upon 'wandering way-side sleepers' and 'hedge-creepers', and never would 'set their camps beside such peddling way-side tramps'.[19]

Francis Hindes Groome (1851–1902), another leading Gypsylorist, filled his memoir *In Gipsy Tents* (1880) with anecdotes of spirited encounters. Groome's Gypsies preferred tents to caravans, though some had two-wheeled carts, and always invited the author to sit for a meal and a story. His principal informants came from the Lovell family, though he also mentioned Boswells, Stanleys, Hearnes, and Chilcotts. From them he learned that 'the truest Gypsy' was 'the deepest speaker of the old Romani tongue', though many had lost that ability. Silvanus Lovell, according to Groome, complained that '*gorgios* fancy all Gypsies are the same...Nay, worse than that, they take for Gypsies the nailers, potters, besom-makers, all the tag, rag, and bobtail travelling on the roads.' 'Nasty Irish breed!' was Lementina Lovell's comment on some travellers who left a field full of litter. 'Irish crinks' was Dimiti Lovell's dismissive judgement, one that the Gypsylorist was at pains to publicize. In Groome's opinion, 'the Romani look, language, habits, and mode of thought' were the markers of Gypsy identity, which for him were a blazon of honour.[20]

Echoing Leland and Groome, and sometimes copying them, Vernon Morwood, *Our Gipsies in City, Tent and Van* (1885), offered 'amusing anecdotes' about these 'separate and mysterious people'. Like other Gypsylorists, Morwood distinguished between 'the pure remnants of the Gypsy people' and others 'who lead roving and Gypsy-like lives'. He admitted, however, 'that some of this people have amalgamated with our own and other races', and that many endured 'a state of moral and mental destitution'.[21]

Several of the self-proclaimed 'Romany rais' came together in the 1880s to form the Gypsy Lore Society, whose *Journal* from 1887 to 1892 published articles on the 'affairs of Egypt', past and present, at home and abroad, with an eclectic mixture of anecdotes and theories. They preferred to glean information from Gypsy families in the green lanes of rural England, rather than the brickfield camps of suburban London or the Black Patch encampment near Birmingham. Modern critics have chastised the Gypsylorists for their antiquarianism, their obsession with race and pedigree, and their condescending claims to intimacy with Gypsies, but their earnest industriousness yielded research that remains the baseline for modern Gypsy studies. Generations of scholars are indebted to the Manchester lawyer Henry T. Crofton (1848–1928), whose 'Early Annals of the Gypsies in England' (1888) remains indispensible.[22] David MacRitchie (1851–1925), another founding member of the Gypsy Lore Society, similarly gathered everything that could be known about the early history of Gypsies in Scotland.[23]

Quite unlike the other 'experts' was George Smith of Coalville (1831–95), an indefatigable campaigner for the moral and material improvement of Gypsy children. In *Gipsy Life: Being an Account of our Gipsies and their Children, with Suggestions for their Improvement* (1880), *I've Been a Gipsying: Or, Rambles among our Gipsies and their Children in their Tents and Vans* (1881), and in countless letters to the press, he railed at Gypsy brutishness and squalor. George Smith scorned Gypsies, but he could not keep away from them. He found nothing picturesque in their encampments, nothing romantic in their way of life, but saw them only as 'wandering, wastrel, ragamuffin vagabonds... drifting into a state of savagery and barbarism'. Visiting racecourses, fairs, and encampments on the fringes of London, Smith made little distinction between 'the genuine Gypsy tribe', whom he believed to be shrinking and degenerate, and other kinds of travellers: they were all 'gutter-scum Gypsies' and 'offscourings of the lowest form of society'. He shared the opinion of a ranger in Epping Forest, that 'there were no real Gypsies at the present time; they have been mixed up with other vagabonds'. Smith's mean and angry mission

put him at odds with the Gypsylorists, but won support from moral reformers. He would not rest until Gypsies became civilized, and found their way
to God.[24]

A philanthropist, not a philologist, George Smith devoted his career to
the registration of moveable dwellings, and the schooling of canal-boat and
Gypsy children. Amid the bile and bombast, he buttressed his case with
observations on the size and arrangement of sleeping tents (7 feet 6 inches
wide, 16 feet long, and 4 feet 6 inches high at the top, with a fire in a tin
bucket on the damp ground), the numbers of caravans and children on a
particular squalid patch (twenty tents and vans at Hackney Wick, with forty
men and women and about seventy children, 'entirely devoid of all sanitary
arrangements'), and the inadequacy of caravans (a 'wooden tumble-down
house upon wheels, about 9 feet long by 5 feet wide, and 6 feet high', housing a 'man, wife, and seven children in a most dirty and heartrending condition').[25] Smith also remarked on the loss of the Gypsy language, of which
he himself acquired a smattering. In one camp of twenty-five adults and
forty children he found 'not three that could talk Romany'. The Gypsies he
met in Oxfordshire 'could "*rocker*" a little only'.[26]

Rich in Romani expressions and Gypsy lore is *No. 747: Being the Autobiography
of a Gipsy* (1890), purportedly the memoir of Samson Loveridge, a Gypsy
prisoner, but actually the work of the Eton-educated Arthur Way, masquerading as Dr F. W. Carew. The author was evidently familiar with the Gypsy
language (which by this time could be learned from books), and was charmed
by Gypsy roguery (especially the 'cokering' of horses to alter their appearance and value). A neglected curiosity, *No. 747* belongs more to the tradition
of picaresque tale-telling than Gypsy studies.[27]

Common to many of these works was the problem of Gypsy identity.
Most authors agreed that Gypsies formed a distinctive race, with common-
alities across time and space. They believed that Gypsies in the green lanes
of Victorian England shared a heritage with European Gypsies past and
present. English Gypsies, however, were subject to mixing and intermarriage
over many generations, so that 'pure-blooded' Gypsies were rare. The Gypsy
'race', went the consensus, still survived, as distinct as ever, but shared the
road with Irish travellers, half-breeds, *poshrats*, *didicoys*, and 'mumpers'. Debating
the Moveable Dwellings Bill in parliament in August 1885, one member
claimed that it was 'aimed, not so much at genuine Gypsies, as at people
who pretended to be Gypsies', and that it would be 'greatly welcomed by
the people of the districts infested by persons masquerading as Gypsies'. He

could as readily have used the word 'counterfeit'.[28] A writer in the *Morning Post* in September 1894 allowed that 'many of the van dwellers are no doubt of Gypsy origin, but the comparative purity of the Romany blood, as the race existed fifty years ago, has been destroyed by intermarriage'.[29] Through such articles in the press, the late Victorian public was exposed to Gypsylorism, even without reading the Society's *Journal*. Tests for authentic Gypsyness included attachment to Gypsy culture, which seemed inextricably bound up with language, itinerancy, genealogy, and blood.

The Arm of the State

Admirers of the 'liberty' of Gypsies often remarked on their independence from the encroaching power of the state. 'The inspector of nuisances, the tax-gatherer, the rate-collector, the school-board officer, the representatives of the Board of Health, all pass them by as beyond the range of their attentions', declared one observer in 1883.[30] That this was only partially true is shown by the many entanglements of Victorian Gypsies with courts of law, local authorities, and public regulations.

The population of England and Wales was close to fourteen and a half million at Queen Victoria's accession in 1837, and over thirty-two million by her death in 1901. During this time Great Britain achieved its position as the leading industrial nation and the greatest imperial power, despite the swings of economic depression and competition from abroad. Parliamentary democracy expanded, and bureaucratic tentacles tightened. Policing became more intrusive, and more professional. The British state sought oversight of its people, and subjected Gypsies increasingly to its gaze. Half-heartedly at first, Census officials took note of itinerant populations, and made efforts to enumerate vagrants and Gypsies. State authorities took an interest in the behaviour of Gypsies on the highways, their places of stopping, the condition of their dwellings, the well-being of their animals, and the welfare of their children. Philanthropists, philologists, and folklorists were by no means alone in subjecting Gypsies to scrutiny, as landowners, constables, and magistrates responded to the so-called Gypsy menace.

Deservedly or not, and despite the efforts of Gypsylorists, Victorian Gypsies had a bad reputation. Their unshackled lifestyle affronted bourgeois sensibilities. The nuisance was 'moral as well as physical', declared the Board of Guardians of Epping Forest in August 1892.[31] Local authorities blamed Gypsies for litter, trespass, damage, deceitful dealing, poaching, and theft. Ratepayers and men of property complained of their disorderly conduct and unsanitary conditions. Indignant householders seethed at their apparent fecklessness. Fighting, drunkenness, neglect of children, and cruelty to animals darkened the picture. Not surprisingly, police and magistrates used all available methods to harass Gypsies, to prevent their stopping on town lands or commons, and to dislodge their temporary encampments.

Though Gypsies were no longer criminalized simply for being Gypsies, a battery of statutory instruments bore down on unfortunate travellers.[32] The Vagrancy Act of 1824 could be used against anyone sleeping in a tent or caravan, not giving a good account of his or herself or not having a regular place of abode.[33] Gypsies caught in its net might be fined ten shillings, or spend a week or two in prison in lieu of payment. Repeat offenders faced a month of hard labour.[34] The law was used with discretion, but local governors demanded stricter enforcement. Officials in Lincolnshire in 1846, for example, requested that the Vagrancy Act be used against 'the great number of Gypsies who... were so powerful that they set the parochial authorities at defiance'.[35] In 1864 a member of parliament questioned 'the committal of a whole family for three weeks, with hard labour, for the offence of sleeping under a tent', and was told that this was proper under the Vagrancy Act, especially for Gypsies who continued to create a nuisance.[36]

The Vagrancy statute also criminalized Gypsy fortune-tellers. 'Every person pretending or professing to tell fortunes, of using any subtle craft, means, or device, by palmistry or otherwise, to deceive and impose on any of his majesty's subjects' could be deemed a rogue and vagabond, to be punished by a month of hard labour.[37] Dozens of Gypsy women were charged with 'a breach of the Vagrancy Act by pretending to tell fortunes'.[38] Magistrates could also invoke the statute of 1736 that repealed the laws against witchcraft. 'For the more effectual preventing and punishing of any pretences to such powers', and to prevent the defrauding of ignorant persons, it was made illegal to use 'any kind of witchcraft, sorcery, enchantment, or conjuration, or undertake to tell fortunes'.[39] Even a century and a half after its enactment, prosecutors could threaten Gypsy fortune-tellers with punishment under this law.[40]

Highway regulations put pressure on itinerants. They could be fined for obstructing the road with their tents, vans, camps or equipment, allowing horses or donkeys to stray or graze on the highway, and for lighting a fire within fifty feet of the centre of the road. The law applied to all highways, roads, cartways, horseways, and bridleways—anywhere a Gypsy might travel. Gypsies with carts or wagons could also be fined for not having lights on their vehicle, and for not having their names and 'place of trade or abode' painted on the side.[41] These provisions were made for the benefit of all road-users, but they could be used vindictively to harass Gypsies.

Other instruments in the Victorian regulatory arsenal impinged upon the life of Gypsies. The Dog Licences Act of 1867, though not primarily aimed at Gypsies, was sometimes used against them. Every domestic dog over six months of age required a licence, which cost five shillings, with a penalty of five pounds for non-compliance. It was another hurdle for Gypsies, who loved their lurchers but were averse to filling in forms.[42] The Commons Act of 1876 allowed local authorities to deem any interference with a town or village green a public nuisance, and to seek remedy for activities, such as the presence of Gypsies, that affected 'the health, comfort, and convenience' of local inhabitants.[43] The Housing of the Working Classes Act of 1885 empowered sanitary and health inspectors to seek out nuisances in any 'tent, van, shed, or similar structure used for human habitation'. Further enactments on behalf of public health and the welfare of children had consequences for Gypsy camps.[44] The state would have reached even more deeply into Gypsy culture if the Moveable Dwellings Bill, long promoted by George Smith of Coalville, had been enacted into law. Smith and his backers wanted the registration and regulation of Gypsy caravans and the compulsory education of Gypsy children.[45]

The Eye of the Press

The Victorian reading public gained much of its knowledge of Gypsies from the press. National and provincial newspapers proliferated in the nineteenth century, and regularly reported incidents involving Gypsies and other newsworthy characters. Attentive readers might learn that Gypsies were not all of one sort, and not all engaged in depredations. Some were law-abiding, others shady; some commanded rich resources, while others were mired in poverty. They experienced different registers of exclusion, prejudice, and acceptance. Reporters generally perpetuated prevailing stereotypes, but sometimes recorded details obtainable nowhere else.

To survey every issue of the hundreds of Victorian newspapers is beyond any individual scholar. Even finding copies poses difficulties. In recent years, however, access to the content of nineteenth-century newspapers has been transformed by digitalization. Much of the material in the following section is derived from 'British Library Newpapers 1800–1950', a database from the British Library and Gale Cengage Learning. This includes searchable copies of full runs of forty-eight newspapers from all parts of Great Britain, including such titles as the *Norfolk Chronicle and Norwich Gazette*, the *Leicestershire Mercury and General Advertiser*, and the *Sheffield and Rotherham Independent*. Similar searching is made possible by *The Times Digital Archive 1785–1985*, also from Gale Cengage Learning.[46] These databases yield over one and a half million entries or articles over the course of Queen Victoria's reign that include the words 'Gypsy' or 'Gypsies', 'Gipsy' or 'Gipsies'. Many of these refer to vessels named *Gypsy*, places named 'Gypsy Lane' or 'Gypsy Hill', or racehorses named 'Gypsy Queen'. Some relate to concerts, pantomimes, or fancy-dress balls with entertainers impersonating Gypsies. The great bulk, however, refer to travelling people identified as Gypsies who were embroiled in situations deemed worthy of report. There was much repetition, as newspapers copied each other or covered the same story, but never a week went by without some reference to Gypsies. The following account is based on a systematic search through the first and final decades of Victoria's reign, and a sampling of intervening years. It is no longer necessary to rely on collections of press cuttings.[47]

The newspapers present us with thousands of named Gypsies in myriad engagements with their neighbours. While exemplifying many of the themes already sketched by Gypsylorists and modern scholars, they offer details, variations, and counter-examples that allow us to complicate the narrative and thicken the description. They put human faces on histories of prejudice, privation, harassment, criminality, credulity, and curiosity. Many of the articles report the appearances of Gypsies in courts of law, and expose their dealings with the Victorian state. Some give indications of the Gypsies' material circumstances and wealth.

An extraordinarily detailed account in the *Examiner* reveals the goods and chattels of one group of Gypsies—three adults and seven children— apprehended near Chester in August 1838. They travelled with three horses—'a dark brown filly, rising three years old; a dark brown horse, aged, hind legs white; a light bay mare, aged with a white blaze down her face; and a cart on springs, colour green'. Found in their possession were a pair of silver sugar tongs; eleven silver spoons; an engraved silver watch; three pepper box tops; forty-two pocket knives, some inlaid with silver; nine pairs of silver-hafted knives and forks; six pairs of green-hafted knives and forks; two new daggers; two steels (for sharpening knives); ten pairs of black-hafted knives and forks; a large carving knife; a percussion gun; a pistol; thirty-three ale taps; a silver bucket; an old-fashioned cream jug; twenty-three printed gowns; four blue and one red silk handkerchiefs; four shawls; a tablecloth; two bolster cases; five pillowcases; four shirts; two bags; seven frocks; a fancy straw bonnet; fourteen blankets; two pairs of breeches; a new green body coat; a white Canton crepe shawl; a large silver ring with a pearl stone; five brooches; a small silver snuff box; sundry other snuff boxes; a box of percussion caps; a riding saddle, nearly new; and various other articles. The press described these items as 'fruits of plunder', and noted that some had monograms of previous owners, but there was no proof that they were stolen. Though not assigned an overall value, the hoard was easily worth several hundred pounds.[48] Andrew Boswell, by contrast, 'the celebrated King of the Gypsies' in Nottinghamshire, left little more than an old fiddle, a broken-down ass, and the three halfpence in his pocket when he died aged 99 in 1837.[49]

Journalists often referred to Gypsies as 'the wandering tribe', as if they inhabited ancient Israel or dark spaces of the British Empire. They confidently identified individuals as members of the Gypsy 'tribe' or 'fraternity', 'the class commonly called Gypsies', or 'that mysterious class of persons denominated Gypsies'. Most agreed with landowners and magistrates that these people were 'a pest to society'.[50] Some of the people they wrote about were well-known Gypsies, but the ascription in other cases may have been made by the police or the courts.

One did not have to be a Gypsylorist to know that Gypsies shared the roads with tramps and drifters, seasonal crop-pickers, itinerant navvies, and travelling hawkers and showmen, some of whom exhibited a Gypsy style of living, countenance, or mode of dress. One newspaper in October 1839 referred to 'imitators of Gypsies'. Another in January 1840 reported the claim of 'an experienced travelling vagrant', that 'the women who travel about with the trampers...sometimes disguise themselves as Gypsies and go fortune telling'.[51] The categories were unstable, and became further blurred in the course of the nineteenth century. Sylvester Lee, as much a Gypsy as anyone, added to the confusion when he told a court in Hampshire in March 1891 that he preferred to be styled a 'traveller'.[52]

Sylvester (or Silvester)'s untidy life can be reconstructed from local newspapers from the 1860s to the beginning of the twentieth century. Most reports referred to him as a Gypsy, though sometimes the papers described him as a pedlar or hawker. Lee and his family moved around the Isle of Wight, with occasional forays on the mainland. He was apparently born at Brighton around 1840. He appeared at Ryde police court in July 1868, charged with sleeping in the open air on Niton Down, and was discharged on promising to leave the island. He was in court at Portsmouth in October 1868, charged with destroying a fence and assaulting a policeman, and was fined forty shillings. This set the pattern for many future confrontations. He may have been the Sylvester Lee 'belonging to a gang of Gypsies' who was sent to prison for a month at Greenwich in February 1869 for assaulting a police officer, and perhaps the Silvester Lee gaoled for two months for purse-snatching at Weymouth, Dorset, in November 1870. Earlier in 1870 he was arrested in Hampshire following a fight with another Gypsy family, the Stanleys. He was fined for drunkenness on the Isle of Wight several times in the 1870s, and again in April 1880, this time identified as a pedlar.[53]

Sylvester Lee's clashes with authority continued in the later Victorian period. The case in March 1891 when he styled himself a 'traveller' involved the attempted ravishment by the Gypsy Sampson Light (also described as a 'dealer') of Kate Barney, aged 17, who had gone out to sell clothes pegs near Cowes. Kate lived as wife to Sylvester's son George Lee, who was in prison for stealing ferrets. Sylvester addressed the court on behalf of his family, but the jury found for Light, because the story was 'got up by the Lees'.[54] It would take a novelist to untangle the background.

Sylvester was fined a pound, plus costs, along with his son George Lee, in September 1892, for 'damaging underwood growing on the Ward estate' and for threatening a woodman. The Lees cut wood to make clothes pegs, and were repeatedly in trouble for their depredations. In June 1893 Sylvester and George Lee, identified as Gypsies with previous convictions, were fined for lighting fires too close to the highway. The elder Gypsy's affairs seemed to deteriorate, for in October 1895 Sylvester Lee, 55, now described as a hawker of Newport on the Isle of Wight, was fined for vagrancy and begging. Sylvester and George, father and son, were convicted in December 1897 of taking wood from a hedge, and George, with twenty-nine previous convictions, was sentenced to three weeks in prison. Sylvester Lee, Gypsy, of Brading, Isle of Wight, was fined again in September 1898 for taking sticks to make clothes pegs, after the police found incriminating evidence in the Gypsy encampment in Rowborough Lane. The newspaper headline read 'What a Gypsy Did'.[55]

Sylvester Lee's career was not over, for a month later he was fined 2s. 6d. plus costs for obstructing the footway, lying across it in his little tent. In

February 1901 he was fined a total of £1 7s. for damaging underwood, 'the property of Mr Oglander, JP'. The 1901 census found him aged 62, a widower, sharing tents with George Lee and his family in the 'Gypsy encampment' at Brading. The enumerator listed both George and Sylvester as 'general labourers'. The family tradition continued in January 1904 when Sylvester's grandson, also Sylvester, described as 'a Gypsy boy', was charged with poaching rabbits.[56]

Some of the newspaper stories showed that Gypsies had admirers, as well as critics. Some landowners welcomed them in small numbers for short periods, and preferred Gypsies to tramps and riff-raff. In the vicinity of the New Forest, *The Times* reported in October 1843, some farmers considered the Gypsy 'a good watch dog' against organized poachers, and felt 'safe when Gypsies are encamped near them'.[57] Townsfolk and visitors were said to have 'flocked' to Gypsy encampments to learn more from this fascinating and mysterious people. When 'several tribes of Gypsies' set up tents near Crediton, Devon, in April 1840, the *Western Times* reported that crowds were drawn thither to see the spectacle.[58] One young clothier visiting Gypsy camps in Yorkshire in 1842 went there, he said, to take 'pleasure in their conversation and the recital of their adventures'.[59] Gypsies were commended from time to time for fighting fires, thwarting thieves, and assisting distressed travellers. Hundreds of people turned to them voluntarily to know their fortunes. A piece in the *Pall Mall Gazette* in August 1894 encouraged sympathizers to approach Gypsies at seaside resorts 'with a pleasant mixture of familiarity and politeness'.[60]

Journalism focused on violations of the law. In a sample of reported cases involving fifty-two Gypsies in the year 1850 the offences included crimes against property (26), crimes of violence (12), highway offences (10), being drunk and disorderly (7), and deceitful fortune-telling (4). The property crimes ranged from horse theft, through poaching, to the unlawful taking of osiers to make baskets. The most serious offences could result in a year or more in prison, or sentence to transportation, but could be difficult to prove. When seven Gypsies of the Lee family were charged with horse theft in Hertfordshire 1850, they were mostly found not guilty. When Sorrendar Boswell was charged in Yorkshire with stealing a plough coulter, and Plato and Phinial Smith were charged in Leicestershire with stealing a donkey, the cases against them collapsed in contradictions. The young Gypsy Adelaide Rix, however, was found guilty of picking pockets (she stole ninepence) and was sentenced to six months' hard labour. More straightforward, and more likely to lead to conviction, were arrests for irregular camping, fighting and assault, or being drunk and disorderly. George Chilcott in Leicestershire was among those charged in 1850 with pitching a tent and lighting a fire on the highway, for which he was fined £1 plus £1 3s. costs. Anson Byles in Buckinghamshire was fined £1 3s. 6d. for cruel usage of a horse. Delity Buckland in Lancashire and Matilda Cooper in Warwickshire were among the women charged in 1850 with fortune-telling and obtaining money by false pretences, for which the usual punishment was prison with hard labour.[61]

A similar survey of newspapers of 1900 retrieved the names of 210 Gypsies facing a variety of charges. The greatest number (105) were cited for highway offences: obstructing the roadway, allowing animals to stray, leaving a wagon unattended, cruelty to horses or donkeys, lighting prohibited fires, and cutting brush for firewood. Lazarus Gray in Suffolk was fined 2s. plus 7s. 6d. costs for driving his cart without a light. Sansom Hughes in Somerset was fined 10s. plus 5s. costs for not having his name and address on his van. The next largest category was crimes against property (46). These were mostly minor offences involving poaching or the breaking of fences for firewood. None was charged that year with horse theft. Charges of drunken disorder (25) and violent assault (24) were often linked together. Only four cases involved fortune-telling. Two Gypsies were charged that year with child neglect, one with having an unlicensed dog, and another with possessing an unlicensed gun. William Cakewell in Warwickshire was charged with manufacturing explosives, which became known when he was injured in an explosion.

Battles of the Roads and Commons

The struggle of Gypsies to travel with impunity, and of communities to prevent them stopping, pre-dated the Victorian period, and continues into the present. The enclosure and fencing of commons, the proliferation of by-laws, and enforcement activities by police produced friction and sometimes violence. Arrests and fines for minor violations of the highway laws were sometimes explicitly intended 'to drive the Gypsies out of the district', as one magistrate in Derbyshire acknowledged in 1892.[62]

Dozens of communities declared Gypsies unwelcome. The Chairman of the Leicester Sessions demanded in October 1837 'that Gypsy encampments should be put down'. Another magistrate in Lincolnshire in 1840 insisted that the Chief Constable was duty bound 'to see these nuisances removed'.[63] The keepers of Putney Heath and Wimbledon Common, south-west of London, attempted to ban Gypsies and impound their horses, but found the task overwhelming.[64] County councils in Essex tried similarly to expel Gypsies from Epping Forest.[65] Magistrates in Dorset in August 1842 threatened fines of up to five pounds for constables and tithingmen who suffered 'Gypsies and other vagrants' to camp 'on the sides of roads and lanes' within their jurisdiction.[66]

At Sheffield the Town Council adopted by-laws in 1844 to prevent 'any hawker, higgler, showman, mountebank, equestrian, Gypsy or other person or persons, travelling with or having any caravan, cart, wagon, carriage, vehicle, circus, stage, show, tent, stall, booth, stand or machine, either with or without any horse, mule, or ass', from stopping 'in any street, road, lane, or public place, without the consent of the Mayor or two justices', except at times of regularly held fairs. The fine could be as much as forty shillings for a first offence, and five pounds for subsequent infractions.[67]

Despite these efforts, few communities succeeded in completely excluding Gypsies. Keepers of forests, guardians of commons, and governors of municipalities passed restrictive ordinances, but they had little binding effect. Local opposition to Gypsies did not extinguish the liberties of the subject and the protections of common law. Nor did it prevent Gypsies from returning to their accustomed haunts. In a case at Winchester in 1859, involving resistance by Gypsies to attempts to remove them, the judge advised that 'the police, in this case, had no right to interfere with the Gypsies, except at the order of the owner of the land, and their resistance, without the use of weapons, would have been justifiable'.[68] Short of outright expulsion, authorities could put pressure on Gypsies by redefining them as vagrants, and by treating their gathering of kindling, cutting of wood, and 'damaging the growing grass' as crimes against property.[69] Everyday activities were thereby recast as deviance.

Pressure mounted in the later Victorian period, with no resolution of the problem. In May 1890 the Clacton Landowners Association in Essex decided to erect notice boards warning Gypsies they would be prosecuted as trespassers; but the Gypsies were mostly illiterate, and were not put off by a sign.[70] Posts and fences were not much more effective, and were easily disposed of as firewood. Officials at Bakewell, Derbyshire, demanded action against Gypsies in October 1890, 'not only to drive them away, but to keep them away'; but the 'nuisance' of Gypsy camping continued.[71] The managers of the common at West Tilbury, Essex, protested in June 1891 against the 'depredation and nuisance' caused by Gypsies, including insanitary conditions and the lowering of property values, but found themselves powerless to act.[72] A common tactic, used at Southampton Common, Hampshire, and Brierly Common, Yorkshire, was to declare the land restricted to ratepayers, or 'open only to tenants having holdings in the township'.[73]

Several local authorities sought greater powers against Gypsies, but most were thwarted in their efforts. Essex County Council drew up a by-law in July 1893, aimed at Gypsies in Epping Forest, that 'no tent, van, etc. shall be pitched, erected, drawn onto, or remain on any common or the unenclosed waste of any manor, under a penalty not exceeding £5'. But the Secretary of State refused confirmation.[74] Similar proposals by other councils were vetoed by the Home Office because they violated principles of public access.[75] Stroud Rural District Council in Gloucestershire discovered 'it was a very thorny question' whether they had power under the Local Government Act to regulate encampments of Gypsies'.[76] The Fortune Green Preservation Society also encountered legal obstacles to their expulsion of Gypsies at Hampstead.[77] Parishioners at Milton, Hampshire, sought to dislodge a Gypsy encampment of seven vans and a dozen tents in December 1899, but were told that 'neither the sanitary officers nor the police have any power to interfere with the Gypsies, so long as they conform to the law'.[78] The member of parliament for south-east Essex fumed that 'there was no atrocity the Gypsies did not commit'—littering, allowing their horses to roam at large, and damaging trees and gardens—but was told that 'the matter is not one in which the Home Office can take any action'.[79] Local councils argued that 'fresh legislation is urgently required' to deal with 'the nuisance and inconvenience caused by the Gypsy class', but parliament was otherwise engaged.[80]

A case before Surrey magistrates in September 1897 exposed the pressure from local authorities and the resilient response of some Gypsies. James ('Dozer') Smith was cited for 'wilfully and maliciously damaging the turf on Arbrook Common by lighting fires thereon', and was fined a pound for his offence. The bailiff for the manor of Thames Ditton told the court that the defendant 'was a well-known Gypsy who practically lived on Arbrook Common'. His removal was essential to protect the space 'for the enjoyment of the public'. The chairman of the magistrates told Smith that 'Gypsies must not frequent this common any more', to which Smith responded, 'then what is to become of us?' The magistrate answered that they must either 'seek some private land' or 'give up living in caravans this way, and lead respectable lives'. 'Dozer' Smith then declared to the court (the newspaper says 'with dignity'): 'I was bred and born a Gypsy, and I hope I shall remain a Gypsy as long as I live.' He then slapped down the money for his fine, and left the court saying loudly, 'I should like to make a quid as quick as that!' His action was more compliance than resistance, but one can imagine his supporters cheering. The view of officialdom was that 'if Gypsies are to survive in this country they will have to face the inevitable and live like other people', but ingenuity and persistence made other outcomes possible.[81]

Fortune Follies

Nineteenth-century England was still a partially enchanted world, in which supernatural forces seemingly operated independently of human action, and in which Gypsies could be credited with insight into fate and luck. The rational, pragmatic, and educated leaders of Victorian society disparaged such views (while reserving their faith in angels, miracles, and life after death), but the belief persisted, especially among country people, that Gypsies could foretell the future, and even influence it by 'ruling the planets'. Dozens of incidents brought before the courts suggest that many people were in awe of Gypsies, believed in their powers, and feared that they could do a person harm.

There seemed no end to the procession of victims who allowed themselves to be deceived by claims that Gypsies could bring them wealth and happiness. The pattern of deception went beyond the routine reading of palms and promising of good fortune in exchange for a sixpence or a shilling. One Gypsy in late Victorian Somerset claimed that she had a globe that would bring people money out of Chancery, and obtained thirty pounds in one month by false pretences.[82] The fortune-tellers were invariably female, and most of their clients were servant girls or married women.

Fortune-tellers often turned up at a shop or farm, and observed a 'lucky' face. Sensing opportunity, they cultivated their victim's anxiety or greed, and hinted at skills or charms with potent consequences. Often they made repeated visits, building confidence and promising to 'rule the planets'. The trick continued much as it always had done: raising the stakes from shillings to pounds, and requiring the handing-over of gold or silver valuables; the ritual sealing of these items in a package or bag, with jiggling or incantation, promising their multiplication; and insistence that the bundle not be opened for several days, to allow the charm to work. Variants included dropping the money in a jug of water, or wrapping it with leaves from a Bible or Prayer book, before making it disappear. Invariably, when the fortune-teller failed to return, the package turned out to be worthless, the money transformed to rags, the precious metal switched for scraps of lead.

Some of the losses were minor, like a servant's clothes or a housemaid's wages, but the pain of discovery was no less. One cheat in 1837 took £40 from 'a simpleton' in Cumberland, that was supposed to be returned to him in thousands. Another Gypsy 'enchantress' took 180 sovereigns from a Derbyshire client in 1838. A Lancashire Gypsy switched £132 in gold for lead in 1839. And so on, across the decades.[83]

So common was the Gypsy fortune trick that some authorities referred to it by its presumed Romani name as *hokkeny baro* or *bori hokani*, the great swindle. By one account, vouchsafed by 'a London detective police officer' in the 1880s, the Gypsies would persuade a 'poor ignorant woman as how they can make money breed money' by wrapping and hiding a parcel of gold sovereigns, after speaking 'some gibberish' and acting 'some games' over it: 'But don't you see, sir, they had another parcel with 'em...filled with lead dumps, or such like, and by a fakement...a slight of hand like...they change the packet.' When the victim looks for her multiplied sovereigns she finds only rubbish, 'and that's the "*Bori Hokani*," sir'.[84]

The perpetrators of these tricks were not always found, and if tried were not always convicted. Sometimes the victims were too embarrassed to bring charges. If the matter came to court, a skilful defence could claim that 'the money had been freely given', or the items only borrowed, so 'the felony could not be supported'.[85] Those found guilty faced a month to a year of hard labour. The Gypsy Louisa Dalton, who tricked a young shop girl in Essex of her family's savings, and may have had previous offences, was sentenced in 1842 to ten years' transportation.[86]

Judges and journalists often reserved harsher words for the victims in these cases than for the perpetrators. Several expressed astonishment that such gullible simplicity persisted in this modern era. One judge at Exeter in 1842 lamented 'the dreadful ignorance that still spreads itself like a dark cloud over many parts of the agricultural districts'.[87] The *Bristol Mercury* commented in September 1845 that 'it is almost beyond the range of belief that at the present day the stale trick of doubling an amount of money, by some pretended hocus-pocus practice, could be successful'. Yet a 'wily tan-skinned Gypsy' conjured a Somerset couple of their savings, and when 'these silly folks opened the precious package, nought but a parcel of rubbish was found'.[88] 'Let the simple beware', declared the *Leeds Mercury* in November 1846, commenting on another successful fortune trick.[89] 'Where is the schoolmaster?' demanded the *Western Times* later that year when another Devonshire woman allowed herself to be cheated by 'some lying Gypsies'.[90]

Later Victorian comments were similarly censorious. When a domestic servant at Hampstead allowed the Gypsy Elizabeth Roster to take her silver watch and chain in February 1890 in exchange for help with her 'planet', the judge told her 'that she almost deserved to lose her watch for having been so foolish'.[91] Sentencing the Gypsy Patience Wood to two months' hard labour for a similar deception in Pimlico in February 1891, the judge declared it 'a sad thing to learn that there were still many people foolish and credulous enough to believe the jargon about fortune-telling by planets and palmistry'.[92] It was astonishing, opined the *Manchester Courier* a year later, 'how many silly girls...are entrapped by that class of people who make their living from simpletons'.[93] It was amazing, declared the *Evening Telegraph and Star* in November 1893, after yet another Gypsy deception at Leeds, 'that such things can happen in enlightened, practical, nineteenth century England'.[94] Sentencing the Gypsy Amelia Stanley to fourteen days' hard labour in November 1899 for 'pretending to tell fortunes', the judge told her victim, a Devonshire shopkeeper, 'that she had acted very foolishly in the matter', and warned her 'not to listen to such foolish rot in the future'.[95]

Rituals and Celebrations

Though mostly concerned with entanglements with the law, the newspapers also took note of Gypsy social observances. Though Gypsy customs and practices remained mysterious, closed to outsiders, the public sometimes witnessed their more extravagant public weddings and funerals. The press generally focused on the costumes of those involved and the refreshments provided, assigning the principals titles like 'King of the Gypsies'.

Several papers reported the wedding in a Somerset parish church in November 1840 'between Miss Eliza Small, a lovely scion of the dark-eyed tribe, and Mr Boswell, a member of the Zingaree royal family'.[96] In September 1844 they reported the wedding of 'Matthew, son of Joshua Stanley, King of the Gypsies, to Martha, second daughter of John Broadway, of the same tribe'. The ceremony was followed by a grand reception for some 400 guests, with church bells ringing and the town band playing. The party returned 'to their camp on Blagdon hill at about twelve o'clock in the evening', and kept the day following as a holiday.[97] Another Somerset wedding in May 1854 united Valentine Stanley with a bride from the Coopers, both 'old Gypsy families' with 'pedigrees as long as your proud English baron'.[98]

A double Gypsy wedding at Plymouth in January 1887 joined Robert Penfold's two sons James and William to Plato Buckland's two daughters Sophy and Jenty. The register recorded all as 'general travelling dealers', which the newspaper claimed was 'the legal definition of a Gypsy'.[99] The well-attended wedding of the Gypsies William Lee and Ada Boswell at Bunbury, Cheshire, in December 1882 was noteworthy because 'toasts were proposed in the Romany dialect'.[100] These were church weddings, performed by licence, temporarily uniting the parish and the camp. They were occasions for hospitality and gift-giving, with everyone on their best behaviour. They were, by their nature, extraordinary, for most Gypsy rituals were private affairs.[101]

Like the weddings, Gypsy funerals became visible only in special circumstances. It is not known how many Gypsies were buried secretly, nor how many in unconsecrated ground. The newspapers reported grand occasions in parish churches, when mourners gathered from across the community. Reports generally noted that such funerals 'created a great deal of curiosity', that the coffins and accoutrements were of the highest quality, and that those in attendance were 'very respectably dressed'.[102] When Wisdom Smith, 'Prince of the Gypsies', was buried in Rutland in April 1839, the local paper reported that 'about one hundred of the wandering tribe were present at the ceremony'.[103] When the Gypsy Cecilia Chilcott was buried at Little Coggeshall, Essex, in October 1842, The Times reported 'between 4,000 and 5,000 persons' in attendance. The Chilcotts were wealthy Gypsies, and spared no expense to bury their 28-year-old daughter. The report noted that 'the deceased's watch and a purse of money' were placed in the coffin by the body, 'for the protection of which a person is appointed to watch the grave for some weeks'.[104]

The Gypsylorist Charles Leland had heard that an older generation of Gypsies 'carefully burned the clothes and bed of the deceased, and, indeed, most objects closely connected with them', and sometimes buried their dead with money and jewelry. Smart and Crofton also noted the destruction of everything belong to a dead Gypsy, including horses and dogs.[105] Customs of this sort had been observed in the reign of George III, and Victorian newspapers periodically branded such Gypsy practices 'strange' and 'superstitious'. On a humble level, when a nine-week-old Gypsy child died in Lincolnshire in 1845, 'the clothes and everything that had been used for the infant [were] buried, in conformity with the belief among the tribe that such should be the case directly the breath left the body'. The local newspaper declared this to be 'ignorant superstition', though it also had sanitary benefits.[106]

A thorough and meticulous purging followed the burial of Aaron Boswell at Long Whatton, Leicestershire, in 1866. The mourners torched his clothes, bedding, tent, cart, grinding barrow, and harness; they pounded his crockery, implements, and utensils to fragments, and buried them in the earth; and they arranged for his animals to be disposed of by a man who did not belong to the group. According to one member of this well-known Gypsy family, it was requisite that anything touched by a dying man had to be destroyed.[107]

Reports in the *Bradford Observer* in December 1873 and the *Hull Packet and East Riding Times* in January 1884 described the burning or destruction of carts, tents, clothes, and goods following a Gypsy's death.[108] After another Gypsy had been buried at Withernsea, Yorkshire, in September 1894, with full Church of England ceremony, 'the caravan and everything belonging to the deceased was burnt... the unusual sight being, of course, the subject of considerable attention and discussion'.[109] Similarly at Slough, Buckinghamshire, in March 1896, following a female Gypsy's death, 'the van in which the old woman lived was totally destroyed', and 'her horse was shot and buried'. Reporters were curious about this destruction of valuable property, but the woman's son explained that had he not followed custom 'he would have been scorned by his tribe'.[110]

The burning of the possessions of the deceased was a distinctive custom that distinguished traditional Gypsies from the rest of the population, including casual travellers. As twentieth-century anthropologists observed, these practices were 'making statements about an ethnic boundary', separating Gypsies from the *gorgio* world. Field ethnographers learned that many Gypsies observed strict pollution taboos, and feared the powers of the *mulo* or ghost.[111] But even among Gypsies the destruction of the goods of the dead was not universal, and could give rise to dispute. When one of the Gypsies in Epping Forest died in 1900, his son Harkless Smith dutifully burned his travelling van, worth thirty pounds, and destroyed his clothes and tools. But his widow Rhoda Smith, also a Gypsy, believed the goods to be hers, and had the incendiary, her stepson, committed to Quarter Sessions.[112]

Playing at Gypsies

While moralists berated the 'savagery' of 'uncivilized' Gypsies, and Gypsylorists pursued their language and customs, some members of the Victorian public imagined Gypsies as carefree wanderers, even subjects for emulation. Fancy and fashion could play with the Gypsy motif, so long as its darker side was eclipsed. One reporter in 1891 captured the conundrum when he noted that the Gypsies looked 'so delightfully picturesque in the distance, and so disgustingly dirty and degraded close at hand'.[113]

Queen Victoria, who had visited real Gypsies, attended a performance of 'The Gypsy's Warning' at the Drury Lane theatre in January 1839.[114] A concert at Buckingham Palace in April 1846 featured the ditty 'Two merry Gypsies are we'.[115] The repertoire of touring concert parties included 'The Gypsy poacher', 'The Gypsy monarch', and 'The merry Gypsy band'.[116] The Music Hall entertainer Edwin Ransford's famed 'Gypsy concerts' included 'impressions of a Gypsy encampment…intermixed with anecdotes and numerous songs'.[117] Applause greeted the Newark Amateur Musical Society's rendition of 'The Gypsy's life is a joyous life' in January 1850, while the singing of 'Two merry Gypsies' at Blandford that month 'was rapturously enjoyed'.[118] The singing of 'We Gypsies live a life of ease' earned an encore at a concert in Birmingham later that year.[119] Meanwhile, not many miles away, Gypsy families were routed from their camping places, and fined for grazing their horses along the highway. 'A select and appreciative audience' at Little Missenden, Buckinghamshire, applauded a rendition of 'A merry Gypsy girl am I' in March 1893, while nearby Gypsies were being harassed as nuisances.[120] The melodrama 'The Romany's Revenge' toured provincial theatres later in Victoria's reign.[121]

One of the most curious adoptions of a mock-Gypsy identity was the cricket team 'I Zingari', comprised of members of parliament. They played at Lords in July 1850 against Lord Burghley's eleven, clad in 'full Zingarian costume'.[122] Successors to 'I Zingari' continued this tradition into the twentieth century. Other teams adopting the 'Gypsy' name were wandering players with no settled ground of their own.

No Victorian fancy-dress ball was without its 'Gypsy' king or queen. Merrymakers costumed as Gypsies enjoyed the New Year 'ice carnival' at Coggeshall, Essex, in 1893, while Gypsies at nearby Lambourne Common were suffering frostbite.[123] Respectable young women in search of 'an effective fancy dress' could do worse than copy the design for the 'Esmeralda' outfit, with 'a cream silk muslin blouse' and 'zouave...in black velvet, trimmed with gold sequins'.[124] In November 1893 the fund-raising bazaar for the Methodists at Northampton featured 'a capital representation of a Gypsy encampment', with 'a warm, cosy appearance', where 'the children looked very charming in their Gypsy costumes'.[125] Parish fêtes and bazaars featured 'Gypsy' tables or 'Gypsy' tents, and social groups went on 'Gypsy' rambles or participated in 'Gypsy' frolics. Gypsylorists were not the only Victorians to go 'Gypsying'. Recreational caravanners set out in 'quaint Gypsy-house[s] on wheels' to explore the summer countryside.[126] The public appetite for pastiche coexisted with news of nuisances and depredations.

Enumeration

Nobody knew how many Gypsies there were in Victorian England. Estimates foundered on difficulties of definition and inadequacies of enumeration. The problem was ideologically inflected, since numbers tell stories and figures affect policies. Accurate figures are as elusive as the Gypsies themselves, so it might be better to treat all estimates of their population as rhetorical devices rather than expressions of statistical precision.

Guesses of the nineteenth-century English Gypsy population ranged from 12,000 to 250,000, with figures of 20,000 to 30,000 commonly accepted. There was little improvement on pre-Victorian estimates of 'about 18,000', no less than 40,000, and 'above 100,000'.[127] Henry Woodcock was content to count 12,000 Gypsies in England in 1865, but Walter and James Simson, publishing in the same year, suggested that 'there cannot be less than 250,000 Gypsies of all castes, colours, characters, occupations, degrees of education, culture, and position in life, in the British Isles alone, and possibly double that number'. Such a huge total was imaginable only by considering itinerants of all sorts as Gypsies, as well as everyone with a trace of Gypsy blood.[128]

Gypsylorists believed that the population of 'true' Gypsies was shrinking, while increasing numbers of ragtag travellers took to the roads. Charles Leland, for example, declared that 'Gypsies in England are passing away as rapidly as Indians in North America'.[129] Early Victorian police authorities shared this opinion, though their later nineteenth-century counterparts complained that the menace was growing. Apparently crediting his own efforts, the Chief Constable for Norfolk boasted in October 1841 that 'the

hordes of Gypsies that once infested the country were not now to be found'.[130]
His counterparts in Suffolk and Essex also reported shrinkage in 'the class
of persons denominated Gypsies'.[131] The census provided only the crudest
of measures for judging these observations. Poverty, meanwhile, was growing among the settled population, with over 800,000 men, women, and
children relieved as paupers in January 1851.[132]

Beginning in 1801 the British state began to number its people, but only
in 1841 did the Registrar General show interest in itinerants.[133] In that year
the enumerators found 20,348 people sleeping in barns, shed, tents, and the
open air, of whom only 439 were specifically identified as Gypsies. The enumerators at Morcott, Rutland, counted forty-eight Gypsies in tents, but in
several counties where Gypsies were known to be active they numbered
none at all.[134] Most of the people sleeping casually in barns and sheds were
single males, who may have been down-and-outs or migrant workers,
whereas many in tents and caravans belonged to family groups. Whether
they were Gypsies, and what that meant in the nineteenth century, remain
matters for conjecture.

David Mayall's study of *Gypsy-Travellers in Nineteenth-Century Society* suggests that 'the census returns provide the best numerical guide available' to
the travelling or 'nomadic' population. Official figures show a fall from
20,348 itinerants in England and Wales in 1841 to 15,764 in 1851, and a further reduction to 11,444 in 1861. The numbers remained steady in 1871 and
1881, at 10,383 and then 10,924, before rising to 15,983 in 1891. In 1901 they
were down to 14,219, but then more than doubled to 30,642 in 1911. Among
these travellers the enumerators listed 7,130 in tents, vans, or the open air in
1861, 8,569 in 1881, and 12,574 in 1901, and these may be better proxies for
the Gypsy population.[135]

Official figures were based on where people slept on the night of the
census, which was usually a Sunday in late March or early April. Because
'Gypsies and vagrants produce nothing valuable', and belonged to the 'unproductive classes', in the words of the Registrar General, there was little incen-
tive to include them. Census-takers worked house to house, street to street,
and may have lacked the knowledge, inclination, or energy to seek out transient or mobile dwellings. There may have been an unspoken belief that
Gypsies were not worth counting, because they were fleeting, itinerant, and
did not belong. And the Gypsies themselves were adept at lying low, and
may have seen no reason to cooperate with authorities whom they generally regarded as hostile. In 1861, out of more than 11,000 listed itinerants,

including some 7,000 in tents or vans, only 738 were entered as Gypsies, including 9 born elsewhere in Europe.[136]

Critics could claim that Gypsies were undercounted, misrepresented, or found ways to avoid inclusion. In 1871 the Registrar General himself conceded as much, reporting that 'vagrants, Gypsies, criminals, prostitutes and the like, are so imperfectly returned that no advantage could have been derived from the publication of their statements'.[137] The Gypsylorist Francis Groome declared the census of 1871 'utterly valueless' for the study of Gypsies, and modern scholars are inclined to agree.[138] Enumerators in subsequent decades looked out for 'caravan dwellers, Gypsies, those living in canal barges, and the jetsam and flotsam of society who creep into outhouses or behind haystacks', but the results were no more convincing.[139]

Where someone slept was an observable fact, but how they were identified and to what group they belonged required assessment. If discrepancies arose from variable labelling, who was applying the labels? Were occupational identifications, for example, a product of self-ascription or external attribution by census workers? There is no way to know how many of the clothes-peg makers, basket-makers, broom-makers, scissor-grinders, tin men, or hawkers included in the census could alternatively have been entered as Gypsies, nor how many such people escaped enumeration altogether. International experts in 1901 put the British Gypsy population at 20,000, but there is no firm basis for that figure.[140]

Though unsatisfactory as a source for overall numbers, the census returns yield remarkable information about Gypsy family structure, sociability, and itinerancy, as well as the shiftiness of identity and the fluidity of social ascription. It was not unusual for people located in Gypsy camps, and housed in tents or caravans, to be written down as hawker, general dealer, basket-maker, chair-caner, grinder, or tin man, the designation shifting from decade to decade. Several of the Gypsies mentioned in Victorian newspapers can also be traced in census records, which sometimes assigned them different occupations.

The curiously named Sorrendar Boswell, who was charged in 1850 with stealing a plough, appeared in the 1841 census as one of the nine children of Moses Boswell, encamped near Cheadle, Staffordshire.[141] Adelaide Rix, who was imprisoned for theft in 1850, surfaced in the census of 1851 among a family of Gypsies at Old Buckenham, Norfolk.[142] Aaron Boswell, whose possessions were ritually destroyed after his death in 1866, appeared in 1861 in a tent in a forest lane at Belton, Leicestershire, identified as a scissor-grinder cutler. He shared the tent with his deceased wife's sister (who lived by selling clothes pegs), five children born in four different counties, and a 4-year-old granddaughter born locally.[143] If others remain untraced, it may be because they were elusive and deliberately kept out of sight.

The celebrity Gypsy Sylvester Boswell, who helped the Gypsylorists learn the Romani language, appeared in three successive censuses. In 1861 enumerators found him and his family 'travelling in vans' on Blue Mill Hill, Witham, Essex, describing him as a chair cane-maker. Boswell's itinerancy was apparent in the birthplaces of his children: in Berkshire, Essex, Suffolk, Cambridgeshire, and Lancashire. The year 1871 found him in Binsey Lane, Abingdon, Berkshire, still a 'cane worker'. By 1881, aged 77, in company with his adult sons Byron and Bruce, he was at Birkenhead, Cheshire, described as a 'worker in cane/strolling musician'.[144] He died in Walton workhouse at West Derby, Lancashire, in April 1890.[145]

Though census enumerators missed many Gypsies, and gave others alternative occupational designations, their manuscript returns reveal concentrations of Gypsies, so named, around the country. One of the largest, though transient and seasonal, was on the downs at Epsom, Surrey, close to the course of the Derby horse race held each Whitsun. In early April 1891 the census recorded the names, ages, relationships, and places of birth of 232 people identified as 'travelling Gypsies' on Epsom Downs, belonging to 43 nuclear families. The oldest head of a household was Henry Pitchley, aged 70; the youngest Charles Matthews, 23. The number of children per family ranged from zero to ten, with the mean household size 5.4. These families slept in caravans and tents, in rows or clusters, perhaps close to their friends or kin. Especially revealing was their place of origin. Members of James Murray's family had been born in Surrey, Kent, or Essex. Thomas and Mary Smith were the only members of the group born outside England, in Cork, Ireland, though their children were born in Surrey and Essex. Of 200 of these Gypsies whose place of birth was recorded, exactly 100 had been born in Surrey, not many miles from where they were counted. Indeed, 17 were said to have been born in Epsom; 28 came from Middlesex, 19 from Kent, 16 from Sussex, 11 from Essex, and 10 from London. The rest came in small numbers from Hampshire and Berkshire, with one each from Bedfordshire, Buckinghamshire, Gloucestershire, Hertfordshire, Staffordshire, Warwickshire, and Wiltshire. These Gypsies were nearly all English, and mostly from the south. The evidence points to a limited circuit of travel, with Epsom, Surrey, as its hub. If these late Victorian Gypsies were typical, they were localized, predictable, and unthreatening. None appeared in the newspapers or had known trouble with the law.

The Sussex Diaries

Another glimpse of Gypsy itinerancy may be obtained from the notebooks or 'Gypsy diaries' maintained by police authorities in some parts of late-Victorian and early twentieth-century Sussex. In 1898 the chief constable instructed officers in each division to note the sites where Gypsies and van-dwellers encamped, the numbers in each party, and the dates of their arrivals and departures. They were also supposed to record whether the travellers camped on waste land or private property, and whether complaints had been made against them.[146]

These Sussex police notebooks invite further questions about Gypsy demography and mobility, as well as the perennial problem of identity. Constables at Burwash, Burwash Weald, Glynde, Fernhurst, and Upper Beeding recorded 105 incidents of Gypsy camping between 1898 and 1915, and many more comings and goings by van-dwellers. 'Gypsies' may have connoted an ethnicity, and 'van-dwellers' a mode of living, but most of these travellers of all sorts had horse-drawn caravans and carts. It was left to individual policemen to register the distinction. Gypsies and van-dwellers alike travelled in nuclear family units, sometimes sharing sites with others of the same surname. Several of the van-dwellers were apparently travelling show-men, attending spring or summer fairs with their roundabouts and swings, rather than traditional Gypsies, though distinctions were by no means rigid.

When various combinations of the Ripley family—Mark senior, Mark junior, Moses, and their wives and children—camped several times at Burwash in the summer and autumn of 1898, PC MacNeill described them as 'van-dwellers'. He recorded their arrival at the Bear Hotel field on 14 June, and their departure the next day; their return to the Bear field on 8 August for two nights, and their stays at Court Lodge Farm from 16 to 18 August, and again from 23 to 26 August. Between visits to Burwash, they told him, they had been at Coursely Wood, Sevenoaks, Hurst Green, and Heathfield. They camped again at Court Lodge Farm from 17 to 24 October 1898, after another visit to Coursely Wood, near Wadhurst, Kent.

Other notebooks show that when Mark Ripley with his wife and two children, their van and two horses, camped at Elmers Marsh, Fernhurst, on the night of 31 January 1900, and again at Linchmere Common for two nights from 6 February, another policeman, PC Wakeford, recorded them as Gypsies. Three weeks later Mark Ripley and his wife were at Beeding, camped at Small Dole 'on wasteland by the side of the road leading from Beeding to Henfield', where PC Ford wrote them down as 'van-dwellers'. Their recent travels had also taken them to Lodsworth, Hollywater, Haslemere, and Brighton, in a circuit connected with other members of the Ripley family. They seemed constantly on the move, through Sussex, Surrey, and Kent, across tens rather than hundreds of miles. They usually stopped no more than two or three days in any location, although the cold and snow of January and February might have induced them to settle for longer. Although Gypsies could be found in lanes and woods, on roadside waste, they were just as likely to camp on private property with a local farmer's permission.

The 1891 census found Mark Ripley, 'licensed hawker', with his wife and children, in a van at Amberstone, Leap Cross, Hellingly, Hailsham, Sussex. The family spent census night 1901 in a van on Magham Down, near Hailsham. Moses Ripley, perhaps Mark's brother, appeared as a 'working cutler' in 1891, which may have indicated a knife-grinder, and a 'travelling hawker' in 1901. They would be designated Gypsies only if policemen or census enumerators deemed them so.[147]

New Migrations

Despite its reputation for inwardness and separateness, the English Gypsy community had flexible boundaries. There had always been mixing, with some Gypsies becoming sedentary and others joining the group, but the scale of this blending is unmeasurable.

Another source of admixture, rarely remarked upon by scholars, was the intermittent arrival of Gypsies from abroad. Since England's borders were unpoliced, and nobody needed passports, it was as easy as ever in the nineteenth century for travellers to land on English shores. There are over 7,000 miles of coastline in England and Wales, with innumerable harbours, havens, and beaches on which to disembark. Informal immigration was essentially invisible, so there is no way to take its measure. It is known, however, that foreign Gypsies were sometimes driven by wars and persecution to escape their home countries, and that some were lured westward by prospects of advantage. The great magnet was America, and England was a step in that direction.

Among the Romanian Gypsies freed from slavery by decrees in 1855 and 1856 a few are believed to have made their way to England.[148] Some of the Hungarian coppersmith Roma, who settled in the Netherlands from 1868 onward, also crossed the Channel.[149] Writing in the early 1870s, Charles Leland noted that 'a large party' of German Gypsies 'appeared at an English racecourse' a few years earlier, 'where they excited much attention, but greatly disgusted the English Roms'. 'They were the dirtiest Gypsies I ever saw', said one of Leland's informants.[150]

In 1886 a band of about a hundred Gypsies from south-east Europe landed at Liverpool. Thwarted in their efforts to find passage to America, they dispersed into the English countryside. Travelling across England, they found it possible to communicate with English Gypsies by use of Romani.[151] One group of so-called Greek Gypsies, encamped at Hull, became 'a serious burden to the inhabitants and ratepayers'. Responding to local concerns, the Home Secretary told parliament that 'the law of this country affords very imperfect protection against the landing of destitute and unsanitary aliens'.[152] More Gypsy refugees from the Balkans made their way across northern England in 1897.[153] Yet more followed from northern and eastern Europe at the beginning of the twentieth century. Though poorly documented, and demographically insignificant, these newcomers may have reinfused Romani elements into English Gypsy culture.[154]

Gypsy arrivals from the Continent were greatly outnumbered by the emigration of English Gypsies to America. Several families took ship in 1850, and were followed by more in the decades that followed. More than 25,000 English passengers a year migrated to the United States in the 1850s, with higher numbers in subsequent decades, and it should not be surprising that Gypsies were among them.[155] Their names and numbers are not readily determined, but newspapers on both sides of the Atlantic sometimes noted their exploits.

One group of Gypsies from north-east England attracted considerable attention in America in 1851, prompting the Boston Daily Atlas to question the possibility of assimilating 'a strange order of cosmopolites, who have, immemoriably, been nomadic in habit, and intolerant of any admixture with a different people'.[156] In April 1852 a Baltimore paper reported the presence of Gypsies 'encamped in the neighborhood of Hunting Creek bridge. They tell fortunes and sell trinkets to visitors.' Another 'strolling band' appeared near Albany, New York: 'The men profess to be cutlers and tinkers in general, while the women are adepts at fortune telling and curers of diseases. They have three wagons, a cow, dogs without number, a parrot, and musical instruments by way of pastime. We have heard that they are particularly fond of poultry.'[157]

More English Gypsies circulated in the Chesapeake region in the autumn of 1852. By January 1853 they were camped along the Potomac in Virginia, and then moved north-west into Pennsylvania, Ohio, and New York. One newspaper observed that, besides English, 'they have a language of their own, which they use *sotto voce* in addressing each other before strangers'. As in the old country, they supported themselves by 'mending tin, pewter and copper ware and utensils, old umbrellas, and tinkering generally'. The women drummed up business as fortune-tellers, and gained a reputation for 'conjurer swindling'. The 'fortune trick' found gullible new world victims, and Betsy Cooper, 'the queen of the troop', was arrested at Buffalo, New York, after cheating people by promising to find them hidden treasure. Taking stock of English Gypsy deceits, the *North American and United States Gazette* in June 1853 pontificated: 'America is, very clearly, not the country for such a class of people.'[158]

Three more families of English Gypsies arrived in New York in August 1855, 'almost destitute', by newspaper report.[159] Most found a niche in the peripatetic economy, and a few grew wealthy through horse-trading. In March 1869 the *Boston Investigator* estimated there were 12,000 Gypsies from England and other countries in the United States. Immigration of Roma from other parts of Europe was gathering pace, and would soon outnumber the English *Romanichals*.[160]

English Gypsies in New England attracted the attention of American Gypsylorists. Eager to learn their language, the Boston lawyer Albert Thomas Sinclair (1844–1911) took to visiting members of the Stanley and Cooper families, who traded horses, sold baskets, and told fortunes. On one occasion in 1880 he found them with 'four tents, three large gaudily painted wagons . . . and had with them eight or ten horses, some very good ones'. Like some of his counterparts in Victorian England, Sinclair noted their 'dislike to talk Gypsy before strangers', and soon concluded that he 'could talk Gypsy easier than they could'. The Gypsy patriarch Richard Cooper had arrived in America in 1852, and by 1882 presided over a stable establishment at East Somerville, Massachusetts. By Sinclair's observation, these Gypsies 'seemed to have plenty of money'.[161]

Newspaper readers could marvel at the success of English Gypsies who achieved their version of the 'American dream'. Owen Stanley, a Gypsy born in England in 1794, became commercially successful in Ohio and Indiana, and was reputed 'King of the Gypsies' when he died in 1860.[162] Originally from Devon, 'Prince Williams', leader of the Connecticut Gypsies, died in 1885 worth over $100,000 acquired from the horse trade. Another successful English Gypsy, Thomas Blythe, died intestate a millionaire in San Francisco in 1889, precipitating an international scramble of claims on his estate.[163]

Discerning Victorians learned that Gypsies were many and varied, and that few conformed exactly to expectations. Some appeared to be Romany aristocrats, while others lived lives of squalor and privation. Squatters in the wasteland camps around London were less 'romantic', though no less 'authentic', than the lightsome wanderers of the rural green lanes. Sylvester Lee was no more typical than Sylvester Boswell; Amelia Stanley was no less a Gypsy than Lementina Lovell, although they occupied different worlds. Those who came to public attention through friction with local authorities or tussles with the law were not necessarily more representative than the Gypsies pursued by the Gypsylorists and Romany rais. Their characteristics were protean, for whenever anyone tried to nail down Gypsy identity, the Gypsies got up and walked away with the nail.

9

Travels and Troubles
in Modern Britain

The closer one approaches the present, the greater is the risk that History is harnessed for current political purposes. There is relatively little at stake for today's living communities in debate about the sixteenth century, but discussion of more recent conditions touches sensitive nerves. Historical research on the experience, identity, and even the numbers of English Gypsies and Travellers has implications for the legal, social, cultural, and economic prospects of those groups. ('Travellers' may henceforward be capitalized, in recognition that they too may be construed as an ethnic group with advocates and aspirations—an illustration of the problem here mentioned.) Recent decades have seen an explosion of writing on Gypsies, as anthropologists, historical linguists, political scientists, popular sensationalists, local governments, members of parliament, international agencies, and advocates for Roma rights and social justice have contributed their measure. This chapter represents a historian's entry into this contested ground.

The Gypsy Lore legacy, passed down from the heyday of the British Empire, harboured a mixture of certainties and speculations, few of them now unchallenged. It was generally agreed that the Gypsies came originally from India, although the timing and circumstances of their departure remained contentious. By modern times they were Europeanized, indeed anglicized, but primordial characteristics were still allegedly discernible. British Imperial India offered opportunities for comparative observation and analysis, but no obvious forebears of the Gypsies could be discovered. The Gypsies were held to be a race, in the same way that the English, Irish, and Germans were considered races, meaning that they shared a common culture and genealogical heritage, with readily identifiable manners and customs. Ethnicity might be a better term, provided we acknowledge its unstable and contingent characteristics. The Gypsy race, the Gypsylorists claimed, had endured for hundreds of years, so, whether it was observed in the sixteenth century or the nineteenth, in England or elsewhere, its members could be recognized as Gypsies by their appearance, their way of life, and their use of the Gypsy language, which was known to be derived from Sanskrit. Variations could be explained by admixture and assimilation, a regrettable falling-away whereby Gypsy culture and bloodlines became adulterated. The Gypsylorists posited a hierarchy from true or pure-blooded Gypsies, through half-breeds, poshrats, and didicoys with diminishing traces of Gypsy blood, down to tramps and mumpers, who merely emulated the itinerant Gypsy lifestyle.[1] None of these distinctions remains creditable today. The truest Gypsies, from the Gypsylorist perspective, and therefore the ones most worthy of study, were those with the blackest hair and darkest eyes, the brightest spark and liveliest demeanour, and the greatest command of the deep Romani tongue. Most Gypsylorists were convinced that they witnessed the Gypsy race declining. They made it an urgent matter to record the language and customs of prominent Gypsy families, and to trace their pedigrees. Recoil from this legacy, and critical digestion of its impact, dominated academic Gypsy studies in the later twentieth century.

Far from remaining unaltered, as a racial and cultural relic, the English Gypsy community has changed radically in its economic activities, cultural practices, and social composition. It has absorbed, or been joined by, other streams of itinerants, especially Irish Travellers. It has become motorized and diversified, and has found advocates among social workers, lawyers, and scholarly activists. Many Gypsies have become settled, or travel only seasonally. Some cherish their Romany roots, while others have denied or forgotten them. Popular sentiment still regards the Gypsies with a mixture of loathing and curiosity. Ignorance and misperceptions abound, sometimes whipped · up by the press. Gypsy voices are still hard to hear. Many questions remain about their engagement with their neighbours, their dealings with the state, and their status in law. Controversy still surrounds discussion of Gypsy identity, and questions remain about its coherence and constructedness. Even the legitimacy of the term 'Gypsy' remains contentious and unresolved.[2]

Alien Gypsies

Imperial Britain became exercised in the opening decade of the twentieth century by the arrival of alien Gypsies on English soil. Ripples of migration from the Balkans to the Baltic brought Macedonian, Serbian, Hungarian,

and other continental Gypsies to the British Isles. Many of them sought shipping to America, but were denied passage. Their numbers were small—
rarely approaching a hundred at a time—but their incursion was magnified
by the press. Foreign Office officials became alarmed that Macedonian Gypsies
with false papers claimed to be British Indian subjects.[3] Members of parliament spoke of an alien invasion, amid a mood of quickening xenophobia.
Gypsylorists seized the opportunity to examine the language and customs
of exotic Gypsies, and compared their movement to wanderings of the fifteenth century.[4] English Gypsies appeared familiar, homely, even domesticated, compared to these strangely garbed and strangely mannered foreigners.
Indeed, English Gypsies were active in disparaging the newcomers.

Among the first to arrive in the reign of Edward VII were Hungarian
gypsies found destitute at Dover in August 1902.[5] A group of Serbian
Gypsies with performing bears landed from France in the summer of 1903,
and set up camp in Surrey. Police sent to remove them from Arbrook Common,
near Esher, 'beat a hasty and undignified retreat' when confronted by six loose
bears.[6] 'Fifteen Serbians with six or seven bears' were later driven off by
English Gypsies at the Black Patch site at Handsworth, Staffordshire. Russian,
Armenian, and Polish Gypsies were also reported in the Birmingham area in
1904. The *Manchester Guardian* reported in December 1904 that some sixty
Gypsies from southern Russia had taken shelter at Leeds after being shipped
back to England from America, where they had not been permitted to land.[7]
Another group of refugee Gypsies, believed to be Macedonians expelled from
Holland, set up camp on Tower Hill, London, much to the perplexity of the
police. Newspapers described them as 'repulsively dirty' and almost destitute,
a spectacle for curious eyes. Numbering between thirty-five and forty, with
vans drawn by half-starved horses, they toiled through Essex and
Cambridgeshire, Suffolk and Norfolk, before being escorted back towards
London. Some of the Macedonians were expelled from England in February
1905, but small bands continued to rove around Hertfordshire and East Anglia.[8]

In August 1905 parliament passed 'An Act to Amend the Law with Regard
to Aliens' in an attempt to secure the kingdom's borders. It applied to steer-
age passengers on immigrant ships carrying more than twenty such aliens,
though not to more prosperous travellers or smaller groups. The new law
empowered the government to deem 'undesirable' anyone without 'the means
of decently supporting himself and his dependants', and to expel criminal
aliens and anyone 'found wandering without ostensible means of subsistence,
or...living under insanitary conditions'. The statute was not specifically

directed against Gypsies, but the recent Gypsy incursions secured its passage.[9] Loopholes in the law, and difficulties of enforcement, allowed more
foreign Gypsies to step ashore. Deportation proved difficult when the aliens
were uncooperative, in large numbers, and without funds.

The British press expressed alarm at the wanderings of Gypsies described
as German, Bohemian, or Hungarian between the spring and autumn of
1906. Members of parliament demanded action. The aliens landed at Leith
and other North Sea ports with their caravans and paraphernalia, and were
said to be escaping oppression on the Continent. Some travelled north
through Scotland towards Perth and Aberdeen, while others drifted south
into England, supporting themselves by acrobatic shows, fortune-telling,
and horse-dealing. Like Gypsies everywhere, they were suspected of petty
theft, but, unlike their English counterparts, they engaged in persistent begging. Some reports noted that the older Gypsies spoke Hungarian, others
German, and a few were learning English. Passing through Cheshire, some
declared themselves Bulgarian. On several occasions they clashed with English
Gypsies, who allegedly tried to steal their horses. A cavalcade of seventy-five
so-called Bohemians passing through West Yorkshire in July with their vans
and horses were said to be 'tired and sick and sad'. By the time they reached
Lincolnshire in November they were almost destitute, and had to rely on
charitable provisions from the Salvation Army. Local authorities provided
police escorts to hustle them into the next jurisdiction. Cooperation was
limited, as the Gypsies insisted that they knew no English, 'and pattered on
in their unintelligible tongue'. A dramatic illustration in the *Penny Illustrated
Paper* in November 1906, with the caption 'Pillage and Plunder—German
Gipsies Harassing the Countryside', showed burly policemen arm to arm
with Gypsy women. A stand-off between the Leicestershire police, who were
escorting the Gypsies, and the constabulary of Warwickshire, who would not
let them pass, recalled the division between justices in Nottinghamshire in
the 1590s, when one faction wanted the Gypsies imprisoned and the other
sought to move them to an adjacent county.[10] One member of parliament
suggested sending a Romani-speaking police officer to persuade the foreigners to leave, and the Society of Friends of Foreigners in Distress joined
the negotiations. Eventually 125 of these Gypsies took ship from Grimsby,
to be returned to Hamburg and Stettin. When a member of parliament asked
the Home Secretary if he intended to introduce legislation to prevent the
Gypsies from coming in again, the minister responded: 'I can hold out no
hope of that.'[11]

PILLAGE AND PLUNDER—German Gipsies Harassing the Countryside.

Amazing scenes were witnessed in Warwickshire, Leicestershire, and Northamptonshire on Saturday. The gipsies, who had slept overnight in the cattle pens of Leicester Market, were escorted outside the borough by the police. When the borough boundary was reached, the county police supplied the escort, and conducted the gipsies, who wanted to go to Rugby, to the Warwickshire boundary. Here they found a cordon of between twenty and thirty Warwickshire police drawn up across the road and barring the way into Warwickshire. For an hour the Leicestershire police stood parleying with the Warwickshire police, but the latter would not budge an inch. Then the Leicester police forced the gipsies to proceed up Watling Street. At each turn into Warwickshire the band, encouraged by some of the police, attempted to force a passage, but they were unsuccessful. At one place the women rushed at the Warwickshire police with sticks, but they were disarmed before they could inflict any injury. Eventually the Leicestershire police managed to end the struggle by deftly moving all the caravans into Northamptonshire, whose police had not put in an appearance.

Figure 9. 'Pillage and Plunder—German Gipsies Harassing the Countryside', *Penny Illustrated Paper and Illustrated Times,* 17 November 1906

More European Gypsies reached England in 1907. One group who landed at Tilbury in May 1907 included female acrobats, 'very scantily clad'. Others arriving at London Bridge in July 'were dressed in picturesque Serbian costumes, and had a bear with them'. As they travelled into Surrey and Kent, with their vans, children, and animals, they were escorted by policemen on bicycles. Another group of so-called Serbian Gypsies reached Hull in November aboard a Danish steamer but were denied permission to land.[12] Other Serbian Gypsies had more success, and were able to set off with their horses, bears, and monkeys. They travelled around eastern England in the summer of 1908, linking up with other eastern Europeans who had arrived a few years earlier. When they reached Scotland in July, newspapers remarked that they were 'very dark skinned' but 'much better behaved than the German Gypsies'. They lived by entertainment and trickery, and said they were on their way to Brazil.[13]

More exotic Gypsies would follow. Some eventually returned to the Continent, some made it to America, and a few blended into the domestic itinerant population. Especially picturesque was a party of Galacian Gypsies from Poland, about eighty in number, who found lodging at Battersea and Wandsworth, south London, in August 1911. *The Times* observed that 'the women were garishly dressed and loaded with barbaric jewelry'. They were not without funds, and expressed the intention of finding passage to America. An illustration in the *Western Gazette* in September showed well-dressed Gypsy men with beards, and the caption noted their gilt and silver drinking vessels and gold and silver rings.[14] These proved to be the advance party of the Gypsy coppersmiths, whose 'invasion' of 1911–13 allowed Gypsylorists to observe in them 'all the barbaric glamour of the East'. Mostly likely originating in Romania, Transylvania, or Hungary, the coppersmiths were intent on joining a transatlantic Roma diaspora that stretched from Montevideo to Montreal, with branches in Mexico and Cuba. According to Eric Winstedt, who spent a month in their company, 'they despised almost all other Gypsies, and had little to do with them'. The men fashioned exquisite hammered copper bowls, and the women were more inclined to begging than fortune-telling.[15]

The Gypsylorists were partially right to compare these early twentieth-century incursions to Gypsy migrations in the age of the Renaissance. Roma newcomers were once again colliding with settled societies further west. Newspapers did the work of early chronicles in relating their comings and goings, while people looked on with curiosity and alarm. The aliens were strange in their looks, strange in their language, and were said to be despicable in their behaviour. Not since the sixteenth century had such large and exotic cavalcades appeared in England. There was confusion about their origins— Galacian, Macedonian, German, or Bohemian—but no doubt at all that they were Gypsies. Media coverage of the Gypsy aliens reflected poorly on Gypsies in general, although they had little in common with established English itinerants.

Foreign Gypsy immigration slowed to a trickle in the era of the two world wars, but became a matter of public concern again in the late twentieth century, especially after Roma from Eastern Europe took advantage of the fall of communism to move to more prosperous countries further west.[16]

New waves of Roma reached the United Kingdom after 2004, when several East European countries joined the European Union. One overview in 2006 put the number of European Roma in Britain between 4,000 and 5,000, but a study from the University of Salford in 2013 estimated that there were over 193,000 migrant Roma in England alone, mostly in private housing in multi-ethnic urban areas.[17]

Camps, Caravans, and Laws

Much of the interaction between Gypsies and their neighbours in twentieth-century England came down to control of stopping places and camping sites. Itinerant Gypsies needed places to halt, sites to set their tents and vans, and areas where they could work and shelter. Local authorities and land-owners wanted to prevent or limit their presence, and to remove Gypsies from their jurisdiction. Early twentieth-century struggles repeated those of the Victorian period, and presaged confrontations yet to come. The venom and antipathy directed against Gypsies changed little over time, notwithstanding evolution in the technologies of transport and administration. The charge was repeated ad nauseam that Gypsies constituted a 'nuisance', that they were unsightly, disorderly, and dirty, a danger to public health, and a threat to public morality. Supporters upheld the Gypsies' right to travel, householders still made use of their services, and writers occasionally commended them as traditional and picturesque. As one defender said in a case in 1905, 'it is unfair to hound these people...because they belong to the Romany class. After all, they are Englishmen, and not aliens.'[18]

The opening decades of the twentieth century saw endless squabbles about the right of itinerants to camp. Local authorities set up signs and barriers, declared camping to be trespassing, and brought actions at law against Gypsies and van-dwellers who refused to leave. The central government declined to become involved. Making use of existing laws regarding highways and commons, the Council at Tavistock, Devon, warned Gypsies to leave Dartmoor, and threatened prosecution of any who remained.[19] The Corporation at Southend, Essex, blocked Gypsies camping at Hind's Green for the annual fair.[20] Continuing battles at Lambourne Common, Essex, led to forcible evictions and Gypsy resistance. On several occasions the authorities employed traction engines to shift Gypsy vans that had been chained together by the wheels. The pattern was repeated in many parts of England.[21]

Figure 10. 'Gypsy Encampment in Essex', early 1900s

Landowners and their agents attempted to clear the notorious Black Patch site at Handsworth, Staffordshire, a former industrial wasteland where Gypsies had camped for several decades. A force of thirty-five policemen and fifty volunteers worked to oust the Gypsies, and barbed-wire fences and earth embankments were erected to prevent their return. One newspaper called the 1905 campaign a 'war against the Gypsies', but despite intimidation a few itinerant families managed to relocate nearby.[22] Local authorities elsewhere used legal injunctions and restraining orders to dislodge Gypsies, and prosecuted individuals for trespass or for damage to herbage and pasturage. Struggles of this sort went on year after year, in a dance of exclusion and eviction, temporary accommodation, and passive resistance. There was little let-up in the citing of Gypsies for 'camping on the highway', 'damaging turf', 'allowing horses to stray', or driving a 'cart or van without lights'. Foraging for food could be classed as 'poaching', while the feeding of fires occasioned the offence of 'taking wood'. Every year Gypsies were charged with obscene language, drunkenness, and obstructing or assaulting the police, although there is no evidence that they were more disorderly than other members of the disreputable classes.[23]

The Law of Property Act of 1925 provided new measures for control of commons or waste land. The law guaranteed public access to such land 'for air and exercise', but made it an offence to draw or drive 'any carriage, cart, caravan, truck, or other vehicle' onto such land without permission, or to camp or light a fire thereon.[24] It was another weapon to use against Gypsies, and local councils and keepers of commons were quick to test its powers.

In April 1929 the Epsom Grandstand Association, managers of the land around the famous racecourse, decided that 'so-called Gypsies' would no longer be permitted to camp on Epsom Downs. Any Gypsy who drew a caravan onto the grass would be prosecuted under the Law of Property. Generations of Gypsies were accustomed to gathering at Epsom, and their camps, entertainments, and fortune-telling booths were established elements of the Derby horse-race spectacle. The Gypsies would not leave without a fight, on the ground and in the courts. The Grandstand Association used traction engines to remove Gypsy caravans, and on one occasion a protester 'placed himself on the ground between the wheels and put his right arm through one of the spokes, and defied anyone to move the van'. Reports of the confrontation divided public opinion, as they would in similar battles in Kent in the 1950s and at Dale Farm, Essex, in 2011.[25]

In 1929 the Gypsies found a friend in the race-going fraternity, when the Eton-educated Conservative member of parliament Oliver Locker-Lampson championed their cause. Standing up for 'the principle of fair play and liberty', he interceded in court to secure 'freedom of the downland' for people who were 'homeless and hunted'. Dozens of Gypsy families defied the ban, in a struggle that dragged on for years. A compromise was proposed in 1938 that Gypsies should pay for limited access to their traditional sites on the Epsom Downs. The Gypsies responded by threatening to block all the Derby Day traffic with their caravans unless they were allowed on the Downs.[26]

By that time the ancient vagrancy laws were partially repealed (by legislation in 1935), allowing Gypsies to travel with their caravans and tents without being deemed rogues and vagabonds. Like other citizens, they were free to roam (though not to halt), provided they caused no damage.[27] The Public Health Act of 1936, however, gave local authorities the powers they had long sought to control and exclude moveable dwellings. The new law allowed councils to move against 'filthy or verminous premises', including tents and vans used for human habitation.[28] Rarely was it used to the Gypsies' benefit. A contributor to the *Nottingham Evening Post* expressed the mainstream view that the Gypsies were 'shiftless, worthless people ... whose presence in a civilized community is a most doubtful asset ... Their morals are not bounded by ordinary rules, and nearly all of them are thieves, no matter what their apologists may say.'[29] This opinion was shared, apparently, by most of the officials responsible for local law enforcement.

Disputes over Gypsy campsites rumbled on for decades. Less was heard of Gypsies in the Second World War, when many were conscripted for service and a few decamped to Ireland, but grievances erupted anew amid the austerities and readjustments of the post-war peace.[30] By this time Gypsylorism had mostly run its course, and England's itinerant population was expanded and transformed. Popular books by Brian Vesey-Fitzgerald (1944), Rupert Croft-Cooke (1955), and G. E. C. Webb (1960) perpetuated notions of 'true' Gypsies, Romany bloodlines, and their unfortunate dilution, but were increasingly distant from changing social realities.[31] A new activism emerged to secure social justice and self-determination for Gypsy people, though few of the campaigners were themselves Gypsies. Among the most influential were the countrywoman Ellen Wilmot-Ware, who agitated for Gypsies in the 1950s, the Labour politician Norman Dodds, who raised awareness of their plight in parliament from 1951 to 1965, the militant Grattan Puxon, who helped establish The Gypsy Council in 1966, Donald Kenrick, the promoter of Romani scholarship, and the sociologist Thomas Acton, whose publications, speeches, and committee work advanced English Gypsy studies from the 1960s onward.[32]

Public discussion was handicapped by false notions and preconceptions. According to the parliamentary secretary to the Ministry of Local Government and Planning, debating in 1951, 'genuine' Gypsies were 'a first-class set of folk' who were 'very much blackguarded and abused by the use of the term in reference to other types who are not Gypsies at all'.[33] *The Times* in April 1952 distinguished 'genuine nomadic Gypsies', who lived 'in a quite decent way', from 'other travellers', who did not.[34] Conservative members of parliament in 1961 distinguished 'real' Gypsies from 'mumpers, the more worthless people', and observed that 'true Gypsies or Romanies' were only a small minority of the people who lived in caravans.[35] Returning to the topic in the early 1990s, one Conservative member wanted it noted that 'many of those so-called Gypsies are not Gypsies at all, but ne'er-do-wells who are anxious to move from one site to another, to avoid paying their community charge'. Another observed that 'new age travellers' and 'people who have just taken up the way of life' confused the issue by calling themselves Gypsies. Bob Cryer, the Labour member for South Bradford, wisely pointed out that 'Gypsies are an amalgam of various kinds of people; like all people, they defy ready classification'.[36]

A series of parliamentary statutes addressed the problem of itinerancy, though never from the itinerant point of view. The Town and Country Planning Act of 1947 made it easier to dislodge Gypsies from semi-permanent camps and unapproved winter quarters. High-profile evictions at Belvedere Marshes, Erith, and Corkes Meadow, St Mary Cray, both in Kent, were based on this authority.[37] The Highways Act of 1959 made it an offence if 'a hawker or other itinerant trader or a Gypsy pitches a booth, stall or stand, or encamps, on a highway', including its lay-bys and verges. Similar action by non-Gypsies would not constitute an offence. Travellers with horses could also be penalized for any dung they deposited within fifteen feet of the centre of a carriageway.[38]

This legislation was followed by the Caravan Sites and Control of Development Act of 1960, which required caravan sites to be licensed subject to planning control. The law empowered local authorities to provide sites for Gypsies, with 'working space and facilities for the carrying on of such activities as are normally carried on by them', but there was no obligation to provide such sites, and no assistance with funding. It also empowered rural district councils to ban caravans from commons and village greens, a provision they had long demanded. Since Gypsies were among the targets of this statute it was thought necessary for the first time to define them. Parliament understood Gypsies to be 'persons of nomadic habit of life, whatever their race or origin', but not 'members of an organized group of travelling showmen, or persons engaged in travelling circuses, travelling together as such'. From the legal, political, and administrative point of view, all Gypsies were itinerants, and all habitual itinerants, other than showmen or circus workers, were Gypsies. Ignoring ethnicity, cultural traits, heritage, and particular circumstances, it reinforced the confusion between Gypsies and other kinds of travellers, and perpetuated that notion in law.[39] 'In law,' Lord Kennet explained, 'Gypsies, didekais, travellers and tinkers are all "Gypsies"'.[40] A sympathetic survey in 1967 concluded that the post-war legislation amounted to the virtual outlawing of the travelling way of life. The law subjected Gypsies to harassment and exclusion, though, as with previous measures, enforcement was erratic, and some authorities effectively turned a blind eye.[41]

Several widely publicized confrontations occurred in the 1960s. As many as 200 Gypsies were evicted from Darenth Wood, near Dartford, Kent, in January 1962. But, instead of dispersing, they moved, or were moved, to the roadside verge of the main trunk road into London. There they stayed with their vans and families for the best part of a year, while government authorities attempted to sidestep the problem.[42] Gypsy families at other camps defied bulldozers sent to clear them away. Some formed human barriers with their babies in their arms, and others tied children to lorries to prevent them being moved. Supporters made sure that photojournalists captured the drama.[43]

Introduced by the Liberal Eric Lubbock, and passed by a socially progressive Labour government, the Caravan Sites Act of 1968 *obligated* local authorities to set up caravan sites 'to provide adequate accommodation for Gypsies residing in or resorting to their area'. The statute referred to 'Gypsies and other persons of nomadic habit', but defined Gypsies in exactly the same words as in the Act of 1960. It imagined the creation of a national network of sites and facilities that would accommodate the needs of itinerants, while also subjecting them to supervision. There were, however, limitations. London boroughs and county boroughs (designated major towns and cities) were obliged to accommodate only fifteen caravans at a time, and none at all if they could persuade the central government that they had no land suitable for the purpose, or that the number of Gypsies in their area was 'not such as to warrant the provision by the council of accommodation for them'. The government could order local authorities to establish sites, but in practice there was delay and obfuscation. Once the state-approved sites were designated, it became difficult, and in some cases illegal, for Gypsies to camp elsewhere. It became an offence, subject to a fine, 'for any person being a Gypsy to station a caravan for the purpose of residing for any period on any land situated within the boundaries of a highway; or on any other unoccupied land; or any occupied land without the consent of the owner'. The Act set forth procedures for removing 'unlawful encampments' by due process, and protected occupiers of caravans from immediate eviction if they could prove that they had stopped 'in consequence of illness, mechanical breakdown, or other immediate emergency'.[44] Advocates for Gypsies broadly welcomed this legislation because it recognized the legitimacy of itinerancy, and required local authorities to set up permanent and transitory sites. In Thomas Acton's opinion, 'the English Gypsy community began to experience more prosperity after the 1968 Caravan Sites Act took the edge off earlier persecution'. Later critics remarked that 'the Gypsies were certainly fooled into thinking there was to be some rapid improvement in their living conditions'.[45]

Problems, of course, persisted. Local authorities found endless excuses not to provide the mandatory sites, and Gypsies continued to be evicted from private land and commons. If they attempted to settle caravans on land that they owned, they collided with the planning authorities. 'Being a Gypsy' attracted trouble, as did living a Gypsy lifestyle. The statutory language acknowledged the need to accommodate travelling Gypsies, but made no provision for 'other persons of nomadic habit' who did not accept that label. Legal, political, and sociological minds became embroiled in the vexed problem of Gypsy identity, and asked how social justice was served if Gypsies received discriminatory consideration that was not extended to other itinerants and travellers. A report by John Cripps in 1977 on the workings of the Caravan Sites Act proposed minor adjustments. It observed that site provision was seriously inadequate, and that many were 'excessively close to sewage plants, refuse destructors, traffic-laden motorways', and the like, where no 'non-Gypsy family would be expected to live'. At this time, Cripps observed, Gypsies were 'not identifiable as an ethnic group in law or in fact', but could be described as a 'migrant and mercurial minority with a totally different standard of moral codes and values'.[46]

A long-drawn-out legal case in the late 1980s hinged on problems of definition. It asked whether the posting of a sign saying 'Sorry, no travellers' in an East London public house constituted racial discrimination. The Commission for Racial Equality, established under the Race Relations Act of 1976,[47] argued that Travellers and Gypsies were synonymous, and constituted an ethnic group, and that the law banning discrimination on grounds of colour, race, nationality, or ethnic origins applied to them. The trial judge in 1987 used the old definition in the Caravan Sites Act of 1968 to determine that Gypsies were merely people 'of a nomadic habit of life', so that discrimination against them was not grounded on race or ethnicity. But when the case went to appeal in 1988 the judges favoured an alternative argument. Recognizing that many Gypsies shared a historically determined social identity, including separateness and self-awareness of a common culture and customs, the court ruled that the Gypsies were 'an identifiable group defined by reference to ethnic origins within the meaning of the Act'. Greeted as a victory by advocates for Gypsies, this landmark ruling would have significance for campsites and caravans as well as for access to pubs.[48]

With Conservatives in power from 1979 to 1997, official policies became gradually more restrictive. Government was much more inclined to treat Gypsies as a nuisance to be repressed than a minority to be countenanced. Using the 1968 act to harass Gypsies rather than assist them, a series of statutory instruments between 1987 and 1994 designated areas where unauthorized camping was prohibited, and where 'unlawfully stationed caravans and their occupants may be removed'.[49] Pressure mounted to relieve local authorities of their obligation to provide caravan sites, as Gypsies found it harder and harder to find a place to park without penalty. Some members of parliament grew indignant that casual itinerants such as 'new age travellers' took advantage of provisions intended for 'traditional Gypsies', and others argued that many Gypsies nowadays were wealthy enough to provide for themselves: they should be left to their own shift, and punished if they broke the law. Bowen Wells, the Conservative member for East Hertfordshire, wanted local authorities to sell their designated caravan sites for development. Others reiterated stereotypes of the Gypsy 'menace'.[50] Controversially, but not surprisingly, the Criminal Justice and Public Order Act of 1994 repealed the duty of local authorities to provide campgrounds for Gypsies, who were still perceived as feckless nomads.[51] The Commission for Racial Equality observed that, under this Act, Gypsies would have to choose 'either to become house dwellers or to be criminalized for following a nomadic way of life'.[52]

In another twist of policy, the Housing Act of 2004 placed a duty on local housing authorities to undertake regular assessments of the accommodation needs of Gypsies and Travellers either living in or resorting to their area. It was not clear what action would follow these assessments. For the purposes of the Act, Gypsies and Travellers were defined as 'persons with a tradition of living in a caravan, and all other persons of a nomadic habit of life, whatever their race or origin'. But, recognizing that not all Gypsies were actively itinerant, and that many lived in settled accommodation, the legislation included 'such persons who, on grounds only of their own or their family's or dependants' educational or health needs or old age, have ceased to travel temporarily or permanently'.[53] A Gypsy petition to parliament in 2004 asserted that 'we are a distinct ethnic group sharing common ancestors, a distinct language, cultural beliefs and a common oral history', who had lived in Britain for centuries. Supporters of other groups, however, admitted no historical distinction between Gypsies and Travellers, arguing instead for universal human rights and entitlements.[54]

Claims for the ethnic distinctiveness of Gypsies and Travellers were slow to gain acceptance among politicians, and statutory instruments continued to define them as nomads.[55] The Equality Act of 2010, which included protection for racial and ethnic origins, made no mention of Gypsies, but case law established that Roma Gypsies and Irish Travellers were covered by its provisions.[56] A series of cases concerning caravan sites and planning permission acknowledged the ethnicity of Gypsies and Travellers, but disallowed any differential treatment on those grounds. Confusion continued among local authorities, government agencies, journalists, and court-appointed experts.[57]

Though mostly invisible to the general public, a trickle of cases concerning English Gypsies came before the European Court of Human Rights. Britain's Human Rights Act of 1998 incorporated the European Convention on Human Rights, which, among other provisions, guaranteed the right to respect for a person's private and family life and home (article 8), and prohibited discrimination on such grounds as race, birth, or other status (article 14).[58] English cases brought before the European court had limited success. Lawyers agreed that Gypsies belonged to a recognized minority, but argued whether this gave them legal privileges and protections. Were they entitled to put caravans on land that they owned, even if this violated planning controls that would prevent anyone else from doing the same? Did enforcement of planning laws or eviction orders against Gypsies constitute infringement of their human rights? Human Rights law provided another arena for argument about camps, caravans, and the cultural needs of Gypsies and travellers.[59]

The European court dealt sympathetically with Gypsies from Cambridgeshire, Hertfordshire, Surrey, Kent, and Lancashire who were forced to remove caravans from land they owned, after planning permission was denied, but found no violation of the European Convention.[60] In 2004, however, the Court ruled that the eviction of James Connors from a local-authority caravan site in West Yorkshire, on allegations of his family's anti-social behaviour, was a violation of his rights. The case entailed a thorough review of British government policy towards a population of Gypsies and Travellers that had become increasingly settled. Connors, an Irish Traveller who was recognized in European law as a Gypsy, had once 'led a traditional travelling lifestyle', but had lived with his family at the Cottingley Springs site, Leeds, for almost fifteen years. Most of the Travellers on the site were permanently settled, or only occasionally nomadic. The court observed that in England 'a substantial majority of Gypsies no longer travel for any material period', although Gypsy culture remained 'nomadic in spirit if not in actual or constant practice'. Government efforts to provide for the needs of Gypsies were predicated on their definition as itinerants, and were increasingly out of touch with Travellers who were no longer travelling. A report conducted by the Centre for Urban and Regional Studies at the University of Birmingham noted that, 'for many residential site residents, nomadism appears to be a spiritual and cultural state of mind, rather than a day-to-day reality'. In the case of Connors, the court found that his eviction constituted 'serious interference' with his Human Rights under article 8 of the European Convention, and that the government action against him was unnecessary and disproportionate. One of the ironies of the case was that someone classed as a Gypsy, from a group once renowned for its estrangement from mainstream society, should now be aggrieved by being made 'homeless', and by 'loss of access to educational facilities, recreational facilities, medical and health services, and basic sanitation and refuse disposal occasioned by the eviction'. Connors was awarded 14,000 euros for 'non-pecuniary damage through feelings of frustration and injustice', plus costs of 21,643 euros to pay for his lawyers.[61]

Media and political responses to the application of the Human Rights Act to Gypsies and Travellers have mostly been indignant. Conservative members of parliament, in particular, have complained that it became 'increasingly difficult for local councils to enforce planning laws, stop unauthorized developments and evict illegal occupants'. The *Sun* newspaper campaigned in 2005 to 'Stamp on the Camps', while its competitors whipped up anti-Gypsy prejudice.[62] Gypsies and Travellers continued to be vilified, and their ability to travel, halt, or settle remained fraught with difficulties.

The clash at Dale Farm, near Billericay, Essex, in the summer and autumn of 2011 encapsulated all of the problems of the preceding century. The Travellers who established an encampment on land they owned on the site of a former scrapyard were evicted in October 2011, after a much-publicized struggle, because the land had Green Belt protection, and the campers lacked planning permission. After legal recourse had been exhausted, and despite the entrenchment of activists, a force of 150 police and bailiffs stormed the site and routed the residents. Public opinion, fuelled by the press, displayed the usual mixture of prejudice, misrepresentation, and anxiety, with some sections of the left expressing solidarity with the oppressed. The crisis raised questions of equity, ethnicity, and identity, and exposed division between English Gypsies and Irish Travellers. Although the press referred to them as Gypsies and Travellers, the Dale Farm occupants were predominantly Irish, and English Gypsies with Romany ancestry gave them minimal support.[63]

Conflicts over caravan and camps were far from being settled in the early twenty-first century, when planning appeals came regularly before the courts.[64] Middle England would make no concession to Gypsy ethnicity, and clung to the notion that Travellers traditionally travelled. New laws introduced in 2015 threatened to expel Gypsies and Travellers from permanent sites, unless they could prove that they were still itinerant. The Commission for Racial

Equality countered that the ethnic minorities of Romany Gypsies and Irish Travellers were not simply defined by mobility, and studies showed that the majority of Gypsies were now sedentary. Recent estimates suggest that as many as two-thirds of England's Gypsies and Travellers now live in 'bricks and mortar' housing. Gypsies remained as controversial and vulnerable as ever, as lawyers, academics, and activists outside their community argued about their identity and their destiny.[65]

Irish Travellers

The greatest change to affect English Gypsies in the second half of the twentieth century was the influx of Irish Travellers. Occupying a similar economic niche, though with different cultural traditions, large numbers of Irish itinerants entered post-war Britain in search of economic opportunity. Their presence affected the response of the state and the public towards Gypsies and other travellers. Observers in the 1970s reported pockets of tolerance for 'genuine' Gypsies, but noted that 'prejudice against Irish Travellers is especially strong'.[66]

Itinerants from Ireland had trickled into mainland Britain during several previous centuries. Charles I's government in the 1630s considered the problem of Irish immigration to be new, and nineteenth-century authorities became familiar with hundreds of families searching for work or fleeing distress. Some Victorian Gypsies treated the newcomers as intruders, and spoke dismissively of Irish tinkers as a 'nasty...breed'.[67] Migration across the Irish Sea was unregulated and unmeasured, and continued without restriction after Ireland had gained independence.

Anthropologists considered the community of Irish Tinkers or Travellers within Ireland in the 1960s and 1970s to be a self-perpetuating group of white, indigenous, English-speaking, Roman Catholic itinerants. Some employed the traveller dialects of Gammon, Shelta, or cant, but not Romani. In Ireland they were not called Gypsies, though the Gypsy label was attached to them when they became established in England. Many adopted Gypsy modes of work, transport, and accommodation, and some may also have copied the practice of fortune-telling.[68] Judith Okely, the anthropologist who worked most closely with Travellers in England in the 1970s, reported that some newcomers from Ireland even adopted such traditional Romany surnames as Lee and Loveridge, and by rules of self-ascription would henceforth be taken as Gypsies.[69]

The largest waves of migration arrived in the late 1950s and 1960s. By 1981 it was estimated that there were 5,200 Irish Travellers in Britain. The increase in the recorded number of Gypsy caravans in England, from 4,750 in 1965 to 13,500 in 1993, was widely attributed to 'the increase in the number of Irish itinerants'.[70] The Traveller families who settled at Dale Farm, Essex, in the early twenty-first century, and were evicted in 2011, were mostly of Irish origin, named Egan, Flynn, McCarthy, O'Brien, and Sheridan.[71]

British reactions to Irish Travellers were generally hostile, although social agencies attempted to respond to their needs. A government study published in 1967 claimed that 'indigenous travellers despise the low standards and dirty conditions of the tinkers which cause trouble for all groups of travellers . . . some English travellers think they should be sent home'.[72] Later accounts report less animosity, and, indeed, a degree of intermarriage. Joanna Richardson and Andrew Ryder observe that 'Gypsies and Irish Travellers have differing origins and cultural traditions', but share 'striking similarities', and have moved toward 'a degree of cultural and political cohabitation'.[73] As far as the sociologists Derek Hawes and Barbara Perez were concerned, the Irish Travellers became 'so closely identified, interbred and integrated with the Gypsies' that there was no point in distinguishing between them.[74] Other scholars are ecumenical and permissive in this regard, recognizing the valency of the various terms, but preferring to allow people to define themselves.[75] Few go so far as the Traveller activist Brian Belton, who deems the 'notion' of ethnicity to be a product of 'emotional, sentimental and psychological considerations', and a false creation of 'the academic and juridical gaze'. There is no place for history or heritage in such accounts, only observation of the narratives of current lived experience.[76]

It was no doubt the effort to find an inoffensive vocabulary that induced one member of parliament in 1998 to speak of 'real travellers', avoiding reference to Gypsies of any kind.[77] Irish Travellers gained legal recognition as an ethnic minority in an English court case in 2000, a status already accorded to Romany Gypsies. The victory was celebrated by 'The Irish Traveller Movement in Britain', established in 1999, which by 2013 was renamed 'The Traveller Movement'.[78] Leaving aside New Age Travellers and recreational caravanners, modern policy discussions often lump Gypsies, Roma, and Travellers together as 'GRT', as if they were an entity, not a compendium. The groups are fused in the popular imagination, and may be increasingly intermarried, but cultural frictions between them persist. Gypsies identifying themselves as English Romanies were among the most vocal critics of the television series *My Big Fat Gypsy Wedding*, withheld support from the Travellers at Dale Farm, and continue to occupy separate pitches at gatherings like Appleby Fair.[79] A mixed group of Romanies and Travellers now adheres to the Light and Life Gypsy Church, which attempts to replace traditional religious eclecticism and indifference with pentecostal discipline.[80]

Contested Numbers

The size of the Gypsy population is as much of a mystery as ever. Modern estimates range from under 15,000 to more than 300,000. The census for England and Wales in 1901 counted 14,219 itinerants, including 12,574 sleeping in tents, caravans, and the open air, at a time when international experts put the British Gypsy population at 20,000.[81] Nobody knows how many Gypsies were uncounted or misclassified. When a member of parliament asked the Home Secretary in 1925 for 'any estimate of the number of Gypsies moving about England and Wales at the present time', Sir William Joynson-Hicks could only answer: 'I have no figures, and should be sorry to have to make any guess in the matter.'[82]

'Pure guesswork' enabled the campaigning politician Norman Dodds to estimate in 1951 that there might be 'about 100,000' travellers in Great Britain, of whom '20,000 are real Romany Gypsies'. Official census figures were useless, he complained, and sociological research was no more helpful in understanding itinerant groups. There needed to be a survey, he believed, 'to find out how many Romanies there are and how many of the "travellers" are not Romanies at all'. When asked in parliament in 1961 whether his concern was Romanies, didicoys, or other travellers, Dodds replied: 'I am concerned with all of them. They are all human beings.'[83]

Partly in response to Dodds's efforts, the British government conducted a survey in 1965 that yielded an estimate of 15,000 Travellers and Gypsies in England and Wales, spread among some 3,400 families. The figures fell far short of the numbers that advocates for Travellers and Gypsies imagined. Officials admitted that some families disappeared as soon as the interviewing started, and others 'were trailed but never found'. Judith Okely commented that the undercount was 'not surprising', given that 'the survey was conducted often by persons responsible for dispersing the Gypsies', including local officials and the police. Designed to guide state policy, the analysis also included a forecast of the size of the Gypsy–Traveller population twenty years into the future, when a figure approaching 28,000 was projected for 1985.[84] At the time of the Cripps report in 1977 the best estimate was that there were some 40,000 Gypsies in England and Wales, more than twice as many as a decade earlier, and that the number was increasing.[85]

Local authorities needed to know how many itinerants to provide for, or to deflect, in face of legislation regarding caravan sites.[86] The heritage and background of these people were not their immediate concern. Recognizing the varied composition of the travelling community, one member of parliament declared in 1993 that 'we are now faced with some 13,500 people—if one can count them—who purport to be Gypsies, but who in no sense are part of the original number'.[87] Another estimate that year, based on a count of caravans, posited a population approaching 40,000, assuming 4 persons per household in 9,900 travelling families. Missing from this were uncounted caravans, and the growing number of settled and semi-settled Gypsies in bricks and mortar accommodation.[88]

Writing in the 1990s, Angus Fraser estimated somewhere above 50,000 Gypsies in the United Kingdom.[89] European statistics from the same period put the number of Gypsies and Travellers in Great Britain between 90,000 and 120,000, and this estimate has often been repeated.[90] The variability of figures is reflected in the work of Donald Kenrick, who in *On the Verge* (with Sian Bakewell, 1990, revised 1995) estimated an English Gypsy population of 63,000, including 53,000 Romanies and 8,000 Irish Travellers.[91] Kenrick's *Historical Dictionary* a few year later estimated the Gypsy population in England as 110,000, with 3,000 more in Wales, just over 1,000 in Northern Ireland, and 30,000 Romanies and Travellers in Scotland and elsewhere, making a total of 144,000. Kenrick's appendix reduced the Gypsy and Traveller population of the United Kingdom to 105,000, but this was still two or three times the total recognized in parliament.[92]

Kenrick and Clark, publishing in 1999, ventured a total of 120,000 Gypsies and Travellers in Britain, comprising 63,000 'Romanies', 1,000 Welsh Gypsies or 'Kalé', 19,000 Irish Travellers, 20,0000 Scottish Travellers, 15,000 so-called New Travellers, and 2,000 relatively recently arrived Roma. These are plausible figures, but the sources behind them are nowhere specified; they are said to come from 'a mixture of official statistics (e.g. census counts) and various other sources (e.g. non-governmental organizations)'.[93] They are, in other words, like all other numbers, guesses.

More recent estimates are just as fanciful and elastic. A social study published in 2004 puts 'the total number of Gypsies and Travellers in England' at 'probably not less than 100,000 or more than 250,000', and cites a recent estimate as high as 300,000.[94] Favouring this maximalist view, David Mayall reported 'the British travelling' in 2005 to have totalled 200,000 to 300,000 people. Joanna Richardson and Andrew Ryder also estimated the number of Gypsies and Travellers in Britain around 300,000, roughly a third of them mobile and two-thirds settled.[95] Several Traveller websites consider even this high figure to be an underestimate.[96]

The 2001 census provided a fresh opportunity to ascertain Gypsy and Traveller numbers, but only added confusion. When individuals were invited to describe their ethnic group in any way they wished, only 1,710 respondents in England and Wales wrote 'Gypsy' or 'Romany', and a further 509 described themselves as 'Traveller' (a total of 2,219). Most Gypsies, it seems, ignored the question or simply identified themselves as 'white'.[97]

Pressed for greater precision, officials responsible for the 2011 census included, for the first time, a tick box for the ethnic group 'Gypsy or Irish Traveller'. There was no box for 'Romany' or 'Roma', and anyone who wrote those words was allocated to 'other white'. Because 'Gypsy and Irish Travellers' (considered together) were now recognized as an ethnic minority, officials wanted to know their numbers. The census found 58,000 Gypsies and Irish Travellers, comprising 20,500 households, in England and Wales. Confounding expectations, 61 per cent of these Gypsies and Irish Travellers lived in built accommodation, and only 24 per cent in caravans. Among caravan-dwellers, 62 per cent owned or shared ownership in their rig. Analysis confirmed that these people 'experienced high levels of discrimination, deprivation and inequality', in terms of qualifications, economic activity, and health.[98] But there was no attempt to disaggregate the category, to enquire about heritage, customs, or origins.

The census figure of 58,000 established a minimum register on which interested parties could build, but it quickly engendered criticism. The Irish Traveller Movement in Britain (now renamed The Traveller Movement) argued that the figures were 'a significant undercount', for the usual reasons of marginalization, distrust, and the invisibility of unauthorized sites. They offered instead a figure of 119,000, more than twice as high, based on interpolations from Gypsy Traveller Accommodation Assessments, counts of caravans by the Department for Communities and Local Government, and a modicum of wishful thinking. This still falls short of the estimate of 300,000 for the United Kingdom, which the Traveller Movement and others continue to promote.[99] Adding this figure to its estimate of 200,000 recently arrived migrant Roma, a controversial University of Salford study of 2013 found as many as '500,000 "Roma", as defined by the Council of Europe, living in the UK'.[100]

Government figures have always been lower than those set forth by more sympathetic investigators. But the guesswork is ideologically shaded as well as volatile and erratic. Alarmists have sometimes inflated numbers to exaggerate the scale of the imagined Gypsy menace. Activists and advocates for Travellers' rights also favour high figures to indicate a large constituency with a claim on public resources. State agencies, on the other hand, cite low numbers to minimize a problem they would prefer to ignore. Determining the size and dynamics of the population of Gypsies and Irish Travellers proves a hazardous enterprise, since not all Travellers are Gypsies, and not all Gypsies are Travellers. The categories are radically unstable. Estimation becomes all the more difficult when Gypsies cease to be itinerant, and itinerants cease to be Gypsies. The difficulty lies not just in the technology of enumeration, or in Gypsy resistance to being counted, but in the fundamental and perennial problem of identity, definition, and inclusion. Since numbers tell stories, and statistics affect policies, it may be better to treat all population figures as rhetorical expressions rather than statements of certainty.[101]

England changed profoundly over the 500 years that Gypsies shared its history. The country became vastly more populous, more prosperous, imperial and post-imperial, industrial and post-industrial, international and multicultural, metropolitan and suburban. Its people, for the most part, experienced improvements in education and literacy, health and longevity, affluence and social security, within their British, European, and globalized worlds. Mainstream culture became dechristianized, or at least more secular, amid moral and material transformations. The media of information and entertainment became much more abundant, inescapable, amid the transformed technologies of leisure and living. What hope for Gypsies in such changed conditions?

Though still marginal, still hounded, and short of acceptance, the Gypsy population of the early twenty-first century was itself multicultural and multiethnic. Though resistant, as ever, to glib definition, Gypsies continued and adapted, variegated and persistent, an anomaly and an enigma, amid the patchwork of British diversity.[102]

IO

Lives and Livelihoods

The authors, authorities, and inhabitants of England have always held strong opinions about the nature and business of Gypsies. These assumptions were often stereotypical, prejudicial, and ill-founded. Gypsies lived in the social imagination, and were victims of false perception, cultural construction, and sentimental misrepresentation. Most of what we know about them comes from people who did not understand them, who were hostile, suspicious, or at best confused. It is hard to unravel the mysteries of Gypsy culture, and almost impossible to write their history on their own terms, when most of our evidence comes from literary sources or from the records of journalism, law, and administration. The enthusiasms of Gypsylorism shed only a filtered light on the subject. Modern activist scholarship is only marginally more helpful. Many of the things we might wish to know about Gypsies—about their historical beliefs, values, and domestic practices—remain unknowable. None the less, it seems worthwhile to pursue questions about the lives and livelihoods of English Gypsies over time. This final chapter takes stock of what was known and believed about Gypsies over half a millennium.

Appearances

Early laws against Gypsies assumed that they could be known by 'their apparel, speech or other behaviour'. Their manner, appearance, language, and 'trade of life' supposedly gave them away. Constables and justices were supposed to be able to recognize 'Gypsies wandering in the form or habit of Egyptians' by how they looked, how they talked, and how they made their living. Though they were similar to travelling vagrants, a frisson of danger and exoticism attached to 'Gypsy people'. Unfortunately, the criteria of identification were never defined, and were almost certainly inadequate.[1]

The continental chroniclers who first noticed Gypsies described them as dark or tawny skinned, with dark curly hair and silver earrings. They stood out as foully or strangely dressed, the women swathed in exotic shawls and crowned with turbans. Sixteenth-century artists recorded these details in drawings and paintings. Tudor and early Stuart commentators also remarked on the 'strange robes' of the Gypsies, and 'the strangeness of the attire of their heads'.[2] Thomas Dekker's depiction of their 'odd and fantastic apparel... like morris-dancers' set the pattern.[3] Other creative writers sustained the stereotype, so that theatre audiences learned how to recognize a character 'attired like an Egyptian'.[4] 'Our women look like Gypsies... Their clothes and fashions beggarly and bankrupt, base, old, and scurvy', observes a character in *The Wild-Goose Chase* by Beaumont and Fletcher.[5] The popular author Richard Head in the 1670s described Gypsies 'very oddly clad with bells, and long sticks with ribbons hanging at the end dangling, with many other mad contrived toys, merely to draw the country people about them', but this description owed less to observation than to plagiarism of Dekker.[6]

It is questionable, however, whether Gypsies conformed to their literary sartorial image. Early modern authorities penalized 'persons wandering in the habit, form, or attire of counterfeit Egyptians',[7] but their records rarely referred to the costumes of the Gypsies they apprehended. The blue coat of the Gypsy leader in Nottinghamshire in 1591 stands out as an exception.[8] Commenting on the wiliness of Gypsies in 1596, the Somerset justice Edward Hext complained that, when brought to the assizes or sessions, they 'will so clothe themselves, for that time, as any should deem him to be an honest husbandman',[9] in this case counterfeiting ordinariness.

In the eighteenth century, whenever the clothing of Gypsies was mentioned, they mostly appeared like common travellers. The Gypsy George Squires in 1753 had 'a blue coat and a red waistcoat', and a greatcoat good enough to lend to a revenue officer; his sister Lucy 'had a white gown on and a red cloak, it was a sort of Holland gown, very clean and neat'. Their mother, the Gypsy Mary Squires, wore 'a sort of drab-coloured cloak' and 'a sort of serge gown', neither of them ragged. If people expected Gypsies to look more exotic, they were disappointed. Only cartoonists represented Mary Squires with a pointed witch's hat and broomstick.[10] When Stanley the horse-stealer, known as 'king of the Gypsies', was hanged at Ilchester in 1794, with his wife and daughter in attendance, newspapers remarked on 'the singular elegance of their persons and the costliness of their dress'.[11] Leading male Gypsies sometimes flashed their wealth, and several reports mention the silver buckles and buttons they wore at funerals.[12] Authorities pursuing 'the daring gang of Gypsies' blamed for a string of burglaries in Essex in 1796 were able to identify the ringleader, Richard Chilcott alias Lee, 'by the singularity of wearing silver buttons on his fustian coat, made out of reduced dollars'. 'He had on his coat, when he was apprehended, forty-four dollars instead of buttons.'[13] When Gypsies were depicted in Hanoverian paintings and drawings, they looked little different from ordinary poor travellers—the men with slouch hats, waistcoats, and gaiters, the women wearing scarves or bonnets, aprons, and shawls. Sprawled around campfires or engaged in fortune-telling, they were identified by their activity, not their dress.

Meeting a woman of the Boswell clan in Yorkshire about 1820, the minister Thomas Blackley was pleased to find her 'dressed in the highest order of Gypsy fashion', but any countrywoman might have dressed the same.[14] The pre-Victorian philanthropist Samuel Roberts saw Gypsy clothing 'equal in quality and colour to what one would expect to be worn by decent trades-people', though one of the women wore a 'coloured handkerchief as a kind of bandeau or turban round the head'.[15] All that stood out for the evangelist James Crabb was the flashing silver buttons.[16] Gypsy showmen and fortune-tellers may have cultivated an exotic appearance, to meet customer expectations, but otherwise Gypsy clothing was unexceptional. The Gypsies at Tilbrook Fair, Huntingdonshire, in 1822, wore frock smocks common to rural labourers.[17] Two Gypsy women in Westmorland in 1826, going out to tell fortunes, were 'dressed quite in costume, having short red cloaks and large low hats, tied down with a ribbon or string'.[18] Two Gypsy men suspected of theft in Lancashire in 1833 'wore drab single-breasted coats with long skirts', and one had 'a drab hat'. One female in their company 'wore a blue printed gown, cotton velvet bonnet trimmed with black lace, and a darkish drab long cloak'. Another 'had on a red printed gown, velvet bonnet, and sometimes a drab cloak, and occasionally a scarlet cloak'.[19] Horse thieves in Yorkshire in 1844 were described as 'dressed in the usual Gypsy fashion', which was a flamboyant version of the ordinary costume of horsemen and country folk.

Nineteenth-century photographs show Gypsies costumed like the ordinary labouring poor, the men with waistcoats and mufflers, the women with aprons and scarves. But some self-styled 'Romany rais' believed they could tell Gypsies by their outfits. The Victorian 'expert' Charles Leland reported that one of his principal informants 'always affected the old Gypsy style, in striped corduroy coat, leather breeches and gaiters, red waistcoat, yellow neck-handkerchief, and a frightfully dilapidated old white hat'. The way a Romany wore his hat, according to Leland, was distinctively 'foreign, Bohemian, and poetic'.[20] As usual, the Gypsylorists saw what they expected.

Francis Groome described his Gypsy acquaintance Silvanus Lovell as dressed like 'a debauched gamekeeper', with 'a yellow silk neckerchief, brown velvet coat with crown-piece buttons, red waistcoat with spade-guinea ditto, cord breeches, and leather leggings', the ensemble topped by 'a high-crowned ribbon-decked hat'. His partner, Lementina Lovell, wore 'a parti-coloured apron over a short blue woollen dress', nailed boots, hooped gold ear-rings, and 'a gorgeous handkerchief' over her 'coal-black curiously-plaited hair'. These were show costumes or 'holiday attire', advertising Gypsy identity, but their ingredients came from the ordinary wardrobe of the working poor.[21] Two more Gypsy women, suspected of crimes in Victorian Cambridgeshire, were identified by their clothing: 'one with a red and green tartan shawl, and yellow handkerchief on her head; the other with a cloak, striped brown and green, and a blue and crimson handkerchief under a black beaver bonnet.'[22] The outfits would not have been out of place at any fair or market.

Though modern Gypsies were sometimes said to be dressed distinctively, with subtle signs of membership in the group, their clothing was usually 'closer to house-dwellers' fashion'.[23] Twentieth-century photographs show Gypsy men in jackets and trousers, accessorized with scarves and caps, like other members of the working class. Gypsy women's costumes changed from long dresses in the era of the First World War, to shorter floral printed frocks after the second, and pants and sweaters closer to the present. If some of their daughters affected short shorts, bare midriffs, heavy jewelry, and eye make-up, it may have been because they had watched too much television. Gypsy dress may have been more a marker of class than of ethnicity, as the anthropologist Judith Okely discovered in the 1970s, when she switched from her fieldwork persona to dress for Oxford seminars.[24]

Conventional commentary characteristically made Gypsies dark eyed and dark skinned.[25] To be 'as tawny as a Gypsy' or 'as tanned as a Gypsy'[26] denoted a light shade of brown. Early modern authors described this as 'dun or tawny', and attributed the skin tone more to a walnut juice dye than natural colouration.[27] John Melton in the seventeenth century described Gypsies as 'black and ill-favoured people', who used artificial means to 'venom their skins' and 'discolour their faces'. The 'tawny-visaged' Gypsies, by this account, were counterfeit through and through.[28]

Later observers recognized dark hair and tawny skin as natural Gypsy attributes rather than marks of deception. A clerical contributor to the *Christian Guardian* in 1813 understood Gypsy faces to be 'coloured by the smoke and the sun', rather than stained with anything 'to give them a tawny colour'. Encountering a Gypsy child in Yorkshire about 1820, Thomas Blackley remarked that 'its swarthy face, its black hair and eyes, plainly bespoke its family and its people'.[29] 'They are betrayed by their very faces; the countenance of a Gypsy is recognized in England almost as readily as that of a negro', remarked another philanthropist in 1828.[30]

Victorian newspapers commented unreflectingly on the 'strange appearances and curious accompaniments' of travelling Gypsies.[31] They sometimes described people as 'Gypsy looking', 'with the lineaments of a Gypsy', or 'having the appearance of Gypsies', when their actual identity was uncertain. Gypsyness, it was suggested, was made manifest by outward signs. When the highway robber 'Gypsy Jack' Britten was captured in 1843, his features and complexion made it 'evident that he belongs to the Gypsy tribe'.[32] Equally identifiable was 'a gang of the original long black curly-haired Gypsies' responsible for deceptions in Cumberland in 1845.[33] The stereotypical Victorian Gypsy was always dusky, though observers also encountered Gypsies with fair hair and blue eyes. 'To this day', insisted one observer in 1896, 'the pure remnants of the Gypsy people are known by the same swarthy complexion, coal black hair, and wild eye'.[34] Thirty years later an observer in northern England wrote stereotypically of 'the dark-skinned, raven-haired' members of the Gypsy 'tribe'.[35] Anyone fairer had to be a half-breed or imposter, or perhaps a victim of child theft. It was a preposterous proposition, since countenance was no more a predictor of Gypsyness than costume.

Families, Companies, and Accommodation

Gypsies from the earliest times have travelled in family groups, with gatherings of extended kin. Early modern authors described them ranged in assemblages of fifty to a hundred at a time, with their offspring, entourage, and followers. There were, guessed Edward Hext in 1596, 'three or four hundred in a shire'.[36] Thomas Dekker's Jacobean Gypsies made up 'commonly an army about four score strong', with smaller bands foraging 'up and down countries, four, five or six in a company', with their children 'horsed, seven or eight upon one jade'.[37] Samuel Rid remarked on Gypsy companies 'above two hundred rogues and vagabonds in a regiment'.[38] These numbers are consistent with early archival accounts, though they do not apply so much to the centuries that followed. Tudor authorities intercepted concentrations of eighty Gypsies in Lincolnshire in 1540, more than a hundred in Nottinghamshire in 1591, and almost two hundred in Yorkshire in 1596, all with children, but these may have been temporary agglomerations of groups who were normally more scattered.[39]

Seventeenth-century sources typically report smaller companies of a dozen to two dozen members. They shared a variety of common English surnames—Clifford, Johnson, Valentine, and so on, and gave ordinary names to their children—Richard, Thomas, Elizabeth, and Jane. It is sometimes claimed that Gypsies had 'aliases and double names', some for use within their community and others for outsiders,[40] but our sources offer no corroboration. Biblical names such as Samson and Moses appeared more commonly in the nineteenth century, as well as female contractions such as Delity, Jenty, and Lementina. Documentary records shed little light on the domestic culture, family life, and demography of pre-Victorian Gypsies. Information about their encounters with authority is abundant, but what went on within their camps and tents remains unknown. Only imagination fills the void.

Early modern Gypsies moved on foot, sometimes with small strings of horses, pack ponies, or donkeys. Families thus equipped could easily move twenty or more miles a day. Few were seen with wheeled carts before the nineteenth century, and only in the Victorian era were Gypsies commonly associated with living wagons or caravans. The Romany word *vardo* for wagon first entered print about 1819. Vans converted into dwellings first appeared in the 1830s, and were enlarged and elaborated in the decades that followed, for those who could afford them. A covered cart could be had for £30, whereas a full-equipped caravan cost up to five times that amount. The bow-topped or barrel-topped wagons that appeared in the Victorian era could cost up to £60 or £70, and a custom-built travelling van, ten feet long, with stove and fittings, cost as much as £150. These were substantial investments in ostentatious mobility, fit only for aristocrats of the road. The golden age of the Gypsy caravan lasted only a hundred years, from the 1850s to the 1950s, and they soon became objects of nostalgia or items for exhibition.[41]

Most Gypsies before the modern era slept in tents. Descriptions of their framing with poles or hoops, their awnings of canvas or sacking, and their arrangement into long low rooms for shelter, cooking, and sleeping, can be augmented with nineteenth-century photographs. There they lay, wrote George Smith of Coalville, 'in such a state as would shock the modesty of South African savages, to whom we send missionaries to show them the blessings of Christianity'. Smith saw only 'filth' where others observed domestic order, and would have been amazed by reports of Gypsy protocols for cleanliness.[42] Portable tents were used in all weathers, though many Gypsies found more substantial winter quarters.

Nineteenth-century Gypsies travelled in small family groups, but sometimes gathered in strength at favoured stopping places, or on special occasions. When police raided a Gypsy camp on Martlesham Heath, near Ipswich, Suffolk, in November 1841, they found thirteen or fourteen tents, occupied by about sixty men, women, and children of all ages. 'The gang was composed of the families of Chilcott, Lee, Cooper, Smith, Boswell, and Brown.'[43] Another gathering in the New Forest in October 1842 numbered 'between 300 and 400 Gypsies, belonging to different tribes, including the Lees, Stanleys, and Coopers'.[44] There were 'upwards of fifty' men, women, and children, twelve horses, 'and a vast quantity of baggage' at a camp of Chilcotts and Smiths in Essex in May 1843.[45] Dozens more families came and went in the New Forest and the Forest of Dean, and camped on the brickfields and heaths on the outskirts of major cities. Observers in the environs of London noted seasonal or semi-permanent clusterings of Gypsies on Plumstead and Hackney marshes, on the brickfields of Shepherd's Bush and West Kensington, among the dust heaps near Finsbury Park, and around the wastelands and rail yards of Wandsworth and Battersea.[46]

Townsfolk encountered Gypsies singly or in pairs, as they sold pegs from door to door or offered to tell fortunes. But they also saw Gypsies in strength at fairs and race meetings. Later Victorian encampments ranged from a lone van with a couple of tents to large and ever-changing compounds of caravans and temporary huts. Medical inspectors found thirty Gypsy tents near the Beehive Inn on Lambourne Common, Essex, in February 1893, the occupants suffering from cold and disease.[47] That summer saw 'no less than thirty vans and up to twenty tents' on the edge of Epping Forest at Chigwell.[48] More than forty families of Gypsies could be found from time to time on Epsom Downs. The average size of these families in the 1881 census was 5.4, significantly larger than the national average of 4.6. Almost two-thirds of the

Figure 11. Appleby Fair Roma, 2015

Epsom Gypsies were children.[49] Gypsy children were said to be generally well loved, through denied the benefits of literate or spiritual education and the comforts of a settled hearth and home. Late Victorian health inspectors worried that Gypsy children were excessively exposed to illness and privation. George Smith campaigned to get them into school. Most would continue in the life to which they were born. A century and more later would see Gypsies in even greater numbers in private and informal campsites, and on local-authority pitches.

Most itinerant Gypsies were motorized by the later decades of the twentieth century. The horse fairs at Appleby and Stow-on-the-Wold continued, and indeed grew as social occasions, but most attendees arrived by car.[50] Most of the remaining horse-drawn wagons and bow-tops were retained only for seasonal use, or for sentimental cultural display. The motor replaced the work horse, with lorries or trucks for haulage and transport. Decrepit cars or 'bangers' were common—the equivalent of the 'lean jade' of yesteryear—while the most prosperous Travellers sported Jaguars and Range Rovers.[51] Comfortable trailers replaced cramped vans and tents, and increasing numbers moved into semi-permanent mobile homes. Their sites, both private and licensed, could be home to isolated individuals as well as communities numbering in the hundreds.

The eighteenth-century German scholar Heinrich Grellmann claimed that 'a Gypsy never marries a person who is not of the true Gypsy breed',[52] but this was evidently false. Victorian commentators also claimed that 'they marry within the line of consanguinity', but this was by no means the rule.[53] John Clare's familiarity with Gypsies in early nineteenth-century Northamptonshire taught him that 'the young girls...sometimes marry with the villagers, but it is very rarely', though it was more common for 'village clowns...to go away with the Gypsy girls'.[54] The pedigrees so assiduously constructed by Gypsylorists contained dozens of examples of marriages between *gorgios* and Gypsies, though no major dilution of Gypsy identity.[55] There is no telling to what degree the Gypsies kept to themselves, or opened their tents to outsiders. Endogamy seems to have been the norm, but neither racial purity nor genealogical inbreeding was essential to Gypsy social reproduction.

Though modern observers found evidence of marrying out, and of the incorporation of non-Gypsy spouses, most marriages took place within the Gypsy–Traveller community, between partners who had known each other from childhood.[56] Gypsies apparently disapproved of marriages with *gorgios*, unless the new spouse could conform to a Gypsy lifestyle. Judith Okely reported that 'ethnic endogamy was both the ideal and the practice of the majority of travelling families who recognized themselves as Gypsies' in the 1970s.[57] Gypsies bred Gypsies, and transmitted their culture through a loose lineal descent.

Though it is sometimes claimed that Gypsies preserved their inherited customs from time immemorial, their intimate beliefs and practices were mostly invisible to outsiders before the modern era. Nobody until the nineteenth century knew that Gypsies adhered to rituals and taboos about purity and pollution. The early modern record is silent in this regard. Later reports of funeral practices involving the burning or destruction of possessions were simply regarded as strange. Only recent observers with extraordinary access learned about items that were ritually unclean (*mockadi*), or the dangers of *mulo* (ghosts).[58]

The modern ethnographic record of Gypsy taboos and practices strengthens belief that they were (and are) a people, rather than a concept. The evidence, however, is both theoretically and empirically problematic. It is hard to gauge the meaning, significance, and vitality of customs that were internal to the group or closed to outside observation. Scholarly accounts inevitably depend upon inference, presumption, or shades of interpretation.

However, we can at least say that observation of similar purity protocols among Gypsies in Europe and America indicates their importance as cultural traits across the Gypsy diaspora.[59]

Employments and Avocations

Pre-modern England encountered Gypsies as itinerant entertainers, dancers, or showmen; petty traders, horse-dealers, and performers of odd jobs; and sometimes as carriers or fences of stolen goods. Popular culture made them pickpockets, thieves, and masters of deceit, given to pilferage, and petty crime, though Gypsies were by no means the only offenders in this regard. Above all, Gypsies were renowned as tellers of destinies, or deceitful pretenders at divination.

The Tudor statutes against Gypsies denounced them for their 'naughty, idle and ungodly life' and their 'idle and false trade, conversation and behaviour', and accused them of 'using no craft nor fact of merchandize'.[60] Popular commentators similarly branded them lazy and good for nothing. The eighteenth-century authority Grellmann extended a long tradition by commenting on Gypsy 'indolence'.[61] More recent commentators have called them parasites. Yet, notwithstanding these strictures, Gypsies worked hard to secure their living. They occupied a niche in the economy of wayfaring as makers and menders of household equipment, and dealers in horses, and in casual and seasonal employment. Versatile and self-reliant, they were purposeful travellers, not mindless wanderers, who followed circuits of sociability, business, and opportunity. Gypsies were fixtures at fairs.[62] Early Gypsies seem to have ranged widely across long distances, but later groups travelled within narrower local areas.

By the nineteenth century the Gypsy economy had diversified to include handicrafts and repairs, basketry, straw-work, metalwork, and tinkering. In an age when little was thrown away, damaged pots, pans, china, and chairs needed mending, and Gypsies excelled in these tasks. John Hoyland's list of twenty-six families of Gypsies in the London area in 1815 finds them engaged in tinkering, knife-grinding, chair-bottoming, basket-making, wire-working, bellows-mending, rat-catching, street trading, and fiddling.[63] Colonel John Staples Harriot, who knew Gypsies in early nineteenth-century Hampshire, listed 'their employments, avocations and customs' as follows:

1. Basket and mat making; fabricating needles, bodkins, nets, carpets, sieves, besoms, and foot-bosses; grinding and cutlery; turning or making troughs, trenchers, dishes, and spoons; farriery and horse-dealing; braziery; and in the summer they are occasionally employed in the fields, reaping, weeding, and hop-picking. 2. Feats of dexterity, as jugglers' tricks, wrestling, single stick, dancing, singing, and music. 3. Palmistry and soothsaying, fortune-telling, astrology, chiromancy, and exorcism. 4. Begging, poaching, pilfering, and stealing: although, on the latter head, it may be observed that they are countenanced by their more settled neighbours.[64]

Other observers mention knife-grinding, razor-sharpening, bellows-mending, and the manufacture of wooden skewers, pins, and clothes pegs, as well as hawking of trinkets and pottery seconds. Little of this work required much capital or equipment, and the raw materials were often readily available from woodland or hedges. The Victorian Gypsies observed by Charles Leland and George Smith included licensed hawkers, opportunistic traders, simple craftsmen, and entertainers. They peddled pottery, made and sold pegs and baskets, dealt in horses, and operated coconut shies and 'knock-'em-downs' at fairs and races.[65] Others foraged for furze roots to make handles for walking sticks and umbrellas, or gathered wild flowers, ferns, and ornamental foliage, which they sold to Covent Garden middlemen.[66] Since little of this work was illegal (apart from trespass, poaching, and deceptive fortune-telling), it is barely noticed in the records of the courts and the press, which constitute the bulk of the Gypsy archive. The descriptions are always external, a gazing-in or a looking-down, by educated, clerical, or professional observers.

'How do they live?' was an often-asked question, and 'the frequent losses of sheep, lambs, and poultry' suggested an answer.[67] Gypsies were credited with the deaths of farm animals—for example, by cramming wool down the throat of a sheep to make it suffocate—so that they could obtain the carcass for a feast.[68] Multiple nefarious practices were laid at their door. The 'mottled avocations' of the Gypsy patriarch Joseph Lee, who died in the New Forest aged 86 in 1844, allegedly included 'smuggling, deer stealing, poaching, and occasionally selling a few ponies at the various fairs'.[69] Gypsies were renowned for their knowledge of horses, and were not immune from charges of 'cokering', the alteration of an animal's health or appearance for deceitful advantage. Unscrupulous dealers could reportedly mask an animal's defects, induce lameness or sickness to alter its value, or change its colour or condition to hide its identity. They were even known to have gelded a stallion to deceive former owners or prospective purchasers.[70]

Gypsies were occasionally accused of obtaining money by false pretences, though perhaps no more frequently than other criminal chancers. A police report from 1839 claimed that the Gypsies 'make rings out of brass buttons and pewter, and the wives sell them for gold and silver'. Reports of such deceptions appeared from time to time in the press.[71] Several were accused of 'ringing the changes', a sleight of hand defrauding shopkeepers by shuffling coins and banknotes. A scam repeated in several nineteenth-century accounts involved Gypsies bargaining to buy food and supplies for an upcoming festivity, thereby securing good will, then putting the deal on hold while swindling the supplier with worthless or overpriced trinkets.

Popular culture represented Gypsies as foragers and pilferers, who found little difficulty in feeding their families. They were renowned, and sometimes envied, for their stores of 'good cheer'. It was rare for anyone to suggest that Gypsies were undernourished. In early modern Somerset, it was said, instead of scattering before the law, 'they did roast all kinds of good meat'.[72] The wildlife and woodland of rural England provided foodstuffs for those who knew how to use them, and farmland yielded bounty for gleaning, poaching, or theft. England teemed with birds and rabbits, which could be converted into food. The cooking of hedgehogs is well attested in nineteenth-century accounts, while badger ham is rated delicious by those who have tried it. Outside the agrarian market economy, with no visible means of support, 'they boast that they can make bread of beans, of acorns, nay of knots of straws rather than they will starve', wrote the seventeenth-century preacher John Randol.[73] Heinrich Grellmann thought that Gypsies ate carrion, and the late Hanoverian Quaker John Hoyland was excited to learn that Gypsies in England would eat 'animals they might find dead on the road', an observation that corresponded 'exactly with that of the Continental Gypsies', as related by the German author.[74] Several stories tell of Gypsies making it appear that a sheep or pig they had killed died of natural causes, then begging or scrounging the carcass from the farmer they had cheated.[75]

Gypsy resourcefulness was legendary, filling pots, plates, and stomachs. They were never short of 'beef or bacon, geese or hens', declared a popular ballad.[76] By imposing on gullible countryfolk, one Restoration treatise asserted, 'here they get a sheep, there a goat, here a kid, there a pig or a young calf: sometimes wine, oil, butter, pulse, milk, cheese, eggs, hens, wool, linen, and money; as it were plunder and prey upon the whole country where they go, returning home laden with the rich spoils of their villainy'.[77] If we take accounts like this at face value, then an inundation of Gypsies could clearly have had a deleterious effect on the local rural economy.

However, many Gypsies did in fact have money, earned from fortune-telling and trade, and could purchase their meat, bread, beer, and shelter, rather than acquire it by other, less legal, means. The Squires family of the eighteenth century, for example, paid cash for their meat and poultry, tobacco, tea, gin, and lodgings.

Visitors interested in Gypsies sometimes sat by their fires. John Clare described their 'two forked sticks with cordage tied', which held their pot above a fire of 'pilfer'd fuel'.[78] An observer in the Lake District described their 'kettle or pan' suspended by a chain from a tripod of poles. 'For seats they roll around the fire large stones, and for table they make use of their knees... When they retire to rest, they spread straw beneath their carts, and cover it with blankets. Under these coverings they repose themselves unmindful of storms or tempests.'[79] Charles Leland, Francis Groome, and others shared tobacco, tea, snail soup, and baked hedgehog in Gypsy camps, using the occasion to learn Romani.[80] Detailed ethnographic commentary of this sort was rare before the age of Victorian Gypsylorism, when much of a Gypsy's diet could be harvested, caught, or foraged.

Today's Gypsy economy appears to be as varied as ever. Observers describe a host of opportunist activities, trading, scrap-dealing, small-scale contracting, fixing things.[81] By the late twentieth century Gypsies were more likely to trade machinery than animals, more likely to fix roofs than make clothes pegs. Some of the skill involved in 'cokering' a horse may have transferred to extending the life and raising the value of old cars. Reputation placed Gypsies outside the formal economy, with a casual attitude to paperwork, but reputation is often undeserved.

It cannot be overemphasized that not all Gypsies were alike, and that the Gypsy community included every variety of wealth and poverty, honesty and dishonesty, probity and deceit. Journalists were often surprised that members of 'the Gypsy fraternity' had cash in hand to pay fines and costs imposed for vagrancy or transportation offences. Their various enterprises, shady or legitimate, allowed some Gypsy families to spend lavishly on weddings and funerals, while others were reduced to the workhouse. Generalizations about Gypsies were invariably wrong.

Gypsies and Vagrants

Since some scholars still insist that Gypsies were simply a substream of vagrants, or that Gypsy and other itinerant identities merged,[82] it may be useful to review more of the characteristics that historically made Gypsies Gypsies. Notwithstanding the porosity, ambivalence, and constructedness of Gypsy identity, it may be possible to delineate some of the features that helped people differentiate them from vagrants and other undesirables. It is neither essentialist nor primordialist to recognize the distinctiveness, as well as the fluidity, of Gypsy ethnicity.

Gypsies and vagrants differed in their social presentation, their legal position, and the cultural sympathies they elicited. Just because the words used to describe them have been loaded with meaning and layered with signification does not mean that Gypsies and vagrants were simply figures of discourse. There was an underlying social reality, a lived experience that coped with the exigencies of eating and sleeping, living and dying. Villagers, householders, and local officials reacted differently to Gypsies and vagrants because they were different kinds of people. Both Gypsies and vagrants were socially constructed, yet both were real presences on England's roads. Vagrants may have been casualties of demographic and social structural change, but Gypsies were heirs to a tradition, to which their offspring were acculturated and socialized.

Every economic system has casualties, and every population has vagrants, temporary or permanent dropouts who are unable to find work or are morally or constitutionally disinclined to seek it. Distinctions between the deserving poor and the feckless poor were well established, separating those who were indigent through little fault of their own from those deemed idle, evil, and worthless. Old age, illness, and disability reduced people to dependency, while economic depressions and dislocations pushed people into itinerancy. The rising population and increasing economic polarization of the sixteenth and early seventeenth century drove a growing number over the edge. Eighteenth- and nineteenth-century depressions added to the population of the migrant and the homeless. Some were rogues with criminal proclivities, and many were identified as beggars. A series of Acts of Parliament from 'An acte against vacabounds and beggars' in 1495 to 'An act for the punishment of idle and disorderly persons, and rogues and vagabonds' in 1824 set forth the legal and administrative response to vagrancy, roguery, and poverty, placing primary responsibility on the local parish.[83] Modern welfare systems provide more comprehensive coverage, but are still biased in favour of people deemed responsible and settled.

Gypsies posed a challenge to these arrangements, at first because they arrived as outsiders, and always because of their deviant resourcefulness and marginality. They were neither unemployed nor seekers of employment, but supported themselves by a variety of skills and mysteries. They usually had money, and where necessary paid their way. Only on the rarest of occasions was a Gypsy accused of begging. They did not fit the provisions of the vagrancy laws, though after Gypsies were established in England the vagrancy laws expanded to include them. Hence the Elizabethan statute of 1598 added persons 'wandering and pretending themselves to be Egyptians, or wandering in the habit, form or attire of counterfeit Egyptians' to a long list of offenders 'deemed rogues, vagabonds and sturdy beggars'.[84] Similar phrasing in later statutes made Gypsies and vagrants subject to the same provisions, but never identified the one with other. Any notion that vagrants would turn Gypsy and 'counterfeit cultural difference in order to evade anti-vagrant legislation' is entirely unfounded. It is, indeed, absurd to imagine, as have some literary scholars, that Gypsies enjoyed 'protected status', that 'they could not be prosecuted as vagrants', or that becoming a Gypsy placed one 'beyond the law's reach'.[85] The vast majority of vagrants were likely to have been baptized, could claim parishes of origin, and were eligible for Christian burial. Gypsies, by contrast, were notoriously remote from the benefits and obligations of the early modern church and state.

Gypsies were uniquely vulnerable to strictures and sanctions that were never designed for mere vagrants or other subjects. The statutes of 1531, 1554, and 1563, as we have seen, made so-called Egyptians liable to exclusion, expulsion, confiscation, and criminalization by virtue of who they were.[86] These laws were used only sparingly, and were mostly forgotten by the mid-seventeenth century, but they exposed Gypsies to risks of arrest and prosecution that were rarely experienced by other itinerants. Even after those laws had been repealed, some magistrates continued to express the view that Gypsies, qua Gypsies, deserved to be punished.[87]

From the sixteenth century to the nineteenth, the business, activity, and avocations of Gypsies set them apart. Few other travellers matched the Gypsies' skills or practised their itinerant crafts, and very few shared their reputation for fortune-telling. People found them interesting, and sometimes useful, as well as menacing and repulsive. Nobody but ne'r-do-wells welcomed vagrants into their communities, but Gypsies attracted a variety of favours and clients. Some people even admired them and emulated them; but Gypsies also stimulated a visceral hostility, sharper and more extreme than conventional disdain for vagrants and vagabonds.

Bands of Gypsies were differently constituted from other gatherings of itinerants. They travelled in family groups, often with large numbers of children, often in company with kin. Vagrants, on the other hand, were more likely to be single, or to rove in small and mostly adult clusters. The distinction drawn in the late Victorian census between tramps and seasonal workers sleeping rough, and Gypsy families in vans and tents, seemed to perpetuate this pattern. Whereas many of the Gypsies, perhaps most, were born into Gypsy families, and experienced a lifetime of acculturation, vagrants included many who had fallen on hard times, or otherwise found themselves in distress, for whom travel was a strategy for survival. Gypsies were also distinguished from vagrants by their equipage, gear, and accoutrements. They were more likely to travel with horses and baggage, more likely to have money at their disposal, more likely to be respectably dressed. Even more important than behaviour and lifestyle were cultural characteristics such as language and values, which were specific to the Gypsy heritage.

Speaking Gypsy

The Gypsy use of the Angloromani language, with a vocabulary rich in Romani words, was another marker of difference. Non-Gypsies may have picked up a few Romani words, and incorporated them as slang, but there was very little correspondence between the Gypsy tongue and underworld cant. The preservation of an exotic language, over multiple generations, is a sign of cultural separateness and cultural survival. Its loss in more recent years bespeaks another modulation in Gypsy identity.

Victorian Gypsylorists believed that knowledge of the Romani language was the 'principal badge of membership' and 'the primary test of Gypsydom'.[88] Some modern analysts agree that language is the key 'marker and badge' of Roma ethnic identity, and that language has replaced blood as the test of authenticity.[89] That may be true in parts of Eastern Europe, where language, culture, and ethnicity are closely entwined, but it does not necessarily apply historically within the British Isles. Early Tudor Gypsies appear to have spoken an inflected Romani, but over time their language changed. By the seventeenth century, it seems, an anglicized Romani (Angloromani) was in use, combining Romani words and phrases with English syntax and grammar. Angloromani provided a vocabulary of difference, a restricted code that was functionally similar but linguistically distinct from the argot or cant of the criminal underworld.[90] Nearly all the Gypsies that people encountered spoke serviceable English, for without it they could not trade or tell fortunes.

To what degree they spoke Romani among themselves, and passed that ability to their offspring, remains a mystery. By the nineteenth century, though
still collectable, the language was in severe decline; in the course of the
twentieth century it shrank to little more than a relic.

Andrew Boorde's *Fyrst Boke of the Introduction of Knowledge* preserved
fragments of inflected Romani from the reign of Henry VIII.[91] Few other
transcriptions are known before the seventeenth century, by which time the
language had changed. The famous cony-catching pamphlets, which did so
much to falsify the image of Gypsies, completely misrepresented their speech.
The early Elizabethan official Thomas Harman identified the 'unlawful language' of the 'rascal rabblement' of vagabonds as 'pedlar's French, or canting',
and believed that it 'began within these thirty years, little above'. His examples
of 'the lewd, lousy language of these loitering lusks and lazy lorels' was
clearly based on English. With words like 'fambles' for hands, 'stampers' for
shoes, 'bung' for purse, 'bouse' for drink, and 'prancer' for a horse, Harman's
list sampled the argot of cant, but contained not a word of Romani. (More
appropriate Romani words would have been *vast* or *dokrapen, chakka, putsi,
pani*, and *grah*.) Either Harman had no acquaintance with Romani-speaking
Gypsies, or the language was not spoken in his presence.[92] His *Caveat for
Commen Cursetors Vulgarely Called Vagabones* (1567) may have been the source
for Sir Thomas Smith's remark in 1568 that among Gypsies 'a different and
distinct language is current, unknown to others and serving only themselves
and their impostures'.[93] And it may have launched a tradition that denied
authenticity to the speech of Gypsies. William Harrison's debt to Harman is
explicit when he notes in his 'Description of England' (1577) that counterfeit Egyptians speak with 'a great number of odd words of their own devising, without all order or reason; and yet such is it as none but themselves are
able to understand'.[94] These authors recognized that Gypsies spoke strangely,
but shed no light on the actual language they used.

Jacobean pamphleteers referred to England's Egyptians 'framing to themselves an unknown language' of 'gibberish or gibble gabble', but left few
clues to its character or content.[95] Thomas Dekker knew it only as 'pedlar's
French' 'or canting'. The criminal fraternity, he believed, invented this vocabulary to keep their dealings secret from spies or outsiders. Dekker's dictionary
of canting was no more extensive than Harman's, though arranged alpha-
betically and accompanied by a canting song.[96] Indeed, it was entirely
dependent on Harman, according to Dekker's contemporary Samuel Rid,
who offered his own examples of 'the right Egyptian language', which

rogues adopted to hide 'their cozening, knaveries, and villainies'.[97] Ignorance of the use of Romani, and the misidentification of Gypsy speech as cant, were symptomatic and long-lasting errors.

It was illegal, by Elizabethan legislation, to adopt the 'counterfeit speech' of 'counterfeit Egyptians', but officials were ignorant of its elements. Though their peculiar language distinguished Gypsies from ordinary itinerants, and was technically grounds for prosecution, it was rarely mentioned by judicial authorities. Gypsies were sometimes detained for 'using certain disguised apparel and forged speech, contrary to the laws and statutes of this realm', but few details of that 'forged speech' were recorded.[98]

Archival sources reveal almost nothing about the speech of Gypsies until the remarkable testimony in Hampshire in 1616 of 'such canting words as the counterfeit Egyptians use amongst themselves as their language'. This listing of more than a hundred Romani words and phrases would have remained hidden but for the diligence of officials at Winchester gaol.[99] Thereafter, for many years, the record is mostly silent. Court records contain hints and fragments, while literary sources are as unreliable as ever. Laconic entries refer to Gypsy use of a 'strange' and incomprehensible language, but none of that speech was transcribed.[100]

Later seventeenth century sources echoed the vulgarities of cony-catching, foisting on Gypsies 'a barbarous language more confused than all the dialects of Babel, which they call canting'.[101] They used canting, wrote Thomas Tryon, to 'bewitch poor people to admire and run after them', and 'to juggle your money out of your pockets. For to gain the greater veneration and esteem, they have invented abundance of hard words, or speak in unknown tongues, making the people believe thereby, that they know the more of God and nature.' It was not only a device for secret communication, by this argument, but an instrument of deceit, part of the *modus operandi* of mystification.[102]

Restoration fiction described how this canting or thieves' slang could be learned. When Richard Head's *English Rogue* joined a Gypsy company, his initiation supposedly included language lessons. He learned to say 'boose' for drink and 'bouzing ken' for an alehouse, 'bleating cheat' for a sheep, 'cackling cheat' for a chicken, 'cove' for a man, 'doxy' for a wench, 'glimmer' for fire, and 'prigger of prancers' for a horse thief. All were established words of low-life cant, but none was associated with Romani. Either the Gypsies had forgotten their original language by Head's time, or, more likely, he had no idea how Gypsies communicated among themselves.[103]

Historical linguists talk of dialects and subdialects, lexicons and sociolects, as well as jargon, idiom, patois, and slang, but their use among eighteenth-century Gypsies is unknown. Angloromani may have continued as a private supplementary tongue, and may have been invigorated by Romani-speaking immigrants from Europe, but no documentation survives. Joseph Addison's foil Sir Roger de Coverly, in the *Spectator* in 1711, was no better informed than Dekker a century earlier, denouncing 'this race of vermin' of Gypsies for speaking 'uncouth gibberish' as well as picking pockets.[104] The *Discoveries* of the villainous John Poulter, published after his execution in 1753, report that 'Gypsies are a people that talk Romney, that is, a cant that nobody understands but themselves'. This may be the earliest English reference to the language as Romani, but no examples were provided.[105] 'You must cant to her, talk Gypsy to her', one alehouse drinker advised another when attempting conversation with the Gypsy Mary Squires in 1753. But nowhere in the extensive testimony about her travels does Mary Squires use any language but English.[106]

International interest in the language of Gypsies quickened at the end of the eighteenth century after German philologists demonstrated its Indic roots. Linguistic analysis strongly indicated that the Gypsies were remnants of a Romani diaspora, not just off-scourings of an English proletariat.[107] But, despite the demonstration of the Indian origins of the Gypsy language, the belief persisted that it was nothing but cant. Mary Saxby (1738–1801), who claimed to have run off with the Gypsies, and to have borne a child by one of them, related that she acquired their manners 'and could use their cant terms fluently'.[108] The poet John Clare (1793–1864) made an effort to learn the 'mystic language' of the Gypsies with whom he socialized, but concluded that it was 'nothing more than things called by slang names like village provincialisms, and that no two tribes spoke the same dialect exactly'.[109] The constable of Frome, Somerset, related how Gypsy women 'struck up in their cant phrases' when he broke up their camp in 1814, and he could not tell if they were summoning their husbands or warning them to take cover.[110]

According to a police informant in 1839, there were different sorts of cant among beggars, thieves, and Gypsies, and 'the Gypsies have a cant word for every word they speak'.[111] Outsiders heard it on rare occasions, such as the outdoor ceremony in 1842 when the New Forest Gypsies expelled an offender, and their leader 'addressed the culprit for nearly an hour, but in a tongue that was perfectly strange to the bystanders',[112] or at the gathering of Lees and Boswells in Cheshire in 1882, when wedding toasts 'were proposed in the Romany dialect'.[113]

Writing his novel about Gypsies, Walter Scott attempted to penetrate 'that great mystery, their language', but found it 'impossible to procure a few words'. Corresponding with the Gypsy expert Walter Simson, he expressed uncertainty 'whether it is likely to prove really a corrupt eastern dialect, or whether it has degenerated into a mere jargon'. Scott had some familiarity with 'the cant language, or slang, used by thieves or flash men', but remained unsure that 'the Gypsies have a distinct and proper language' of their own. 'It would be important to know', he wrote to Simson, 'whether they have a real language, with the usual parts of speech, or whether they have a collection of nouns, combined by our own language'. Without knowing it, Scott was distinguishing 'deep' or inflected Romani from Angloromani, which employed English grammar. Resolving the matter among Gypsies would be difficult, Scott acknowledged, because 'the knowledge of their language is the secret' of which they were most protective.[114]

The most persuasive evidence for the persistence of a Gypsy language across multiple generations is the discovery of its apparent vitality by nineteenth-century evangelicals and Gypsylorists. Visiting Gypsy camps in Northamptonshire in 1814, the Quaker John Hoyland discovered that 'the Gypsies really had a language peculiar to themselves', which was spoken by children and adults 'with great fluency'. Equipped with a vocabulary taken from Grellmann, augmented by gleanings from British officials in India, Hoyland was delighted to discover that he could communicate with Gypsies in Essex. The more that was learned of the Gypsy vocabulary the more it seemed to confirm their Indian origin.[115]

A succession of Victorian philanthropists and Gypsylorists competed to compile the most comprehensive lists of Gypsy words and phrases before they were forever lost. Most believed that the Gypsies 'spoke English and Gypsy indiscriminately among each other', or used Romani only 'in their own households and among their kindred'.[116] Most believed that the language was fast disappearing. By the 1870s it was matter of urgency, perhaps the last chance, to preserve 'specimens of a rapidly-vanishing language . . . a language in extreme decay'. Considering himself 'a boro rye rakkerin Romanis' ('a true expert speaking Romani'), Charles Leland was greatly grieved that so many Gypsies were ignorant of their language, 'which I myself, albeit a stranger, knew very well and would fain teach them'.[117]

LaterVictorian authors found the Gypsy language in 'a state of rapid deteri-
oration', though it survived among traditionalists. Most English Gypsies had
lost their use of Romani or spoke only fragments and remnants. Francis
Groome observed how few of his Gypsy friends could manage 'deep'
Romani, and even George Smith of Coalville noted how very few Gypsies
could *rocker* a little.[118] The fortune-teller Lucy Lee told a journalist in 1895,
'we all speak Romany among ourselves, though the language and those who
use it are dying out fast'.[119] The brothers Joshua, Esau, and Gus Gray, described
as remnants of 'the true Romany breed' in late-Victorian East Anglia, 'seldom
or never used [the ancient tongue] amongst themselves', though they had
picked it up from their parents. They still found it useful sometimes when
engaged in horse-dealing, and on one occasion, when Greek Gypsies were
travelling across England, 'the old Romany tongue' provided a workable *lingua
franca*.[120] The 'deepest' Romani in the 1890s apparently survived among isolated Welsh Gypsies, especially the family of Abraham Wood.[121] Within a
generation or two it would be gone.

Experts report that 'the indigenous variety of Romani with Indic grammar' became extinct by the 1920s, but that 'Angloromani' endured as 'a special
lexis' that mixed a Romani vocabulary with English grammatical forms. It
served, some suggest, as a 'lexical reservoir' and 'a conversational device',
though the number of speakers was unknown. Anthropological fieldwork-
ers in the 1970s found little more than a miscellany of remnant words and
phrases, some buried deep in memory.[122]

Oral history collected at the end of the twentieth century found considerable interest in the Romani language among Gypsies in Yorkshire, but
diminished ability to speak it. One young member of the Lee family, who
took pride in being 'Romanichal', recalled that his grandfather Nelson
Lee 'could speak Romany fluent…the real old stuff'. Bobby Lee, a member of the next generation, who described himself as 'a full Gypsy, a full
Lee', claimed knowledge of Romani, but his son 'young' Bobby Lee, born
in 1956, commented that 'it's not used at all now, really, just odds and ends
and bits and bats… it's a thing of the past now'.[123] Keywords such as *mush*,
chavo, kushti, romanichal, gorgio, rocker, dukker, mockadi, mulo, vardo, and a
couple of dozen more, remained in common use, and found some cur-
rency outside the Romany Gypsy community.[124] Linguists have recorded
several thousand words and expressions from users of Angloromani,
though most come from historical rather than living informants.[125] The
language may have received stimulus from recent academic study, as well

as from the arrival in England of Romani speakers from other parts of Europe.[126]

Gypsy Fortunes

Fortune-telling was, historically, the quintessential activity of Gypsy women, and perhaps their primary source of income. Their boast was to discern the future, not to shape it, so they mostly avoided spells or magic that might be construed as witchcraft. From the sixteenth century to the nineteenth, Gypsy fortune-tellers offered some of the counselling and therapeutic services commonly associated with 'cunning folk' or village 'wise women'. They advised on matters of the heart, and indicated the location of lost or stolen goods. It mattered little whether Gypsies truly possessed arcane knowledge, so long as people credited them with skill in the 'crafty sciences' and 'the dark and secret mysteries of nature'.[127] Despite repeated strictures that their 'art is impudence and lying',[128] the popular belief persisted that Gypsies possessed supernatural powers that enabled them to see the future, warn of ill fortune, or assist in the recovery of hidden treasure. Only the most gullible

Figure 12. Fortune-Teller, Appleby Fair, 2015

believed that Gypsy women could 'rule the planets' to achieve the multiplication of wealth.

Early modern commentators reported that 'the multitude' of 'ignorant
common people' flocked about the Gypsies when they arrived in a parish,
and were 'delighted' to be told their futures. Young people and servants, in
particular, patronized Gypsy women who used palmistry and physiognomy,
'to make their prognostics concerning the strength, health, disposition and
several events of any man's life'.[129] Later sources reported continuing gullibility, especially among people who were young, poorly educated, or simple
minded. It was shocking, wrote a stream of Victorian commentators, that
people in this modern age 'should be found credulous enough to put faith
in these imposters'.[130] Religious instructors had long denounced fortune-
telling as a mocking of God, who alone knew how the future would unfold.
'Fortune tellers...do impiously derogate from God, and from his providence', declared the Jacobean minister Edward Elton. It was 'a kind of cozenage, and the devil therein sought to', William Slatyer concurred in the
1640s.[131] It was desertion of faith, preached the Hanoverian minister William
Davy, 'to trust in uncertain tokens and lying vanities' of the kind purveyed
by fortune-tellers.[132] It was 'folly and wickedness' to encourage Gypsy
fortune-telling, preached the early nineteenth-century 'advocate' of Gypsies
James Crabb.[133]

Though Gypsies may have advertised their skills and solicited customers,
their reputations preceded them, and people *expected* Gypsies to be able to
read their hands. Samuel Pepys was amused when his wife and her companions went 'to see the Gypsies at Lambeth and have their fortunes told', but
he himself found it hard to resist when encountering 'some Gypsies who
would needs tell me my fortune' for the price of ninepence.[134] One of the
witnesses to the travels of Mary Squires 'asked her if she could tell fortunes;
she said no, she was no fortune teller'. But on other occasions she told fortunes for twopence.[135] The daughters of the vicar of Wakefield, in the eighteenth-century novel of that name, paid a shilling apiece to be told their
futures, which of course, being fiction, came true.[136] Higher up the social
scale, the adulteress Mary Eleanor Bowes, Countess of Strathmore, admitted
in 1784 to consulting 'some Gypsies in a barn three summers ago, at Paul's
Walden [Hertfordshire], and three near there at different sets'. As much as
any troubled young woman, the countess wanted to know her future, and
which of her lovers loved her best.[137] When William Cobbett encountered
Gypsies in 1822, it was he, not they, who initiated talk of fortune-telling.[138]

As soon as the process began, however, the fortune-teller took control, in a temporary inversion of customary relationships of gender and power.

Nineteenth-century fortune-tellers were at greater risk of prosecution than their Tudor and Stuart predecessors. The legislation of 1736 that repealed the earlier witchcraft statutes enacted a new clause that made fortune-telling a crime. The law was designed to protect 'ignorant persons' from being 'deluded and defrauded' by pretended 'arts and powers', and provided a spell in the pillory and a year of imprisonment for any who 'undertake to tell fortunes'.[139] Gypsy fortune-tellers were rarely charged under this Act, but the law gave magistrates a weapon to use against outrageous offenders. More potent because more widely applied was the Vagrancy Act of 1824, which treated 'every person pretending or professing to tell fortunes, or using any subtle craft, means, or device, by palmistry or otherwise, to deceive or impose on any of [the monarch's] subjects', as a rogue and vagabond.[140] It was under this Act that the Gypsy Leticia Buss was imprisoned for a month in Yorkshire in 1838 for 'vagrancy and offering to tell fortunes'.[141] Ann Nichols, described as 'one of the Gypsy tribe and a pest to society', was sentenced to a month at hard labour for 'defrauding a servant girl out of two half sovereigns and one half crown, under pretense of telling her her fortune' in Sussex in 1839.[142] Almost a century later the Vagrancy Act was still being used to bring charges against fortune-tellers at Bournemouth in 1934.[143]

Victorian newspapers denounced both the deceptiveness of Gypsy prognosticators and the folly of people who paid them money. Magistrates charged fortune-tellers with 'imposing upon the credulous', but the Gypsies could argue that their dealings were consensual. When the Gypsy Rose Lee was charged at Greenwich in April 1841 for telling fortunes at Blackheath, she protested in court: 'I am innocent, your worship. The lady asked me to tell her fortune, and forced the money into my hand.' Unpersuaded, the judge sentenced her to fourteen days on the treadmill in the Brixton house of correction, saying she was lucky not to have received three months at hard labour.[144]

Newly emergent seaside resorts, at Blackpool, Clacton, and elsewhere, sprouted clusters of fortune-telling tents, often patronized by holidaymakers but sometimes raided by the police.[145] The crackdown prompted an unresolved debate about the justice of punishing Gypsy fortune-tellers while the 'professional medium' or the fashionable 'drawing-room fortune teller' could operate with impunity. Fortune-telling that was 'just a bit of fun' could be regarded as harmless, but not if it affected people's lives and pockets.[146]

There are still modern Gypsies, and perhaps pseudo-gypsies, who make a living as fortune tellers. One, whose sign declares her 'A True Born Romany Gypsy' is a fixture at gatherings like Appleby Fair. There is still money to be made, and expectations to be met, by 'dukkering'. But many among the Romany Gypsy community have given it up. Anthropological observation in the 1970s showed that some of the women who went out hawking found willing clients for 'their allegedly magical powers of clairvoyance', but fortune-telling had become a secondary activity.[147] It has all but disappeared in more recent accounts of the livelihoods of Gypsy and Traveller women.[148] The Gypsy Sakie Lee recalled in Yorkshire in 2000 that 'dukkering' or fortune-telling 'would be handed down from centuries and centuries...my mum can, well not now...she's give it all up. My sisters didn't want to know nothing.' Another member of the Lee family, who declared herself a Christian, rejected the art, saying 'its wicked, telling people things'.[149]

A special category of fortune-telling commanded the attention of the police and the press because of the criminal ingenuity of its adepts and the covetous simplicity of its victims. In dozens of examples from the sixteenth to the twentieth centuries, a fortune-teller gained the confidence of a servant or householder and told them that they were due for good fortune. When the victims sought further details, they would be instructed to provide a sample of jewelry, plate, or money to act as seed or investment. This usually involved a second visit to the house, to raise the stakes, and for the trickster to supervise the wrapping and hiding of the selected articles or money. Special spells and incantations would then be deployed, with stories of supernatural helpers, requiring large degrees of patience and trust. Needless to say, when the victim went to retrieve the valuables, they found them switched for dross or rubbish, no miraculous new wealth, and the fortune-teller well out of sight. One reason for its recurrence was that the fortune trick so often worked, with a seemingly endless supply of dupes to be swindled. The tricksters were not always Gypsies, though Gypsies were perennially blamed for the scam.

In America too, where English Gypsies travelled in the 1850s, the fortune trick found willing victims. Around Christmas 1852 a Gypsy woman persuaded a farmer at West River, Maryland, to gather $800 in a handkerchief to draw out hidden money. After 'sundry cabalistic words and doings', she said the sum was not sufficient, so the farmer borrowed more, and put $1,035 into a 'magic trunk', which miraculously disappeared.[150] When the same band of Gypsies showed up at Tully, New York, about eighteen miles south of Syracuse, in May 1853, 'the queen of the troop', Betsy Cooper, tried the trick again and earned $485 more. This time her luck ran out, and she was arrested, but reports from Ohio in 1854 showed similar deceptions being deployed.[151] It was easy money for the Gypsies, for once the gull was hooked the *bori hokani* almost always worked.

The supposedly rational, educated, worldly society of twentieth-century Britain had not seen the last of the fortune trick. The 'great credulity' of a Lancashire woman in 1912 persuaded her to give £13 to a Gypsy named Elsie Leah Lovell, who promised 'plenty of money coming to her'. In 1915 a domestic servant at Windsor, Berkshire, gave £4 10s. to the Gypsy fortune-teller Sarah Greenfield, in hopes of 'strengthening' her planet. A palmist billed as 'the original Gypsy Leah' defrauded an Exeter man of £300 in 1926 by promising to bring back the wife who had left him. Dealing with a similar fraud in North Wales in 1928, the lawyer for the Gypsy Miranda Evans said 'that if people had sufficient credulity to part with their money in this way, they had only themselves to blame'.[152]

More cases came to light in the decade following the Second World War. In 1948 a village shopkeeper in South Wales lost nearly £2,000 to the Gypsy Geraldine Worrall, who promised her a husband and a fortune. In 1950 Rosina Smith, 'a Gypsy living in a caravan at Rashwood, near Droitwich', obtained £22 1s. and a pair of earrings from a woman at Mosely, Worcestershire, by claiming that she could put her unlucky house 'under a planet, and remove the curse'. In 1954 a Gypsy 'known as Rose Mary Ann Lee, but actually named Mrs Lucy Price', obtained £905 from a shopkeeper at Ipswich, Suffolk, by persuading her that she 'had consulted the crystal' and could 'lift the veil' to make her wishes come true.[153] Modern accounts of Gypsy culture rarely remark on these cases, perhaps out of care not to discredit the community or to sensationalize the subject. Though infrequent and atypical, they belong to an ancient tradition associating Gypsies with supernatural power and a penchant for deception.

Stealing Children

It was long believed, and in some quarters may still be credited, that Gypsies stole children, and sometimes switched abducted babies for their own. Their alleged propensity for kidnapping was part of an international black legend that rendered Gypsies guilty of all manner of crimes and villainies. The legend had deep roots in popular anxiety and was nourished in early modern Europe by rumour and fiction. It flourished again in the nineteenth century, and still reappears from time to time in sensational media panics. It is grimly ironic that the only documented cases of abduction in modern times involved not Gypsy kidnappers stealing babies, but police and protection officers removing children from Gypsy and Traveller families. As recently as 2013 the international media became exercised about the likelihood that Roma families in Greece and Ireland harboured stolen children and passed them off as their own.[154]

Stories about Gypsies stealing children date back to their earliest years in Western Europe. They incorporated myths of 'changeling' children, familiar from the Middle Ages, in which demons, fairies, dwarfs, or fauns stole babies from their cradles. Literary productions from the Renaissance to the Romantics included tales of aristocratic children stolen by Gypsies, whose true identity and character were later dramatically revealed. Early examples include Gigio Artemio Giancarli, *La Zingara* (Mantua, 1545), Lope de Rudea, *Medora* (Madrid, 1567), and the story of 'La Gitanilla' by Miguel de Cervantes (Madrid, 1613), where the comedy turns on the revelation of Gypsy kidnapping. It was an effective plot device, but pernicious misrepresentation. English versions included Middleton and Rowley, *The Spanish Gipsie* (1653), and Thomas D'Urfey, *Trick for Trick* (1678).[155] The sensationalist eighteenth-century compendium *The Thief-Catcher* (1753) perpetuated the unsubstantiated belief that Gypsies stole children and made them cripples, in order 'to excite compassion' as beggars.[156]

The abduction of children by Gypsies remained a recurrent motif in nineteenth-century literature, especially in publications for young readers. Plots involving foundlings, changelings, and Gypsies made frequent appearances in Victorian poetry and novels, testifying to a residue of dread and suspicion.[157] Walter Scott's *Guy Mannering* (1815) exploited the genre while vindicating the Gypsies, in the story of a missing heir. When the artist William Allen was commissioned a few years later to depict Scott's fictional Meg Merrilies, he was found 'studying a sketch of the recovery of a child which had been stolen by Gypsies'.[158] Another literary fantasy entitled *The Stolen Child; or, Twelve Years with the Gypsies* (1868) enjoyed transatlantic circulation. Here too a fair-haired blue-eyed boy found in the company of 'dark-haired, dark-faced' Gypsies turned out to have been taken from the house of a pious gentleman, to which he was providentially restored.[159] Generations of children were warned to be careful, lest the Gypsies take them. Victorian children played the 'game of the Gypsy', a variant of hide-and-seek, which involved hiding from the Gypsy kidnapper.[160] Editorializing on Gypsies in 1879, the *Birmingham Daily Mail* recalled that families were 'frightened with tales of their child-thieving propensities', though these were stories for the nursery rather than courts of law. [161]

Popular familiarity with the legend of Gypsy kidnapping was so deeply entrenched that writers and politicians could use it for rhetorical effect. Andrew Marvell, in his poem 'Upon Appleton House' (1651), referred to nuns 'who guiltily their prize bemoan, | Like Gypsies that a child hath stol'n', as if that practice was common knowledge.[162] Gypsies 'tell fortunes, and steal children too', repeated the Restoration poet Robert Dixon.[163] The eighteenth-century playwright Richard Brinsley Sheridan alluded to the legend in *The Critic* (1779), when a character complained of ideas being altered, 'as Gypsies do stolen children, disfigure them to make 'em pass for their own'.[164] Speaking in parliament in 1812, on the topic of Protestant schools in Catholic Ireland, Lord Byron said that they were filled in the same manner as 'the Gypsies of the present day with stolen children'.[165] A generation later another member of parliament complained that 'Mr Cobden had taken every word of his original motion, as Gypsies do stolen children, and made them pass for his own'.[166] Henry Berkley spoke similarly in 1858, telling the House that aristocratic interests treated certain Liberals 'as Gypsies are reported to treat stolen children, disfiguring them to make them pass as their own'.[167]

It needs to be stressed that no documented case of child theft by Gypsies can be found in English records. But evidence was not needed for such notions to flourish. Discussing the depredations of vagabonds and Gypsies in Elizabethan England, William Harrison remarked: 'What notable robberies, pilferies, murders, rapes, and stealing of young children... I need not rehearse'. Harrison suggested that infants were at risk from marauding child-stealers, although he supplied no details or evidence.[168] Judicial authorities in Gloucestershire repeated the canard in 1591 when they apprehended a group of fifty travelling Gypsies, some of them believed to be 'young children and stolen from sundry persons of that country by the Egyptians'. Despite appeals to the Privy Council and to learned counsellors at law, no parents came forward to claim their missing offspring.[169]

Several early modern celebrities were alleged to have experienced Gypsy kidnapping, though none of the claims can be verified. The legend still circulates that as a child Sir John Popham (1531–1607), Attorney General and

Lord Chief Justice under Elizabeth I, 'was stolen by a band of Gypsies, and remained some months in their society'. The episode was said to have shaped 'the irregular habits and little respect for the rules of property which afterwards marked one period of his life'. The experience of 'the wandering life he had led with these lawless associates' was said to have strengthened Popham's constitution, but could not erase 'a cabalistic mark' that his captors had burnt on his left arm. The abduction apparently occurred in Somerset during Popham's childhood in the 1530s, and is said to have prefigured his 'profligate' period as a student at Oxford. The fullest version of this story appears in Lord John Campbell's nineteenth-century account of *The Lives of the Chief Justices*. It recurs in a modern biography and in an essay by the historian Christopher Hill, despite the assertion by A. V. Judges in 1930 that this story 'is now discredited'. The late Victorian *Dictionary of National Biography* relates the story that young Popham was stolen by Gypsies but treats it with scepticism, and it is not mentioned at all in the more recent *Oxford Dictionary of National Biography*. No sixteenth- or seventeenth-century source supports this story, which appears to have been a fanciful elaboration of a somewhat unflattering character sketch in John Aubrey's late-Stuart 'brief lives'.[170] There is no evidence of Gypsy child theft in Tudor England, and Popham was not its victim.

A similar story is told about the Jesuit martyr Robert Southwell (1561–95, canonized 1970), that as an infant he was 'stolen by Gypsies' and then recovered. It appears uncritically in the original *Dictionary of National Biography* and in pious modern hagiographies. According to Southwell's twentieth-century biographer, 'the sensational event of his infancy was being kidnapped by a Gypsy woman who had been captivated herself, so she said, by the beauty of his countenance as he lay in his cradle. In the panic that followed he was recovered by the devotion of a maidservant, whom he sought out long afterwards and cared for.'[171] The seventeenth-century source for this story, however, does not mention Gypsies. Henry More, *Historia Provinciae Anglicanae Societas Iesu* (St Omer, 1660), simply says that 'abstulit vaga mulier' ('a wandering or vagrant woman removed him'), and he was quickly recovered. The Jesuit historian Francis Edwards renders this: 'one day a woman stole him', with no mention of Gypsies.[172]

In Southwell's case the story offered the kind of providential marvel that foreshadowed the career of a saint. St Lawrence, St Bartholomew, and St Stephen were among other saints supposedly snatched soon after birth by devils, and then miraculously recovered.[173] The son of the legendary hero

Guy of Warwick was also supposedly taken from his cradle in his infancy, as was Titania's 'changeling boy' in *A Midsummer Night's Dream*, who was stolen from an Indian king.[174] Narratives like these became attached to the black legend of Gypsy child abduction.

A surprisingly similar story about a later celebrity concerns the childhood of the economist Adam Smith (1723–90). According to Smith's biographer John Rae, 'in his fourth year, while on a visit to his grandfather at Strathendry ... the child was stolen by a passing band of Gypsies, and for a time could not be found. But presently a gentleman arrived who had met a Gypsy woman a few miles down the road carrying a child that was crying piteously. Scouts were immediately dispatched', and the child was recovered, though the abductress managed to escape. This well-known story appeared in the religious tract *The Stolen Child*; it is repeated in the late-Victorian *Dictionary of National Biography*, though not in its modern successor.[175]

Whether this really happened to the infant Smith, or was rather a romantic addition to the life of a 'genius', is hard to determine. The source on which it is based, however, like the foundation for the story about Robert Southwell, does not actually mention Gypsies. The writer Dugald Stewart gave 'an account of the life ... of Adam Smith' to the Royal Society of Edinburgh in 1793, and published it in 1795 with a collection of Smith's essays. In this account, the future economist 'was stolen by a party of that set of vagrants who are known in Scotland by the name of tinkers', and he was recovered 'by his uncle, who hearing that some vagrants had passed, pursued them' and recovered the child, thereby 'preserving to the world a genius, who was destined, not only to extend the boundaries of science, but to enlighten and reform the commercial policy of Europe'.[176] Poorly founded to begin with, tales of Gypsy kidnapping only grew in the telling, with wandering vagrants, tinkers, and Gypsies fused together in some popular imaginations.

By his own account the Victorian Gypsy enthusiast and self-declared 'Romany Rye' George Borrow (1803–81) was yet another victim of Gypsy child theft. An entry in the *Journal of the Gypsy Lore Society* for 1889 reports the reminiscence of the secretary of the British and Foreign Bible Society, that, at their first meeting in the 1830s, Borrow told him 'that he had been stolen by Gypsies in his boyhood, had passed several years with them, but had been recognized at a fair in Norfolk, and brought home to his family by his uncle'.[177] No such incident can be corroborated. The young Borrow spent much of his life in an army family, but none of it as a captive or changeling. A taste for fantasy may explain this report, as if the author wished it were true and was nourishing a legend.

No one has effectively explained why Gypsies might want to steal children. One would have thought they had enough mouths to feed, though they might have been driven to replace a child that had perished. It is conceivable that some Gypsies went in for childcare, and perhaps relieved settled society of some of its unwanted bastards, but evidence of this practice is wanting. The closest approximation is in Richard Head's account of Restoration roguery, which relates a Gypsy trade in 'bantlings', illegitimate children of the gentry, 'who for a good round sum are sent to us to be nursed, where they are never like to come to the knowledge of their true parents'.[178] Fearful and fanciful, but easily repeated, this connects with tales of evil wetnurses, changeling children, and babies stolen by Gypsies, whose subsequent recovery of status and identity drives the plots of picaresque fiction. Heinrich Grellmann recognized that 'many authors' mention the Gypsies stealing children, though others deny it, saying that 'the Gypsies have brats enough of their own'.[179]

Several publications early in the reign of George III reported the story of a Hampshire farmer 'who had lost a favourite little boy two years before', and, approaching some Gypsies,

> seeing a child along with them whom he suspected to be his, went up to them and insisted upon stripping him. This being after some difficulty complied with, he soon discovered, by a mark on the boy's thigh, that it was his own child, and carried him home. The Gypsies, apprehensive of the consequences, made off, and though immediate pursuit was made after them, it was without success.

No reference to this matter appears in records of law enforcement, but it appears in *The Universal Museum* in 1762 and in the *Polite Magazine of History, Politicks, and Literature* the year after. The *Gentleman's Magazine* commented, wisely: 'this story is told in so romantic a manner, that we doubt the truth of it, and should be glad of better information.'[180]

Another story told that year, though set in an earlier era, related the tale of the child John Rooke, who was sold to the Gypsies for 'two sauce pans and a tin pot'. These Gypsies, the adult John Rooke later related, taught him how 'to live hard, to keep a steady countenance, to know the value of money, and how, on all occasions, to supply my wants'. They also taught him 'to treat all mankind like enemies', and 'to make free with a stray goose, turkey or lamb'. Though purportedly a true account, the story is pure fiction.[181]

Stories of Gypsy child theft revived in the eighteenth century, along with popular interest in the deeds or misdeeds of Gypsies. They were stimulated by the sensational case of Elizabeth Canning, who claimed to have been imprisoned by the Gypsy Mary Squires. Much was made of the mother's distress, and her joy when the lost girl returned, though many believed Miss Canning to be a fantasist.[182] Stories of this sort helped to sell papers, and further fanned fears of kidnapping.

The *Oracle and Public Advertiser* stirred similar emotions in May 1796 in reporting that 'Ann Gammon, of the city of Gloucester, a fine girl, about nine years of age, was a few days since inveigled and carried off towards Bristol, by a gang of monster Gypsies, infesting the neighbourhood, to the pungent grief of her disconsolate mother, a poor and unfortunate widow'.[183] Other publications made assertions about Gypsies who 'kidnap little children whenever an opportunity presents'. They were said to have stripped their victims of their clothing, dressed them in rags, darkened their skin, and set them about Gypsy chores. One such claim was based on an incident in June 1802 when 'a party of Gypsies was ... charged with kidnapping a female child named Mary Kellen, who was discovered in a most wretched state' near Lewisham, Kent. Mary reported that she had just escaped 'from some Gypsies who had stolen her from her friends at Plymouth', and had been forced to wander with them for seven months. Diligent officials arrested the Gypsies and held them in the House of Correction, until it transpired that the child had run away from the Rotherhithe poorhouse, was sheltered by the Gypsies at Kennington at her own request, and spent only ten days in their company. The tale of kidnapping was entirely false, and the Gypsies emerged exonerated. This did not stop a later writer from retelling the story as one of child theft and torment by notorious Gypsies.[184]

Similar stories surfaced in succeeding generations, with similar absence of documentation. Public authorities and even some journalists could be sceptical, but the stories played on deeply entrenched assumptions about the vulnerability of children and the villainy of Gypsies. Press reports in October 1822 presented another 'extraordinary fact' of the 'alleged sale of children to Gypsies'. It emerged in the course of a matrimonial dispute in London that a father who refused to support his infant son threatened 'to dispose of the child to a Gypsy gang at Norwood'. The Norwood Gypsies, it was claimed, trafficked in such children, and stained their skin so that they would never again 'be heard of in society'. The mother and grandmother of the child in question evidently believed the legend that Gypsies stole or bought babies. Parish officers, however, assured the court 'that they did not believe that such a practice existed', and that 'the mother's fears sprung merely from imagination'.[185]

According to popular opinion, the Gypsy practice of child-stealing was not just to augment their numbers, buts also to hold children for ransom. This belief featured in a report in *The Times* in September 1824 about the theft and recovery of a 5-year-old boy on the outskirts of London. The disappearance was blamed on 'a strange woman, and an itinerant tinker', the woman being named as Margaret Parker, 'an active member in the celebrated Gypsy gang that are known to infest the roads from Hounslow to London'. The newspaper claimed that she turned kidnapper after 'decrepitude and age' barred her from normal Gypsy activities. She was said to have 'carried off several children with the view of inducing the parents to offer large rewards for their restoration', and, when that failed, had them trained as Gypsy entertainers. In this case 'the poor father, by dint of inquiry, and the offer of a considerable reward', managed to find his son, but by this time the alleged perpetrators had disappeared. Margaret Parker was not apprehended and was never brought to trial, so her story, if there is one, was never told. We are left with a sensational report in the form of a morality tale, fuelled by popular prejudice.[186]

Evangelical activists of the early nineteenth century alluded to child theft as an indicator that the Gypsies needed 'moral and religious reformation'. 'How many respectable families have been rendered wretched by their common practice of stealing and mutilating children to move pity!' wrote an essayist in the *Scottish Missionary and Philanthropic Register* in 1828, claiming that 'many instances of this crime still occur in England annually'.[187] The appearance that year of a Gypsy child 'whose gentle looks and engaging behaviour seemed to bespeak a better origin than the condition in which he was found, and the rags in which he was enveloped', encouraged suspicion that it had happened again.[188] When the Victorian 'expert' Walter Simson encountered a family of 'swarthy and barbarous looking' Gypsies with 'two beautiful children ... with light flaxen hair, and very fair complexions', he surmised 'that they might have been stolen from different parents'. Despite the complete lack of evidence, Simson accepted the belief that Gypsy practices 'led to many children being kidnapped'.[189] Visiting Gypsy tents a generation later, the philanthropist George Smith noticed 'many strange-looking children' who seemed 'quite out of their element', and was ready to assume the worst.[190]

The Methodist James Crabb, who considered himself a friend of the Gypsies, insisted in 1832 that their reputation as kidnappers was unjust. 'The Gypsies in this country have for centuries been accused of child-stealing; and therefore it is not to be wondered at, that, when children have been missing, the Gypsies should be taxed with having stolen them.' Crabb gave several examples where Gypsies were blamed for the disappearance of children who were subsequently found drowned, or who had been enticed away, 'but *not by a Gypsy*'.[191]

The appetite for such stories remained undiminished. In December 1832 several newspapers reported the alleged abduction near Bristol of two girls aged 13 and 15, who 'were overtaken in their way home by several lock-up Gypsy carts...and threatened that if they made the least noise they should be murdered'. One of the girls allegedly escaped when the Gypsies neared Worcester, and was reunited with her parents. The newspapers informed readers that, 'when children are stolen, they are stripped, their faces blacked, and ragged clothes given to disguise them'. It was 'regretted that means were not adopted to apprehend' the perpetrators, of whom nothing more was discovered. No abductor was identified, and nobody was punished. Nor is it known whether any of these stories involved troubled runaways who later blamed their absence on the Gypsies, as Elizabeth Canning pinned her kidnapping on Mary Squires.[192]

News reports of this nature faded from view in the Victorian period, perhaps as worries about the white slave trade supplanted fears of Gypsies. But suspicion fell briefly on itinerant Gypsies whenever a child went missing.[193] One teenage boy exploited this suspicion later in the nineteenth century when he ran away from home, and claimed to have been taken by Gypsies. A magistrate at Bow Street surmised that 'the boy had evidently been reading trashy and pernicious literature'.[194] But popular literature, and popular culture in general, kept the myth of Gypsy child theft alive. Pioneer cinema in the early twentieth century featured the drama *Stolen by Gypsies* (1905), in which a child in company with Gypsies is subsequently recognized and retrieved. British cinema-goers also saw *Kidnapped for Revenge* (1913), in which a dog saves a baby from being kidnapped by a Gypsy.[195] In October 1980, and again in July 2008, BBC television viewers were treated to a documentary about Gypsies with the ironically intended title *They Steal Children, Don't They?*[196]

It bears repeating that the records of English law enforcement yield no cases in which Gypsies were found to have stolen children. The author of a recent study of child abduction in the late eighteenth and early nineteenth centuries concludes that, 'in reality, children were not abducted so that their parents could be held to ransom', despite streams of fiction to this effect.[197] Yet readers and media consumers in the past and the present have been willing to believe reports of Gypsy abductions, however untrue. Some of the errors in cultural perception perennially applied against Gypsies may be akin to other delusional, phobic, aberrant, and racist beliefs examined by social psychologists.[198] The willingness to believe ill of Gypsies is evidently deep rooted, long lasting, and extremely difficult to eradicate.

Changes and Continuities

English Gypsies, we have seen, experienced change over time. They were not 'a people without history', but were caught up in the histories of their environment. It is possible to chart changes in their numbers and activities, their mode of living, their preferences for shelter and transportation, with at least a modicum of confidence. Far more difficult, given problems of access and documentation, is to discern developments in their interiority and self-perception. Much easier is to trace alterations in their treatment in law.

Gypsies were never—neither now nor in the past—a coherent category with uniform characteristics. As individuals and families, they exhibited the varieties of human nature. Generalization about them is perilous, especially across half a millennium. Nevertheless, some features have endured over time. The name 'Gypsy', first coined in the sixteenth century and always problematic, continues to represent people of itinerant tendencies, or at least nomadic memories or aspirations, many of them linked, at least notionally, to the historic Romani diaspora. Gauging their identity has always posed problems, yet elements of a Gypsy culture survive. They have always been separate, though never rigidly enclosed. The Gypsies known to history have interacted, and sometimes intermarried with members of the mainstream community, but have always, to a great degree, kept themselves to themselves. Pamphleteers, creative writers, evangelicals, Gypsylorists, anthropologists, and journalists have attempted to explain them, but the Gypsies have resisted intimate analysis. Historians must be content with documentary traces, external indications, and markers of social interaction.

Complaints could be heard in almost every decade from the reign of Henry VIII to the present that Gypsies were idle and disorderly, dirty and deceitful, parasitical outsiders. The nastiness of Jacobean cony-catching pamphleteers could be matched by commentary in the modern tabloids. The charge by the Jacobean bishop Lancelot Andrewes that Gypsies were 'idle and will not take pains in a calling', and were 'against the public good of mankind', recurred in the statement of the Registrar General in 1861 that Gypsies 'produce nothing valuable' and belonged to the 'unproductive classes'.[199]

Alongside general condemnation, the fantasy flourished of Gypsy liberty and romance. The adoption of Gypsy chic in early modern courts and play-houses could be compared to the modern fascination with Gypsy style in fashion and popular culture. From the Jacobean masque to the air-conditioned Gypsies of rock and roll, the long history of playing at Gypsies has been a privilege of the elite. Earrings, scarves, and bodices do not make one a Gypsy, nor does travel or pretending to tell fortunes. If Gypsies were aware of this emulation, it is not known whether they were outraged, amused, or indif-ferent to the appropriation of their image.

Gypsy culture appears to have been malleable and renewable, maintaining key elements and incorporating others. Gypsy ethnicity was fluid and self-replicating, and could be inherited, inhabited, and absorbed by those described as 'Gypsy people'. Processes of assimilation may have weaned some from the road, to settled or semi-sedentary lives, and courtship, friend-ship, opportunity, or adventure may have brought newcomers to the Gypsy ranks, but Gypsy identity was perpetuated. Adapting to change, Gypsies acquired new skills and technologies, and altered their circuits of itinerancy. Their children ensured that Gypsy culture would survive, even as successive generations recast their relations to state authorities and the mainstream society around them.

Paying attention to Gypsies over five centuries reveals much more about 'us' than them. Throughout their history Gypsies have provoked sharp responses, in politics, policing, administration, and law. They have revealed the anxieties of the powerful, and the concerns of the mainstream. Generations of householders and local officials have construed them as a 'nuisance' or a 'menace'. Religious leaders from the sixteenth century to the twentieth have charged them with being unchristian and unchurched. Their occasional participation in religious services and sacraments only demonstrated their estrangement from the fold. A series of laws sought to discipline Gypsies, either to intensify their exclusion by making them felons, or to encourage their assimilation. Laws against vagrancy, fortune-telling, and roadside camping bore disproportionately on Gypsies. More recent regulations governing caravan sites and planning controls have turned Gypsies into litigants, outlaws, and pariahs.

The hope that the Gypsy problem could be resolved by their absorption into the mainstream has resurfaced every few decades. Tudor legislation allowed Gypsies to escape penalties if they 'shall leave that naughty, idle and ungodly life and company' and take up 'some lawful work, trade or occupation'.[200] Later Elizabethan officials allowed Gypsies to go free if they promised 'to reform their lives' and 'to demean themselves in some honest faculty'.[201] It was the hope of early nineteenth-century reformers that Gypsies would be taught their letters and catechism, and settle into ordinary lives. Christian charity would lift them out of Gypsydom.[202] George Smith of Coalville wanted to end the Gypsy way of life by educating their children and registering their vehicles.[203] Even admirers of the Gypsies, like the Victorian Gypylorists, hoped for some amelioration of their condition. A comment in the *Morning Post* in October 1897 expressed the common sentiment that 'if Gypsies are to survive in this country they will have to face the inevitable and live like other people'.[204] Twentieth-century members of parliament never tired of saying that the age of wandering was over, and that Gypsies would have to settle down to homes and responsibilities like everybody else. Norman Dodds, who campaigned for their better treatment, endorsed the goal of 'helping the Gypsies to become ordinary members of the community', if that was what they wanted.[205] Government intentions in the 1970s were not to pressure Gypsies to settle or assimilate 'unless and until' they wished it themselves, 'but the opportunity is to be provided'.[206]

Gypsies have always attracted commentary, and have periodically become objects of analysis. A burgeoning body of scholarship has expanded Gypsy studies, though the academic gaze is no more benign than any other. Early modern encyclopedists sought to place Gypsies among the peoples of mankind, in primitive ethnological comparisons. Seventeenth-century writers piled on the stereotypes. Enlightenment philologists and their Victorian successors employed comparative linguistics and a modicum of fieldwork to make Gypsies appear eastern, ancient, and interesting. The Gypsylorists were nothing if not indefatigable in pursuit of Gypsy essences and origins. The problem of Gypsy identity, and questions about their Indian ancestry, continue to exercise some authors almost to the point of obsession. Whether conducted in the library, the archives, or the field, the study of Romany Gypsies, Gypsy Travellers, Traveller Gypsies, Roma, and other combinations of GRT (Gypsy–Roma–Travellers) has led to greater sophistication in discourse.

Racialized commentary, mostly a Victorian invention, has all but disappeared. Nobody now takes seriously the bogus distinction between 'pure bred' and 'half-breed' Gypsies, or between Gypsies, didicoys, and mumpers. Recognition of Gypsy ethnicity came late to English law, but the generic equation of Gypsies with other kinds of customary travellers has robbed the term of any cultural precision. Today you are a Gypsy if you say you are, and perhaps still a Gypsy if you prefer the less loaded term Traveller. Self-ascription rules. The 1988 judgment that declared Gypsies an ethnic minority included the recognition that 'the common use of "Gypsy" as a term of abuse has caused both Gypsies and the settled population to use the non-pejorative alternative "Traveller"'.[207] The index of an important study of twentieth-century developments contains the revealing entry 'Gypsies, see Travellers', which echoes the eighteenth-century entry 'Egyptians, see Vagrants'.[208]

Family historians looking for their Gypsy heritage are now advised to regard anyone who seems to be a Gypsy to be one. Genealogists 'need have no doubts' about identifying an ancestor as a Gypsy if they can find a traditional Gypsy forename and surname, a typical Gypsy occupation, and evidence of mobility.[209] Ecumenism of this sort enlists all sorts of people who might have been labelled differently by record-keepers in the past. The predilection for self-ascription allows people to be Gypsies, or not Gypsies, according to the context and dynamics of conversation, as if identity was a choice as much as a predicament. A Gypsy can be a Romany or a Traveller, according to the needs of the moment, and an adherent of the modern Traveller community can present himself, without irony, as 'a true didicoy'. Some of Judith Okely's informants in the 1970s identified themselves as 'Travellers' in interactions with officials and outsiders, 'but among themselves, in trusting contexts, they used the word "Gypsy" with pride'.[210] The Yorkshire Gypsy Bobby Lee remarked in the 1990s, 'we're Gypsies, Romanichals... We're proud of being Gypsies', but his son Young Bobby identified as 'a Traveller... a Romany Traveller'.[211]

Definitions, by definition, pin things down. They buttress a term with certainty that might not be justified in the messier and more shaded world of daily interactions. The definitions of Gypsies in twentieth-century statutes are no more stable or authoritative than Renaissance encyclopedias or early modern dictionaries. The well-intentioned stiffness of the post-war statutory definition was clearly inadequate. If English Gypsies in the 1960s were simply 'persons of nomadic habit of life, whatever their race or origin' (though not travelling showmen or circus workers), then nearly everybody on the road or in transient camps could be a Gypsy. The problem of distinguishing Gypsies from vagrants, casual van-dwellers, and Irish itinerants seemingly disappeared.[212] The apparently more nuanced definition of the early twenty-first century was only a marginal improvement. Following judicial decisions that both Gypsies and Travellers belonged to ethnic minorities, and that travelling was no longer requisite so long as the parties remained 'nomadic in spirit if not in actual or constant practice', regulators defined both groups together as 'persons with a tradition of living in a caravan, and all other persons of a nomadic habit of life, whatever their race or origin', including 'such persons who, on grounds only of their own or their family's or dependants' educational or health needs or old age, have ceased to travel temporarily or permanently'. Such definitions could be written only by committees. Gypsies did not need to be Travellers if they had settled in housed accommodation; and Travellers did not need to be Gypsies if they preferred not to label themselves by that term.[213]

The most awkward, most comprehensive, and most historically deficient definition was adopted by the Council of Europe in 2010. At the request of international Roma associations who judged the word 'Gypsy' to be 'an alien term, linked with negative, paternalistic stereotypes' and which was 'felt to be pejorative and insulting by most of the people concerned', the Council recommended that the term 'Gypsy' no longer be used. The vocabulary had to be adjusted, or 'harmonized', in the light of 'recent developments with regard to usage and acceptance in everyday language'. An exception was allowed, however, in countries like the United Kingdom, where connotations of the word 'Gypsy' were not necessarily negative, and where the usage was accepted as appropriate by the people concerned. In general, in official communications, the word 'Roma' was preferred and was taken to refer to 'Roma, Sinti, Kale and related groups, including Travellers and the Eastern groups (Dom and Lom), and includes persons who identify themselves as Gypsies'. The Council of Europe recognized 'Travellers' as an ethnic identity, but noted that in Ireland and Great Britain they are 'ethnically distinct from the Roma/Sinti/Kale', and 80 per cent were no longer travelling.[214] A revised definition is no doubt under consideration.

The international struggle for Roma rights and empowerment puts further strain on the history and identity of Gypsies by focusing on their present condition. By various counts, none of them definitive, the European

Gypsy population is estimated to range from six million to sixteen million.[215] Stimulated by the horrors of the Holocaust, in which more than a quarter of a million Gypsies (some say as many as 500,000) were murdered, and energized by the post-war liberal movement for human rights, activists have joined councils, agencies, associations, congresses, and centres to rally and represent the Roma people of today. Organizations including the European Roma Rights Centre, the European Roma and Travellers Forum, the International Roma Union, and the World Romani Congress have generated a Romani flag, a Romani anthem, an International Romani Day (8 April), and a non-territorial Romani bureaucracy. Neither Roma nationalism nor Gypsy internationalism has much purchase in Britain, and English Travellers appear to take little interest in initiatives supposedly taken on their behalf.[216] The media and the mainstream continue to manifest stereotypical prejudice, but with little of the violence or venom that has inflamed anti-Gypsy sentiments elsewhere in Europe.[217]

Conditions have changed dramatically in Britain since the sixteenth century, but Gypsies remain a problem for local, national, and international authorities. Social policy and scholarly enquiry still strive to comprehend Gypsies and to deal with their issues. Whether seen as a nuisance to be curbed or injustice to be righted, the Gypsy 'problem' generates studies, proposals, memoranda, and reports without end. Approached by tolerant and present-minded observers, the various communities of English Gypsies, Irish Travellers, immigrant Roma, and others on the social margins appear as people in need of resources and understanding. The cultural, ethnic, demographic, and historical differences between them pale in the face of continuing prejudice and deprivation, though widespread ignorance about their background and circumstances compounds the problem.

It should not be surprising that modern activists subordinate discussion of the origin and history of Gypsies and Travellers to the struggle for current necessities. History, however, provides the long view, revealing continuities, comparisons, and changes over time. It is simply not true that Gypsies are a 'people without history' or who have lived 'outside history', as some authors have suggested.[218] People known as Gypsies have troubled the English establishment since the age of Henry VIII, sparking legal, social, and cultural responses with varying ferocity and effect. By placing Gypsies within the long march of English history, we can better see how the past has shaped the present. By tracing interactions over half a millennium, we restore lost elements of England's cultural heritage and potentially empower participants for the future. Though not its original intent, which was strictly historical, this study may provide information and inspiration of value to Gypsies and Travellers today. If there is any truth in the observation that 'the past is neg-ated' in modern popular culture, and that the history of Gypsies in England had been 'deleted from national memory',[219] this book is a step towards its restoration.

Scholars and Gypsies

A Bibliographical Sketch

Conventional surveys of Gypsy history rely on a limited number of sources, many of questionable reliability. The story is often compressed or garbled in its telling. None of the historical evidence presents Gypsies on their own terms or from a Romani point of view. The gaze is always external and often hostile, seeing Gypsies as a 'problem' of exoticism, idleness, vagrancy, deviancy, disorder, crime, and deceit. Whether registered in the language of legislators or the fulminations of popular pamphleteers, the Gypsies were always separate from the ordered, hierarchical, and settled structures of Renaissance, Enlightenment, and modern commercial Europe. Gypsies remained marginal and mysterious through most of their history, as they are, in many respects, today. Some modern scholars have deconstructed them almost out of existence, preferring to treat Gypsies as a literary trope or a subset of vagrants rather than people with a troubled history.

The social marginality of Gypsies, past and present, is matched by their marginality in modern scholarship. References to Gypsies are rare in works of social history, while the general literature on Gypsies in the past tends to be slight, inward-looking, and harnessed to other agendas. Scholars have sometimes remarked on the 'isolation' of Gypsy studies, where specialists argue mainly with each other.[1] Research on the period before the nineteenth century is especially limited and untrustworthy. Popular fascination with Gypsies continues apace, but myths and misunderstandings abound. A comprehensive history is wanting, but the recent quickening of interest in Britain and Europe offers both a stimulus and a model.[2]

Historians of early modern England have paid Gypsies no more than glancing attention, usually with regard to poverty, vagabondage, divination, or deceit. They are absent from the general national narrative. Historians of vagrancy, crime, and deviance, to be sure, have briefly noted Gypsies, but their remarks are tangential to their primary concerns.[3] It was possible for

English historians in the 1970s to write about 'the wayfaring community' of the sixteenth and seventeenth centuries without mentioning Gypsies, and it is still possible to leave Gypsies out of accounts of early modern 'British travellers'.[4] Pioneering work on poverty and vagrancy cited Gypsies only as people 'misunderstood from the beginning', with 'an air of mystery', who survived legislative attempts to contain them.[5] The historian Paul Slack (characteristically using the lower case) observed in 1974 that vagrants practising fortune-telling 'were occasionally called "gypsies" but very few genuine gypsies have been discovered'. Slack's later work located Gypsies among the 'dangerous poor' who stimulated 'emotions of fear and disgust'.[6] Joan Kent's 1986 study of village constables, who dealt locally with migrants and wanderers, made no reference to Gypsies, even though the accounts she used cited Gypsies and 'Egyptians'.[7]

Very little has been written on early modern Gypsies since A. L. Beier devoted five pages to them in his classic 1985 study *Masterless Men*. Influenced by the antiquarian studies of the Gypsy Lore Society, he offered a guardedly sympathetic assessment. Beier's Gypsies appear as 'a shadowy group' who nonetheless formed 'a genuine alternative society', distinct from the ordinary vagabond poor. With their dark skin, 'fantastic' dress, and exotic language, they 'remained alien in many respects' from the host society and the rest of the vagrant community. Travelling in 'large troops' with 'recognized leaders', and engaging in fortune-telling and trickery, these Gypsies belonged to an ethnic community with transnational and transhistorical connections. Beier recognized them to be 'Romanies' with Indian origins, though that was unknown in the early modern era. Tudor legislation threatened Gypsies with expulsion and death, but magistrates tended to lump them together with ordinary rogues and vagabonds. Gypsy distinctiveness faded by the seventeenth century, according to Beier's influential study, as 'Gypsies and English vagrants merged' in legal, official, and popular perception.[8]

Apart from Beier there is mostly a void until studies of the nineteenth century. As David Smith recognized, in his work on the forest economy, 'there is no substantial work on the history of Gypsies in England and the investigator finds himself working at the margins of other people's subjects'.[9] A recent study of racism in Britain referred to 'the marginalization, if not . . . the exclusion of Gypsies in modern historical scholarship'.[10] David Mayall, one of the few historians concerned with Gypsies, observed that 'the history of the group has mostly been written from an alarmingly ahistorical perspective'. Mayall's own survey includes a suggestive chapter on 'the

Gypsy in early modern England'.[11] Apart from these entries, and passing references to 'hereditary vagrants' and 'tellers of destinies', Gypsies are almost invisible in studies of Tudor and Stuart England or Hanoverian Britain.[12] Only Christopher Hill, in one of his last essays, celebrated 'Gypsy liberty', and applauded 'their resolute rejection of wage-labour', as if they were hippies or revolutionaries.[13] Other social historians pay Gypsies even less attention. They are entirely absent from most scholars' footnotes and indices on the sixteenth, seventeenth, or eighteenth centuries. Only recently has research been renewed on Gypsies in pre-modern England.[14]

Though scholarship on the subject remains limited, a consensus seems to have emerged among English historians that immigrant Gypsies of the six-teenth century soon became indistinguishable from home-bred vagrants, whose appearance, activity, and self-presentation made them seem Gypsy-like; and, that being so, there is little point in trying to untangle their history. Later Gypsies, by these lights, were little more than especially colourful itinerants. These conclusions rest on a limited selection of sources and a shallow range of investigation, mediated through the antiquarianism of the Victorian era and the ideological concerns of the present. They sit uneasily with the views of some modern Romani activists who posit a robust Gypsy identity and an unbroken ethnic heritage, and may need modification in the light of new research. They may find favour, however, among cultural con-structionist critics of the concept of ethnicity, and supporters of today's 'Gypsy Roma Traveller' movement, for whom Gypsy identity is circumstan-tial, self-ascribed, and essentially ahistorical.[15]

The history of Gypsies in modern Britain rests on much firmer founda-tions thanks to George Behlmer's essay on the Victorian 'Gypsy problem' (1985), and Mayall's research on *Gypsy-Travellers in Nineteenth-Century Society* (1988).[16] Valuable surveys by Angus Fraser, Yaron Matras, and Becky Taylor set English Gypsy history in its wider European context. More recent work has brought the history up to the present. However, as Mayall and others recognize, scholarship on Gypsies is marked by 'considerable controversy and... heated and volatile debate'.[17] The question of Gypsy identity has energized numerous scholars and activists almost to the point of obsession, and of necessity is a major theme in this book.

Activists and academics in various disciplines and traditions disagree whether Gypsies originated as migrants from Asia or emerged, mysteriously, from domestic conditions; whether they were (and are) a people or a lifestyle, an ethnicity or a cultural construction; whether they should be written with a small or capital 'G'; and whether to use the word 'Gypsy' at all. Many of the arguments about the origins, ancestry, ethnicity, identity, and heritage of Gypsies depend upon hypotheses that may be proposed, but never definitively proved.

Though cultural, historical, linguistic, and genetic evidence all point to an immigrant origin, it is still possible to suggest that English Gypsies were home-grown misfits who emerged from the collapse of feudalism and 'the transition from manorialism to capitalism', and refused to be 'proletarianised'.[18] This claim is often repeated, though never documented. If Gypsies indeed emerged domestically from the ashes of the old agrarian order, one might expect historians of social and economic change in the fifteenth and sixteenth centuries to have noticed them. Few, however, speak glibly of the decline of feudalism, the collapse of manorialism, or resistance to proletarianization, and none can convincingly relate these matters to the emergence of Gypsies.[19] Chronological correspondence does not indicate origins.

As is often the case with cultural history, especially for the early modern period, the most creative work has been done by literary historicists, critics, and theorists, who are typically associated with academic departments of English. Primarily interested in the literary Renaissance—the world of William Shakespeare and Ben Jonson—they have based their commentary on representations in plays, masques, satires, and tales of picaresque adventure, buttressed by citations from Elizabethan rogue literature and Jacobean 'cony-catching' pamphlets. Those focusing on later periods bring a similar sensibility to novels from Henry Fielding to George Eliot, and to English poetry from John Clare to Matthew Arnold.

Among early modernists, Thomas Harman's *A Caveat or Warening for Commen Cursetors Vulgarely Called Vagabones* (1567) and Jonson's masque *The Gypsies Metamorphos'd* (first performed in 1621) are touchstone texts.[20] The literary tradition runs from the 'old' historicism of Frank Aydelotte, A. V. Judges, and Gamini Salgado, through the cultural criticism of 'new' historicism and postmodernism, to its theoretically fractured successors. Most literary practitioners saw Gypsies as their original creative authors described them: deceitful, disreputable, but curiously beguiling, though many of the Gypsies in literature turn out to be noble changelings or aristocrats in disguise.[21]

Recent work by literary theorists treats Gypsies as members of a 'dissident criminal sub-culture' with 'subversive potential', or else as opportunist vagabonds whose 'feigned identity' was a matter of imposture and self-fashioning.

Elizabethan cony-catching pamphlets and Jacobean court entertainments provide evidence, they claim, of 'the evasive character of Gypsy cultural difference' and the 'transversal performativity' of Gypsy identity. Their work exposes an underground sub-culture inhabited by 'Gypsies, vagabonds, beggars, cony-catchers, cutpurses, and prostitutes', whose image was 'attractive and potent'. But they also suggest that Gypsies were primarily a literary or discursive phenomenon, a 'floating signifier' with 'a fabricated historical reality'. Paola Pugliatti suggests, perhaps too pessimistically, that 'there is probably no new discovery to be made about these issues', though perhaps more to be 'unveiled... to be gleaned and discussed... between the lines'.[22] Deborah Epstein Nord, *Gypsies and the British Imagination, 1807–1930* (2006), and Sarah Houghton-Walker, *Representations of the Gypsy in the Romantic Period* (2014), pursue literary treatments of the figure of the Gypsy from the eighteenth to the twentieth century, with substantial historical framing.[23]

Social scientists have contributed valuable scholarship on Gypsies and Travellers, with greater interest in the observable present than the researchable past. A recent survey of 'Roma and Gypsy "Ethnicity" as a Subject of Anthropological Inquiry' notes that 'historical approaches have won little favor'.[24] The anthropologist Judith Okely, who conducted pioneer research among English Traveller–Gypsies in the 1970s, prefaced her account with a brief historical sketch that acknowledged past attempts by mainstream society 'to exoticise, disperse, control, assimilate or destroy them'. Sceptical of claims for their racialized, Indian, Romany, or immigrant origin, Okely suggested instead that English Gypsies 'emerged from the indigenous vagrant population as an ethnic group using the principle of descent and other self-defining features'. Gypsies, by this interpretation, were products of socio-economic distress, flavoured with the mystification of romance. Using the Romani word for non-Gypsies, she concludes that 'the separation between Gypsy and *Gorgio* is socially constructed and can never be absolute'.[25] Another anthropologist in this tradition resisted the historical, linguistic, or ethnic approach to Gypsies because, she said, it placed them in a past over which they had no control.[26]

Congruent with this approach, the Dutch sociologists Leo Lucassen and Wim Willems have been influential in advancing the notion that the Gypsy legacy of 'poverty, mendacity, vagabondage, marginality and criminality' is primarily a matter of representation and social construction. For them the 'gypsies' (uncapitalized) are not so much a 'people... as persons who have been labelled as such over the course of time'. While recognizing that 'hardly any revaluation of extant historical knowledge has yet taken place', Willems suggests that there is little to be gained by attending to the ethnic or linguistic history of 'Gypsies', who constitute a discursive category rather than a particular population. The historians David Mayall and Frances Timbers have generally endorsed this cultural constructionist approach.[27]

Much of the modern work on Gypsies that incorporates historical material serves other agenda with legal, moral, or political preoccupations. It is often flavoured by the scholarship of commitment, seeking justice for today's Gypsies and Travellers, or dignity and redress for Roma people. Activist accounts move briskly from the Renaissance to the Holocaust, in which at least a quarter of a million Gypsies died, and then to modern confrontations over caravans and camps, to expose a heritage of prejudice and persecution. History, from this perspective, is primarily a chronology of oppression.[28] It has even been suggested 'that all Gypsy historiography had been completed, and that the history of their past persecution had been exhaustively described and scientifically documented', so that there is no point in following 'the old paths of Gypsiology' by undertaking further research.[29] The gap has been filled by popular sensationalists and partisans of Romani rights. Though well intentioned, this work is too often shaded by amateurism, romanticism, outrage, and uncritical recycling of limited information. The website of the Gypsy Lore Society warns that 'much of the material published on Gypsies and Travellers on the internet is misleading due either to stereotyping, antiquated perspectives on ethnicity or culture, poor scholarship, excessive political correctness or other biases and, in some cases, outright fabrication'.[30] Similar warnings apply to work presented in print.

Gypsies have posed a puzzle for as long as people have been interested in them. They have been labelled, discussed, reproved, and romanticized by people external to their experience. Though historians have mostly held back, there has been no shortage of pundits, experts, and commentators ready to pronounce. Gypsies are indeed a discursive category, a textual phenomenon, but behind the cultural construction lies the material embodiment of families and individuals. Rather than offering a generalized and reified history of 'the Gypsies', I have tried in this book, as much as possible, to relate the experience of named individuals, and to treat English Gypsies as people rather than as constructs or categories. This fresh approach, based on a wide range of evidence, may augment the work of other scholars and set the subject on firmer historical foundations.

The sources, though sometimes opaque and scattered, are more abundant and more rewarding than might conventionally be thought. Materials for the history of Gypsies in England survive in State Papers, Privy Council act books, and the archives of local law and government. More appear in judicial proceedings, provincial and national newspapers, and the records of parliamentary legislation and debate. Sermons, ballads, plays, paintings, pamphlets, chronicles, and private writings expose relationships and attitudes. Speeches, tracts, and government reports add data and documentation. Some of these materials were unearthed by Gypsylorist antiquarians a century or more ago, but others are recent discoveries and previously unpublished. It is simply not true that Gypsy history is complete, and that there are no new stories to tell.

Missing, unfortunately, are the voices of Gypsies themselves. Like other maligned and marginal people, the Gypsies in the past were subjects of commentary by authors and authorities external or hostile to their experience. None of the surviving documentation comes from Gypsy or Romani sources, and all of the legislation, law enforcement, journalistic and literary representation emanates from settled mainstream culture. Only occasionally are fragments of Gypsy testimony preserved. Moving within environments of derogation and suspicion, the Gypsies were always liable to misunderstanding. In the absence of first-hand accounts, we are forced to rely on remarks by their neighbours, investigators, prosecutors, and enemies. This is not necessarily disabling, for historians have developed strategies for recovering 'the voices of the voiceless' and 'reading against the grain'.

In writing this book I have benefited from the comments, support, advice, and criticism of the following friends and scholars: Thomas Acton, Jeffrey Auerbach, Gordon Boswell, Dympna Callaghan, Andrew Connell, Valerie Cressy, Robert Davis, Lori Anne Ferrell, Paul Hammer, Ian Hancock, Tim Harris, Karen Harvey, Steve Hindle, Norman Jones, Chris Kyle, Yaron Matras, Anne Minken, Lee Monroe, Elisa Novi Chavarria, Judith Okely, Ann Ostendorf, Gerald Power, Wilfrid Prest, Becky Taylor, and the anonymous reviewers for Oxford University Press. I am grateful to the Liguria Study Centre of the Fondazione Bogliasco for a month by the Mediterranean to devise this book, and to Christ Church, Oxford, for the award of a visiting fellowship to complete it. The work would have been nigh impossible without continuing access to research databases at the Ohio State University Library, resource-sharing at the Honnold Library of the Claremont Colleges, and above all to the staff and community of the Huntington Library, San Marino, California. Although I aim to be as authoritative and comprehensive as possible, my work no doubt has errors and omissions, for which I alone am responsible.

Notes

CHAPTER I

1. Useful overviews appear in Angus Fraser, *The Gypsies*, 2nd edn (1995); Yaron Matras, *I Met Lucky People: The Story of the Romani Gypsies* (2014); Becky Taylor, *Another Darkness, Another Dawn: A History of Gypsies, Roma and Travellers* (2014).

2. Arguments indicating an indigenous origin appear in Judith Okely, *The Traveller-Gypsies* (Cambridge, 1983; repr. 1993), 2–5, 15; Judith Okely, 'Ethnic Identity and Place of Origin: The Traveller Gypsies in Great Britain', in Hans Vermeulen and Jeremy Boissevain (eds), *Ethnic Challenge: The Politics of Ethnicity in Europe* (Gottingen, 1984), 53–9; Judith Okely, 'Some Political Consequences of Theories of Gypsy Ethnicity: The Place of the Intellectual', in Allison James, Jennifer Hockey, and Andrew Dawson (eds), *After Writing Culture: Epistemology and Praxis in Contemporary Anthropology* (1997), 227, 241; Judith Okely, 'Deterritorialised and Spatially Unbounded Cultures within Other Regimes', *Anthropological Quarterly*, 76 (2003), 152. See also Leo Lucassen, 'Eternal Vagrants? State Formation, Migration and Travelling Groups in Western Europe, 1350–1914', in Leo Lucassen, Wim Willems, and Annemarie Cottaar (eds), *Gypsies and Other Itinerant Groups: A Socio-Historical Approach* (Basingstoke, 1998), 55–73; David Mayall, *Gypsy Identities 1500–2000: From Egipcyans and Moon-Men to the Ethnic Romany* (2004), 59–60. Following Okely, Michael Stewart, *The Time of the Gypsies* (Oxford, 1997), 236, claims that Gypsies evolved from 'the landless poor who had refused to become proletarians'. Frances Timbers, *'The Damned Fraternitie': Constructing Gypsy Identity in Early Modern England, 1500–1700* (2016), 3, 23–5, 28, 39–45, derides the theory of Indian origins as 'primordialist' and romantic, and promotes the idea that Gypsy identity coalesced locally amid socio-economic upheavals.

3. Fraser, *Gypsies*, 10–32; Donald Kenrick, 'Romany Origins and Migration Patterns', *International Journal of Frontier Missions*, 17 (2000), 37–40, 56; Adrian Marsh, 'The Origins of the Gypsy Peoples: Identity and Influence in Romani History', *Kuri' Journal of the Dom Research Center*, 1 (2003) <http://www.domresearchcenter.com/journal/19/index.html> (accessed October 2017); Donald Kenrick, *Gypsies: From the Ganges to the Thames* (Hatfield, 2004); Ian Hancock, 'On Romany Origins and Identity—Questions for Discussion', in Adrian Marsh and Elin Strond (eds), *Gypsies and the Problem of Identities: Contextual, Constructed and Contested* (Istanbul, 2006), 69–92; Shulamith Shahar, 'Religious Minorities, Vagabonds and Gypsies in Early Modern Europe', in Roni Stauber and Raphael Vago (eds), *The Roma—A*

Minority in Europe: Historical, Political and Social Perspectives (Budapest, 2007), 1–18; Ronald Lee, 'Roma in Europe: "Gypsy" Myth and Romani Reality—New Evidence for Romani History', in Valentina Glajar and Domnica Radulescu (eds), *'Gypsies' in European Literature and Culture* (Basingstoke and New York, 2008), 1–9; Yaron Matras, 'Scholarship and the Politics of Romani Identity: Strategic and Conceptual Issues', *European Yearbook of Minority Issues*, 10 (2011), 213–16; Matras, *I Met Lucky People*, 104–12, 122; Taylor, *Another Darkness*, 18–30. For further review of competing theories, see David Cressy, 'Marginal People in a Stressful Culture: Gypsies and "Counterfeit Egyptians"', in Trevor Dean, Glyn Parry, and Edward Valance (eds), *Faith, Place, and People in Early Modern England* (forthcoming).

4. Fraser, *Gypsies*, 75; Donald Kenrick, 'The Origins of Anti-Gypsyism: The Outsiders' View of Romanies in Western Europe in the Fifteenth Century', in Nicholas Saul and Susan Tebbutt (eds), *The Role of the Romanies* (Liverpool, 2004), 79–84; Richard J. Pym, *The Gypsies of Early Modern Spain, 1425–1783* (Basingstoke and New York, 2007), 5, 8; Elisa Novi Chavarria, *Sulle tracce degli zingari: Il popolo rom nel Regno di Napoli (secoli XV–XVIII)* (Naples, 2007), 1–19; David Abulafia, 'The Coming of the Gypsies: Cities, Princes and Nomads', in P. Hoppenbrouwers, Antheun Janse, and Robert Stein (eds), *Power and Persuasion: Essays on the Art of State Building in Honour of W. P. Blockmans* (Turnhout, 2010), 325–42.

5. Agrippa von Nettesheim (Heinrich Cornelius), *The Vanity of Arts and Sciences* (1676), 213–14.

6. Paul Batillard, 'Immigration of the Gypsies into Western Europe in the Fifteenth Century', *Journal of the Gypsy Lore Society* (henceforth *JGLS*) 1 (1889), 336–8; Fraser, *Gypsies*, 72.

7. Heinrich Moritz Gottlieb Grellmann, *Dissertation on the Gipsies, Being an Historical Enquiry Concerning the Manner of Life, Oeconomy, Customs and Conditions of these People in Europe, and their Origin* (1787), trans. Matthew Raper from H. G. Grellmann, *Die Zigeuner* (Dessau and Leipzig, 1783); Yaron Matras, 'Johann Rüdiger and the Study of Romani in 18th Century Germany', *JGLS*, 5th ser., 9 (1999), 89–116; Yaron Matras, *Romani: A Linguistic Introduction* (Cambridge, 2002), 14–22; Yaron Matras, *Romani in Britain: The Afterlife of a Language* (Edinburgh, 2010), 31–40.

8. Recent claims and counter-claims are summarized in Yaron Matras, 'Transnational Policy and "Authenticity" Discourses on Romani Language and Identity', *Language in Society*, 44 (2015), 309–11.

9. Mayall, *Gypsy Identities*, 11, 225–6.

10. Sarabjit S. Mastana and Surinder S. Papiha, 'Origins of the Romany Gypsies: Genetic Evidence', *Zeitschrift für Morphologie und Anthropologie*, 79 (1992), 43–51; Luba Kalaydjieve et al., 'Genetic Studies of the Roma (Gypsies): A Review', *BMC Medical Genetics*, 2 (2001) <https://doi.org/10.1186/1471-2350-2-5> (accessed October 2017); David Gresham et al., 'Origins and Divergence of the Roma (Gypsies)', *American Journal of Human Genetics*, 69 (2001), 1314–31; Radu P. Iovita and Theodore G. Schurr, 'Reconstructing the Origins and Migrations

of Diasporic Populations: The Case of the European Gypsies', *American Anthropologist*, 106 (2004), 267–81; Bharti Morar et al., 'Mutation History of the Roma/Gypsies', *American Journal of Human Genetics*, 75 (2004), 596–609; Maria Regueiro et al., 'Divergent Patrilineal Signals in Three Roma Populations', *American Journal of Physical Anthropology*, 144 (2011), 80–91; Horolma Pamjav et al., 'Genetic Structure of the Paternal Lineage of the Roma People', *American Journal of Physical Anthropology*, 145 (2011), 21–9; Peter Bakker, 'Romani Genetic Linguistics and Genetics: Results, Prospects and Problems', *Romani Studies*, 5th ser., 22 (2012), 91–111; Niraj Rai et al., 'The Phylogeography of Y-Chromosome Haplogroup H1a1a-M82 Reveals the Likely Indian Origin of the European Romani Populations', *PLoS One*, 7/11 (2012) <http://e48477.doi.10.1371> (accessed October 2017).

11. Isabel Mendizabal et al., 'Reconstructing the Population History of European Romani from Genome-Wide Data', *Current Biology*, 22 (2012), 2342–9. Broadly consistent findings appear in Priya Moorjani et al, 'Reconstructing Roma History from Genome-Wide Data', *PLoS One*, 8/3 (2013), <https://doi.org/10.1371/journal.pone.0058633> (accessed October 2017). See also Begoña Martinez-Cruz et al., 'Origins, Admixture and Founder Lineages in European Roma', *European Journal of Human Genetics*, 24 (2016), 937–43.

12. Joachim S. Hohmann, *Geschichte der Zigeuner Verfolgung in Deutschland* (Frankfurt and New York, 1981), 13–16; Henriette Asséo, 'Marginalité et exclusion: Le Traitement adminstratif des Bohémiens dans la societé Française du XVIIe siècle', in Henriette Asséo and Jean-Paul Vittu (eds), *Problèmes socio-culturels au XVIIe au XVIIe siècle* (Paris, 1974), 9–87; Batillard, 'Immigration of the Gypsies', 40 n.; O. Van Kappen, 'Three Dutch Safe-Conducts for "Heidens"', *JGLS*, NS 41 (1962), 89.

13. Peter Pett, *The Happy Future State of England* (1688), 235.

14. B.E., *A New Dictionary of the Terms Ancient and Modern of the Canting Crew* (1699), preface.

15. John Ray, *A Collection of Curious Travels & Voyages*, 2 vols (1693), ii. 73.

16. George C. Soulis, 'The Gypsies in the Byzantine Empire and the Balkans in the Late Middle Ages', *Dumbarton Oaks Papers*, 15 (1961), 146–7; Fraser, *Gypsies*, 46–8; David M. Crowe, *A History of the Gypsies of Eastern Europe and Russia* (New York, 1996), 1; Elena Marushiakova and Vesselin Popov, *Gypsies in the Ottoman Empire* (Hatfield, 2001), 15.

17. Benedetto Fassanelli, ' "Piccoli Egitti" tra Cristianita e Islam: Prezenze zingare nel mediterraneo orientale (secc. XV–XVII)', *Quaderni storici*, 146 (2014), 349–82.

18. Fraser, *Gypsies*, 58–9; Crowe, *History of the Gypsies of Eastern Europe*, 107–23; Viorel Achim, *The Roma in Romanian History* (Budapest and New York, 2004); Fassanelli, ' "Piccoli Egitti" ', 366–74.

19. Taylor, *Another Darkness*, 24–5; Fraser, *Gypsies*, 61; Crowe, *History of the Gypsies of Eastern Europe*, 196–7; Lech Mróz, *Roma–Gypsy Presence in the Polish–Lithuanian Commonwealth 15th–18th Centuries* (Budapest, 2015), 17, 36, 46.

20. Batillard, 'Immigration of the Gypsies', 205–6, 260–1, 270; Reimer Gronemeyer, *Zigeuner im Spiegel Früher Chroniken und Abhandlungen: Quellen von 15 bis zum 18 Jarhundert* (Geissen, 1987), 15–28; Hohmann, *Geschichte der Zigeuner*, 13–16.

21. Fraser, *Gypsies*, 63–8; Batillard, 'Immigration of the Gypsies', 275, 324–45.

22. Batillard, 'Immigration of the Gypsies', 210, 337–41

23. Batillard, 'Immigration of the Gypsies', 338–42.

24. Asséo, 'Marginalité et exclusion'; Batillard, 'Immigration of the Gypsies', 340 n.

25. Asséo, 'Marginalité et exclusion', 17.

26. Batillard, 'Immigration of the Gypsies', 325–8.

27. Batillard, 'Immigration of the Gypsies', 327.

28. Fraser, *Gypsies*, 69–70.

29. Batillard, 'Immigration of the Gypsies', 330–5; David MacRitchie, 'Gypsies at Geneva in the 15th, 16th, and 17th Centuries', *JGLS*, NS 6 (1912–13), 81–6; Fraser, *Gypsies*, 92–4.

30. Batillard, 'Immigration of the Gypsies', 8; Paul Batillard, 'Immigration of the Gypsies into Western Europe in the Fifteenth Century' (continued), *JGLS* 2 (1890), 28–31. *London Magazine: Or, Gentleman's Monthly Intelligencer* for August 1747, 366–8, tells this story in English from French sources. See also Asséo, 'Marginalité et exclusion', 14; Fraser, *Gypsies*, 73–4, 77–8; *Journal d'un Bourgeois de Paris* (Paris, 1881); *A Parisian Journal 1405–1449*, trans. Janet Shirley (Oxford, 1968), 216–19.

31. Batillard, 'Immigration of the Gypsies' (cont.), 31–2.

32. Batillard, 'Immigration of the Gypsies' (cont.), 33–4.

33. Asséo, 'Marginalité et exclusion', 16–18; Fraser, *Gypsies*, 73–4, 77–8, 9–4.

34. Batillard, 'Immigration of the Gypsies', 334–6; Bronislaw Geremek, 'L'Arrivée des tsiganes en Italie: De l'assistance a las répression', in Giorgi Politi, Maria Rosa, and Franco della Peruta (eds), *Timore e carita: I poveri nell' Italia moderna* (Cremona, 1982), 27–44; Giorgio Viaggio, *Storia degli zingari in Italia* (Rome, 1997), 13–29; Novi Chavarria, *Sulle tracce degli zingari*, 22–5.

35. Batillard, 'Immigration of the Gypsies', 336–8; Viaggio, *Storia degli zingari in Italia*, 16–27; Fraser, *Gypsies*, 72.

36. A. G. Spinelli, 'Gli zingari nel Modenese', *JGLS*, NS 3 (1909), 42–57, 88–111; Fraser, *Gypsies*, 73, 105–6; Novi Chavarria, *Sulle tracce degli zingari*, 25.

37. Elisa Novi Chavarria, 'I cognomi del popolo rom', in Andrea Addobbati, Roberto Bizzocchi, and Gregorio Salinero (eds), *L'Italia dei cognomi: L'antroponimia italiana nel quadro mediterraneo* (Pisa, 2013), 3.

38. Viaggio, *Storia degli zingari in Italia*, 15–16; Novi Chavarria, *Sulle tracce degli zingari*, 25–30, 35–8.

39. Fraser, *Gypsies*, 76–7; Pym, *Gypsies of Early Modern Spain*, 2, 4. See also Aaron C. Taylor, 'A Possible Early Reference to Gypsies in Spain Prior to 1420: MS 940 of the Trivulziana Library in Milan, Italy', *Romani Studies*, 5th ser., 26 (2016), 79–86.

40. Soulis, 'Gypsies in the Byzantine Empire', 154; Pym, *Gypsies of Early Modern Spain*, 9; Marushiakova and Popov, *Gypsies in the Ottoman Empire*, 34–6, 41–2

41. Fernanda Baroco and David Lagunas, 'Another Otherness: The Case of the Roma in Mexico', in Premysel Macha and Eloy Gomez-Pellon (eds), *Masks of Identity: Representing and Performing Otherness in Latin America* (Newcastle upon Tyne, 2014), 97.

42. Kenrick, *Gypsies: From the Ganges to the Thames*, 36, 39, 56. See also the chronology in Donald Kenrick, *Historical Dictionary of the Gypsies (Romanies)* (Lanham, MD, and London, 1988), pp. xvii–xxi.

43. Sebastian Münster, *La Cosmographie universelle, contenant la situation de toutes les parties du monde, avec leurs proprietez et appartenances* (Basle, 1552), 286–8; Sebastian Münster, *Cosmographia Universalis* (Basle, 1572), 357–8; D. M. M. Bartlett, 'Münster's *Cosmographia Universalis*', *JGLS*, 3rd ser., 31 (1952), 83–90. First published in 1544, with twenty-one editions in German by 1628, Münster's encyclopedia became an international bestseller well into the seventeenth century. See also Jacob Thomasius, *Curiöser Tractat von Zigeunern* (Dresden, 1702); Nicholas Saul, *Gypsies and Orientalism in German Literature and Anthropology of the Long Nineteenth Century* (2007), 2–4.

44. See Chapter 2 for comments by Thomas Dekker, Samuel Rid, and others.

45. Jean Talpin, La Police chrétienne (Paris, 1572), trans. Geoffrey Fenton as *A Forme of Christian Pollicie* (1574), 167.

46. Philip Camerarius, *The Living Librarie, or, Meditations and Observations Historical, Natural, Moral, Political, and Poetical* (1621), 54–5. First published in Latin in 1615, and soon after in French and German, this encyclopedic work appeared in English in 1621 and 1625, translated by John Molle. See also the Tuscan lawyer Antonia Maria Cospi, *Il giudice criminalista* (Florence, 1643), describing Gypsies as 'thieves by nature...They make deception, changes, and prognostication from the lines of the hand, and earn their living by these amusing frauds...The women steal chickens, and while they pretend to tell one's fortune by the signs of the hand, rob the peasants and steal the women's purses and handkerchiefs', in Andrew Graham-Dixon, *Caravaggio: A Life Sacred and Profane* (New York, 2011), 106.

47. For the Italian version of fast and loose, 'il gioco della correzuola', see Benedetto Fassanelli, 'Una prezenza inammissibile: I cingani nella terraferma veneta durante il secolo dei bandi', *Italia romani*, 5 (2008), 54–5. The trick is illustrated on the title page of *Comedia llamada Aurelia* (Valencia, 1564), where one of the *gitanos* holds the rope and stick. For an eye-witness description from seventeenth-century Yorkshire, see John Webster, *The Displaying of Supposed Witchcraft: Wherein it is affirmed that there are many sorts of Deceivers and Impostors* (1677), 61–2. See also Reginald Scot, *The Discouerie of Witchcraft* (1584), 336–7; *Hocus Pocus Iunior. The Anatomie of Legerdemain* (1634), 1–2.

48. Gronemeyer, *Zigeuner im Spiegel Früher Chroniken und Abhandlungen*, 88; Hohmann, *Geschichte der Zigeuner*, 16–31; Daniel Strauss, 'Anti-Gypsyism in German-Speaking Society and Literature', in Susan Tebbutt (ed.), *Sinti and Roma in German-Speaking Society and Literature* (New York and Oxford, 1998; paperback edn 2008), 81–9; Leo Lucassen, 'Between Hobbes and Locke: Gypsies and the

Limits of the Modernization Paradigm', *Social History*, 22 (2008), 433; Fraser, *Gypsies*, 85, 87–90.

49. Mróz, *Roma–Gypsy Presence in the Polish–Lithuanian Commonwealth*, 78, 127.

50. Fraser, *Gypsies*, 90; MacRitchie, 'Gypsies at Geneva', 81–5.

51. Crowe, *History of the Gypsies of Eastern Europe*, 34, 155; Fraser, *Gypsies*, 111, 121. The English legislation is examined in Chapter 3.

52. Van Kappen, 'Three Dutch Safe-Conducts for "Heidens"', 89–100; O.Van Kappen, 'A Contribution to the History of the Gypsies in the Bishopric of Liège (1540–1726)', *JGLS*, NS 46 (1967), 142–50.

53. Spinelli, 'Gli zingari nel Modenese', 48–57; 'Andreas', 'Two Italian Gypsy Edicts', *JGLS*, 3rd ser., 13 (1934), 45–9; Maria Zuccon, 'La legislazione sugli Zingari negli stati Italiania prima della rivoluzione', *Lacio Drom*, 15 (1979), 1–68; Geremek, 'L'Arrivée des tsiganes en Italie', 43; Fraser, *Gypsies*, 106–7.

54. 'Venetian Edicts Relating to the Gypsies of the Sixteenth, Seventeenth, and Eighteenth centuries. (Extracted from the Archivio dei Frari, at Venice)', *JGLS* 2 (1889), 358–62; Benedetto Fassanelli, '"Considerata la mala qualità delli Cingani erranti": I Rom nella repubblica di Venezia: Retoriche e stereotipi', *Acta Histriae*, 15 (2007), 139–54; Fassanelli, 'Una prezenza inammissibile'.

55. Zuccon, 'La legislazione sugli Zingari', 44–9; Viaggio, *Storia degli zingari in Italia*, 51–4; Novi Chavarria, *Sulle tracce degli zingari*, 121–31.

56. Adriano Colocci, 'The Gypsies in the Marches of Ancona during the 16th, 17th, and 18th Centuries', *JGLS* 2 (1889), 213–20.

57. Zuccon, 'La legislazione sugli Zingari', 50–2; Novi Chavarria, *Sulle tracce degli zingari*, 35–42, 126–31, 145–60; Elisa Novi Chavarria, 'Pluralita di appartenenze: Gruppi e individui "Di Nazione Zingara" nel mezzogiorno spagnolo', *Quaderni storici*, 146 (2014), 383–406.

58. Fassanelli, '"Considerata la mala qualità delli Cingani erranti"'; Fassanelli, 'Una prezenza inammissibile'; Benedetto Fassanelli, '"Andar con Cigani" o "Viver Christianamente"? Tipi, icone e visioni del mondo attraverso un *Costituto* cinquecentesco', in Felice Gambin (ed.), *Alle radici dell'Europa: Mori, giudei e zingari nel paesi del Mediterraneao Occidentale (secoli XV–XVII)* (Florence, 2008), 79–92; Benedetto Fassanelli, '"In Casa del Boldu Siamo Stati una Sera": Pratiche relazaione di una compagnia di "Cingani in Viazo" nella terraferma veneta di fine cinquecento', *Quaderni storici*, 129 (2008), 691–723.

59. Spinelli, 'Gli zingari nel Modenese', 96. On England, see Chapters 3 and 4.

60. J. Moreno Casado, 'Los gitanos de España bajo Carlos I', *Chronica nova*, 4–5 (1969), 183–5; Pym, *Gypsies of Early Modern Spain*, 24–5; Fraser, *Gypsies*, 96–100; Enrique Garrido and Díez de Baldeón, 'Estudio aproximativo de la legislación relativa a la etnia gitana en los siglos XV, XVI y XVII: Dificultades, controversias, aplicación y escritos de los memorialistas y arbitristas', *Tiempos modernos*, 23 (2011), 1–40.

61. Casado, 'Los gitanos de España', 186–94. On galley manpower, see John F. Guilmartin, *Gunpowder and Galleys: Changing Technology and Mediterranean Warfare at Sea in the Sixteenth Century* (New York, 1974).

62. Pym, *Gypsies of Early Modern Spain*, 29, 33, 36, 53, 61, 86–92, 106–18.

63. Niccolo Guasti, 'The Debate on the Expulsion of the Gypsies in the Castilian *Arbitrismo* of the Early Seventeenth Century', in Sina Rauschenbach and Christian Windler (eds), *Reforming Early Modern Monarchies: The Castilian Arbitristas in Comparative European Perspective* (Wiesbaden, 2016), 157–76, quoting Pedro Salazar de Mendoza, *Memorial de el hecho de los Gitanos* (Toledo, 1618), and Juan de Quinones, *Discurso contra los Gitanos* (Madrid, 1631).

64. Robert Treswell, *A Relation of Such Things as were Observed to Happen in the Iourney of the Right Honourable Charles Earle of Nottingham* (1605), 27.

65. Bill M. Donovan, 'Changing Perceptions of Social Deviance: Gypsies in Early Modern Portugal and Brazil', *Journal of Social History*, 26 (1992), 33–53; Fraser, *Gypsies*, 100; Taylor, *Another Darkness* 54, 88–91.

66. Casado, 'Los gitanos de España', 194–8; 'Notes and Queries: Gipsies in America, 1581', *JGLS*, NS 6 (1912), 61.

67. Asséo, 'Marginalité et exclusion', 19, 24; Fraser, *Gypsies*, 95.

68. Asséo, 'Marginalité et exclusion', 22–3; Frederick Christian Wellstood, 'A Contribution to French Gypsy History', *JGLS*, NS 3 (1909), 20; Jean-Pierre Liégeois, *Gypsies and Travellers: Socio-Cultural Data. Socio-Political Data* (Strasbourg, 1987), 91–2; Fraser, *Gypsies*, 94–5.

69. Cornwall Record Office, Truro, AR/26/2; Sally L. Joyce and Evelyn S. Newlyn (eds), *Records of Early English Drama: Cornwall* (Toronto, 1999), 530.

70. See Chapter 3.

71. Asséo, 'Marginalité et exclusion', 23. Gypsies at Nîmes in 1521 were feared to be carriers of the plague.

72. Asséo, 'Marginalité et exclusion', 23–4, 42.

73. Asséo, 'Marginalité et exclusion', 24; F. C. Wellstood, 'Some French Edicts against the Gypsies', *JGLS*, NS 5 (1911), 313–14.

74. Asséo, 'Marginalité et exclusion', 18, 25.

75. Fenton, *Forme of Christian Pollicie*, 167.

76. Fraser, *Gypsies*, 119–20; Timbers, *'Damned Fraternitie'*, 16. The drawing is in the municipal archives at Arras, France. James V visited France in 1536–7.

77. Pechon de Ruby, *La Vie généreuse des Mercelots, Geux et Boemiens* (Paris, 1586; repr. 1596, 1612, 1618, 1627).

78. Asséo, 'Marginalité et exclusion', 25–6; 33–4; Wellstood, 'Some French Edicts against the Gypsies', 314.

79. Henriette Asséo, '"Bohesmiens du Royaume": L'insediamento dinastico dei "Capitaines Égyptiens" nella Francia di Antico Regime (1550–1660)', *Quaderni storici*, 146 (2014), 453.

80. Asséo, 'Marginalité et exclusion', 35–7, 46; Asséo, '"Bohesmiens du Royaume"', 457.

81. Asséo, 'Marginalité et exclusion', 50; Asséo, '"Bohesmiens du Royaume"', 446.

82. François de Vaux de Foletier, 'Recherches sur l'histoire des Tsiganes dans les anciens registres paroissiaux', *Etudes Tsiganes*, 2 (1956), 3–11.

83. Asséo, '"Bohesmiens du Royaume"'; Tallement des Réaux, *Historiettes*, 2 vols (Paris, 1960–1), ii. 844–5.

84. Asséo, 'Marginalité et exclusion', 27–9, 60; Wellstood, 'Contribution to French Gypsy History', 201; Wellstood, 'Some French Edicts against the Gypsies', 315.

85. Lucassen, 'Eternal Vagrants?', 62.

86. Asséo, 'Marginalité et exclusion', 31; Wellstood, 'Some French Edicts against the Gypsies', 315–16.

87. Asséo, 'Marginalité et exclusion', 31–3, 61–5.

88. François de Vaux de Foletier, *Les Tsiganes dans l'Ancienne France* (Paris, 1961), 152–60.

89. Asséo, 'Marginalité et exclusion', 58.

90. Asséo, 'Marginalité et exclusion', 72–5.

91. Ann Ostendorf, 'A Bohémian Community in Colonial Louisiana', paper presented at the Gyspy Lore Society Conference on Romani Studies, Stockholm, September 2016. The names of 'bohemians' and 'women who became bohemians' who sailed aboard *Le Tilleul* in May 1720 are listed in Albert J. Robichaux, Jr, *German Coast Families: European Origins and Settlement in Colonial Louisiana* (Rayne, LA, 1997), 432–7.

92. Thomas Acton, 'Categorising Irish Travellers', in May McCann, Séamas O Síocháin, and Joseph Ruane (eds), *Irish Travellers: Culture and Ethnicity* (Belfast, 1994), 36, 43, 45.

93. The history of Gypsies in Scotland has been well served by the Victorian Gypsylorist David MacRitchie, *Scottish Gypsies under the Stewarts* (Edinburgh, 1894), and by his predecessors Walter Simson and James Simson, *A History of the Gipsies: With Specimens of the Gipsey Language* (1865; London and New York, 1866). Although their interpretations were flawed by their quest for the 'true' Gypsy soul, their antiquarian research uncovered a wide range of documents. They were aided by the early nineteenth-century publication of *Criminal Trials in Scotland*, and by editions of Burgh and Privy Council records. All subsequent commentators are indebted to their work. The sections on Scotland in Fraser, *Gypsies*, are based almost entirely on MacRitchie and the Simsons. A fresh approach, in a broader British context, offers an expanded and updated revision of a familiar narrative.

94. Simson and Simson, *History of the Gipsies*, 99–100; MacRitchie, *Scottish Gypsies*, 29–30; Fraser, *Gypsies*, 111–12.

95. Fraser, *Gypsies*, 117.

96. Gerald Power, 'Gypsies and Sixteenth-Century Ireland', *Romani Studies*, 5th ser. 24 (2014), 204–6.

97. Lambeth Palace Library, Carew Manuscripts, MS 614, p. 260, MS 629, p. 29.

98. MacRitchie, *Scottish Gypsies*, 32–6; Fraser, *Gypsies*, 116–17.

99. Simson and Simson, *History of the Gipsies*, 101–3; MacRitchie, *Scottish Gypsies*, 37–9; Fraser, *Gypsies*, 117–18; Timbers, 'Damned Fraternitie', 83–7, 98.

100. MacRitchie, *Scottish Gypsies*, 40–4; Fraser, *Gypsies*, 118, 120.

101. Simson and Simson, *History of the Gipsies*, 104–5.

102. Simson and Simson, *History of the Gipsies*, 106; MacRitchie, *Scottish Gypsies*, 41; Fraser, *Gypsies*, 118.

103. Simson and Simson, *History of the Gipsies*, 107; MacRitchie, *Scottish Gypsies*, 44.

104. G. W. Shirley, 'A Loan to a Scottish Gypsy', *JGLS*, NS 8 (1914), 10–11.

105. MacRitchie, *Scottish Gypsies*, 62–7.

106. Simson and Simson, *History of the Gipsies*, 110; MacRitchie, *Scottish Gypsies*, 67–72.

107. Simson and Simson, *History of the Gipsies*, 111, 119; Eric Otto Winstedt, 'Early British Gypsies', *JGLS*, NS 7 (1913–14), 24, 26. See Chapter 3 for discussion of the word 'counterfeit'.

108. Robert Pitcairn (ed.), *Criminal Trials in Scotland from A.D. MCCCCLXXXVIII to A.D. MDCXXIV* (Edinburgh, 1833), 201; Simson and Simson, *History of the Gipsies*, 111–12; MacRitchie, *Scottish Gypsies*, 80–1.

109. David Masson (ed.), *The Register of the Privy Council of Scotland. Volume X: 1613–1616* (Burlington, Ontario, 2004), 655–7; MacRitchie, *Scottish Gypsies*, 94–6.

110. Pitcairn (ed.), *Criminal Trials in Scotland*, 90 (my modernization from the Scots).

111. Masson (ed.), *Register of the Privy Council of Scotland. Volume X: 1613–1616*, 556, 559, 579, 620; Pitcairn (ed.), *Criminal Trials in Scotland*, 202; MacRitchie, *Scottish Gypsies*, 82–3.

112. Masson (ed.), *Register of the Privy Council of Scotland. Volume X: 1613–1616*, 132; MacRitchie, *Scottish Gypsies*, 84, 87,

113. MacRitchie, *Scottish Gypsies*, 53, 86; John R. Tudor, *Orkneys and Shetland: Their Past and Present* (1883), 117.

114. Pitcairn (ed.), *Criminal Trials in Scotland*, 398–9; MacRitchie, *Scottish Gypsies*, 88–94.

115. MacRitchie, *Scottish Gypsies*, 99.

116. Pitcairn (ed.), *Criminal Trials in Scotland*, 559–62; MacRitchie, *Scottish Gypsies*, 99.

117. David Masson (ed.), *The Register of the Privy Council of Scotland. Second Series. Volume I: 1625–1627* (Burlington, Ontario, 2004), 217–18.

118. Masson (ed.), *Register of the Privy Council of Scotland…1625–1627*, 542–3, 546–7, 565–6; MacRitchie, *Scottish Gypsies*, 101.

119. P. Hume Brown (ed.), *The Register of the Privy Council of Scotland. Second Series. Volume II: 1627–1628* (Burlington, Ontario, 2004), 444.

120. Simson and Simson, *History of the Gipsies*, 119; MacRitchie, *Scottish Gypsies*, 100–1.

121. MacRitchie, *Scottish Gypsies*, 101.

122. MacRitchie, *Scottish Gypsies*, 102.

123. MacRitchie, *Scottish Gypsies*, 102–3; Winstedt, 'Early British Gypsies', 29; Fraser, *Gypsies*, 170–1.

124. Winstedt, 'Early British Gypsies', 30.

125. MacRitchie, *Scottish Gypsies*, 108–9; Winstedt, 'Early British Gypsies', 30–3.

126. David Dobson, *Directory of Scots Banished to the American Plantations, 1650–1775* (Baltimore, 1983), 6.

127. Simson and Simson, *History of the Gipsies*, 119–20; MacRitchie, *Scottish Gypsies*, 113–17.

128. Fraser, *Gypsies*, 171; Gwendon Morgan and Peter Rushton, *Eighteenth-Century Criminal Transportation: The Formation of the Criminal Atlantic* (Basingstoke and New York, 2004), 14–15; Timbers, *'Damned Fraternitie'*, 83.

129. Ian Hancock, *The Pariah Syndrome: An Account of Gypsy Slavery and Persecution* (Ann Arbor, 1987), 58; Lee, 'Roma in Europe: "Gypsy" Myth and Romani Reality', 6; http://romafacts.uni-graz.at/index.php/history/early-european-history-first-discrimination/western-europe (accessed 4 November 2014).

130. R. A. Scott MacFie, 'Gypsy Persecutions: A Survey of a Black Chapter in European History', *JGLS*, NS 22 (1943), 65–78; Hohmann, *Geschichte der Zigeuner*, 27–43; Liégeois, *Gypsies and Travellers*, 92–3; Wim Willems and Leo Lucassen, 'The Church of Knowledge: Representation of Gypsies in Dutch Encyclopedias and their Sources (1724–1984)', in Matt. T. Salo (ed.), *100 Years of Gypsy Studies* (Cheverly, MD, 1900), 31–50; Taylor, *Another Darkness*, 72–86, 100–11.

131. O. Van Kappen, *Geschiedenis der Zigeuners in Nederland: De Ontwikkeling van de Rechtspositie der Heidens of Egyptenaren in de Noordelijke Nederlanden (1420–±1750)* (Assen, 1965), 463–73, 551–2; Pieter Spierenburg, *The Spectacle of Suffering: Executions and the Evolution of Repression: From a Preindustrial Metropolis to the European Experience* (Cambridge, 1984), 173–5.

132. Van Kappen, *Geschiedenis der Zigeuners in Nederland*, 463–6.

133. Van Kappen, *Geschiedenis der Zigeuners in Nederland*, 463–6.

134. Richard Andree, 'Old Warning-Placards for Gypsies', *JGLS*, NS 5 (1911), 202–4; Eva Lacour, 'Faces of Violence Revisited. A Typology of Violence in Early Modern Rural Germany', *Journal of Social History*, 34 (2001), 658–9.

135. Stephan Steiner, ' "Making Short Work by Flogging, Hanging and Beheading": A "Gypsy" Trial and its Pitfalls', *Frühneuzeit-Info* (Early Modern Studies Institute, Vienna), 25 (2014), 154–60.

136. Hohmann, *Geschichte der Zigeuner*, 27–36; Eric Otto Winstedt, 'Some Records of the Gypsies in Germany', *JGLS*, 3rd ser., 11 (1932), 97–111; 12 (1933), 123–31, 189–96; 13 (1934), 98–116; Taylor, *Another Darkness*, 76–9.

137. Leo Lucassen and Wim Willems, 'The Weakness of Well-Ordered Societies: Gypsies in Western Europe, the Ottoman Empire, and India, 1400–1914', *Review of the Fernand Braudel Center*, 26 (2003), 295–8; MacFie, 'Gypsy Persecutions: A Survey of a Black Chapter', 68; Grellmann, *Dissertation on the Gipsies*, 4.

138. Jules Admant, 'Les Bohémiens et leurs juges en Lorraine au XVIIIe siècle', *Revue transversales du Centre Georges Chevrier*, 8 (2016) <http://tristan.u-bourgogne.fr/CGC/publications/transversales/Entre_confrontation_reconnaissance-rejet/J_Admant.html> (accessed November 2016).

139. Novi Chavarria, *Sulle tracce degli zingari*, 171–2.

140. 'Venetian Edicts Relating to the Gypsies', 360–2; Viaggio, *Storia degli zingari in Italia*, 54; Alice Vezzoli, 'Migration, Non-Integration and Integration of *Cingani* (Gypsies) in the Republic of Venice during the Early Modern Age', University of Leiden, MA thesis, 2013.

141. Grellmann, *Dissertation on the Gipsies*, 82–8; Hohmann, *Geschichte der Zigeuner*, 43–4; James Crabb, *The Gipsies' Advocate; or Observations on the Origin, Character,*

Manners, and Habits, of the English Gipsies, 3rd edn (1832), 95; Saul, *Gypsies and Orientalism in German Literature*, 4–8; Taylor, *Another Darkness*, 102–3. See also Tara Zahra, '"Condemned to Rootlessness and Unable to Budge": Roma, Migration Panics, and Internment in the Habsburg Empire', *American Historical Review*, 122 (2017), 702–26.

142. Donovan, 'Changing Perceptions of Social Deviance', 38–40; Taylor, *Another Darkness*, 88.

143. Pym, *Gypsies of Early Modern Spain*, 152–64; Antonio Gomez Alfaro, *The Great Gypsy Round-Up. Spain: The General Imprisonment of the Gypsies in 1749* (Madrid, 1993); Ruth MacKay, '*Lazy Improvident People': Myth and Reality in the Writing of Spanish History* (Ithaca, NY, and London, 2006), 187–8.

144. *Pragmatica-Sancion en Fuerza de Ley, En que se dan Nuevas Reglas para contener y castigar la vagancia de los que hasta aqui se han conocido con el nombre de Gitanos, o Castellanos nuevos, con lo demes que expresa* (Seville, 1783).

145. See Chapter 6.

146. Margarita Torrione, 'El Traje Antiguo de los Gitanos: Aletrida y Castigo', *Cuadernos Hispanoamericanos*, 536 (1995), 19–42; Erwin Pokorny, 'The Gypsies and their Impact on Fifteenth-Century Western European Iconography', in Jaynie Anderson (ed.), *Crossing Cultures: Conflict, Migration and Convergence: The Proceedings of the 32nd International Congress of the History of Art* (Melbourne, 2009), 597–601; Erwin Pokorny, 'Das Ziegeunerbild in der Altdeutschen Kunst: Ethnographisches Interesse und Antiziagnismus', in Andreas Tacke and Stefan Heinz (eds), *Menschenbilder Beiträge zur Altdeutschen Kunst* (Petersberg, 2011), 97–110.

147. John F. Moffitt, *Caravaggio in Context: Learned Naturalism and Renaissance Humanism* (Jefferson, NC, 2004), 45; Tom Nichols, *The Art of Poverty: Irony and Ideal in Sixteenth-Century Beggar Imagery* (Manchester, 2008), 49.

148. Hans Burgkmair, *Gypsies in the Market*, National Museum, Stockholm; Tilman Falk, *Hans Burgkmair Studien zu Leben und Werke des Augsburger Malers* (Munich, 1968), 23–4, 134; Andrew Morrall, 'Soldiers and Gypsies: Outsiders and their Families in Early Sixteenth Century German Art', in Pia Cuneo (ed.), *Artful Armies, Beautiful Battles: Art and Warfare in Early Modern Europe* (Leiden, 2002), 159–80; Tom Nichols, 'The Vagabond Image: Depictions of False Beggars in Northern Art of the Sixteenth Century', in Tom Nichols (ed.), *Others and Outcasts in Early Modern Europe: Picturing the Social Margins* (Aldershot and Burlington, VT, 2007), 37–60.

149. Edward J. Sullivan, 'Jacque Callot's *Les Bohémiens*', *Art Bulletin*, 59 (1977), 217–21; Musée Historique Lorrain, *Jacques Callot 1592–1635* (Paris, 1992), 282–5; Dena Woodall and Diane Wolfthal, *Princes and Paupers: The Art of Jacques Callot* (New Haven, 2013); Ruby, *La Vie généreuse des Mercelots, Geux et Boemiens*.

150. Rheinhold Regensburger, 'Gypsy Fortune-Tellers as a Subject of the Italian Baroque Painters', *JGLS*, 3rd ser., 45 (1966), 1–6; Moffitt, *Caravaggio in Context*, 41–62.

151. John Barrell, *The Dark Side of the Landscape: The Rural Poor in English Painting 1730–1840* (Cambridge, 1980); K. D. M. Snell, 'In or Out of their Place: The

Migrant Poor in English Art, 1740–1900', *Rural History*, 24 (2013), 73–100. See also Gypsies in paintings by Henrick Avercamp, Philips Wouwerman, David Teniers, and Thomas Gainsborough.

152. Gil Vicente, *Farça das Ciganas* (Lisbon, 1521); Gigio Artemio Giancarli, *La Zingara* (Mantua, 1545); Lope de Rueda, *Comedia Llamada Medora* (Madrid, 1567); Lou Charnon-Deutsch, *The Spanish Gypsy: The History of a European Obsession* (College Park, PA, 2004), 18.

153. Miguel de Cervantes, *Novelas Exemplares* (Madrid, 1613); Miguel de Cervantes, *La Gitanilla: The Little Gypsie* (1709); Charnon-Deutsch, *Spanish Gypsy*, 19, 27. See also Walter Starkie, 'Cervantes and the Gypsies', *Huntington Library Quarterly*, 26 (1963), 337–49.

154. Thomas Middleton and William Rowley, *The Spanish Gypsie* (performed 1623; printed 1653).

155. Thomas D'Urfey, *Trick for Trick* (1678), Act 2, scene 1.

156. James F. Gaines (ed.), *The Molière Encyclopedia* (Westport, CT, 2002), 211–12.

157. See Chapter 2. See also Sarah Houghton-Walker, *Representations of the Gypsy in the Romantic Period* (Oxford, 2014); Katie Trumpener, 'The Time of the Gypsies: A "People without History" in the Narratives of the West', *Critical Inquiry*, 18 (1992), 843–84.

158. Claus Schreiner (ed.), *Flamenco Gypsy Dance and Music from Andalusia* (Portland, OR, 1990), 16, 42–3; Bernard Leblon, *Gypsies and Flamenco: The Emergence of the Art of Flamenco in Andalusia* (Hatfield, 2003), 3–10, 37–43; Carol Silverman, *Romani Routes: Cultural Politics and Balkan Music in Diaspora* (Oxford, 2012); Anna G. Piotrowska, *Gypsy Music in European Culture from the Late Eighteenth to the Early Nineteenth Centuries* (Boston, 2013); Petra Gelbart, 'Gypsyness and the Uhrovska Manuscript', *Transactions of the Royal Historical Society*, 22 (2012), 209.

159. See Crowe, *History of the Gypsies of Eastern Europe*, 4, for wars in 1736–9, 1768–74, and 1787–91.

160. Lucassen, 'Between Hobbes and Locke', 437; Crowe, *History of the Gypsies of Eastern Europe*, 8, 11

161. Fraser, *Gypsies*, 58–9; Crowe, *History of the Gypsies of Eastern Europe*, 119.

162. Jim MacLaughlin, 'European Gypsies and the Historical Geography of Loathing', *Review of the Fernand Braudel Center*, 22 (1999), 31–59; Margaret Brearley, 'The Persecution of Gypsies in Europe', *American Behavioral Scientist*, 45 (2001), 588–99; Angus Bancroft, *Roma and Gypsy-Travellers in Europe: Modernity, Race, Space and Exclusion* (Aldershot, 2005); Peter Vermeersch, *The Romani Movement: Minority Politics and Ethnic Mobilization in Contemporary Central Europe* (Oxford and New York, 2006); Nando Sigona and Nidhi Trehan (eds), *Romani Politics in Contemporary Europe: Poverty, Ethnic Mobilization, and the Neoliberal Order* (Basingstoke and New York, 2009).

163. Kenrick, *Historical Dictionary of the Gypsies*, pp. xiii, 1; European Commission, *The Situation of Roma in an Enlarged European Union* (Luxembourg, 2004);

Commission on Security and Cooperation in Europe, *The Human Rights Situation of Roma: Europe's Largest Ethnic Minority* (Washington, 2008), 28–9.

164. *Council of Europe Descriptive Glossary of Terms Relating to Roma Issues* (Strasbourg, 2012), 8; Jean-Pierre Liégeois, *The Council of Europe and Roma: 40 Years of Action* (Strasbourg, 2012), 7, 11–12.

CHAPTER 2

1. Samuel Rid, *The Art of Iugling or Legerdemaine* (1612), sig. B; Thomas Harman, *A Caveat or Warening for Commen Cursetors Vulgarely Called Vagabones* (1567, 1573), sig. Aiii^v; Thomas Dekker, *The Belman of London. Bringing to Light the Most Notorious Villanies that are now Practiced in the Kingdome* (1608), sig. C^v.

2. Thomas More, *A Dyaloge of Syr Thomas More* (1529), otherwise known as *A Dialogue Concerning Heresies*, bk 3, fo. 91; Henry Thomas Crofton, 'Early Annals of the Gypsies in England', *JGLS* 1 (1888), 7.

3. Arthur Ogle, *The Tragedy of the Lollards' Tower: The Case of Richard Hunne, with its Aftermath in the Reformation Parliament* (Oxford, 1949), 94–9; Richard Marius, *Thomas More: A Biography* (New York, 1984), 135–41.

4. *The Complete Poems of John Skelton Laureate,* ed. Philip Henderson (1959), 114, 391. Cf. Pontius Pilate, in John 19:22: 'What I have written, I have written.'

5. Crofton, 'Early Annals', 7; Edward Hall, *Union of the Two Noble and Illustrate Famelies of Lancastre & Yorke* (1548), fo. lxviii.

6. Andrew Boorde, *The Fyrst Boke of the Introduction of Knowledge* (1542; repr. 1562), ch. 38, sigs Nii–Nii^v. On the linguistic significance of Boorde's word list, see Ian Hancock, 'Romani and Angloromani', in Peter Trudgill (ed.), *Language in the British Isles* (Cambridge, 1984), 368, 378–9; Matras, *Romani in Britain*, 58.

7. John Awdeley, *The Fraternitie of Vacabondes* (1565); Thomas Harman, *A Caveat for Commen Cursetors Vulgarely Called Vagabones* (1567); Dekker, *Belman of London*; Thomas Dekker, *Lanthorne and Candle-Light. Or the Bell-mans Second Nights Walke* (1608); Samuel Rid, *Martin Mark-all, Beadle of Bridewell: His Defence and Answere to the Belman of London* (1610); and Rid, *Art of Iugling.*

8. Bryan Reynolds, *Becoming Criminal: Transverse Performance and Cultural Dissidence in Early Modern England* (Baltimore and London, 2002), 22, 24, 29, 34, 43, 47, 64. The mostly literary discussion of cony-catching texts includes Frank Aydelotte, *Elizabethan Rogues and Vagabonds* (Oxford, 1913); A. V. Judges, *The Elizabethan Underworld: A Collection of Tudor and Early Stuart Tracts and Ballads Telling of the Lives and Misdoings of Vagabonds, Thieves, Rogues and Cozeners, and Giving Some Account of the Operation of the Criminal Law* (1930; repr. 1965); Arthur F. Kinney (ed.), *Rogues, Vagabonds, & Sturdy Beggars: A New Gallery of Tudor and Early Stuart Rogue Literature* (Barre, MA, 1973); Gamini Salgado, *The Elizabethan Underworld* (1977; repr. 1997); John L. McMullan, *The Canting Crew: London's Criminal Underworld 1550–1700* (New Brunswick, 1984); Pascale Drouet, *Le Vagabond dans l'Angleterre de Shakespeare: Ou l'art de contrefaire à la*

ville at à la scène (Paris, 2003); Paola Pugliatti, *Beggary and Theatre in Early Modern England* (2003); Anna Bayman, 'Rogues, Conycatching and the Scribbling Crew', *History Workshop Journal*, 63 (2007), 1–17; Anupam Basu, ' "Like Very Honest and Substantial Citizens": Cony-Catching as Social Performance', *English Literary Renaissance*, 44 (2014), 36–55. For more sceptical assessments of early modern 'rogue' literature, see also David Mayall, 'Egyptians and Vagabonds: Representations of the Gypsy in Early Modern Official and Rogue Literature', *Immigrants and Minorities*, 16 (1997), 55–82; Mayall, *Gypsy Identities*, 63–76; Linda Woodbridge, *Vagrancy, Homelessness, and English Renaissance Literature* (Urbana, IL, and Chicago, 2001), and Patricia Fumerton, *Unsettled: The Culture of Mobility and the Working Poor in Early Modern England* (Chicago and London, 2006).

9. Awdeley (sometimes Awdely or Awdelay) was the printer and presumably also the author of *The Fraternitie of Vacabondes*. Said to be first published in 1561, there were reprints in 1575 and 1603. His influence endures in the title of Frances Timbers, *'Damned Fraternitie'*.

10. Harman's *A Caveat for Commen Cursetors Vulgarely Called Vagabones*, also titled *A Caveat or Warening for Commen Cursetors Vulgarely Called Vagabones*, may have been first printed late in 1566. The title page of the two impressions of 1567 announces it be 'augmented and enlarged'. A reprint in 1573 was followed by another in 1592 retitled *The Groundworke of Conny-Catching*, this time without the epistle that mentions Gypsies. The 1573 edition has 'banished' instead of 'vanished'. Quotations are from *A Caveat for Commen Cursetors* (1567), sigs Aii–Aiii (also fos 3–7). See also A. L. Beier, 'New Historicism, Historical Context, and the Literature of Rogues: The Case of Thomas Harman Reopened', in Craig Dionne and Steve Mentz (eds), *Rogues and Early Modern English Culture* (Ann Arbor, 2004), 98–119.

11. Thomas Smith, *De Recta & Emendata Linguae Anglicae Scriptione, Dialogus* (Paris, 1568), 6.

12. William Harrison, *The Description of England by William Harrison*, ed. Georges Edelen (Ithaca, NY, 1968), 180–6.

13. Scot, *The Discouerie of Witchcraft*, 197.

14. John Harvey, *A Discoursive Probleme Concerning Prophesies* (1588), 63–4.

15. Thomas Nashe, *A Pleasant Comedie, Called Summers Last Will and Testament* (1600), sig. G.

16. George Abbot, *A Brief Description of the Whole World* (1605), sig. K4ᵛ. This passage does not appear in the 1599 or 1600 editions of Abbot's work, but is in all subsequent editions. See also George Abbot, *An Exposition Vpon the Prophet Ionah* (1600), 79, denouncing the 'heathenish superstition' of 'the counterfeit Egyptians in telling of fortunes'.

17. John Cowell, *The Interpreter* (1607), sub. 'Egyptians'.

18. Dekker, *Belman of London* (repr. 1620), 640; Dekker, *Lanthorne and Candle-Light*; Rid, *Martin Mark-all*; Rid, *Art of Iugling*. Thomas Dekker, *English Villanies* (1632; repr. 1638), recycles earlier material, and refers on the title page to 'cunning canting Gypsies and all the scum of our nation'. Later plagiarized versions

include *A New Plot Newly Discovered, By the Help of the London Bell-Man* (1685).

19. Dekker, *Belman of London*, sigs A4ᵛ, B4ᵛ; Dekker, *Lanthorne and Candle-Light*, sigs G4ᵛ–G5.

20. Dekker, *Lanthorne and Candle-Light*, sigs G5–G5ᵛ.

21. Dekker, *Lanthorne and Candle-Light*, sig. G6.

22. Dekker, *Lanthorne and Candle-Light*, sigs G6–G6ᵛ. Priggers, anglers, cheaters, and morts, are cant terms for various wandering criminals.

23. W. Carew Hazlitt, 'Notes on Popular Antiquities', *Antiquary*, 18 (1886), 217.

24. Dionne and Mentz (eds), *Rogues and Early Modern English Culture*, 11. For sceptical reflection on Jacobean rogue writing, see Paul Griffiths, *Lost Londons: Change, Crime and Control in the Capital City, 1550–1660* (Cambridge, 2008), 140; and Anna Bayman, *Thomas Dekker and the Culture of Pamphleteering in Early Modern London* (Farnham and Burlington, VT, 2014), 97, where the cony-catching underworld is associated with 'other forms of early modern deviance, disorder, carnival, and inversion'.

25. Rid, *Martin Mark-all*, sigs G4–G4ᵛ; Rid, *Art of Iugling*, sigs Bᵛ–B2. Awdelay and Harman also mention Cock Lorel, who is best known from the early Tudor poem 'Cock Lorel's Boat'.

26. Rid, *Art of Iugling*, sigs B2–B2ᵛ.

27. Dekker, *Belman of London*, sig. Cᵛ. Cf. the language of statutes, 22 Henry VIII, c. 12 (1531), and 1 and 2 Philip and Mary, c. 4 (1554).

28. 'An Homylee against Idlenesse', in John Jewel, *The Second Tome of Homilees* (1570), 497–508.

29. Henry Crosse, *Vertues Common-Wealth: or The Highway to Honour* (1603), sig. R; Thomas Adams, *The Workes of Tho: Adams. Being the Summe of his Sermons* (1629), 419.

30. Lancelot Andrewes, *The Pattern of Catechistical Doctrine at Large: Or a Learned and Pious Exposition of the Ten Commandments* (1650), 469. This was an expanded edition of a text first published in 1630.

31. Thomas Barnes, *Vox Belli, or, An Alarum to Warre* (1626), 1. For more in this vein, see Crosse, *Vertues Common-wealth*, sig. R.

32. John Randol, *Noble Blastus: The Honor of a Lord Chamberlaine: and of a Good Bed-Chamber-Man* (1633), 32–5. Randol's sermon was preached at Burford, 'with special relation to…the plague and dearth then among the people'.

33. Anthony Munday, *A Briefe Chronicle, of the Successe of Time, from the Creation of the World to this Instant* (1611), 105.

34. John Minsheu, *Hegemon eis tas Glossas. Id est, Ductor in Linguas, The Guide into Tongues* (1617), 168, 215.

35. Dionys Fitzherbert, *Women, Madness and Sin in early Modern England: The Autobiographical Writings of Dionys Fitzherbert*, ed. Katherine Hodgkin (Farnham and Burlington, VT, 2010), 206–7.

36. John Melton, *Astrologaster, or, the Figure-Caster. Rather the Arraignment of Artless Astrologers, and Fortune-Tellers, that Cheat many Ignorant People* (1620), 47–8. See

also Sir Thomas Overbury, *Sir Thomas Overbury His Wife, with Additions of New Characters*, 16th edn (1638), sig. I2, for the tinker's companion, 'som fould sunburnt quean, that since the terrible statute recanted gyspyism, and is turned pedlaress'.

37. John Abernathy, *A Christian and Heavenly Treatise* (1622), 467.
38. Nicholas Breton, *The Court and the Country* (1618), sig. B2.
39. Richard Head, *The Canting Academy, Or, the Devils Cabinet Opened* (1673), 5.
40. Thomas Culpeper, *The Necessity of Abating Usury Re-asserted* (1670), 27. Other later Stuart authors lumped together 'scullions, cobblers, colliers, jakes-farmers, fiddlers, ostlers, oysterers, rogues, Gypsies, players, panders, punks, and all': J. H., *Two Broad-Sides against Tobacco* (1672), 55; and 'highwaymen, bawds and common strumpets, Gypsies, witches and conjurers': Thomas Cock, *Kitchin-Physick, or, Advice to the Poor* (1676), 18; or grouped Gypsies indiscriminately with all 'sorts of crafty rogues and canting beggars': *New Plot Newly Discovered, By the Help of the London Bell-Man*, title page, 1.
41. *Strange and Certain News from Warwick* (1673), in William E. A. Axon (ed.), 'A Gypsy Tract from the Seventeenth Century', *JGLS*, NS 1 (1907–8), 68–72. In English folklore 'Hern' was a ghostly huntsman, associated with the green forest. A Robert Hern and Elizabeth Boswell, described as 'king and queen of the Gypsies', were married at Camberwell, Surrey in June 1687: Eric Otto Winstedt, 'The Norwood Gypsies and their Vocabulary', *JGLS*, NS 9 (1915–16), 129.
42. Ben Jonson, *The Masque of the Gypsies* (1640); W. W. Greg, *Jonson's Masque of Gipsies in the Burley, Belvoir, and Windsor Versions: An Attempt at Reconstruction* (1952).
43. Dale B. J. Randall, *Jonson's Gypsies Unmasked: Background and Theme of* The Gypsies Metamorphos'd (Durham, NC, 1975); Mark Netzloff, '"Counterfeit Egyptians" and Imagined Borders: Jonson's *The Gypsies Metamorphosed*', *ELH* 68 (2001), 763, 765; Reynolds, *Becoming Criminal*, 26–31; James Knowles, '"Songs of baser alloy": Jonson's *Gypsies Metamorphosed* and the Circulation of Manuscript Libels', *Huntington Library Quarterly*, 69 (2006), 159, 166–7; Sujat Iyengar, *Shades of Difference: Mythologies of Skin Color in Early Modern England* (Philadelphia, 2005), 187–91. Bancroft, *Roma and Gypsy-Travellers*, 36–7, discusses the 'racialization' of Gypsies by reference to Jonson's masque.
44. John P. Cutts, 'Seventeenth-Century Illustrations of Three Masques by Jonson', *Comparative Drama*, 6 (1972), 130.
45. Jonson, *Masque of the* Gypsies, 45–104; Johannes Indagine, *Brief Introductions, both Naturall, Pleasaunte, and also Delectable unto the Art of Chiromancy, or Manual Divination* (1558 and many later editions); Richard Saunders, *Palmistry, the Secrets thereof Disclosed* (1663).
46. George Whetstone, *The Right Excellent and Famous Historye of Promos and Cassandra* (1578), Act 2, scenes 5 and 6.
47. John Lyly, *Euphues and his England Containing his Voyage and his Aduentures, myxed with sundrie pretie discourses of honest loue, the discription of the countrey, the court, and the manners of that isle* (1580), 53.

48. William Shakespeare, *Antony and Cleopatra* (first performed c.1607), Act 4, scene 12.

49. Edmund Spenser, *Prosopopoia: Or Mother Hubberds Tale* (1591), line 86.

50. George Chapman, *The Gentleman Usher* (1606), Act 5, scene 1.

51. James Shirley, *A Contention for Honour and Riches* (1633), sigs B3ᵛ, B4.

52. Richard Zouch, *The Sophister* (1639), Act 1, scene 2.

53. William Shakespeare, *Othello* (performed c.1602), Act 3, scene 4. References to Gypsies also appear in William Shakespeare, *As You Like It* (performed c.1600), Act 5, scene 3; *Romeo and Juliet* (performed c.1604), Act 2, scene 3, and Act 4, scene 1; and *Antony and Cleopatra*, Act 1, scene 1, and Act 4, scene 12.

54. Thomas Middleton, *A Game at Chess* (1625), Act 3.

55. Lodowick Carlell, *The Deseruing Fauorite* (1629), Act 5, scene 1.

56. Robert Herrick, *Hesperides: Or, the Works both Humane & Divine of Robert Herrick Esq.* (1648), 69.

57. Jonson, *Masque of the Gypsies*, 48, 56; Ben Jonson, *The Staple of Newes* (1640), Act 4, scene 1.

58. Ben Jonson, *The New Inne* (1631), Act 1, scene 5.

59. Thomas Middleton, *More Dissemblers besides Women* (1657), Act 3, scene 2; Act 4, scene 2. The nonsense words are copied exactly in John Leanerd, *The Rambling Justice, or the Jealous Husbands* (1678), 20.

60. Barten Holyday, *Technogamia: or the Marriages of the Arts* (1618), Act 2, scene 6.

61. Middleton and Rowley, *The Spanish Gipsie*, dramatis personae, Act 2, Act 3, scene 2.

62. Henry Chettle and John Day, *The Blind-Beggar of Bednal Green* (1659), Act 3, scene 4. Disguise, imposture, and elective vagabondage also move the plot and amuse the spectators in Richard Brome, *A Jovial Crew, or, The Merry Beggars* (1652), which features professional beggars, not Gypsies.

63. Aphra Behn, *The Rover* (1677), Act 1, scene 2; Act 3, scene 1.

64. Aphra Behn, *The Lives of Sundry Notorious Villains* (1678). 28.

65. Leanerd, *Rambling Justice*, 23. See also Urfey, *Trick for Trick* (1678), Act 2, scene 1; Robert Dixon, *Canidia, or the Witches* (1683), canto 2.

66. Peter *Motteux, Love's a Jest* (1696), Act 4, lines 45–7.

67. John Corye, *The Generous Enemies, or, the Ridiculous Lovers* (1672), Act 5, scene 1.

68. B.E., *New Dictionary of the Terms Ancient and Modern*, preface.

69. *The Brave English Jipsie* (1625?), broadsheet in University of California, Santa Barbara, Broadside Ballad Archive, ID 30360; also in W. Chappell (ed.), *The Roxburghe Ballads. Part VII, or Vol. III, Part I* (Hertford, 1975), 329–33.

70. *The Gypsie Loddy* (1720?), broadsheet in University of California, Santa Barbara, Broadside Ballad Archive, ID 31420; in Chappell (ed.), *Roxburghe Ballads*, 685.

71. <www.bodley.ox/ac/uk/ballads/>, subject 'Gypsies' (accessed April 2016).

72. See, e.g. John Lilburne, *Liberty Vindicated against Slavery* (1646); Henry Care, *English Liberty, or, The Free-Born Subjects Inheritance* (1703).

73. Robert Naunton, *Fragmenta Regalia, Or Observations on the Late Queen Elizabeth, her Times and Favorits* (1641), 17,

74. Richard Harvey, *A Theologicall Discourse of the Lamb of God and his Enemies* (1590), 97.

75. Somerset Heritage Centre, Taunton, DD/PH/219, no. 42

76. Somerset Heritage Centre,, D/D/Cd. 66, fo. 173.

77. Richard Ames, *The Female Fire-Ships: A Satyr Against Whoring* (1691), 13; William Burnaby, *The Modish Husband* (1702), Act 3, scene 1. See also John Wilmot in 1679 on women 'who, born like monarchs free, | Turn Gypsies for a meaner liberty', in *The Complete Poems of John Wilmot, Earl of Rochester*, ed. David M. Vieth (New Haven and London, 1968), 105–6.

78. Thomas Bell, *The Catholique Triumph, Conteyning a Reply to the Pretended Answer of B. C. (a Masked Iesuite)* (1610), 123, 237,

79. Thomas Thompson, *Antichrist Arraigned in a Sermon at Pauls Crosse* (1618), 182.

80. Huntington Library, San Marino, California, MS HM 60666, 'A New Ballad Called the Northamptonshire High Constable', fo. 13.

81. Henry Burton, *Vindiciae Veritatis: Truth Vindicated against Calumny* (1645), 19 (imperfect pagination), responding to John Bastwick, *Independency Not Gods Ordinance* (1645).

82. Stephen Proudlove, *Truths Triumph over Errour: or, The Routing of the Seven False Prophets* (1653), title page.

83. Richard Brathwait, *The Honest Ghost, or a Voice from the Vault* (1658), 320. See also George Whitehead, *An Antidote against the Venom of the Snake in the Grass* (1697), 67, 70, for comparison of Quakers to Gypsies.

84. John Milton, *The Life and Reigne of King Charles, or, The Pseudo-Martyr Discovered* (1651), 126.

85. Fabian Phillips, *King Charles the First, no Man of Blood: but a Martyr for his People* (1649), 65; Fabian Phillips, *The Antiquity, Legality, Reason, Duty and Necessity of Præ-emption and Pourveyance, for the King* (1663), sig. b2.

86. *The Mad-Merry Merlin: The Black Almanack* (1653), 6.

87. Traiano Boccalini, *Advertisements from Parnassus* (1656), 186.

88. British Library, Thomason Tracts, E. 538 (8). The collector George Thomason acquired his scribal copy on 12 January 1648, just days before King Charles went on trial.

89. Lewis Griffin, *Essays and Characters* (1661), 24–5.

90. John Collop, *Itur Satyricum: In Loyall Stanzas* (1660), 10.

91. John Tillotson, *The Rule of Faith, or, An Answer to the Treatise of Mr I. S.* (1676), 250.

92. Edmund Hickeringill, *Gregory, Father-Greybeard, with his Vizard off; Or, News from the Cabal* (1673), 251, 258.

93. *A Choice Collection of Wonderful Miracles, Ghosts, and Visions* (1681), 4.

94. Boccalini, *Advertisements from Parnassus*, 170.

95. *Mourt's Relation. A Journal of the Pilgrims at Plymouth*, ed. Dwight B. Heath (Bedford, MA, 1963), 53.

96. Philip Ford, *The Vindication of William Penn* (1683), 2.

97. Samuel Purchas, *Purchas His Pilgrimes in Five Books* (1625), 1509, 1570. Christoph Frick, *A Relation of Two Several Voyages* (1700), 238, compared African Hottentots to Gypsies.

98. John Fryer, *A New Account of East India and Persia* (1698), 192.

99. William Bruton, *Newes from the East-Indies; or, a Voyage to Bengalla* (1638), 27.

100. Ray, *A Collection of Curious Travels & Voyages*, ii. 150, 165,

101. Frick, *Relation of Two Several Voyages*, 238

102. Aylett Sammes, *Britannia Antiqua Illustrata: or, the Antiquities of Ancient Britain* (1676), 45, 112–13.

103. Thomas Heywood, *Gynaikeion: or, Nine Bookes of Various History. Concerninge Women* (1624), 103.

104. See Chapter 1.

105. William Perkins, *A Golden Chaine, or the Description of Theologie* (1591), sig. H2ᵛ; Alexander Ross, *Medicus Medicatus, or, The Physicans Religion Cured* (1645), 70.

106. Alexander Ross, *Pansebeia, or, a View of all Religions in the World* (1655), 169.

107. R. M., *Micrologia. Characters or Essayes, of Persons, Trades, and Places* (1629), sig. C3.

108. Wye Saltonstall, *Picturae Loquentes. Or Pictures Drawne Forth in Characters* (1631), not paginated. The hack writer John Taylor made the same charge against 'a crew of strolling rogues and whores that took upon them the name of Egyptians, jugglers and fortune-tellers', which he allegedly met in Germany: John Taylor, *Three Weekes, Three Daies, and Three Houres: Observations and Travel from London to Hamburgh in Germanie* (1617), sigs E4ᵛ–F.

109. Ysbrand van Diemerbroeck, *The Anatomy of Human Bodies, comprehending the most modern discoveries and curiosities in that art* (1694), 494.

110. Agrippa von Nettisham, *The Vanity of Arts and Sciences*, 214; *Strange and Certain News from Warwick*, 70; N. H., *The Ladies Dictionary* (1694), 278.

111. *The Severall Notorious and Lewd Cousenages of Iohn West, and Alice West, falsely called the King and Queene of Fayries* (1614).

112. *Strange and Certain News from Warwick*, 70.

113. Thomas Gataker, *Thomas Gataker B.D. his Vindication of the Annotations by him Published* (1653), 56. Gataker became a fellow of Sidney Sussex, Cambridge, in 1596, soon after its foundation. He dates this episode to the time when 'the college, whereof I was to be a fellow, was building'.

114. Melton, *Astrologaster*, 48–51.

115. Head, *Canting Academy*, 5, 32.

116. Hickeringill, *Gregory, Father-Greybeard*, 258.

117. 'A Poem in Praise of Rambling', attributed to J.H. of Exeter College, Oxford, in John Dunton, *A Voyage around the World*, 3 vols (1691), i, not paginated.

118. N. H., *Ladies Dictionary*, 277–8.

119. Fynes Moryson, *An Itinerary Written by Fynes Moryson* (1617), part 3, 45.

120. Richard Thornton, *The Aegyptian Courtier. Delivered in Two Sermons* (1635), sig. A2, 10, 12, 47. See also Joannes Boemus, *The Manners, Lawes, and Customes of all Nations* (1611), 19–37, on the arcane wisdom of the ancient Egyptians.

121. Sammes, *Britannia Antiqua Illustrata*, 45.

122. Head, *Canting Academy*, 2, 7, 8.

123. John Gaule, *Pusmantia the Mag-Astro-Mancer, or, The Magicall-Astrollogicall-Diviner Posed, and Puzzled* (1652), 197. See also William Ramesey, *Lux Veritatis. Or, Christian Judicial Astrology Vindicated* (1652), title page.

124. Thomas Ady, *A Candle in the Dark Shewing the Divine Cause of the Distractions of the Whole Nation of England* (1655), 24.

125. Saunders, *Palmistry*, 'to the reader', 11.

126. John Butler, *Hagiastrologia, or, The Most Sacred and Divine Science of Astrology* (1680), 39.

127. *Strange and Certain News from Warwick*, 70.

128. Thomas Browne, *Religio Medici* (1642), 117, repeated in Edward Leigh, *A Treatise of Religion & Learning* (1656), 51–2. See, however, Thomas Browne, *Pseudodoxia Epidemica: or, Enquiries into Very Many Received Tenents and Commonly Presumed Truths* (1658), 285, which recognizes that Gypsies 'are no Egyptians'.

129. *The Diary of Samuel Pepys*, ed. Robert Latham and William Matthews, 11 vols (Berkeley and Los Angeles, 1970–83), iv. 284, 296.

130. Robert Boyle, *Some Considerations Touching the Usefulnesse of Experimental Naturall Philosophy* (1663), 216, 301.

131. Joseph Glanvill, *The Vanity of Dogmatizing: Or, Confidence in Opinions* (1661), 196–8; Cambridge University Library, Add. MS 3996, fo. 109; Matthew Arnold, 'The Scholar-Gypsy', in Matthew Arnold, *Poems* (1853), 199–216.

132. Rid, *Art of Iugling*, sig. B^v.

133. The genre follows Matheo Aleman, *The Rogue: Or the Life of Guzman de Alfarache* (1623; repr. 1630, 1634), and Carlos Garcia, *The Sonne of the Rogue, or the Politick Theefe* (1638), both translated from Spanish. See also Carlos Garcia, *Lavernae, or The Spanish Gipsy: The Whole Art, Mystery, Antiquity, Company, Noblenesse, and Excellency of Theeves and Theeving* (1650).

134. *The Run-awayes Answer, to a Booke called, A Rodde for Runne-awayes* (1625), 1; Chapman, *The Gentleman Usher*, Act 5, scene 1; Jonson, *Staple of Newes*, following Act 2; John Fletcher, *Love's Pilgrimage* (1647), Act 1, scene 1; Laurence Price, *Witty William of Wilt-shire* (1674), sigs A2–A2^v.

135. Head, *Canting Academy*, 3–4.

136. Richard Head, *The English Rogue Containing a Brief Discovery of the most Eminent Cheats, Robberies, and other Extravagancies, by him Committed* (1665; repr. 1688), 5.

137. Head, *Canting Academy*, 6–8, 31.

138. Head, *Canting Academy*, 3.

139. Head, *Canting Academy*, 5, 6.

140. *The German Princess Revived: or The London Jilt: Being the True Account of the Life and Death of Jenney Voss* (1684), 3; *Ordinary of Newgate's Account*, December 1684 <www.oldbaileyonline.org> (accessed June 2013).

141. B.E., *New Dictionary of the Terms Ancient and Modern*, title page, sub 'Gypsies', 'strowlers'.

CHAPTER 3

1. Louis XII ordered so-called *Egyptiens* to be expelled from France in 1504. See Chapter 1.

2. Cornwall Record Office, Truro, AR/26/2; Joyce and Newlyn (eds), *Records of Early English Drama: Cornwall*, 530.

3. Crofton, 'Early Annals', 7, 8; Henry Ellis (ed.), *Original Letters Illustrative of English History* 3 vols (1825), ii. 101; *Oxford English Dictionary*, sub 'gipsy/gypsy'. The churchwardens' accounts for Lydd, Kent, include 7s. 6d. in 1533 'receuyd of the gypcons for brekyng of the ground in the churche for one of ther company', and 18d. 'receuyd of the gypcous' for wax candles: Arthur Finn (ed.), *Records of Lydd* (Ashford, Kent, 1911), 361, checked against Kent History and Library Center MS Ly15/2/1/1.

4. C. H. Cooper, *Annals of Cambridge*, 5 vols (Cambridge, 1842–52), i. 298.

5. More, *A Dyaloge of Syr Thomas More*, otherwise known as *A Dialogue Concerning Heresies*, bk 3, fo. 91.

6. Taylor, *Another Darkness*, 49–50, citing Herefordshire Archives, BG/11/28, Misc. Papers, 6/18.

7. 22 Henry VIII, c. 10.

8. Stanford E. Lehmberg, *The Reformation Parliament 1529–1536* (Cambridge, 1970), 123.

9. Simon Fish, *A Supplication for the Beggars* (1528), in G. R. Elton (ed.), *The Tudor Constitution* (Cambridge, 1962), 322; G. R. Elton, *Reform and Renewal: Thomas Cromwell and the Common Weal* (Cambridge, 1973), 122–6.

10. 22 Henry VIII, c. 12.

11. 27 Henry VIII, c. 25.

12. Finn (ed.), *Records of Lydd*, 361.

13. *Letters and Papers, Foreign and Domestic, of the Reign of Henry VIII* (henceforth *LP*), 21 vols (1862–1910), xii, pt 2, 79.

14. Cheryl Butler (ed.), *The Book of Fines: The Annual Accounts of the Mayors of Southampton, Volume I, 1488–1540* (Southampton Record Series, 41, 2007), 165, xix, n. 40.

15. *LP* xii, pt 2, 349.

16. Fraser, *Gypsies*, 117–18.

17. Simson and Simson, *History of the Gipsies*, 101–3; MacRitchie, *Scottish Gypsies*, 37–9; Fraser, *Gypsies*, 117–18.

18. Ellis (ed.), *Original Letters*, ii. 100–3, transcribed (says Ellis) from British Library, Cotton MS Tiberius B. I. rather than from Cotton MS Titus B. I, fo. 407. Ellis mistakes the bishop 'lord' of Chester for the earl. Bishop Rowland Lee was President of the Council of the Marches from 1534 to 1543.

19. The National Archives, Kew (henceforth TNA), REQ 2/5/322. Undated, this petition can be no later than 1539, when Rowland Messenger, vicar of Wycombe, who had a claim on the silver, died or left his post.

20. *LP* xiv, pt 1, 84; TNA: SP1/142, fo. 220; TNA: E 199/41/46. European Gypsies claimed similar questionable letters of protection. It is possible that 'the Egyptians that danced before the king at Holyrood House' in 1529, and received safe-conduct from King James V of Scotland in 1530, subsequently displayed their credentials in England: Fraser, *Gypsies*, 117; MacRitchie, *Scottish Gypsies*, 29–39.

21. *LP* xiv, pt 1,21; TNA: SP1/153, fo. 40.

22. *LP* xiv, pt 2, 109, 303.

23. *LP* xv. 325; TNA: SP 1/160, fo. 49. Crofton, 'Early Annals', 11, dates this episode to 1544.

24. John Sampson, 'Early Records of the Gypsies in England', *JGLS*, 3rd ser., 3 (1927), 34.

25. TNA: E 101/518/28; Sampson, 'Early Records', 32–4, citing Exchequer K. R. Accounts Misc. 524/5. 'Egyptians' reported in Essex in 1543, and twenty more in Norfolk in 1544, were ordered to be sent overseas: *LP* xviii, pt 1, 106, 217, 305; William Hudson and John Cottingham Tingey (eds), *The Records of the City of Norwich*, 2 vols (Norwich and London, 1910), ii. 172.

26. *LP* xix, pt 2, 112; TNA: SP 1/192, fo. 51–51ᵛ. Crofton, 'Early Annals', 11.

27. *LP* xix, pt 2, 112. 159.

28. E. Lodge, *Illustrations of British History, Biography and Manners in the Reigns of Henry VIII, Edward VI, Mary, Elizabeth, and James I*, 3 vols (1838), iii. 148; Lambeth Palace Library, Talbot MS 3206, fo. 5.

29. *Journal of the House of Lords*, 10 vols (1802), i. 272–4 (December 1545).

30. *LP* xxi, pt 1, 46; *Acts of the Privy Council of England, 1542–1631*, ed. J. R. Dasent et al., 45 vols (1890–1964) (henceforth *APC*), i. 320.

31. *LP* xxi, pt 1, 217; *APC* i. 358.

32. *APC* i. 555; *LP* xxi, pt 2, 259; TNA: E 315/255, fo. 116: *APC* ii. 448, 452.

33. Power, 'Gypsies and Sixteenth-Century Ireland', 204–6; Timbers, *'Damned Fraternitie'*, 81–2; TNA: SP 60/1, fos 137, 139.

34. *Journal of the House of Lords*, i. 310–11 (December 1547); *Journal of the House of Commons*, 10 vols (1802), i. 1–3.

35. See, e.g. Hancock, *Pariah Syndrome*, 89–90; Ian Hancock, *We Are the Romani People* (Hatfield, 2002), 27; Katherine Quarmby, *No Place to Call Home: Inside the Real Lives of Gypsies and Travellers* (2013), 15.

36. 1 Edward VI, c. 3; Paul Slack, *Poverty and Policy in Tudor and Stuart England* (1988), 122. The most thorough treatment remains C. S. L. Davies, 'Slavery and Protector Somerset: The Vagrancy Act of 1547', *Economic History Review*, NS 19 (1966), 533–49.

37. *The Journal of King Edward's Reign, Written with his Own Hand* (Clarendon Historical Society, Edinburgh, 1884), 22.

38. Lambeth Palace Library, Talbot MS 3198, fo. 540; Crofton, 'Early Annals', 12.

39. *APC* iv. 18, 59, 165.

40. Imtiaz Habib, *Black Lives in English Archives, 1500–1677: Imprints of the Invisible* (Aldershot, 2008), 255, 258.

41. Boorde, *The Fyrst Boke of the Introduction of Knowledge*, ch. 38, sigs Nii–Nii^v.
Boorde, a former Carthusian monk, was a renowned physician who travelled
extensively in Britain and Europe. On the linguistic significance of Boorde's
word list, see Henry Thomas Crofton, 'Borde's Egipt Speche', *JGLS*, NS 1 (1907),
157–68; Hancock, 'Romani and Angloromani', 368, 378–9; Matras, *Romani in
Britain*, 58. For earlier fragments, see Georg Nicolaus Knauer, 'The Earliest
Vocabulary of Romani Words (*c.* 1515) in the *Collectanea* of Johannes ex Grafing,
a Student of Johannes Reuchlin and Conrad Celtis', *Romani Studies*, 5th ser., 20
(2010), 1–15.

42. This often-repeated figure appears in John Hoyland, *A Historical Survey of the
Customs, Habits, and Present State of the Gypsies* (1816), 82, and Crofton, 'Early
Annals', 17. Its apparent source is William Harrison's description of Elizabethan
England, where he includes 'Egyptian rogues' with the 'thriftless poor' and
vagrant beggars 'to amount unto above 10,000 persons, as I have heard reported':
Raphael Holinshed, William Harrison, et al., *The First and Second Volumes of
Chronicles* (1587), 182–4; Harrison, *Description of England*, 184. Hancock, *Pariah
Syndrome*, 89, renders this as 'ten thousand Gypsies in the British Isles' and dates
it to 1528.

43. More traces of mid-Tudor Gypsies appear in Lambeth Palace Library, Talbot
MS 3198, fo. 540; Talbot MS 3206, fo. 5; *Journal of the House of Lords*, i. 272–4,
310–11; *Journal of the House of Commons*, i. 1–3; *LP* xxi, pt 1, 46; *APC* i. 320, 358,
555; *APC* ii. 448, 452; *APC* iv. 4, 18, 59, 16; *LP* xxi, pt 1, 217, pt 2, 259; TNA: E
315/255, fo. 116.

44. 1 and 2 Philip and Mary, *c.* 4, repealed 1820.

45. *APC* v. 185.

46. Folger Shakespeare Library, MS L.b.210; St George Kiernan Hyland, *A Century
of Persecution under Tudor and Stuart Sovereigns from Contemporary Records* (1920),
346–7.

47. Margaret Pelling and Francis White, 'Valentine, Lawrence', in *Physicians and
Irregular Practitioners in London 1550–1640* (2004) <http://www.british-history.
ac.uk/no-series/london-physicians/1550-1640> (accessed May 2016). Valentine
was a common Gypsy surname later in the sixteenth century.

48. TNA: SP 12/6, fo. 63–63^v; SP 12/51, fo. 27.

49. Judith Ford, '"Egyptians" in Early-Modern Dorset', *Proceedings of the Dorset
Natural History and Archaeological Society*, 130 (2009), 2.

50. TNA: SP 12/6, fos 82, 109.

51. TNA: SP 12/6, fo. 108; SP 12/7, fo. 37; Historical Manuscripts Commmission
(henceforth HMC), *Twelfth Report*, appendix, pt 9, 468; Crofton, 'Early Annals',
16.

52. British Library, Additional MS 32243, fos 62–5; Joyce and Newlyn (eds), *Records
of Early English Drama: Cornwall*, 521–2. There is a similar reference to Gypsy
use of the church house at Yeovil, Somerset, in 1564: G. W. Saunders, 'Notes and
Queries: Gypsies in Somerset', *JGLS*, 3rd ser., 11 (1932), 47. It is possible that the
Gypsies were putting on a sale or an entertainment.

53. *The Diary of Henry Machyn*, ed. J. G. Nichols (Camden Society, no. 42, 1848), 265.

54. *APC* vii. 112, 124. The arresting magistrate was Richard Fenys, esquire.

55. 5 Elizabeth I, c. 20; *Anno Quinto Reginae Elizabethe. At the Parliament Holden at Westmynster* (1563), fos 55−55ᵛ; *Journal of the House of Lords*, i. 595−8; *Journal of the House of Commons*, i. 66−7, 71; *Proceedings in the Parliaments of Elizabeth I. Volume 1. 1558−1581*, ed. T. E. Hartley (Leicester, 1981), 64, 83; *The Journals of All the Parliaments during the Reign of Queen Elizabeth*, ed. Simonds D'Ewes (1682), 6, 19, 70; G. R. Elton, *The Parliament of England 1559−1581* (Cambridge, 1986), 233.

56. See Chapter 6 for eighteenth-century repeal of the Elizabethan law.

57. Overbury, *Sir Thomas Overbury His Wife*, sig. I2.

58. 23 Geo. III, c. 51; Sir Samuel Romilly, *Observations on the Criminal Law of England* (1810), 5; George Borrow, *The Zincali; or, An Account of the Gypsies of Spain*, 2 vols (1841; 2nd edn, 1843), i. 17; George Smith, *Gipsy Life: Being an Account of our Gipsies and their Children with Suggestions for their Improvement* (1880), 142. Hancock, *Pariah Syndrome*, 90, remarks that 'by Cromwell's time in the 1600s, it had become a hanging offense not only to be born a Gypsy, but for non-Gypsies to associate with Gypsies', and echoes earlier claims about executions of Gypsies.

59. Taylor, *Another Darkness*, 66.

60. Okely, *The Traveller-Gypsies*, 3−5; Angus Fraser, 'Counterfeit Egyptians', *Tsiganologische Studien*, 2 (1990), 43−69; Wim Willems, *In Search of the True Gypsy: From Enlightenment to Final Solution* (1997), 3, 293, 301; Mayall, *Gypsy Identities*, 61−3. See also Tobias B. Hug, *Impostures in Early Modern England: Representations and Perceptions of Fraudulent Identities* (Manchester and New York, 2009), 112−15; Miriam Eliav-Feldon, *Renaissance Imposters and Proofs of Identity* (2012), 127−9; John Morgan, ' "Counterfeit Egyptians": The Construction and Implementation of a Criminal Identity in Early Modern England', *Romani Studies*, 5th ser., 26 (2016), 105−28.

61. Thomas Middleton, *A Mad World, My Masters* (1608), Act 5; John Benbrigge, *Usura Accomodata, or A Ready Way to Rectifie Usury* (1646), 13. See also William Shakespeare, *Henry V* (performed *c.*1599), Act 3, scene 6, where Pistol is described 'an arrant counterfeit rascal'.

62. Scot, *The Discouerie of Witchcraft*, 464; John Gaule, *Select Cases of Conscience Touching Witches and Witchcrafts* (1646), 177. See also Jean Calvin, *An Admonicion against Astrology Iudiciall and other Curiosities that Raigne now in the World* (1561), sig. c iiii, on 'counterfeit astrologians'.

63. Walter Haddon, *A Dialogue Agaynst the Tyrannye of the Papists* (1562), sig. Cᵛ. An opponent of Charles I's fiscal policy in 1638 charged that 'Ship Money was but counterfeit and not just': Bodleian Library, Oxford, MS Bankes 37/54, fo. 112.

64. TNA: SP 12/77/60.

65. Taylor, *Another Darkness*, 56.

66. Mayall, *Gypsy Identities*, 60.

67. *Calendar of State Papers Domestic* (henceforth *CSPD*), ed. Mary Anne Everett Green et al., 84 vols (1856–2006), *1547–1580*, 334; Surrey History Centre, Woking, 6729/11/52, Council to Sheriff of Surrey, March 1569.

68. 39 Elizabeth I, c. 4; N. A. M. Rodger, *The Safeguard of the Sea: A Naval History of Britain 660–1649* (New York, 1998), 208, 478–80.

CHAPTER 4

1. *Proceedings in the Parliaments of Elizabeth I. Volume. 1. 1558–1581*, ed. Hartley, 111–12; British Library, Lansdowne MS 102, fo. 25; Elton, *Parliament of England*, 223. Secretary Cecil also expressed pride in the 'good laws' passed in this session.

2. G. W. Saunders, 'Notes and Queries, Gypsies in Somerset'.

3. Essex Record Office, Chelmsford, Q/SR 19A/24, 30, 34, 61, 76.

4. Essex Record Office, Q/SR/19A; J. S. Cockburn (ed.), *Calendar of Assize Records. Essex Indictments Elizabeth I* (1978), 47.

5. J. S. Cockburn (ed.), *Calendar of Assize Records. Kent Indictments Elizabeth I* (1979), 88.

6. Cockburn (ed.), *Calendar of Assize Records. Essex*, 81, 83; Philip Jenkins, 'From Gallows to Prison? The Execution Rate in Early Modern England', *Criminal Justice History*, 7 (1986), 51–71. See also Cynthia B. Herrup, *The Common Peace: Participation and the Criminal Law in Seventeenth-Century England* (Cambridge, 1987), 165–6.

7. Frederick G. Blair, 'Forged Passports of British Gypsies in the Sixteenth Century', *JGLS*, 3rd ser., 28 (1950), 131–7; *APC* ix. 304. Early in the seventeenth century a forged pass cost 2s. in Dorset, 3s. in London: Paul. A. Slack, 'Vagrants and Vagrancy in England, 1598–1664', *Economic History Review*, 27 (1974), 364.

8. HMC, *Report on Manuscripts in Various Collections*, i (1901), 88, 92.

9. Essex Record Office, Q/SR 79/92. Edward Symson, who was examined regarding these seals, had travelled through Warwickshire, Bedfordshire, Hertfordshire, and Essex, but was not identified as a Gypsy.

10. John Awdelay, *The Fraternitye of Vacabondes* (1575), sig Aiii.

11. *APC* x. 6.

12. *APC* ix. 304, 311, 313; TNA: KB 8/44 (*Baga de Secretis*), fos 6–11; *Fourth Report of the Deputy Keeper of the Public Records* (1843), 271–2; Cockburn (ed.), *Calendar of Assize Records. Essex*, 175; T. W. Thompson, 'Consorting with and Counterfeiting Egyptians', *JGLS*, 3rd ser., 2 (1923), 81–92.

13. J. S. Cockburn (ed.), *Calendar of Assize Records. Sussex Indictments Elizabeth I* (1975), 168, 172. James and Margaret Valentine would appear in subsequent indictments of vagrants in Sussex in 1582.

14. Cockburn (ed.), *Calendar of Assize Records. Essex*, 175. For more discussion of Gypsy names, see Winstedt, 'Early British Gypsies'.

15. Surrey History Centre, 6729/11/5 (1569); LM/COR/3/561 (1596). I am grateful to Sue Jones for supplying these references.

16. *APC* viii. 113.

17. *APC* xvii. 278.

18. *APC* xi. 361.

19. *APC* xxi. 62–3.

20. William Lambard, *Eirenarcha: or of the Office of the Iustices of Peace* (1581), 198, 332.

21. *William Lambarde and Local Government: His 'Ephemeris' and Twenty-Nine Charges to Juries and Commissions*, ed. Conyers Read (Ithaca, NY, 1962), 21.

22. E. O. Winstedt, 'Notes and Queries: Early Annals', *JGLS* 6 (1912), 63.

23. TNA: E 199/24/38; E 199/24/40.

24. TNA: E 199/4/50; Peter Edwards, *Horse and Man in Early Modern England* (London and New York, 2007), 194–8.

25. Essex Record Office, Q/SR/113/40 and 40a; John Tucker Murray, *English Dramatic Companies 1558–1642*, 2 vols (1910), ii. 69–70, 391. There is no need to speculate that 'Lord Staff' refers to one of the characters in a 'play-game', with reference to 'the staff or stick in Morris dancing': Timbers, *'Damned Fraternitie'*, 105.

26. The following account is based on TNA: STAC 5/R36/15; STAC 7/10/20; STAC 10/1/132; *APC* xxi. 61–3. For the regional political background, see W. T. MacCaffery, 'Talbot and Stanhope: An Episode in Elizabethan Politics', *Bulletin of the Institute of Historical Research*, 33 (1960), 73–85.

27. *APC* xxi. 62–3.

28. Douglas Walthew Rice, *The Life and Achievements of Sir John Popham 1531–1607* (Madison, NJ, 2005), 18–19. See Chapter 10 on the myth of Gypsy child-stealing.

29. 39 Elizabeth I, c. 3 and 4.

30. Crofton, 'Early Annals', 20; *CSPD 1581–90*, 672; *CSPD 1591–4*, 146; John Cordy Jeaffreson (ed.), *Middlesex County Records…to the End of the Reign of Queen Elizabeth* (Clerkenwell, 1886), 221, also 253, 267.

31. *CSPD 1581–90*, 672; *CSPD 1591–4*, 146; Crofton, 'Early Annals', 20. The Durham victims were named Simson, Arington, Fetherstone, Fenwicke, and Lancaster.

32. *APC* xxiii. 290.

33. Jeaffreson (ed.), *Middlesex County Records…Elizabeth*, 221; Huntington Library, MS Ellesemere 4123.

34. Surrey History Center, LM/COR/3/561, Council to Sheriff and Justices of Surrey, October 1596; *APC* xxvi. 314.

35. R. O. Jones, 'The Mode of Disposing of Gipsies and Vagrants in the Reign of Elizabeth', *Archaeologia Cambrensis*, 4th ser., 13 (1882), 226–9.

36. Edward Hext to Lord Burghley, 25 September 1596, in British Library, Lansdowne MS 81, fos 161–2; John Strype, *Annals of the Reformation,* 4 vols (1738), iv. 290–5.

37. Crofton, 'Early Annals', 23.

38. Jeaffreson (ed.), *Middlesex County Records…Elizabeth*, 253, 266–7.

39. James Tait (ed.), *Lancashire Quarter Sessions Records…1590–1606* (Chetham Society, NS 77, 1917), 161.

40. Winstedt, 'Notes and Queries: Early Annals', 63–4.

41. 'Robert an Egyptian bastard' was buried at Bury St Edmunds, Suffolk, in 1563: Eric Otto Winstedt, 'Records of Gypsies in the Eastern Counties of England', *JGLS*, 3rd ser., 40 (1961), 28.

42. Crofton, 'Early Annals', 14, 17; Thomas Wainwright (ed.), *Barnstable Parish Register. 1538 A.D to 1812 A.D* (Exeter, 1903), 16.

43. Henry Thomas Crofton, 'Supplementary Annals of the Gypsies in England, before 1700', *JGLS*, NS 1 (1907–8), 32.

44. Crofton, 'Early Annals', 19.

45. Crofton, 'Supplementary Annals', 32.

46. T. W. Thompson, 'Gleanings from Constables' Accounts and Other Sources', *JGLS*, 3rd ser., 7 (1928), 42.

47. East Riding Archives, Beverley, PE158/1, fo.. 37. I am grateful to Helen Good for supplying this reference.

48. Blackburn parish register, cited in Onyeka, *Blackamoores: Africans in Tudor England, their Presence, Status and Origins* (2013), 36. I am grateful to Miranda Kaufmann for this reference.

49. HMC, *Calendar of the Manuscripts of . . . the Marquis of Salisbury, Preserved at Hatfield House*, 24 vols (1883–1976), v, *1591–1595* (1894), 81–2; Hatfield House, Hertfordshire, Cecil MSS 5/162–4; *The Brideling, Sadling and Ryding of a Rich Churle in Hampshire, by the Subtill Practise of one Judeth Philips, a Professed Cunning Woman, or Fortune Teller* (1595). The story is also told in Alec Ryrie, *The Sorcerer's Tale: Faith and Fraud in Tudor England* (Oxford, 2008), 101–7, without mention of Gypsies. See also *The Severall Notorious and Lewd Cousenages of Iohn West, and Alice West*, for similar exploitation of 'covetous simplicity'.

CHAPTER 5

1. Lambarde, *Eirenarcha*, 198–9, 277, 279, 332; Michael Dalton, *The Countrey Iustice: Conteyning the Practice of the Iustices of the Peace* (1618), 97, 244. See also Huntington Library, MS HM 17298, 'What a Justice of Peace may do. 1627', fo. 45; John Layer, *The Office and Dutie of Constables, Churchwardens, and Other the Overseers of the Poore* (Cambridge, 1641), 31–3; Richard Gardiner, *The Compleat Constable* (1692), 31–2.

2. Francis Beaumont and John Fletcher, *The Coxcombe* (performed 1612), Act 2, scene 1, in Francis Beaumont and John Fletcher, *Fifty Comedies and Tragedies* (1679), 325.

3. *Strange and Certain News from Warwick*, 70.

4. J. C. Atkinson (ed.), *North Riding of the County of York. Quarter Sessions Records*, 4 vols (1884–6), i. 11, 21; iii. 119–20.

5. H. Hampton Copnall (ed.) *Nottinghamshire County Records: Notes and Extracts from the Nottinghamshire County Records of the 17th Century* (Nottingham, 1915), 50, 116.

6. Thompson, 'Gleanings from Constables' Accounts', 32, 33.

7. Marjorie Masten (ed.), *Woodstock Chamberlains' Accounts, 1609–50* (Oxfordshire Record Society, vol. 58, 1993), 1, 2, 95.

8. David Smith, 'Gypsies, Tinkers, Travellers and the Forest Economy', in John Langton and Graham Jones (eds), *Forests and Chases of England and Wales c.1500 to c.1850* (Oxford, 2005), 65, citing Hampshire Record Office, Winchester, 27M74/DBCs, Lymington Town Book, 1613–1729.

9. Crofton, 'Supplementary Annals', 32.

10. Winstedt, 'Notes and Queries: Early Annals', 64; Saunders, 'Notes and Queries: Gypsies in Somerset'.

11. J. H. Bettey (ed.), *The Casebook of Sir Francis Ashley JP Recorder of Dorchester 1614–35* (Dorset Record Society, vol. 7, 1981).

12. Robin Blades (ed.), *Oxford Quarter Sessions Order Book, 1614–1637* (Oxford Historical Society, NS 29, 2009).

13. John Lister (ed.), *West Riding Sessions Records. Vol. II. Orders, 1611–1642. Indictments, 1637–1642* (Yorkshire Archaeological Society, vol. 54, 1915), 7.

14. J. S. Cockburn (ed.), *Calendar of Assize Records. Indictments. Essex. James I* (1982), 46; Tait (ed.), *Lancashire Quarter Sessions Records*, 161.

15. Essex Record Office, Q/SR 196/16–18.

16. Essex Record Office, T/A 418/84/89 (transcribed from TNA: ASSI 33/55/1).

17. *CSPD 1611–18*, 168.

18. W. H. Overall and H. C. Overall (eds), *Analytical Index to the Series of Records Known as the Remembrancia: 1579–1664* (1878), 269.

19. Francis Blomefield, *An Essay towards a Topographical History of the County of Norfolk*, 5 vols (1739), i. 742–3; Fraser, 'Counterfeit Egyptians', 60.

20. Alan McGowan (ed.), *The Winchester Confessions 1615–1616: Depositions of Travellers, Gypsies, Fraudsters, and Makers of Counterfeit Documents, Including a Vocabulary of the Romany Language* (Romany and Traveller Family History Society, South Chailey, Sussex, 1996), checked against Hampshire Record Office, Winchester, Jervoise of Herriard Collection, 44 M69/G3/159; Peter Bakker, 'An Early Vocabulary of British Romani (1616): a Linguistic Analysis', *Romani Studies*, 5th ser., 5 (2002), 75–101. See Chapter 10 for more on the Gypsy language.

21. Ernest Axon (ed.), *Manchester Sessions. Notes of Proceedings…Vol. 1, 1616–1622/23* (Record Society of Lancashire and Cheshire, vol. 42, 1901), 70; J. P. Earwaker (ed.), *The Constables' Accounts of the Manor of Manchester from the Year 1612 to the Year 1647*, 2 vols (Manchester, 1891), i. 57.

22. Joan R. Kent, 'Population Mobility and Alms: Poor Migrants in the Midlands during the Early Seventeenth Century', *Local Population Studies*, 27 (1981), 36, 38, 51.

23. W. J. Hardy (ed.), *Hertfordshire County Records. Notes and Extracts from the Sessions Rolls 1591 to 1698* (Hertford, 1905), 56–8; Helen Stocks and W. H. Stevenson (eds), *Records of the Borough of Leicester…1603–1688* (Cambridge, 1923), 201; HMC, *Fifth Report* (1876), appendix, 410; Thompson, 'Gleanings from Constables' Accounts', 35.

24. Ford, ' "Egyptians" in Early-Modern Dorset', 3.

25. Bodleian Library, Firth MS C 4, fo. 498; *APC* xlv. 23.

26. Layer, *Office and Dutie of Constables*, 30–3.

27. Huntington Library, MS HM 17298, 'What a Justice of Peace may do. 1627', fo. 45.

28. James F. Larkin (ed.), *Stuart Royal Proclamations: Volume II. Royal Proclamations of King Charles I 1625–1646* (Oxford, 1983), 233–5, 412–14.

29. HMC, *Calendar of the Manuscripts of . . . the Marquis of Salisbury, Preserved at Hatfield House*, xxii. 213.

30. Cheshire Record Office, Chester, QJB 1/6, fo. 46; J. W. Willis Bund (ed.), *Worcestershire County Records . . . Calendar of the Quarter Sessions Papers . . . 1591–1643* (Worcester, 1900), 577.

31. *APC* xli. 288; *APC* xlii. 158, 185.

32. J. Charles Cox (ed.), *Three Centuries of Derbyshire Annals: As Illustrated by the Records of the Quarter Sessions*, 2 vols (1890), 152–3; Slack, 'Vagrants and Vagrancy', 360–79, esp. 364.

33. B. W. Quintrell (ed.), *Proceedings of the Lancashire Justices of the Peace at the Sheriff's Table during Assizes Week, 1578–1694* (Record Society of Lancashire and Cheshire, vol. 121, 1981), 94.

34. Winstedt, 'Notes and Queries: Early Annals', 64.

35. Essex Record Office, Q/SR/256/49; T/A 418/101/113.

36. Essex Record Office, Q/SR/258/95; T/A 418/102/34 and 88.

37. Hancock, *Pariah Syndrome*, 90; Fraser, *Gypsies*, 133.

38. Sir Matthew Hale, *Historia Placitorum Coronae. The History of the Pleas of the Crown*, 2 vols (1736), i. 671. Note that he calls them 'Gypsies' rather than 'Egyptians'. Hale's remarks are repeated in Hoyland, *Historical Survey*, 86–7, and in many subsequent surveys.

39. Essex Record Office, D/Y 2/9, Microfilm of Morant MSS, vol. 9, CXLVIII, 253.

40. J. H. E. Bennett and J. C. Dewhurst (eds), *Quarter Sessions Records . . . for the County Palatine of Chester 1559–1760* (Record Society of Lancashire and Cheshire, vol. 94, 1940), 96; Willis Bund (ed.), *Worcestershire County Records . . . 1591–1643*, 577

41. Lister (ed.), *West Riding Sessions Records*, 23.

42. *A Looking-Glasse for City and Countrey* (1630).

43. TNA: SP 16/123/5; SP 16/131/1; SP 16/139/1; SP 16/181/123; Slack, 'Vagrants and Vagrancy', 365; Patrick Fitzgerald, ' "Like Crickets to the Crevice of a Brew-House": Poor Irish Migrants in England, 1560–1640', in Patrick Fitzgerald (ed.), *Patterns of Migration* (Leicester, 1992), 13–35.

44. TNA: SP 16/141/75; SP 16/234/57; Larkin (ed.), *Stuart Royal Proclamations*, ii. 233–5, 412–14, quotation at 233.

45. Earwaker (ed.), *Constables' Accounts of the Manor of Manchester*, ii. 3.

46. Slack, 'Vagrants and Vagrancy', 365.

47. Gráinne Henry, 'Ulster Exiles in Europe, 1605–1641', in Brian MacCuarta (ed.), *Ulster 1641: Aspects of the Rising* (Belfast, 1993), 39–40.

48. Charles Herbert Mayo (ed.), *The Municipal Records of the Borough of Dorchester Dorset* (Exeter, 1908), 653–6.
49. J. S. W. Gibson and E. R. C. Brinkworth (eds), *Banbury Corporation Records: Tudor and Stuart* (Banbury Historical Society, vol. 15, 1997), 152.
50. John M. Wasson (ed.), *Records of Early English Drama: Devon* (Toronto, 1986), 299.
51. TNA: SP 16/194, fo. 73.
52. TNA: SP 16/281/83.
53. Winstedt, 'Notes and Queries: Early Annals', 64.
54. Bedfordshire and Luton Archives and Records Service, Bedford, P 44/5/2.
55. Thompson, 'Gleanings from Constables' Accounts', 32.
56. Crofton, 'Early Annals', 24.
57. Hampshire Record Office, 1 M 70/PW 1.
58. Thompson, 'Gleanings from Constables' Accounts', 32–3; Winstedt, 'Notes and Queries: Early Annals', 64; Martyn Bennett (ed.), *A Nottinghamshire Village in War and Peace: The Accounts of the Constables of Upton 1640–1666* (Thoroton Society Record Series, vol. 39, Nottingham, 1995), 7.
59. Essex Record Office, Q/SR 304/152.
60. London Metropolitan Archives, London, 'Middlesex County Records. Calendar of the Sessions Books', 51 vols (typescript, 1911), i, fos 45, 49.
61. Devon Record Office, Exeter, 2021 A/PW1.
62. Devon Record Office, Q/SB Box 46.
63. HMC, *Sixth Report* (1877), appendix, 215.
64. Thompson, 'Gleanings from Constables' Accounts', 33, 36.
65. Thompson, 'Gleanings from Constables' Accounts', 31; 'Notes and Queries: Gypsies at Helmdon, Northants', *JGLS*, NS 4 (1910–11), 307; Bennett (ed.), *Nottinghamshire Village*, 50, 79, 87.
66. Ford, '"Egyptians" in Early-Modern Dorset', 3.
67. T. W. Thompson, 'English Gypsy Death and Burial Customs', *JGLS*, 3rd ser., 3 (1924), 68.
68. Abiezer Coppe, *A Second Fiery Flying Roule* (1650), 9–10.
69. Barbara Blaugdone, *An Account of the Travels, Sufferings and Persecutions of Barbara Blaugdone* (1691), 15–16.
70. TNA: ASSI 45/3/2/141.
71. TNA: ASSI 45/3/2/142.
72. TNA: ASSI 45/3/2/143.
73. Thomas Forster, *The Lay-Mans Lawyer, Reviewed & Enlarged* (1656), 72–3.
74. John Cordy Jeaffreson (ed.), *Middlesex County Records. Volume III … 1 Charles I to 18 Charles II* (Clerkenwell, 1888), 289.
75. Bethlem Royal Hospital Archives, London, Bcp 9, fos 637, 677.
76. D. E. Howell James (ed.), *Norfolk Quarter Sessions Order Book 1650–1657* (Norfolk Record Society, vol. 26, 1955), 70.
77. HMC, *Report on Manuscripts in Various Collections*, i. 129.
78. HMC, *Report on Manuscripts in Various Collections*, i. 136; Thompson, 'Gleanings from Constables' Accounts', 39.

79. Hardy (ed.), *Hertfordshire…Sessions Rolls 1591 to 1698*, 112.

80. William Le Hardy (ed.), *Hertfordshire County Records. Calendar to the Sessions Books…1619–1657* (Hertford, 1928), 471.

81. Crofton, 'Supplementary Annals', 33.

82. Somerset Heritage Centre, Q/SR/93/135.

83. Steven Hobbs (ed.), *Gleanings from Wiltshire Parish Records* (Wiltshire Record Society, vol. 63, 2010), 295.

84. Eric Otto Winstedt, 'Notes and Queries: The Squires Family', *JGLS*, NS 16 (1937), 147; Hilary Jenkinson and Dorothy L. Powell (eds), *Surrey Quarter Sessions Records: The Order Book for 1659–1661 and the Sessions Rolls for Easter and Midsummer, 1661* (Surrey Record Society, vol. 13, 1934), 12–13.

85. Richard Young, *The Poores Advocate* (1654), pt 2, 9–11.

86. See Chapter 2.

87. Gregory King, 'Scheme of the Income and Expence of the Several Families of England, Calculated for the Year 1688', in Peter Laslett, *The World We Have Lost—Further Explored* (1983), 32; Thomas Arkell, 'Illuminations and Distortions: Gregory King's Scheme Calculated for the Year 1688 and the Social Structure of Later Stuart England', *Economic History Review*, 59 (2006), 32–69.

88. Bodleian Library, MS Rawlinson C 948, 63; W. M. Palmer, 'The Reformation of the Corporation of Cambridge, July 1662', *Proceedings of the Cambridgeshire Antiquarian Society*, 17 (1914), 91.

89. *The Diary of Samuel Pepys*, ed. Latham and Matthews, ix. 278.

90. *The Diary of Samuel Pepys*, ed. Latham and Matthews, iv. 284, 296.

91. Bennett (ed.), *Nottinghamshire Village*, 118.

92. Walter Money, 'The Gypsies', *Berks, Bucks and Oxon Archaeological Journal*, 4 (1898), 28.

93. David Hitchcock, *Vagrancy in English Culture and Society, 1650–1750* (2016), 107.

94. 'Notes and Queries, Gypsies at Helmdon, Northants', 307.

95. Gardiner, *The Compleat Constable*, 30–3.

96. TNA: ASSI 23/3, fo. 198ᵛ.

97. J. S. Cockburn (ed.), *Calendar of Assize Records. Kent Indictments. Charles II. 1660–1675* (1995), 216.

98. HMC, *Report on Manuscripts in Various Collections*, i. 151.

99. Smith, 'Gypsies, Tinkers, Travellers and the Forest Economy', 65.

100. Dorset History Centre, Dorchester, PE/HOL/OV 1/1.

101. S. A. Peyton (ed.), *Minutes of Proceedings in the Quarter Sessions Held for the Parts of Kesteven in the County of Lincoln 1674–1695* (Lincoln Record Society, vol. 26, 1931), 472, 477.

102. Somerset Heritage Centre, Q/SR/193/11–14.

103. Hobbs (ed.), *Gleanings from Wiltshire Parish Records*, 168, citing a Quarter Sessions order of April 1678 entered into the parish register of Netheravon.

104. I. E. Gray and A. T. Gaydon (eds), *Gloucestershire Quarter Sessions Archives 1660–1889* (Gloucester, 1958), 16.

105. Somerset Heritage Centre, Q/SR/124/13.

106. Lancashire Archives, Preston, Kenyon of Peel MSS DDKE/acc. 7840 HMC/888.

107. *CSPD 1668–9*, 361.

108. 'An Early Gypsey', *Virginia Magazine of History and Biography*, 2 (1894), 100; Ann Marguerite Ostendorf, ' "An Egiptian and noe Xtian Woman": Gypsy Identity and Race Law in Early America', *Journal of Gypsy Studies*, 1 (2017), 5–15

109. Steve Hindle, *On the Parish? The Micro-Politics of Poor Relief in Rural England, 1550–1750* (Oxford, 2004); David Hitchcock, 'A Typology of Travellers: Migration, Justice, and Vagrancy in Warwickshire, 1670–1730', *Rural History*, 23 (2012), 21–39.

110. *A True Account of the Proceedings at the Sessions for London and Middlesex, Begun in the Old-Bailey on Wednesday the Twenty Sixth of May. 1680* (1680), 4.

111. <www.oldbaileyonline.org>, ref. t16950828–53 and 54, s16950828–1, OA16950918 (accessed April 2013). The unfortunate Buckley may have been related to the Gypsy John Buckle who was buried in 1657, or the fortune-telling Elizabeth Buckley who was cited in 1675. Other 'strolling Gypsies' named Buckley were recorded in Oxfordshire in the eighteenth century: <http://rom-anygenes.com/#/hearn-family/4524765491> (accessed October 2014).

112. <www.oldbaileyonline.org>, ref. t16950703–8 (accessed April 2013).

113. Somerset Heritage Centre, Q/SR/206/6.

114. Somerset Heritage Centre, Q/SR/206/7.

115. <www.oldbaileyonline.org>, ref. t169912131–2 (accessed June 2011).

CHAPTER 6

1. MacFie, 'Gypsy Persecutions: A Survey of a Black Chapter in European History'; Van Kappen, *Geschiedenis der Zigeuners in Nederland*, 463–73, 551–2; Asséo, 'Marginalité et exclusion'; Hohmann, *Geschichte der Zigeuner*, 27–43; Alfaro, *The Great Gypsy Round-Up. Spain*; Pym, *Gypsies of Early Modern Spain*, 152–64. Frank McLynn, *Crime and Punishment in Eighteenth-Century England* (Oxford, 1991), 105, claims 'there was a violent prejudice against Gypsies at the time' in England, but the evidence for this is uncertain.

2. David Mayall, *English Gypsies and State Policies* (Hatfield, 1995), 46; Mayall, *Gypsy Identities*, 41. Houghton-Walker, *Representations of the Gypsy in the Romantic Period*, attends to cultural developments from the late eighteenth century.

3. *Spectator*, 30 July 1711. See also *Spectator*, 9 October 1712, for 'wizards, Gypsies and cunning men' who thrive on the curiosity of the gullible.

4. *A New Canting Dictionary: Comprehending All the Terms, Antient and Modern, Used in the Several Tribes of Gypsies, Beggars, Shoplifters, Highwaymen, Foot-Pads, and all Other Clans of Cheats and Villains* (1725).

5. 'By a Lover of his Country', *The Thief-Catcher; or, Villainy Detected* (1753), 22.

6. Alexander Pope, 'Bounce to Fob. An Heriock Epistle', in *Alexander Pope: Minor Poems*, ed. Norman Ault (1954), 366. Pope later substituted 'Sturdy vagrants' for 'Idle Gypsies'.

7. *The Brave English Jipsie.*

8. *Poetical Reflexions Moral, Comical, Satyrical, etc. On the Vice and Follies of the Age* (1708), 5.

9. *Jolly Gipsies: A New Song* (1770?), broadside. A verse about Gypsies published in 1776 described their delight 'to plunder all day, and get drunk every night', living happily every day, with never a thought of tomorrow: *Norfolk Chronicle: or, the Norwich Gazette*, 1 June 1776.

10. Jane Barker, *The Lining of the Patch Work Screen* (1726), 84–6, 91–2.

11. *The Life and Humorous Adventures of William Grigg* (1733), 38–9.

12. *Memoirs of Mary Saxby, a Female Vagrant* (1807), 4, 5.

13. *The Life and Adventures of Bampfylde-Moore Carew* (1745), 4–6. The fictional autobiographer John Rooke also claimed to have served an apprenticeship with some Gypsies: *Universal Museum, or, Gentleman's and Ladies Polite Magazine of History, Politicks, and Literature* (1763), 427.

14. Henry Fielding, *The History of Tom Jones, A Foundling*, 4 vols (1749), iii. 192–203.

15. Samuel Richardson, *Pamela: Or, Virtue Rewarded*, 2 vols, 4th edn (1741), ii. 4–7.

16. Oliver Goldsmith, *The Vicar of Wakefield: A Tale. Supposed to be Written by Himself*, 2 vols (1766), i. 90–1.

17. Winstedt, 'Norwood Gypsies, 132–3; *Edinburgh Magazine and Literary Miscellany*, 59 (1797), 179.

18. *The Diary of the Late George Bubb Dodington, Baron of Melcombe Regis: From March 8, 1749, to February 6, 1761*, ed. Henry Penruddocke Wyndham (1784), 80. The tourist habit continued in July 1801, when a family from Birmingham took 'a journey of pleasure to see the Gypsies at Norwood': <www.oldbaileyonline.org>, ref. t18010701–36> (accessed 7 August 2015).

19. 'Notes and Queries, Foreign Gypsies in England', *JGLS*, NS 4 (1910–11), 307; Winstedt, 'Norwood Gypsies', 129–65.

20. 5 Elizabeth I, c. 20 (1563). This followed legislation in 1531 and 1554 that banished Gypsies and forbade their entering into England. See Chapter 3.

21. Hale, *Historia Placitorum Coronae*, i. 670–1. See also William Blackstone, *Commentaries on the Laws of England*, 4 vols (Oxford, 1765–9), iv. 166.

22. Tim Hitchcock, 'Vagrant Lives', in Joanne McEwan and Pamela Sharpe (eds), *Accommodating Poverty: The Housing and Living Arrangements of the English Poor, c. 1600–1850* (Basingstoke and New York, 2012), 152–44; Audrey Eccles, *Vagrancy in Law and Practice under the Old Poor Law* (Farnham and Burlington, VT, 2012); Hitchcock, *Vagrancy in English Culture and Society*.

23. Dalton, *The Countrey Iustice*, 97, 244; Michael Dalton, *The Country Justice: Containing the Practice of the Justices of the Peace* (1705), 65, 386; Michael Dalton, *The Country Justice: Containing the Practice, Duty and Power of the Justices of the Peace* (1746), 73, 361.

24. Jacob Giles, *The Compleat Parish Officer* (1744), 86–7; Richard Burn, *The Justice of the Peace, and Parish Officer*, 2 vols (1755), i. 276.

25. 13 Anne, c. 26 (1714).

26. 17 George II, c. 5 (1744); Henry Boult Cay, *An Abridgement of the Publick Statutes now in Force and of General Use* (1766), sub 'Vagrants'.

27. W. J. Hardy (ed.), *Hertfordshire County Records. Notes and Extracts from the Sessions Rolls 1699 to 1850* (Hertford, 1905), 34.

28. Essex Record Office, Q/SR 532/6 (1707); Cumbria Record Office, Carlisle, Q/11/1/161/3 and 4 (1732); Bedfordshire and Luton Archives, P 69/13/2, Overseers Removal Papers, Southill, 1723–1833.

29. Essex Record Office, Q/SR 532/6. Elizabeth Bicknell was committed to the House of Correction after defrauding the barber of Great Dunmow of six shillings.

30. Bedfordshire and Luton Archives, P 69/13/2, Overseers Removal Papers, Southill, 1723–1833.

31. TNA: SP 36/48, fos 142–144^v.

32. <www.oldbaileyonline.org>, ref. t17510703–16> (accessed April 2013).

33. Hampshire Record Office, 44 M69/G3/797/1–2; *World*, 9 September 1790; *Albion and Evening Advertiser*, 4 August 1800.

34. Surrey History Centre, QS 2/6/1713/62. The offenders were William Lee and Mary his wife, and Francis Lee and his wife Dina alias Diana. I am grateful to Sue Jones for this reference.

35. e.g. William Le Hardy (ed.), *Hertfordshire County Records. Calendar to the Sessions Books...1752 to 1799* (Hertford, 1935), 344; TNA: HO 47/11, fos 79–83^v; Somerset Heritage Centre, Q/SR/360/2/29; *The Newgate Calendar*, ed. Andrew Knapp and William Baldwin, 5 vols (*c.*1800), iii. 447–8. News accounts include *Lloyd's Evening Post*, 20–2 May 1765; *London Magazine*, 38 (1769), 486; *Oracle and Public Advertiser*, 29 September 1794; Eric Otto Winstedt, 'Notes and Queries: Gypsies at Aylesbury', *JGLS*, NS 6 (1912), 74.

36. TNA: SP 36/48, fo. 106.

37. Surrey History Centre, QS 2/6/1764/Mic/3.

38. Buckinghamshire Archives, Aylesbury, Quarter Sessions, R 50/24 and 84, Michaelmas 1714 and Epiphany 1714/5 <http://www.bucksrecsoc.org.uk/QS-VOLUMES/QS4.html> (accessed September 2016).

39. Morgan and Rushton, *Eighteenth-Century Criminal Transportation*, 14–15, 68.

40. *A Journal of the Proceedings of J. Hewitt, Senior Alderman, of the City of Coventry* (1790), 130, 152, 160, 163, 190.

41. Morgan and Peter, *Eighteenth-Century Criminal Transportation*, 96, 196; *Maryland Gazette,* 1149 and 1150, 17 and 27 September 1767.

42. *Mist's Weekly Journal*, 12 March 1726.

43. *Grub Street Journal*, 6 May 1731; *London Daily Post and General Advertiser*, 30 December 1735.

44. Eccles, *Vagrancy in Law and Practice*, 183.

45. Essex Record Office, D/P4/18/20.

46. *A Compleat Collection of Remarkable Tryals, of the Most Notorious Malefactors* (1721), 147–8.

47. *Life and Adventures of Bampfylde-Moore Carew*, 6–7.

48. <www.oldbaileyonline.org>, ref. t17510703–16 (accessed April 2013).

49. *Oracle and Daily Advertiser*, 30 December 1799; *Sun*, 17 January 1800; <www.oldbaileyonline.org>, ref. s18000115–1 (accessed 18 February 2014).

50. Printed sources include *The Arguments on Both Sides the Question in the Intricate Affair of Elizabeth Canning* (1753); *The Controverted Hard Case: Or Mary Squires's Magazine of Facts Re-Examined* (1753); *Thief-Catcher: or, Villainy Detected; The Truth of the Case: Or, Canning and Squires Fairly Opposed* (1753); *Canning's Magazine; or, A Review of the Whole Evidence that has been hitherto offered for or against Elizabeth Canning, and Mary Squires* (1754); *The Chronicle of the Canningites and Gipseyites* (1754); *A Full Relation of Every Thing that has Happened to Elizabeth Canning, since Sentence has been passed upon her about the Gypsy* (1754); *An Inquiry of Sir Crisp Gascoyne…Into the Cases of Canning and Squires*, 2nd edn (Dublin, 1754); *Miss Canning and the Gypsey* (1754); *A Refutation of Sir Crisp Gascoyne's Account of his Conduct in the Cases of Elizabeth Canning and Mary Squires* (1754); *A True Draught of Eliz: Canning* (1754); *Truth Triumphant: Or, the Genuine Account of the Whole Proceedings against Elizabeth Canning* (1754); and *A True Narrative of the Proceedings, with General Remarks on the Evidence given upon the Memorable Trials of Mary Squires, and Elizabeth Canning* (1755). The case was reported in *London Magazine*, *London Evening Post*, and *London Examiner*, and also in the provincial and Scottish press—e.g. *Derby Mercury* and *Caledonian Mercury*.

51. Modern studies and speculations include Barrett R. Wellington, *The Mystery of Elizabeth Canning* (New York, 1940); R. Lillian de la Torre (pseudonym of Lillian Bueno McCue), *'Elizabeth Is Missing' or, Truth Triumphant: An Eighteenth Century Mystery* (New York, 1945); John Treherne, *The Canning Enigma* (1989); Roger Guttridge, *Ten Dorset Mysteries* (Southampton, 1989), 27–52; Judith Moore, *The Appearance of Truth: The Story of Elizabeth Canning and Eighteenth-Century Narrative* (Newark, DE, and London, 1994); Kristina Straub, 'Heteroanxiety and the Case of Elizabeth Canning', *Eighteenth-Century Studies*, 30 (1997), 296–304; Amy L. Masciola. ' "The Unfortunate Maid Exemplified": Elizabeth Canning and Representations of Infanticide in Eighteenth-Century England', in Mark Jackson et al. (eds), *Infanticide: Historical Perspectives on Child Murder and Concealment, 1550–2000* (Aldershot, 2002), 52–72; Bevis Hillier, 'The Mysterious Case of Elizabeth Canning', *History Today*, 53/3 (March 2003), 47–5; Judith Moore, 'Elizabeth Canning and Mary Squires: Representations of Guilt and Innocence in Legal and Literary Texts, 1753–1989', in Katherine Kittredge (ed.), *Lewd and Notorious: Female Transgression in the Eighteenth Century* (Ann Arbor, 2003), 197–209; Dana Rabin, 'The Sorceress, the Servant, and the Stays: Sexuality and Race in Eighteenth-Century Britain', in Antoinette Burton and Tony Ballantyne (eds), *Moving Subjects: Gender, Mobility, and Intimacy in an Age of Global Empire* (Urbana, IL, 2009), 252–73; Dana Y. Rabin, 'Seeing Jews and Gypsies in 1753', *Cultural and Social History*, 7 (2012), 35–58. The only attempt to consider the Gypsy point of view is Frances Timbers, 'Mary Squires: A Case Study in Constructing Gypsy Identity in Eighteenth-Century England', in Kim Kippen and Lori Woods (eds), *Worth and Repute: Valuing Gender in Late Medieval and*

Early Modern Europe (Toronto, 2011), 153–77, which makes little use of the witness statements. For the judicial context, see James Oldham, 'Truth-Telling in the Eighteenth-Century English Courtroom', *Law and History Review*, 12 (1994), 95–121; David Lemmings, *Professors of the Law: Barristers and English Legal Culture in the Eighteenth Century* (Oxford, 2000).

52. T. B. Howell (comp.), *A Complete Collection of State Trials and Proceedings for High Treason and Other Crimes and Misdemeanors*, 33 vols (1811–26), xix. 261–76, 283–92. The following account is taken from this source unless otherwise specified. The transcript of the 1754 Old Bailey trial was 'taken in short-hand by Thomas Gurney, Samuel Rudd and Isaac Harman, all eminent short-hand writers, appointed by the court for this purpose; and after being carefully examined together, faithfully transcribed by the said Thomas Gurney, many years short-hand writer to the said court': *The Trial of Elizabeth Canning, Spinster, for Wilful and Corrupt Perjury* (1754), title page and 205 pp., reproduced in *Complete Collection of State Trials*. The version in *Old Bailey Online* is little more than a summary.

53. Nicholas Rogers, *Mayhem: Post-War Crime and Violence in Britain, 1748–53* (London and New Haven, 2013); David Lemmings and Claire Walker (eds), *Moral Panics, the Media and the Law in Early Modern England* (Basingstoke and New York, 2009), 1–40.

54. *Controverted Hard Case*, 13.

55. *Truth Triumphant*, 16; Tobias Smollett, *Continuation of the Complete History of England*, 5 vols (1763), i. 156.

56. Howell (comp.), *Complete Collection of State Trials*, xix. 19, 275–84.

57. Henry Fielding, *A Clear State of the Case of Elizabeth Canning, who hath sworn that she was robbed and almost starved to death by a gang of gipsies and other villains* (1753), 11, 58; *London Magazine, or, Gentleman's Monthly Intelligencer*, 22 (March 1753), 143–4; *Arguments on Both Sides the Question*, 4.

58. *Controverted Hard Case*, 32.

59. Winstedt, 'The Squires Family', 146–8. 'A Journal of the Towns the Gipsey came through', derived from the trial testimony, appears in *Truth Triumphant*, 23–4.

60. *Inquiry of Sir Crisp Gascoyne*, 1.

61. *London Evening Post*, 15–17 February 1753; *Controverted Hard Case*, 13; *Inquiry of Sir Crisp Gascoyne*, 13; *Arguments on Both Sides the Question*, 29; *A True Draught of Eliz: Canning*.

62. *Arguments on Both Sides the Question*, 4.

63. *Truth of the Case*, 3.

64. *Full Relation of Every Thing that has happened to Elizabeth Canning*, 15; *Thief-Catcher; or, Villainy Detected*, 74.

65. *Refutation of Sir Crisp Gascoyne's Account*, 13, 18–19.

66. De la Torre, 'Elizabeth Is Missing', 124; Moore, *Appearance of Truth*, 123–4; *Canning's Magazine*, 82.

67. *London Evening Post*, 31 March–3 April 1753; *London Examiner*, April 1753; *London Magazine*, April 1753.

68. *Controverted Hard Case*, 13; *London Evening Post*, 15–17 February 1753.

69. *Inquiry of Sir Crisp Gascoyne*, 10.

70. Rabin, 'Seeing Jews and Gypsies', 39, draws on Thomas Dekker's *Lantern and Candle-Light* of 1608 to remark on the 'odd and fantastic' garb of the Gypsies.

71. Eccles, *Vagrancy in Law and Practice*, 183, 184.

72. F. J. Harvey Darton, *The Marches of Wessex: A Chronicle of England* (1922), 204–22; F. J. Harvey Darton, *The Soul of Dorset* (New York, 1922), 204 ff.

73. *Inquiry of Sir Crisp Gascoyne*, 47.

74. *Whitehall Evening Post*, 11 October 1766.

75. Hugh Walpole to Richard Bentley, 18 May 1754, *The Yale Edition of Horace Walpole's Correspondence*, ed. W. S. Lewis et al., 48 vols (New Haven, 1937–83), xxxv. 175.

76. See also *Virtue Triumphant, or, Elizabeth Canning in America* (1757), for a far-fetched tale of the heroine's adventures in the New World.

77. Smollett, *Continuation of the Complete History of England*, i. 157; *Arguments on Both Sides the Question*, 35; *Inquiry of Sir Crisp Gascoyne*; *Refutation of Sir Crisp Gascoyne's Account*; *True Narrative of the Proceedings*.

78. *Chronicle of the Canningites and Gipseyites*, 16. For development of this association, see Timbers, 'Mary Squires: A Case Study in Constructing Gypsy Identity'.

79. *Yale Edition of Horace Walpole's Correspondence*, xxxv. 175.

80. *Truth Triumphant*, 5; *Refutation of Sir Crisp Gascoyne's Account*, 13, 18–19.

81. *Virtue Triumphant, or, Elizabeth Canning in America*, 54; *Full Relation of Every Thing that has happened to Elizabeth Canning*, 15.

82. *London Evening News*, 20–3 February 1762; *St James Chronicle, or the British Evening Post*, 23–5 February 1762.

83. Surrey History Centre, LS/536/13. Cf. Grellmann, *Dissertation on the Gipsies*, 2: 'Some say they call themselves Moors.'

84. *Northern Liberator*, 3 February 1838.

85. Thomas Gainsborough, *Landscape with Gipsies*, Tate Britain ref. N05845. See also Snell, 'In or Out of their Place'.

86. Blackstone, *Commentaries on the Laws of England*, iv. 165–6.

87. William Eden (Lord Auckland), *Principles of Penal Law*, 2nd edn (1771), 19, 305–6.

88. Romilly, *Observations on the Criminal Law of England*, 5.

89. *Scots Magazine*, August 1772, 402; *The Parliamentary History of England, from the Earliest Period to the Year 1803*, 36 vols. (1813), vol. 17, 448–50; Leon Radzinowicz, *A History of English Criminal Law and its Administration from 1750*, 4 vols. (1948–68), i. 427–9, 518, 552; Hansard, *House of Lords Debates*, 17 July 1820, vol. 2, cols 491–623; 23 George III, c. 51 (1783).

90. Crabb, *Gipsies' Advocate*, 17 n. The speaker was William Marsden.

91. Hansard, *House of Lords Debates*, 17 July 1820, vol. 2, cols 491–623; 1 George IV, c. 116 (1820).
    Hansard, *House of Commons Debates*, 12 April 1824, vol. 11, cols 361–84. The 1531 law against 'Egyptians' was formally removed by 'An Act to repeal certain statutes which are not in use', 19 and 20 Victoria, c. 64 (1856).

92. See Chapter 1.

93. Thompson, 'English Gypsy Death and Burial Customs', 76; *The Annual Register, or a View of the History, Politics, and Literature for the Year 1773* (1774), 142–3.

94. Thompson, 'Gypsy Marriage in England', *JGLS*, 3rd ser., 6 (1927), 124, 126, citing *London Chronicle*, 20–2 August 1771, and *Lincoln Gazetteer*, 29 July 1785. The parties to the Isleworth wedding were Joseph Lovell and Diana Boswell; those marrying at Leicester were Phoenix Hearne and Sarah Boswell.

95. Winstedt, 'Norwood Gypsies', 149; Dorset History Centre, PE/Yet/RE 1/4. Many records of Gypsy baptisms have been collected on the websites <http://www.gypsyjib.com/> and >http://romanygenes.com/> (both accessed April 2016).

96. K. D. M. Snell, *Parish and Belonging: Community, Identity and Welfare in England and Wales 1700–1950* (Cambridge, 2006), 54, 137.

97. William Marsden, 'Observations on the Language of the People Commonly Called Gypsies. In a Letter to Sir Joseph Banks', in *The Annual Register, or a View of the History, Politics, and Literature, for the years 1784 and 1785* (1787), 81–3; Jacob Bryant, 'Collections on the Zingara or Gypsey Language', in *The Annual Register…1784 and 1785*, 83–8; John Staples Harriot, 'Observations on the Oriental Origin of the Romnichal, or Tribe Miscalled Gypsey and Bohemian', *Transactions of the Royal Asiatic Society of Great Britain*, 2 (1829), 518–58; Crabb, *Gipsies' Advocate*, 17 n.

98. Heinrich Moritz Gottlieb Grellmann, *Dissertation on the Gipsies*, pp. ix–x. The German original, *Die Zigeuner. Ein Historicher Versuch über die Lebensart und Verfassung, Sitten und Schicksale dieses Volks in Europa, nebast ihren Ursprunge* (Dessau and Leipzig, 1783), was largely plagiarized from Johann Rűdiger, *Von der Sprache und Herkunft der Zigeuner aus Indien* (Leipzig, 1782). See Matras, 'Johann Rűdiger and the Study of Romani'; Ken Lee, 'Orientalism and Gypsylorism', *Social Analysis*, 44 (2000), 129–56, esp. 134–8 on 'Grellmann's paradigm shift'.

99. *British Chronicle, or, Pugh's Hereford Journal*, 29 November 1787; *The Times*, 30 November 1787.

100. Kent History and Library Centre, P 178/1.

101. *Edinburgh Magazine and Literary Miscellany*, 59 (1797), 178.

102. *English Chronicle or Universal Evening Post*, 4–6 August 1789.

103. *Courier and Evening Gazette*, 13 October 1795; *Oracle and Public Advertiser*, 16 October 1795.

104. Bedfordshire and Luton Archives, BC 512/11.

105. Snell, 'In or Out of their Place'; Houghton-Walker, *Representations of the Gypsy in the Romantic Period*, 229–43.

106. *The Diary of Thomas Fenwick Esq. of Burrow Hall, Lancashire, and Nunridiing, Northumberland, 1774 to 1784*, ed. Jennifer S. Holt, 4 vols (List and Index Society, 2011–12), i. 266.

107. *The Diary of a Country Parson: The Reverend James Woodforde, 1758–1802*, ed. John Beresford, 5 vols (1924–31), v. 179.

108. William Cowper, *The Task. A Poem, in Six Books* (1785), bk 1, 30–2. The most insightful recent commentary is Houghton-Walker, *Representations of the Gypsy in the Romantic Period*, 72–93.

109. *York Chronicle, and Weekly Advertiser*, 20 (April 1773).

110. *London Chronicle*, 25–7 November 1777; *Public Advertiser*, 26 November 1777; *Airs, Duets, etc. in the New Pantomime, Called the Norwood Gypsies. Performing at the Theatre-Royal in Covent-Garden* (1777); David Garrick, *May-Day: or, The Little Gipsy* (Dublin, 1777).

111. Charles Dibdin, *The Gipsies. A Comick Opera, in Two Acts* (1778).

112. Peter Pindar, *The Wandering Gipsy: A Ballad, Sung by a Young Lady in the Character of a Gipsy, at the Ranelagh Masquerade, and by Mrs Clendening at the Theatre Royal Covent Garden* (1795).

113. *Sun*, 16 July 1800.

114. *Morning Chronicle*, 4 April 1804.

115. Huntington Library, RB 633790, 'The New Gypsy Fan' (*c.*1790); RB 633789, 'The Wheel of Fortune' (a fan decorated with images of four Gypsy heads) (*c.*1805).

116. *St James's Chronicle or the British Evening Post*, 1–3 September 1789.

117. Somerset Heritage Centre, Q/SR/360/2/29.

118. Essex Record Office, D/P 202/12/33, resolution to prosecute Gypsies, 1797; East Sussex Record Office, Lewes, PAR 412/37/2, order of Quarter Sessions, 22 February 1798.

119. TNA: HO 47/18/8, fos 30–4.

120. Thomas Tattershall, *An Extraordinary Account of Tobias Smith, a Gipsy, who was Executed at Bedford, April 3d, 1792* (1792); Thomas Tattershall, *An Account of Tobias Smith, a Gipsy, who was Executed at Bedford, April 3d, 1792* (1792).

121. Tattershall, *Extraordinary Account*, 3.

122. Tattershall, *Extraordinary Account*, 4.

123. Tattershall, *Extraordinary Account*, 4

124. Tattershall, *Extraordinary Account*, 5, 7

125. Tattershall, *Extraordinary Account*, 6.

126. Tattershall, *Extraordinary Account*, 7–24.

127. Tattershall, *Extraordinary Account*, 17–18.

128. Eric Otto Winstedt, 'The Cost of Hanging a Gypsy', *JGLS*, 3rd ser., 10 (1931), 55, citing Haynes parish records. An appeal to the Home Secretary to save Tobias from the gallows, on the grounds of extenuating circumstances, fell on deaf ears. An unsigned letter dated 1 April 1792 claims that 'from his birth he has herded with those persons called Gypsies, and been brought up in total ignorance of everything but vice', making him 'less culpable' because he lacked 'a proper sense right and wrong': TNA: HO 47/14/11, fo. 83.

CHAPTER 7

1. James Peller Malcolm, *Anecdotes of the Manners and Customs of London* (1811), 350–1.

2. 'A Clown' [a country curate], 'The Poor Man's Friend: A Dialogue between a Clergyman and some Gypsies', *Christian Guardian and Church of England Magazine*, 4 (1812), 98–101; *Critical Review, or Annals of Literature* (1816), 575.

3. William Hone, *The Year Book of Daily Recreation and Information* (1832), 1485; *Christian Observer*, 28 (1828), 339; *The Prose of John Clare*, ed. J. W. Tibble and Anne Tibble (New York, 1970), 38.

4. Frederick W. Spackman, *An Analysis of the Occupations of the People Showing the Relative Importance of the Agricultural, Manufacturing, Shipping, Colonial, Commercial & Mining Interests* (1847), 31; 1,657,980 acres were enclosed 1801–10, 1,410,930 acres 1811–20, yielding a rental value some 30% higher.

5. Malcolm, *Anecdotes of the Manners and Customs of London*, 350.

6. Samuel Roberts, *The Gypsies: Their Origin, Continuance, and Destination, as Clearly Foretold in the Prophecies of Isaiah, Jeremiah, and Ezekiel*, 4th edn (1836), 125; Hoyland, *Historical Survey*, 254; Crabb, *Gipsies' Advocate*, 24. According to a contributor to the *Christian Observer* in 1828, 'the number of Gypsies in England was estimated, sixty years ago, at 40,000, and it is not thought to have since decreased': *Christian Observer*, 28 (1828), 339.

7. 'Scoto-Montanus', 'On the Influence which the State of the Gypsies has on the Moral Condition of England', *Scottish Missionary and Philanthropic Register*, 1 January 1828.

8. 'Observations, Enumeration and Parish Register Abstracts, 1821', 100 <www.histpop.org/ohpr/servlet> (accessed 9 September 2015); 'Abstracts of the Answers and Returns made Pursuant to an Act...for Taking an Account of the Population', *House of Commons Parliamentary Papers*, 139 (1833), 264, 406, 607.

9. Hardy (ed.), *Hertfordshire...Sessions Books...1752 to 1799*, 344; TNA: HO 47/18/8; HO 47/18/37. When Lord Salisbury heard of 'a great number of people who pass for Gypises' encamped in Hertfordshire in 1802, he asked the Home Secretary what could be done 'to get rid of them', and suggested that 'many able bodied young men among them' might be enlisted in the militia 'for the defence of the realm': TNA: HO 44/45, fo. 336.

10. *Prose of John Clare*, ed. Tibble and Tibble, 35; Jonathan Bate, *John Clare: A Biography* (New York, 2003), 95–6.

11. Crabb, *Gipsies' Advocate*, 65.

12. Isaac Gregory, *Crime and Punishment in Regency Frome: The Journals of Isaac Gregory, Constable of Frome 1813–14 and 1817–18*, ed. Michael McGarvie (Frome Society for Local Study, 1984), 23–4. I am grateful to Neil Howlett for supplying this reference.

13. 3 George IV, c. 126, sect. 121 (1822), revised by 4 George IV, c. 95 (1823). A parliamentary report in 1818 recorded 19,725 miles of turnpike roads and paved streets, and 95,104 miles of 'other roads in the kingdom': William Knight Dehany, *The General Turnpike Acts* (1823), p. xxx.

14. 5 George IV, c. 83, sect. 4 (1824). Contrast 3 George IV, c. 40, sect. 3 (1822), which includes 'persons pretending to be Gypsies'.

15. 'Returns of Persons Committed under the Vagrant Laws...from the 1st January 1820 to the 1st January 1824', *House of Commons Parliamentary Papers*, 357 (1824), 6, 43, 67.

16. *Cobbett's Annual Register* (1822), 617–18.
17. Huntingdonshire Archives, Huntingdon, KHCP/1/8/5; KHCP/1/9/3.
18. The following account is based on TNA: HO 17/53/234 (IN 32), plus reports in *Salisbury and Winchester Journal*, 28 April, 21 July, 28 July, and 15 September 1828; *Hampshire Chronicle*, 28 July 1828; and *Devizes and Wiltshire Gazette*, 24 April and 11 September 1828.
19. 'First Annual Report of the Commissioners under the Poor Law Amendment Act', *House of Commons Parliamentary Papers*, 255 (1835), Appendix B, 145.
20. 'First Annual Report of the Commissioners under the Poor Law Amendment Act', *House of Commons Parliamentary Papers*, 255 (1835), Appendix A, 402.
21. For example, allegations of kidnapping in *The Times*, 8 June 1802; *Yorkshire Gazette*, 5 October 1822, and *The Times*, 1 October 1824; a 'fatal fight on Wimbledon Common', in *The Times*, 21 March 1831; and the funeral of the 'king of the Gypsies' [Henry Boswell] in the *Derby Mercury*, 20 October 1824.
22. *The Times*, 17 September 1816.
23. *Devizes and Wiltshire Gazette*, 26 January 1832; *Leicester Chronicle*, 28 January 1832; *Hampshire Telegraph and Sussex Chronicle*, 30 January 1832.
24. *Morning Post*, 26 October 1822.
25. *Lincoln, Rutland and Stamford Mercury*, 13 January 1832.
26. *Bath Chronicle*, 29 March 1832. The same vacuous report appeared as a filler in the *Devizes and Wiltshire Gazette*, the *Berkshire Chronicle*, the *Bristol Mercury*, and the *Salisbury and Winchester Journal* between 29 March and 3 April 1832.
27. *Morning Post*, 10 November 1821.
28. *Westmorland Gazette*, 6 May 1826.
29. *Police Gazette; or, Hue and Cry*, 6 July 1833. See also similar reports of fraud in the *Morning Chronicle*, 3 November 1828, and in *Leeds Times*, 31 May 1834.
30. *Derby Mercury*, 25 May 1815. Experiment might show how many guineas fill a pint pot.
31. *Examiner*, 8 January 1832.
32. *The Poetical Works of Wordsworth*, ed. Thomas Hutchinson and Ernest de Selincourt (Oxford, 1964), 152–3. Important criticism includes David Simpson, *Wordsworth's Historical Imagination: The Poetry of Displacement* (London and New York, 1987), 25–55; Deborah Epstein Nord, *Gypsies and the British Imagination, 1807–1930* (New York, 2006), 50–6, 185–6; Houghton-Walker, *Representations of the Gypsy in the Romantic Period*, 134–53. See also Regina Hewitt, '"Wild Outcasts of Society": Stigmatization in Wordsworth's "Gipsies"', *Nineteenth-Century Contexts: An Interdisciplinary Journal*, 12 (1988), 19–28; Trumpener, 'The Time of the Gypsies'; Anne F. Janowitz, '"Wild Outcasts of Society": The Transit of the Gypsies in Romantic Period Poetry', in Gerald MacLean, Donna Landry, and Joseph P. Ward (eds), *The Country and the City Revisited: England and the Politics of Culture, 1550–1850* (Cambridge, 1999), 213–30; Alexandra Drayton, '"The poor tawny wanderers": The Coleridges, Wordsworth, Arnold and the Gypsies', *Coleridge Bulletin*, 34 (2009), 17–24.

33. Samuel Taylor Coleridge, *Biographia Literaria: Or Biographical Sketches of my Literary Life and Opinions*, ed. James Engell and W. Jackson Bate, 2 vols (London and Princeton, 1983), ii. 137.

34. *The Poems of John Clare*, ed. J. W. Tibble, 2 vols (1935), i. 116, 158, 180, 236; ii. 210–12, 379. See also Clare's autobiography in *Prose of John Clare*, ed. Tibble and Tibble, 35–8. For commentary and criticism, see Angus M. Fraser, 'John Clare's Gypsies', *JGLS*, 3rd ser., 50 (1971), 85–100; Nord, *Gypsies and the British Imagination*, 46–50; Bate, *John Clare*, 93–8; Sarah Houghton-Walker, 'John Clare's Gypsies', *Romani Studies*, 5th ser., 19 (2009), 125–45; Houghton-Walker, *Representations of the Gypsy in the Romantic Period*, 92–125.

35. Walter Scott, *Guy Mannering; or, The Astrologer* (1815). Quotations are from the Penguin Classics edition, ed. P. D. Garside (2003), 35, 43, 149, 340. See also W(alter) S(cott), 'Anecdotes of the Fife Gypsies', *Blackwood's Edinburgh Magazine*, 2 (November 1817), 282–5. Valuable commentary includes Peter Garside, 'Picturesque Figure and Landscape: Meg Merrilies and the Gypsies', in Stephen Copley and Peter Garside (eds), *The Politics of the Picturesque: Literature, Landscape and Aesthetics since 1770* (Cambridge, 1994), 145–74; Nord, *Gypsies and the British Imagination*, 21–42; Houghton-Walker, *Representations of the Gypsy in the Romantic Period*, 5–7.

36. *The Novels of Jane Austen*, ed. R. W. Chapman, 5 vols (Oxford, 1960), iv (*Emma*), 333–4. Commentary includes Michael Kramp, 'The Woman, the Gypsies, and England: Harriet Smith's National Role', *College Literature*, 31 (2004), 147–68; Nord, *Gypsies and the British Imagination*, 4–5, 15; Houghton-Walker, *Representations of the Gypsy in the Romantic Period*, 155–85.

37. 'Evangelism' is the spreading of the Gospel, 'Evangelicalism' the organization of that activity. For the theology, purposes, and politics of the British movement, see D. W. Bebbington, *Evangelicalism in Modern Britain: A History from the 1730s to the 1980s* (1989); Mark Smith and Stephen Taylor (eds), *Evangelicalism in the Church of England c. 1790–1890* (2004); John Wolffe, *The Expansion of Evangelicalism: The Age of Wilberforce, More, Chalmers and Finney* (Downers Grove, IL, 2007). For tracts relating to Gypsies, see John S. Andrews, 'Missionary and Allied Material in the Romany Collection of the University of Leeds', *International Review of Missions*, 46 (1957), 424–31.

38. John Rudall, *A Memoir of the Rev. James Crabb, late of Southampton* (1854), 136.

39. 'Scoto-Montanus', 'On the Influence which the State of the Gypsies has'.

40. David Mayall, *Gypsy-Travellers in Nineteenth-Century Society* (Cambridge, 1988), 97–129; Fraser, *Gypsies*, 198–9; Willems, *In Search of the True Gypsy*, 137–49; Mayall, *Gypsy Identities*, 154–5; David Cressy, 'Evangelical Ethnographers and English Gypsies from the 1790s to the 1830s', *Romani Studies*, 5th ser., 26 (2016), 63–77.

41. 'A Clown', 'The Poor Man's Friend', 101.

42. Grellmann, *Dissertation on the Gipsies*, title page, pp. iii–vi, 123–4, 231, 241.

43. Hoyland, *Historical Survey*, 151–4.

44. Hoyland, *Historical Survey*, 156.

45. Hoyland, *Historical Survey*, 158–64.
46. Hoyland, *Historical Survey*, 178–9, 190.
47. Hoyland, *Historical Survey*, 165–8.
48. Hoyland, *Historical Survey*, 169.
49. William E. A. Axon, 'The English Gipsies in 1818', *Antiquary*, 43 (1907), 181–4; John Sampson, 'English Gypsies in 1818', *JGLS*, NS 1 (1907), 183–5.
50. Thomas Blackley, *The Gypsies, or, a Narrative, in Three Parts, of Several Communications with that Wandering and Scattered People: With some Thoughts on the Duty of Christians to Attempt their Instruction & Conversion* (York, 1822), preface. Blackley's authorship is indicated by a manuscript note in the copy at Leeds University Brotherton Library; it is confirmed by the author's acknowledgement in Thomas Blackley, *The Hallowed Harp* (London and Rotherham, 1833). There are lengthy unattributed extracts in Crabb, *Gipsies' Advocate*, 165–75, and Roberts, *Gypsies*, 103–27.
51. Blackley, *Gypsies*, 6–9; Roberts, *Gypsies*, 106, 108.
52. 'Polypragmon', 'A Short Account of the Potters of Natland—a Retired village near Kendal', *Lonsdale Magazine, or Kendal Repository*, 2 (September 1821), 343–7.
53. Blackley, *Gypsies*, 9–18; Roberts, *Gypsies*, 106–7, 114, 121, 125.
54. Blackley, *Gypsies*, 12–18; Roberts, *Gypsies*, 113, 121.
55. Mark Bryant, 'Dr Who? The First Cartoon Character', *History Today*, 57 (July 2007), 60–1; Thomas Rowlandson, *Dr Syntax and the Gypsies*, in William Combe, *The Second Tour of Doctor Syntax. In Search of Consolation*, 3rd edn (1820), facing 80. Rowlandson's print went through many editions in the nineteenth century.
56. Samuel Roberts, *The Blind Man and his Son: A Tale for Young People. The Four Friends: A Fable. And a Word for the Gipsies* (1816), 99–104; Samuel Roberts, *Parallel Miracles; or, the Jews and the Gypsies* (1830), 46–50.
57. Roberts, *Parallel Miracles*, pp. vi, 39; Roberts, *Gypsies*, preface; Samuel Roberts, *The Autobiography and Select Remains of the Late Samuel Roberts* (1849), 141.
58. Roberts, *Blind Man and his Son*, 107, 119–20. A bibliography and memoir appear in Samuel Roberts, 'Samuel Roberts of Park Grange, Sheffield AD 1763–1848', *JGLS*, NS 5 (1911–12), 161–6.
59. Roberts, *Parallel Miracles*, 79–81; Roberts, *Gypsies*, 84, 85.
60. Roberts, *Gypsies*, 78.
61. Roberts, *Gypsies*, 75, 77, 80.
62. Roberts, *Parallel Miracles*, pp. 31, ix; Roberts *Gypsies*, 86, 89–103; George Hall, 'Roberts's Vocabulary', *JGLS*, NS 5 (1911), 177–91. See also Colin Holmes, 'Samuel Roberts and the Gypsies', in Sidney Pollard and Colin Holmes (eds), *Essays in the Economic and Social History of South Yorkshire* (Barnsley, 1976), 233–46.
63. Crabb, *Gipsies' Advocate*, pp. viii, 63–6; Rudall, *Memoir of the Rev. James Crabb*, 135, 139, 141; *Christian Observer*, 28 (1828), 277.
64. *Woolmer's Exeter and Plymouth Gazette*, 8 September 1838.

65. *Letters of George Borrow to the British and Foreign Bible Society*, ed. T. H. Darlow (1911), 8;Viscount Esher (ed.), *The Girlhood of Queen Victoria: A Selection from Her Majesty's Diaries between the years 1832 and 1840*, 2 vols (1912), i. 182.
66. Crabb, *Gipsies' Advocate*, pp. ix, 139.
67. Crabb, *Gipsies' Advocate*, 11, 12, 48, 54.
68. Crabb, *Gipsies' Advocate*, 14, 26, 31, 36, 38, 48.
69. Crabb, *Gipsies' Advocate*, 31, 48, 137; Hoyland, *Historical Survey*, 212 n.
70. *Children's Friend*, 1 February 1836.
71. Rowland Hill to the Southampton Committee, 24 November 1827), in Rudall, *Memoir of the Rev. James Crabb*, 139.
72. Esher (ed.), *Girlhood of Queen Victoria*, i. 179–82.
73. *Bradford Observer*, 23 November 1837, and other papers.

CHAPTER 8

1. George K. Behlmer, 'The Gypsy Problem in Victorian England', *Victorian Studies*, 28 (1985), 231–53. See also Raphael Samuel, 'Comers and Goers', in H. J. Dyos and M. Wolff (eds), *The Victorian City, Images and Reality*, 2 vols (1976), i. 123–60, on Gypsy encampments on the outskirts of London.
2. Mayall, *Gypsy-Travellers*; Mayall, *Gypsy Identities*. See also Mayall, *English Gypsies and State Policies*.
3. Willems, *In Search of the True Gypsy*. See also Leo Lucassen, Wim Willems, and Annemarie Cottaar (eds), *Gypsies and Other Itinerant Groups: A Socio-Historical Approach* (New York, 1998).
4. Jodie Matthews, ' "Tsiganes on the Brain": The "Last Gypsy" as a Case of Archive Fever', *Immigrants and Minorities*, 31 (2013), 290, citing Jacques Derrida, *Archive Fever: A Freudian Impression* (Chicago, 1998).
5. Nord, *Gypsies and the British Imagination*; Houghton-Walker, *Representations of the Gypsy in the Romantic Period*. See also Trumpener, 'The Time of the Gypsies'; Abby Bardi, 'The Gypsy as Trope in Victorian and Modern British Literature', *Romani Studies*, 5th ser., 16 (2006), 31–42; Jodie Matthews, 'Mobilising the Imperial Uncanny: Nineteenth-Century Textual Attitudes to Travelling Romani People, Canal-Boat People, Showpeople and Hop-Pickers in Britain', *Nineteenth-Century Contexts*, 37 (2015), 359–75.
6. *The Works of John Ruskin*, ed. E. T. Cooke and Alexander Wedderburn, 39 vols (1903–12), ii. 27–41. See also Arthur Penrhyn Stanley, *The Gipsies: A Prize Poem* (Oxford, 1837), for similar sentiments.
7. Charlotte Brontë, *Jane Eyre* (1847); Emily Brontë, *Wuthering Heights* (1847); Arnold, 'The Scholar-Gypsy'; George Eliot, *The Mill on the Floss* (1860); George Eliot, *The Spanish Gypsy* (1868); George Meredith, *The Adventures of Harry Richmond* (1871).
8. Simson and Simson, *History of the Gipsies*, 302; Charles G. Leland, *The English Gipsies and their Language* (1873), 152, 155.

9. Judith Okely, 'Retrospective Reading of Fieldnotes: Living on Gypsy Camps', *Behemoth: A Journal on Civilisation*, 4 (2011), 18–42, esp. 22 on 'faked or dodged answers to absurdly intrusive questions' and 'what the questioner wanted to hear'; Jeremy Harte, 'Romance and the Romany', *History Today*, 66/1 (January 2016), 35. Cf. reports of American Indian and African villager informants who relayed the findings of classic anthropology: George E. Marcus and Michael M. J. Fischer, *Anthropology as Cultural Critique: An Experimental Moment in the Human Sciences* (Chicago and London, 1986), 36.

10. Borrow, *The Zincali; Lavengro: The Scholar—The Gypsy—The Priest* (1851), preface; *Romany Rye: A Sequel to 'Lavengro'* (1857); *Romano Lavo-Lil: Word Book of the Romany; or, English Gypsy Language*(1874).

11. Behlmer, 'Gypsy Problem', 240–1; Willems, *In Search of the True Gypsy*, 93–137, 156–9; Mayall, *Gypsy Identities*, 156–62. See also Ian Hancock, 'George Borrow's Romani', in Hancock, *Danger! Educated Gypsy* (Hatfield, 2010), 160–76; Ian Duncan, 'George Borrow's Nomadology', *Victorian Studies*, 41 (1998), 381–403.

12. Henry Woodcock, *The Gipsies: Being a Brief Account of their History, Origin, Capabilities, Manners and Customs; with Suggestions for the Reformation and Conversion of the English Gipsies* (1865), 2 and *passim*.

13. Simson and Simson, *History of the Gipsies*, 302.

14. Simson and Simson, *History of the Gipsies*, 4, 9, 93–4, 375.

15. Simson and Simson, *History of the Gipsies*, 6, 9–10, 12–14, 22, 72, 94, 302, 341–2, 375–6, 499, 532.

16. Leland, *English Gipsies*, pp. x, 143, 170, 173, 174, and *passim*. See also Regenia Gagnier, 'Cultural Philanthropy, Gypsies and Interdisciplinary Scholars: Dream of a Common Language', *19: Interdisciplinary Studies in the Long Nineteenth Century*, 1 (2005) <http://doi.org/10.16995/ntn.433> (accessed October 2017).

17. B. C. Smart and H. T. Crofton, *The Dialect of the English Gypsies* (1875), pp. vii–ix, xxiii, 191–204. See also Bath C. Smart, 'The Dialect of the English Gypsies', *Transactions of the Philological Society* (Berlin, 1862–3), appendix.

18. S. B. James, 'English Gipsies: A Monograph. In Five Chapters', *Church of England and Lambeth Magazine*, 79 (1875), 97–100, 161–4, 225–30, 289–4, 353–7, quotations at 100, 294.

19. David Townsend, *The Gipsies of Northamptonshire: Their Manner of Life, Festive Amusements, and Fortune-Telling, Fifty Years Ago* (Kettering, 1877), 10.

20. Francis Hindes Groome, *In Gipsy Tents* (1880; repr. 1973), 2, 26, 55–6, 101–2, 252, 386. Francis Hindes Groome, *The Gipsies: Reminiscences and Social Life of their Extraordinary Race: Their Manners, Customs, and Wanderings* (Edinburgh, 1881), is the same work retitled. See also Francis H. Groome, 'Gipsies', in *Encyclopedia Britannica*, 9th edn, 25 vols (Edinburgh, 1875–88), x. 611–18; Francis Hindes Groome, *Gypsy Folk Tales* (1899); Willems, *In Search of the True Gypsy*, 176–80.

21. Vernon Morwood, *Our Gipsies in City, Tent and Van* (1885), 2–6.

22. Willems, *In Search of the True Gypsy*, 172–4; Mayall, *Gypsy Identities*, 120–79. Michael Hayes, 'Nineteenth-Century Gipsilorism and the Exoticisation of the

Roma (Gypsies)', in Michael Hayes (ed.), *Road Memories: Aspects of Migrant History* (Newcastle, 2007), 20–35. The *Journal of the Gypsy Lore Society* (1887–92) was revived in 1907, and in 2000 became *Romani Studies*. Crucial articles in this tradition include Crofton, 'Early Annals'; Crofton, 'Supplementary Annals'; Winstedt, 'Early British Gypsies'; Thompson, 'Gleanings from Constables' Accounts'; Thompson, 'Consorting with and Counterfeiting Egyptians'; Winstedt, 'Records of Gypsies in the Eastern Counties of England'.

23. MacRitchie, *Scottish Gypsies*.

24. Smith, *Gipsy Life*, pp. xii, 42, 73, 99, 110; George Smith, *I've Been a Gipsying: Or, Rambles among our Gipsies and their Children* (1881), 28, 349–51. See also Behlmer, 'Gypsy Problem', 244–51; Mayall, *Gypsy-Travellers*, 130–49.

25. Smith, *Gipsy Life*, 97, 261–2; Smith, *I've Been a Gipsying*, 276. See also James Ewing Ritchie (Christopher Crayon), 'In a Gipsy Camp', *Christian World*, 19 December 1879; repr. in Stephen Donovan and Matthew Rubery (eds), *Secret Commissions: An Anthology of Victorian Investigative Journalism* (Peterborough, Ontario, 2012), 144–8.

26. Smith, *Gipsy Life*, 195–6; Smith, *I've Been a Gipsying*, 130, 197–8. *Rokker* (variously spelled) is the Romany verb 'to talk'.

27. [Arthur Edward Gregory Way], *No. 747. Being the Autobiography of a Gipsy, Edited by F. W. Carew, MD* (1890); Henry J. Francis, 'No. 747. Being the Autobiography of a Gypsy', *JGLS*, NS 33 (1954), 88–107; Behlmer, 'Gypsy Problem', 234–5.

28. Hansard, *House of Commons Debates*, 10 August 1885, vol. 300, col. 1705.

29. *Morning Post*, 15 September 1894.

30. W. Maurice Adams, 'The Wandering Tribes of Great Britain', *Cassell's Family Magazine*, 9 (November 1883), 731.

31. *Essex County Chronicle*, 26 August 1892, 23 June 1893, 29 June 1894.

32. See Mayall, *Gypsy-Travellers*, 189–92, and Mayall, *English Gypsies and State Policies*, 23–6, for more than two dozen statutes relating to Gypsies.

33. 5 George IV, c. 83, sect. 4 (1824). The legislation echoed earlier acts against rogues and vagabonds, especially 39 Elizabeth 1, c. 4 (1598), and 13 Anne, c. 26 (1714).

34. *Chelmsford Chronicle*, 25 February 1842; *Bath Chronicle*, 12 May 1842.

35. *Lincoln, Rutland and Stamford Mercury*, 9 January and 10 July 1846.

36. Hansard, *House of Commons Debates*, 9 and 13 May 1864, vol. 175, cols 193, 461.

37. 5 George IV, c. 83 (1824).

38. e.g. Madonna Gibbs in Staffordshire: *Birmingham Daily Post*, 22 December 1891; Caroline Gray at Boston: *Nottinghamshire Guardian*, 7 May 1898.

39. 9 George II, c. 5, sect. 4 (1736).

40. *North Devon Journal*, 23 August 1900.

41. 5 and 6 William IV, c. 50, sects 72, 76 (1835). See also The Metropolitan Police Act, 2 and 3 Victoria, c. 47, sect. 54 (1839), on the 'prohibition of nuisances by persons in the thoroughfares'.

42. 30 and 31 Victoria, c. 5 (1867).

43. 39 and 40 Victoria, c. 56 (1876).

44. 48 and 49 Victoria, c. 72, sect. 9; 52 and 53 Victoria, c. 17, sect. 13 (1889); 54 and 55 Victoria, c. 76, sect. 95 (1891).

45. Hansard, *House of Commons Debates*, 10 August 1885, vol. 300, col. 1705); Mayall, *English Gypsies and State Policies*, 31–40.

46. I am grateful to Ohio State University for continuing access to these databases, which are available through various subscribing libraries. See also The British Newspaper Archive <https://www.britishnewspaperarchive.co.uk/> (accessed October 2017).

47. Mayall, *Gypsy Identities*, 46.

48. *Examiner*, 19 August 1838.

49. *Derby Mercury*, 8 February 1837.

50. *Brighton Patriot and South of England Free Press*, 16 April 1839; *Lincoln, Rutland and Stamford Mercury*, 19 April 1839; *Jackson's Oxford Journal*, 6 June 1840.

51. *Morning Post*, 9 October 1839; *Devizes and Wiltshire Gazette*, 2 January 1840.

52. *Evening News* (Portsmouth), 12 March 1891.

53. *Hampshire Telegraph and Sussex Chronicle*, 4 July 1868, 21 October 1868, 18 February 1870; *Hampshire Advertiser*, 24 October 1868, 16 May 1877, 18 September 1878; *Bucks Herald*, 20 February 1869; *Western Gazette*, 18 November 1870; *Isle of Wight Observer*, 3 April 1880.

54. *Evening News* (Portsmouth), 12 March 1891.

55. *Evening News* (Portsmouth), 19 September 1892, 19 June 1893, 16 October 1895; *Hampshire Advertiser*, 22 December 1897; *Isle of Wight Observer*, 10 September 1898.

56. *Isle of Wight Observer*, 8 October 1898; *Evening News* (Portsmouth), 19 February 1901, 27 January 1904; TNA: RG 13/1028.

57. *The Times*, 12 October 1842.

58. *Western Times*, 25 April 1840.

59. *Sheffield and Rotherham Independent*, 1 October 1842.

60. *Pall Mall Gazette*, 15 August 1894.

61. Information extracted from all newspapers from 1850 in 'British Library Newspapers, 1800–1950'.

62. *Derbyshire and Chesterfield Herald*, 9 January 1892, quoting a superintendant at the Wirksworth petty sessions.

63. *Leicester Chronicle; or, Commercial and Agricultural Advertiser*, 21 October 1837; *Lincoln, Rutland and Stamford Mercury*, 17 April 1840.

64. *Standard*, 20 July 1841,

65. *Essex County Standard*, 8 July 1893; *Essex County Chronicle*, 3 August 1894.

66. *Woolmer's Exeter and Plymouth Gazette*, 6 August 1842,

67. *Sheffield and Rotherham Independent*, 11 May 1844, 27 July 1844. The language was borrowed from the Highway Act of 1835.

68. *Regina v. Rachel Cox*, in 175 *English Reports*, 897 <http://www.commonlii.org/uk/cases/EngR/1859/120.pdf> (accessed October 2017).

69. *Hampshire Advertiser*, 2 April 1890; *Essex County Chronicle*, 6 March 1891; *Essex County Standard*, 24 August 1895; *Trewman's Exeter Flying Post*, 5 May 1897; *Illustrated Police News*, 9 October 1897; *Cheltenham Chronicle*, 16 September 1899.

70. *Essex Standard*, 10 May 1890.

71. *Sheffield and Rotherham Independent*, 2 October 1890.

72. *Essex County Chronicle*, 5 June 1891.

73. *Yorkshire Evening Post*, 2 April 1892; *Hampshire Advertiser*, 5 November 1892.

74. *Essex County Standard*, 8 July 1893; *Essex County Chronicle*, 3 August 1894.

75. *Reynold's Newspaper*, 10 January 1897.

76. *Citizen* (Gloucester), 3 August 1895.

77. *Morning Post*, 25 December1893.

78. *Evening News* (Portsmouth), 15 December 1899.

79. *Yorkshire Evening Post,* 17 January 1899; Hansard, *House of Commons Debates*, 24 February 1899, vol. 67, col. 455.

80. *Bury and Norwich Post*, 13 September 1898.

81. *Evening Telegraph and Star,* 1 October 1897; *Morning Post*, 2 October 1897.

82. *Western Gazette,* 11 November 1898. The fortune-teller was Sarah Stokes, who was sentenced to six months in prison.

83. *Bradford Observer*, 23 November 1837; *The Times*, 18 April 1838; *Berkshire Chronicle*, 29 January 1839. See also the case of *Regina* v. *Bunce*, in which a housewife feared that a Gypsy would do her evil unless she gave her everything of value: 175 *English Reports*, 836–7, spring 1859 <http://www.common-lii.org/uk/cases/EngR/1859/94.pdf> (accessed October 2017).

84. Leland, *English Gipsies*, 141; Morwood, *Our Gipsies*, 303–4. George Borrow may be responsible for misuse and mistranslation of the phrase 'hokkano baro': Hancock, 'George Borrow's Romani', 170–1.

85. *Woolmer's Exeter and Plymouth Gazette*, 23 July 1842.

86. *The Times*, 19 May 1842.

87. *Devizes and Wiltshire Gazette*, 28 July 1842.

88. *Bristol Mercury*, 8 September 1845.

89. *Leeds Mercury,* 21 November 1846,

90. *Western Times*, 12 December 1846.

91. *Lloyd's Weekly Newspaper*, 9 March 1890. Elizabeth Roster was sentenced to two months' hard labour.

92. *Standard*, 14 February 1891.

93. *Manchester Courier and Lancashire General Advertiser*, 20 February 1892.

94. *Evening Telegraph and Star* (Sheffield), 27 November 1893.

95. *Evening News* (Portsmouth), 14 November 1899.

96. *Hereford Journal*, 4 November 1840.

97. *Hereford Journal*, 25 September 1844.

98. *Berrow's Worcester Journal*, 20 May 1854.

99. *Star* (Saint Peter Port), 15 January 1887.

100. *Evening News* (Portsmouth), 20 December 1882.

101. T. W. Thompson, 'Gypsy Marriage in England', *JGLS*, 3rd ser., 5 (1926), 9–37; 3rd ser., 6 (1927), 101–29, 151–82.

102. *Royal Leamington Spa Courier*, 7 March 1846; *Nottinghamshire Guardian*, 25 March 1862; *Western Gazette*, 1 April 1879; *Devon and Exeter Daily Gazette*, 28

July 1891. The most thorough survey is Thompson, 'English Gypsy Death and Burial Customs', 5–38, 60–93; T. W. Thompson, 'Additional Notes on English Gypsy Death and Burial Customs', *JGLS*, 3rd ser., 9 (1930), 34–8.

103. *Lincoln, Rutland and Stamford Mercury*, 19 April 1839. Wisdom Smith was John Clare's Gypsy companion.

104. *The Times*, 18 October 1842.

105. Leland, *English Gipsies*, 56, 59; Smart and Crofton, *Dialect of the English Gypsies*, 202–3.

106. *Lincoln, Rutland and Stamford Mercury*, 1 August 1845.

107. The death of Aaron Boswell, age 74, was announced in the *Leicestershire Chronicle and Leicestershire Mercury*, 9 June 1866. For the ritual destruction of his possessions, see Thompson, 'English Gypsy Death and Burial Customs', 78.

108. *Bradford Observer*, 10 December 1873; *Hull Packet and East Riding Times*, 4 January 1884.

109. *Hull Daily Mail*, 17 September 1894.

110. *Edinburgh Evening News*, 21 March 1896.

111. Thompson, 'English Gypsy Death and Funeral Customs', 87–90; Okely, *The Traveller-Gypsies*, 216, 222.

112. *Essex County Chronicle*, 12 October 1900; *Essex Newsman*, 13 October 1900; and *Essex County Standard*, 13 and 27 October 1900.

113. *Daily News*, 6 October 1891.

114. *Standard*, 25 January 1839.

115. *Morning Post*, 2 April 1846.

116. *Hampshire Advertiser and Salisbury Guardian*, 4 April 1846.

117. *Hampshire Advertiser and Salisbury Guardian*, 14 November 1846.

118. *Bury and Norwich Post*, 16 January 1850; *Salisbury and Winchester Journal*, 26 January 1850.

119. *Aris's Birmingham Gazette*, 25 November 1850.

120. *Bucks Herald*, 11 March 1893.

121. *Sunderland Daily Echo*, 21 August 1900.

122. *Lincoln, Rutland and Stamford Mercury*, 12 July 1850.

123. *Essex County Chronicle*, 6 January and 24 February 1893.

124. *Leeds Times*, 23 December 1893.

125. *Northampton Mercury*, 3 November 1893.

126. *Sheffield and Rotherham Independent*, 6 May 1892.

127. See Chapter 7.

128. Woodcock, *Gipsies*, 3; Simson and Simson, *History of the Gipsies*, 4.

129. Leland, *English Gipsies*, preface.

130. *Ipswich Journal*, 30 October 1841.

131. *Bury and Norwich Post*, 13 April 1842; *Essex Standard and General Advertiser*, 8 April 1842.

132. Snell, *Parish and Belonging*, 307–8.

133. Richard Lawton (ed.), *The Census and Social Structure: An Interpretative Guide to Nineteenth Century Censuses of England and Wales* (1978); Edward Higgs,

A Clearer Sense of the Census: The Victorian Censuses and Historical Research (1996), 46.

134. Registrar General, *1841 Census, Abstracts of Answers and Returns* (1841), 240 and *passim*.

135. Mayall, *Gypsy-Travellers*, 23–6.

136. Registrar General, *General Report, England and Wales. 1861. VII. Occupations of the People* (1861), 225; Registrar General, *Population Tables, England and Wales, vol. II, part I* (1861), pp. xli, lvi, lxv, lxxix.

137. Registrar General, *General Report. England and Wales, 1871* (1871), p. liii.

138. Groome, 'Gipsies', 545.

139. *Sheffield and Rotherham Independent*, 28 March 1891.

140. Norman N. Dodds, *Gypsies, Didikois and Other Travellers* (1966), 17.

141. TNA: HO 107/1004/10.

142. TNA: HO 107/1822.

143. TNA: RG 9/2276.

144. TNA: RG 9/1107; RG 10/1264; RG 11/3591.

145. John Sampson, 'Notes and Queries: Death of a Well-Known English Gypsy', *JGLS* 2 (1890), 191.

146. Janet Keet-Black (ed.), *The Sussex Gypsy Diaries 1896–1926* (Romany and Traveller Family History Society, 1999). Similar records for Burgess Hill survive from 1912 to 1915.

147. TNA: RG 12/777, p. 20; RG 13/890, p. 32.

148. Crowe, *History of the Gypsies of Eastern Europe*, 121.

149. Leo Lucassen and Wim Willems, 'Wanderers or Migrants? Gypsies from Eastern to Western Europe, 1860–1940', in Robin Cohen (ed.), *The Cambridge Survey of World Migration* (Cambridge, 1995), 137–89.

150. Leland, *English Gipsies*, 131–2.

151. Batillard, 'Immigration of the Gypsies into Western Europe', 204; William A. Dutt, 'With the East-Anglian Gypsies', *Good Words*, 37 (1896), 120–6.

152. Hansard, *House of Commons Debates*, 22 September 1886, vol. 309, cols 1269–79; Henry Thomas Crofton, 'Affairs of Egypt, 1892–1906', *JGLS*, NS 1 (1907), 370.

153. *Evening Telegraph and Star* (Sheffield), 21 August 1897.

154. Ian Hancock, 'Marko: Stories of my Grandfather', *Lacio Drom*, 6 (1985), 54–5, cites an example of intermarriage and cultural transfer between Hungarian Gypsies and Victorian Romanichal.

155. Stanley C. Johnson, *A History of Emigration from the United Kingdom to North America, 1763–1912* (1913), 347.

156. *Boston Daily Atlas*, 5 August 1851. The English Gypsy experience in North America is best approached through Matt T. Salo and Sheila Salo, 'Romnichel Economic and Social Organization in Urban New England', *Urban Anthropology*, 11 (1982), 273–313. See also Anne Sutherland, *Gypsies: The Hidden Americans* (Prospect Heights, IL., 1975; repr. 1986); Marlene Sway, *Familiar Strangers: Gypsy Life in America* (Urbana, IL, and Chicago, 1988).

157. *Sun* (Baltimore), 1 April 1852; *Albany Journal*, 24 April 1852.

158. *Ripley Bee* (Ripley, Ohio), 8 January 1853; *Daily National Intelligencer* (Washington), 17 January 1853; *North American and United States Gazette* (Philadelphia), 19 January 1853, 15 June 1853; *Daily Cleveland Herald*, 2 June 1853, 4 March 1854.

159. *Daily Morning News* (Savannah, Georgia), 18 August 1855; *Daily South Carolinian*, 21 August 1855.

160. *Boston Investigator*, 31 March 1869; *Nottingham Evening Post*, 14 November 1888; Salo and Salo, 'Romnichel Economic and Social Organization', 280, 287–92, 303–5.

161. Albert Thomas Sinclair, *American Gypsies* (New York, 1917), 4–12. See also Riley M. Fletcher Berry, 'The American Gypsy', *Frank Leslie's Popular Monthly*, 53 (1902), 560–72.

162. *Milwaukee Daily Sentinel*, 4 April 1860.

163. Crofton, 'Affairs of Egypt, 1892–1906', 359. *Hampshire Advertiser*, 8 January 1890, was among several English papers to report the death of Thomas Blythe.

CHAPTER 9

1. John Sampson (ed.), *The Wind on the Heath: A Gypsy Anthology* (1930), offers a sentimental Gypsylorist compendium.

2. Glimpses of modern Gypsy life may be found in Elwood B. Trigg, *Gypsy Demons and Divinities: The Magic and Religion of the Gypsies* (Secaucus, NJ, 1973); 'Some Notes on Gypsies in North Britain', in Farnham Rehfisch (ed.), *Gypsies, Tinkers and other Travellers* (1975), 85–121; Okely, *The Traveller-Gypsies*; Sylvester Gordon Boswell, *The Book of Boswell: The Autobiography of a Gypsy*, ed. John Seymour (1970); Manfri Frederick Wood, *In the Life of a Romany Gypsy*, ed. John A. Brune (1973); Peter Saunders, Jim Clarke, Sally Kendall, Anna Lee, Sakie Lee, and Freda Matthews (eds), *Gypsies and Travellers in Their Own Words* (Leeds, 2000); and Jeremy Sandford, *Rokkering to the Gorjios: In the Early Nineteen Seventies British Romany Gypsies Speak of their Hopes, Fears and Aspirations* (Hatfield, 2000).

3. British Library, India Office, IOR/L/PJ/6, items 816, 844, 855.

4. Eric Otto Winstedt, 'The Gypsy Coppersmiths "Invasion" of 1911–13', *JGLS*, NS 6 (1912), 244.

5. *Nottingham Evening Post*, 25 August 1902.

6. *Northampton Mercury*, 5 June 1903; Crofton, 'Affairs of Egypt, 1892–1906', 367.

7. Crofton, 'Affairs of Egypt, 1892–1906', 369, 370.

8. *Daily Mail*, 2 December 1904; *Cambridge Independent Press*, 16 December 1904; *Essex Newsman*, 24 December 1904; *Manchester Courier and Lancashire General Advertiser*, 10 February 1905; *Nottingham Evening Post*, 14 February 1905; *Cambridge Independent Press*, 2 June 1905; Colin Holmes, 'The German Gypsy Question in Britain, 1904–1906', in Kenneth Lunn (ed.), *Hosts, Immigrants and Minorities: Historical Responses to Newcomers in British Society 1870–1914* (New

York, 1980), 138–42. See also Colin Holmes, *John Bull's Island: Immigration and British Society 1871–1971* (Basingstoke, 1988).

9. 5 Edward VII, c. 13 (An Act to Amend the Law with Regard to Aliens). Aliens Act, 1905.

10. *Nottingham Evening Post*, 23 July, and 3 and 5 October 1906; *Derby Daily Telegraph*, 2 October 1906; *Tamworth Herald*, 27 October 1906; *Lincoln, Rutland and Stamford Mercury*, 16 November 1906; *Penny Illustrated Paper and Illustrated Times*, 17 November 1906. See Chapter 4 for the episode in Elizabethan Nottinghamshire.

11. Hansard, *House of Lords Debates*, 30 April 1906, vol. 156, col. 205; Hansard, *House of Commons Debates*, 2 May 1906, vol. 156, col. 554, 2 August 1906, vol. 162, col. 1356, 26 November 1906, vol. 165, cols 1236–7, 4 December 1906, vol. 166, col. 749; Crofton, 'Affairs of Egypt, 1892–1906', 373–84; Holmes, 'German Gypsy Question', 142–4.

12. Henry Thomas Crofton, 'Affairs of Egypt, 1907', *JGLS*, NS 2 (1908), 132–3.

13. *Daily Mail* (Hull), 17 June 1908; *Cambridge Independent* Press, 26 June 1908; Henry Thomas Crofton, 'Affairs of Egypt, 1908', *JGLS*, NS 3 (1909), 287–8.

14. *The Times*, 26 August 1911; *Western Gazette*, 8 September 1911.

15. Winstedt, 'Gypsy Coppersmiths "Invasion"', 244–302.

16. *Sunday Times*, 19 October 1997, 18 January 2004; Donald Kenrick, 'Foreign Gypsies and British Immigration Law after 1945', in Thomas Acton (ed.), *Gypsy Politics and Traveller Identity* (Hatfield, 1997), 100–10; Colin Clark and Elaine Campbell, '"Gypsy Invasion": A Critical Analysis of Newspaper Reaction to Czech and Slovak Romani Asylum-Seekers in Britain, 1997', *Romani Studies*, 5th ser., 10 (2000), 23–47.

17. Colin Clark and Margaret Greenfields (eds), *Here to Stay: The Gypsies and Travellers of Britain* (Hatfield, 2006), 17; Philip Brown, Lisa Scullion, and Philip Martin, *Migrant Roma in the United Kingdom* (Manchester, 2013); David Smith, 'The Political Context of Migration in the UK: The Case of Roma Gypsies', in *Handbook of Research on Impacts of International Business and Political Affairs in the Global Economy* (2016), 367–80.

18. *Derby Daily Telegraph*, 11 February 1905.

19. *Daily Mail*, 28 January and 11 February 1902; *Western Times,* 21 March 1902.

20. *Essex Newsman*, 24 May 1902.

21. *Essex Newsman*, 16 May 1903; *Sheffield Daily Telegraph*, 20 May 1903; *Essex County Chronicle*, 31 July 1903; *Western Times*, 10 January 1905.

22. *Derby Daily Telegraph*, 8 October 1904, 26 July 1905; *Western Times*, 27 July 1905; Mayall, *English Gypsies and State Policies*, 79–83.

23. *Devon and Exeter Daily Gazette*, 13 July 1905, 11 October 1907, 28 April 1909; *Nottingham Evening Post*, 15 March 1909; *Western Gazette*, 29 January 1915. See also 'Notes and Queries: British Gypsy Crimes, 1911', *JGLS*, NS 6 (1912), 71.

24. Law of Property Act 1925 (15 and 16 George V, c. 11), sect. 193.

25. *The Times*, 6 April 1929; *Western Gazette*, 12 April 1929; *Courier and Advertiser* (Dundee), 22 April 1929; *Nottingham Evening Post*, 23 April 1929.

26. *Nottingham Evening Post*, 23 April 1929. The struggle can be followed in the *Daily Mail* from 9 to 27 April 1929, 23 May 1930, 23 April 1937, 24 May 1938; Thomas Acton, *Gypsy Politics and Social Change: The Development of Ethnic Ideology and Pressure Politics among British Gypsies from Victorian Reformism to Romany Nationalism* (1974), 102, citing *News Chronicle*, 1 June 1938; Becky Taylor, *A Minority and the State: Travellers in Britain in the Twentieth Century* (Manchester, 2008), 66–9.

27. Vagrancy Act 1935 (25 George V, c. 20).

28. Public Health Act 1936 (25 George V and 1 Edward VIII, c. 49), sects 268–9.

29. *Nottingham Evening Post*, 8 July 1931.

30. Taylor, *Minority and the State*, 37–48, 69–70.

31. Brian Vesey-Fitzgerald, *Gypsies of Britain: An Introduction to their History* (1944); Rupert Croft-Cooke, *A Few Gypsies* (1955); and G. E. C. Webb, *Gypsies: The Secret People* (1960). See also Angus M. Fraser, 'The Gypsy Problem: A Survey of Post-War Developments', *JGLS* NS 32 (1953), 82–100.

32. *Evening Telegraph*, 14 September 1950; *Citizen* (Gloucester), 15 September and 15 November 1950; *The Times*, 14 October 1953 and 2 December 1961; Dodds, *Gypsies, Didikois and Other Travellers*; Grattan Puxon, 'The Romani Movement: Rebirth and the First World Romani Conference in Retrospect', in Thomas Acton (ed.), *Scholarship and the Gypsy Struggle: Commitment in Romani Studies* (Hatfield, 2000), 94–113; Thomas Acton, 'The Life and Times of Donald Kenrick', in Acton (ed.), *Scholarship and the Gypsy Struggle*, pp. xi–xxxi; Acton, *Gypsy Politics and Social Change*, 137–72; Derek Hawes and Barbara Perez, *The Gypsy and the State: The Ethnic Cleansing of British Society* (Bristol, 1995), 18–19.

33. Hansard, *House of Commons Debates*, 20 April 1951, vol. 486, col. 2260; 12 March 1956, vol. 566, col. 962.

34. *The Times*, 18 April 1952.

35. *The Times*, 2 December 1961.

36. Hansard, *House of Commons Debates*, 5 February 1993, vol. 218, cols 587–651, and 1 April 1993, vol. 222, col. 525.

37. 10 and 11 George VI, c. 51 (Town and Country Planning Act, 1947); *The Times*, 18 April 1952; Taylor, *Minority and the State*, 115, 123.

38. Highways Act, 1959 (7 and 8 Elizabeth II, c. 25), sect. 127; Barbara Adams, Judith Okely, David Morgan, and David Smith, *Gypsies and Government Policy in England* (1975), 9.

39. Caravan Sites and Control of Development Act of 1960 (1960, c. 62); Donald Kenrick and Colin Clark (eds), *Moving On: The Gypsies and Travellers of Britain* (1999), 87–8.

40. Acton, *Gypsy Politics and Social Change*, 203. Lord Kennet was the progressive politician and author Wayland Young.

41. Sociological Research Section of the Ministry of Housing and Local Government, *Gypsies and Other Travellers* (1967), 17–19.

42. *The Times*, 20 January 1962; *Daily Mail*, 20 January 1962; Dodds, *Gypsies, Didikois and Other Travellers*, 59–72, 81–7; Simon Evans, *Stopping Places: A Gypsy History*

of South London and Kent (Hatfield, 1999), 79–99; Taylor, *Minority and the State*, 124–5.

43. *The Times*, 14 May and 6 December 1968.

44. Caravan Sites Act 1968 (1968, c. 52) sect. 16. For the background to this legislation, see Acton, *Gypsy Politics and Social Change*, 179–82, and Adams, Okely, Morgan, and Smith, *Gypsies and Government Policy*, 16–22.

45. Thomas Acton, 'Human Rights as a Perspective on Entitlements: The Debate over "Gypsy Fairs" in England', in Michael Hayes and Thomas Acton (eds), *Travellers. Gypsies, Roma: The Demonisation of Difference* (Cambridge, 2007), 6; Donald Kenrick and Sian Bakewell, *On the Verge: The Gypsies of England* (Hatfield, 1990; repr. 1995), 39. See also Hawes and Perez, *Gypsy and the State*, 22–3, 28–9; Kenrick and Clark (eds), *Moving On*, 89–101; Margaret Greenfields, 'Stopping Places', in Clark and Greenfields (eds), *Here to Stay*, 57–89; David M. Smith and Margaret Greenfields, *Gypsies and Travellers in Housing: The Decline of Nomadism* (Bristol, 2013), pp. xv, 18–27.

46. John Cripps, *Accommodation for Gypsies: A Report on the Working of the Caravan Sites Act 1968* (1977), 1, 4, 11, 34.

47. Race Relations Act 1976 (1976, c. 74).

48. *The Law Reports (Queen's Bench Division)*, 27 July 1988, *Commission for Racial Equality v. Dutton*; *Guardian*, 18 August 1988; Stephen J. Roth, 'Are Gypsies an Ethnic Group?' *Patterns of Prejudice*, 22 (1988), 51–2; Kenrick and Clark (eds), *Moving On*, 70–1; Mayall, *Gypsy Identities*, 200–2.

49. e.g. Statutory Instruments 1987, no. 73, 'Gypsy Encampments (Designation of the Borough of Maidstone) Order'; Statutory Instruments 1990, no. 1928, 'Gypsy Encampments (Designation of East Cambridgeshire) Order'.

50. *Guardian*, 15 July 1992; *Observer*, 17 January 1993; Hansard, *House of Commons Debates*, 5 February 1993, vol. 218, cols 587–651, 1 April 1993, vol. 222, col. 525; Hansard, *House of Lords Debates*, 7 June 1994, vol. 555, cols 1166–218; Royce Turner, 'Gypsies and British Parliamentary Language: An Analysis', *Romani Studies*, 5th ser., 12 (2002), 1–34.

51. The Criminal Justice and Public Order Act 1994 (1994, c. 33), sect. 80.

52. Sue Campbell, 'Gypsies: The Criminalization of a Way of Life?', *Criminal Law Review*, 1 (1995), 28; Luke Clements and Sue Campbell, 'The Criminal Justice and Public Order Act and its Implications for Travellers', in Acton (ed.), *Gypsy Politics and Traveller Identity*, 61–9; Diana Allen, 'Gypsies and Planning Policy', in Acton (ed.), *Scholarship and the Gypsy Struggle*, 114–28; Pat Niner, 'Accommodating Nomadism? An Examination of Accommodation Options for Gypsies and Travellers in England', *Housing Studies*, 19 (2004), 141–59.

53. Hansard, *House of Commons Debates*, 9 February 2004, vol. 417, cols 1358–9; Housing Act 2004 (2004, c. 34), sect. 225; *The Housing (Assessment of Accommodation Needs) (Meaning of Gypsies and Travellers) (England) Regulations 2006*, regulation 2.

54. Acton, 'Human Rights as a Perspective on Entitlements', 1–4.

55. Statutory Instruments 2001, no. 1002 (c. 40).

56. Equality Act 2010 (2010, c. 15), sect. 9.

57. Taylor, *Minority and the State*, 188–91. See also Bancroft, *Roma and Gypsy-Travellers*, 65–72, 95–92, 98, on 'legal imbalances in the rights of British Gypsy-Travellers and settled people'.

58. Human Rights Act 1998 (1998, c. 42); *European Convention on Human Rights* (Strasbourg, 2010).

59. Joke Kusters, 'Criminalising Romani Culture through Law', in Marie-Clare Foblets and Alison Dundes Renteln (eds), *Multicultural Jurisprudence: Comparative Perspectives on the Cultural Defense* (Oxford and Portland, OR., 2009), 199–227.

60. European Court of Human Rights, applications 24876/94, 24882/94, 25154/94, 25289/94, 27238/95.

61. European Court of Human Rights, *Connors v. United Kingdom* (Application 66746/01), final judgment, 27 August 2004; Taylor, *A Minority and the State*, 151. For photographs of the Cottingley Springs site in the 1990s, and comments by residents, see Saunders et al. (eds), *Gypsies and Travellers in their own Words*, 232–40.

62. David Mayall, ' "Britain's Most Demonised People?": Political Responses to Gypsies and Travellers in Twentieth Century England', in Michael Zimmermann (ed.), *Zwischen Erziehung und Vernichtung: Zigeunerpolitik und Ziegeunerforschung im Euopea des 20 Jarhunderts* (Stuttgart, 2007), 255; Kalwant Bhopal and Martin Myers, *Insiders, Outsiders and Others: Gypsies and Identity* (Hatfield, 2008), 145–74; Joanna Richardson and Richard O'Neil, ' "Stamp on the Camps": The Social Construction of Gypsies and Travellers in Media and Political Debate', in Joanna Richardson and Andrew Ryder (eds), *Gypsies and Travellers: Empowerment and Inclusion in British Society* (Bristol and Chicago, 2012), 169–86.

63. Becky Taylor, 'A People on the Outside', *History Today*, 61/6 (June 2011), 17–19; *Weekly Law Reports: Egan v. Basildon Borough Council*, 19 September 2011; *Daily Mail*, 13 and 19 October, 1 November 2011; *Evening Standard*, 19 October 2011; *Guardian*, 20 November 2011; *The Times*, 20 October 2011; Judith Okely, 'The Dale Farm Eviction', *Anthropology Today*, 27 (December 2011), 24–7; Quarmby, *No Place to Call Home*, pp. vii–viii, 4–11, 99–160.

64. *Weekly Law Reports: Conners v. Secretary of State for Communities and Local Government*, 11 July 2014; *Regina v. Secretary of State*, 21 January 2015; *Wenman v. Secretary of State,* 21 April 2015.

65. *Independent*, 19 September 2015; Smith and Greenfields, *Gypsies and Travellers in Housing*, 1 and *passim*; <http://travellerstimes.org.uk/Blogs--Features/Losing-my-Ethnicity-When-is-a-Gypsy-not-a-Gypsy.aspx> (accessed December 2016). See also Peter Kabachnik, 'Place Invaders: Constructing the Nomadic Threat in England', *Geographic Review*, 100 (2010), 90–108; Peter Kabachnik and Andrew Ryder, 'Nomadism and the 2003 Anti-Social Behaviour Act: Constraining Gypsy and Traveller Mobilities in Britain', *Romani Studies*, 5th ser., 23 (2013), 83–106.

66. Cripps, *Accommodation for Gypsies*, 2. Lower-case 'travellers' was standard usage before the late twentieth century.

67. Groome, *In Gipsy Tents*, 386.

68. Adams, Okely, Morgan, and Smith, *Gypsies and Government Policy*, 172–87; Bettina Barnes, 'Irish Travelling People', in Farnham Rehfisch (ed.), *Gypsies, Tinkers and Other Travellers* (1975), 231–56; Sharon Bohn Gmelch and George Gmelch, 'The Emergence of an Ethnic Group: The Irish Tinkers', *Anthropological Quarterly*, 49 (1976), 225–38; George Gmelch, *The Irish Tinkers: The Urbanization of an Itinerant People* (Menlo Park, CA, 1977), 3, 21–6, 49; Acton, 'Categorising Irish Travellers', 36, 53; Aoife Bhreatnach, *Becoming Conspicuous: Irish Travellers, Society and the State 1922–1977* (Dublin, 2006), 7–29. See also Jane Leslie Helleiner, *Irish Travellers: Racism and the Politics of Culture* (Toronto, 2000); Sinéad ní Shinéar, 'Apocrypha to Canon: Inventing Irish Traveller History', *History Ireland*, 12 (2004), 15–9; and Mary Burke, *'Tinkers': Synge and the Cultural History of the Irish Traveller* (Oxford, 2009).

69. Okely, 'Ethnic Identity and Place of Origin', 61–2.

70. George Gmelch and Sharon Bohn Gmelch, 'The Cross-Channel Migration of Irish Travellers', *Economic and Social Review*, 16 (1985), 287; Hansard, *House of Commons Debates*, 5 February 1993, vol. 218, cols 587–651

71. Quarmby, *No Place to Call Home*, 4, 12–13, 39.

72. Sociological Research Section, *Gypsies and Other Travellers*, 3.

73. Richardson and Ryder (eds), *Gypsies and Travellers*, 7.

74. Hawes and Perez, *Gypsy and the State*, 7; Taylor, *Minority and the State*, 113–15.

75. Okely, *The Traveller-Gypsies* (Cambridge, 1993), 18–21, 66–76; Royce Turner, 'Gypsies and Politics in Britain', *Political Quarterly*, 71 (2000), 68–77.

76. Brian A. Belton, *Gypsy and Traveller Ethnicity: The Social Generation of an Ethnic Phenomenon* (2005), 1, 4; Brian A. Belton, *Questioning Gypsy Identity: Ethnic Narratives in Britain and America* (Oxford and Walnut Creek, CA, 2005), 133, 146, 169. See also Martin Shaw, *Narrating Gypsies, Telling Travellers: A Study of the Relational Self in Four Life Stories* (Umeå, 2006), 13, 47–50; Smith and Greenfields, *Gypsies and Travellers in Housing*, 37–43, 57–62.

77. Hansard, *House of Commons Debates*, 8 July 1998, vol. 315, col. 1030.

78. *Independent*, 29 and 30 August 2000; <http://www.travellermovement.org.uk/> (accessed 12 October 2015).

79. Thomas Acton and Andrew Ryder, 'Recognising Gypsy, Roma and Traveller History and Culture', in Richardson and Ryder (eds), *Gypsies and Travellers*, 135–49; Richardson and O'Neill, '"Stamp on the Camps"', 179–83; Anca Pusca, 'Representing Romani Gypsies and Travelers: Performing Identity from Early Photography to Reality Television', *International Studies Perspectives*, 16 (2015), 327–44, esp. 336–40; Andrew Connell, *Appleby Gypsy Horse Fair: Mythology, Origins, Evolution and Evaluation*, (Cumberland and Westmorland Antiquarian and Archaeological Society, extra series no. 44, 2015), 54, 63, 74–5, 83; personal communication from Gordon Boswell, Spalding, Lincolnshire, June 2015.

80. <http://www.lightandlifegypsychurch.com/> (accessed March 2017); <http://travellerstimes.org.uk/Blogs--Features/Romanies-Religion-and-Revival-.aspx> (accessed March 2017).

81. Mayall, *Gypsy-Travellers*, 23; Hansard, *House of Commons Debates*, 1 December 1961, vol. 650, col. 790 (Norman Dodds, citing the work of Arthur Thesleff).

82. Hansard, *House of Commons Debates*, 5 March 1925, vol. 181, col. 622.

83. Hansard, *House of Commons Debates*, 20 April 1951, vol. 486, col. 2250; 1 December 1961, vol. 650, cols 789–889; Dodds, *Gypsies, Didikois and Other Travellers*, 17, 33–4, 144–5, 149.

84. Sociological Research Section, *Gypsies and Other Travellers*, 4, 7, 9, 10; Okely, *Traveller-Gypsies*, 22. See also Angus M. Fraser, 'A Government Survey of Travellers in England and Wales', *JGLS*, ns 46 (1967), 9–23.

85. Cripps, *Accommodation for Gypsies*, 8–9.

86. Hazel Green, *Counting Gypsies* (Office of Population Censuses and Surveys, 1991).

87. Hansard, *House of Commons Debates*, 1 April 1993, vol. 222, col. 525.

88. Hansard, *House of Commons Debates*, 5 February 1993, vol. 218, col. 588.

89. Fraser, *Gypsies*, 301.

90. Hawes and Perez, *Gypsy and the State*, 146; Peter Kabachnik, 'To Choose, Fix, or Ignore Culture? The Cultural Politics of Gypsy and Traveler Mobility in England', *Social and Cultural Geography*, 10 (2009), 465.

91. Kenrick and Bakewell, *On the Verge*, 11.

92. Kenrick, *Historical Dictionary of the Gypsies*, 50, 147, 178, 188.

93. Kenrick and Clark (eds), *Moving On*, 19–22. The figure in the *Independent*, 15 September 2015, of 'the UK's 120,000 Gypsies and Travellers' is most likely derived from Kenrick and Clark.

94. Niner, 'Accommodating Nomadism?', 143, 157.

95. Mayall, '"Britain's Most Demonised People?"', 256; Richardson and Ryder (eds), *Gypsies and Travellers* (2012), 4. See also Clark and Greenfields (eds), *Here to Stay*, 20, offering an 'educated estimate' of 250,000.

96. <http://www.travellermovement.org.uk/> (accessed 12 October 2015).

97. Hansard, *House of Lords Debates*, 23 February 2004, vol. 658, col. 16.

98. Office of National Statistics, *What does the 2011 Census Tell us about the Characteristics of Gypsy or Irish Travellers in England and Wales?* (2014). Actual totals were 54,895 in England and 2,785 in Wales.

99. Irish Traveller Movement in Britain, *Gypsy and Traveller Population in England and the 2011 Census* (2013).

100. Brown, Scullion, and Martin, *Migrant Roma in the United Kingdom*, 7. For criticism, see Judit Durst (ed.), 'Network Discussion 2: Roma Migrants in the UK and the Numbers Games' <http://romanistudies.edu/documents/email-list-archive/> (accessed May 2016). The term *Roma* used by the Council of Europe refers to Roma, Sinti, Kale, and related groups in Europe, including Travellers and the Eastern groups (Dom and Lom), and covers the wide diversity of the groups concerned, including persons who identify themselves as Gypsies.

101. A similar point is made in Paul Slack, *The Invention of Improvement: Information and Material Progress in Seventeenth-Century England* (Oxford, 2015), 262.

102. Clark and Greenfields (eds), *Here to Stay*, 289.

CHAPTER 10

1. See Chapter 3.
2. Harman, *A Caveat for Commen Cursetors*, fo. 6; Cowell, *The Interpreter*, sub. 'Egyptians'.
3. Dekker, *Lanthorne and Candle-Light*, sig. G5. Writing about the eighteenth century, Dana Rabin draws on Dekker to remark on the 'odd and fantastic' garb of the Gypsies: Rabin, 'Seeing Jews and Gypsies', 39.
4. B. E., *New Dictionary of the Terms Ancient and Modern*, sub 'Gypsies'.
5. John Fletcher and Francis Beaumont, *The Wild-Goose Chase* (1652), Act 5, scene 2.
6. Head, *Canting Academy*, 60.
7. Layer, *Office and Dutie of Constables*, 30–3.
8. See Chapter 4.
9. Edward Hext to Lord Burghley, 25 September 1596, in Strype, *Annals of the Reformation*, iv. 295.
10. See Chapter 6.
11. *Oracle and Public Advertiser*, 29 September 1794.
12. Winstedt, 'Norwood Gypsies', 144.
13. *Sun*, 20 January 1796; *True Briton*, 21 January 1796; *Oracle and Public Advertiser*, 21 January 1796.
14. Blackley, *Gypsies*, 9.
15. Roberts, *Parallel Miracles*, 79–81; Roberts, *Gypsies*, 84, 85.
16. Crabb, *Gipsies' Advocate*, 26.
17. Huntingdonshire Archives, KHCP/1/8/5.
18. *Westmorland Gazette*, 6 May 1826.
19. *Police Gazette: or, Hue and Cry*, 6 July 1833.
20. Leland, *English Gipsies*, 37, 148.
21. Groome, *In Gipsy Tents*, 2–4, 323.
22. Groome, *In Gipsy Tents*, 354.
23. Adams, Okely, Morgan, and Smith, *Gypsies and Government Policy*, 47.
24. Okely, *Traveller-Gypsies*, 43.
25. Grellmann, *Dissertation on the Gipsies*, 8
26. *Vox Graculi, or Iacke Dawes Prognostication* (1622), not paginated; B. E., *New Dictionary of the Terms Ancient and Modern*, sub 'Gypsies'.
27. Abbot, *A Brief Description of the Whole World* (1605), sig. K4^v.
28. Melton, *Astrologaster*, 47–8; Dekker, *Belman of London*, sigs A4^v, B4^v; Dekker, *Lanthorne and Candle-Light*, sigs G4^v–G5.
29. 'A Clown', 'The Poor Man's Friend', 413; Blackley, *Gypsies*, 6–7.
30. 'Scoto-Montanus', 'On the Influence which the State of the Gypsies has', 46.
31. *Liverpool Mercury*, 19 July 1850.
32. *Examiner*, 30 September 1843.
33. *Morning Post*, 17 March 1845.
34. *Cornishman*, 9 April 1896.

35. J. Fairfax Blakeborough, 'Gypsy Fortune-Tellers', *Notes and Queries*, 18 November 1926, 207.

36. Hext to Burghley, 1596, in Strype, *Annals of the Reformation*, iv. 290–5.

37. Dekker, *Lanthorne and Candle-Light*, sig. G5.

38. Rid, *Martin Mark-all*, sigs G4–G4ᵛ; Rid, *Art of Iugling*, sigs Bᵛ–B2.

39. See Chapters 3 and 4.

40. Smith, *Gipsy Life*, 94.

41. Ferdinand Gerard Huth, 'Gypsy Caravans', *JGLS*, 3rd ser., 19 (1940), 113–46; C. H. Ward-Jackson and Denis E. Harvey, *The English Gypsy Caravan: Its Origins, Builders, Technology and Conservation*, 2nd edn (Newton Abbot and Pomfret, VT. 1986). Caravans may be seen at the Gordon Boswell Romany Museum, Spalding, Lincolnshire, and various museums of 'rural life'.

42. Smith, *Gipsy Life*, 97–8,

43. *The Times*, 30 November 1841.

44. *The Times*, 5 October 1842.

45. *Essex Standard and General Advertiser*, 4 May 1843.

46. Samuel, 'Comers and Goers', i. 129–31.

47. *Essex County Chronicle*, 24 February 1893.

48. *Essex County Chronicle*, 23 June 1893.

49. TNA: RG 11/761–2; Peter Laslett, 'Size and Structure of the Household in England over Three Centuries', *Population Studies*, 23 (1969), 199–223.

50. Clark and Greenfields (eds), *Here to Stay*, 37, 282–8; Connell, *Appleby Gypsy Horse Fair*, 75–86.

51. Okely, *Traveller-Gypsies*, 145–9; Taylor, *Minority and the State*, 110–11.

52. Grellmann *Dissertation on the Gipsies*, 46.

53. *Hull Packet and East Riding Times*, 26 December 1845.

54. *Prose of John Clare*, ed. Tibble and Tibble, 36.

55. Okely, *Traveller-Gypsies*, 16. Notes and files of Gypsy pedigrees survive in bulk in the papers of T. W. Thompson, in the Bodleian Library, Oxford.

56. Adams, Okely, Morgan, and Smith, *Gypsies and Government Policy*, 30, 62; Clark and Greenfields (eds), *Here to Stay*, 13, 15, 36–7; Judith Okely, 'Gypsies Travelling in Southern England', in Farnham Rehfisch (ed.), *Gypsies, Tinkers and Other Travellers* (1975), 60–1.

57. Okely, *Traveller-Gypsies*, 154–6

58. Okely, *Traveller-Gypsies*, 43, 81–3, 193, 196, 215–30; Clark and Greenfields (eds), *Here to Stay*, 41–2, 301; Trigg, *Gypsy Demons and Divinities*, 67–70, 158–62; Fraser, *Gypsies*, 242–6. Speakers of Angloromani used the word *mockadi* rather than the East European Vlax Roma *mahrime* to mean ritually unclean.

59. Matt T. Salo, 'Gypsy Ethnicity: Implications of Native Categories and Interactions for Ethnic Classification', *Ethnicity*, 6 (1979), 78; Sutherland, *Gypsies*, 8–30; Sway, *Familiar Strangers*, 51–3; Carol Silverman, 'Negotiating "Gypsiness": Strategy in Context', *Journal of American Folklore*, 1012 (1988), 262–4; Isabel Fonseca, *Bury Me Standing: The Gypsies and their Journey* (New York, 1995, 2010), 104–7; Matras, *I Met Lucky People*, 69–76.

60. 22 Henry VIII, c. 10; 1 and 2 Philip and Mary, c. 4; 5 Elizabeth I, c. 20.

61. Grellmann, *Dissertation on the Gipsies*, 67.

62. The dates and locations of fairs commonly appear in early modern almanacs, such as Samuel Ashwell, *A New Almanacke and Prognostication for the Year of our Lord God 1642* (1642), sigs C8–D4. For 'A brief remembrance of the principal fairs in England and Wales', see Arthur Hopton, *A Concordancy of Yeares* (1612), 169–80. See also Ian Mitchell, 'The Changing Role of Fairs in the Long Eighteenth Century: Evidence from the North Midlands', *Economic History Review*, 60 (2007), 545–73.

63. Hoyland, *Historical Survey*, 184–5.

64. Harriot, 'Observations on the Oriental Origin of the Romnichal', 522.

65. Leland, *English Gipsies*, 3; Smith, *I've Been a Gipsying*, 283.

66. *Dover Express*, 24 April 1891; *Hampshire Telegraph and Sussex Chronicle*, 11 January 1896.

67. *Lincoln, Rutland and Stamford Mercury*, 7 June 1844.

68. *The Times*, 14 November 1842.

69. *Morning Post*, 5 September 1844.

70. [Way], *No. 747. Being the Autobiography of a Gipsy*, tells stories to this effect.

71. *Leicester Chronicle: or, Commercial and Agricultural Advertiser*, 1 June 1839.

72. Hext to Burghley, 1596, in Strype, *Annals of the Reformation*, iv. 295.

73. Randol, *Noble Blastus*, 32–3.

74. Grellmann, *Dissertation on the Gipsies*, 111; Hoyland, *Historical Survey*, 151–4.

75. [Way], *No. 747. Being the Autobiography of a Gipsy*, echoes stories in newspapers.

76. *The Brave English Jipsie*.

77. Agrippa von Nettesheim, *The Vanity of Arts and Sciences*, 213.

78. *Poems of John Clare*, ed. Tibble, i. 158.

79. 'Polypragmon', 'A Short Account of the Potters of Natlandl', 343.

80. Leland, *English Gipsies*, 8–9; Groome, *In Gipsy Tents*, 338–46.

81. Clark and Greenfields (eds), *Here to Stay*, 50–2.

82. For a recent example, see Timbers, *'Damned Fraternitie'*, 4, 28, 39, 56, 71, 143.

83. 11 Henry VII, c. 2 (1485); 22 Henry VIII, c. 12 (1531); 27 Henry VIII, c. 25 (1536); 1 Edward VI, c. 3 (1547); 14 Elizabeth I, c. 5 (1572); 39 Elizabeth I, c. 3 and 4 (1598); 43 Elizabeth I, c. 2 (1601); 13 Anne, c. 26 (1713); 17 George II, c. 5 (1744); 3 George IV, c. 40 (1822); 5 George IV, c. 83 (1824).

84. 39 Elizabeth I, c. 4 (1598).

85. Mark Netzloff, *England's Internal Colonies: Class, Capital, and the Literature of Early Modern English Colonialism* (2003), 149, 155.

86. 22 Henry VIII, c. 10 (1531); 1 and 2 Phillip and Mary, c. 4 (1554); 5 Elizabeth, c. 20 (1563).

87. TNA: HO 47/18/8, fos 30–4; Crabb, *Gipsies' Advocate*, 65; Bate, *John Clare*, 95–6.

88. Simson and Simson, *A History of the Gipsies*, 10, 12; Groome, *In Gipsy Tents*, 250, 253.

89. Matras, *I Met Lucky People*, 105; Matras, 'Transnational Policy and "Authenticity" Discourses'.

90. For scholarship on Romani in England, see Donald Kenrick, ' Romani English', *International Journal of the Sociology of Language*, 19 (1979), 111–20; Hancock, 'Romani and Angloromani'; Peter Bakker, 'The Genesis of Anglo-Romani', in Acton (ed.), *Scholarship and the Gypsy Struggle*, 14–31; Yaron Matras, *Romani: A Linguistic Introduction* (Cambridge, 2002); Yaron Matras, Hazel Gardener, Charlotte Jones, and Veronica Schulman, 'Angloromani: A Different Kind of Language?' *Anthropological Linguistics*, 49 (2007), 142–84; Peter Bakker and Donald Kenrick, 'Angloromani', in David Britain (ed.), *Language in the British Isles* (Cambridge, 2007), 368–74; Matras, *Romani in Britain*. On canting, see Lee Beier, 'Anti-Language or Jargon? Canting in the English Underworld in the Sixteenth and Seventeenth Centuries', in Peter Burke and Roy Porter (eds), *Languages and Jargons: Contributions to a Social History of Language* (Cambridge, 1995), 64–101; Maurizio Gotti, 'The Origins of 17th Century Canting Terms', *Costerus*, 141 (2002), 163–96; Janet Sorensen, 'Vulgar Tongues: Canting Dictionaries and the Language of the People in Eighteenth-Century Britain', *Eighteenth Century Studies*, 37 (2004), 435–54.

91. Boorde, *The Fyrst Boke of the Introduction of Knowledge*, sig. Nii–Nii^v; Crofton, 'Borde's Egipt Speche'; Hancock, 'Romani and Angloromani', 368, 378–9; Matras, *Romani in Britain*, 58.

92. Harman, *A Caveat for Commen Cursetors*, sigs Aii^v–Aiiii, Gii^v–Giiii. Cf. the 'lexicon of Angloromani' in Matras, *Romani in Britain*, 176–217.

93. Smith, *De Recta & Emendata Linguae Anglicae Scriptione*, 6 (my translation from Latin).

94. Harrison, *Description of England*, 184.

95. Cowell, *The Interpreter*, sub. 'Egyptians'; Minsheu, *Hegemon eis tas Glossas*, 215.

96. Dekker, *Belman of London*, sig. C; Dekker, *Lanthorne and Candle-Light*, sigs B3, C.

97. Rid, *Martin Mark-all*, sigs C^v–C4; Rid, *Art of Iugling*, sig. B^v. The sceptic Thomas Browne believed that the first Gypsies to enter Western Europe spoke 'the Sclavonian tongue', and it is indeed plausible that some Gypsies from the east used a form of Slavic: Browne, *Pseudodoxia Epidemica*, 387.

98. Jones, 'The Mode of Disposing of Gipsies and Vagrants'.

99. McGowan (ed.), *Winchester Confessions 1615–1616*, 20–3, transcribed from Hampshire Record Office, 44 M69/G3/159; Bakker, 'An Early Vocabulary of British Romani (1616)'; Matras et al., 'Angloromani: A Different Kind of Language?', 150–1. See Chapter 5 for discussion of the Winchester depositions.

100. TNA: ASSI 45/3/2/141–3; Somerset Heritage Centre, Q/SR/93/135; Winstedt, 'Early British Gypsies', 34–5.

101. *Strange and Certain News from Warwick*, 70.

102. Thomas Tryon, *The Way to Health, Long Life and Happiness* (1691), 431.

103. Richard Head, *The English Rogue Containing a Brief* Discovery, 5–7; Head, *Canting Academy*, 3–4, 34–57. See also Gotti, 'Origins of 17th Century Canting Terms', 163–96.

104. *Spectator*, 130 (30 July 1711).

105. *The Discoveries of John Poulter, Alias Baxter*, 11th edn (1754), 40; E. O. Winstedt, 'Notes and Queries: An Early Mention of the Language "Romney"', *JGLS*, NS 5 (1910–11), 78–9.

106. Howell (comp.), *Complete Collection of State Trials*, xix. 261–76, 283–692.

107. Grellmann, *Dissertation on the Gipsies*, 61, 131–64; Matras, 'Johann Rüdiger and the Study of Romani'.

108. *Memoirs of Mary Saxby*, 4.

109. Clare's autobiography, in *Prose of John Clare*, ed. Tibble and Tibble, 35.

110. Gregory, *Crime and Punishment in Regency Frome*, 23–4.

111. *Leicester Chronicle: or, Commercial and Agricultural Advertiser*, 1 June 1839, citing the report of the Constabulary Force Commissioners.

112. *The Times*, 5 October 1842. Modern ethnographers might refer to the forum of Gypsy justice as a '*kris*'.

113. *The Evening News* (Portsmouth), 20 December 1882.

114. *Letters of Sir Walter Scott*, ed. H. J. C. Grierson, 12 vols (1932–7), iv. 4, 319, 544; v. 283–4.

115. Hoyland, *Historical Survey*, introduction, 148–51, 178–9, 188–90.

116. Roberts, *Parallel Miracles*, pp. ix, 31; Roberts, *Gypsies*, 86, 89–103; Simson and Simson, *History of the Gipsies*, 10, 12. On nineteenth-century collectors of Gypsy speech, see Matras, *Romani in Britain*, 58–9.

117. Leland, *English Gipsies*, preface, 10, 70, 100, 152, 155. See also Smart, 'Dialect of the English Gypsies', appendix; Smart and Crofton, *Dialect of the English Gypsies*.

118. Groome, *In Gipsy Tents*, 252–3; Smith, *Gipsy Life*, 195–6; Smith, *I've Been a Gipsying*, 130, 197–8.

119. *Derby Daily Telegraph*, 3 August 1895.

120. Dutt, 'With the East-Anglian Gypsies'.

121. *Liverpool Mercury*, 20 June 1896; *Wrexham Advertiser, and North Wales News*, 27 June 1896; John Sampson, *The Dialect of the Gypsies of Wales: Being the Older Form of British Romani Preserved in the Speech of the Clan of Abram Wood* (Oxford, 1926).

122. Okely, *Traveller-Gypsies*, 43.

123. Saunders et al. (eds), *Gypsies and Travellers in their own Words*, 94–5, 109, 121. See also Clark and Greenfields (eds), *Here to Stay*, 15, 361, 365.

124. The words mean man, child, good, Gypsy man, non-Gypsy, speak, tell fortunes, unclean, ghost, and wagon. Spelling conventions vary for words transcribed from speech.

125. Matras, *Romani in Britain*, 176–217.

126. Bakker and Kenrick, 'Angloromani', 368–9; Matras et al., 'Angloromani: A Different Kind of Language?' 173.

127. 22 Henry VIII, c. 10; Head, *Canting Academy*, 6.

128. John Barnard, *Theologo-Historicus, or the True Life of...Peter Heylin* (1683), 24.

129. Ady, *A Candle in the Dark*, 24; B.E., *New Dictionary of the Terms Ancient and Modern*, sub 'Gypsies'.

130. *Brighton Patriot and South of England Free Press*, 16 April 1839.

131. Edward Elton, *The Great Mystery of Godlinesse* (1653), 79; William Slatyer, *The Compleat Christian* (1643), 429.

132. William Davy, *A System of Divinity, in a Course of Sermons*, 26 vols (Lustleigh, Devon, 1795–1807), ii. 317, 319.

133. *Hampshire Advertiser and Salisbury Guardian*, 28 December 1844, reporting on Crabb's annual festival for reformed Gypsies.

134. *The Diary of Samuel Pepys*, ed. Latham and Matthews, iv. 284, 296.

135. See Chapter 6.

136. See Chapter 6.

137. 'A Civilian of Doctors Commons', *A New and Complete Collection of Trials for Adultery*, 4 vols (1796), i. 38.

138. *Cobbett's Annual Register* (1822), 617–18.

139. 9 George II, c. 5 (1736), sect. 4.

140. 5 George IV, c. 83 (1824), sect. 4.

141. *York Herald, and General Advertiser*, 19 January 1839.

142. *Brighton Patriot and South of England Free Press*, 16 April 1839.

143. *Western Gazette*, 1 June 1934.

144. *Standard*, 14 April 1841.

145. *Sheffield Daily News*, 26 May 1891; *Manchester Times*, 29 May 1891.

146. *Cheltenham Chronicle*, 23 May 1891; *Birmingham Daily Post*, 10 December 1891; *Yorkshire Evening Post*, 27 May 1896. See also Maureen Perkins, 'The Trial of Joseph Powell, Fortune-Teller: Public and Private in Early Nineteenth-Century Magic', *Journal of Victorian Culture*, 6 (2001), 27–45. The Vagrancy Act of 1824 was used against spiritualist fortune-tellers in London as late as 1921: *The Law Reports (King's Bench Division)*, 19 April 1921 (*Stonehouse* v. *Masson*).

147. Adams, Okely, Morgan, and Smith, *Gypsies and Government Policy*, 123.

148. Clark and Greenfields (eds), *Here to Stay*, 49–50.

149. Saunders et al. (eds), *Gypsies and Travellers in their own Words*, 125, 145; Adams, Okely, Morgan, and Smith, *Gypsies and Government* Policy, 43.

150. *Daily National Intelligencer* (Washington), 17 January 1853.

151. *Daily Cleveland Herald*, 2 June 1853, 4 March 1854.

152. *Courier and Argus* (Dundee), 20 November 1912; *Derby Daily Telegraph*, 29 May 1915; *Western Times*, 5 March 1926; *Nottingham Evening Post*, 18 December 1928.

153. *Press and Journal* (Aberdeen), 27 February 1948; *Citizen* (Gloucester), 22 September 1950; *Daily Mail*, 12 October 1954.

154. Mayall, *Gypsy-Travellers in Nineteenth-Century Society*, 5; Sheila Salo, ' "Stolen by Gypsies": The Kidnap Accusation in the United States', *Papers from the Eighth and Ninth Annual Meetings, Gypsy Lore Society, North American Chapter* (New York, 1988), 25–40, reviews sensational claims of child-stealing by Gypsies in the American press from 1867 to 1972. A police raid on a Roma camp near Athens in October 2103 revealed a blond-haired pale-skinned 4-year-old girl who looked suspiciously different from the other Gypsies. Dubbed 'the blond

angel' by the popular press, the girl was taken into custody as a likely victim of abduction or child-trafficking. It later transpired that the young Maria had been informally adopted, not stolen, and that the couple charged with her kidnapping were distraught at separation from the girl they were raising as a daughter. Within a week of the incident in Greece, amid more rumours of child slavery, adoption rings, and the wicked practices of Gypsies, a blue-eyed blond girl of 7 was removed from a Roma couple in Dublin on similar fears that she must have been stolen. DNA tests proved, however, that she was their biological daughter, and embarrassed authorities returned her to her parents <http://www.bbc.com/news/world-europe-24589614> (accessed 28 May 2015);,<http://www.theguardian.com/commentisfree/2013/oct/22/angel-kidnapped-by-gypsies-libel-replayed> (accessed 28 May 2015); <http://www.telegraph.co.uk/news/worldnews/europe/ireland/10396991/Irish-police-find-blonde-haired-blue-eyed-girl-in-Dublin-Roma-camp.html> (accessed 28 May 2015); <http://www.bbc.com/news/world-europe-24645947> (accessed 28 May 2015). See also Judith Okely, 'Recycled (Mis)representations: Gypsies, Travellers or Roma Treated As Objects, Rarely Subjects', *People, Place and Policy*, 8 (2014), 72–6; Huub van Baar, 'The Emergence of a Reasonable Anti-Gypsyism in Europe', in Timofey Agarin (ed.), *When Stereotype Meets Prejudice: Antiziganism in European Societies* (Stuttgart, 2014), 28–30.

155. See also Charnon-Deutsch, *Spanish Gypsy*.

156. *Thief-Catcher; or, Villainy Detected*, 74.

157. Jodie Matthews, 'Back where they Belong: Gypsies, Kidnapping and Assimilation in Victorian Children's Literature', *Romani Studies*, 5th ser., 20 (2010), 137–59; Nord, *Gypsies and the British Imagination*, 10–12, 23, 107.

158. *Letters of Sir Walter Scott*, vi. 469.

159. 'An English Clergyman of Lady Huntingdon's Connection', *The Stolen Child: or, Twelve Years with the Gypsies* (New York, 1868). In this story, distributed by the American Tract Society, the child grows up to become a Methodist minister.

160. *Leeds Times*, 5 November 1892.

161. *Birmingham Daily Mail*, 8 October 1879, quoted in George Smith, *Gipsy Life*, 102.

162. Andrew Marvell, 'Upon Appleton House, to my Lord Fairfax', in *Miscellaneous Poems by Andrew Marvell, Esq* (1681), stanza 34.

163. Dixon, *Canidia*, canto 2.

164. Richard Brinsley Sheridan, *The Critic* (1779), Act 1, scene 1.

165. Hansard, *House of Lords Debates*, 21 April 1812, vol. 22, col. 646.

166. *Morning Post*, 14 March 1845.

167. Hansard, *House of Commons Debates*, 8 June 1858, vol. 150, cols 1735–6.

168. Harrison, *Description of England*, 185.

169. *APC* xxiii. 290.

170. John Campbell, *The Lives of the Chief Justices*, 3 vols (1849–51), i. 209; Lord Campbell, *The Lives of the Chief Justices of England*, 4 vols (Boston, 1873), i. 214;

Crofton, 'Early Annals', 10; *Dictionary of National Biography* (1896); Judges, *Elizabethan Underworld*, 507; Rice, *The Life and Achievements of Sir John Popham*, 18–19; Christopher Hill, *Liberty against the Law: Some Seventeenth-Century Controversies* (1996), 134.

171. Christopher Devlin, *The Life of Robert Southwell: Poet and Martyr* (1956), 6. Versions of this story appear in Christobel M. Hood, *The Book of Robert Southwell: Priest, Poet, Prisoner* (Oxford, 1926), 8, and *Dictionary of National Biography* (1897), though not *Oxford Dictionary of National Biography* (2004).

172. Henry More, *Historia Provinciae Anglicanae Societas Iesu* (St Omer, 1660), 172–3; Francis Edwards, *English Jesuits* (1981), 228.

173. Jean-Claude Schmitt, *The Holy Greyhound: Guinefort, Healer of Children since the Thirteenth Century* (Cambridge, 1983), 74–81.

174. *The Romances of Sir Guy of Warwick, and Rembrun his Son*, ed. William B. D. D. Turnbull (Edinburgh, 1840), pp. xx, 426; William Shakespeare, *A Midsummer Night's Dream* (performed *c*.1598), Act 2, scene 1.

175. John Rae, *Life of Adam Smith* (1895), 1; 'English Clergyman', *Stolen Child*, 23; *Dictionary of National Biography* (1897), sub 'Smith'.

176. Adam Smith, *Essays on Philosophical Subjects...To which is Prefixed An Account of the Life and Writings of the Author* (1795), p. x.

177. Wentworth Webster, 'Stray Notes on George Borrow's Life in Spain', *JGLS* 1 (1889), 150–3.

178. Head, *Canting Academy*, 32.

179. Grellmann, *Dissertation on the Gipsies*, 14.

180. *Universal Museum* (1763), 297.

181. *Universal Museum* (1763), 427.

182. See Chapter 6.

183. *Oracle and Public Advertiser*, 17 May 1796.

184. *The Times*, 7 and 8 June 1802, 3; Eric Otto Winstedt, 'Notes and Queries: Cases of Kidnapping', *JGLS*, NS 6 (1912), 58–9.

185. *Yorkshire Gazette*, 5 October 1822.

186. *The Times*, 1 October 1823, 3.

187. 'Scoto-Montanus', 'On the Influence which the State of the Gypsies has', 45–7.

188. *Manchester Courier and Lancashire General Advertiser*, 24 May 1828.

189. Simson and Simson, *History of the Gipsies*, 9, 94.

190. Smith, *Gipsy Life*, 281.

191. Crabb, *Gipsies' Advocate*, 50, 55–6, emphasis in original.

192. *Berrow's Worcester Journal*, 20 December 1832; *Jackson's Oxford Journal*, 22 December 1832; Winstedt, 'Notes and Queries: Cases of Kidnapping', 60.

193. e.g. *London Dispatch and Peoples' Political and Social Reformer*, 22 July 1838; *Lincolnshire, Rutland and Stamford Mercury*, 11 June 1841; *Lloyd's Weekly Newspaper*, 28 September 1890; *Evening Telegraph and Star* (Sheffield), 18 July 1894; *Evening Telegraph*, 23 August 1900.

194. *Illustrated Police News*, 6 February 1892.

195. British Film Institute reference numbers 32313 and N-150463.

196. British Film Institute reference number 225852.

197. Elizabeth Foyster, 'The "New World of Children" Reconsidered: Child Abduction in Late Eighteenth- and Early Nineteenth-Century England', *Journal of British Studies*, 52 (2013), 679.

198. Niall Galbraith (ed.) *Aberrant Beliefs and Reasoning* (London and New York, 2015); Sharyn Clough and William E. Loges, 'Racist Value Judgments as Objectively False Beliefs: A Philosophical and Social-Psychological Analysis', *Journal of Social Philosophy*, 39 (2008), 77–95.

199. Andrewes, *The Pattern of Catechistical Doctrine at Large*, 469; Registrar General, *General Report, England and Wales. 1861*, 225; Rachel Morris, 'Nomads and Newspapers', in Clark and Greenfields (eds), *Here to Stay*, 236–58.

200. 1 and 2 Philip and Mary, c. 4; 5 Elizabeth I, c. 20.

201. Jones, 'The Mode of Disposing of Gipsies and Vagrants'.

202. See Chapter 7.

203. See Chapter 8.

204. *Morning Post*, 2 October 1897.

205. Dodds, *Gypsies, Didikois and Other Travellers*, 106, 109.

206. Cripps, *Accommodation for Gypsies*, 1.

207. *Weekly Law Report: Commission for Racial Equality v. Dutton*, 788. Neither 'Gypsy' nor 'Traveller' is capitalized in the original report.

208. Taylor, *Minority and the State*, 241; Burn, *The Justice of the Peace, and Parish Officer*, i. 276.

209. Sharon Sillers Floate, *My Ancestors were Gypsies*, 3rd edn (2010), 7–10.

210. Belton, *Questioning Gypsy Identity*, 37; Okely, 'Recycled (Mis)representations', 83–4.

211. Saunders et al. (eds), *Gypsies and Travellers in their Own Words*, 95,

212. Caravan Sites and Control of Development Act of 1960 (1960, c. 62); Caravan Sites Act 1968 (1968, c. 52); Cripps, *Accommodation for Gypsies*, 2.

213. *The Housing (Assessment of Accommodation Needs) (Meaning of Gypsies and Travellers) (England) Regulations 2006* (2006), regulation 2.

214. *Council of Europe Descriptive Glossary of Terms Relating to Roma Issues*, 8; Liégeois, *Council of Europe*, 7, 11–12.

215. Liégeois, *Council of Europe and Roma*, 19–21.

216. Colin Clark, 'Europe', in Clark and Greenfields (eds), *Here to Stay*, 259–80. See also Fonseca, *Bury Me Standing*, 293–305; Vermeersch, *The Romani Movement*; Yaron Matras, 'Scholarship and the Politics of Romani Identity: Strategic and Conceptual Issues', *European Yearbook of Minority Issues*, 10 (2011), 217–28; Hristo Kyuchukov (ed.), *New Faces of Antigypsyism in Modern Europe* (Prague, 2012); Matras, 'Transnational Policy and "Authenticity" Discourses'.

217. Michael Stewart (ed.), *The Gypsy 'Menace': Populism and the New Anti-Gypsy Politics* (2012).

218. Trumpener, 'The Time of the Gypsies'; Fonseca, *Bury Me Standing*, 5, 8.

219. Judith Okely, 'Foreword', to Smith and Greenfields, *Gypsies and Travellers in Housing*, pp. viii, x.

SCHOLARS AND GYPSIES: A BIBLIOGRAPHICAL SKETCH

1. On 'the splendid isolation of Gypsy studies', see Willems, *In Search of the True Gypsy*, 305–9.
2. Useful points of entry include Fraser, *Gypsies*; Taylor, *Another Darkness*; and Matras, *I Met Lucky People*. Work on European Gypsies includes Henriette Asséo, *Les Tsiganes: Une destinée européenne* (Paris, 1994); Crowe, *History of the Gypsies of Eastern Europe*; Tebbutt (ed.), *Sinti and Roma in German-Speaking Society and Literature*; Marushiakova and Popov, *Gypsies in the Ottoman Empire*; Pym, *Gypsies of Early Modern Spain*; Novi Chavarria, *Sulle tracce degli zingari*; Benedetto Fassanelli, *Vite al bando: Storie di cingari nella terrferma veneta all fine del cinquecento* (Rome, 2011); Mróz, *Roma–Gypsy Presence in the Polish–Lithuanian Commonwealth*. See also David Cressy, 'Trouble with Gypsies in Early Modern England, *Historical Journal*, 59 (2016), 45–70.
3. John Pound, *Poverty and Vagrancy in Tudor England* (1971), 29; Slack, 'Vagrants and Vagrancy', 364; A. L. Beier, *Masterless Men: The Vagrancy Problem in England 1560–1640* (1985); Paul Slack, *Poverty and Policy in Tudor and Stuart England* (1988).
4. Alan Everitt, *Change in the Provinces: The Seventeenth Century* (Leicester, 1972), 38–43; Anthony Fletcher, *A County Community in Peace and War: Sussex 1600–1669* (1975), 165–70; John Cramsie, *British Travellers and the Encounter with Britain, 1450–1700* (2015).
5. Pound, *Poverty and Vagrancy in Tudor England*, 29.
6. Slack, 'Vagrants and Vagrancy', 364; Slack, *Poverty and Policy in Tudor and Stuart England*, 23, 96, 98.
7. Joan R. Kent, *The English Village Constable 1580–1642: A Social and Administrative Study* (Oxford, 1986); Kent, 'Population Mobility and Alms'. Contrast Thompson, 'Gleanings from Constables' Accounts', 32, 33.
8. Beier, *Masterless Men*, 10, 31, 58–62, 104, 125. See also A. L. Beier, 'Vagrants and the Social Order in Elizabethan England', *Past & Present*, 64 (1974), 3–29.
9. Smith, 'Gypsies, Tinkers, Travellers and the Forest Economy', 61.
10. Miriam Eliav-Feldon, 'Vagrants or Vermin? Attitudes towards Gypsies in Early Modern England', in Miriam Eliav-Feldon, Benjamin Isaac, and Joseph Ziegler (eds), *The Origins of Racism in the West* (Cambridge, 2009), 277.
11. Mayall, *Gypsy Identities*, 26, 54–83.
12. William Hunt, *The Puritan Moment: The Coming of Revolution to an English County* (Cambridge, MA, 1983), 51–4; Hug, *Impostures in Early Modern England*, 112–15.
13. Christopher Hill, *Liberty against the Law: Some Seventeenth-Century Controversies* (1996), 131–41.
14. The topic is reopened in Cressy, 'Trouble with Gypsies'; Timbers, *'Damned Fraternitie'*; and Morgan, '"Counterfeit Egyptians"'.
15. Acton and Ryder, 'Recognising Gypsy, Roma and Traveller History and Culture', 136, 142; Thomas Acton and Garry Mundy (eds), *Romani Culture and Gypsy Identity* (Hatfield, 1997), introduction.

16. Behlmer, 'Gypsy Problem'; Mayall, *Gypsy-Travellers in Nineteenth-Century Society*.
17. Fraser, *Gypsies*; Matras, *I Met Lucky People*; Taylor, *Another Darkness*; Mayall, *Gypsy Identities*, 3.
18. Okely, *The Traveller-Gypsies*, 4, 14–15; Lucassen, 'Eternal Vagrants?', 56, 71; Mayall, *Gypsy Identities*, 59; Timbers, 'Damned Fraternitie', 40.
19. None of the classic studies mentions Gypsies: R. H. Tawney, *The Agrarian Problem in the Sixteenth* Century (1912); Maurice Dobb, *Studies in the Development of Capitalism*, 6th impression (1954); R. H. Hilton. *The English Peasantry in the Later Middle Ages* (Oxford, 1975); T. H. Aston and C. H. E. Philpin (eds), *The Brenner Debate: Agrarian Class Structure and Economic Development in Pre-Industrial Europe* (Cambridge, 1985); Richard Lachmann, *From Manor to Market: Structural Change in England, 1536–1640* (Madison, WI, 1987); Maurice Keen, *English Society in the Later Middle Ages 1348–1500* (1990); Rosemary Horrox (ed.), *Fifteenth Century Attitudes: Perceptions of Society in Late Medieval England* (Cambridge, 1994); Spencer Dimmock (ed.), *The Origins of Capitalism in England, 1400–1600* (Leiden, 2014).
20. Thomas Harman, *A Caveat or Warening for Commen Cursetors Vulgarely Called Vagabones* (1567), claiming on the title page to be 'augmented and enlarged', repr. 1573, 1592; Ben Jonson, 'The Gypsies Metamorphos'd' (performed 1621), in Ben Jonson, *The Gypsies Metamorphosed*, ed. George Watson Cole, New York, 1931); Jonson, *The Masque of the Gypsies*.
21. Aydelotte, *Elizabethan Rogues and Vagabonds*; Judges, *Elizabethan Underworld*; James A. S. McPeek, *The Black Book of Knaves and Unthrifts in Shakespeare and other Renaissance Authors* (Storrs, CT, 1969); Salgado, *Elizabethan Underworld*; Kinney (ed.), *Rogues, Vagabonds, & Sturdy Beggars*; McMullan, *The Canting Crew*. Newer work includes Trumpener, 'The Time of the Gypsies'; Reynolds, *Becoming Criminal*; Bayman, 'Rogues, Conycatching and the Scribbling Crew'.
22. Netzloff, '"Counterfeit Egyptians" and Imagined Borders', 763; Reynolds, *Becoming Criminal*, 22, 24, 29, 34, 43, 47, 64; Paola Pugliatti, 'A Lost Lore: The Activity of Gypsies as Performers on the Stage of Elizabethan–Jacobean Street Theatre', in Paola Pugliatti and Alessandro Serpieri (eds), *English Renaissance Scenes: From Canon to Margins* (Oxford, Bern, and Berlin, 2008), 259–310, quotation at 271. Literary scholars and historians interested in race, ethnicity, and immigration in Tudor and Stuart England have rarely considered Gypsies. Neither Mary Floyd-Wilson, *English Ethnicity and Race in Early Modern Drama* (Cambridge, 2003), nor Nigel Goose and Lien Luu (eds), *Immigrants in Tudor and Early Stuart England* (Brighton and Portland, OR, 2005), mentions Gypsies. See, however, Jeffrey Knapp, *Shakespeare's Tribe: Church, Nation, and Theater in Renaissance England* (Chicago and London, 2002), 75–6. Eliav-Feldon, 'Vagrants or Vermin?' 277, 288, comments on the 'marginalization', 'exclusion', and 'verminization' of Gypsies, while noting that they 'are seldom discussed in studies of early modern attitudes to minorities and aliens'.
23. Nord, *Gypsies and the British Imagination*; Houghton-Walker, *Representations of the Gypsy in the Romantic Period*.

24. Michael Stewart, 'Roma and Gypsy "Ethnicity" as a Subject of Anthropological Inquiry', *Annual Review of Anthropology*, 42 (2013), 415–32, quotation at 419. See also Thomas Acton, 'Academic Success and Political Failure: A Review of Modern Social Science Writing in English on Gypsies', *Ethnic and Racial Studies*, 2 (1979), 231–41.

25. Okely, *Traveller-Gypsies*, 1, 3, 10–16, 231.

26. Sarah Buckler, *Fire in the Dark: Telling Gypsiness in North East England* (New York and Oxford, 2007), 9–10.

27. Wim Willems, 'Ethnicity as a Death-Trap: The History of Gypsy Studies', in Lucassen, Willems, and Cottaar (eds), *Gypsies and Other Itinerant Groups*, 18, 34. See also Lucassen and Willems, 'Wanderers or Migrants?', 136–41; Lucassen and Willems, 'The Weakness of Well-Ordered Societies'; Marsh and Strond (eds), *Gypsies and the Problem of Identities*; Annabel Tremlett, Aidan McGarry, and Timofey Agarin, 'The Work of Sisyphus: Squaring the Circle of Roma Recognition', *Ethnicities*, 14 (2014), 727–36; Mayall, *Gypsy Identities*; Timbers, *'Damned Fraternitie'*.

28. Hancock, *Pariah Syndrome*; Ian Hancock, 'Duty and Beauty, Possession and Truth: Lexical Impoverishment as Control', in Acton and Mundy (eds), *Romani Culture and Gypsy Identity*, 182–9; MacLaughlin, 'European Gypsies and the Historical Geography of Loathing'; Acton (ed.), *Scholarship and the Gypsy Struggle*; Angus Fraser, 'The Present and Future of the Gypsy Past', *Cambridge Review of International Affairs*, 13 (2000), 17–31; Brearley, 'Persecution of Gypsies in Europe'; Bancroft, *Roma and Gypsy-Travellers*; Vermeersch, *The Romani Movement*; Xavier Rothéa, 'Piste pour une histographe des Tsiganes en France', *Études tsiganes*, 39–40 (2009), 14–42; Sigona and Trehan (eds), *Romani Politics in Contemporary Europe*; Donald Kenrick and Grattan Puxon, *Gypsies under the Swastika* (Hatfield, 2009).

29. Fraser, 'Counterfeit Egyptians', 43, quoting Joachim S. Hohmann, '"Gypsiology", an Instrument of Persecution?', *Newsletter of the Gypsy Lore Society, North American Chapter*, 11 (1988), 1–4.

30. http://www.Gypsyloresociety.org/additional-resources/external-links (accessed May 2011).

Bibliography

MANUSCRIPT SOURCES

Bedfordshire and Luton Archives and Records Service, Bedford
BC 512/11, Flitton records
P 44/5/2, Shillington register
P 69/13/2, Southill overseers' accounts

Bethlem Royal Hospital Archives, London
Court of Governors, Bcp 9

Bodleian Library, Oxford
Bankes 37/54
Firth C 4
Rawlinson C 948
T. W. Thompson papers

British Library, London
Additional 32243
Cotton Titus B
Lansdowne 81, 102
Thomason E. 538 (8)
India Office, IOR/L/PJ/6, items 816, 844, 855

Buckinghamshire Archives, Aylesbury
Sess. R 50/24 and 84, Quarter Sessions, 1714–1715

Cambridge University Library, Cambridge
Add. MS 3996

Cheshire Record Office, Chester
QJB 1/6, Quarter Sessions

Cornwall Record Office, Truro
AR/26/2 Arundell of Lanhere accounts

Cumbria Record Office, Carlisle

Q/11/1/161 Quarter Sessions

Devon Record Office, Exeter

2021 A/PW1 Lapford accounts
Q/SB Box 46 Quarter Sessions

Dorset History Centre, Dorchester

PE/HOL/OV 1/1 Holwell overseers' accounts
PE/Yet/RE 1/4, Yetminster register

East Riding Archives, Beverley

PE158/1, Hull Trinity register

East Sussex Record Office, Lewes

PAR 412/37/2, Quarter Sessions

Essex Record Office, Chelmsford

D/P4/18/20 Hatfield Broad Oak overseers' accounts
D/P 202/12/33 Resolution to prosecute Gypsies
D/Y 2/9 Microfilm of Morant MSS
Q/SR 19–532 Quarter Sessions
T/A 418 Assize transcripts

Folger Shakespeare Library, Washington, DC

MS L.b.210

Hampshire Record Office, Winchester

1 M 70/PW 1 Chawton accounts
44M69/G3/159 Jervoise of Herriard MS 'Winchester Depositions'
44 M69/G3/797, Quarter Sessions

Hatfield House, Hertfordshire

Cecil MSS 5/162–4

Huntingdonshire Archives, Huntingdon

KHCP/1/8 and 9, Quarter Sessions

Huntington Library, San Marino, California

MS Ellesemere 4123, Pardons
MS HM 17298, 'What a Justice of Peace may do. 1627'
MS HM 60666, 'A New Ballad Called the Northamptonshire High Constable'
RB 633789, 'The Wheel of Fortune' (c.1805)
RB 633790, 'The New Gypsy Fan' (c.1790)

Kent History and Library Centre, Maidstone

Ly15/2/1/1 Lydd records
P 178/1 Hawkhurst register

Lambeth Palace Library, London

Carew MSS 614 and 629
Talbot MSS 3198 and 3206

Lancashire Archives, Preston

Kenyon of Peel MSS

London Metropolitan Archives, London

Calendar of the Sessions Books, 51 vols (typescript, 1911)

The National Archives, Kew

ASSI 23/3; 45/3/2 Assize records
E 101/518; E 199/4, 24 and 41; E 315/255 Exchequer records
HO 17/53, HO 44/45, HO 47/11, HO 47/14, HO 47/18, HO 107/1004, HO
    107/1822 Home Office
KB 8/44 King's Bench
REQ 2/5/322 Court of Requests
RG 9, 10, 11, 12, 13 Registrar General
SP1, 12, 13, 14, 16, 36, 60 State Papers
STAC 5, 7, 10 Star Chamber

Somerset Heritage Centre, Taunton

D/D/Cd. 66 Diocesan records
DD/PH/219 Phelips MSS
Q/SR/93–360 Quarter Sessions

Surrey History Centre, Woking

MS 6729/11/5 and 52
LM/COR/3/561 Council to Sheriff of Surrey
LS/536/13 Farnham register
QS 2/6/1713 and 1764 Quarter Sessions

PRINTED PRIMARY SOURCES

(place of publication is London unless otherwise indicated)

Abbot, George, *An Exposition Vpon the Prophet Ionah* (1600).
Abbot, George, *A Brief Description of the Whole World* (1605, 1617).
Abernathy, John, *A Christian and Heavenly Treatise* (1622).
Acts of the Privy Council of England, 1542–1631, ed. J. R. Dasent et al., 45 vols (1890–1964).

Adams, Thomas, *The Workes of Tho: Adams. Being the Summe of his Sermons* (1629).

Ady, Thomas, *A Candle in the Dark Shewing the Divine Cause of the Distractions of the Whole Nation of England* (1655).

Agrippa von Nettesheim (Heinrich Cornelius), *The Vanity of Arts and Sciences* (1676).

Airs, Duets, etc. in the New Pantomime, Called the Norwood Gypsies. Performing at the Theatre-Royal in Covent-Garden (1777).

Aleman, Matheo, *The Rogue: Or the Life of Guzman de Alfarache* (1623; repr. 1630, 1634).

Ames, Richard, *The Female Fire-Ships: A Satyr Against Whoring* (1691).

Andrewes, Lancelot, *The Pattern of Catechistical Doctrine at Large: Or a Learned and Pious Exposition of the Ten Commandments* (1650).

Anno Quinto Reginae Elizabethe. At the Parliament Holden at Westmynster (1563).

The Annual Register, or a View of the History, Politics, and Literature for the Year 1773 (1774).

The Arguments on Both Sides the Question in the Intricate Affair of Elizabeth Canning (1753).

Aristotle's Legacy: or, His Golden Cabinet of Secrets Opened (1698).

Arnold, Matthew, 'The Scholar-Gypsy', in Matthew Arnold, *Poems* (1853), 199–216.

Ashwell, Samuel, *A New Almanacke and Prognostication for the Year of our Lord God 1642* (1642).

Atkinson, J. C. (ed.), *North Riding of the County of York. Quarter Sessions Records*, 4 vols (1884–6).

Austen, Jane, *The Novels of Jane Austen*, ed. R. W. Chapman, 5 vols (Oxford, 1960).

Awdeley, John, *The Fraternitie of Vacabondes* (1565).

Awdeley, John, *The Fraternitye of Vacabondes* (1575).

Axon, Ernest (ed.), *Manchester Sessions. Notes of Proceedings... Vol. 1, 1616–1622/23* (Record Society of Lancashire and Cheshire, vol. 42, 1901).

Barker, Jane, *The Lining of the Patch Work Screen* (1726).

Barnard, John, *Theologo-Historicus, or the True Life of... Peter Heylin* (1683).

Barnes, Thomas, *Vox Belli, or, An Alarum to Warre* (1626).

Bastwick, John, *Independency Not Gods Ordinance* (1645).

Beaumont, Francis, and John Fletcher, *Fifty Comedies and Tragedies* (1679).

Behn, Aphra, *The Rover* (1677).

Behn, Aphra, *The Lives of Sundry Notorious Villains* (1678).

Bell, Thomas, *The Catholique Triumph, Conteyning a Reply to the Pretended Answer of B. C. (a Masked Iesuite)* (1610).

Benbrigge, John, *Usura Accomodata, or A Ready Way to Rectifie Usury* (1646).

Bennett, J. H. E., and J. C. Dewhurst (eds), *Quarter Sessions Records... for the County Palatine of Chester 1559–1760* (Record Society of Lancashire and Cheshire, vol. 94, 1940).

Bennett, Martyn (ed.), *A Nottinghamshire Village in War and Peace: The Accounts of the Constables of Upton 1640–1666* (Thoroton Society Record Series, vol. 39, Nottingham, 1995).

Bettey, J. H. (ed.), *The Casebook of Sir Francis Ashley JP Recorder of Dorchester 1614–35* (Dorset Record Society, vol. 7, 1981).

Blackley, Thomas, *The Gypsies, or, a Narrative, in Three Parts, of Several Communications with that Wandering and Scattered people: With some Thoughts on the Duty of Christians to Attempt their Instruction & Conversion* (York, 1822).

Blackley, Thomas, *The Hallowed Harp* (London and Rotherham, 1833).

Blackstone, William, *Commentaries on the Laws of England*, 4 vols (Oxford, 1765–9).

Blades, Robin (ed.), *Oxford Quarter Sessions Order Book, 1614–1637* (Oxford Historical Society, NS 29, 2009).

Blaugdone, Barbara, *An Account of the Travels, Sufferings and Persecutions of Barbara Blaugdone* (1691).

Blomefield, Francis, *An Essay towards a Topographical History of the County of Norfolk*, 5 vols (1739).

Boccalini, Traiano, *Advertisements from Parnassus* (1656).

Boemus, Joannes, *The Manners, Lawes, and Customes of all Nations* (1611).

Boorde, Andrew, *The Fyrst Boke of the Introduction of Knowledge* (1542; repr. 1562).

Borrow, George, *The Zincali; or, An Account of the Gypsies of Spain*, 2 vols (1841; 2nd edn 1843).

Borrow, George, *Lavengro: The Scholar—The Gypsy—The Priest* (1851).

Borrow, George, *Romany Rye: A Sequel to 'Lavengro'* (1857).

Borrow, George, *Romano Lavo-Lil: Word Book of the Romany; or, English Gypsy Language* (1874).

Borrow, George, *Letters of George Borrow to the British and Foreign Bible Society*, ed. T. H. Darlow (1911).

Boswell, Sylvester Gordon, *The Book of Boswell: The Autobiography of a Gypsy*, ed. John Seymour (1970).

Boyle, Robert, *Some Considerations Touching the Usefulnesse of Experimental Naturall Philosophy* (1663).

Brathwait, Richard, *The Honest Ghost, or a Voice from the Vault* (1658).

The Brave English Jipsie (1625?), broadsheet in University of California Santa Barbara, Broadside Ballad Archive, ID 30360; also in W. Chappell (ed.), *The Roxburghe Ballads. Part VII, or Vol. III, Part I* (Hertford, 1975), 329–33.

Breton, Nicholas, *The Court and the Country* (1618).

The Brideling, Sadling and Ryding of a Rich Churle in Hampshire, by the Subtill Practise of one Judeth Philips, a Professed Cunning Woman, or Fortune Teller (1595).

Brome, Richard, *A Joviall Crew, or, The Merry Beggars* (1652).

Brontë, Charlotte, *Jane Eyre* (1847).

Brontë, Emily, *Wuthering Heights* (1847).

Browne, Thomas, *Religio Medici* (1642).

Browne, Thomas, *Pseudodoxia Epidemica: or, Enquiries into Very Many Received Tenents and Commonly Presumed Truths* (1658).

Bruton, William, *Newes from the East-Indies; or, a Voyage to Bengalla* (1638).

Bryant, Jacob, 'Collections on the Zingara or Gypsey Language', *The Annual Register, or a View of the History, Politics, and Literature, for the years 1784 and 1785* (1787), 83–8.

Burn, Richard, *The Justice of the Peace, and Parish Officer*, 2 vols (1755).

Burnaby, William, *The Modish Husband* (1702).

Burton, Henry, *Vindiciae Veritatis: Truth Vindicated against Calumny* (1645).

Butler, Cheryl (ed.), *The Book of Fines: The Annual Accounts of the Mayors of Southampton, Volume I, 1488–1540* (Southampton Record Series, 41, 2007).

Butler, John, *Hagiastrologia, or, The Most Sacred and Divine Science of Astrology* (1680).

Calendar of State Papers, Domestic, ed. Mary Anne Everett Green et al., 84 vols (1856–2006).

Calvin, Jean, *An Admonicion against Astrology Iudiciall and other Curiosities that Raigne now in the World* (1561).

Camerarius, Philip, *The Living Librarie, or, Meditations and Observations Historical, Natural, Moral, Political, and Poetical* (1621).

Canning's Magazine; or, A Review of the Whole Evidence that has been hitherto offered for or against Elizabeth Canning, and Mary Squires (1754).

Care, Henry, *English Liberty, or, The Free-Born Subjects Inheritance* (1703).

Carew, Bampfylde-Moore, *The Life and Adventures of Bampfylde-Moore Carew* (1745).

Carlell, Lodowick, *The Deseruing Fauorite* (1629).

Cay, Henry Boult, *An Abridgement of the Publick Statutes now in Force and of General Use* (1766).

Cervantes, Miguel de, *Novelas Exemplares* (Madrid, 1613).

Cervantes, Miguel de, *La Gitanilla: The Little Gypsie* (1709).

Chapman, George, *The Gentleman Usher* (1606).

Chappell, W. (ed.), *The Roxburghe Ballads. Part VII, or Vol. III, Part I* (Hertford, 1975).

Chettle, Henry, and John Day, *The Blind-Beggar of Bednal Green* (1659).

A Choice Collection of Wonderful Miracles, Ghosts, and Visions (1681).

The Chronicle of the Canningites and Gipseyites (1754).

'A Civilian of Doctors Commons', *A New and Complete Collection of Trials for Adultery,* 4 vols (1796).

Clare, John, *The Poems of John Clare,* ed. J. W. Tibble, 2 vols (1935).

Clare, John, *The Prose of John Clare,* ed. J. W. Tibble and Anne Tibble (New York, 1970).

'A Clown' [a country curate], 'The Poor Man's Friend: A Dialogue between a Clergyman and some Gypsies', *Christian Guardian and Church of England Magazine,* 4 (1812), 98–101; 5 (1813), 412–15.

Cock, Thomas, *Kitchin-Physick, or, Advice to the Poor* (1676).

Cockburn, J. S. (ed.), *Calendar of Assize Records. Sussex Indictments Elizabeth I* (1975).

Cockburn, J. S. (ed.), *Calendar of Assize Records. Essex Indictments Elizabeth I* (1978).

Cockburn, J. S. (ed.), *Calendar of Assize Records. Kent Indictments Elizabeth I* (1979).

Cockburn, J. S. (ed.), *Calendar of Assize Records. Indictments. Essex. James I* (1982).

Cockburn, J. S. (ed.), *Calendar of Assize Records. Kent Indictments. Charles II. 1660–1675* (1995).

Coleridge, Samuel Taylor, *Biographia Literaria: Or Biographical Sketches of my Literary Life and Opinions,* ed. James Engell and W. Jackson Bate, 2 vols (London and Princeton, 1983).

Collop, John, *Itur Satyricum: In Loyall Stanzas* (1660).

Combe, William, *The Second Tour of Doctor Syntax. In Search of Consolation*, 3rd edn (1820).

Comedia llamada Aurelia (Valencia, 1564).

A Compleat Collection of Remarkable Tryals, of the Most Notorious Malefactors (1721).

The Controverted Hard Case: Or Mary Squires's Magazine of Facts Re-Examin'd (1753).

Copnall, H. Hampton (ed.), *Nottinghamshire County Records: Notes and Extracts from the Nottinghamshire County Records of the 17th Century* (Nottingham, 1915).

Coppe, Abiezer, *A Second Fiery Flying Roule* (1650).

Corye, John, *The Generous Enemies, or, the Ridiculous Lovers* (1672).

Cospi, Antonia Maria, *Il giudice criminalista* (Florence, 1643).

Cowell, John, *The Interpreter* (1607).

Cowper, William, *The Task: A Poem, in Six Books* (1785).

Cox, J. Charles (ed.), *Three Centuries of Derbyshire Annals: As Illustrated by the Records of the Quarter Sessions*, 2 vols (1890).

Crabb, James, *The Gipsies' Advocate; or Observations on the Origin, Character, Manners, and Habits, of the English Gipsies*, 3rd edn (1832).

Critical Review, or Annals of Literature (1816),

Crosse, Henry, *Vertues Common-Wealth: or The Highway to Honour* (1603).

Culpeper, Thomas, *The Necessity of Abating Usury Re-asserted* (1670).

Dalton, Michael, *The Countrey Iustice: Conteyning the Practice of the Iustices of the Peace* (1618).

Dalton, Michael, *The Country Justice: Containing the Practice of the Justices of the Peace* (1705).

Dalton, Michael, *The Country Justice: Containing the Practice, Duty and Power of the Justices of the Peace* (1746).

Davy, William, *A System of Divinity, in a Course of Sermons*, 26 vols (Lustleigh, Devon, 1795–1807).

Dehany, William Knight, *The General Turnpike Acts* (1823).

Dekker, Thomas, *Satiro-Mastix. Or the Untrussing of the Humorous Poet* (1602).

Dekker, Thomas, *The Belman of London. Bringing to Light the Most Notorious Villanies that are now Practiced in the Kingdome* (1608).

Dekker, Thomas, *Lanthorne and Candle-Light. Or the Bell-mans Second Nights Walke* (1608).

Dekker, Thomas, *English Villanies* (1632; repr. 1638).

Dibdin, Charles, *The Gipsies. A Comick Opera, in Two Acts* (1778).

The Discoveries of John Poulter, Alias Baxter, 11th edn (1754).

Dixon, Robert, *Canidia, or the Witches* (1683).

Dodington, George, *The Diary of the Late George Bubb Dodington, Baron of Melcombe Regis: From March 8, 1749, to February 6, 1761*, ed. Henry Penruddocke Wyndham (1784).

Dunton, John, *A Voyage around the World*, 3 vols (1691).

E., B., *A New Dictionary of the Terms Ancient and Modern of the Canting Crew* (1699).

Earwaker, J. P. (ed.), *The Constables' Accounts of the Manor of Manchester from the Year 1612 to the Year 1647*, 2 vols (Manchester, 1891).

Eden, William (Lord Auckland), *Principles of Penal Law*, 2nd edn (1771).

Eliot, George, *The Mill on the Floss* (1860).

Eliot, George, *The Spanish Gypsy* (1868).

Ellis, Henry (ed.), *Original Letters Illustrative of English History*, 3 vols (1825).

Elton, Edward, *The Great Mystery of Godlinesse* (1653).

'An English Clergyman of Lady Huntingdon's Connection', *The Stolen Child: or, Twelve Years with the Gypsies* (New York, 1868).

English Reports, 1220–1873 <http://www.commonlii.org/uk/cases/EngR/> (accessed October 2017).

Esher, Viscount (ed.), *The Girlhood of Queen Victoria: A Selection from Her Majesty's Diaries between the Years 1832 and 1840*, 2 vols (1912).

Fenton, Geoffrey, *A Forme of Christian Pollicie* (1574).

Fenwick, Thomas, *The Diary of Thomas Fenwick Esq. of Burrow Hall, Lancashire, and Nunriding, Northumberland, 1774 to 1784*, ed. Jennifer S. Holt, 4 vols (List and Index Society, 2011–12).

Fielding, Henry, *The History of Tom Jones, A Foundling*, 4 vols (1749).

Fielding, Henry, *A Clear State of the Case of Elizabeth Canning, who hath sworn that she was robbed and almost starved to death by a gang of gipsies and other villains* (1753).

Finn, Arthur (ed.), *Records of Lydd* (Ashford, Kent, 1911).

Fish, Simon, *A Supplication for the Beggars* (1528), in G. R. Elton (ed.), *The Tudor Constitution* (Cambridge, 1962), 422–4.

Fitzherbert, Dionys, *Women, Madness and Sin in Early Modern England: The Autobiographical Writings of Dionys Fitzherbert*, ed. Katherine Hodgkin (Farnham and Burlington, VT, 2010).

Fletcher, John, *Love's Pilgrimage* (1647).

Fletcher, John, and Francis Beaumont, *The Wild-Goose Chase* (1652).

Ford, Philip, *A Vindication of William Penn* (1683).

Forster, Thomas, *The Lay-Mans Lawyer, Reviewed & Enlarged* (1656).

Christoph Frick, *A Relation of Two Several Voyages* (1700).

Fryer, John, *A New Account of East India and Persia* (1698).

A Full Relation of Every Thing that has Happened to Elizabeth Canning, since Sentence has been passed upon her about the Gypsy (1754).

Garcia, Carlos, *The Sonne of the Rogue, or the Politick Theefe* (1638).

Garcia, Carlos, *Lavernae, or The Spanish Gipsy: The Whole Art, Mystery, Antiquity, Company, Noblenesse, and Excellency of Theeves and Theeving* (1650).

Gardiner, Richard, *The Compleat Constable* (1692).

Garrick, David, *May-Day: or, The Little Gipsy* (Dublin, 1777).

Gataker, Thomas, *Thomas Gataker B.D. his Vindication of the Annotations by him Published* (1653).

Gaule, John, *Select Cases of Conscience Touching Witches and Witchcrafts* (1646).

Gaule, John, *Pusmantia the Mag-Astro-Mancer, or, The Magicall-Astrollogicall-Diviner Posed, and Puzzled* (1652).

Geographia Magnae Britanniae. Or, Correct Maps of All the Counties in England, Scotland and Wales (1748).

The German Princess Revived: or The London Jilt: Being the True Account of the Life and Death of Jenney Voss (1684).

Giancarli, Gigio Artemio, *La Zingara* (Mantua, 1545).

Gibson, J. S. W, and E. R. C. Brinkworth (eds), *Banbury Corporation Records: Tudor and Stuart* (Banbury Historical Society, vol. 15, 1997).

Giles, Jacob, *The Compleat Parish Officer* (1744).

Glanvill, Joseph, *The Vanity of Dogmatizing: Or, Confidence in Opinions* (1661).

Goldsmith, Oliver, *The Vicar of Wakefield: A Tale. Supposed to be Written by Himself*, 2 vols (1766).

Gray, I. E., and A. T. Gaydon (eds), *Gloucestershire Quarter Sessions Archives 1660–1889* (Gloucester, 1958).

Gregory, Isaac, *Crime and Punishment in Regency Frome: The Journals of Isaac Gregory, Constable of Frome 1813–14 and 1817–18*, ed. Michael McGarvie (Frome Society for Local Study, 1984).

Grellmann, H. M. G., *Die Zigeuner. Ein Historicher Versuch über die Lebensart und Verfassung, Sitten und Schicksale dieses Volks in Europa, nebst ihren Ursprunge* (Dessau and Leipzig, 1783).

Grellmann, Heinrich Moritz Gottlieb, *Dissertation on the Gipsies, Being an Historical Enquiry Concerning the Manner of Life, Oeconomy, Customs and Conditions of these People in Europe, and their Origin*, trans. Matthew Raper (1787).

Griffin, Lewis, *Essays and Characters* (1661).

Grigg, William, *The Life and Humorous Adventures of William Grigg* (1733).

The Gypsie Loddy (1720?), broadsheet in University of California Santa Barbara, Broadside Ballad Archive, ID 31420.

H., J., *Two Broad-Sides against Tobacco* (1672).

H., J. (of Exeter College, Oxford), 'A Poem in Praise of Rambling', in John Dunton, *A Voyage around the World*, 3 vols (1691), vol. 1, not paginated.

H., N., *The Ladies Dictionary* (1694).

Haddon, Walter, *A Dialogue Agaynst the Tyrannye of the Papists* (1562).

Hale, Sir Matthew, *Historia Placitorum Coronae. The History of the Pleas of the Crown*, 2 vols (1736).

Hall, Edward, *Union of the Two Noble and Illustrate Famelies of Lancastre & Yorke* (1548).

Hansard, *House of Commons Debates*.

Hansard, *House of Lords Debates*.

Hardy, W. J. (ed.), *Hertfordshire County Records. Notes and Extracts from the Sessions Rolls 1591 to 1698* (Hertford, 1905).

Hardy, W. J (ed.), *Hertfordshire County Records. Notes and Extracts from the Sessions Rolls 1699 to 1850* (Hertford, 1905).

Hardy, William Le (ed.), *Hertfordshire County Records. Calendar to the Sessions Books … 1619–1657* (Hertford, 1928).

Hardy, William Le (ed.), *Hertfordshire County Records. Calendar to the Sessions Books … 1752 to 1799* (Hertford, 1935).

Harriot, John Staples, 'Observations on the Oriental Origin of the Romnichal, or Tribe Miscalled Gypsey and Bohemian', *Transactions of the Royal Asiatic Society of Great Britain*, 2 (1829), 518–58.

Harman, Thomas, *A Caveat for Commen Cursetors Vulgarely Called Vagabones* (1567).

Harman, Thomas, *A Caveat or Warening for Commen Cursetors Vulgarely Called Vagabones* (1567, 1573).

Harman, Thomas, *The Groundworke of Conny-Catching* (1592).

Harrison, William, *The Description of England by William Harrison*, ed. Georges Edelen (Ithaca, NY, 1968).

Harvey, John, *A Discoursive Probleme Concerning Prophesies* (1588).

Harvey, Richard, *A Theologicall Discourse of the Lamb of God and his Enemies* (1590).

Head, Richard, *The Canting Academy, Or, the Devils Cabinet Opened* (1673).

Head, Richard, *The English Rogue Containing a Brief Discovery of the most Eminent Cheats, Robberies, and other Extravagancies, by him Committed* (1665; repr. 1688).

Head, Richard, *The English Rogue Described in the Life of Meriton Latroon* (1665, 1666).

Herrick, Robert, *Hesperides: Or, the Works both Humane & Divine of Robert Herrick Esq.* (1648).

Heywood, Thomas, *Gynaikeion: or, Nine Bookes of Various History. Concerninge Women* (1624).

Hickeringill, Edmund, *Gregory, Father-Greybeard, with his Vizard Off; Or, News from the Cabal* (1673).

Historical Manuscripts Commission, *Fifth Report* (1876).

Historical Manuscripts Commission, *Sixth Report* (1877).

Historical Manuscripts Commission, *Ninth Report* (1883).

Historical Manuscripts Commission, *Twelfth Report* (1891).

Historical Manuscripts Commission, *Report on Manuscripts in Various Collections*, i (1901).

Historical Manuscripts Commission, *Calendar of the Manuscripts of ... the Marquis of Salisbury, Preserved at Hatfield House,* 24 vols (1883–1976).

Hobbs, Steven (ed.), *Gleanings from Wiltshire Parish Records* (Wiltshire Record Society, vol. 63, 2010).

Hocus Pocus Iunior. The Anatomie of Legerdemain (1634).

Holinshed, Raphael, William Harrison, et al., *The First and Second Volumes of Chronicles* (1587).

Holyday, Barten, *Technogamia: or the Marriages of the Arts* (1618).

Hone, William, *The Year Book of Daily Recreation and Information* (1832).

Hopton, Arthur, *A Concordancy of Yeares* (1612)

House of Commons Parliamentary Papers (1824).

Howell, T. B. (comp.), *A Complete Collection of State Trials and Proceedings for High Treason and Other Crimes and Misdemeanors,* 33 vols (1811–26).

Hoyland, John, *A Historical Survey of the Customs, Habits, and Present State of the Gypsies* (1816).

Hudson, William, and John Cottingham Tingey (eds), *The Records of the City of Norwich*, 2 vols (Norwich and London, 1910).

Hume Brown, P. (ed.), *The Register of the Privy Council of Scotland. Second Series. Volume II: 1627–1628* (Burlington, Ontario, 2004).

Indagine, Johannes, *Brief Introductions, both Naturall, Pleasaunte, and also Delectable unto the Art of Chiromancy, or Manual Divination* (1558).

An Inquiry of Sir Crisp Gascoyne ... Into the Cases of Canning and Squires, 2nd edn (Dublin, 1754).

James, D. E. Howell (ed.), *Norfolk Quarter Sessions Order Book 1650–1657* (Norfolk Record Society, vol. 26, 1955).

Jeaffreson, John Cordy (ed.), *Middlesex County Records ... to the End of the Reign of Queen Elizabeth* (Clerkenwell, 1886).

Jeaffreson, John Cordy (ed.), *Middlesex County Records. Volume III ... 1 Charles I to 18 Charles II* (Clerkenwell, 1888).

Jenkinson, Hilary, and Dorothy L. Powell (eds), *Surrey Quarter Sessions Records: The Order Book for 1659–1661 and the Sessions Rolls for Easter and Midsummer, 1661* (Surrey Record Society, vol. 13, 1934).

Jewel, John, *The Second Tome of Homilees* (1570).

Jolly Gipsies: A New Song (1770?).

Jonson, Ben, *The Masque of the Gypsies* (1640).

Jonson, Ben, *The Staple of Newes* (1640).

Jonson, Ben, *The New Inne* (1631).

Jonson, Ben, 'The Gypsies Metamorphos'd' (performed 1621), in Ben Jonson, *The Gypsies Metamorphosed*, ed. George Watson Cole (New York, 1931).

Journal d'un bourgeois de Paris (Paris, 1881).

The Journal of King Edward's Reign, Written with his Own Hand (Clarendon Historical Society, Edinburgh, 1884).

Journal of the House of Commons, 10 vols (1802).

Journal of the House of Lords, 10 vols (1802).

The Journals of All the Parliaments during the Reign of Queen Elizabeth, ed. Simonds D'Ewes (1682).

A Journal of the Proceedings of J. Hewitt, Senior Alderman, of the City of Coventry (1790).

Joyce, Sally L., and Evelyn S. Newlyn (eds), *Records of Early English Drama: Cornwall* (Toronto, 1999).

Keet-Black, Janet (ed.), *The Sussex Gypsy Diaries 1896–1926* (Romany and Traveller Family History Society, 1999).

King, Gregory, 'Scheme of the Income and Expence of the Several Families of England, Calculated for the Year 1688', in Peter Laslett, *The World We Have Lost—Further Explored* (1983), 32.

Lambard, William, *Eirenarcha: or of the Office of the Iustices of Peace* (1581).

Lambard, William, *William Lambarde and Local Government: His 'Ephemeris' and Twenty-Nine Charges to Juries and Commissions,* ed. Conyers Read (Ithaca, NY, 1962).

Larkin, James F. (ed.), *Stuart Royal Proclamations: Volume II. Royal Proclamations of King Charles I 1625–1646* (Oxford, 1983).

The Law Reports (King's Bench Division) (1921).

The Law Reports (Queen's Bench Division) (1988).

Layer, John, *The Office and Dutie of Constables, Churchwardens, and Other the Overseers of the Poore* (Cambridge, 1641).

Leigh, Edward, *A Treatise of Religion & Learning* (1656).

Leanerd, John, *The Rambling Justice, or the Jealous Husbands* (1678).

Letters and Papers, Foreign and Domestic, of the Reign of Henry VIII, 21 vols (1862–1910).

Lilburne, John, *Liberty Vindicated against Slavery* (1646).

Lister, John (ed.), *West Riding Sessions Records. Vol. II. Orders, 1611–1642. Indictments, 1637–1642* (Yorkshire Archaeological Society, vol. 54, 1915).

Lodge, E., *Illustrations of British History, Biography and Manners in the Reigns of Henry VIII, Edward VI, Mary, Elizabeth, and James I*, 3 vols (1838).

A Looking-Glasse for City and Countrey (1630).

'By a Lover of his Country', *The Thief-Catcher; or, Villainy Detected* (1753).

Lyly, John, *Euphues and his England Containing his Voyage and his Aduentures, myxed with sundrie pretie discourses of honest loue, the discription of the countrey, the court, and the manners of that isle* (1580).

Lysons, Daniel, *The Environs of London*, 4 vols (1792).

M., R., *Micrologia. Characters or Essayes, of Persons, Trades, and Places* (1629).

Machyn, Henry, *The Diary of Henry Machyn*, ed. J. G. Nichols (Camden Society, no. 42, 1848).

The Mad-Merry Merlin: The Black Almanack (1653).

Malcolm, James Peller, *Anecdotes of the Manners and Customs of London* (1811).

Masson, David (ed.), *The Register of the Privy Council of Scotland. Volume X: 1613–1616* (Burlington, Ontario, 2004).

Masson, David (ed.), *The Register of the Privy Council of Scotland. Second Series. Volume I: 1625–1627* (Burlington, Ontario, 2004).

Marsden, William, 'Observations on the Language of the People Commonly Called Gypsies. In a Letter to Sir Joseph Banks', *The Annual Register, or a View of the History, Politics, and Literature, for the Years 1784 and 1785* (1787), 81–3.

Marvell, Andrew, *Miscellaneous Poems by Andrew Marvell, Esq.* (1681).

Masten, Marjorie (ed.), *Woodstock Chamberlains' Accounts, 1609–50* (Oxfordshire Record Society, vol. 58, 1993).

Mayo, Charles Herbert (ed.), *The Municipal Records of the Borough of Dorchester Dorset* (Exeter, 1908).

McGowan, Alan (ed.), *The Winchester Confessions 1615–1616: Depositions of Travellers, Gypsies, Fraudsters, and Makers of Counterfeit Documents, Including a Vocabulary of the Romany Language* (Romany and Traveller Family History Society, South Chailey, Sussex, 1996).

Melton, John, *Astrologaster, or, the Figure-Caster. Rather the Arraignment of Artless Astrologers, and Fortune-Tellers, that Cheat many Ignorant People* (1620).

Mennes, John, *Recreation for Ingenious Head-Peeces* (1650).

Meredith, George, *The Adventures of Harry Richmond* (1871).

Middleton, Thomas, *A Mad World, My Masters* (1608).

Middleton, Thomas, *A Game at Chess* (1625).

Middleton, Thomas, *More Dissemblers besides Women* (1657).

Middleton, Thomas, and William Rowley, *The Spanish Gipsie* (1653).

Milton, John, *The Life and Reigne of King Charles, or, The Pseudo-Martyr Discovered* (1651).

Minsheu, John, *Hegemon eis tas Glossas. Id est, Ductor in Linguas, The Guide into Tongues* (1617).

Miss Canning and the Gypsey (1754).

More, Henry, *Historia Provinciae Anglicanae Societas Iesu* (St Omer, 1660).

More, Thomas, *A Dyaloge of Syr Thomas More* (*A Dialogue Concerning Heresies*) (1529).

Moryson, Fynes, *An Itinerary Written by Fynes Moryson* (1617).

Motteux, Peter, *Love's a Jest* (1696).

Mourt's Relation. A Journal of the Pilgrims at Plymouth, ed. Dwight B. Heath (Bedford, MA, 1963).

Munday, Anthony, *A Briefe Chronicle, of the Successe of Times, from the Creation of the World, to this Instant* (1611).

Münster, Sebastian, *La Cosmographie universelle, contenant la situation de toutes les parties du monde, avec leurs proprietez et appartenances* (Basle, 1552).

Münster, Sebastian, *Cosmographiae Universalis* (Basle, 1572).

Nashe, Thomas, *A Pleasant Comedie, Called Summers Last Will and Testament* (1600).

Naunton, Robert, *Fragmenta Regalia, Or Observations on the Late Queen Elizabeth, her Times and Favorits* (1641).

Nelson, William, *The Office and Authority of a Justice of Peace*, 2 vols (1745).

A New Canting Dictionary: Comprehending All the Terms, Antient and Modern, Used in the Several Tribes of Gypsies, Beggars, Shoplifters, Highwaymen, Foot-Pads, and all Other Clans of Cheats and Villains (1725).

A New Plot Newly Discovered, By the Help of the London Bell-Man (1685).

The New Newgate Calendar, ed. Andrew Knapp and William Baldwin, 5 vols (c. 1800).

Overall, W. H., and H. C. Overall (eds), *Analytical Index to the Series of Records Known as the Remembrancia: 1579–1664* (1878).

Overbury, Sir Thomas, *Sir Thomas Overbury His Wife. With Additions of New Characters*, 16th edn (1638).

Oxford English Dictionary.

A Parisian Journal 1405–1449, trans. Janet Shirley (Oxford, 1968).

The Parliamentary History of England, from the Earliest Period to the Year 1803, 36 vols (1813).

Pepys, Samuel, *The Diary of Samuel Pepys*, ed. Robert Latham and William Matthews, 11 vols (Berkeley and Los Angeles, 1970–83).

Perkins, William, *A Golden Chaine, or the Description of Theologie* (1591).

Pett, Peter, *The Happy Future State of England* (1688).

Peyton, S. A. (ed.), *Minutes of Proceedings in the Quarter Sessions Held for the Parts of Kesteven in the County of Lincoln 1674–1695* (Lincoln Record Society, vol. 26, 1931).

Phillips, Fabian, *King Charles the First, no Man of Blood: but a Martyr for his People* (1649).

Phillips, Fabian, *The Antiquity, Legality, Reason, Duty and Necessity of Præ-emption and Pourveyance, for the King* (1663).

Pindar, Peter, *The Wandering Gipsy: A Ballad, Sung by a Young Lady in the Character of a Gipsy, at the Ranelagh Masquerade, and by Mrs Clendening at the Theatre Royal Covent Garden* (1795).

Pitcairn, Robert (ed.), *Criminal Trials in Scotland from A.D. MCCCCLXXXVIII to A.D. MDCXXIV* (Edinburgh, 1833).

Poetical Reflexions Moral, Comical, Satyrical, etc. On the Vice and Follies of the Age (1708).

'Polypragmon', 'A Short Account of the Potters of Natland—a Retired Village near Kendal', *Lonsdale Magazine, or Kendal Repository*, 2 (September 1821), 343–7.

Pope, Alexander, *Alexander Pope: Minor Poems*, ed. Norman Ault (1954).

Pragmatica-Sancion en Fuerza de Ley, En que se dan Nuevas Reglas para contener y castigar la vagancia de los que hasta aqui se han conocido con el nombre de Gitanos, o Castellanos nuevos, con lo demes que expresa (Seville, 1783).

Price, Laurence, *Witty William of Wilt-shire* (1674).

Proceedings in the Parliaments of Elizabeth I. Volume 1. 1558–1581, ed. T. E. Hartley (Leicester, 1981).

Proudlove, Stephen, *Truths Triumph over Errour: or, The Routing of the Seven False Prophets* (1653).

Purchas, Samuel, *Purchas His Pilgrimes in Five Books* (1625).

Quintrell, B. W. (ed.), *Proceedings of the Lancashire Justices of the Peace at the Sheriff's Table during Assizes Week, 1578–1694* (Record Society of Lancashire and Cheshire, vol. 121, 1981).

Ramesey, William, *Lux Veritatis. Or, Christian Judicial Astrology Vindicated* (1652).

Randol, John, *Noble Blastus: The Honor of a Lord Chamberlaine: and of a Good Bed-Chamber-Man* (1633).

Ray, John, *A Collection of Curious Travels & Voyages*, 2 vols (1693).

Réaux, Tallement des, *Historiettes*, 2 vols (Paris, 1960–1).

A Refutation of Sir Crisp Gascoyne's Account of his Conduct in the Cases of Elizabeth Canning and Mary Squires (1754).

Registrar General, *1841 Census, Abstracts of Answers and Returns* (1841).

Registrar General, *General Report, England and Wales. 1861. VII. Occupations of the People* (1861).

Registrar General, *Population Tables, England and Wales, vol. II, part I* (1861).

Registrar General, *General Report. England and Wales, 1871* (1871).

Richardson, Samuel, *Pamela: Or, Virtue Rewarded*, 2 vols, 4th edn (1741).

Rid, Samuel, *Martin Mark-all, Beadle of Bridewell: His Defence and Answere to the Belman of London* (1610).

Rid, Samuel, *The Art of Iugling or Legerdemaine* (1612).

Ritchie, James Ewing (Christopher Crayon), 'In a Gipsy Camp', *Christian World*, 19 December 1879; repr. in Stephen Donovan and Matthew Rubery (eds), *Secret Commissions: An Anthology of Victorian Investigative Journalism* (Peterborough, Ontario, 2012), 144–8.

Roberts, Samuel, *The Blind Man and his Son: A Tale for Young People. The Four Friends: A Fable. And a Word for the Gipsies* (1816).

Roberts, Samuel, *Parallel Miracles; or, the Jews and the Gypsies* (1830).

Roberts, Samuel, *The Gypsies: Their Origin, Continuance, and Destination, as Clearly Foretold in the Prophecies of Isaiah, Jeremiah, and Ezekiel*, 4th edn (1836).

Roberts, Samuel, *The Autobiography and Select Remains of the Late Samuel Roberts* (1849).

The Romances of Sir Guy of Warwick, and Rembrun his Son, ed. William B. D. D. Turnbull (Edinburgh, 1840).

Ross, Alexander, *Medicus Medicatus, or, The Physicans Religion Cured* (1645).

Ross, Alexander, *Pansebeia, or, a View of all Religions in the World* (1655).

Ruby, Pechon de, *La Vie généreuse des Mercelots, Geux et Boemiens* (Paris, 1586; repr. 1596, 1612, 1618, 1627).

Rudall, John, *A Memoir of the Rev. James Crabb, Late of Southampton* (1854).

Rüdiger, Johann, *Von der Sprache und Herkunft der Zigeuner aus Indien* (Leipzig, 1782).

Rueda, Lope de, *Comedia Llamada Medora* (Madrid, 1567).

The Run-awayes Answer, to a Booke called, A Rodde for Runne-awayes (1625).

Ruskin, John, *The Works of John Ruskin*, ed. E. T. Cooke and Alexander Wedderburn, 39 vols (1903–12).

Saltonstall, Wye, *Picturae Loquentes. Or Pictures Drawne Forth in Characters* (1631).

Sammes, Aylett, *Britannia Antiqua Illustrata: or, the Antiquities of Ancient Britain* (1676).

Saunders, Richard, *Palmistry, the Secrets thereof Disclosed* (1663).

Saxby, Mary, *Memoirs of Mary Saxby, a Female Vagrant* (1807).

Scot, Reginald, *The Discouerie of Witchcraft* (1584).

'Scoto-Montanus', 'On the Influence which the State of the Gypsies has on the Moral Condition of England', *Scottish Missionary and Philanthropic Register*, 1 January 1828.

Scott, Walter, *Guy Mannering; or, The Astrologer* (1815).

Scott, Walter, *Guy Mannering; or, The Astrologer*, ed. P. D. Garside (2003).

S(cott), W(alter), 'Anecdotes of the Fife Gypsies', *Blackwood's Edinburgh Magazine*, 2 (November 1817), 282–5.

Scott, Walter, *Letters of Sir Walter Scott*, ed. H. J. C. Grierson, 12 vols (1932–7).

The Severall Notorious and Lewd Cousnages of Iohn West, and Alice West, falsely called the King and Queene of Fayries (1614).

Shakespeare, William, *A Midsummer Night's Dream* (performed c.1598).

Shakespeare, William, *Henry V* (performed c.1599).

Shakespeare, William, *As You Like It* (performed c.1600).

Shakespeare, William, *Othello* (performed c.1604)

Shakespeare, William, *Romeo and Juliet* (performed c.1604).

Shakespeare, William, *Antony and Cleopatra* (performed c.1607)

Sheridan, Richard Brinsley, *The Critic* (1779).

Shirley, James, *A Contention for Honour and Riches* (1633).

Skelton, John, *The Complete Poems of John Skelton Laureate*, ed. Philip Henderson (1959).

Slatyer, William, *The Compleat Christian* (1643).

Smith, Adam, *Essays on Philosophical Subjects . . . To which is Prefixed An Account of the Life and Writings of the Author* (1795).

Smith, George, *Gipsy Life: Being an Account of our Gipsies and their Children with Suggestions for their Improvement* (1880).

Smith, George, *I've Been a Gipsying: Or, Rambles among our Gipsies and their Children* (1881).

Smith, Thomas, *De Recta & Emendata Linguae Anglicae Scriptione, Dialogus* (Paris, 1568).

Smollett, Tobias, *Continuation of the Complete History of England*, 5 vols (1763).

Spackman, Frederick W., *An Analysis of the Occupations of the People Showing the Relative Importance of the Agricultural, Manufacturing, Shipping, Colonial, Commercial & Mining Interests* (1847).

Spenser, Edmund, *Prosopopoia: Or Mother Hubberds Tale* (1591).

Stanley, Arthur Penrhyn, *The Gipsies: A Prize Poem* (Oxford, 1837).

Stocks, Helen, and W. H. Stevenson (eds), *Records of the Borough of Leicester... 1603–1688* (Cambridge, 1923).

Strange and Certain News from Warwick (1673), in William E. A. Axon (ed.), 'A Gypsy Tract from the Seventeenth Century', *Journal of the Gypsy Lore Society*, NS 1 (1907–8), 68–72.

Strype, John, *Annals of the Reformation*, 4 vols (1738).

Tait, James (ed.), *Lancashire Quarter Sessions Records... 1590–1606* (Chetham Society NS 77, 1917).

Talpin, Jean, *La Police chrétienne* (Paris, 1572).

Tattershall, Thomas, *An Account of Tobias Smith, a Gipsy, who was Executed at Bedford, April 3d, 1792* (1792).

Tattershall, Thomas, *An Extraordinary Account of Tobias Smith, a Gipsy, who was Executed at Bedford, April 3d, 1792* (1792).

Taylor, John, *Three Weekes, Three Daies, and Three Houres: Observations and Travel from London to Hamburgh in Germanie* (1617).

Thomasius, Jacob, *Curiöser Tractat von Zigeunern* (Dresden, 1702).

Thompson, Thomas, *Antichrist Arraigned in a Sermon at Pauls Crosse* (1618).

Thornton, Richard, *The Aegyptian Courtier. Delivered in Two Sermons* (1635).

Tillotson, John, *The Rule of Faith, or, An Answer to the Treatise of Mr I. S.* (1676).

Treswell, Robert, *A Relation of Such Things as were Observed to Happen in the Iourney of the Right Honourable Charles Earle of Nottingham* (1605).

The Trial of Elizabeth Canning, Spinster, for Wilful and Corrupt Perjury (1754).

A True Account of the Proceedings at the Sessions for London and Middlesex, Begun in the Old-Bailey on Wednesday the Twenty Sixth of May. 1680 (1680).

A True Draught of Eliz: Canning (1754).

A True Narrative of the Proceedings, with General Remarks on the Evidence given upon the Memorable Trials of Mary Squires, and Elizabeth Canning (1755).

The Truth of the Case: Or, Canning and Squires Fairly Opposed (1753).

Truth Triumphant: Or, the Genuine Account of the Whole Proceedings against Elizabeth Canning (1754).

Tryon, Thomas, *The Way to Health, Long Life and Happiness* (1691).

The Unfortunate Maid Exemplified, in the Story of Elizabeth Canning (1754).

Urfey, Thomas D', *Trick for Trick* (1678).

van Diemerbroeck, Ysbrand, *The Anatomy of Human Bodies, comprehending the most modern discoveries and curiosities in that art* (1694).

'Venetian Edicts Relating to the Gypsies of the Sixteenth, Seventeenth, and Eighteenth Centuries (Extracted from the Archivio dei Frari, at Venice)', *Journal of the Gypsy Lore Society*, 2 (1889), 358–62.

Vicente, Gil, *Farça das Ciganas* (Lisbon, 1521).

Virtue Triumphant, or, Elizabeth Canning in America (1757).

Vox Graculi, or Iacke Dawes Prognostication (1622).

Wainwright, Thomas (ed.), *Barnstable Parish Register. 1538 A.D to 1812 A.D* (Exeter, 1903).

Walpole, Horace, *The Yale Edition of Horace Walpole's Correspondence*, ed. W. S. Lewis et al., 48 vols (New Haven, 1937–83).

Wasson, John M. (ed.), *Records of Early English Drama: Devon* (Toronto, 1986).

[Way, Arthur Edward Gregory], *No. 747. Being the Autobiography of a Gipsy, Edited by F. W. Carew, MD* (1890).

Webster, John, *The Displaying of Supposed Witchcraft: Wherein it is affirmed that there are many sorts of Deceivers and Impostors* (1677).

Welsh, Thomas, *The Merry Gypsies: A Glee for Three Voices* (1825).

Whetstone, George, *The Right Excellent and Famous Historye of Promos and Cassandra* (1578).

Whitehead, George, *An Antidote against the Venome of the Snake in the Grass* (1697).

Willis Bund, J. W. (ed.), *Worcestershire County Records . . . Calendar of the Quarter Sessions Papers . . . 1591–1643* (Worcester, 1900).

Wilmot, John, *The Complete Poems of John Wilmot, Earl of Rochester*, ed. David M. Vieth (New Haven and London, 1968).

Wood, Manfri Frederick, *In the Life of a Romany Gypsy*, ed. John A. Brune (1973).

Woodforde, James, *The Diary of a Country Parson: The Reverend James Woodforde, 1758–1802*, ed. John Beresford, 5 vols (1924–31).

Wordsworth, William, *The Poetical Works of Wordsworth*, ed. Thomas Hutchinson and Ernest de Selincourt (Oxford, 1964).

Young, Richard, *The Poores Advocate* (1654).

Zouch, Richard, *The Sophister* (1639).

STATUTES OF THE REALM

11 Henry VII, c. 2 (1485) Vagrancy Act
22 Henry VIII, c. 10 (1531) Egyptians
22 Henry VIII, c. 12 (1531) Vagrancy Act
27 Henry VIII, c. 25 (1536) Vagrancy Act
1 Edward VI, c. 3 (1547) Vagrancy Act
1 and 2 Philip and Mary, c. 4 (1554) Egyptians
5 Elizabeth I, c. 20 (1563) Egyptians
14 Elizabeth I, c. 5 (1572) Vagrancy Act
39 Elizabeth I, c. 3 (1598) Poor Law
39 Elizabeth I, c. 4 (1598) Vagrancy Act
43 Elizabeth I, c. 2 (1601) Poor Law
13 Anne, c. 26 (1714) Vagrancy Act

4 George I, c. 11 (1718) Transportation Act
9 George II, c. 5 (1736) Witchcraft Repeal
17 George II, c. 5 (1744) Vagrancy Act
23 George III, c. 51 (1783) Egyptians Repeal
50 George III, c. 41 (1810) Hawkers and Pedlars
1 George IV, c. 116 (1820) Egyptians Repeal
3 George IV, c. 40 (1822) Vagrancy Act
3 George IV, c. 126 (1822) Turnpike Act
4 George IV, c. 95 (1823) Turnpike Act
5 George IV, c. 83 (1824) Vagrancy Act
5 and 6 William IV, c. 50 (1835) Highways Act
2 and 3 Victoria, c. 47 (1839) Metropolitan Police Act
19 and 20 Victoria, c. 64 (1856) Obsolete Statutes Repeal
25 and 26 Victoria, c. 114 (1862) Prevention of Poaching
30 and 31 Victoria, c. 5 (1867) Dog Licences Act
34 and 35 Victoria, c. 96 (1871) Pedlars Act
39 and 40 Victoria, c. 56 (1876) Commons Act
44 and 45 Victoria, c. 5 (1881) Pedlars Act
48 and 49 Victoria, c. 72 (1885) Housing of the Working Classes Act
51 and 52 Victoria, c. 45 (1881) Hawkers Act
54 and 55 Victoria, c. 76 (1891) Public Health Act
56 and 57 Victoria, c. 73 (1894) Local Government Act
62 and 63 Victoria, c. 30 (1899) Commons Act
5 Edward VII, c. 13 (1905) Aliens Act
15 and 16 George V, c. 11 (1925) Law of Property Act
25 George V, c. 20 (1935) Vagrancy Act
25 George V and 1 Edward VIII, c. 49 (1936) Public Health Act
10 and 11 George VI, c. 51 (1947) Town and Country Planning Act
7 and 8 Elizabeth II, c. 25 (1959) Highways Act
(1960, c. 62) Caravan Sites and Control of Development Act
(1968, c. 52) Caravan Sites Act
(1976, c. 74) Race Relations Act
(1994, c. 33) Criminal Justice and Public Order Act
(1998, c. 42) Human Rights Act
(2004, c. 34) Housing Act
(2010, c. 15) Equality Act
Statutory Instruments 1987, 1990, 2001, 2011

NEWSPAPERS AND PERIODICALS

Albion and Evening Advertiser, 1800.
Aris's Birmingham Gazette, 1850.
Bath Chronicle, 1828–1900.
Bell's Life in London or Sporting Chronicle, 1826.

Berkshire Chronicle, 1832–60.

Berrow's Worcester Journal, 1832–91.

Birmingham Daily Mail, 1879.

Birmingham Daily Post, 1891.

Blackwood's Edinburgh Magazine, 1817–18.

Birmingham Daily Post, 1891–4.

Blackburn Standard and Weekly Express, 1891.

Boston Daily Atlas (US), 1851.

Boston Investigator (US), 1869.

Bradford Observer, 1837–74.

Brighton Patriot and South of England Free Press, 1839.

Bristol Mercury, 1832–98.

British Chronicle, or, Pugh's Hereford Journal, 1787.

British Critic, 1793–1828.

British Review and London Critical Review, 1819.

Bucks Herald, 1869–93.

Bury and Norwich Post, 1842–98.

Caledonian Mercury, 1753–4.

Cambridge Independent Press, 1891–1905.

Cassell's Family Magazine, 1883.

Chelmsford Chronicle, 1842.

Cheltenham Chronicle, 1891–99.

Cheltenham Chronicle and Gloucestershire Graphic, 1946.

Cheshire Observer, 1891–9.

Christian Guardian and Church of England Magazine, 1812.

Christian Observer, 1828.

Christian World, 1879.

Church of England and Lambeth Magazine, 1875.

Citizen (Gloucester), 1891–1950.

Cobbett's Annual Register, 1822.

Cornishman, 1896–9.

Courier and Argus (Dundee), 1912.

Courier and Advertiser (Dundee), 1929.

Courier and Evening Gazette, 1795–9.

Critical Review, or, Annals of Literature, 1812–16.

Daily Cleveland Herald (US), 1853–4.

Daily Mail, 1902–2011.

Daily Morning News (Savannah, Georgia), 1855.

Daily National Intelligencer (Washington), 1853.

Daily News, 1890–8.

Daily Post, 1730.

Daily South Carolinian, 1855.

Derby Daily Telegraph, 1895–1915.

Derby Evening Telegraph, 1940–50.

Derby Mercury, 1753–1837.

Derbyshire Times and Chesterfield Herald, 1892.

Devizes and Wiltshire Gazette, 1828–42.

Devon and Exeter Daily Gazette, 1891–1909, 1950.

Dover Express, 1891.

Dundee Chronicle and Argus, 1895.

Edinburgh Evening News, 1892–6.

Edinburgh Magazine and Literary Miscellany, 1797–1816.

English Chronicle or Universal Evening Post, 1789.

Era, 1898.

Essex County Chronicle, 1890–1903.

Essex County Standard, 1893–1900.

Essex Newsman, 1891–1904.

Essex Standard, 1890–1.

Essex Standard and General Advertiser, 1842–3.

Evening News (Portsmouth), 1882–1901.

Evening Standard, 2011.

Evening Telegraph, 1897–1950.

Evening Telegraph and Star (Sheffield), 1891–7.

Examiner, 1832–43.

Good Words, 1896.

Grantham Journal, 1882–99.

Grub Street Journal, 1731.

The Guardian, 1988–2011.

Hampshire Advertiser and Salisbury Guardian, 1844–6.

Hampshire Advertiser, 1843–97.

Hampshire Chronicle, 1828.

Hampshire Telegraph and Sussex Chronicle, 1832–96.

Hereford Journal, 1840–1944.

Huddersfield Chronicle and West Yorkshire Advertiser, 1890–1.

Huddersfield Daily Chronicle, 1893–9.

Hull Daily Mail, 1893–8.

Hull Packet and East Riding Times, 1845–84.

Illustrated London News, 1879.

Illustrated Police News, 1892–97.

Independent, 2000–15.

Ipswich Journal, 1841–91.

Isle of Wight Observer, 1880–98.

Jackson's Oxford Journal, 1832–40.

Journal of the Gypsy Lore Society, 1888–1982.

Leamington Spa Courier, 1832–96.

Leeds Mercury, 1846–96.

Leeds Times, 1834–93.

Leicestershire Chronicle and Leicestershire Mercury, 1866–94.

Leicester Chronicle; or, Commercial and Agricultural Advertiser, 1832–9.

Lincoln Gazetteer, 1785.

Lincoln, Rutland and Stamford Mercury, 1832–1906.

Liverpool Mercury, 1850–96.

Lloyd's Evening Post, 1765.

Lloyd's Weekly Newspaper, 1890–99.

London Chronicle, 1771–7.

London Daily Post and General Advertiser, 1735.

London Dispatch and Peoples' Political and Social Reformer, 1838.

London Examiner, 1753–4.

London Evening News, 1762.

London Evening Post, 1753–4.

London Magazine, 1753–69.

London Magazine: Or, Gentleman's Monthly Intelligencer, 1747.

Lonsdale Magazine, or Kendal Repository, 1821.

Manchester Courier and Lancashire General Advertiser, 1828–1905.

Manchester Times, 1891.

Maryland Gazette, 1767.

Milwaukee Daily Sentinel, 1860.

Mist's Weekly Journal, 1726.

Morning Advertiser, 1796.

Morning Chronicle, 1804–28.

Morning Post, 1821–99.

Morpeth Herald, 1891.

Newcastle Weekly Courant, 1894.

Norfolk Chronicle: or, the Norwich Gazette, 1776.

North American and United States Gazette (Philadelphia), 1853.

North Devon Journal, 1900.

Northampton Mercury, 1843–1903.

North-Eastern Daily Gazette, 1892–6.

Northern Echo, 1892.

Northern Liberator, 1838.

Nottingham Evening Post, 1888–1931.

Nottinghamshire Guardian, 1852–98.

Observer, 1993.

Oracle and Daily Advertiser, 1799.

Oracle and Public Advertiser, 1794–6.

Pall Mall Gazette, 1866–94.

Penny Illustrated Paper and Illustrated Times, 1906.

Police Gazette; or, Hue and Cry, 1833.

Press and Journal (Aberdeen), 1948.

Public Advertiser, 1777.

Reynold's Newspaper, 1890–7.

Ripley Bee (Ripley, Ohio), 1853.

Royal Cornwall Gazette, 1854–98.

Royal Leamington Spa Courier, 1846–51.

Salisbury and Winchester Journal, 1828–50.

Scots Magazine, 1772.

Scottish Missionary and Philanthropic Register, 1828.

Sheffield and Rotherham Independent, 1842–92.

Sheffield Daily News, 1891.

Sheffield Daily Telegraph, 1856–1903.

St James Chronicle, or the British Evening Post, 1762–89.

Spectator, 1711–12, 1879, 1911.

Standard, 1828–1900.

Star (Saint Peter Port), 1887–95.

Sun, 1796–1800.

Sun, 2004–9.

Sunday Times, 1997–2005.

Sunderland Daily Echo, 1898–1900.

Tamworth Herald, 1906.

The Times, 1787–2011.

Trewman's Exeter Flying Post, 1897–8.

True Briton, 1796.

Universal Museum, or, Gentleman's and Ladies Polite Magazine of History, Politicks, and Literature (1763).

Weekly Standard and Express, 1898.

Western Gazette, 1870–1950.

Western Times, 1840–1926.

Westmorland Gazette, 1826–1915.

Whitehall Evening Post, 1766.

Woolmer's Exeter and Plymouth Gazette, 1838–42.

World, 1790.

World and Fashionable Advertiser, 1787.

Wrexham Advertiser, and North Wales News, 1896.

York Chronicle, and Weekly Advertiser, 1773.

York Herald, and General Advertiser, 1839.

Yorkshire Evening Post, 1892–9.

Yorkshire Gazette, 1822.

Yorkshire Herald, 1894.

Yorkshire Telegraph and Star, 1899.

MODERN SOURCES

(place of publication is London unless otherwise indicated)

Abulafia, David, 'The Coming of the Gypsies: Cities, Princes and Nomads', in P. Hoppenbrouwers, Antheun Janse, and Robert Stein (eds), *Power and Persuasion:*

Essays on the Art of State Building in Honour of W. P. Blockmans (Turnhout, 2010), 325–42.

Achim, Viorel, *The Roma in Romanian History* (Budapest and New York, 2004).

Acton, Thomas, *Gypsy Politics and Social Change: The Development of Ethnic Ideology and Pressure Politics among British Gypsies from Victorian Reformism to Romany Nationalism* (1974).

Acton, Thomas, 'Academic Success and Political Failure: A Review of Modern Social Science Writing in English on Gypsies', *Ethnic and Racial Studies*, 2 (1979), 231–41.

Acton, Thomas, 'Categorising Irish Travellers', in May McCann, Séamas O Síocháin, and Joseph Ruane (eds), *Irish Travellers: Culture and Ethnicity* (Belfast, 1994), 36–53.

Acton, Thomas (ed.), *Gypsy Politics and Traveller Identity* (Hatfield, 1997).

Acton, Thomas (ed.), *Scholarship and the Gypsy Struggle: Commitment in Romani Studies* (Hatfield, 2000).

Acton, Thomas, 'The Life and Times of Donald Kenrick', in Thomas Acton (ed.), *Scholarship and the Gypsy Struggle: Commitment in Romani Studies* (Hatfield, 2000), pp. xi–xxxi.

Acton, Thomas, 'Human Rights as a Perspective on Entitlements: The Debate over "Gypsy Fairs" in England', in Michael Hayes and Thomas Acton (eds), *Travellers. Gypsies, Roma: The Demonisation of Difference* (Cambridge, 2007), 1–16.

Acton, Thomas, 'Scientific Racism, Popular Racism and the Discourse of the Gypsy Lore Society', *Ethnic and Racial Studies*, 32 (2016), 1187–1204 <http://dx.doi.org/10.1080/01419870.2015.1105988> (accessed October 2017).

Acton, Thomas, and David Gallant, *Romnichal Gypsies* (Hove, 1997).

Acton, Thomas, and Gary Mundy (eds), *Romani Culture and Gypsy Identity* (Hatfield, 1997).

Acton, Thomas, and Andrew Ryder, 'Recognising Gypsy, Roma and Traveller History and Culture', in Joanna Richardson and Andrew Ryder (eds), *Gypsies and Travellers: Empowerment and Inclusion in British Society* (Bristol and Chicago, 2012), 135–49.

Adams, Barbara, Judith Okely, David Morgan, and David Smith, *Gypsies and Government Policy in England* (1975).

Adams, W. Maurice, 'The Wandering Tribes of Great Britain', *Cassell's Family Magazine*, 9 (November 1883), 731.

Admant, Jules, 'Les Bohémiens et leurs juges en Lorraine au XVIIIe siècle', *Revue transversales du Centre Georges Chevrier*, 8 (2016) <http://tristan.u-bourgogne.fr/CGC/publications/transversales/ Entre_confrontation_reconnaissance-rejet/J_Admant.html> (accessed November 2016).

Agarin, Timofey (ed.), *When Stereotype Meets Prejudice: Antiziganism in European Societies* (Stuttgart, 2014).

Alfaro, Antonio Gomez, *The Great Gypsy Round-Up. Spain: The General Imprisonment of the Gypsies in 1749* (Madrid, 1993).

Allen, Diana, 'Gypsies and Planning Policy', in Thomas Acton (ed.), *Scholarship and the Gypsy Struggle: Commitment in Romani Studies* (Hatfield, 2000), 114–28.

'An Early Gypsey', *Virginia Magazine of History and Biography*, 2 (1894), 100.

'Andreas', 'Two Italian Gypsy Edicts', *Journal of the Gypsy Lore Society*, 3rd ser., 13 (1934), 45–9.

Andree, Richard, 'Old Warning-Placards for Gypsies', *Journal of the Gypsy Lore Society*, NS 5 (1911), 202–4.

Andrews, John S., 'Missionary and Allied Material in the Romany Collection of the University of Leeds', *International Review of Missions*, 46 (1957), 424–31.

Arkell, Thomas, 'Illuminations and Distortions: Gregory King's Scheme Calculated for the Year 1688 and the Social Structure of Later Stuart England', *Economic History Review*, 59 (2006), 32–69.

Asséo, Henriette, 'Marginalité et exclusion: Le Traitement adminstratif des Bohémiens dans la societé Française du XVIIe siècle', in Henriette Asséo and Jean-Paul Vittu (eds), *Problèmes socio-culturels au XVIIe au XVIIe siècle* (Paris, 1974), 9–87.

Asséo, Henriette, *Les Tsiganes: Une destinée européenne* (Paris, 1994).

Asséo, Henriette, ' "Bohesmiens du Royaume" : L'insediamento dinastico dei "Capitaines Égyptiens" nella Francia di Antico Regime (1550–1660)', *Quaderni storici*, 146 (2014), 439–69.

Aston, T. H., and C. H. E. Philpin (eds), *The Brenner Debate: Agrarian Class Structure and Economic Development in Pre-Industrial Europe* (Cambridge, 1985).

Axon, William E. A., 'The English Gipsies in 1818', *Antiquary*, 43 (1907), 181–4.

Axon, William E. A. (ed.), 'A Gypsy Tract from the Seventeenth Century', *Journal of the Gypsy Lore Society*, NS 1 (1907–8), 68–72

Aydelotte, Frank, *Elizabethan Rogues and Vagabonds* (Oxford, 1913).

Bakker, Peter, 'The Genesis of Anglo-Romani', in Thomas Acton (ed.), *Scholarship and the Gypsy Struggle: Commitment in Romani Studies* (Hatfield, 2000), 14–31.

Bakker, Peter, 'An Early Vocabulary of British Romani (1616): A Linguistic Analysis', *Romani Studies*, 5th ser., 5 (2002), 75–101.

Bakker, Peter, 'Romani Genetic Linguistics and Genetics: Results, Prospects and Problems', *Romani Studies*, 5th ser., 22 (2012), 91–111.

Bakker, Peter (ed.), *The Typology and Dialectology of Romani* (Amsterdam and Philadelphia, 1998).

Bakker, Peter, and Hristo Kyuchukov (eds), *What is the Romani Language?* (Hatfield, 2000).

Bakker, Peter, and Donald Kenrick, 'Angloromani', in David Britain (ed.), *Language in the British Isles* (Cambridge, 2007).

Bancroft, Angus, *Roma and Gypsy-Travellers in Europe: Modernity, Race, Space and Exclusion* (Aldershot, 2005).

Bardi, Abby, 'The Gypsy as Trope in Victorian and Modern British Literature', *Romani Studies*, 5th ser., 16 (2006), 31–42.

Barnes, Bettina, 'Irish Travelling People', in Farnham Rehfisch (ed.), *Gypsies, Tinkers and Other Travellers* (1975), 231–56.

Baroco, Fernanda, and David Lagunas, 'Another Otherness: The Case of the Roma in Mexico', in Premysel Macha and Eloy Gomez-Pellon (eds), *Masks of Identity: Representing and Performing Otherness in Latin America* (Newcastle upon Tyne, 2014), 95–108.

Barrell, John, *The Dark Side of the Landscape: The Rural Poor in English Painting 1730–1840* (Cambridge, 1980).

Bartlett, D. M. M., 'Münster's *Cosmographia Universalis*', *Journal of the Gypsy Lore Society*, 3rd ser., 31 (1952), 83–90.

Basu, Anupam, ' "Like Very Honest and Substantial Citizens": Cony-Catching as Social Performance', *English Literary Renaissance*, 44 (2014), 36–55.

Bate, Jonathan, *John Clare: A Biography* (New York, 2003).

Batillard, Paul, 'Immigration of the Gypsies into Western Europe in the Fifteenth Century', *Journal of the Gypsy Lore Society*, 1 (1889), 185–212, 260–86, 324–45.

Batillard, Paul, 'Immigration of the Gypsies into Western Europe in the Fifteenth Century', (continued), *Journal of the Gypsy Lore Society*, 2 (1890), 27–41.

Bayman, Anna, 'Rogues, Conycatching and the Scribbling Crew', *History Workshop Journal*, 63 (2007), 1–17.

Bayman, Anna, *Thomas Dekker and the Culture of Pamphleteering in Early Modern London* (Farnham and Burlington, VT, 2014).

Bebbington, D. W., *Evangelicalism in Modern Britain: A History from the 1730s to the 1980s* (1989).

Behlmer, George K., 'The Gypsy Problem in Victorian England, *Victorian Studies*, 28 (1985), 231–53.

Beier, A. L., 'Vagrants and the Social Order in Elizabethan England', *Past & Present*, 64 (1974), 3–29.

Beier, A. L., *Masterless Men: The Vagrancy Problem in England 1560–1640* (1985).

Beier, A. L., 'New Historicism, Historical Context, and the Literature of Rogues: The Case of Thomas Harman Reopened', in Craig Dionne and Steve Mentz (eds), *Rogues and Early Modern English Culture* (Ann Arbor, 2004), 98–119.

Beier, A. L., and Paul Ocobock (eds), *Cast Out: Vagrancy and Homelessness in Global and Historical Perspective* (Athens, OH, 2008).

Beier, Lee, 'Anti-Language or Jargon? Canting in the English Underworld in the Sixteenth and Seventeenth Centuries', in Peter Burke and Roy Porter (eds), *Languages and Jargons: Contributions to a Social History of Language* (Cambridge, 1995), 64–101

Belton, Brian A., *Gypsy and Traveller Ethnicity: The Social Generation of an Ethnic Phenomenon* (2005).

Belton, Brian A., *Questioning Gypsy Identity: Ethnic Narratives in Britain and America* (Oxford and Walnut Creek, CA, 2005).

Berry, Riley M. Fletcher, 'The American Gypsy', *Frank Leslie's Popular Monthly*, 53 (1902), 560–72.

Bhopal, Kalwant, and Martin Myers, *Insiders, Outsiders and Others: Gypsies and Identity* (Hatfield, 2008).

Bhreatnach, Aoife, *Becoming Conspicuous: Irish Travellers, Society and the State 1922–1977* (Dublin, 2006).

Blair, Frederick G., 'Forged Passports of British Gypsies in the Sixteenth Century', *Journal of the Gypsy Lore Society*, 3rd ser., 28 (1950), 131–7.

Blakeborough, J. Fairfax, 'Gypsy Fortune-Tellers', *Notes and Queries*, 18 November 1926, 207.

Bowers, Jake, 'Gypsies and Travellers Accessing their Own Past: The Surrey Project and Aspects of Minority Representation', in Michael Hayes and Thomas Acton (eds), *Travellers. Gypsies, Roma: The Demonisation of Difference* (Cambridge, 2007), 18–20.

Boyce, George, James Curran, and Pauline Wingate (ed.), *Newspaper History from the Seventeenth Century to the Present Day* (1978).

Brantlinger, Patrick, and Donald Ulin, 'Policing Nomads and Social Control in Early Victorian England', *Cultural Critique*, 25 (1993), 33–63.

Brearley, Margaret, 'The Persecution of Gypsies in Europe', *American Behavioral Scientist*, 45 (2001), 588–99.

Brown, Philip, Lisa Scullion, and Philip Martin, *Migrant Roma in the United Kingdom* (Manchester, 2013).

Bryant, Mark, 'Dr Who? The First Cartoon Character', *History Today*, 57 (July 2007), 60–1.

Buckler, Sarah, *Fire in the Dark: Telling Gypsiness in North East England* (New York and Oxford, 2007).

Burke, Mary, *'Tinkers': Synge and the Cultural History of the Irish Traveller* (Oxford, 2009).

Camden, Carol, 'Elizabethan Chiromancy', *Modern Language Notes*, 62 (1947), 1–7.

Campbell, John, *The Lives of the Chief Justices*, 3 vols (1849–51).

Campbell, Lord, *The Lives of the Chief Justices of England*, 4 vols (Boston, 1873).

Campbell, Sue, 'Gypsies: The Criminalization of a Way of Life?', *Criminal Law Review*, 1 (1995), 28–37.

Carroll, William C., *Fat King, Lean Beggars: Representations of Poverty in the Age of Shakespeare* (Ithaca, NY, and London, 1996).

Carter, Helen Ruth, 'Responses to Gypsies in Britain 1900–1939', University of Northumbria, Ph.D. thesis, 2002.

Casado, J. Moreno, 'Los gitanos de España bajo Carlos I', *Chronica nova*, 4–5 (1969), 181–98.

Charnock, Richard S., 'On the Origins of the Gypsies', *Anthropological Review*, 12 (1866), 89–96.

Charnon-Deutsch, Lou, *The Spanish Gypsy: The History of a European Obsession* (College Park, PA, 2004).

Clark, Colin, 'Europe', in Colin Clark and Margaret Greenfields (eds), *Here to Stay: The Gypsies and Travellers of Britain* (Hatfield, 2006), 259–80.

Clark, Colin, and Elaine Campbell, '"Gypsy Invasion": A Critical Analysis of Newspaper Reaction to Czech and Slovak Romani Asylum-Seekers in Britain, 1997', *Romani Studies*, 5th ser., 10 (2000), 23–47.

Clark, Colin, and Margaret Greenfields (eds), *Here to Stay: The Gypsies and Travellers of Britain* (Hatfield, 2006).

Clements, Luke, and Sue Campbell, 'The Criminal Justice and Public Order Act and its Implications for Travellers', in Thomas Acton (ed.), *Scholarship and the Gypsy Struggle: Commitment in Romani Studies* (Hatfield, 2000), 61–9.

Clough, Sharyn, and William E. Loges, 'Racist Value Judgments as Objectively False Beliefs: A Philosophical and Social-Psychological Analysis', *Journal of Social Philosophy*, 39 (2008), 77–95.

Colocci, Adriano, 'The Gypsies in the Marches of Ancona during the 16th, 17th, and 18th Centuries', *Journal of the Gypsy Lore Society*, 2 (1889), 213–20.

Commission on Security and Cooperation in Europe, *The Human Rights Situation of Roma: Europe's Largest Ethnic Minority* (Washington, 2008).

Connell, Andrew, *Appleby Gypsy Horse Fair: Mythology, Origins, Evolution and Evaluation* (Cumberland and Westmorland Antiquarian and Archaeological Society, extra ser. no. 44, 2015).

Cooper, C. H., *Annals of Cambridge*, 5 vols (Cambridge, 1842–52).

Council of Europe Descriptive Glossary of Terms Relating to Roma Issues (Strasbourg, 2012).

Cramsie, John, *British Travellers and the Encounter with Britain, 1450–1700* (2015).

Crawford, John, 'On the Origin of the Gypsies', *Anthropological Review*, 1 (1863), 445–7.

Cressy, David, 'Evangelical Ethnographers and English Gypsies from the 1790s to the 1830s', *Romani Studies*, 5th ser., 26 (2016), 63–77.

Cressy, David, 'Trouble with Gypsies in Early Modern England, *Historical Journal*, 59 (2016), 45–70.

Cressy, David, 'Marginal People in a Stressful Culture: Gypsies and "Counterfeit Egyptians"', in Trevor Dean, Glyn Parry, and Edward Valance (eds), *Faith, Place, and People in Early Modern England* (forthcoming).

Cripps, John, *Accommodation for Gypsies: A Report on the Working of the Caravan Sites Act 1968* (1977).

Croft-Cooke, Rupert, *A Few Gypsies* (1955).

Crofton, Henry Thomas, 'Early Annals of the Gypsies in England', *Journal of the Gypsy Lore Society*, 1 (1888), 5–25.

Crofton, Henry Thomas, 'Supplementary Annals of the Gypsies in England, before 1700', *Journal of the Gypsy Lore Society*, NS 1 (1907–8), 31–4.

Crofton, Henry Thomas, 'Borde's Egipt Speche', *Journal of the Gypsy Lore Society*, NS 1 (1907), 157–68.

Crofton, Henry Thomas, 'Affairs of Egypt, 1892–1906', *Journal of the Gypsy Lore Society*, NS 1 (1907), 358–84.

Crofton, Henry Thomas, 'Affairs of Egypt, 1907', *Journal of the Gypsy Lore Society*, NS 2 (1908), 121–41.

Crofton, Henry Thomas, 'Affairs of Egypt, 1908', *Journal of the Gypsy Lore Society*, NS 3 (1909), 276–98.

Crowe, David M., *A History of the Gypsies of Eastern Europe and Russia* (New York, 1996).

Cutts, John P., 'Seventeenth-Century Illustrations of Three Masques by Jonson', *Comparative Drama*, 6 (1972), 125–34.

Darton, F. J. Harvey, *The Marches of Wessex: A Chronicle of England* (1922).

Darton, F. J. Harvey, *The Soul of Dorset* (New York, 1922).

Davies, C. S. L., 'Slavery and Protector Somerset: The Vagrancy Act of 1547', *Economic History Review*, NS 19 (1966), 533–49.

Davies, Owen, *Cunning Folk: Popular Magic in English History* (2003).

Dawson, Robert, *Times Gone: Gypsies and Travellers* (Alfreton, Derbyshire, 2007).

Devlin, Christopher, *The Life of Robert Southwell: Poet and Martyr* (1956).

Dictionary of National Biography.

Dimmock, Spencer (ed.), *The Origins of Capitalism in England, 1400–1600* (Leiden, 2014).

Dionne, Craig, and Steve Mentz (eds), *Rogues and Early Modern English Culture* (Ann Arbor, 2004).

Dobb, Maurice, *Studies in the Development of Capitalism*, 6th impression (1954).

Dobson, David, *Directory of Scots Banished to the American Plantations, 1650–1775* (Baltimore, 1983).

Dodds, Norman N., *Gypsies, Didikois and Other Travellers* (1966).

Donovan, Bill M., 'Changing Perceptions of Social Deviance: Gypsies in Early Modern Portugal and Brazil', *Journal of Social History*, 26 (1992), 33–53.

Drayton, Alexandra, ' "The poor tawny wanderers": The Coleridges, Wordsworth, Arnold and the Gypsies', *Coleridge Bulletin*, 34 (2009), 17–24.

Drouet, Pascale, *Le Vagabond dans l'Angleterre de Shakespeare: Ou l'art de contrefaire à la ville at à la scène* (Paris, 2003).

Duncan, Ian, 'George Borrow's Nomadology', *Victorian Studies*, 41 (1998), 381–403.

Durst, Judit (ed.), 'Network Discussion 2: Roma Migrants in the UK and the Numbers Games', <http://romanistudies.edu/documents/email-list-archive/> (accessed May 2016).

Dutt, William A., 'With the East Anglian Gypsies', *Good Words*, 37 (1896), 120–6.

Eccles, Audrey, *Vagrancy in Law and Practice under the Old Poor Law* (Farnham and Burlington, VT, 2012).

Edwards, Francis, *English Jesuits* (1981).

Edwards, Peter, *Horse and Man in Early Modern England* (London and New York, 2007).

Eliav-Feldon, Miriam, 'Vagrants or Vermin? Attitudes towards Gypsies in Early Modern England', in Miriam Eliav-Feldon, Benjamin Isaac, and Joseph Ziegler (eds), *The Origins of Racism in the West* (Cambridge, 2009), 276–91.

Eliav-Feldon, Miriam, *Renaissance Imposters and Proofs of Identity* (2012).

Elton, G. R., *Reform and Renewal: Thomas Cromwell and the Common Weal* (Cambridge, 1973).

Elton, G. R., *The Parliament of England 1559–1581* (Cambridge, 1986).

End, Markus, 'Antigypsyism: What's Happening in a Word?' in Jan Selling, Markus End, Hristo Kyuchukov, Pia Laskar, and Bill Templer (eds), *Antiziganism: What's in a Word?* (Newcastle upon Tyne, 2015), 99–113.

European Commission, *The Situation of Roma in an Enlarged European Union* (Luxembourg, 2004).

European Convention on Human Rights (Strasbourg, 2010).

European Court of Human Rights, applications 24876/94, 24882/94, 25154/94, 25289/94, 27238/95, 66746/01.

Evans, Simon, *Stopping Places: A Gypsy History of South London and Kent* (Hatfield, 1999).

Everitt, Alan, *Change in the Provinces: The Seventeenth Century* (Leicester, 1972).

Falk, Tilman, *Hans Burgkmair Studien zu Leben und Werke des Augsburger Malers* (Munich, 1968).

Fassanelli, Benedetto, ' "Considerata la mala qualità delli Cingani erranti": I Rom nella repubblica di Venezia: Retoriche e stereotipi', *Acta Histriae*, 15 (2007), 139–54.

Fassanelli, Benedetto, ' "Andar con Cigani" o "Viver Christianamente"? Tipi, icone e visioni del mondo attraverso un *Costituto* cinquecentesco', in Felice Gambin (ed.), *Alle radici dell'Europa: Mori, giudei e zingari nel paesi del Mediterraneo Occidentale (secoli XV–XVII)* (Florence, 2008), 79–92.

Fassanelli, Benedetto, ' "In Casa del Boldu Siamo Stati una Sera": Pratiche relazaione di una compagnia di "Cingani in Viazo" nella terraferma veneta di fine cinquecento', *Quaderni storici*, 129 (2008), 691–723.

Fassanelli, Benedetto, 'Una prezenza inammissibile: I cingani nella terraferma veneta durante il secolo dei bandi', *Italia romani*, 5 (2008), 41–70.

Fassanelli, Benedetto, *Vite al bando: Storie di cingari nella terrferma veneta all fine del cinquecento* (Rome, 2011).

Fassanelli, Benedetto, ' "Piccoli Egitti" tra Cristianita e Islam: Prezenze zingare nel mediterraneo orientale (secc. XV–XVII)', *Quaderni storici*, 146 (2014), 349–82.

Fitzgerald, Patrick, ' "Like Crickets to the Crevice of a Brew-House": Poor Irish Migrants in England, 1560–1640', in Patrick Fitzgerald (ed.), *Patterns of Migration* (Leicester, 1992), 13–35.

Fletcher, Anthony, *A County Community in Peace and War: Sussex 1600–1669* (1975).

Floate, Sharon Sillers, *My Ancestors were Gypsies*, 3rd edn (2010).

Floyd-Wilson, Mary, *English Ethnicity and Race in Early Modern Drama* (Cambridge, 2003).

Fonseca, Isabel, *Bury Me Standing: The Gypsies and their Journey* (New York, 1995, 2010).

Ford, Judith, ' "Egyptians" in Early-Modern Dorset', *Proceedings of the Dorset Natural History and Archaeological Society*, 130 (2009), 1–8.

Fourth Report of the Deputy Keeper of the Public Records (1843).

Foyster, Elizabeth, 'The "New World of Children" Reconsidered: Child Abduction in Late Eighteenth- and Early Nineteenth-Century England', *Journal of British Studies*, 52 (2013), 669–92.

Francis, Henry J., 'No. 747: Being the Autobiography of a Gypsy', *Journal of the Gypsy Lore Society*, NS 33 (1954), 88–107.

Fraser, Angus, 'Counterfeit Egyptians', *Tsiganologische Studien*, 2 (1990), 43–69.

Fraser, Angus, *The Gypsies* (Oxford, 1992, 1995).

Fraser, Angus, 'The Present and Future of the Gypsy Past', *Cambridge Review of International Affairs*, 13 (2000), 17–31.

Fraser, Angus M., 'The Gypsy Problem: A Survey of Post-War Developments', *Journal of the Gypsy Lore Society*, NS 32 (1953), 82–100.

Fraser, Angus M., 'A Government Survey of Travellers in England and Wales', *Journal of the Gypsy Lore Society*, NS 46 (1967), 9–23.

Fraser, Angus M., 'John Clare's Gypsies', *Journal of the Gypsy Lore Society*, 3rd ser., 50 (1971), 85–100.

Fumerton, Patricia, *Unsettled: The Culture of Mobility and the Working Poor in Early Modern England* (Chicago and London, 2006).

Gagnier, Regenia, 'Cultural Philanthropy, Gypsies and Interdisciplinary Scholars: Dream of a Common Language', *19: Interdisciplinary Studies in the Long Nineteenth Century*, 1 (2005), 1–24 <http://doi.org/10.16995/ntn.433> (accessed October 2017).

Gaines, James F. (ed.), *The Molière Encyclopedia* (Westport, CT, 2002).

Galbraith, Niall (ed.), *Aberrant Beliefs and Reasoning* (London and New York, 2015).

Garrett, James. M., 'The Unaccountable "Knot" of Wordsworth's "Gipsies" ', *Studies in English Literature*, 40 (2000), 603–20.

Garrido, Enrique, and Díez de Baldeón, 'Estudio aproximativo de la legislación relativa a la etnia gitana en los siglos XV, XVI y XVII: Dificultades, controversias, aplicación y escritos de los memorialistas y arbitristas', *Tiempos modernos*, 23 (2011), 1–40.

Garside, Peter, 'Picturesque Figure and Landscape: Meg Merrilies and the Gypsies', in Stephen Copley and Peter Garside (eds), *The Politics of the Picturesque: Literature, Landscape and Aesthetics since 1770* (Cambridge, 1994), 145–74.

Gelbart, Petra, 'Gypsyness and the Uhrovska Manuscript', *Transactions of the Royal Historical Society*, 22 (2012), 199–221.

Geremek, Bronislaw, 'L'Arrivée des Tsiganes en Italie: De l'assistance a la répression', in Giorgi Politi, Maria Rosa, and Franco della Peruta (eds), *Timore e carita: I poveri nell' Italia moderna* (Cremona, 1982), 27–44.

Glajar, Valentina, and Domnica Radulescu (eds), *'Gypsies' in European Literature and Culture* (Basingstoke and New York, 2008).

Gmelch, George, *The Irish Tinkers: The Urbanization of an Itinerant People* (Menlo Park, CA, 1977).

Gmelch, George, and Sharon Bohn Gmelch, 'The Cross-Channel Migration of Irish Travellers', *Economic and Social Review*, 16 (1985), 287–96.

Gmelch, Sharon Bohn, and George Gmelch, 'The Emergence of an Ethnic Group: The Irish Tinkers', *Anthropological Quarterly*, 49 (1976), 225–38.

Goose, Nigel, and Lien Luu (eds), *Immigrants in Tudor and Early Stuart England* (Brighton and Portland, OR, 2005).

Gotti, Maurizio, 'The Origins of 17th Century Canting Terms', *Costerus*, 141 (2002), 163–96.

Graham-Dixon, Andrew, *Caravaggio: A Life Sacred and Profane* (New York, 2011).

Green, Hazel, *Counting Gypsies* (Office of Population Censuses and Surveys, 1991).

Greenfields, Margaret, 'Stopping Places', in Colin Clark and Margaret Greenfields (eds), *Here to Stay: The Gypsies and Travellers of Britain* (Hatfield, 2006), 57–89.

Greg, W. W., *Jonson's Masque of Gipsies in the Burley, Belvoir, and Windsor Versions: An Attempt at Reconstruction* (1952).

Gresham, David, et al., 'Origins and Divergence of the Roma (Gypsies)', *American Journal of Human Genetics*, 69 (2001), 1314–31.

Griffiths, Paul, *Lost Londons: Change, Crime and Control in the Capital City, 1550–1660* (Cambridge, 2008).

Groome, Francis H., 'Gipsies', in *Encyclopedia Britannica*, 9th edn, 25 vols (Edinburgh, 1875–88), x. 611–18.

Groome, Francis Hindes, *In Gipsy Tents* (1880; repr. 1973).

Groome, Francis Hindes, *The Gipsies: Reminiscences and Social Life of their Extraordinary Race: Their Manners, Customs, and Wanderings* (Edinburgh, 1881).

Groome, Francis Hindes, *Gypsy Folk Tales* (1899).

Gronemeyer, Reimer, *Zigeuner im Spiegel Früher Chroniken und Abhandlungen: Quellen von 15 bis zum 18 Jarhundert* (Geissen, 1987).

Guasti, Niccolo, 'The Debate on the Expulsion of the Gypsies in the Castilian *Arbitrismo* of the Early Seventeenth Century', in Sina Rauschenbach and Christian Windler (eds), *Reforming Early Modern Monarchies: The Castilian Arbitristas in Comparative European Perspective* (Wiesbaden, 2016), 157–76.

Guilmartin, John F., *Gunpowder and Galleys: Changing Technology and Mediterranean Warfare at Sea in the Sixteenth Century* (New York, 1974).

Guttridge, Roger, *Ten Dorset Mysteries* (Southampton, 1989).

Habib, Imtiaz, *Black Lives in English Archives, 1500–1677: Imprints of the Invisible* (Aldershot, 2008).

Hall, George, 'Clara Heron', *Journal of the Gypsy Lore Society*, NS 5 (1911), 167–77.

Hall, George, 'Roberts's Vocabulary', *Journal of the Gypsy Lore Society*, NS 5 (1911), 177–91.

Hancock, Ian, 'Romani and Angloromani', in Peter Trudgill (ed.), *Language in the British Isles* (Cambridge, 1984), 367–83.

Hancock, Ian, 'Marko: Stories of my Grandfather', *Lacio Drom*, 6 (1985), 53–60.

Hancock, Ian, *The Pariah Syndrome: An Account of Gypsy Slavery and Persecution* (Ann Arbor, 1987).

Hancock, Ian, 'Duty and Beauty, Possession and Truth: Lexical Impoverishment as Control', in Thomas Acton and Gary Mundy (eds), *Romani Culture and Gypsy Identity* (Hatfield, 1997), 182–9.

Hancock, Ian, 'George Borrow's Romani', in Ian Hancock, *Danger! Educated Gypsy* (Hatfield, 2010), 169–76.

Hancock, Ian, *We Are the Romani People* (Hatfield, 2002).

Hancock, Ian, 'On Romany Origins and Identity—Questions for Discussion', in Adrian Marsh and Elin Strond (eds), *Gypsies and the Problem of Identities: Contextual, Constructed and Contested* (Istanbul, 2006), 69–92.

Hancock, Ian, *Danger! Educated Gypsy* (Hatfield, 2010).

Harriot, John Staples, 'Observations on the Oriental Origin of the Romnichal, or Tribe Miscalled Gypsey and Bohemian', *Transactions of the Royal Asiatic Society of Great Britain*, 2 (1829), 518–58.

Harte, Jeremy, 'Romance and the Romany', *History Today*, 66/1 (January 2016), 32–6.

Hawes, Derek, and Barbara Perez, *The Gypsy and the State: The Ethnic Cleansing of British Society* (Bristol, 1995).

Hayes, Michael, 'Nineteenth-Century Gipsilorism and the Exoticisation of the Roma (Gypsies)', in Michael Hayes (ed.), *Road Memories: Aspects of Migrant History* (Newcastle, 2007), 20–35.

Hayes, Michael, and Thomas Acton (eds), *Travellers, Gypsies, Roma: The Demonisation of Difference* (Cambridge, 2007).

Hazlitt, W. Carew, 'Notes on Popular Antiquities', *Antiquary*, 18 (1886), 217.

Helleiner, Jane Leslie, *Irish Travellers: Racism and the Politics of Culture* (Toronto, 2000).

Henry, Gráinne, 'Ulster Exiles in Europe, 1605–1641', in Brian MacCuarta (ed.), *Ulster 1641: Aspects of the Rising* (Belfast, 1993), 39–40.

Herrup, Cynthia B., *The Common Peace: Participation and the Criminal Law in Seventeenth-Century England* (Cambridge, 1987).

Hewitt, Regina, '"Wild Outcasts of Society": Stigmatization in Wordsworth's "Gipsies"', *Nineteenth-Century Contexts: An Interdisciplinary Journal*, 12 (1988), 19–28.

Higgs, Edward, *A Clearer Sense of the Census: The Victorian Censuses and Historical Research* (1996).

Hill, Christopher, *Liberty against the Law: Some Seventeenth-Century Controversies* (1996).

Hillier, Bevis, 'The Mysterious Case of Elizabeth Canning', *History Today*, 53/3 (March 2003), 47–5.

Hilton, R. H., *The English Peasantry in the Later Middle Ages* (Oxford, 1975).

Hindle, Steve, *On the Parish? The Micro-Politics of Poor Relief in Rural England, 1550–1750* (Oxford, 2004).

Hitchcock, David, 'A Typology of Travellers: Migration, Justice, and Vagrancy in Warwickshire, 1670–1730', *Rural History*, 23 (2012), 21–39.

Hitchcock, David, *Vagrancy in English Culture and Society, 1650–1750* (2016).

Hitchcock, Tim, 'Vagrant Lives', in Joanne McEwan and Pamela Sharpe (eds), *Accommodating Poverty: The Housing and Living Arrangements of the English Poor, c.1600–1850* (Basingstoke and New York, 2012), 152–44.

Hohmann, Joachim S., *Geschichte der Zigeuner Verfolgung in Deutschland* (Frankfurt and New York, 1981).

Hohmann, Joachim S., '"Gypsiology", an Instrument of Persecution?', *Newsletter of the Gypsy Lore Society, North American Chapter*, 11 (1988), 1–4.

Holberton, Paul, 'Giorgione's Tempest or "little landscape with the storm with the gypsy": More on the Gypsy, and a Reassessment', *Art History*, 18 (1995), 383–404.

Holloway, Sarah L., 'Outsiders in Rural Society? Constructions of Rurality and Nature–Society Relations in the Racialisation of English Gypsy-Travellers, 1869–1934', *Environment and Planning D: Society and Space*, 21 (2003), 695–715.

Holmes, Colin, 'Samuel Roberts and the Gypsies', in Sidney Pollard and Colin Holmes (eds), *Essays in the Economic and Social History of South Yorkshire* (Barnsley, 1976), 233–46.

Holmes, Colin, 'The German Gypsy Question in Britain, 1904–1906', in Kenneth Lunn (ed.), *Hosts, Immigrants and Minorities: Historical Responses to Newcomers in British Society 1870–1914* (New York, 1980), 134–59.

Holmes, Colin, *John Bull's Island: Immigration and British Society 1871–1971* (Basingstoke, 1988).

Hood, Christobel M., *The Book of Robert Southwell: Priest, Poet, Prisoner* (Oxford, 1926).

Horrox, Rosemary (ed.), *Fifteenth Century Attitudes: Perceptions of Society in Late Medieval England* (Cambridge, 1994).

Houghton-Walker, Sarah, 'John Clare's Gypsies', *Romani Studies*, 5th ser., 19 (2009), 125–45.

Houghton-Walker, Sarah, *Representations of the Gypsy in the Romantic Period* (Oxford, 2014).

House of Commons, *Report of the Select Committee on the Existing Laws Relating to Vagrants* (1821).

The Housing (Assessment of Accommodation Needs) (Meaning of Gypsies and Travellers) (England) Regulations 2006 (2006).

Hug, Tobias B., *Impostures in Early Modern England: Representations and Perceptions of Fraudulent Identities* (Manchester and New York, 2009).

Hunt, William, *The Puritan Moment: The Coming of Revolution to an English County* (Cambridge, MA, 1983).

Hutchinson, John, and Anthony D. Smith (eds), *Ethnicity* (Oxford and New York, 1996).

Huth, Ferdinand Gerard, 'Gypsy Caravans', *Journal of the Gypsy Lore Society*, 3rd ser., 19 (1940), 113–46.

Hyland, St George Kiernan, *A Century of Persecution under Tudor and Stuart Sovereigns from Contemporary Records* (1920).

Iovita, Radu P., and Theodore G. Schurr, 'Reconstructing the Origins and Migrations of Diasporic Populations: The Case of the European Gypsies', *American Anthropologist*, 106 (2004), 267–81.

Irish Traveller Movement in Britain, *Gypsy and Traveller Population in England and the 2011 Census* (2013).

Iyengar, Sujata, *Shades of Difference: Mythologies of Skin Color in Early Modern England* (Philadelphia, 2005).

Jackson, William (ed.), *The New and Complete Newgate Calendar, or Malefactor's Universal Register*, 7 vols (c. 1810).

James, S. B., 'English Gipsies: A Monograph. In Five Chapters', *Church of England and Lambeth Magazine*, 79 (1875), 97–100, 161–4, 225–30, 289–4, 353–7.

Janowitz, Anne F., ' "Wild Outcasts of Society": The Transit of the Gypsies in Romantic Period Poetry', in Gerald MacLean, Donna Landry, and Joseph P. Ward (eds), *The Country and the City Revisited: England and the Politics of Culture, 1550–1850* (Cambridge, 1999), 213–30.

Jenkins, Philip, 'From Gallows to Prison? The Execution Rate in Early Modern England', *Criminal Justice History*, 7 (1986), 51–71.

Johnson, Stanley C., *A History of Emigration from the United Kingdom to North America, 1763–1912* (1913).

Jones, David, 'Rural Crime and Protest', in G. E. Mingay (ed.), *The Victorian Countryside* (1981), 566–79.

Jones, R. O., 'The Mode of Disposing of Gipsies and Vagrants in the Reign of Elizabeth', *Archaeologia Cambrensis*, 4th ser., 13 (1882), 226–9.

Judges, A. V., *The Elizabethan Underworld: A Collection of Tudor and Early Stuart Tracts and Ballads Telling of the Lives and Misdoings of Vagabonds, Thieves, Rogues and Cozeners, and Giving Some Account of the Operation of the Criminal Law* (1930; repr. 1965).

Kabachnik, Peter, 'To Choose, Fix, or Ignore Culture? The Cultural Politics of Gypsy and Traveler Mobility in England', *Social and Cultural Geography*, 10 (2009), 461–79.

Kabachnik, Peter, 'Place Invaders: Constructing the Nomadic Threat in England', *Geographic Review*, 100 (2010), 90–108.

Kabachnik, Peter, and Andrew Ryder, 'Nomadism and the 2003 Anti-Social Behaviour Act: Constraining Gypsy and Traveller Mobilities in Britain', *Romani Studies*, 5th ser., 23 (2013), 83–106.

Kalaydjieve, Luba, et al., 'Genetic Studies of the Roma (Gypsies): A Review', *BMC Medical Genetics*, 2 (2001) <https://doi.org/10.1186/1471-2350-2-5> (accessed October 2017).

Keen, Maurice, *English Society in the Later Middle Ages 1348–1500* (1990).

Kenrick, Donald, 'Romani English', *International Journal of the Sociology of Language*, 19 (1979), 111–20.

Kenrick, Donald, 'Foreign Gypsies and British Immigration Law after 1945', in Thomas Acton (ed.), *Gypsy Politics and Traveller Identity* (Hatfield, 1997), 100–10.

Kenrick, Donald, *Historical Dictionary of the Gypsies (Romanies)* (Lanham, MD, and London, 1998).

Kenrick, Donald, 'Romany Origins and Migration Patterns', *International Journal of Frontier Missions*, 17 (2000), 37–40, 56.

Kenrick, Donald, *Gypsies: From the Ganges to the Thames* (Hatfield, 2004).

Kenrick, Donald, 'The Origins of Anti-Gypsyism: The Outsiders' View of Romanies in Western Europe in the Fifteenth Century', in Nicholas Saul and Susan Tebbutt (eds), *The Role of the Romanies* (Liverpool, 2004), 79–84.

Kenrick, Donald, and Sian Bakewell, *On the Verge: The Gypsies of England* (Hatfield, 1990; repr. 1995).

Kenrick, Donald, and Colin Clark (eds), *Moving On: The Gypsies and Travellers of Britain* (1999).

Kenrick, Donald, and Grattan Puxon, *Gypsies under the Swastika* (Hatfield, 2009).

Kent, Joan R., 'Population Mobility and Alms: Poor Migrants in the Midlands during the Early Seventeenth Century', *Local Population Studies*, 27 (1981), 35–51.

Kent, Joan R., *The English Village Constable 1580–1642: A Social and Administrative Study* (Oxford, 1986).

Kinney, Arthur F. (ed.), *Rogues, Vagabonds, & Sturdy Beggars: A New Gallery of Tudor and Early Stuart Rogue Literature* (Barre, MA, 1973).

Knapp, Jeffrey, *Shakespeare's Tribe: Church, Nation, and Theater in Renaissance England* (Chicago and London, 2002).

Knauer, Georg Nicolaus, 'The Earliest Vocabulary of Romani Words (*c*.1515) in the *Collectanea* of Johannes ex Grafing, a Student of Johannes Reuchlin and Conrad Celtis', *Romani Studies*, 5th ser., 20 (2010), 1–15.

Knowles, James, '"Songs of baser alloy": Jonson's *Gypsies Metamorphosed* and the Circulation of Manuscript Libels', *Huntington Library Quarterly*, 69 (2006), 153–76.

Kramp, Michael, 'The Woman, the Gypsies, and England: Harriet Smith's National Role', *College Literature*, 31 (2004), 147–68.

Kusters, Joke, 'Criminalising Romani Culture through Law', in Marie-Clare Foblets and Alison Dundes Renteln (eds), *Multicultural Jurisprudence: Comparative Perspectives on the Cultural Defense* (Oxford and Portland, OR, 2009), 199–227.

Kyuchukov, Hristo (ed.), *New Faces of Antigypsyism in Modern Europe* (Prague, 2012).

Kyuchukov, Hristo, and Ian Hancock, *A History of the Romani People* (Honesdale, PA., 2005).

Lachmann, Richard, *From Manor to Market: Structural Change in England, 1536–1640* (Madison, WI, 1987).

Lacour, Eva, 'Faces of Violence Revisited. A Typology of Violence in Early Modern Rural Germany', *Journal of Social History*, 34 (2001), 649–67.

Laslett, Peter, 'Size and Structure of the Household in England over Three Centuries', *Population Studies*, 23 (1969), 199–223.

Lawton, Richard (ed.), *The Census and Social Structure: An Interpretative Guide to Nineteenth Century Censuses of England and Wales* (1978).

Leblon, Bernard, *Gypsies and Flamenco: The Emergence of the Art of Flamenco in Andalusia* (Hatfield, 2003).

Lee, Ken, 'Orientalism and Gypsylorism', *Social Analysis*, 44 (2000), 129–56.

Lee, Ronald, 'Roma in Europe: "Gypsy" Myth and Romani Reality—New Evidence for Romani History', in Valentina Glajar and Domnica Radulescu (eds), *'Gypsies' in European Literature and Culture* (Basingstoke and New York, 2008), 1–28.

Leland, Charles G., *The English Gipsies and their Language* (1873).

Leland, Charles Godfrey, *The English Gipsies and their Language*, 2nd edn. (1874).

Lehmberg, Stanford E., *The Reformation Parliament 1529–1536* (Cambridge, 1970).

Lemmings, David, *Professors of the Law: Barristers and English Legal Culture in the Eighteenth Century* (Oxford, 2000).

Lemmings, David, and Claire Walker (eds), *Moral Panics, the Media and the Law in Early Modern England* (Basingstoke and New York, 2009).

Liégeois, Jean-Pierre, *Mutation tsigane: La Revolution bohémienne* (Brussels, 1976).

Liégeois, Jean-Pierre, *Gypsies and Travellers: Socio-Cultural Data. Socio-Political Data* (Strasbourg, 1987).

Liégeois, Jean-Pierre, *The Council of Europe and Roma: 40 Years of Action* (Strasbourg, 2012).

Lucassen, Leo, 'Eternal Vagrants? State Formation, Migration and Travelling Groups in Western Europe, 1350–1914', in Leo Lucassen, Wim Willems, and Annemarie Cottaar (eds), *Gypsies and Other Itinerant Groups: A Socio-Historical Approach* (Basingstoke, 1998), 55–73.

Lucassen, Leo, 'Between Hobbes and Locke: Gypsies and the Limits of the Modernization Paradigm', *Social History*, 22 (2008), 423–41.

Lucassen Leo, and Wim Willems, 'Wanderers or Migrants? Gypsies from Eastern to Western Europe, 1860–1940', in Robin Cohen (ed.), *The Cambridge Survey of World Migration* (Cambridge, 1995), 137–89.

Lucassen, Leo, and Wim Willems, 'The Weakness of Well-Ordered Societies: Gypsies in Western Europe, the Ottoman Empire, and India, 1400–1914', *Review of the Fernand Braudel Center*, 26 (2003), 283–313.

Lucassen, Leo, Wim Willems, and Annemarie Cottaar (eds), *Gypsies and Other Itinerant Groups: A Socio-Historical Approach* (New York, 1998).

Lunn, Kenneth (ed.), *Hosts, Immigrants and Minorities: Historical Responses to Newcomers in British Society 1870–1914* (New York, 1980).

MacCaffery, W. T., 'Talbot and Stanhope: An Episode in Elizabethan Politics', *Bulletin of the Institute of Historical Research*, 33 (1960), 73–85.

McFarlane, Andrew, 'George Morland as an Illustrator of English Gypsy Life', *Journal of the Gypsy Lore Society*, 3rd ser., 33 (1954), 1–14.

MacFie, R. A. Scott, 'Gypsy Persecutions: A Survey of a Black Chapter in European History', *Journal of the Gypsy Lore Society*, NS 22 (1943), 65–78.

McGowan, Alec, *On the Gypsy Trail: Sources for the Family History of Gypsies* (Romany and Traveller Family History Society, 1998).

MacKay, Ruth, *'Lazy Improvident People': Myth and Reality in the Writing of Spanish History* (Ithaca, NY, and London, 2006).

MacLaughlin, Jim, 'European Gypsies and the Historical Geography of Loathing', *Review of the Fernand Braudel Center*, 22 (1999), 31–59.

McLynn, Frank, *Crime and Punishment in Eighteenth-Century England* (Oxford, 1991).

McMullan, John L., *The Canting Crew: London's Criminal Underworld 1550–1700* (New Brunswick, 1984).

McPeek, James A. S., *The Black Book of Knaves and Unthrifts in Shakespeare and Other Renaissance Authors* (Storrs, CT, 1969).

MacRitchie, David, *Scottish Gypsies under the Stewarts* (Edinburgh, 1894).

MacRitchie, David, 'Gypsies at Geneva in the 15th, 16th, and 17th Centuries', *Journal of the Gypsy Lore Society*, NS 6 (1912–13), 81–6.

Marcus, George E., and Michael M. J. Fischer, *Anthropology as Cultural Critique: An Experimental Moment in the Human Sciences* (Chicago and London, 1986).

Marius, Richard, *Thomas More: A Biography* (New York, 1984).

Marsh, Adrian, 'The Origins of the Gypsy Peoples: Identity and Influence in Romani History', *Kuri' Journal of the Dom Research Center*, 1 (2003) <http://www.domresearchcenter.com/journal/19/index.html> (accessed October 2017).

Marsh, Adrian, and Elin Strond (eds), *Gypsies and the Problem of Identities: Contextual, Constructed and Contested* (Istanbul, 2006).

Martinez-Cruz, Begoňa, et al., 'Origins, Admixture and Founder Lineages in European Roma', *European Journal of Human Genetics*, 24 (2016), 937–43.

Marushiakova, Elena, and Vesselin Popov, *Gypsies in the Ottoman Empire* (Hatfield, 2001).

Marushiakova, Elena, and Vesselin Popov, 'De l'est à l'ouest: Chronologie et typologie des migrations tsiganes en Europe (du XVème siècle jusqu'à présent)', *Études Tsiganes*, 27–8 (2006), 10–25.

Masciola, Amy L., '"The Unfortunate Maid Exemplified": Elizabeth Canning and Representations of Infanticide in Eighteenth-Century England', in Mark Jackson et al. (eds), *Infanticide: Historical Perspectives on Child Murder and Concealment, 1550–2000* (Aldershot, 2002), 52–72.

Mastana, Sarabjit S., and Surinder S. Papiha, 'Origins of the Romany Gypsies: Genetic Evidence', *Zeitschrift für Morphologie und Anthropologie*, 79 (1992), 43–51.

Matthews, Jodie, 'Back where they Belong: Gypsies, Kidnapping and Assimilation in Victorian Children's Literature', *Romani Studies*, 5th ser., 20 (2010), 137–59.

Matthews, Jodie, ' "Tsiganes on the Brain": The "Last Gypsy" as a Case of Archive Fever', *Immigrants and Minorities*, 31 (2013), 289–316.

Matthews, Jodie, 'Mobilising the Imperial Uncanny: Nineteenth-Century Textual Attitudes to Travelling Romani People, Canal-Boat People, Showpeople and Hop-Pickers in Britain', *Nineteenth-Century Contexts*, 37 (2015), 359–75.

Matras, Yaron, 'Johann Rüdiger and the Study of Romani in 18th Century Germany', *Journal of the Gypsy Lore Society*, 5th ser., 9 (1999), 89–116.

Matras, Yaron, *Romani: A Linguistic Introduction* (Cambridge, 2002).

Matras, Yaron, 'The Role of Language in Mystifying and De-Mystifying Gypsy Identity', in Nicholas Saul and Susan Tebbutt (eds), *The Role of the Romanies* (Liverpool, 2004), 53–78.

Matras, Yaron, *Romani in Britain: The Afterlife of a Language* (Edinburgh, 2010).

Matras, Yaron, 'Scholarship and the Politics of Romani Identity: Strategic and Conceptual Issues', *European Yearbook of Minority Issues*, 10 (2011), 211–47.

Matras, Yaron, *I Met Lucky People: The Story of the Romani Gypsies* (2014).

Matras, Yaron, 'Transnational Policy and "Authenticity" Discourses on Romani Language and Identity', *Language in Society*, 44 (2015), 295–316.

Matras, Yaron, Hazel Gardner, Charlotte Jones, and Veronica Schulman, 'Angloromani: A Different Kind of Language?', *Anthropological Linguistics*, 49 (2007), 142–84.

Mayall, David, *Gypsy-Travellers in Nineteenth-Century Society* (Cambridge, 1988).

Mayall, David, 'The Making of British Gypsy Identities, c.1500–1980', *Immigrants and Minorities*, 11 (1992), 21–41.

Mayall, David, *English Gypsies and State Policies* (Hatfield, 1995).

Mayall, David, 'Egyptians and Vagabonds: Representations of the Gypsy in Early Modern Official and Rogue Literature', *Immigrants and Minorities*, 16 (1997), 55–82.

Mayall, David, *Gypsy Identities 1500–2000: From Egipcyans and Moon-Men to the Ethnic Romany* (2004).

Mayall, David, ' "Britain's Most Demonised People?": Political Responses to Gypsies and Travellers in Twentieth Century England', in Michael Zimmermann (ed.), *Zwischen Erziehung und Vernichtung: Zigeunerpolitik und Ziegeunerforschung im Europa des 20 Jarhunderts* (Stuttgart, 2007), 254–67.

Mendizabal, Isabel, et al., 'Reconstructing the Population History of European Romani from Genome-Wide Data', *Current Biology*, 22 (2012), 2342–9.

Mitchell, Ian, 'The Changing Role of Fairs in the Long Eighteenth Century: Evidence from the North Midlands', *Economic History Review*, 60 (2007), 545–73.

Mitchison, Rosalind, *The Old Poor Law in Scotland: The Experience of Poverty, 1574–1845* (Edinburgh, 2000).

Moffitt, John F., *Caravaggio in Context: Learned Naturalism and Renaissance Humanism* (Jefferson, NC, 2004).

Money, Walter, 'The Gypsies', *Berks, Bucks and Oxon Archaeological Journal*, 4 (1898), 28.

Moore, Judith, *The Appearance of Truth: The Story of Elizabeth Canning and Eighteenth-Century Narrative* (Newark, DE, and London, 1994).

Moore, Judith, 'Elizabeth Canning and Mary Squires: Representations of Guilt and Innocence in Legal and Literary Texts, 1753–1989', in Katherine Kittredge (ed.), *Lewd and Notorious: Female Transgression in the Eighteenth Century* (Ann Arbor, 2003), 197–209.

Moorjani, Priya, et al., 'Reconstructing Roma History from Genome-Wide Data', *PLoS One*, 8/3 (2013) <https://doi.org/10.1371/journal.pone.0058633> (accessed October 2017).

Morar, Bharti, et al., 'Mutation History of the Roma/Gypsies', *American Journal of Human Genetics*, 75 (2004), 596–609.

Morgan, Gwendon, and Peter Rushton, *Eighteenth-Century Criminal Transportation: The Formation of the Criminal Atlantic* (Basingstoke and New York, 2004).

Morgan, John, ' "Counterfeit Egyptians": The Construction and Implementation of a Criminal Identity in Early Modern England', *Romani Studies*, 5th ser., 26 (2016), 105–28.

Morrall, Andrew, 'Soldiers and Gypsies: Outsiders and their Families in Early Sixteenth Century German Art', in Pia Cuneo (ed.), *Artful Armies, Beautiful Battles: Art and Warfare in Early Modern Europe* (Leiden, 2002), 159–80.

Morris, Rachel, 'Nomads and Newspapers', in Colin Clark and Margaret Greenfields (eds), *Here to Stay: The Gypsies and Travellers of Britain* (Hatfield, 2006), 236–58.

Morwood, Vernon S., *Our Gipsies in City, Tent, and Van* (1885).

Mróz, Lech, *Roma–Gypsy Presence in the Polish–Lithuanian Commonwealth 15th–18th Centuries* (Budapest, 2015).

Murray, John Tucker, *English Dramatic Companies 1558–1642*, 2 vols (1910).

Musée Historique Lorrain, *Jacques Callot 1592–1635* (Paris, 1992).

Netzloff, Mark, ' "Counterfeit Egyptians" and Imagined Borders: Jonson's *The Gypsies Metamorphosed*', *ELH* 68 (2001), 763–93.

Netzloff, Mark, *England's Internal Colonies: Class, Capital, and the Literature of Early Modern English Colonialism* (2003).

Nichols, Tom, 'The Vagabond Image: Depictions of False Beggars in Northern Art of the Sixteenth Century', in Tom Nichols (ed.), *Others and Outcasts in Early Modern Europe: Picturing the Social Margins* (Aldershot and Burlington, VT, 2007), 37–60.

Nichols, Tom (ed.), *Others and Outcasts in Early Modern Europe: Picturing the Social Margins* (Aldershot and Burlington, VT, 2007).

Nichols, Tom, *The Art of Poverty: Irony and Ideal in Sixteenth-Century Beggar Imagery* (Manchester, 2008).

Niner, Pat, 'Accommodating Nomadism? An Examination of Accommodation Options for Gypsies and Travellers in England', *Housing Studies*, 19 (2004), 141–59.

Nord, Deborah Epstein, *Gypsies and the British Imagination, 1807–1930* (New York, 2006).

'Notes and Queries, Foreign Gypsies in England', *Journal of the Gypsy Lore Society*, NS 4 (1910–11), 307.

'Notes and Queries: Gypsies at Helmdon, Northants', *Journal of the Gypsy Lore Society*, NS 4 (1910–11), 307.

'Notes and Queries: Gipsies in America, 1581', *Journal of the Gypsy Lore Society*, NS 6 (1912), 61.

'Notes and Queries: British Gypsy Crimes, 1911', *Journal of the Gypsy Lore Society*, NS 6 (1912), 70–1.

Novi Chavarria, Elisa, *Sulle tracce degli zingari: Il popolo rom nel Regno di Napoli (secoli XV–XVIII)* (Naples, 2007).

Novi Chavarria, Elisa, 'I cognomi del popolo rom', in Andrea Addobbati, Roberto Bizzocchi, and Gregorio Salinero (eds), *L'Italia dei cognomi: L'antroponimia italiana nel quadro mediterraneo* (Pisa, 2013), 1–15.

Novi Chavarria, Elisa, 'Pluralita di appartenenze: Gruppi e individui "Di Nazione Zingara" nel mezzogiorno spagnolo', *Quaderni storici*, 146 (2014), 383–406.

Office of National Statistics, *What does the 2011 Census Tell us about the Characteristics of Gypsy or Irish Travellers in England and Wales?* (2014).

Ogle, Arthur, *The Tragedy of the Lollards' Tower: The Case of Richard Hunne, with its Aftermath in the Reformation Parliament* (Oxford, 1949).

Okely, Judith, 'Gypsies Travelling in Southern England', in Farnham Rehfisch (ed.), *Gypsies, Tinkers and Other Travellers* (1975), 55–83.

Okely, Judith, *The Traveller-Gypsies* (Cambridge, 1983; repr. 1993).

Okely, Judith, 'Ethnic Identity and Place of Origin: The Traveller Gypsies in Great Britain', in Hans Vermeuelen and Jeremy Boissevain (eds), *Ethnic Challenge: The Politics of Ethnicity in Europe* (Gottingen, 1984), 50–65.

Okely, Judith, *Own and Other Cultures* (1996).

Okely, Judith, 'Some Political Consequences of Theories of Gypsy Ethnicity: The Place of the Intellectual', in Allison James, Jennifer Hockey, and Andrew Dawson (eds), *After Writing Culture: Epistemology and Praxis in Contemporary Anthropology* (1997), 224–43.

Okely, Judith, 'Deterritorialised and Spatially Unbounded Cultures within Other Regimes', *Anthropological Quarterly*, 76 (2003), 151–64.

Okely, Judith, 'Retrospective Reading of Fieldnotes: Living on Gypsy Camps', *Behemoth: A Journal on Civilisation*, 4 (2011), 18–42.

Okely, Judith, 'The Dale Farm Eviction', *Anthropology Today*, 27 (December 2011), 24–7.

Okely, Judith, 'Foreword', to David M. Smith and Margaret Greenfields, *Gypsies and Travellers in Housing: The Decline of Nomadism* (Bristol, 2013), pp. vii–xix.

Okely, Judith, 'Recycled (Mis)representations: Gypsies, Travellers or Roma Treated as Objects, Rarely Subjects', *People, Place and Policy*, 8 (2014), 65–85.

Oldham, James, 'Truth-Telling in the Eighteenth-Century English Courtroom', *Law and History Review*, 12 (1994), 95–121.

Onyeka, *Blackamoores: Africans in Tudor England, their Presence, Status and Origins* (2013).

Ostendorf, Ann, 'A Bohémian Community in Colonial Louisiana', paper presented at the Gyspy Lore Society Conference on Romani Studies, Stockholm, September 2016.

Ostendorf, Ann Marguerite, ' "An Egiptian and noe Xtian Woman": Gypsy Identity and Race Law in Early America', *Journal of Gypsy Studies*, 1 (2017), 5–15.

Oxford Dictionary of National Biography.

Palmer, W. M., 'The Reformation of the Corporation of Cambridge, July 1662', *Proceedings of the Cambridgeshire Antiquarian Society*, 17 (1914), 75–132.

Pamjav, Horolma, et al., 'Genetic Structure of the Paternal Lineage of the Roma People', *American Journal of Physical Anthropology*, 145 (2011), 21–9.

Perkins, Maureen, 'The Trial of Joseph Powell, Fortune-Teller: Public and Private in Early Nineteenth-Century Magic', *Journal of Victorian Culture*, 6 (2001), 27–45.

Piotrowska, Anna G., *Gypsy Music in European Culture from the Late Eighteenth to the Early Nineteenth Centuries* (Boston, 2013).

Pokorny, Erwin, 'The Gypsies and their Impact on Fifteenth-Century Western European Iconography', in Jaynie Anderson (ed.), *Crossing Cultures: Conflict, Migration and Convergence: The Proceedings of the 32nd International Congress of the History of Art* (Melbourne, 2009), 597–601.

Pokorny, Erwin, 'Das Ziegeunerbild in der Altdeutschen Kunst: Ethnographisches Interesse und Antiziganismus', in Andreas Tacke and Stefan Heinz (eds), *Menschenbilder Beiträge zur Altdeutschen Kunst* (Petersberg, 2011), 97–110.

Pound, John, *Poverty and Vagrancy in Tudor England* (1971).

Power, Gerald, 'Gypsies and Sixteenth-Century Ireland', *Romani Studies*, 5th ser., 24 (2014), 203–9.

Pugliatti, Paola, *Beggary and Theatre in Early Modern England* (2003).

Pugliatti, Paola, 'A Lost Lore: The Activity of Gypsies as Performers on the Stage of Elizabethan–Jacobean Street Theatre', in Paola Pugliatti and Alessandro Serpieri (eds), *English Renaissance Scenes: From Canon to Margins* (Oxford, Bern, and Berlin, 2008), 259–310.

Pugliatti, Paola, and Alessandro Serpieri (eds), *English Renaissance Scenes: From Canon to Margins* (Oxford, Bern, and Berlin, 2008).

Pusca, Anca, 'Representing Romani Gypsies and Travelers: Performing Identity from Early Photography to Reality Television', *International Studies Perspectives*, 16 (2015), 327–44.

Puxon, Grattan, 'The Romani Movement: Rebirth and the First World Romani Conference in Retrospect', in Thomas Acton (ed.), *Scholarship and the Gypsy Struggle* (Hatfield, 2000), 94–113.

Pym, Richard J., *The Gypsies of Early Modern Spain, 1425–1783* (Basingstoke and New York, 2007).

Quarmby, Katherine, *No Place to Call Home: Inside the Real Lives of Gypsies and Travellers* (2013).

Rabin, Dana 'The Sorceress, the Servant, and the Stays: Sexuality and Race in Eighteenth-Century Britain', in Antoinette Burton and Tony Ballantyne (eds),

Moving Subjects: Gender, Mobility, and Intimacy in an Age of Global Empire (Urbana, IL, 2009), 252–73.

Rabin, Dana Y., 'Seeing Jews and Gypsies in 1753', *Cultural and Social History*, 7 (2012), 35–58.

Radzinowicz, Leon, *A History of English Criminal Law and its Administration from 1750*, 4 vols (1948–68).

Rae, John, *Life of Adam Smith* (1895).

Rai, Niraj, et al., 'The Phylogeography of Y-Chromosome Haplogroup H1a1a-M82 Reveals the Likely Indian Origin of the European Romani Populations', *PLoS One*, 7/11 (2012) <http://e48477.doi.10.1371> (accessed October 2017).

Randall, Dale B. J., *Jonson's Gypsies Unmasked: Background and Theme of* The Gypsies Metamorphos'd (Durham, NC, 1975).

Rehfisch, Farnham (ed.), *Gypsies, Tinkers and Other Travellers* (1975).

Regensburger, Rheinhold, 'Gypsy Fortune-Tellers as a Subject of the Italian Baroque Painters', *Journal of the Gypsy Lore Society*, 3rd ser., 45 (1966), 1–6.

Regueiro, Maria, et al., 'Divergent Patrilineal Signals in Three Roma Populations', *American Journal of Physical Anthropology*, 144 (2011), 80–91.

Reynolds, Bryan, *Becoming Criminal: Transverse Performance and Cultural Dissidence in Early Modern England* (Baltimore and London, 2002).

Rice, Douglas Walthew, *The Life and Achievements of Sir John Popham 1531–1607* (Madison, NJ, 2005).

Richardson, Joanna, and Andrew Ryder (eds), *Gypsies and Travellers: Empowerment and Inclusion in British Society* (Bristol and Chicago, 2012).

Richardson, Joanna, and Richard O'Neil, '"Stamp on the Camps": The Social Construction of Gypsies and Travellers in Media and Political Debate', in Joanna Richardson and Andrew Ryder (eds), *Gypsies and Travellers: Empowerment and Inclusion in British Society* (Bristol and Chicago, 2012), 169–86.

Roberts, Samuel, 'Samuel Roberts of Park Grange, Sheffield AD 1763–1848', *Journal of the Gypsy Lore Society*, NS 5 (1911–12), 161–6.

Robichaux, Albert J., Jr, *German Coast Families: European Origins and Settlement in Colonial Louisiana* (Rayne, LA, 1997).

Rodger, N. A. M., *The Safeguard of the Sea: A Naval History of Britain 660–1649* (New York, 1998).

Rogers, Nicholas, *Mayhem: Post-War Crime and Violence in Britain, 1748–53* (London and New Haven, 2013).

Romilly, Sir Samuel, *Observations on the Criminal Law of England* (1810).

Roth, Stephen J., 'Are Gypsies an Ethnic Group?', *Patterns of Prejudice*, 22 (1988), 51–2.

Rothéa, Xavier, 'Piste pour une histographe des Tsiganes en France', *Études tsiganes*, 39–40 (2009), 14–42.

Ryrie, Alec, *The Sorcerer's Tale: Faith and Fraud in Tudor England* (Oxford, 2008).

Salgado, Gamini, *The Elizabethan Underworld* (1977; repr. 1997).

Salo, Matt T., 'Gypsy Ethnicity: Implications of Native Categories and Interactions for Ethnic Classification', *Ethnicity*, 6 (1979), 73–96.

Salo, Matt T., and Sheila Salo, 'Romnichel Economic and Social Organization in Urban New England', *Urban Anthropology*, 11 (1982), 273–313.

Salo, Sheila, '"Stolen by Gypsies": The Kidnap Accusation in the United States', *Papers from the Eighth and Ninth Annual Meetings, Gypsy Lore Society, North American Chapter* (New York, 1988), 25–40.

Sampson, John, 'Notes and Queries: Death of a Well-Known English Gypsy', *Journal of the Gypsy Lore Society*, 2 (1890), 191.

Sampson, John, 'English Gypsies in 1818', *Journal of the Gypsy Lore Society*, NS 1 (1907), 183–5.

Sampson, John, *The Dialect of the Gypsies of Wales: Being the Older Form of British Romani Preserved in the Speech of the Clan of Abram Wood* (Oxford, 1926).

Sampson, John, 'Early Records of the Gypsies in England', *Journal of the Gypsy Lore Society*, 3rd ser., 3 (1927), 32–4.

Sampson, John (ed.), *The Wind on the Heath: A Gypsy Anthology* (1930).

Samuel, Raphael, 'Comers and Goers', in H. J. Dyos and M. Wolff (eds), *The Victorian City, Images and Reality*, 2 vols (1976), i. 123–60.

Sandford, Jeremy, *Rokkering to the Gorjios: In the Early Nineteen Seventies British Romany Gypsies Speak of their Hopes, Fears and Aspirations* (Hatfield, 2000).

Sandland, Ralph, 'The Real, the Simulacrum and the Construction of the "Gypsy" in Law', *Journal of Law and Society*, 23 (1996), 383–405.

Saul, Nicholas, *Gypsies and Orientalism in German Literature and Anthropology of the Long Nineteenth Century* (2007).

Saul, Nicholas, and Susan Tebbutt (eds), *The Role of the Romanies* (Liverpool, 2004).

Saunders, G. W., 'Notes and Queries: Gypsies in Somerset', *Journal of the Gypsy Lore Society*, 3rd ser., 11 (1932), 47.

Saunders, Peter, Jim Clarke, Sally Kendall, Anna Lee, Sakie Lee, and Freda Matthews (eds), *Gypsies and Travellers in their own Words* (Leeds, 2000).

Schmitt, Jean-Claude, *The Holy Greyhound: Guinefort, Healer of Children since the Thirteenth Century* (Cambridge, 1983).

Schreiner, Claus (ed.), *Flamenco Gypsy Dance and Music from Andalusia* (Portland, OR, 1990).

Selling, Jan, Markus End, Hristo Kyuchukov, Pia Laskar and Bill Templer (eds), *Antiziganism: What's in a Word?* (Newcastle upon Tyne, 2015).

Shahar, Shulamith, 'Religious Minorities, Vagabonds and Gypsies in Early Modern Europe', in Roni Stauber and Raphael Vago (eds), *The Roma—A Minority in Europe: Historical, Political and Social Perspectives* (Budapest, 2007), 1–18.

Shaw, Martin, *Narrating Gypsies, Telling Travellers: A Study of the Relational Self in Four Life Stories* (Umeå, 2006).

Shinéar, Sinéad ní, 'Apocrypha to Canon: Inventing Irish Traveller History', *History Ireland*, 12 (2004), 15–19.

Shirley, G. W., 'A Loan to a Scottish Gypsy', *Journal of the Gypsy Lore Society*, NS 8 (1914), 10–11.

Sigona, Nando, and Nidhi Trehan (eds), *Romani Politics in Contemporary Europe: Poverty, Ethnic Mobilization, and the Neoliberal Order* (Basingstoke and New York, 2009).

Silverman, Carol, 'Negotiating "Gypsiness": Strategy in Context', *Journal of American Folklore*, 1012 (1988), 261–75.

Silverman, Carol, *Romani Routes: Cultural Politics and Balkan Music in Diaspora* (Oxford, 2012).

Simpson, David, *Wordsworth's Historical Imagination: The Poetry of Displacement* (London and New York, 1987).

Simson, Walter, and James Simson, *A History of the Gipsies: With Specimens of the Gipsy Language* (1865; London and New York, 1866).

Sinclair, Albert Thomas, *American Gypsies* (New York, 1917).

Slack, Paul A., 'Vagrants and Vagrancy in England, 1598–1664', *Economic History Review*, 27 (1974), 360–79.

Slack, Paul, *Poverty and Policy in Tudor and Stuart England* (1988).

Slack, Paul, *The Invention of Improvement: Information and Material Progress in Seventeenth-Century England* (Oxford, 2015).

Smart, B. C., and H. T. Crofton, *The Dialect of the English Gypsies* (1875).

Smart, Bath C, 'The Dialect of the English Gypsies', *Transactions of the Philological Society* (Berlin, 1862–3), appendix, 1–86.

Smith, David, 'Gypsies, Tinkers, Travellers and the Forest Economy', in John Langton and Graham Jones (eds), *Forests and Chases of England and Wales c.1500 to c.1850* (Oxford, 2005), 61–6.

Smith, David, 'The Political Context of Migration in the UK: The Case of Roma Gypsies', in *Handbook of Research on Impacts of International Business and Political Affairs in the Global Economy* (2016), 367–80.

Smith, David M., and Margaret Greenfields, *Gypsies and Travellers in Housing: The Decline of Nomadism* (Bristol, 2013).

Smith, Mark, and Stephen Taylor (eds), *Evangelicalism in the Church of England c.1790–1890* (2004).

Snell, K. D. M., *Parish and Belonging: Community, Identity and Welfare in England and Wales 1700–1950* (Cambridge, 2006).

Snell, K. D. M., 'In or Out of their Place: The Migrant Poor in English Art, 1740–1900', *Rural History*, 24 (2013), 73–100.

Sociological Research Section of the Ministry of Housing and Local Government, *Gypsies and Other Travellers* (1967).

'Some Notes on Gypsies in North Britain', in Farnham Rehfisch (ed.), *Gypsies, Tinkers and Other Travellers* (1975), 85–121.

Sorensen, Janet, 'Vulgar Tongues: Canting Dictionaries and the Language of the People in Eighteenth-Century Britain', *Eighteenth Century Studies*, 37 (2004), 435–54.

Soulis, George C., 'The Gypsies in the Byzantine Empire and the Balkans in the Late Middle Ages', *Dumbarton Oaks Papers*, 15 (1961), 152–5.

Spinelli, A. G., 'Gli zingari nel Modenese', *Journal of the Gypsy Lore Society*, NS 3 (1909), 42–57, 88–111.

Spierenburg, Pieter, *The Spectacle of Suffering: Executions and the Evolution of Repression: From a Preindustrial Metropolis to the European Experience* (Cambridge, 1984),

Starkie, Walter, 'Cervantes and the Gypsies', *Huntington Library Quarterly*, 26 (1963), 337–49.

Steiner, Stephan, '"Making Short Work by Flogging, Hanging and Beheading": A "Gypsy" Trial and its Pitfalls', *Frühunezeit-Info* (Early Modern Studies Institute, Vienna), 25 (2014), 154–60.

Stewart, Michael, *The Time of the Gypsies* (Oxford, 1997).

Stewart, Michael (ed.), *The Gypsy 'Menace': Populism and the New Anti-Gypsy Politics* (2012).

Stewart, Michael, 'Roma and Gypsy "Ethnicity" as a Subject of Anthropological Inquiry', *Annual Review of Anthropology*, 42 (2013), 415–32.

Straub, Kristina, 'Heteroanxiety and the Case of Elizabeth Canning', *Eighteenth-Century Studies*, 30 (1997), 296–304.

Strauss, Daniel, 'Anti-Gypsyism in German-Speaking Society and Literature', in Susan Tebbutt (ed.), *Sinti and Roma in German-Speaking Society and Literature* (New York and Oxford, 1998; paperback edn, 2008), 81–90.

Studen, Andrej, 'Maladjusted and Dangerous Gypsies: A Glimpse at the History of Contamination, Aversion and Despise in the 18th and 19th Century', *Acta Histriae*, 23 (2015), 97–112.

Sullivan, Edward J., 'Jacque Callot's *Les Bohémiens*', *Art Bulletin*, 59 (1977), 217–21.

Sutherland, Anne, *Gypsies: The Hidden Americans* (Prospect Heights, IL, 1975, rerp. 1986).

Sway, Marlene, *Familiar Strangers: Gypsy Life in America* (Urbana, IL, and Chicago, 1988).

Tawney, R. H., *The Agrarian Problem in the Sixteenth* Century (1912).

Taylor, Aaron C., 'A Possible Early Reference to Gypsies in Spain Prior to 1420: MS 940 of the Trivulziana Library in Milan, Italy', *Romani Studies*, 5th ser., 26 (2016), 79–86.

Taylor, Becky, *A Minority and the State: Travellers in Britain in the Twentieth Century* (Manchester, 2008).

Taylor, Becky, 'A People on the Outside', *History Today*, 61/6 (June 2011), 17–19.

Taylor, Becky, *Another Darkness, Another Dawn: A History of Gypsies, Roma and Travellers* (2014).

Tebbutt, Susan (ed.), *Sinti and Roma in German-Speaking Society and Literature* (New York and Oxford, 1998, 2008).

Thompson, T. W., 'Affairs of Egypt, 1909', *Journal of the Gypsy Lore Society*, NS 5 (1911), 113–35.

Thompson, T. W., 'The Ceremonial Customs of the British Gipsies', *Folklore*, 24 (1913), 314–56.

Thompson, T. W. 'Consorting with and Counterfeiting Egyptians', *Journal of the Gypsy Lore Society*, 3rd ser., 2 (1923), 81–92.

Thompson, T. W., 'English Gypsy Death and Burial Customs', *Journal of the Gypsy Lore Society*, 3rd ser., 3 (1924), 5–38, 60–93.

Thompson, T. W., 'Gypsy Marriage in England', *Journal of the Gypsy Lore Society*, 3rd ser., 5 (1926), 9–37; continued in *Journal of the Gypsy Lore Society*, 3rd ser., 6 (1927), 101–29, 151–82.

Thompson, T. W., 'Additional Notes on English Gypsy Death and Burial Customs', *Journal of the Gypsy Lore Society*, 3rd ser., 9 (1930), 34–8.

Thompson, T. W., 'Gleanings from Constables' Accounts and Other Sources', *Journal of the Gypsy Lore Society*, 3rd ser., 7 (1928), 30–47.

Timbers, Frances, 'Mary Squires: A Case Study in Constructing Gypsy Identity in Eighteenth-Century England', in Kim Kippen and Lori Woods (eds), *Worth and Repute: Valuing Gender in Late Medieval and Early Modern Europe* (Toronto, 2011), 153–77.

Timbers, Frances, *'The Damned Fraternitie': Constructing Gypsy Identity in Early Modern England, 1500–1700* (2016).

Tong, Diane (ed.), *Gypsies: An Interdisciplinary Reader* (1998).

Torre, R. Lillian de la (pseudonym of Lillian Bueno McCue), *'Elizabeth Is Missing' or, Truth Triumphant: An Eighteenth Century Mystery* (New York, 1945).

Torrione, Margarita, 'El Traje Antiguo de los Gitanos: Aletrida y Castigo', *Cuadernos Hispanoamericanos*, 536 (1995), 19–42.

Townsend, David, *The Gipsies of Northamptonshire: Their Manner of Life, Festive Amusements, and Fortune-Telling, Fifty Years Ago* (Kettering, 1877).

Treherne, John, *The Canning Enigma* (1989).

Tremlett, Annabel, Aidan McGarry, and Timofey Agarin, 'The Work of Sisyphus: Squaring the Circle of Roma Recognition', *Ethnicities*, 14 (2014), 727–36.

Trigg, Elwood B., 'Magic and Religion amongst the Gypsies of Great Britain', University of Oxford, D. Phil. thesis, 1968.

Trigg, Elwood B., *Gypsy Demons and Divinities: The Magic and Religion of the Gypsies* (Secaucus, NJ, 1973).

Trumpener, Katie, 'The Time of the Gypsies: A "People without History" in the Narratives of the West', *Critical Inquiry*, 18 (1992), 843–84.

Tudor, John R., *Orkneys and Shetland: Their Past and Present* (1883).

Turner, Royce, 'Gypsies and Politics in Britain', *Political Quarterly*, 71 (2000), 68–77.

Turner, Royce, 'Gypsies and British Parliamentary Language: An Analysis', *Romani Studies*, 5th ser., 12 (2002), 1–34.

Van Baar, Huub, 'The Emergence of a Reasonable Anti-Gypsyism in Europe', in Timofey Agarin (ed.), *When Stereotype Meets Prejudice: Antiziganism in European Societies* (Stuttgart, 2014), 27–55.

Van Kappen, O., 'Three Dutch Safe-Conducts for "Heidens"', *Journal of the Gypsy Lore Society*, NS 41 (1962), 89–100.

Van Kappen, O., *Geschiedenis der Zigeuners in Nederland: De Ontwikkeling van de Rechtspositie der Heidens of Egyptenaren in de Noordelijke Nederlanden (1420–±1750)* (Assen, 1965).

Van Kappen, O., 'A Contribution to the History of the Gypsies in the Bishopric of Liège (1540–1726), *Journal of the Gypsy Lore Society*, NS 46 (1967), 142–50.

Vaux de Foletier, François de, 'Recherches sur l'histoire des Tsiganes dans les anciens registres paroissiaux', *Études Tsiganes*, 2 (1956), 3–11.

Vaux de Foletier, François de, *Les Tsiganes dans l'Ancienne France* (Paris, 1961).

Vaux de Foletier, François de, 'Gypsy Captains in Provence and the Rhone Valley in the 16th and 17th Centuries', *Journal of the Gypsy Lore Society*, 3rd ser., 41 (1962), 3–10.

Vermeersch, Peter, *The Romani Movement: Minority Politics and Ethnic Mobilization in Contemporary Central Europe* (Oxford and New York, 2006).

Vermeulen, Hans, and Jeremy Boissevain (eds), *Ethnic Challenge: The Politics of Ethnicity in Europe* (Gottingen, 1984).

Vesey-Fitzgerald, Brian, *Gypsies of Britain: An Introduction to their History* (1944).

Vezzoli, Alice, 'Migration, Non-Integration and Integration of *Cingani* (Gypsies) in the Republic of Venice during the Early Modern Age', University of Leiden, MA thesis, 2013.

Viaggio, Giorgio, *Storia degli zingari in Italia* (Rome, 1997).

Ward-Jackson, C. H., and Denis E. Harvey, *The English Gypsy Caravan: Its Origins, Builders, Technology and Conservation*, 2nd edn (Newton Abbot and Pomfret, VT, 1986).

Webb, G. E. C., *Gypsies: The Secret People* (1960).

Weekly Law Reports, 2011, 2014, 2015.

Webster, Wentworth, 'Stray Notes on George Borrow's Life in Spain', *Journal of the Gypsy Lore Society*, 1 (1889), 150–3.

Wellington, Barrett R., *The Mystery of Elizabeth Canning* (New York, 1940).

Wellstood, Frederick Christian, 'A Contribution to French Gypsy History', *Journal of the Gypsy Lore Society*, NS 3 (1909), 201–4.

Wellstood, F. C., 'Notes and Queries: Foreign Gypsies in England, 1761', *Journal of the Gypsy Lore Society*, NS 4 (1910–11), 307.

Wellstood, F. C, 'Some French Edicts against the Gypsies', *Journal of the Gypsy Lore Society*, NS 5 (1911), 313–16.

Willems, Wim, 'Ethnicity as a Death-Trap: The History of Gypsy Studies', in Leo Lucassen, Wim Willems, and Annemarie Cottaar (eds), *Gypsies and Other Itinerant Groups: A Socio-Historical Approach* (New York, 1998), 17–34.

Willems, Wim, *In Search of the True Gypsy: From Enlightenment to Final Solution* (1997).

Willems, Wim, and Leo Lucassen, 'The Church of Knowledge: Representation of Gypsies in Dutch Encyclopedias and their Sources (1724–1984)', in Matt. T. Salo (ed.), *100 Years of Gypsy Studies* (Cheverly, MD, 1900), 31–50.

Williams, Patrick, *Gypsy World: The Silence of the Living and the Voices of the Dead* (Chicago and London, 2003).

Winstedt, Eric Otto, 'Notes and Queries: An Early Mention of the Language "Romney"', *Journal of the Gypsy Lore Society*, NS 5 (1910–11), 78–9.

Winstedt, Eric Otto, 'Notes and Queries: Cases of Kidnapping', *Journal of the Gypsy Lore Society*, NS 6 (1912), 58–9.

Winstedt, Eric Otto, 'Notes and Queries: Gypsies at Aylesbury', *Journal of the Gypsy Lore Society*, NS 6 (1912), 74–7.

Winstedt, Eric Otto, 'Notes and Queries: Early Annals', *Journal of the Gypsy Lore Society*, 6 (1912), 63–4.

Winstedt, Eric Otto, 'The Gypsy Coppersmiths "Invasion" of 1911–13', *Journal of the Gypsy Lore Society*, NS 6 (1912), 244–302

Winstedt, Eric Otto, 'Early British Gypsies', *Journal of the Gypsy Lore Society*, NS 7 (1913–14), 5–37.

Winstedt, Eric Otto, 'The Norwood Gypsies and their Vocabulary', *Journal of the Gypsy Lore Society*, NS 9 (1915–16), 129–65.

Winstedt, Eric Otto, 'The Cost of Hanging a Gypsy', *Journal of the Gypsy Lore Society*, 3rd ser., 10 (1931), 55.

Winstedt, Eric Otto, 'Some Records of the Gypsies in Germany', *Journal of the Gypsy Lore Society*, 3rd ser., 11 (1932), 97–111; 12 (1933), 123–31, 189–96; 13 (1934), 98–116.

Winstedt, Eric Otto, 'Notes and Queries: The Squires Family', *Journal of the Gypsy Lore Society*, NS 16 (1937), 146–8.

Winstedt, Eric Otto, 'Records of Gypsies in the Eastern Counties of England', *Journal of the Gypsy Lore Society*, 3rd ser., 40 (1961), 23–35.

Wolffe, John, *The Expansion of Evangelicalism: The Age of Wilberforce, More, Chalmers and Finney* (Downers Grove, IL, 2007).

Woodall, Dena, and Diane Wolfthal, *Princes and Paupers: The Art of Jacques Callot* (New Haven, 2013).

Woodbridge, Linda, *Vagrancy, Homelessness, and English Renaissance Literature* (Urbana, IL, and Chicago, 2001).

Woodcock, Henry, *The Gipsies: Being a Brief Account of their History, Origin, Capabilities, Manners and Customs; with Suggestions for the Reformation and Conversion of the English Gipsies* (1865).

Yahav-Brown, Amit, 'Gypsies, Nomadism, and the Limits of Realism', *Modern Language Notes*, 121 (2006), 1124–47.

Zahra, Tara, ' "Condemned to Rootlessness and Unable to Budge": Roma, Migration Panics, and Internment in the Habsburg Empire', *American Historical Review*, 122 (2017), 702–26.

Zuccon, Maria, 'La legislazione sugli Zingari negli stati Italiania prima della rivoluzione', *Lacio Drom*, 15 (1979), 1–68.

INTERNET SOURCES

<http://www.bbc.com/news/world-europe-24589614> (accessed May 2015).

<http://www.bbc.com/news/world-europe-24645947> (accessed May 2015).

<http://www.bodley.ox.ac.uk/ballads/> (accessed April 2016).

<http://www.british-history.ac.uk/no-series/london-physicians/1550-1640> (accessed May 2016).

<https://www.britishnewspaperarchive.co.uk/> (accessed October 2017).

<http://www.bucksrecsoc.org.uk/QS-VOLUMES/> (accessed September 2016).

<http://eebo.chadwyck.com./home> (Early English Books Online) (accessed August 2016).

<http://www.errc.org/> (European Roma Rights Centre) (accessed April 2016).

<http://gale.cengage.co.uk/state-papers-online-15091714.aspx> (accessed May 2015).

http://find.galegroup.com.proxy.lib.ohio-state.edu/bncn/page.do?page=/bncn_
about.jsp&prodId=BNCN&userGroupName=colu44332> (British Library
Newspapers 1800–1950) (accessed October 2015).

<http://www.gale.com/daily-mail-historical-archive-1896-2004> (*Daily Mail*)
(accessed May 2015).

<http://www.gale.com/primary-sources/eighteenth-century-collections-online>
(Eighteenth-Century Collections Online) (accessed April 2015).

<http://www.gale.com/the-times-digital-archive/> (*The Times Digital Archive
1785–1985*) (accessed April 2015).

<http://www.gale.com/17th-and-18th-century-burney-collection> (Newspapers)
(accessed May 2015).

<http://www.gdc.galegroup.com.proxy.lib.ohio-state.edu/gdc/artemis/
NewspapersFullListPage/> (accessed August 2016).

<http://www.gypsyjib.com/> (accessed April 2016).

<http://www.histpop.org/ohpr/servlet> (accessed September 2015).

<http://www.oldbaileyonline.org/> (accessed April 2016).

<http://patrin.org.uk/> (East Midlands Gypsy Heritage Project) (accessed August
2016).

<http://romafacts.uni-graz.at/> (accessed April 2016).

<http://romanistudies.edu/> (accessed May 2016).

<http://romanygenes.com/> (accessed April 2016).

<http://rombase.uni-graz.at/> (accessed August 2016).

<http://www.theguardian.com/commentisfree/2013/oct/22/angel-kidnapped-
by-gypsies-libel-replayed> (accessed May 2015).

<http://www.telegraph.co.uk/news/worldnews/europe/ireland/10396991/Irish-
police-find-blonde-haired-blue-eyed-girl-in-Dublin-Roma-camp.html>
(accessed May 2015).

<http://www.travellermovement.org.uk/> (accessed October 2015).

Picture Acknowledgements

Index